Microeconomics for MBAs

This is the first textbook in microeconomics written exclusively for MBA students. McKenzie and Lee minimize attention to mathematics and maximize attention to intuitive economic thinking, examining key questions such as "How should organizations and incentives be structured to best encourage profit maximization?" The text is structured clearly and accessibly: Part I of each chapter outlines the basic theory with applications to social and economic policies and Part II applies this basic theory to management issues, with a substantial focus on the emerging subdiscipline of organizational economics. The "Perspective" sections in each chapter provide a new line of argument or different take on a business or policy issue. The accompanying DVD contains video modules in which Professors McKenzie and Lee give a personal tutorial on the key microeconomic concepts which MBA students need to understand, as well as elucidating complex lines of argument covered in the chapters and helping students to review for tests. Throughout the text, McKenzie and Lee aim to infuse students with the economic way of thinking in the context of a host of problems that MBA students, as future managers of real-world firms, will find relevant to their career goals.

Richard B. McKenzie is the Gerken Professor of Enterprise and Society in the Paul Merage School of Business at the University of California, Irvine.

Dwight R. Lee is Professor of Economics and Ramsey Chair of Private Enterprise in the Terry College of Business at the University of Georgia.

Microeconomics for MBAs

The Economic Way of Thinking for Managers

RICHARD B. McKENZIE
DWIGHT R. LEE

CAMBRIDGE
UNIVERSITY PRESS

CAMBRIDGE UNIVERSITY PRESS
Cambridge, New York, Melbourne, Madrid, Cape Town, Singapore, São Paulo

Cambridge University Press
The Edinburgh Building, Cambridge CB2 2RU, UK

Published in the United States of America by Cambridge University Press, New York

www.cambridge.org
Information on this title: www.cambridge.org/9780521859813

First published 2006

Printed in the United States of America

A catalogue record for this publication is available from the British Library

ISBN-13 978-0-521-85981-3 hardback
ISBN-10 0-521-85981-6 hardback

There is only one difference between a bad economist and a good one: the bad economist confines himself to the visible effect; the good economist takes into account both the effect that can be seen and those effects that must be foreseen.

Frédéric Bastiat (1801–50)
Selected Essays on Political Economy

CONTENTS

PREFACE

Almost all (if not all) textbooks used in MBA students' first course in microeconomics are designed with undergraduate economics majors or first-year PhD students in mind. Accordingly, MBA students are often treated to a course in intermediate microeconomic theory, often full of arcane mathematical explanations. The applications in such standard textbooks deal mainly with the impact of social or government policies on markets, with little discussion of how managers can make better decisions within their firms in response to market forces or how market forces can be expected to affect firms' institutional and financial structures.

This is because much microeconomic theory simply assumes firms into existence, with little or no discussion of why they are needed in the first place. Managers and their staff are assumed to do exactly what they are employed to do by their firms' owners – maximize owners' profits – with no discussion of how firms' organizational structures affect incentives and how incentives affect firms' production and profit outcomes.

That is to say, little is written in standard textbooks used in MBA courses about exactly how real-world firms pursue the goal of profit maximization. And that void in microeconomics textbooks is a real problem for MBA students, for an obvious reason: MBA students have typically come back to school to learn how to improve their management skills, which involves learning about how they can improve their ability to extract more profits from the scarce resources available to the firms where they work (or the firms where they expect to move after graduation). They do not come back to school to become economic theorists. Standard microeconomic textbooks are of little value to MBA students in helping them achieve their career objectives.

MBA students stand a quantum leap apart from undergraduate students, who typically have little idea of what they want to do with their lives, and have far less real-world business experience to which they can relate. MBA students are also sacrificing far more by attending school than undergraduates and must get value for their time spent reading their textbooks and going to class because of the cost of their education, in terms of both their tuition payments and the valuable work opportunities they have to set aside.

Microeconomics for MBAs breaks dramatically from the standard textbook mold. As the title suggests, we have designed this textbook with only MBA students in mind. In Part I of every chapter, we cover standard microeconomic theory in an accessible way, and we provide an array of applications to government policies which MBA students need to understand. After all, managers everywhere face the constraints of government-imposed laws and regulations that are ever-changing, and managers must work to maximize their firms' profits within those constraints. Moreover, professors in marketing, finance, accounting, strategy, and operations research who teach first- and second-year elective courses in MBA programs will expect their students to have a firm grounding in conventional microeconomic theory.

To help students learn the material covered in these pages and lectures, we have provided a set of video modules on a DVD packaged with the textbook and on the Internet that deal with three classes of topics:

(1) Basic economic concepts that all MBA students should understand at some level upon entering their programs of study
(2) Concepts, principles, and modes of analysis that are often hard to comprehend the first time they are presented in the form of written text or lectures
(3) Topics that have a high probability of being covered in examinations.

Of course, these videos can be stopped at any time to allow for note taking, and can be replayed repeatedly.

In Part II of every chapter, we go where other microeconomics textbooks seldom, if ever, go with such completeness. We drop the usual assumption that firms exist and that they automatically maximize owners' profits by simply following maximization rules. Instead, we bring to the forefront of our analysis a crucial problem faced by firms. This problem (dubbed the "principal–agent problem" within the economics profession and in this textbook) is that both owners and workers are more interested in pursuing their own wellbeing than someone else's wellbeing.

Owners ("principals") want to maximize their income stream and wealth through the firms they create by getting the most they can out of their employees. Similarly, managers and line workers (the owners' "agents") seek to maximize some combination of income, on-the-job perks, and job security, which are often in conflict with maximizing profits for the firm's owners. Without effective firm policies that align the incentives of owners and workers (for their mutual benefit), the work in a firm can be a self-destructive tug of war, with the demise of the firm virtually assured in competitive markets.

In this textbook, we focus MBA students' attention on thinking through the complex problems of getting incentives right. This is mainly because there is as much (maybe more) profit to be made from creatively structuring incentives as there can be made from creatively developing products for sale.

Getting hourly and monthly pay systems right is obviously an important means of aligning the interests of owners and managers. However, we also explain how firms' organizational structure, in terms of both people and finances, can affect the alignment of owners' and workers' incentives. And make no mistake about it, both owners and their employees have a stake in finding the right alignment. Workers' jobs can hang in the balance. Owners' investments can hang just as precariously on a cost-effective, balanced alignment of incentives.

Accordingly, this book places a great deal of emphasis on a field within economics that is growing rapidly in importance, especially as the subject relates directly to the business world – and MBA programs: *organizational economics*, which is the study of the design of firms' organizational and financial structures using the analytical tools of microeconomic analysis. The mode of thinking presented in these pages is crucial for managers – MBAs – who want to move up their corporate hierarchy or go off and create successful companies of their own.

In between Parts I and II of every chapter, we have inserted a "Perspective" – that is, a short section that provides a new or different take on a business or policy issue. For example, everyone *knows*, don't they, that the "first mover" in any market has a competitive advantage. In the Perspective for chapter 9, we discuss a startling observation made by management scholars: There is no first-mover advantage.

Each chapter ends with a section that we have titled "The bottom line," mainly because the section contains listings of "key takeaways" – succinct statements of the most important lessons to be drawn from the chapter. We understand that MBA students, you included, face serious time constraints, especially when you are working full time and have family responsibilities. "The bottom line" section is designed to focus your attention when reviewing the material covered in the chapter, with the hope that your time devoted to studying will be made more productive.

The scholarly and policy literature in economics and management relating to most of the topics considered in this volume is massive. We have tried to give credit where credit is due, especially when "classic," path-breaking treatments by distinguished scholars are concerned, but we have tried hold references and footnotes in check in order that the flow of the argument is not constantly disrupted. Still, our references section at the end of the book is extensive. We have also tried to smooth out the flow of the core material by relegating topics that will be only selectively used in classes to appendixes.

Many textbook authors and their publishers play the development of their course books "safe" by taking up only those topics that have become fixtures in the profession's "conventional wisdom." We see such an approach as sucking the life out of a discipline and its treatment in textbooks. Topics that have not yet been fully settled by decades of professional debate can give life to a discipline by showing students how disciplines have an organic quality, in that they are constantly evolving. As a consequence, you can expect many topics in this book to spark lively, and instructive, debates among student team members and between class members and professors in class. That is how we want the book to be received.

We have appended to each chapter a series of Review questions that we expect will activate discussions within your student teams. In addition, we have set up a web site for the book on which we will, from time to time, post interesting pointers and puzzles that have occurred to us after the book went to press. We also expect to post on that web site video commentaries on management issues and related economic policies that are bound to arise while you are reading this book and taking your course.

* * *

You may be interested in knowing that we – the authors of this book – have between us more than seventy-five years of university teaching experience, with most of our teaching careers spent in business schools. For the last fifteen years, we both have taught *only* MBA students. That should tell you that we have a pretty good fix on our readers and their interests, not the least of which is to have a course of study that is intellectually challenging as well as having practical application.

Each year, we often start our MBA courses in microeconomics with a question that puzzles our students, many of whom are mid- and upper-level managers in firms from a broad range of industries who remain employed while completing their MBA programs. The question seems simple on the surface, "Why are you here?" Invariably, the students' interests are piqued, but typically because they are puzzled by the question, which prompts our elaboration, "Why are you here in graduate school getting your MBA?" To be more precise, "Why are you sitting there in your seat in this classroom, all facing this lectern?"

MBA students are rarely reticent, and the answers are quick in coming and are varied: "I'm here to make more money," one student always confesses with an uneasy laugh. But many other answers share a common theme, "To learn how to *do* business" (with the emphasis on "*do*ing business"). That answer is understandable, mainly because MBA students are a focused lot, their eyes typically fixed on one objective – improving their career paths. Also, much business education encompasses instruction in business skills – for example, how to develop business plans and to secure funding for new business ventures. But invariably the answers leave an important part of our question unanswered because the answer – "to learn how to do business" – doesn't explain why our students are in their seats and we behind the lectern.

The problem with the answer is that neither of us – the authors, that is – has ever "done business." We have spent our entire careers in academe, lecturing to students about business, or other social, political, and economic topics. Indeed, there is a very good reason we have never done business: We don't think we would be very good at it if we ever tried. We figure that our fortes are *thinking, studying, and teaching* – not *doing* – business and then writing about what we have been thinking, studying, and teaching.

If our courses were primarily, if not exclusively, supposed to be about *doing* business, should we not change places with our students? They should come up to the lectern, and we should take their seats and listen to what they have to say. After all, they are actually *doing* business and know more about *doing* it than we could ever hope to know.

Understandably, the students become perplexed at our response. We assuage their concerns by pointing out the obvious, that what we will *do* in class is radically different from what they *do* in business. Indeed, the students come to class on a campus removed from their work to get away from what they do at work, and that means getting away from the multitude of details of business dealings that are a part of their everyday, workaday world.[1] In a literal sense, the class is a world apart from the world of business, and intentionally designed that way for one strategic purpose: to take a look at how business is done from a broad perspective without the clutter of details that our students deal with day in and day out.

In no small way, the purpose of our class (or any other business course worthy of academic respect) is to explore ways to *think* creatively about how

[1] (They also want to take courses from professors who haven't been out there in the "real world" *doing* what they have been doing, or else their professors would have little to offer that they didn't already know.)

business is done and can be done better, not to actually *do* business. In this regard, we take to heart an observation made by the late economist Kenneth Boulding:

> It is a very fundamental principle indeed that knowledge is always gained by the orderly loss of information; that is, by conducing and abstracting and indexing the great buzzing confusion of information that comes from the world around us into a form we can appreciate and comprehend. (1970, 2)

The way of thinking we take up in class, and that which Professor Boulding had in mind, is necessarily *abstract* – that is, without the clutter of many business details. We approach thinking with abstractions principally because no one's brain is sufficiently powerful to handle all the complex details of everyday business life. In no small way, productive thought requires that the complexity of business life be reduced enough to allow us to focus on the few things that are most important to the problems at hand by finding meaningful relationships between those things. That is why Professor Boulding insists that knowledge can so often (if not "always") be gained only "by the orderly loss of information."

Without thinking, many business people often spurn theory on the grounds that it lacks practical value. We insist, "not so at all." The abstract way of thinking that we shall develop in this textbook has a very practical, overriding goal, which is to afford students more *understanding* of the business world than they could have if they tried some alternative approach – that is, if they tried to keep the analysis cluttered up with the "buzzing confusion" of facts MBA students leave behind in their workplaces when they set out for class.

There is another highly practical goal to be achieved by theory (or rather *thinking* with the use of theory). If people can *think* through business problems in some organized way, albeit abstractly, they might be able to avoid mistakes when they actually go out and *do* business. In economic terms, business mistakes imply a regrettable misuse and loss of firm resources. *Thinking* before doing offers the prospect of reducing waste in doing business.

Our main interest in posing our initial question to our students – "Why are you here?" – is to stress the obvious: If the class is about *thinking* (not doing), then we – Richard McKenzie and Dwight Lee and students' other professors – have some justification for being in front of the class. Also, if the class is about the thinking process, there must be some method for thinking through problems, business-related or otherwise. The development of that *method* is the focus of our classes and this textbook.

Our goal in this volume is to develop *the economic way of thinking* in the context of a host of problems that MBA students, as future managers of real-world firm, will find relevant to their career goals.[2]

We understand that some readers may worry about our emphasis on theory because they may have read theory-grounded books that seemed sterile or irrelevant, mainly because of the heavy reliance on highly technical mathematics or complicated charts. That will not be the case in this book. The first principle of economics that has guided the development of this book is one that many readers will appreciate: *Keep the theory as simple as possible and illustrate it with real problems.*

This book carries the subtitle *The Economic Way of Thinking for Managers*, for a very good reason: In the following pages, we bring together a host of large and small ideas that economists have developed over the past several decades that have transformed the way we must think about the way the business world works.

Readers' reactions to large and small ideas will, we expect, have changed radically by the time they have read the last words of this volume. Two of those large questions are:

- How should organizations and incentives be structured to best encourage profit maximization?
- How does the competition in the market for goods and in the market for corporate control discipline executives?

The small questions that can be addressed from studying this volume are no less important and can be just as intriguing:

- Should used cars really be expected to be "better deals" than new ones (as so many people seem to think)?
- If competitive markets are expected to "clear" (with quantity demanded equaling quantity supplied), why are so many queues observed in grocery stores and at concerts?
- If queues are not mutually beneficial to buyers and sellers, then why aren't they eliminated?

Readers who think that these questions have simple, obvious, pat answers need to read on.

[2] (*The Economic Way of Thinking* is the title of a book by the late economist Paul Heyne (1994), which influenced a generation of students with its lucid discussion of basic economic concepts, principles, and theories that form a way of gaining insights about the world.)

We expect that readers of this book will end this book the way our students end our courses: changed for life in the way they see the business world around them. But then that is what MBA students typically want – or should want – from every course in their MBA programs. Readers have our best wishes for the journey of a lifetime.

This book was developed over the last several years as we taught our microeconomics courses for our MBA students at the University of California, Irvine and University of Georgia, Athens. Our students have made innumerable and invaluable suggestions for improvement in the book, and we are indebted to them. We are also indebted to Oxford University Press for allowing us to draw freely from our previously published book with the Press, *Managing Through Incentives.* All excerpts from that book have been substantially revised and updated for inclusion in this textbook.

ABBREVIATIONS AND ACRONYMS

CBA	cost–benefit analysis
CEO	chief executive officer
CPI	consumer price index
EPA	Environmental Protection Agency
FCC	Federal Communications Commission
GDP	gross domestic product
GE	General Electric
JV	joint venture
NTB	non-tariff barrier
LAN	local area network
M&A	mergers and acquisitions
MIS	management information system
MSA	Medical Savings Account
MU	marginal utility
ONS	Office for National Statistics
PBS	Public Broadcasting System
PPC	production possibilities curve
PPP	purchasing power parity
PV	present value
R&D	research and development
RPM	retail price maintenance
S&L	savings and loan
SEC	Securities and Exchange Commission

CHAPTER

1

Microeconomics: a way of thinking about business

In economics in particular, education seems to be largely a matter of unlearning and "disteaching" rather than constructive action. A once-famous American humorist observed that "it's not ignorance that does so much damage; it's knowin' so darn much that ain't so" . . . It seems that the hardest things to learn and to teach are things that everyone already knows. **Frank H. Knight**

The late Frank Knight was a wise professor at the University of Chicago who realized that students – even those who are in advanced business programs – beginning a study of economics, no matter the level, face a difficult task. They must learn many things in a rigorous manner that, on reflection and with experience, amount to common sense. To do that, however, they must set aside – or "unlearn" – many preconceived notions of the economy and of the course itself. The problem of "unlearning" can be especially acute for MBA students who are returning to a university after years of experience in industry. People in business rightfully focus their attention on the immediate demands of their jobs and evaluate their firms' successes and failures with reference to production schedules and accounting statements, a perspective that stands in stark contrast to the perspective developed in an economics class.

You are now one of the many students at whom Knight directed his comments. As all good teachers must do, we intend to challenge you in this course to rethink your views on the economy and the way firms operate. We shall ask you to develop new methods of analysis, maintaining all the while that there is, indeed, an "economic way of thinking" that deserves to be mastered. We shall also ask you to reconsider, in light of the new methods of thinking, old policy issues – both inside and outside the firm – about which you may have fixed views. These tasks will not always be easy for you, but we are convinced that the rewards from the study ahead are substantial. The greatest reward may be that this course of study will help you to better understand the way the business world works and how businesses may be made more efficient and profitable.

Each chapter is divided into two major parts. The first part (Part I) will always develop microeconomic concepts and theories and apply the concepts and theories to social and economic policies. Part II will always apply the theory directly to issues that mid-level and executive-level managers confront all the time. Sandwiched in between those two major sections will be a "Perspective" that covers some policy or management topic new to economics or that provides a novel take on a topic that has been mistakenly accepted among economists and lay people to economics as settled.

We understand that time is a scarce commodity for most MBA students, especially those who have to balance their studies with the demands of a full-time job and a family. Accordingly, we conclude each chapter with a section which we call "The bottom line," which itemizes and crystallizes the most important points developed in the chapter. We have deliberately kept these lists of "key takeaways" short.

Throughout the volume, we have one goal: to change the way you think about the world in large and small ways. When you complete this book, your view of how markets work (and fail to work) should be greatly clarified, with an improved ability to predict market outcomes. You will see more clearly the manager's role as one of coping with, and responding to, the competitive market forces that are ever-present outside the doors of every business, pressing both owners and executives to pay as much attention to the way business organizations and executive and line workers' incentives are structured as to how products are created and developed.

You will naturally be able to make observations that might, without going through this course of study, escape your attention. For example, most people now understand the entire world, not just the United States, faces a growing weight problem, which is giving rise to a growth in obesity-related health problems which, in turn, are driving up firms' health insurance costs and depriving workers of increases in money wages (Brody 2005; Girion 2005).

Having completed this book, you will naturally think about how people's weight problems are founded, at least partially, on the growing openness and competitiveness of the world's food markets, which is driving down the cost of food and driving up people's real incomes, with both effects leading to more food consumption – and people's expanded girths and backsides. You will also naturally wonder how managers will change their pay offers for prospective overweight workers, since the healthcare costs of such workers can be expected to feed into company health insurance costs. Indeed, might not competitive market forces be expected to put downward pressures on the money wages of overweight workers and upward pressures on prospective workers who maintain a healthy weight (and lifestyle)?

On completing this book, you will no longer be able to assess the terrorists' attack on the World Trade Center towers on September 11, 2001 as having only political or military consequences. After all, the 9/11 attack immediately hiked many people's perceived risk of flying, as well as caused a substantial lengthening of security lines at airports – with both factors – risk and wait time – increasing the total cost of plane trips. You will naturally understand why economic academic researchers have looked for, and found, that the greater cost of flying from the terrorists' actions should be expected to lead to – and apparently has led to – more people driving to many destinations, the consequence of which should have been more automobile accidents, injuries, and deaths (Blalock, Kadiyali, and Simon 2005a, 2005b).[1]

Hence, you will understand with greater facility after completing this book how airport security is truly a management problem with life-and-death consequences: Tighter airport security can have two opposing effects. First, it can increase the cost of flying (by increasing the length of the security lines), which can lead to less flying and more driving – and more highway accidents, injuries, and deaths. Second, the greater security can reduce the risk of flying and, thus, can increase the demand for flying (and reduce the demand for driving). Which effect is stronger? To date, the evidence suggests that, on balance, raising the alert status at airports from, say, yellow to orange can lead to more driving and more road deaths (Blalock, Kadiyali, and Simon 2005a, 2005b). Managers of the nation's homeland security system must weigh their actions very carefully and, before they raise the alert status, feel reasonably confident

[1] Cornell business school professors Garrick Blalock, Vrinda Kadiyali, and Daniel Simon found that initially the 9/11 attacks led to more intense screening of air passengers and their baggage. As a consequence, between 2001 and 2003, the greater security measures led to a 5 percent reduction in the volume of air travel at all airports and an 8 percent reduction in the volume of air travel at the country's fifty largest airports. The volume of travel on "short flights" (those less than 500 miles) fell by 16 percent (Blalock, Kadiyali, and Simon 2005a). Blalock, Kadiyali, and Simon (2005b) have also found that some air travelers switched to far more deadly road travel, the net effect of which is that, during the last three months of 2001, there were 726 more deaths on US roads (from noncommercial travel) than would otherwise have been expected had the 9/11 attacks never occurred. They also found that as fears of flying subsided with no additional terrorist attacks in the American skies during the twenty-four months after 9/11, the "9/11 effect" on monthly road travel and deaths began to dissipate. This means that during the twenty-four months after 9/11 there were a total of 1,243 more deaths on American roads than would have been without the terrorists' attacks. The authors consider their estimates of the additional road deaths very "conservative."

that the higher alert status will avert more deaths in the air than will arise on the nation's roads. Hence, we should expect that airport homeland security managers will often not elevate the alert status when the increase in the perceived risk of terrorist attacks is small.

In casual conversations, business people talk as though they *know* many things that few listeners think to challenge:

- "Houses with views sell quicker than houses without views."
- "Buying a house is a better deal than renting a comparable size apartment because houses carry tax advantages (interest on home mortgages is deductible from taxable incomes)."

On completing this textbook and hearing any such comment, you will be inclined to ask reflectively and in earnest, "How can that be?"

The kind of economic thinking that will be central to this book, and evident in the foregoing discussions of obesity and airport security and any assessment of the above statements, springs from an innocuous observation: *People have a basic drive to improve their lot in life because they don't have everything they want and need.* Much of this introductory chapter and the book (and the course), in both theory and in application, is directed at driving home this easily overlooked lesson. Oddly enough, many lessons covered in this book are crystallized in a story of what happened in a German prisoner-of-war (POW) camp during the Second World War, as related by a prisoner who happened to be a trained economist.

PART I THEORY AND PUBLIC POLICY APPLICATIONS

The emergence of a market

A **market** is the process by which buyers and sellers determine what they are willing to buy and sell and on what terms. It is the process by which buyers and sellers decide the prices and quantities of goods that are to be bought and sold.

Economic systems spring from people's drive to improve their welfare. R. A. Radford, an American soldier who was captured and imprisoned during the Second World War, left a vivid account of the primitive **market** for goods and services that grew up in the most unlikely of places, in his POW camp (Radford 1945). Because the inmates had few opportunities to produce the things they wanted, they turned to a system of exchange based on the cigarettes, toiletries, chocolate, and other rations distributed to them periodically by the Red Cross.

The Red Cross distributed the supplies equally among the prisoners, but "very soon after capture ... [the prisoners] realized that it was rather undesirable and unnecessary, in view of the limited size and the quality of supplies, to give away or to accept gifts of cigarettes or food. Goodwill developed into trading as a more equitable means of maximizing individual satisfaction" (Radford 1945, 190).

As the weeks went by, trade expanded, and the prices of goods stabilized. A soldier who hoped to receive a high price for his soap found he had to compete with others who also wanted to trade soap. Soon shops emerged, and middlemen began to take advantage of discrepancies in the prices offered in different prisoners' bungalows.

For example, a priest, one of the few prisoners allowed to move freely among the prison bungalows, found that he could exchange a pack of cigarettes for a pound of cheese in one bungalow, trade the cheese for a pack and a half of cigarettes in a second bungalow, and return home with more cigarettes than he had started with. Although he was acting in his own self-interest (not so much out of religious convictions), he had provided the people in the second bungalow with something they wanted – more cheese than they would otherwise have had. In fact, prices for cheese and cigarettes differed partly because prisoners in different bungalows had different desires and partly because they could not all interact freely. To exploit the discrepancy in prices, the priest moved the camp's store of cheese from the first bungalow, where it was worth less, to the second bungalow, where it was worth more. Everyone involved in the trade benefited from the priest's enterprise.

An **entrepreneur** is an enterprising person who discovers potentially profitable opportunities and organizes, directs, and manages productive ventures.

A few **entrepreneurs** in the camp hoarded cigarettes and used them to buy up the troops' rations shortly after issue, and then sold the rations just before the next issue, at higher prices. Although these entrepreneurs were pursuing their own private interest, like the priest, they were providing a service to the other prisoners. They bought the rations when people wanted to get rid of them and sold them when people were running short. The difference between the low price at which they bought and the high price at which they sold gave them the incentive they needed to make the trades, hold on to the rations, and assume the risk that the price might not rise.

Soon the troops began to use cigarettes as money, quoting prices in packs or fractions of packs. (Only the less desirable brands of cigarette were used this way; the better brands were smoked.) Because cigarettes were generally acceptable, the soldier who wanted soap no longer had to search out those who might want his jam; he could buy the soap with cigarettes. Even nonsmokers began to accept cigarettes in trade.

This makeshift monetary system adjusted itself to allow for changes in the money supply. On the day the Red Cross distributed new supplies of cigarettes, prices rose, reflecting the influx of new money. After nights spent listening to nearby bombing, when the nervous prisoners had smoked up their holdings of cigarettes, prices fell. Radford saw a form of social order emerging in these spontaneous, voluntary, and completely undirected efforts. Even in this unlikely environment, the human tendency toward mutually advantageous interaction had asserted itself.

Today, markets for numerous new and used products spring up spontaneously in much the same way. At the end of each semester, college students can be found trading books among themselves, or standing in line at the bookstore to resell the books they bought at the beginning of the semester. Garage sales are now common in practically all communities (with eBay effectively being the largest global "garage sale"). Indeed, like the priest in the POW camp, many people go to garage sales to buy what they believe they can resell – at a higher price, of course. "Dollar stores" have sprung up all over the country for one purpose, to buy the surplus merchandise from manufacturers and to unload it at greatly reduced prices to willing customers. There are even firms that make a market in getting refunds for other firms on late overnight deliveries. Many firms don't think it is worth their time to seek refunds for late deliveries, mainly because they individually don't have many late deliveries (because the overnight delivery firms have an economic incentive to hold the late deliveries in check). However, there are obviously economies to be had from other firms collecting the delivery notices from several firms and sorting the late ones out, with the refunds shared by all concerned.

Today, we stand witness to what is an explosion of a totally new economy on the Internet that many of the students reading this book will, like the priest in the POW camp, help to develop. More than two hundred years ago, Adam Smith, a moral philosopher considered to be the first economist, outlined a society that resembled these POW camp markets in his classic *Wealth of Nations* (1776) (Smith 1937). Smith asked why firms and markets arise, and how they contribute to social and economic improvement. When Smith wrote his bestseller, many of his points were considered novel and controversial. Now, many of his points are a part of conventional economic wisdom – and have been incorporated, with refinements and updating, in this textbook.

The economic problem

Our world is not nearly as restrictive as Radford's POW camp, but it is no Garden of Eden, either. Most of us are constantly occupied in securing the food, clothing, and shelter we need to exist, to say nothing of those things we

Resources are things used in the production of goods and services. There are only so many acres of land, gallons of water, trees, rivers, wind currents, oil and mineral deposits, trained workers, and machines that can be used in any one period to produce the things we need and want.

would only like to have – a high-definition television, a trip to Taihiti, and a shopping spree. Indeed, if we think seriously about the world around us, we can make two general observations.

First, the world is more or less fixed in size and limited in its **resources**. We can plant more trees, find more oil, and increase our stock of human talent, but there are limits on what we can accomplish with the resources at our disposal.

Economists have traditionally grouped resources into four broad categories: land, labor, capital (also called investment goods), and technology.[2] To this list, some economists would add a fifth category, *entrepreneurial talent*. The entrepreneur is critical to the success of any economy, especially if it relies heavily on markets. Because entrepreneurs discover more effective and profitable ways of organizing resources to produce the goods and services people want, they are often considered a resource in themselves.

Second, in contrast to the world's physical limitations, human wants abound. You yourself would probably like to have books, notebooks, pens and a calculator, perhaps even a computer with a several gigahertz microprocessor and a 200 gigabyte hard-disk drive. A stereo system, a car, more clothes, a plane ticket home, a seat at a big concert or ballgame – you could probably go on for a long time, especially when you realize how many basics, like three good meals a day, you normally take for granted.

Scarcity is the fact that we cannot all have everything we want all the time.

In fact, most people want far more than they can ever have. One of the unavoidable conditions of life is the fundamental condition of **scarcity**. Put simply, there isn't enough of everything to go around. Consequently, society must face four unavoidable questions:

(1) **What** will be produced? More guns or more butter? More schools or more prisons? More cars or more art, more textbooks or more "Saturday night specials"?

(2) **How** will those things be produced, considering the resources at our disposal? Shall we use a great deal of labor and little mechanical power, or vice versa? And how can a firm "optimize" the use of various resources, given their different prices?

[2] Land includes the surface area of the world and everything in nature – minerals, chemicals, plants – that is useful in the production process. Labor includes any way in which human energy, physical or mental, can be usefully expended. Capital (investment goods) includes any output of a production process that is designed to be used later in other production processes. Plants and equipment – things produced to produce other things – are examples of these manufactured means of production. Technology is the knowledge of how resources can be combined in productive ways.

(3) **Who** will be paid what and who will receive the goods and services produced? Shall we distribute them equally? If not, then on what other basis shall we distribute them?
(4) Perhaps most important, **who** will determine how the above questions shall be answered? Shall we allow for individual freedom of choice, or shall we make all these decisions collectively?

These questions have no easy answers. Most of us spend our lives attempting to come to grips with them on an individual level. What should I do with my time today – study or work on company projects (beyond what my job requires)? How should I study – in the library or at home with my MP3 on? Who is going to benefit from my efforts – me or my spouse, who wants me to succeed? Am I going to live by principle or by habit? Take each day as it comes or plan ahead? In a broader sense, these questions are fundamental not just to the individual but to all the social sciences, economics in particular. Indeed, most economists see the fact of scarcity as the foundation of **economics**. More to the point, economics is a way of *thinking* about how people, individually and collectively in various organizations (including firms), cope with scarcity.

> ***Economics*** is the study of how people cope with scarcity – with the pressing problem of how to allocate their limited resources among their competing wants in order to satisfy as many of those wants as possible.

The problem of allocating resources among competing wants is not as simple as it may first appear. You may think that economics is an examination of how one person, or a small group of people, makes fundamental social choices on resource use. That is not the case. The problem is that we have information about our wants and the resources at our disposal that may be known to no one else. This is a point the late Leonard Read made (Read 1983) in a short article concerning what it takes to produce a product as simple as a pencil, and it also is a point that F. A. Hayek stressed in many of his writings that, ultimately, gained him a Nobel Prize in economics (Hayek 1945). (We have included Read's short article in an appendix to this chapter, p. 42.)

For example, as Read and Hayek might note about your own personal context as you read this page, you may know you want a calculator because your statistics class requires you to have one, but even your friends (much less the people at Hewlett-Packard or Samsung) do not yet know your purchase plans. You may also be the only person who knows how much labor you have, which is determined by exactly how long and intensely you are willing to work at various tasks in your MBA program and at work. At the same time, you may know little about the wants and resources that other people around the country and world may have (or even your cohorts in your MBA study groups). Before resources can be effectively allocated, the information we hold about our individual wants and resources must somehow be communicated to others. This means that economics must be concerned with systems of communications – e.g. the priest in the POW camp who used both words and prices to convey information about how the troops in the various bungalows assessed the value he had to offer. Indeed, the field is extensively concerned with how information about wants and resources is transmitted or shared through, for example, prices in the market process and votes in the political process. Indeed, the "information problem" is often acute within firms, given that the CEO often knows little about how to do the jobs at the bottom of the corporate "pyramid." The information problem is one important reason that firms must rely extensively on *incentives* to get their workers (and managers) to pursue firm goals.

Markets like the one in the POW camp and even the firms that operate within markets emerge in direct response to scarcity. Because people want more than is immediately available, they produce some good and services for trade. By exchanging things they like less for things they like more, they reallocate their resources and enhance their welfare as individuals. As we will see, people organize firms, which often substitute command-and-control structures for the competitive negotiations and exchanges of markets, because the firms are more cost-effective than markets. Firms can be expected to expand only as long as things can be done more cost-effectively through firms than through competitive market trades. This means that many firms fail not only because of things they do wrong (allow costs to get out of control), but because market trades between firms become less costly (through improved telecommunications), thus causing firms to outsource their needed services and shed their employees.

The scope of economics

MBA students often associate economics with a rather narrow portion of the human experience: the pursuit of wealth; money and taxes; commercial and industrial life. Critics often suggest that economists are oblivious to the aesthetic and ethical dimensions of human experience. Such criticism is partly justified. Increasingly, however, economists are expanding their horizons and applying the laws of economics to the full spectrum of human activities.

The struggle to improve one's lot is not limited to the attainment of material goals. Although most economic principles have to do with the pursuit of material gain, they can be relevant to aesthetic and humanistic goals as well.

The appreciation of a poem or play can be the subject of economic inquiry. Poems and plays, and the time in which to appreciate them, are also scarce.

Jacob Viner, a distinguished economist active in the first half of the twentieth century, once defined economics as "what economists do." Today, economists study an increasingly diverse array of topics. As always, they are involved in describing market processes, methods of trade, and commercial and industrial patterns. They also pay considerable attention to poverty and wealth; to racial, sexual, and religious discrimination; to politics and bureaucracy; to crime and criminal law; and to revolution. There is even an economics of group interaction, in which economic principles are applied to marital and family problems. And there is an economics of firm organization and the structure of incentives inside firms.

What is the unifying factor in these diverse inquiries? What ties them all together and distinguishes the economist's work from that of other social scientists? Economists take a distinctive approach to the study of human behavior, and they employ a mode of analysis based on certain presuppositions. For example, much economic analysis starts with the general proposition that people prefer more to fewer of those things they value and that they seek to maximize their welfare by making reasonable, consistent choices in the things they buy and sell. These propositions enable economists to derive the "law of demand" (people will buy more of any good at a lower price than at a higher price, and vice versa) and many other principles of human behavior.

One purpose of this book is to describe the economic approach in considerable detail – to develop in precise terms the commonly accepted principles of economic analysis and to demonstrate how they can be used to understand a variety of problems, including pollution, unemployment, crime, and ticket scalping – as well as firms' organizational and financial structures. In every case, economic analysis is useful only if it is based on a sound theory that can be evaluated in terms of real-world experience. This mode of analysis – sometimes dubbed the "economic way of thinking" – will appear time and again as you move through your MBA programs, most prominently in your finance, accounting, marketing, and strategy courses.

Developing and using economic theories

The real world of economics is staggeringly complex. Each day millions of people engage in innumerable transactions, only some of them involving money (about 30 percent), and many of them undertaken for conflicting reasons

> **A theory** is a model of how the world is put together; it is an attempt to uncover some order in the seemingly random events of daily life. Theory is how we make sense of the world.

(McMillan 2002, 168–9). To make sense of all these activities, economists turn to **theory**.

Economic theory is abstract, but not in the sense that its models lack concreteness. On the contrary, good models are laid out with great precision. Economic theories are simplified models *abstracted from* the complexity of the real world. Economists deliberately simplify their models to best concentrate attention on the problems they are most interested in. Just as a map is more useful because it ignores most of the details between the different points we are interested in traveling between, so a model is more useful because it ignores the details not relevant to the questions being investigated.

Although a theory is not a complete and realistic description of the real world, a good theory should incorporate enough data to simulate real life. That is, it should provide some explanation for past experiences and permit reasonably accurate predictions of the future. When you evaluate a new theory, ask yourself:

- Does this theory explain what has been observed?
- Does it provide a better basis for prediction than other theories?

There is a story regarding the classroom interaction of an old and wise economics professor and one of his Ph D students that is relevant to the points on theory we are seeking to make here. The professor was lecturing intently on some esoteric microeconomic theory in the middle of which the student dared to interrupt, "But, professor, in the real world . . ." At that point the good professor quickly cut the student off, only to insist in earnest, "Mr. Griswold, the real world is a special case and we therefore need not consider it!" There is obvious humor in the professor's retort (we heard you snicker), but there is also a good measure of widely unrecognized wisdom in what he said. The real world as it exists right now – as you are reading these words – is indeed a *special case*, with the enormous array of details in it never to be repeated exactly as they are. Similarly, the real world of tomorrow and all following tomorrows will be *special cases*. What we need is some means – some theory (or theories) – that has lasting value to the sequences of special-case real worlds that we will confront every day in the future. Theory helps us generate insights that transcend the special cases that will quickly fade into history. That is why the professor stressed theory in his lecture, not the details of everyday life. That is something of what Professor Knight meant when he noted that students often have to unlearn a lot, not the least of which is that real-world details of business life supersede the importance of theory in understanding the world about us.

Microeconomics and macroeconomics

The discipline of economics is divided into two main parts that are typically covered in two different MBA courses – microeconomics and macroeconomics.[3]

Microeconomics

When economists measure, explain, and predict the demand for specific products such as bicycles and PDAs, they are dealing with microeconomics. This book will deal almost exclusively with microeconomic theory, policy implications, and applications inside firms.

Questions of interest to microeconomists include:

- What determines the price of particular goods and services?
- What determines the output of particular firms and industries?
- What determines the wages workers receive? The interest rates lenders receive? The profits businesses receive?
- How do government policies – such as minimum-wage laws, price controls, tariffs, and excise taxes – affect the price and output levels of individual markets?
- Why do incentives matter inside firms and how can economic theory be used to properly structure a firm's incentives to increase worker productivity and firm profitability?
- How do literally millions of people, each pursuing her own interests with little information on or interest in what others are doing, coordinate their decisions to be consistent with each other, and so serve to promote the general interest?

[3] Economic thinking is often divided into two categories – positive and normative. *Positive economics* is that branch of economic inquiry that is concerned with the world *as it is* rather than as it should be. It deals only with the consequences of changes in economic conditions or policies. A positive economist suspends questions of values when dealing with issues such as crime or minimum wage laws. The object is to predict the effect of changes in the criminal code or the minimum wage rate – not to evaluate the fairness of such changes. *Normative economics* is that branch of economic inquiry that deals with value judgments – with what prices, production levels, incomes, and government policies *ought* to be. A normative economist does not shrink from the question of what the minimum wage rate ought to be. To arrive at an answer, the economist weighs the results of various minimum wage rates on the groups affected by them – the unemployed, employers, taxpayers, and so on. Then, on the basis of value judgments of the relative need or merit of each group, the normative economist recommends a specific minimum wage rate. Of course, values differ from one person to the next. In the analytical jump from recognizing the alternatives to prescribing a solution, scientific thinking gives way to ethical judgment.

These questions are relevant to the performance of the entire economy, but they are also questions that concern the managers of individual firms. Decisions on what goods and services to produce, how to produce them, what prices to sell them for, and how much to pay employees are obviously important to the profitability – and, indeed, viability – of firms.

Unfortunately, microeconomic theory is commonly presented in terms of abstract diagrams and mathematical models with, at best, feeble attempts to relate the concepts to real-world institutions. For example, microeconomics, as commonly presented, assumes that the firm is a single decision maker that:

(1) Buys inputs in markets at prices determined by the impersonal forces of demand and supply
(2) Transforms the least-cost combination of those inputs into an output in accordance with a *given* production function
(3) Given the demand curve for the output, produces the profit maximizing amount of output.

Unfortunately, the firm in a traditional microeconomics course is so general that it is largely useless at shedding light on the day-to-day problems faced by people attempting to actually manage a firm.

The competitiveness of a firm is determined by the decisions its managers make on:

(1) How best to compensate employees (commonly considered a concern of personnel management)
(2) The best mix of debt versus equity financing (commonly considered a concern of financial management)
(3) How best to distribute the product (commonly considered a concern of marketing management)
(4) Whether to purchase a productive input from an outside supplier or expand the firm through vertical integration by producing the input in-house (commonly considered a concern of purchasing and organizational management).

As suggested by the comments in parentheses, these decisions are traditionally examined in completely different courses (taught in completely different academic departments) as ways to address completely different problems. But all of these decisions can be usefully analyzed in terms of solving a pervasive problem – i.e. providing incentives that harmonize the interests of those who work for, invest in, manage, and supply inputs to a firm. Microeconomics has a lot to say about this problem, as we shall see.

In many respects, the business firm faces the same problem faced by the overall economy. In both cases, success depends on somehow motivating a large number of people to take action that promotes the general interest of all when those people have:

(1) Widely different abilities and interests
(2) Little concern for the interests of others
(3) Limited knowledge on how to serve the interests of others, even if they were concerned with doing so.

By keeping this problem in mind when examining the structures, strategies, practices, and procedures of real business firms, and applying the insights provided by the economic way of thinking, we can, and will, take a giant step toward a better understanding of business management.

Macroeconomics

Macroeconomics is the study of the national economy as a whole or of its major components. It deals with the "big picture," not the details, of the nation's economic activity.

Economists also study broad **macroeconomic** subdivisions of the economy, such as the total output of all firms that produce goods and services. Instead of concentrating on how many bicycles or PDAs are sold, macroeconomists watch how many goods and services consumers purchase in total or how much money all producers spend on new plants and equipment. Typical macroeconomic questions include:

- What determines the general price level? The rate of inflation?
- What determines national income and production levels?
- What determines national employment and unemployment levels?
- What effects do government monetary and budgetary policies have on the general price, income, production, employment, and unemployment levels?

These and similar questions are of more than academic interest. The theories that have been developed to answer them can be applied to problems and issues of the real world. They clearly have application to business, given that firm sales are often affected by "macro variables" such as national income and the inflation rate. However, we hasten to repeat that this book and course are devoted primarily to "microeconomic" theory and applications. We make microeconomics our focus because it is generally viewed as being better grounded and more relevant to the interests of MBA students than macroeconomic theory. Besides, we are firmly convinced that an understanding of the "macroeconomy" is necessarily dependent on an understanding of the "microeconomy."

Private property rights and the Prisoner's Dilemma game

Property rights pertain to the permissible use of resources, goods, and services; they define the limits of social behavior – what can and cannot be done by individuals in society. They also specify whether resources, goods, and services are to be used privately or collectively by the state or some smaller group.

In microeconomics, we start with the proposition that all actions are constrained by the fact of *scarcity*. Private "property rights" are one of the institutional mechanisms people have devised to help alleviate the pressing constraints of scarcity, which is why we take them up at this early stage in the course. **Property rights** are a social phenomenon; they arise out of the necessity for individuals to "get along" within a social space in which all wish to move and interact.

Where individuals are isolated from one another by natural barriers or are located where goods and resources are extremely abundant, property rights have no meaning. In the world of Robinson Crusoe, shipwrecked alone on an island, property rights were inconsequential. His behavior was restricted by the resources found on the island, the tools he was able to take from the ship, and his own ingenuity. He had a problem of efficiently allocating his time within these constraints – procuring food, building shelter, and plotting his escape; however, the notion of "property" did not restrict his behavior – it was not a barrier to what he could do. He was able to take from the shipwreck, with impunity, stores that he thought would be most useful to his purposes.[4]

After the arrival of Friday, the native whom Robinson Crusoe saved from cannibals, a problem of restricting and ordering interpersonal behavior immediately emerged. The problem was particularly acute for Crusoe because Friday, prior to coming to Tibago, was himself a cannibal. (Each had to clearly establish property rights to his body.) The system that they worked out was a simple one, not markedly different from that between Crusoe and "Dog" (the name Crusoe gave his dog). Crusoe essentially owned everything. Their relationship was that of master and servant, Crusoe dictating to Friday how the property was to be used.

In common speech, we frequently speak of someone "owning" this land, that house, or these bonds. This conventional style is undoubtedly economical from the viewpoint of quick communications, but it masks the variety and complexity of the ownership relationship. What is owned are *rights* to *use* resources, including one's body and mind, and these rights are always circumscribed,

[4] The absence of human beings also affected his idea of what was useful. Crusoe, in going through the ship, came across a coffer of gold and silver coins: "Thou art not worth to me, no, not taking off the ground; one of these knives is worth all this heap [of gold]." At first, he evaluated the cost of taking the coins in terms of what he could take in their place and decided to leave them. But on second thought, perhaps taking into consideration the probability of being rescued, he took the coins with him! (See *Robinson Crusoe*, by Daniel Defoe.)

often by prohibition of certain actions. To "own land" usually means to have the right to till (or not to till) the soil, to mine the soil, to *offer* those rights for sale, etc. but not to have the right to throw soil at a passer-by, to use it to change the course of a stream, or to force someone to buy it. What are owned are *socially recognized rights of action* (Alchian and Demsetz 1973).

Property rights are not necessarily distributed equally, meaning that people do not always have the same rights to use the same resources. Students may have the right to use their voices (i.e. a resource) to speak with friends in casual conversation in the hallways of classroom buildings, but they do not, generally speaking, have the right to disrupt an organizational behavior class with a harangue on their political views. In other words, property rights can be recast in terms of the *behavioral rules,* which effectively limit and restrict our behavior. Behavioral rules determine what rights we have with regard to the use of resources, goods, and services. The rights we have may be the product of the legislative process and may be enforced by a third party, usually the third party is the government – or, more properly, the agents of government. In this case, property rights emerge from legislation.

Private property rights and the market

In the private market economy people are permitted to initiate trades with one another. Indeed, when people trade, they are actually trading "rights" to goods and services or to do certain things. For example, when a person buys a house in the market, she is actually buying the right to live in the house under certain conditions – as long as she does not disturb others, for example. This market economy is predicated upon establishing patterns of *private* property rights; those patterns have legitimacy because of enforcement by government – and, perhaps just as important, because of certain social norms regarding the limits of individual behavior that are commonly accepted, observed, and self-enforced (with locks and alarm systems, for example). Without recognized property rights there would be nothing to trade – no market.

How dependent are markets on government enforcement for the protection and legitimacy of private property rights? Our answer must of necessity be somewhat speculative. We know that markets existed in the "Old West" when *formally* instituted governments were nonexistent. Further, it is highly improbable that any government can be so pervasive in the affairs of people that it can be the arbiter of all private rights. Cases in which disputes over property rights within a neighborhood are settled by association councils are relatively rare, and the disputes that end up at police headquarters are rarer still. Most conflicts over property rights are resolved at a local level, between two people, and many potential disputes do not even arise because of generally accepted behavioral limits.

Finally, the concept of property rights helps make clear the relationship between the public and private sectors of the economy – that is, between that section of the economy organized by collective action through government and that section which is organized through the actions of independent individuals. When government regulates aspects of the market, it redefines behavioral limits (in the sense that people can no longer do what they once could) and can be thought of as realigning the property rights between the private and public spheres. When the government imposes price ceilings on goods and services (as it does with rent controls), or price floors (as it does with minimum wage legislation and agricultural price support programs), it is redefining the rights that sellers have with regard to the property they sell. One of the purposes of economics is to analyze the effect that such realignment of property rights has on the efficiency of production.

The emergence of private property rights

In an idealized world in which people are fully considerate of each other's feelings and adjust and readjust their behavior to that of others without recourse to anything resembling a dividing line between "mine" and "thine," property rights are likely no more necessary than they were for Robinson Crusoe alone on Tibago. But in the world as it now exists, there is the potential for conflict. Conflict, or the potential for conflict, can be alleviated by the development of property rights, held communally, by the state, or by private individuals. These rights can be established in ways that are similar but which can be conceptually distinguished: (1) *voluntary* acceptance of behavioral norms with no third-party enforcer, such as the police and courts, and (2) the specification of rights in a legally binding "social contract," meaning that a third-party enforcer is established. Most of what we say for the remainder of this chapter applies to both modes of establishing rights. However, for reasons developed later in the book, the establishment of rights through voluntary acceptance of behavioral norms, although important in itself, has distinct limitations, especially in relation to size of the group (with growth in the group's size undermining the behavior norms).

To develop the analysis in the simplest terms possible, consider a model of two people, Fred and Harry, who live alone on an island. They have, at the start, no behavioral rules or anything else that "naturally" divides their spheres of interest – that is, they have nothing that resembles property rights. Further, being rational, they are assumed to want more than they have or can produce by themselves. Their social order is essentially anarchic. Each has two fundamental options for increasing his welfare: He can use his labor and other resources to produce goods and services or he can steal from his fellow man. With no social or ethical barriers restricting their behavior, they should be expected to allocate their resources between these options in the most productive way. This may mean that each should steal from the other as long as more is gained that way than through the production of goods and services.

If Fred and Harry find stealing a reasonable course to take, each will have to divert resources into protecting that which he has produced (*or* stolen). Presumably, their attacks and counterattacks will lead them toward a social equilibrium in which each is applying resources to predation and defense and neither finds any further movement of resources into those lines of activity profitable (Bush 1972, 5–8). This is not an equilibrium in the sense that the state of affairs is a desirable or stable one; in fact, it may be characterized as a "Hobbesean jungle" in which "every man is Enemy to every man" (Hobbes 1968, first published in 1651).

In an economic sense, resources diverted into predatory and defensive behavior are wasted; they are taken away from productive processes. If these resources are applied to production, total production can rise, and both Fred and Harry can be better off – both can have more than if they try to steal from each other. It is only through winding up in a state of anarchy, or seeing the potential for ending up there, that they must question the rationality of continued plundering and unrestricted behavior; and it is because of the prospects of individual improvement that there exists a potential for a "social contract" that spells out legally defined property rights. Through a social contract they may agree to place restrictions on their own behavior, but they will do away with the relatively more costly restraints that, through predation and required defense, each imposes on the other. The fear of being attacked on the streets at night can be far more confining than laws that restrict people from attacking one another. This is what John Locke meant when he wrote, "The end of law is not to abolish or restrain but to preserve and enlarge freedom" (Locke 1690, 23).

Once the benefits from the social contract are recognized, there *may* still be, as in the case of voluntary behavioral norms, an incentive for Fred or Harry to chisel on the contract. Fred may find that although he is "better off" materially by agreeing to property rights than he is by remaining in a state of anarchy, he may be even "better off" by violating the agreed-upon rights of the other. Through stealing, or in other ways violating Harry's rights, Fred can redistribute the total wealth of the community toward himself.

Table 1.1 *The games Fred and Harry can play with property rights*

	Harry respects Fred's rights		Harry violates Fred's rights	
	Cell 1		Cell 2	
Fred respects Harry's rights	Fred	Harry	Fred	Harry
	15 utils	10 utils	8 utils	16 utils
	Cell 3		Cell 4	
Fred violates Harry's rights	Fred	Harry	Fred	Harry
	18 utils	5 utils	10 utils	7 utils

The payoffs (measured in "util" terms) from Fred and/or Harry either respecting or violating the other's rights are indicated in the four cells of the matrix. Each has an incentive to violate the other's rights. If they do violate each other's rights, they will end up in cell 4, the worst of all possible states for both of them. The productivity of the "social contract" can be measured by the increase in Fred and Harry's utility resulting from their moving from cell 4, the "state of nature," to cell 1, a state in which a social contract is agreed upon.

To illustrate, consider table 1.1, which illustrates the kind of "games" – involving actions and reactions of individual players – we and other economists use to draw out strategies people will (or should) use to deal with given situations. Table 1.1 contains a chart or matrix of Fred and Harry's utility (or satisfaction) levels if either respects or fails to respect the rights established for each as a part of the contract. (The actual utility levels are hypothetical, but serve the purpose of illustrating a basic point.) There are four cells in the matrix, representing the four combinations of actions that Fred and Harry can take. They can both respect the agreed-upon rights of the other (cell 1), or they can both violate each other's rights (cell 4). Alternatively, Harry can respect Fred's rights while Fred violates Harry's rights (cell 3), or vice versa (cell 2).

Clearly, by the utility levels indicated in cells 1 and 4, Fred and Harry are both better off by respecting each other's rights than by violating them. However, if Harry respects Fred's rights and Fred fails to reciprocate, Fred has a utility level of 18 utils, which is greater than he will receive in cell 1 – that is, by going along with Harry and respecting his rights. Harry is similarly better off if he violates Fred's rights while Fred respects Harry's rights: Harry has a utility level of 16, whereas he will have a utility level of 10 utils if he and Fred respect each other's rights. The lesson to be learned is that: Inherent in an agreement over property rights is the possibility for each person to gain by violating the rights of the other. If both follow this course, they both will end up in cell 4 – that is, back in the state of anarchy.

There are two reasons why this may happen. First, as we stated above, both Fred and Harry may violate each other's rights in order to improve their own positions; the action may be strictly *offensive.* By the same token, each must consider what the other will do. Neither would want to be caught upholding the agreement while the other one violates it. If Fred thinks that Harry may violate his rights, Fred may follow suit and violate Harry's rights: he will be better off in cell 4, i.e. anarchy, than in cell 2. Fred and Harry can wind up in anarchy for purely *defensive* reasons.

Many wars and battles, at both the street and international levels, have been fought because one party was afraid that the other would attack first in order to get the upper hand. The same problem is basically involved in our analysis of the fragile nature of Fred and Harry's social contract. The problem of contract violation can grow as the community grows in number, because violations by individual persons are more difficult (more costly) to detect.

Prisoner's Dilemma games

Fred and Harry's situation is a classic example of what social scientists call a "Prisoner's Dilemma." This dilemma represents a common problem in achieving cooperation in any number of social settings, not the least of which is business, and a topic that will come up repeatedly in this book.

The name "Prisoner's Dilemma" comes from a standard technique of interrogation employed by police to obtain confessions from two or more suspected partners to a crime. If the method is used, the suspects are taken to different rooms for questioning, and each is offered a lighter sentence if he confesses. But each will also be warned that if the other suspect confesses and he does not, his sentence will be more stringent. The suspect has to try to figure out, without the benefit of communication, how the other will stand up to that kind of pressure. Each may worry that the other will confess and may confess because he cannot trust his partner not to take the easy way out. The problem for the individual suspect becomes more complicated as the number of captured partners to the crime increases. There are more people whom he must count on to hold up under the pressure which he knows is being brought to bear. He must also consider the fact that the others may confess because they cannot count on all their partners to hold under the pressure.

Prisoner's Dilemma solutions: enforcement and trade

To prevent violations of both an offensive and of a defensive nature, a community may agree to the establishment of a police, court, and penal system to

Table 1.2 *Relative satisfaction from marginal units consumed*

	Coconut (utils)	Papaya (utils)
Fred	10	15
Harry	90	30

protect the rights specified in the social contract. The system may be costly, but the drain on its total wealth may be smaller than if it reverts back to anarchy, in which case resources will be diverted into predatory and defensive behavior. The costs associated with making the contract and enforcing it will determine just how extensive the contract will be, and this matter will be considered later in the book

The social contract, which defines property rights, establishes only the limits of permissible behavior; it does not mean that Fred and Harry will be satisfied with the exact combination of property rights they have been given through the contract. To the degree that some other combination or distribution of the existing property held by Fred and Harry will give them both more satisfaction, trades are not only possible, but likely, because the trades can be mutually beneficial. Mutually beneficial exchanges can be expected to emerge.

For example, suppose that the only goods on Fred and Harry's island are coconuts and papayas. The social contract specifies the division of the fruits between them. We need not concern ourselves with the total number of the fruit each has; we need only indicate the relative satisfaction that Fred and Harry receive from the marginal units. Suppose the marginal utilities in table 1.2 represent the satisfaction they received from the last coconut and papaya in their possession.

In table 1.2, Fred receives more utility from the last papaya (15 utils) than from the last coconut (10 utils). He would be on a higher level of utility if he could trade a coconut for a papaya. He would lose 10 utils from the coconut but would more than regain that with the additional papaya. On the other hand, Harry receives more utility from the last coconut than from the last papaya. He would gladly give up a papaya for a coconut; he would be 60 utils of satisfaction better off (90 minus 30) than if he did not engage in the exchange. The two should continue to exchange *rights* to the coconuts and papayas until one or both of them can no longer gain via trade.

In this example, we are not concerned with production of coconuts and papayas; we are concerned merely with the benefits from trade resulting from the initial allotments of the fruits. The trades are comparable to those that took place in the POW camps as described by R.A. Radford at the start of the book.

Table 1.3 *Specializing in production and trade*

	Coconut production	Papaya production
Fred	4	8
Harry	6	24

If the social contract allocates to Fred and Harry rights to *produce* the fruit, we can also demonstrate that both can be better off through specializing in their production and trading with each other. Consider the information in table 1.3; it indicates how many coconuts or papayas Fred and Harry can produce with, say, one hour of labor.

In 1 hour of labor Fred can produce either 4 coconuts or 8 papayas; Harry can produce either 6 coconuts or 24 papayas. Even though Harry is more productive in both lines of work – and thus has an *absolute advantage* in both goods – we can show that they both can gain by specializing and trading with each other. This is because each has a *comparative advantage* in one good. That is, each can produce one good at a relatively lower cost than the other person can.

If Fred produces 4 coconuts, he cannot use that hour of time to produce the 8 papayas. In other words, the cost of the 4 coconuts is 8 papayas, or, which amounts to the same thing, the cost of 1 coconut is 2 papayas. Fred would be better off if he could trade 1 coconut for *more than* 2 papayas, because that is what he has to give up in order to produce the coconut. To determine whether there is a basis for trade, we must explore the cost of coconuts and papayas to Harry. We note that the cost of 1 coconut to Harry is 4 papayas; this is because he has to give up 24 papayas to produce 6 coconuts. If Harry could give up fewer than 4 papayas for a coconut, he would be better off. He could produce the 4 papayas; and if he has to give up fewer than that for a coconut, he will have papayas left over to eat, which he would not have had without the opportunity to trade.

To summarize: Fred would be better off if he could get more than 2 papayas for a coconut; Harry would be better off if he could give up fewer than 4 papayas for a coconut. If, for example, they agree to trade at the exchange rate of 1 coconut for 3 papayas, both would be better off. Fred will produce a coconut, giving up 2 papayas, but he can get 3 papayas for the coconut. Hence, he is better off. Harry can produce 4 papayas, giving up 1 coconut, and trade 3 of the papayas for a coconut. He has the same number of coconuts, but has an additional papaya. Harry is better off.

Although relatively simple, the above example of *exchange* is one of economists' most important contributions to discussions of social interaction.

So many people seem to think that when people trade, one person must gain at the expense of another. If people in the United States trade with people in Japan, someone must be made worse off in the process, or so the argument goes. We will deal with such arguments in more detail in chapter 15; for now, we wish to emphasize that we have demonstrated that, through trade, both Harry and Fred are better off. This was demonstrated even though we postulated that Harry was more efficient than Fred in the production of both fruits!

Communal property rights

To many, the ideal state of affairs may appear to be one in which everyone has the right to use all resources, goods, and services and in which no one (not even the state) has the right to exclude anyone else from their use. We may designate such rights as "communal rights." Many rights to scarce property have been and still are allocated in this way. Rights to the use of a university's facilities are held communally by the students. No one admitted to the university has the right to keep you off campus paths or lawns or from using the library according to certain rules and regulations. (Such rules and regulations form the boundaries, much as if they were natural, within which the rights are truly communal.) The rights to city parks, sidewalks, and streets are held communally. Before the United States was settled, many Indian tribes held communal rights to hunting grounds: that is, at least within the tribe's territory, no one had the right to exclude anyone else from hunting on the land. During most of the first half of the nineteenth century, the rights to graze cattle on the prairies of the western United States were held communally; anyone who wanted to let his cattle loose on the plains could do so. Granted, the US government held by law the right to exclude people from the plains; but as long as it did not exercise that right, the land rights were communal. The same can be said for all other resources whose "owner" does not exercise the right to exclude them.

Communal property rights can be employed with tolerably efficient results so long as one of two conditions holds:

1. There is more of the resource than can be effectively used for all intended purposes (in other words, there is no cost to its use) or
2. People within the community fully account for the effects that their own use of the resources has on others.

Without the presence of one of these conditions, the resources will tend to be "overused."

The late biologist Garrett Hardin (1968) characterized the problem of overused (and abused) communal resources as "the tragedy of the commons" and considered why a pasture might be overgrazed by cattle if ranchers whose access to the pasture were unimpeded by property rights. In deciding on how many cattle to add, each cattleman will likely be compelled to reason that the addition of his cattle – and his cattle alone – to the pasture will make no difference to the amount of feed available to the cattle of other "herdsmen." One person's cattle just don't eat that much, given the size of the pasture. The result is that the cattlemen will collectively face an outcome – a "tragedy" in the form of overly thin cattle – that none of them would want:

> Therein is the tragedy. Each man is locked into a system that compels him to increase his herd without limit – in a world that is limited. Ruin is the destination toward which all men rush, each pursuing his own best interest in a society that believes in the freedom of the commons. Freedom in the commons brings ruin to all. (Hardin 1968)

The prospect of the emergence of a "tragedy" under communal ownership has been a very powerful argument for conversion of communal rights to *private property rights*, which is an institutional setting under which the owners simultaneously have both usage and exclusion rights.[5]

Under communal ownership, if the resource is not presently being used by someone else, no one can be excluded from the use of it. Consequently, once in use, the resource becomes, for that period of time, the private property of the user. The people who drive their cars onto the freeway take up space on the road that is not in use; no one else (they hope!) can then use that space at the same time. Unless the drivers violate the rules of the road, they cannot be excluded from that space; and if they are rational, they will continue to use the resource until their cost of a little additional use equals their benefits from that additional use. They may consider most of the costs involved in their use of the road, but one that they may overlook, especially as it applies to themselves personally, is that their space may have had some *alternative use*: that is, by others. Their presence also increases highway congestion and the discomfort of the other drivers (potentially nontrivial costs). As a result, they may overextend the use of their resource, meaning that they continue to drive as long as the additional benefits *they*, themselves, get from driving additional miles is greater than the additional cost.

The state can make the driver consider the social costs of driving in an indirect way by imposing a tax on the driver's use of the road, causing less driving, and fewer costs that drivers impose on others. This is called "internalizing the social

[5] For extended discussions of how the "tragedy of the commons" has formed the foundation of the property-rights literature, see Bethel (1998). The important point in the "tragedy of the commons" is that the externalities of individual actions have to be managed, or have to be internalized in some way, and private property is only one way to do the managing, as recognized by Gordon (1954), before Hardin wrote his seminal article, and Scott (1955).

cost." Once the state does this – and it is commonly done through gasoline taxes and/or tolls – the rights to the freeway are no longer "communal"; the rights have been effectively attenuated by the state.

There are two additional ways that social costs can be internalized. First, people can be considerate of others and account for the social cost in their behavior. Second, the right to the road can be turned into *private property*, meaning that individuals are given the right to exclude others from the use of the resource (i.e. the road). This may seem to be a totally undesirable turn of events unless we recognize that private owners can then charge for the use of the road: they can sell "use rights," in which case the marginal cost of driving will rise, resulting in an increase in the cost that individual drivers incur.

The prime difference between this private ownership and government taxation is that, with private ownership, the revenues collected go into the coffers of individuals instead of to the state; this is either "good" or "bad," depending upon your attitude toward government vs. private uses of the funds. Furthermore, under private ownership and without viable competitors (and we have an example in which competition *may* not be practical), the owners may attempt to charge an amount that is greater than the social costs in table 1.1; they may attempt, in the jargon of economists, to acquire **monopoly** *profits*, and in so doing cause an *underuse* of the road.[6]

A **monopoly** (see chapter 11) is a single seller of a good or service that can charge higher prices and reap greater profits than if it had to worry about the actions of other competitors.

For that matter, the state-imposed taxes may be greater than the social costs. The state may also act like a monopolist. State agencies may not be permitted to make a "profit" as it is normally conceived, but this does not exclude the use of their revenues for improving salaries and the working conditions of state employees. Monopoly profits may be easy to see on the accounting statements of a firm but may be lost in bureaucratic waste or overexpenditures under state ownership. State ownership does not necessarily lead to waste, but it is a prospect, and one that only the naïve will ignore. More is said on this subject at various points in the book.

We have now considered the distinction between private and communal property. Several examples will enable us to amplify that distinction and to understand more clearly the limitations of communal property rights and the pervasive use of private property.

[6] To provide for competition and to prevent monopoly profits from emerging, private rights can be assigned to similar units of the same resource. Although this may not be practical in road construction, it is quite practical in the cattle business, for example. Many different people can own all the resources necessary for cattle production. If one tries to raise his price to achieve monopoly profits, the others can undercut him, forcing him to lower his price. As a general rule, competition requires the dispersion of property rights among different people and groups.

Pollution

Pollution can be described as a logical consequence of communal property rights to streams, rivers, air, etc. The state and federal governments, by right of eminent domain, have always held rights to these resources; but until very recently they have inadequately asserted their right to exclude people and firms from their use. As a result, the resources have been subject to communal use and to overuse, in the same sense as that discussed above.

By dumping waste into the rivers, people, firms, and local governments have been able to acquire ownership to portions of the communal resource – they use it and pollute it. Furthermore, because of the absence of exclusion, those people doing the polluting do not have to pay to draw the resource away from its alternative uses (such as pretty scenery) or to reimburse the people harmed by the pollution for the damage done. Under communal ownership, in which government does not exercise its control, the firm with smoke billowing from its stacks does not have to compensate the people who live around the plant for the eye irritation they experience or the extra number of times they have to paint their homes.

Pollution is often thought to be the product of antisocial behavior, as indeed it often is. Many who pollute simply do not care about what they do to others. However, much pollution results from the behavior of people who do *not* have devious motives. People may view their behavior as having an inconsequential effect on the environment. The person who throws a cigarette butt on the ground may reason that if this cigarette butt is the only one on the ground, it will not materially affect anyone's sensibilities, and in fact it may not. However, if everyone follows the same line of reasoning, the cigarette butts will accumulate and an eyesore will develop. Even then, there may be little incentive for people to stop throwing their butts on the ground. Again, a person may reason on the basis of the effects of his own individual action: "If I do not throw my butt on the ground here with all the others, will my behavior materially affect the environment quality, *given the fact that other butts are already there?*" This type of reasoning can lead to a very powerful argument for conversion of communal rights to private or state rights, with the implied power for someone to exclude some or all of this kind of use.

Fur trade

According to Harold Demsetz, the hunting grounds of the Indian tribes of the Labrador Peninsula were held in common until the emergence of the fur trade there (Demsetz 1964). The Indians could hunt as they wished without being excluded by other members of their tribe. Presumably, given the cost of hunting and the limited demand for meat, there was no inclination to "overhunt" – that is, they hunted until there was an adverse effect on the stock of animals in the area.

However, when fur trading commenced and the Indians hunted animals for their skins, the demand and therefore the price of animal skins increased. This provided an incentive for the Indians to hunt beyond their demand for meat. Under communal ownership, when a beaver was killed, an Indian hunter did not have to consider the effects that his action had on the ability of the other hunters to trap and hunt. Each hunter, through his own efforts, imposed a cost on the others; when a beaver was killed by one hunter, the task of finding beavers was made more difficult for the other hunters. The cost may be construed as a *social cost*, much like the congestion a driver can impose upon the other drivers around. Furthermore, under a communal rights structure, there was little incentive for hunters to avoid trapping or incurring the costs of increasing the stock of animals. If a hunter refrained from killing a beaver, perhaps someone else would kill it. In addition, if one person tried to increase the stock of animals, perhaps many others would benefit from his efforts in terms of more animals for them to kill. There was, in other words, no assurance that the Indian who built up the stock of animals would reap the benefits. (For the same reason, we doubt that many buildings would be built if the developers could not reap the benefits of their investment or if what they built were to be *communal* property upon completion.) The Indians' solution to the problem of overkill was to assign private property rights to portions of the hunting grounds. Each individual, by virtue of his right to exclude others, had an incentive to control his own take from the land and to take measures, much as ranchers do, to increase the potential stock of furs.

Whales

Whales have been hunted for centuries, but there was never a problem with their possible extinction until the nineteenth and twentieth. Whales have always been more or less communal property. However, because people in former centuries did not have the technology we now have to kill and slaughter whales far out at sea, the sheer cost of hunting them prevented men from exceeding the whales' reproductive capacity. Theoretically, the problem could be solved by applying the same solution to the whale overkill as the Indians applied in their hunting grounds: establish private property rights. However, whales present a special problem. The annual migrations of whales can take them through 6,000 miles of ocean. Establishing and enforcing private property rights to such an expanse of ocean is an onerous task, even without the complications involved in securing agreement among several governments to respect those rights. These costs have, without doubt, been a major reason that whales remain communal property and why some species have been threatened with extinction.

Theft

The prevalence of theft can affect people's willingness to create, invest in, and enhance property. This is because theft reduces the rewards from property. The greater the prevalence of theft of property, the less willing people can be expected to invest in and build up their property. That rule is transparent in the bicycles people ride in Amsterdam, the Netherlands. While bikes are everywhere present, few bikes are less than thirty years old. Bikes without gears (or with no more than three gears) are common, and most show signs of wear. The reason is that bike theft is common. As residents of Amsterdam will freely admit, it simply doesn't pay to buy a modern bike. Indeed, parking a new bike on the sidestreets and alleys of Amsterdam is an invitation to thieves. The working rule among bike owners in Amsterdam is that the amount spent on bike locks should be greater than the amount spent than on a bike.

Perspective The Tragedy of the Anticommons

The *tragedy of the commons* is a powerful justification for the establishment of private property rights (or at least a case for managing a resource so that much of its value is not destroyed with overuse). But the argument for the establishment of property rights must be understood in its proper context. For the tragedy of the commons to be a potential threat, the resource itself must have a characteristic that land has, subject to use by different people for the same or different purposes. This means that the resource is subject to *rivalry* and must be *exhaustible,* much like the pasture in Garrett Hardin's discussion of the commons' problem noted earlier in the chapter. There is no reason for establishing property rights, giving owners rights of exclusion, when the resource is inexhaustible, because there can be no rivalry and the resource cannot be subject to overuse.

Numbers (1, 2, 3, etc.), letters (A, B, C, etc.), and musical notes (or marks on sheet music or sounds from instruments) need not be subject to property right assignment because they are inexhaustible in supply – anyone can use them without reducing the ability of others to use them – they are *nonrivalrous* in use. When these words were typed into a computer, the supply of letters available to everyone else in the world was not diminished. Granted, there is a case to be made for assigning property rights to a book, given that the published copies will be limited by the cost of their production, but the letters themselves from which the words (and paragraphs and arguments) were constructed remain as available as they ever were. Hence, there can be no potential for a "tragedy" of *overuse* in letters. Privatization in this case can lead to a greater tragedy, a monopoly of letters and words, which in turn can lead to the *underuse* of letters and words, which is another form of waste (or, in economists' jargon "resource misallocation"), dubbed the *tragedy of the anticommons* (Heller 1998).

This tragedy of the anticommons would be especially tragic if all letters and words were privately owned by one person or firm. The tragedy might even be more severe if individual letters or words were owned by different people or firms, because there could be enormous costs of people engaging in all the transactions required to make letters into words and words into published documents (which economists call "transaction costs," a topic to be taken up in detail in chapter 6). The assignment of private rights could, in other words, substitute one tragedy – *overuse* – for another – *underuse* – with no convincing argument that the rights assignment has on balance improved welfare.

The tragedy of the anticommons can also be encouraged by the requirement that users seek agreement on *usage rights* from several (or many) agents who control access to the resource. For example, Michael Heller noticed the anticommons tragedy as it played out in the streets of Moscow after the fall of the Soviet Union. The streets were lined with carts of goods outside perfectly good multi-story buildings that stood empty. The buildings remained unused because vendors had to get permission to use the buildings from several agencies, each of which had exclusion rights but not usage rights. The vendors obviously found it less costly to set up their carts and kiosks than to incur the costs involved in obtaining the required use rights (Heller 1998). James Buchanan observed a similar case of the anticommons tragedy in Italy. An entrepreneur in Sardinia was unable to develop a seaside hunting preserve and resort because he was required to get permits from the tourist board, the hotel restaurant agency, and the public wildlife protection agency (as Buchanan reports in Buchanan and Yoon 2000).[7]

What these examples highlight is a point that has been stressed by Lawrence Lessig, a law professor who argues that, as in all other things, we must strive for balance in the privatization process (Lessig 2001). Lessig stresses that the logic underlying the tragedy of the commons has been so widely accepted that analysts no longer harbor the requisite appreciation for having at least *some* resources – especially those that are nonrivalrous in nature – remain under common ownership, to be exploited with a high degree of freedom by all without the need to get the permission of the property owners (especially multiple owners). As a consequence, we may be suffering a growing tragedy of the anticommons, Lessig argues without noticing the damage from underusage that is developing, especially in the growth of ideas and technology.

Lessig points out how in movie scenes almost everything that is used – pictures on the wall, distinctive chairs and couches, computers, place settings, and images of identifiable bystanders, not to mention the images and voices of the actors and actresses in lead and supporting roles – is owned by someone, which means that usage rights from all the various owners must be secured before the movie can be shot. If permission is not secured before the scene is shot, each owner can be expected to bargain strategically (while making a threat of filing a lawsuit), trying to secure a price for his or her agreement that extracts the full value of the scene. This means, of course, that the scene might not be used, even though it is "in the can." To prevent such strategic bargaining, and wastage, the producers can bargain for the rights prior to filming. However, the potential for an anticommons tragedy in the form of fewer films produced still exists, given the multiple resource owners who must give their consent. Again, the transaction costs involved can result in "too few" films being produced.

Similarly, patents (and copyrights) can give rise to a tragedy of the anticommons, especially when products incorporate any number of patented parts held by different owners. The various owners of patented parts to, say, an engine can hike development costs as they each bargain strategically

[7] Buchanan and his George Mason University colleague Yong Yoon have been able to show (with a formal mathematical model) that with more than one person with exclusion rights, the resource will be less utilized than would be the case under a single owner/monopoly. They found this to be the case so long as each person with exclusion rights seeks to maximize his or her gain, subject to what the other person does. That is, multiple exclusion rights result in underutilization of the resource so long as the excluders don't work together with their joint welfare in mind (Buchanan and Yoon 2000).

and seek monopoly profits, in the process increasing transaction costs and the prices of engines, and reducing the number of engines produced and sold.

Lessig, of course, recognizes that patents (and copyrights) are devices that have been developed to provide economic incentives for creativity. However, the incentive for creativity does not need to be unlimited, a fact that has historically been recognized in patent and copyright law by the limited life of patents. Lessig points out that we have extended the life of patents (and copyrights) greatly since the 1950s. These extensions might indeed be required, given the growth in development costs for many products. At the same time, the extensions may have been grounded in special interest politics, not economics, which can imply that the extensions have unnecessarily increased the monopoly rents that patent holders have realized, meaning that the economic reward for many patents exceeds the reward required for creating the products. The extensions, Lessig argues, have given rise to an extended tragedy of the anticommons in the form of too few technological developments in the commons, available for exploitation at no cost by other creative people.

Since patents (and copyrights) embody ideas that are by their nature nonrivalrous, Lessig is concerned about how the continued privatization of ideas will stifle future intellectual developments. We do need some "system of control to *assure the resource is created*" (2001, 97, italics in the original), Lessig writes, which explains the patent and copyright system that enables developers to recover their development costs but that is also imperfect, assuring that not all of the value of any development is appropriated by the developer: "Intellectual property does this by giving the producers a limited exclusive right over their intellectual property... A 'sufficient return,' however, is not perfect control . . . Instead some of the benefits ought to be reserved for the public, in common." Lessig concludes:

> In essence, the changes in the environment of the Internet that we are observing now alter the balance between control and freedom on the Net. The tilt of these changes is pronounced: control is increasing. And while one cannot say in the abstract that increased control is a mistake, it is clear that we are expanding this control with no sense of what is lost. The shift is not occurring with the idea of a balance in mind. Instead, the shift proceeds as if control were the only value. (2001, 97)

Lessig charts the multiple ways that patent and copyright laws have been changed, with the effect being that transaction costs for the development of new ideas and products have been increased.

PART II ORGANIZATIONAL ECONOMICS AND MANAGEMENT

How incentives count in business

We noted above that much of this book and course is concerned with the problem of overcoming a basic condition of life: *scarcity*. Firms are an integral means by which the pressures of scarcity are partially relieved for all those people who either own or work for firms. However, in order to get people involved in firms to work diligently for their firms, they must have some reason or purpose – some *incentive* – to do that which they are supposed to do.

Within the Part II sections of this book that we have titled "Organizational economics and management," we seek to apply the economic principles developed in Part I of the chapter to problems that all MBA students will confront in their "real-world" careers, those of getting incentives within firms right. Doing that is no easy assignment for managers, mainly because incentives are powerful – both when they are wrong as well as when they are right, as we shall see by taking up an array of incentive issues that range from how workers' compensation can affect firm output to how a firm's finances (debt and equity) can affect management risk taking and, hence, firm profitability.[8]

Tying pay to performance

Of course, incentives have been found to be important for more mundane, everyday business reasons. Tying compensation to some objective measure of firm performance can cause the affected workers' productivity to rise substantially. This is because tying pay to performance is a way of giving workers *rights* – a form of property rights – to a portion of the output they produce.

In addition, tying pay to performance can change the type of workers who are attracted to the pay-for-performance jobs. As might be expected, appropriately structured incentive pay can increase a firm's rate of return and stock price, as well as the income of the affected workers.

Productivity increases

When Safelite Auto Glass switched from paying its glass installers by the hour to paying them "piece rates," worker productivity went up by 44 percent, only

[8] Those MBA students that wish to go beyond the basics of the "organizational economics" discussed in this textbook are advised to consider reading (and digesting) three important books: Milgrom and Roberts (1992), P. Rubin (1990), and J. Roberts (2004).

half of which could be attributable to the motivational effect of the piece-rate pay system. The other half was attributable to the fact that Safelite started attracting people who were willing to work hard and began holding onto its more motivated and productive workers, with its less motivated and productive workers leaving the company (Lazear 2000).

One study of thousands of managers of large corporations found that adding a 10 percent bonus for good performance could be expected to add 0.3 to 0.9 percent to the companies' after-tax rate of return on stockholder investment. If managerial bonuses are tied to the market prices of the companies' stock, share prices can be expected to rise by 4–12 percent. The study also found that the greater the sensitivity of management pay to company performance, the better the performance.[9] Another study found that firms don't have to wait around for the incentives to have an impact on the firms' bottom line to get a jump in their stock prices; all they have to do is to *announce* that executives' compensation over the long haul is going to be more closely tied (through stock options or bonuses) to performance measures and the stock will, within days, go up several percentage points, increasing shareholder wealth by tens, if not hundreds, of millions of dollars (depending on firm size) (Brickley, Bhagat, and Lease 1985).

Naturally, if managers are paid just a straight salary, they have less reason to take on risky investments (Roberts 2004, chapter 4). Their potential gain from the higher rates of return associated with risky investments is uncertain and problematic (given that the rise in their future salary from performance may not be clear and direct), which is why they may shy away from risky investments (more so than they would if their pay were clearly tied, in part or in whole, to some measure of firm performance). Accordingly, it should surprise no one to learn that when managers are given bonuses based on performance, they tend to undertake riskier, higher-paying investments (Amihud and Lev 1981; Holmstrom 1979; Shavell 1979; Smith and Watts 1982). But, then, if the bonuses are based on some short-term goal – say, this year's earnings – instead of some longer-term goal – say, some level for the stock price – you can bet that managers will tend to sacrifice investments with higher longer-term payoffs for the smaller payoffs that are received within the performance period. The managers' time horizons can be lengthened by tying their compensation to the firm's stock value and then requiring that they hold the firm's stock until some later date – for example, retirement (Jensen and Meckling 1979).

[9] The study covered the pay of 16,000 managers from 250 large corporations over the 1982–6 period (Abowd 1990).

Although incentives have always mattered, they probably have never been more important to businesses interested in competing aggressively on a global scale. Greater global competition means that producers everywhere must meet the best production standards anywhere on the globe, which requires them to have the best incentive systems anywhere. Incentives will continue to grow in importance in business as the economy becomes more complex, more global, and more competitive. Although incentives are both positive and negative, when structured properly they can ensure that managers, workers, and consumers prosper.

The growing importance of incentives

Like it or not, business people will have to learn to think about incentives with the same rigor that they now contemplate their balance sheets and marketing plans. They will need to justify the incentive structures they devise, which means they will have to understand why they do what they do. High pay and so-called "golden parachutes" (or generous firing packages) for executives and stock options for workers will need to be used judiciously. They can't be employed just because they seem like a nice idea, or because everyone else is using them. Investors who find it easier and easier to move their investment funds anywhere in the world will be less inclined to allow their capital to be used for "nice ideas": Unless well thought out, "nice ideas" can spell wasted investments. The multitude of ways that incentives can matter in business makes a study of them mandatory – if managers want to get them right.

The Lincoln Electric case

Unless policies are carefully considered, *perverse incentives* can be an inadvertent consequence, mainly because people can be very creative in responding to policies. Lincoln Electric is known for achieving high productivity levels among its production workers by tying their pay to measures of how much they produce. But the company went too far. When it tied the pay of secretaries to "production," with counters installed on typewriters to measure how much was typed, the secretaries responded by spending their lunch hours typing useless pages of manuscript to increase their pay, which resulted in that incentive being quickly abandoned (Fast and Berg 1971; Roberts 2004, 42). In seeking to reduce the number of "bugs" in its programs, a software company began paying programmers to find and fix bugs. The goal was noble but the response wasn't: Programmers began creating bugs in order that they could find and fix them, with one programmer increasing his pay $1,700 through essentially fraudulent means. The company eliminated the incentive pay scheme within a week of its introduction (Adam 1995).

Lincoln Electric's experience brings us to a general rule that managers of all companies must keep in mind: Incentives almost always work, but they don't always work well or in the way that is expected (a fact that has led to harsh criticisms of even attempting to use incentives, punishments, or rewards[10]). Economic researchers in Israel have sought to help ten daycare centers in Haifa reduce the number of times parents picked up their children late (Gneezy and Rustichini 2000). For the first four weeks of their twenty-week research experiment, the researchers did not impose a fine for late pickups and observed that the daycare centers had an average of seven late pickups per week. After the fifth week, they imposed a fee of $3 per late pickup. Contrary to their presumption, late pickups jumped to an average of twenty per week per center. The late pickups could have increased for two reasons not considered by the researchers, according to Stephen Levitt and Stephen Dubner who report on the experiment in their best-selling economics book *Freakonomics*: First, the parents considered the $3 fee to be an approved and cheap form of added baby sitting. (Thus, a $20 late fee might have had the expected response, a curb in tardiness, because the fee would then be greater than the cost of babysitting found elsewhere.) Second, the daycare centers had probably lowered, on balance the true cost for tardiness: The money late fee took the place of the "psychic cost" associated with doing something considered "wrong," such as not picking up children on time (Levitt and Dubner 2005, 19–20, 23).

Mitsubishi Motors sought to increase the sales of its cars in 2003 through a promotional campaign dubbed "zero-zero-zero" – for zero down payment, zero interest, and zero car payments for the first twelve months after sale. According to one automobile industry journalist, "[A] hefty number [of car buyers] used this promotion to drive a new car without paying anything for a year, after which they let the car get repossessed," resulting in losses of hundreds of millions of dollars for the company (Ingrassia 2005).

Incentives and managed earnings

Of course, incentive systems can cause managers to manage their earnings. For example, when managers are paid on the basis of *annual* performance targets, research shows that they have been induced to advance the reporting of sales

[10] For criticisms of incentives, see Kohn (1993b) and Pearce (1987).

when they expect to be short of the targets. When they expect to more than make their targets, managers have moved sales to the first quarter of the next year on the grounds that there is no reason for them to "waste" sales (Oyer 1998; Horngren 1999, 937–8). The fact that so many executives at the now-defunct Enron and Worldcom held so much of their companies' stock can go a long way toward explaining the extensive accounting fraud at those companies. By "cooking the books," the managers were able to inflate the value of their stock holdings (Roberts 2004, 156–7), which carries a valuable lesson: Beware of tying managers' pay to performance measures that are easily manipulated (Baker 2000).

In the twenty-first century world economy, business incentives will become even more commonplace, and getting them right will be an even greater concern for managers.

The role of incentives in firm successes and failures

Why do some firms prosper while others fail? An easy answer is that some firms produce a better product or provide a better service. The fortunes of many fast-food restaurants have depended upon the quality of their burgers and the cleanliness of their rest rooms.

Some firms have failed not because they have done anything "wrong," but rather because they have not done as much "right" as their competitors. Many textile firms in the southeast United States have folded since the 1980s in spite of their substantial efforts to improve their productivity and increase quality. The failing firms closed their doors simply because they were not able meet the competition from lower-priced textile imports *and* from textiles produced by even more aggressive (and successful) domestic textile firms.[11]

Many firms have failed because they did not pay attention to their costs, or because their managers were not very smart in setting their firms' product and service strategies to meet the changes in their markets. In the two decades before the 9/11 catastrophe, several major airlines (and scores of smaller ones) folded their wings because their planes and personnel, set when their fares were regulated, were too expensive when fares were deregulated.

We agree that a lot of things are important to success in business, not the least of which are the leadership of managers, worker skills and character,

[11] Indeed, many textile firms have failed because the expanding nontextile economies of their regions have pushed up labor costs, outcompeting some textile firms for the resources they need for continued production.

firm strategies, and cost-control methods. One of the more important points managers must remember is that incentives can be very powerful forces within a firm – for both good and bad! This means that managers must pay attention to the art and logic of getting incentives *right.* In the "Organizational economics and management" sections that are included in every chapter, we shall examine a large number of different questions related to the organization of production within firms, most of which relate to incentives in one way or another:

- How large should firms be?
- Do workers want tough bosses?
- Why don't more firms pay piece rates?
- What difference does debt make?
- What good are corporate raiders?

At the most obvious level, these questions are concerned with the widely different problems firms have to face. But beneath all that is written about these questions, and many others, in the "Organizational economics and management" sections is an important theme:

- Develop incentives so that everyone in your firm is connected with the incentives – owners, executives, managers, workers, suppliers, and customers – and can win from your firm's operation.

Why incentives are important

But such conceptual and factual points beg two critical questions:

- Why are incentives important?
- Why do they work?

Admittedly, the answers are many. One of the more important reasons that incentives matter within firms is that firms are collections of workers whose interests are not always aligned with the interests of the people who employ them – that is, the owners. The major problem facing the owners is how to get the workers to do what the owners want them to do. The owners could just issue directives, but without some incentive to obey them, nothing may happen. Directives may have some value in themselves: people do feel a sense of obligation to do what they were hired to do, and one of the things they may have been hired to do is to obey orders (within limits). However, directives can be costly. Firms may use incentives simply as a cheaper substitute for giving out orders that can go unheeded unless the workers have some reason to heed them.

Firms may also use incentives to clarify firm goals, to spell out in concrete terms to workers what the owners want to accomplish. As every manager knows all too well, it is difficult to establish and write out the firm's strategy that will be used to achieve its stated goals, and it is an even more difficult task to get workers to appreciate, understand, and remember firm goals – and then work toward them. The communication problem typically escalates with the size of the organization.

Goals are always imperfectly communicated, especially by memoranda or through employment manuals that may be read once and tossed away. Workers do not always know how serious the owners and upper managers are: they can remember any number of times when widely circulated memos were nothing but "window dressing." Incentives are a means by which owners and upper managers can validate overall company goals and strategies. They can in effect say through incentives (reinforced regularly in paychecks and end-of-year bonuses): "This is what we think is important. This is what we will be working toward. This is what we will be trying to get everyone else to do. And this is where we will put our money." Even if workers were not sensitive to the pecuniary benefits of work, but were interested only in doing what their companies wanted them to do, incentives, because of the messages they convey, can have a valuable and direct impact on what workers do and how long and hard they work (White 1991; Robins 1996).

But there is a far more fundamental reason that incentives matter: *Managers don't always know what orders or directives to give.* No matter how intelligent, hard working and well informed managers are, they seldom know as much about particular jobs as those who are actually doing them. Knowing about the peculiarities of a machine, the difficulties a fellow worker on the production line is experiencing at home, or the personality quirks of a customer are just a few examples of the innumerable particular bits of localized knowledge that are crucial to the success of a firm. And this knowledge is spread over everyone in the firm without the possibility of its being fully communicated to, and effectively utilized by, those who are primarily responsible for managerial oversight. The only way a firm can fully benefit from such localized knowledge is to allow those who possess the knowledge – the firm's employees – the freedom to use what they know. This is what it means to *empower* workers.

But the benefits from participatory management, or employee empowerment, can be realized only if employees have not only the freedom but also the *motivation* to use their special knowledge in productive cooperation with each other. The crucial ingredient for bringing about the requisite coordination is incentives that align the otherwise conflicting interests of individual employees with the collective interests of all members of the firm. Without such incentives, there can be no real employee empowerment because there is no hope that the knowledge dispersed throughout the firm will be used in a coordinated and constructive way. The only practical alternative to a functioning system of incentives is, again, a top-down, command-and-control approach that, unfortunately, can never allow the full potential of a firm's employees to be realized.

Managers must heed the words of social philosopher Friedrich Hayek: "The more men know, the smaller the share of knowledge becomes that any one mind [the planner's mind included] can absorb. The more civilized we become, the more relatively ignorant must each individual be of the facts on which the working of civilization depends. The very division of knowledge increases the necessary ignorance of the individual of most of this knowledge" (Hayek 1960).

Hayek's ageless insight applies within the firm. With the growing complexity and sophistication of production, knowledge becomes ever more widely dispersed among a growing number of workers. Hence, the importance of incentives has grown with modern-day leaps in the technological sophistication of products and production processes. Incentives will continue to grow in importance as production and distribution processes become ever more complex.

Seen in this light, the problem of the firm is the same as the problem of the general economy. As did Hayek, economists have argued for years that no group of government planners, no matter how intelligent and dedicated, can acquire all the localized knowledge necessary to allocate resources intelligently. The long and painful experiments with socialism and its extreme variant, communism, have confirmed that this is one argument that economists got right. But the freedom for people to use the knowledge that only they individually have has to be coupled with incentives that motivate people to use that knowledge in socially cooperative ways – meaning that the best way for individuals to pursue their own objectives is by making decisions that improve the opportunities for others to pursue their objectives. In a market economy, these incentives are found primarily in the form of *prices* that emerge from the rules of private property and voluntary exchange. Market prices provide the incentive people need to productively coordinate their decisions with each other, thus making it not only possible, but desirable, for people to have a large measure of freedom to make use of the localized information and know-how they have.

A perfect incentive system would assure that everyone could be given complete freedom because it would be in the interest of each to advance the interests of all. No such perfect incentive system exists, not within any firm or within any economy. In every economy there is always some appropriate "mix" of both market incentives and government controls that achieve the best overall results. The argument over just what the right mix is will no doubt continue indefinitely, but few deny that both incentives and controls are needed. Similarly, for any firm made up of more than one person, there is some mix of incentives and direct managerial control that best promotes the objectives of the firm – i.e. the general interests of its members.

Granted, incentives may not seem to matter much at any point in time, but even so the power of incentives can accumulate with time. For example, suppose that without improved incentives firm profits will grow in real-dollar terms by 2 percent a year. Suppose that with more effective incentives firm profits can grow by 2.5 percent a year. The difference is not "much," just a half of a percentage point per year. However, the compound impact of the higher growth rate will mean that after thirty years real profits will be 33 percent higher with the improved incentives (a fact that is likely to be reflected in a higher current stock price). Furthermore, the firm may be able to achieve the relatively higher profits with little or no cost. "Good" incentives may be no more expensive than "bad" incentives. Good incentives are the proverbial "free lunch" that economists typically dismiss.

Of course, if a given firm doesn't pay attention to its incentives, it may lose more than its lunch; it may be forced out of business by those firms that do recognize the importance of incentives. Seen from this perspective, incentives can be a critical component of firm survival – perhaps just as critical as product development or technological sophistication.

The problem is in getting the incentives right and using the full range of potential incentives. Unfortunately, we can't say exactly what incentives your firm should employ. The precise incentives chosen depend on local conditions that can vary greatly across firms. You would not want us to write about *particular incentives* for your particular circumstances, mainly because we can be assured of only one constant fact about business: Particular circumstances – yours included – will change with time and markets. Here, we offer a *way of thinking* about incentives that, if employed with diligence, will enable managers and owners to get their firms' incentives more in line with their desire for increased productivity and profits.

THE BOTTOM LINE

In the concluding section of each chapter, we will lay out "key takeaways" from the chapter. By using the word "key," we obviously don't intend to list every significant point covered in the chapter. Rather, we intend to restrict the list of key takeaways to those relatively few overarching points that every student should understand on concluding the chapter and should emphasize in reviewing the chapter for an examination. We have dubbed this section "The bottom line" because in it we seek to draw the wide-ranging discussion in the chapter into sharp focus. The key takeaways from chapter 1 are the following:

(1) Economics is a discipline best described as the study of human interaction in the context of scarcity. It is the study of how, individually and collectively, people use their scarce resources to satisfy as many of their wants as possible. The economic method is founded in a set of presuppositions about human behavior on which economists construct theoretical models.
(2) Economics is a way of thinking about virtually everything, including the issues that managers confront daily.
(3) Private property rights matter because they affect people's incentives to use scarce resources. This is because they affect the people's rewards from effectively utilizing scarce resources. They also affect the costs they incur from misusing and abusing scarce resources.
(4) Communally owned property is a not uncommon cause of resource misuse and overuse.
(5) For trade to reoccurr and be systematic, it must be mutually beneficial to the trading partners, and trade can be mutually beneficial even when one party to the trades is more efficient in both goods subject to trade.
(6) In general, incentives of all kinds matter in how effectively (or ineffectively) scarce resources are utilized. There is obviously profit to be made from developing better, improved goods and services. Less widely recognized, is the fact that there is also profit to be made from developing better, more cost-effective incentives systems.
(7) Overcoming Prisoner's Dilemmas is a pervasive problem in the development of social and management policies.

REVIEW QUESTIONS

(1) In the prison camp described on p. 4, rations were distributed equally. Why did trade within and among bungalows result?
(2) Recall the priest who traded the cigarettes for cheese, and cheese for cigarettes, so that he ended up with more cigarettes than he had initially. Did someone else in the camp lose by the priest's activities? How was the priest able to end up better off than when he began? What did his activities do to the price of cheese in the different bungalows?
(3) Theories may be defective, but economists continue to use them. Why?
(4) A microeconomics book designed for MBA students could include theories more complex than those in this book. What might be the trade offs in dealing with more complex theories?
(5) Most MBA students study in "groups." (If you are not in a study group, imagine yourself in one.) What incentive problems do these groups have to overcome? How has your group sought to overcome the incentive problems?
(6) What are the economic consequences of extending the copyright term for a book from fourteen to 150 years?

Appendix: "I, Pencil"[12]

Leonard E. Read (1983)

I am a lead pencil – ordinary wooden pencil familiar to all boys and girls and adults who can read and write. (My official name is "Mongol 482." My many ingredients are assembled, fabricated and finished by Eberhard Faber Pencil Company, Wilkes-Barre, Pennsylvania.)

Writing is both my vocation and my avocation; that's all I do.

You may wonder why I should write a genealogy. Well, to begin with, my story is interesting. And, next, I am a mystery – more so than a tree or a sunset or even a flash of lightning. But, sadly, I am taken for granted by those who use me, as if I were a mere incident and without background. This supercilious attitude relegates me to the level of the commonplace. This is a species of the grievous error in which mankind cannot too long persist without peril. For, as a wise man, G.K. Chesterton, observed, "We are perishing for want of wonder, not for want of wonders."

[12] The late Leonard Read was the founder of the Foundation for Economic Education. Permission for use in this volume has been granted by Donald Boudreaux, President, Foundation for Economic Education (May 4, 1999).

I, Pencil, simple though I appear to be, merit your wonder and awe, a claim I shall attempt to prove. In fact, if you can understand me – no, that's too much to ask of anyone – if you can become aware of the miraculousness that I symbolize, you can help save the freedom mankind is so unhappily losing. I have a profound lesson to teach. And I can teach this lesson better than can an automobile or an airplane or a mechanical dishwasher because – well, because I am seemingly so simple.

Simple? Yet, not a single person on the face of this earth knows how to make me. This sounds fantastic, doesn't it? Especially when you realize that there are about one and one-half billion of my kind produced in the US each year.

Pick me up and look me over. What do you see? Not much meets the eye – there's some wood, lacquer, the printed labeling, graphite lead, a bit of metal, and an eraser.

Innumerable antecedents

Just as you cannot trace your family tree back very far, so is it impossible for me to name and explain all my antecedents. But I would like to suggest enough of them to impress upon you the richness and complexity of my background.

My family tree begins with what in fact is a tree, a cedar of straight grain that grows in Northern California and Oregon. Now contemplate all the saws and trucks and rope and the countless other gear used in harvesting and carting the cedar logs to the railroad siding. Think of all the persons and the numberless skills that went into their fabrication: the mining of ore, the making of steel and its refinement into saws, axes, motors; the growing of hemp and bringing it through all the stages to heavy and strong rope; the logging camps with their beds and mess halls, the cookery and the raising of all the foods. Why, untold thousands of persons had a hand in every cup of coffee the loggers drink!

The logs are shipped to a mill in San Leandro, California. Can you imagine the individuals who make flat cars and rails and railroad engines and who construct and install the communication systems incidental thereto? These legions are among my antecedents.

Consider the millwork in San Leandro. The cedar logs are cut into small, pencil-length slats less than one-fourth of an inch in thickness. These are kiln-dried and then tinted for the same reason women put rouge on their faces. People prefer that I look pretty, not a pallid white. The slats are waxed and kiln-dried again. How many skills went into the making of the tint and kilns, into supplying the heat, the light and power, the belts, motors, and all the other things a mill requires? Are sweepers in the mill among my ancestors? Yes, and also included are the men who poured the concrete for the dam of a Pacific Gas & Electric company hydroplant, which supplies the mill's power. And don't overlook the ancestors present and distant who have a hand in transporting sixty carloads of slats across the nation from California to Wilkes-Barre.

Complicated machinery

Once in the pencil factory – $4,000,000 in machinery and building, all capital accumulated by thrifty and saving parents of mine – each slat is given eight grooves by a complex machine, after which another machine lays leads in every other slat, applies glue, and places another slat atop – a lead sandwich, so to speak. Seven brothers and I are mechanically carved from this "wood-clinched" sandwich.

My "lead" itself – it contains no lead at all – is complex. The graphite is mined in Ceylon. Consider the miners and those who make their many tools and the makers of the paper sacks in which the graphite is shipped and those who make the string that ties the sacks and those who put them aboard ships and those who make the ships. Even the lighthouse keepers along the way assisted in my birth – and the harbor pilots.

The graphite is mixed with clay from Mississippi in which ammonium hydroxide is used in the refining process. Then wetting agents are added such as sulfonated tallow – animal fats chemically reacted with sulfuric acid. After passing through numerous machines, the mixture finally appears as endless extrusions – as from a sausage grinder – cut to size, dried, and baked for several hours at 1,850 degrees Fahrenheit. To increase their strength and smoothness the leads are then treated with a hot mixture, which includes candililla wax from Mexico, paraffin wax and hydrogenated natural fats.

My cedar receives six coats of lacquer. Do you know all of the ingredients of lacquer? Who would think that the growers of castor beans and the refiners of castor oil are a part of it? They are. Why, even the processes by which the lacquer is made a beautiful yellow involves the skills of more persons than one can enumerate!

Observe the labeling. That's a film formed by applying heat to carbon black mixed with resins. How do you make resins and what, pray, is carbon black?

My bit of metal – the ferrule – is brass. Think of all the persons who mine zinc and copper and those who have the skills to make shiny sheet brass from these products of nature. Those black rings on my ferrule are black nickel. What is black nickel and how is it applied? The complete story of why the center of my ferrule has no black nickel on it would take pages to explain.

Then there's my crowning glory, inelegantly referred to in the trade as "the plug," the part man uses to erase the errors he makes with me. An ingredient called "factice" is what does the erasing. It is a rubber-like product made by reacting grape seed oil from the Dutch East Indies with sulfur chloride. Rubber, contrary to the common notion, is only for binding purposes. Then, too, there are numerous vulcanizing and accelerating agents. The pumice comes from Italy; and the pigment which gives "the plug" its color is cadmium sulfide.

Vast web of know-how

Does anyone wish to challenge my earlier assertion that no single person on the face of this earth knows how to make me?

Actually, millions of human beings have had a hand in my creation, no one of whom even knows more than a very few of the others. Now, you may say that I go too far in relating the picker of a coffee berry in far-off Brazil and food growers elsewhere to my creation; that this is an extreme position. I shall stand by my claim. There isn't a single person in all these millions, including the president of the pencil company, who contributes more than a tiny, infinitesimal bit of know-how. From the standpoint of know-how the only difference between the miner of graphite in Ceylon and the logger in Oregon is in the type of know-how. Neither the miner nor the logger can be dispensed with, any more than the chemist at the factory or the worker in the oil field – paraffin being a by-product of petroleum.

Here is an astounding fact: Neither the worker in the oil field nor the chemist nor the digger of graphite or clay nor anyone who mans or makes the ships or trains or trucks nor the one who runs the machine that does the knurling on my bit of metal nor the president of the company performs his singular task because he wants *me*. Each one wants me less, perhaps, than does a child in the first grade. Indeed, there are some among this vast multitude who never saw a pencil nor would they know how to use one. Their motivation is other than me. Perhaps it is something like this: Each of these millions sees that he can thus exchange his tiny know-how for the goods and services he needs or wants. I may or may not be among these items.

No human master-mind

There is a fact still more astounding: The absence of a master-mind, of anyone dictating or forcibly directing these countless actions that bring me into being. No trace of such a person can be found. Instead, we find the Scottish economist and moral philosopher Adam Smith's famous "Invisible Hand" at work in the marketplace. This is the mystery to which I earlier referred.

It has been said that "only God can make a tree." Why do we agree with this? Isn't it because we realize that we ourselves could not make one? Indeed, can we even describe a tree? We cannot, except in superficial terms. We can say, for instance, that a certain molecular configuration manifests itself as a tree. But what mind is there among men that could even record, let alone direct, the constant changes in molecules that transpire in the life span of a tree? Such a feat is utterly unthinkable!

I, Pencil, am a complex combination of miracles: a tree, zinc, copper, graphite, and so on. But to these miracles which manifest themselves in Nature an even more extraordinary miracle has been added: the configuration of creative human energies – millions of tiny bits of know-how configurating naturally and spontaneously in response to human necessity and desire and in the absence of any human master-minding! Since only God can make a tree, I insist that only God could make me. Man can no more direct millions of bits of know-how so as to bring a pencil into being than he can put molecules together to create a tree.

That's what I meant when I wrote earlier, "If you can become aware of the miraculousness that I symbolize, you can help save the freedom mankind is so unhappily losing." For, if one is aware that these bits of know-how will naturally, yes, automatically, arrange themselves into creative and productive patterns in response to human necessity and demand – that is, in the absence of governmental or any other coercive master-minding – then one will possess an absolutely essential ingredient for freedom: a faith in free men. Freedom is impossible without this faith.

Once government has had a monopoly on a creative activity – the delivery of the mail, for instance – most individuals will believe that the mail could not be efficiently delivered by men acting freely. And here is the reason: Each one acknowledges that he himself doesn't know how to do all the things involved in mail delivery. He also recognizes that no other individual could. These assumptions are correct. No individual possesses enough know-how to perform a nation's mail delivery any more than any individual possesses enough know-how to make a pencil. In the absence of a faith in free men – unaware that millions of tiny kinds of know-how would naturally and miraculously form and cooperate to satisfy this necessity – the individual cannot help but reach the erroneous conclusion that the mail can be delivered only by governmental master-minding.

Testimony galore

If I, Pencil, were the only item that could offer testimony on what men can accomplish when free to try, then those with little faith would have a fair case. However, there is testimony galore; it's all about us on every hand. Mail delivery is exceedingly simple when compared, for instance, to the making of an automobile or a calculating machine or a grain combine or a milling machine, or to tens of thousands of other things.

Delivery? Why, in this age where men have been left free to try, they deliver the human voice around the world in less than one second; they deliver an event visually and in motion to any person's home when it is happening; they deliver 150 passengers from Seattle to Baltimore in less than four hours; they deliver gas from Texas to one's range or furnace in New York at unbelievably low rates and without subsidy; they deliver each four pounds of oil from the Persian Gulf to our Eastern Seaboard – halfway around the world – for less money than the government charges for delivering a one-ounce letter across the street! (*Some things have changed since this essay first ran in 1958 and 1983!*)

Leave men free

The lesson I have to teach is this: Leave all creative energies uninhibited. Merely organize society to act in harmony with this lesson. Let society's legal apparatus remove all obstacles the best it can. Permit creative know-how to freely flow. Have faith that free men will respond to the "Invisible Hand." This faith will be confirmed. I, Pencil, seemingly simple though I am, offer the miracle of my creation as testimony that this is a practical faith, as practical as the sun, the rain, a cedar tree, and the good earth.

CHAPTER

2

Competitive product markets and firm decisions

Competition, if not prevented, tends to bring about a state of affairs in which: first, everything will be produced which somebody knows how to produce and which he can sell profitably at a price at which buyers will prefer it to the available alternatives: second, everything that is produced is produced by persons who can do so at least as cheaply as anybody else who in fact is not producing it: and third, that everything will be sold at prices lower than, or at least as low as, those at which it could be sold by anybody who in fact does not do so.

Friedrich A. Hayek

In the heart of New York City, Fred Lieberman's small grocery is dwarfed by the tall buildings that surround it. Yet it is remarkable for what it accomplishes. Lieberman's carries thousands of items, most of which are not produced locally, and some of which come thousands of miles from other parts of this country or abroad. A man of modest means, with little knowledge of production processes, Fred Lieberman has nevertheless been able to stock his store with many if not most of the foods and toiletries his customers need and want. Occasionally Lieberman's runs out of certain items, but most of the time the stock is ample. Its supply is so dependable that customers tend to take it for granted, forgetting that Lieberman's is one small strand in an extremely complex economic network.

How does Fred Lieberman get the goods he sells, and how does he know which ones to sell and at what price? The simplest answer is that the goods he offers and the prices at which they sell are determined through the *market process* – the interaction of many buyers and sellers trading what they have (their labor or other resources) for what they want. Lieberman stocks his store by appealing to the private interests of suppliers – by paying them competitive prices. His customers pay him extra for the convenience of purchasing goods in their neighborhood grocery – appealing to his private interests in the process. To determine what he should buy, Fred Lieberman considers his suppliers' prices. To determine what and how much they should buy, his customers consider the prices he charges. The economist Friedrich Hayek (1945) has suggested that the market process is manageable for people such as Fred Lieberman, his suppliers, and his customers, precisely because prices condense a great deal of information into a useful form, signaling quickly what people want, what goods cost, and what resources are readily available. Prices guide and coordinate the sellers' production decisions and consumers' purchases.

How are prices determined? That is an important question for people in business, simply because an understanding of how prices are determined can help business people understand the forces that will cause prices to change in the future and, therefore, the forces that affect their businesses' bottom lines. There's money to be made in being able to understand the dynamics of prices. Our most general answer to the question of how prices are determined is deceptively simple: In competitive markets, the forces of supply and demand establish prices. However, there is much to be learned through the concepts of supply and demand. Indeed, we suspect that most MBA students will find supply and demand the most useful business concepts and tools of analysis developed in this book (and perhaps their entire MBA program). However, to understand supply and demand, you must first understand that the market process is inherently competitive.

PART I THEORY AND PUBLIC POLICY APPLICATIONS

The competitive market process

So far, our discussion of markets and their consequences has been rather casual. In this section, we shall define precisely such terms as "market" and "competition". In later sections, we shall examine the way markets work and learn why, in a limited sense, markets can be considered efficient systems for determining what and how much to produce.

The market setting

Most people tend to think of a market as a geographical location – a shopping center, an auction hall, a business district. From an economic perspective, however, it is more useful to think of a market as a process. You may recall from chapter 1 that a market is defined as the process by which buyers and sellers determine what they are willing to buy and sell and on what terms. That is, it is the process by which buyers and sellers decide the prices and quantities of goods to be bought and sold.

In this process, individual market participants search for information relevant to their own interests. Buyers ask about the models, sizes, colors, and quantities available and the prices they must pay for them. Sellers inquire about the types of goods and services buyers want and the prices they are willing to pay.

This market process is *self-correcting*. Buyers and sellers routinely revise their plans on the basis of experience. As economist Israel Kirzner has written:

> The overly ambitious plans of one period will be replaced by more realistic ones; market opportunities overlooked in one period will be exploited in the next. In other words, even without changes in the basic data of the market, the decision made in one period one time generates systematic alterations in corresponding decisions for the succeeding period. (Kirzner 1973, 10)

The market is made up of people, consumers, and entrepreneurs, attempting to buy and sell on the best terms possible. Through the groping process of give and take, they move from relative ignorance about others' wants and needs to a reasonably accurate understanding of how much can be bought and sold and at what price. The market functions as an ongoing *information and exchange system*.

Competition is the process by which market participants, in pursuing their own interests, attempt to outdo, outprice, outproduce, and outmaneuver each other. By extension, competition is also the process by which market participants attempt to avoid being outdone, outpriced, outproduced, or outmaneuvered by others.

Competition among buyers and among sellers

Part and parcel of the market process is the concept of **competition**. Competition does not occur *between* buyer and seller, but *among* buyers or among sellers. Buyers compete with other buyers for the limited number of goods on the market. To compete, they must discover what other buyers are bidding and offer the seller better terms – a higher price or the same price for a lower-quality product. Sellers compete with other sellers for the consumer's dollar. They must learn what their rivals are doing and attempt to do it better or differently – to lower the price or enhance the product's appeal.

This kind of competition stimulates the exchange of information, forcing competitors to reveal their plans to prospective buyers or sellers. The exchange of information can be seen clearly at auctions. Before the bidding begins, buyers look over the merchandise and the other buyers, attempting to determine how high others might be willing to bid for a particular piece. During the auction, this specific information is revealed as buyers call out their bids and others try to top them. Information exchange is less apparent in department stores, where competition is often restricted. Even there, however, comparison-shopping will often reveal some sellers who are offering lower prices in an attempt to attract consumers.

In competing with each other, sellers reveal information that is ultimately of use to buyers. Buyers likewise inform sellers. From the consumer's point of view:

> The function of competition is here precisely to teach us who will serve us well: which grocer or travel agent, which department store or hotel, which doctor or solicitor, we can expect to provide the most satisfactory solution for whatever particular personal problem we may have to face. (Hayek 1948, 97)

From the seller's point of view – say, the auctioneer's – competition among buyers brings the highest prices possible.

Competition among sellers takes many forms, including the price, quality, weight, volume, color, texture, poor durability, and smell of products, as well as the credit terms offered to buyers. Sellers also compete for consumers' attention by appealing to their hunger and sex drives or their fear of death, pain, and loud noises. All these forms of competition can be divided into two basic categories – *price* and *nonprice* competition. Price competition is of particular interest to economists, who see it as an important source of information for market participants and a coordinating force that brings the quantity produced into line with the quantity consumers are willing and able to buy. In the following sections, we shall construct a model of the competitive market and use it to explore the process of *price* competition. Nonprice competition will be covered in a later section.

Supply and demand: a market model

A fully competitive market is made up of many buyers and sellers searching for opportunities or ready to enter the market when opportunities arise. To be described as "competitive," therefore, a market must include a significant number of actual or potential competitors. A fully competitive market offers freedom of entry: There are no legal or artificial barriers to producing and selling goods in the market.

Our market model assumes **perfect competition** – an idealized situation that is seldom, if ever, achieved in real life but that will simplify our calculations. This kind of market is well suited to graphic analysis. Our discussion concentrates on how buyers and sellers interact to determine the price of tomatoes, a product Fred Lieberman almost always carries. It will employ two curves. The first represents buyers' behavior, which is called their demand for the product.

Perfect competition is a market composed of numerous independent sellers and buyers of an identical product, such that no one individual seller or buyer has the ability to affect the market price by changing the production level. Entry into and exit from a perfectly competitive market is unrestricted. Producers can start up or shut down production at will. Anyone can enter the market, duplicate the good, and compete for consumers' dollars. Since each competitor produces only a small share of the total output, the individual competitor cannot significantly influence the degree of competition or the market price by entering or leaving the market.

Demand is the assumed inverse relationship between the price of a good or service and the quantity consumers are willing and able to buy during a given period, all other things held constant.

The elements of demand

To the general public, **demand** is simply what people want, but to economists, demand has much more technical meaning. The concept of demand is important because it is so widely applicable to human behavior, not just in business, but everyday life.

Demand as a relationship

The relationship between price and quantity is normally assumed to be *inverse.* That is, when the price of a good rises, the quantity sold, *ceteris paribus* (Latin for "everything else held constant"), will go down. Conversely, when the price of a good falls, the quantity sold goes up. Demand is not a quantity but a relationship. A given quantity sold at a particular price is properly called the *quantity demanded.*

Both tables and graphs can be used to describe the assumed inverse relationship between price and quantity.

Demand as a table or a graph

Demand may be thought of as a *schedule* of the various quantities of a particular good consumers will buy at various prices. As the price goes down, the quantity purchased goes up and vice versa. Table 2.1 contains a hypothetical schedule of the demand for tomatoes in the New York area during a typical week. Column (2) shows prices that might be charged. Column (3) shows the number of bushels consumers will buy at those prices. Note that as the price rises from zero to $11 a bushel, the number of bushels purchased drops from 110,000 to zero.

Demand may also be thought of as a *curve.* If price is scaled on a graph's vertical axis and quantity on the horizontal axis, the demand curve has a negative slope (downward and to the right), reflecting the assumed inverse relationship between price and quantity. The shape of the market demand curve is shown in figure 2.1, which is based on the data from table 2.1. Points *a* through *l* on the graph correspond to the price–quantity combinations *A* through *L* in the table. Note that as the price falls from P_2 ($8) to P_1 ($5), consumers move down their demand curve from a quantity of Q_1 (30,000) to the larger quantity Q_2 (60,000).[1]

[1] Mathematically, a linear demand relationship may be stated as $Q_d = a - bP$, where Q_d is the quantity demanded at every price; *a* is the quantity consumers will buy when the price is zero; *b* is the slope of the demand curve; and *P* is the price of the good. Thus the demand function for tomatoes described in table 2.1 and figure 2.1 may be written as $Q_d = 110{,}000 - 10{,}000\,P$.

Table 2.1 *Market demand for tomatoes*

Price–quantity combinations (1)	Price per bushel ($) (2)	No. (000) of bushels (3)
A	0	110
B	1	100
C	2	90
D	3	80
E	4	70
F	5	60
G	6	50
H	7	40
I	8	30
J	9	20
K	10	10
L	11	0

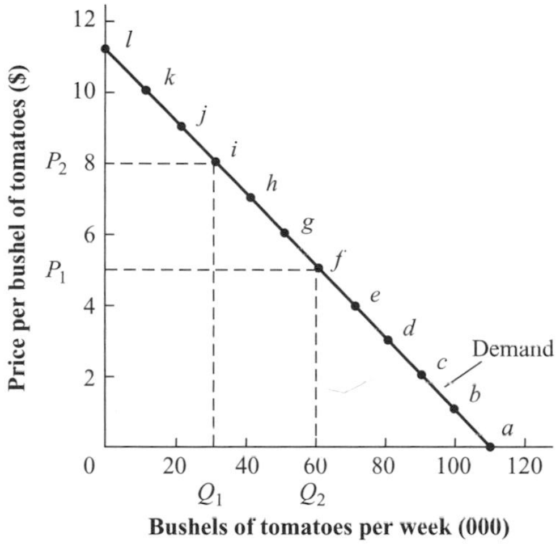

Figure 2.1 Market demand for tomatoes
Demand, the assumed inverse relationship between price and quantity purchased, can be represented by a curve that slopes down toward the right. Here, as the price falls from $11 to zero, the number of bushels of tomatoes purchased per week rises from zero to 110,000.

The slope and determinants of demand

Price and quantity are assumed to be inversely related, for two reasons. First, as the price of a good decreases (and the prices of all other goods stay the same – remember *ceteris paribus*), the purchasing power of consumer incomes rises.

More consumers are able to buy the good, and many will buy more of most goods. This response is called the "income effect."

In addition, as the price of a good decreases (and the prices of all other goods remain the same), the good becomes relatively cheaper, and consumers will substitute that good for others. This response is called the "substitution effect."

In sum, when the price of tomatoes (or razor blades, or any other good) falls, more tomatoes will be purchased because more people will be buying them for more purposes.

Although price is an important part of the definition of demand, it is not the only determinant of how much of a good people will want. It may not even be the most important. The major factors that affect market demand are called the *determinants of demand.* They are:

- Consumer tastes or preferences
- The prices of other goods
- Consumer incomes
- The number of consumers
- Expectations concerning future prices and incomes.

A host of other factors, such as weather, may also influence the demand for particular goods – ice cream, for instance.

A change in any of these determinants of demand will cause either an increase or a decrease in demand:

- An *increase in demand* is an increase in the quantity demanded at each and every price. It is represented graphically by a rightward, or outward, shift in the demand curve.
- A *decrease in demand* is a decrease in the quantity demanded at each and every price. It is represented graphically by a leftward, or inward, shift of the demand curve.

Figure 2.2 illustrates the shifts in the demand curve that result from a change in one of the determinants of demand. The outward shift from D_1 to D_2 indicates an increase in demand: consumers now want more of a good at each and every price. For example, they want Q_3 instead of Q_2 tomatoes at price P_2. Consumers are also now willing to pay a higher price for any quantity. For example, they will pay P_3 instead of P_2 for Q_2 tomatoes. The inward shift from D_1 to D_3 indicates a decrease in demand: Consumers want less of a good at each and every price – Q_1 instead of Q_2 tomatoes at price P_2. And they are willing to pay less than before for any quantity – P_1 instead of P_2 for Q_2 tomatoes.

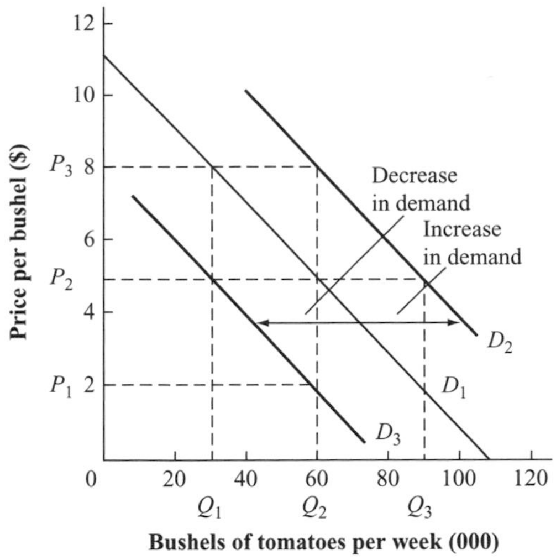

Figure 2.2 Shifts in the demand curve

An increase in demand is represented by a rightward, outward, shift in the demand curve, from D_1 to D_2. A decrease in demand is represented by a leftward, or inward, shift in the demand curve, from D_1 to D_3.

A change in a determinant of demand may be translated into an increase or decrease in market demand in numerous ways. An increase in market demand can be caused by:

- *An increase in consumers' desire or taste for the good* If people truly want the good more, they will buy more of the good at any given price or pay a higher price for any given quantity.
- *An increase in the number of buyers* If, because more people consume the good, more of the good will be purchased at any given price, then the price will be higher at any given quantity.
- *An increase in the price of substitute goods* (which can be used in place of the good in question). If the price of oranges increases, the demand for grapefruit will increase.
- *A decrease in the price of complement goods* (which are used in conjunction with the good in question) If the price of stereo systems falls, the demand for records, tapes, and CDs will rise.
- *Generally speaking (but not always), an increase in consumer incomes* An increase in people's incomes may increase the demand for luxury goods, such as new cars. It may also decrease demand for low-quality goods (such

as hamburger) because people can now afford better-quality products (such as steak).

- *An expected increase in the future price of the good in question* If people expect the price of cars to rise faster than the prices of other goods, then (depending on exactly when they expect the increase) they may buy more cars now, thus avoiding the expected additional cost in the future.
- *An expected increase in the future price of a substitute good* If people expect the price of oranges to fall in the future, then (depending on exactly when they expect the price decrease) they may reduce their current demand for grapefruit, so that they can buy more oranges in the future.
- *An expected increase in future incomes of buyers* College seniors' demand for cars tends to increase as graduation approaches and they anticipate a rise in income.

The determinants of a decrease in market demand are just the opposite:

- *A decrease in consumers' desire or taste for the good*
- *A decrease in the number of buyers*
- *A decrease in the price of substitute goods*
- *An increase in the price of complement goods*
- *Generally speaking (but not always), a decrease in consumer incomes*
- *An expected decrease in the future price of the good in question*
- *An expected decrease in the future price of a substitute good*
- *An expected increase in the future price of the good in question*
- *An expected decrease in the future incomes of buyers.*

As will be noticeable throughout this book, much attention will be placed on how changes in price affect the quantity demanded, while little attention will be given to how changes in "tastes" affect the quantity demanded. The differential treatment of price and tastes is not due to the presumption that price is more important than tastes in determining the consumption level of any good. Rather, economists concentrate on price because they seek a theory of price determination (not a theory of taste determination). In addition, the effect of price changes on quantity demanded is viewed as being highly predictable, given extensive consumer theory and empirical observation. The inverse relationship between price and quantity consumed that is it is viewed as a "law," or the "law of demand." "Tastes," on the other hand, are an amorphous, subjective concept. Hence, predicting the impact of changes in "tastes" on quantity demanded is, for economists (maybe not as much so for psychologists), problematic.

Similarly, as will be discussed in chapter 7, the impact of a change in buyer's real income on quantity bought has an element of uncertainty. Granted, for most normal goods, the relationship between income and quantity of a good bought can be, as indicated above, positive. However, the relationship can be inverse for some goods (so-called "inferior goods"). When low-income people experience an increase in real income, they may switch between low-quality sources of, say, protein – beans – to high-quality sources – meat. In this case, an increase in real income leads to a reduction in the demand for (and quantity purchased of) beans.

The elements of supply

On the other side of the market are the producers of goods. The average person thinks of supply as the quantity of a good producers are willing to sell. To economists, however, **supply** means something quite different. As with demand, supply is not a "given quantity" – that is called the "quantity supplied." Supply is a *relationship between price and quantity.* As the price of a good rises, producers are generally willing to offer a larger quantity. The reverse is equally true: as price decreases, so does quantity supplied. Like demand, supply can be described in a table or a graph.

Supply is the assumed relationship between the quantity of a good producers are willing to offer during a given period and the price, everything else held constant. Generally, because additional costs tend to rise with expanded production, this relationship is presumed to be positive.

Supply as a table or a graph

Supply may be described as a *schedule of the quantity that producers will offer* at various prices during a given period of time. Table 2.2 shows such a supply schedule. As the price of tomatoes goes up from zero to \$11 a bushel, the quantity offered rises from zero to 110,000, reflecting the assumed positive relationship between price and quantity.

Supply may also be thought of as a *curve.* If the quantity producers will offer is scaled on the horizontal axis of a graph and the price of the good is scaled on the vertical axis, the supply curve will slope upward to the right, reflecting the assumed positive relationship between price and quantity. In figure 2.3, which was plotted from the data in table 2.2, points *a* through *l* represent the price–quantity combinations *A* through *L*. Note how a change in the price causes a movement along the supply curve.[2]

[2] Mathematically, the supply relationship may be stated as $Q_s = a + bP$, where Q_s is the quantity supplied; *a* is the quantity producers will supply when the price is zero; *b* is the slope; and *P* is the price. Thus the supply function of tomatoes represented in table 2.2 and figure 2.3 may be written as $Q_s = 0 + 10{,}000\ P$. However, do note that the supply curve need not be linear. All that is needed for the analysis in figure 2.3 is that the supply curve be upward sloping.

Table 2.2 *Market supply of tomatoes*

Price–quantity combinations (1)	Price per bushel ($) (2)	No. (000) of bushels (3)
A	0	0
B	1	10
C	2	20
D	3	30
E	4	40
F	5	50
G	6	60
H	7	70
I	8	80
J	9	90
K	10	100
L	11	110

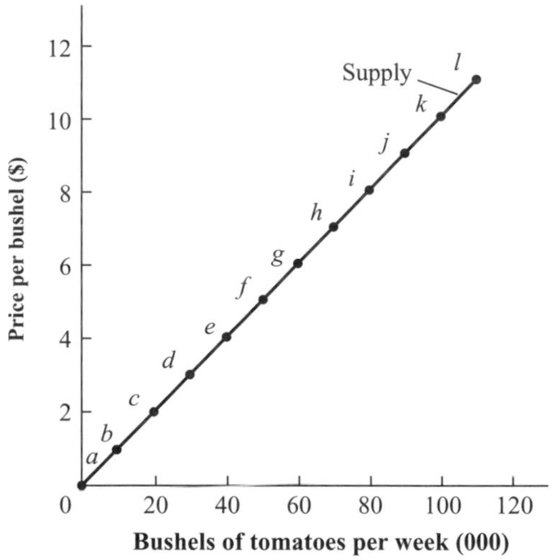

Figure 2.3 Supply of tomatoes

Supply, the assumed relationship between price and quantity produced, can be represented by a curve that slopes up toward the right. Here, as the price rises from zero to $11, the number of bushels of tomatoes offered for sale during the course of a week rises from zero to 110,000.

The slope and determinants of Supply

The quantity producers will offer on the market depends on their *production costs*. Obviously the total cost of production will rise when more is produced because more resources will be required to expand output. The additional or marginal cost of each additional bushel produced also tends to rise as total output expands. In other words, it costs more to produce the second bushel of tomatoes than the first, and more to produce the third than the second. Firms will not expand their output unless they can cover their higher unit costs with a higher price. This is the reason the supply curve is thought to slope upward.

Anything that affects production costs will influence supply and the position of the supply curve. Such factors, which are called *determinants of supply*, include:

- *Change in productivity due to a change in technology*
- *Change in the profitability of producing other goods*
- *Change in the scarcity (and prices) of various productive resources.*

Many other factors, such as the weather, can also affect production costs. A change in any of these determinants of supply can either increase or decrease supply:

- An *increase in supply* is an increase in the quantity producers are willing and able to offer at each and every price. It is represented graphically by a rightward, or outward, shift in the supply curve.
- A *decrease in supply* is a decrease in the quantity producers are willing and able to offer at each and every price. It is represented graphically by a leftward, or inward, shift in the supply curve.

In figure 2.4, an increase in supply is represented by the shift from S_1 to S_2. Producers are willing to produce a larger quantity at each price – Q_3 instead of Q_2 at price P_2, for example. They will also accept a lower price for each quantity – P_1 instead of P_2 for quantity Q_2. Conversely, the decrease in supply represented by the shift from S_1 to S_3 means that producers will offer less at each price – Q_1 instead of Q_2 at price P_2. They must also have a higher price for each quantity – P_3 instead of P_2 for quantity Q_2.

A few examples will illustrate the impact of changes in the determinants of supply. If firms learn how to produce more goods with the same or fewer resources, the cost of producing any given quantity will fall. Because of the technological improvement, firms will be able to offer a larger quantity at any

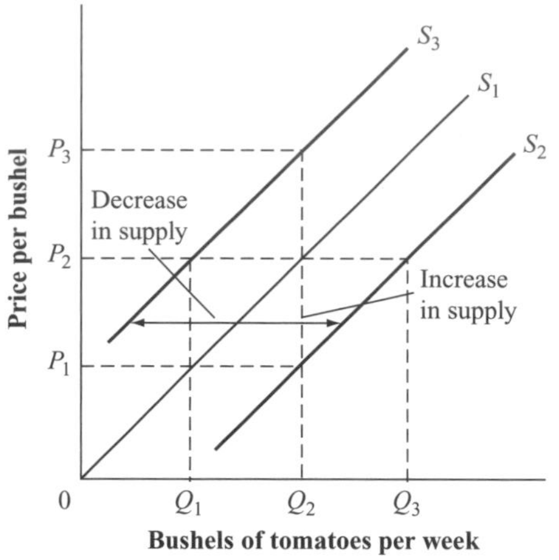

Figure 2.4 Shifts in the supply curve

A rightward, or outward, shift in the supply curve, from S_1 to S_2, represents an increase in supply. A leftward, or inward, shift in the supply curve, from S_1 to S_3, represents a decrease in supply.

given price or the same quantity at a lower price. The supply will increase, shifting the supply curve outward to the right.

Similarly, if the profitability of producing oranges increases relative to grapefruit, grapefruit producers will shift their resources to oranges. The supply of oranges will increase, shifting the supply curve to the right. Finally, if lumber (or labor or equipment) becomes scarcer, its price will rise, increasing the cost of new housing and reducing the supply. The supply curve will shift inward to the left.[3]

Market equilibrium

Supply and demand represent the two sides of the market – sellers and buyers. By plotting the supply and demand curves together, as in figure 2.5, we can explain why the decisions of buyers and sellers will be inconsistent with each other, and why a market surplus or shortage of tomatoes will result.

[3] Not all demand and supply curves are alike (or like the ones we have drawn in our figures to this point). A decrease in the price of all goods can result in an increase in the quantity demanded and a decrease in the quantity supplied. However, the quantity responses can be different for different goods. While this point is an important one, we shall reserve treatment of differences in quantity responses until later chapters. In this chapter, our intent is to cover only the basics of supply and demand.

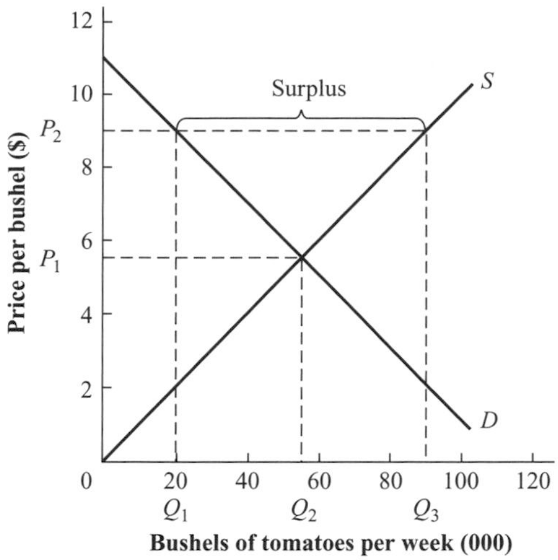

Figure 2.5 Market surplus

If a price is higher than the intersection of the supply and demand curves, a market surplus – a greater quantity supplied, Q_3, than demanded, Q_1 – results. Competitive pressure will push the price down to the equilibrium price P_1, the price at which the quantity supplied equals the quantity demanded (Q_2).

Market surpluses

A **market surplus** is the amount by which the quantity supplied exceeds the quantity demanded at any given price.

Suppose that the price of a bushel of tomatoes is $9, or P_2 in figure 2.5. At this price, the quantity demanded by consumers is 20,000 bushels, much less than the quantity offered by producers – 90,000. There is a **market surplus**, or excess supply, of 70,000 bushels. Graphically, an excess quantity supplied occurs at any price above the intersection of the supply and demand curves.

What will happen in this situation? Producers who cannot sell their tomatoes will have to compete by offering to sell at a lower price, forcing other producers to follow suit. As the competitive process forces the price down, the quantity that consumers are willing to buy will expand, while the quantity that producers are willing to sell will decrease. The result will be a contraction of the surplus, until it is finally eliminated at a price of $5.50 or P_1 (at the intersection of the two curves). At that price, producers will be selling all they want; they will see no reason to lower prices further. Similarly, consumers will see no reason to pay more; they will be buying all they want. This point at which the wants of buyers and sellers intersect is called the *equilibrium*, with the price and quantity at that point called *equilibrium price* and *equilibrium quantity*.

- The *equilibrium price* is the price toward which a competitive market will move, and at which it will remain once there, everything else held constant. It is the price at which the market "clears" – that is, at which the quantity demanded by consumers is matched exactly by the quantity offered by producers. At the equilibrium price, the quantity sellers are willing to supply and the quantity buyers want to consume are equal. This is the equilibrium quantity.
- The *equilibrium quantity* is the output (or sales) level toward which the market will move, and at which it will remain once there, everything else held constant.

In sum, a surplus emerges when the price asked is above the equilibrium price. It will be eliminated, through competition among sellers, when the price drops to the equilibrium price.

Market shortages

A **market shortage** is the amount by which the quantity demanded exceeds the quantity supplied at any given price.

Suppose that the price asked is below the equilibrium price, as in figure 2.6. At the relatively low price of \$1, or P_1, buyers want to purchase 100,000 bushels – substantially more than the 10,000 bushels producers are willing to offer. The result is a **market shortage**. Graphically, a market shortage is the shortfall that occurs at any price below the intersection of the supply and demand curves.

As with a market surplus, competition will correct the discrepancy between buyers' and sellers' plans. Buyers who want tomatoes but are unable to get them at a price of \$1 will bid higher prices, as at an auction. As the price rises, a larger quantity will be supplied because suppliers will be better able to cover their increasing production costs. Simultaneously, the quantity demanded will contract as buyers seek substitutes that are now relatively less expensive compared with tomatoes. At the equilibrium price of \$5.50, or P_2, the market shortage will be eliminated. Buyers will have no reason to bid prices up further; they will be getting all the tomatoes they want at that price. Sellers will have no reason to expand production further; they will be selling all they want to at that price. The equilibrium price will remain the same until some force shifts the position of either the supply or the demand curve. If such a shift occurs, the price will move toward a new equilibrium at the new intersection of the supply and demand curves.

In our graphical treatment of supply and demand, movement toward equilibrium can be thought of as instantaneous. Real-world movements in price will necessarily take some time, which means that the equilibrium price and

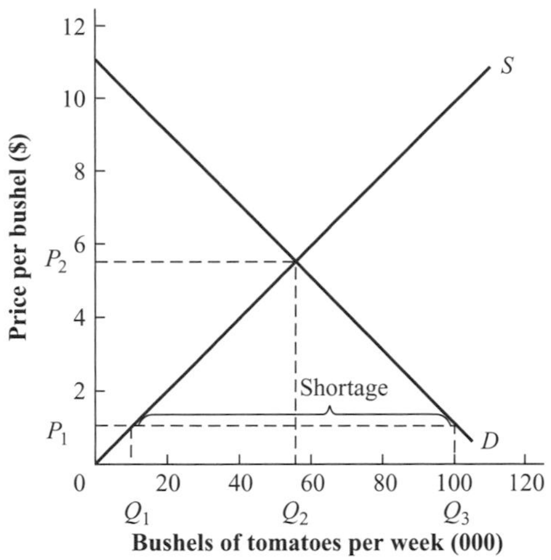

Figure 2.6 Market shortages

A price that is below the intersection of the supply and demand curves will create a shortage – a greater quantity demanded, Q_3, than supplied, Q_1. Competitive pressure will push the price up to the equilibrium price P_2, the price at which the quantity supplied equals the quantity demanded (Q_2).

quantity toward which the market will ultimately settle can shift with changes in supply and demand.

The effect of changes in demand and supply

Figure 2.7 shows the effects of shifts in demand and supply on the equilibrium price and quantity. In figure 2.7(a), an increase in demand from D_1 to D_2 raises the equilibrium price from P_1 to P_2 and quantity from Q_1 to Q_2. Figure 2.7(b) shows the reverse effects of a decrease in demand.

An increase in supply from S_1 to S_2 – figure 2.7(c) – has a different effect. The equilibrium quantity rises from Q_1 to Q_2, but the equilibrium price falls from P_2 to P_1. A decrease in supply from S_1 to S_2 – figure 2.7(d) – causes the opposite effect: the equilibrium quantity falls from Q_2 to Q_1, and the equilibrium price rises from P_1 to P_2.

Price ceilings and price floors

Political leaders have occasionally objected to the prices charged in open, competitive markets and have mandated the prices at which goods must be sold.

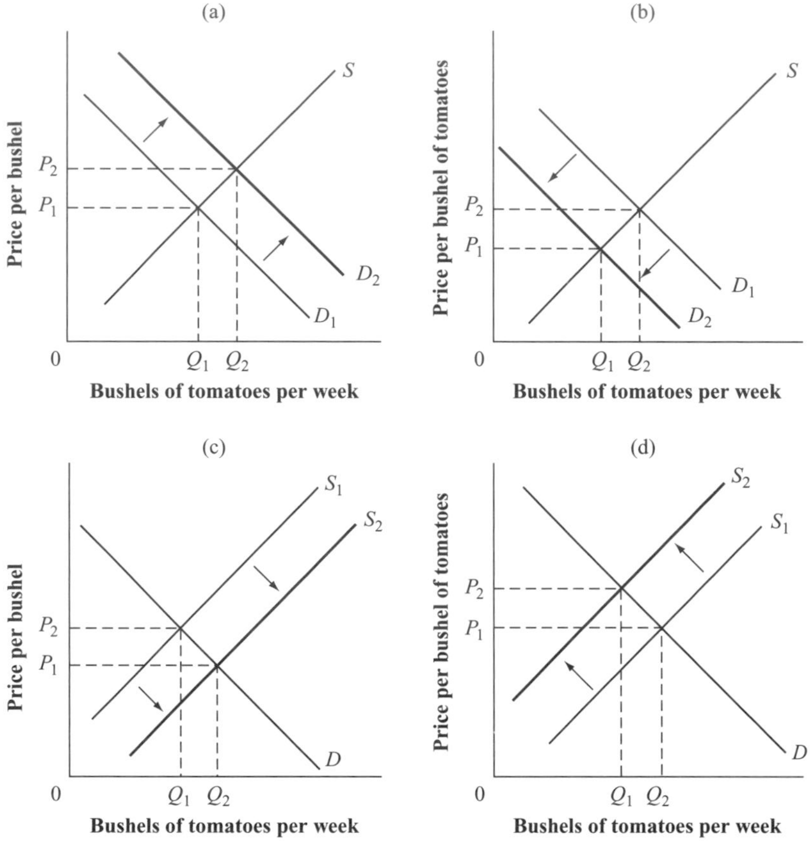

Figure 2.7 The effects of changes in supply and demand

An increase in demand – panel (a) – raises both the equilibrium price and the equilibrium quantity. A decrease in demand – panel (b) – has the opposite effect: a decrease in the equilibrium price and quantity. An increase in supply – panel (c) – causes the equilibrium quantity to rise but the equilibrium price to fall. A decrease in supply – panel (d) – has the opposite effect: a rise in the equilibrium price and a fall in the equilibrium quantity.

> A **price ceiling** is a government-determined price above which a specified good cannot be sold. A **price floor** is a government-determined price below which a specified good cannot be sold.

That is, the government has enforced **price ceilings** and **price floors**. Supply and demand graphs can illustrate the consequences of price ceilings and price floors.

For example, some cities impose ceilings on the rents (or prices) for apartments. Such a ceiling must be below the equilibrium price – somewhere below P_1 in figure 2.8(a). (If the ceiling were above equilibrium, it would be above the market price and would have no effect.) As the graph shows, such a price control creates a market shortage. The number of people wanting apartments, Q_2, is greater than the number of apartments available, Q_1. Because of the

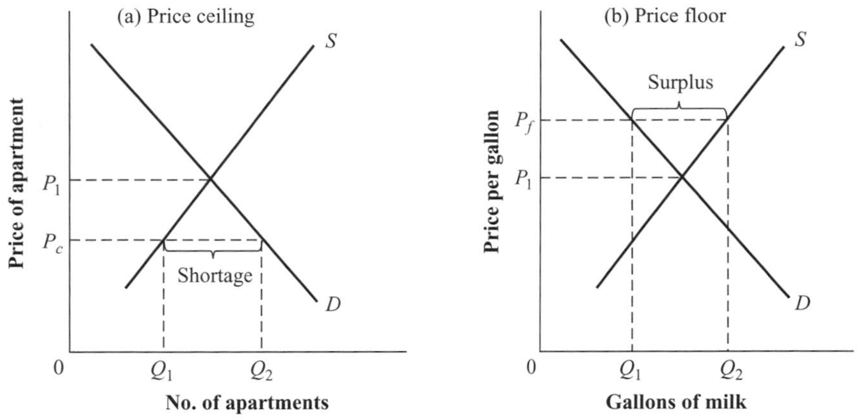

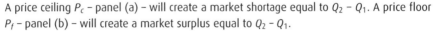

Figure 2.8 Price ceilings and floors
A price ceiling P_c – panel (a) – will create a market shortage equal to Q_2 - Q_1. A price floor P_f – panel (b) – will create a market surplus equal to Q_2 - Q_1.

shortage, landlords will be less concerned about maintaining their units, for they will be able to rent them in any case.

If the government imposes a price *floor* – on a commodity such as milk, for example – the price must be above the equilibrium price, P_1 in figure 2.8b. (A price floor below P_1 would be irrelevant, because the market would clear at a higher level on its own.) The result of such a price edict is a market surplus. Producers want to sell more milk, Q_2, than consumers are willing to buy, Q_1. Some producers – those caught holding the surplus (Q_2 – Q_1) – will be unable to sell all they want to sell. Eventually, someone must bear the cost of destroying or storing the surplus – and in fact the government holds vast quantities of a number of agricultural commodities because of efforts to support an equilibrium price for those commodities above their market clearing price.

More will be said about government price and wage controls in chapter 5.

The efficiency of the competitive market model

Early in this chapter we asked how Fred Lieberman knew what prices to charge for the goods he sold. The answer is now apparent: He adjusts his prices until his customers buy the quantities that he wants to sell. If he cannot sell all the fruits and vegetables he has, he lowers his price to attract customers and cuts back on his orders for those goods. If he runs short, he knows that he can raise his prices and increase his orders. His customers then adjust their purchases accordingly. Similar actions by other producers and customers all over the city

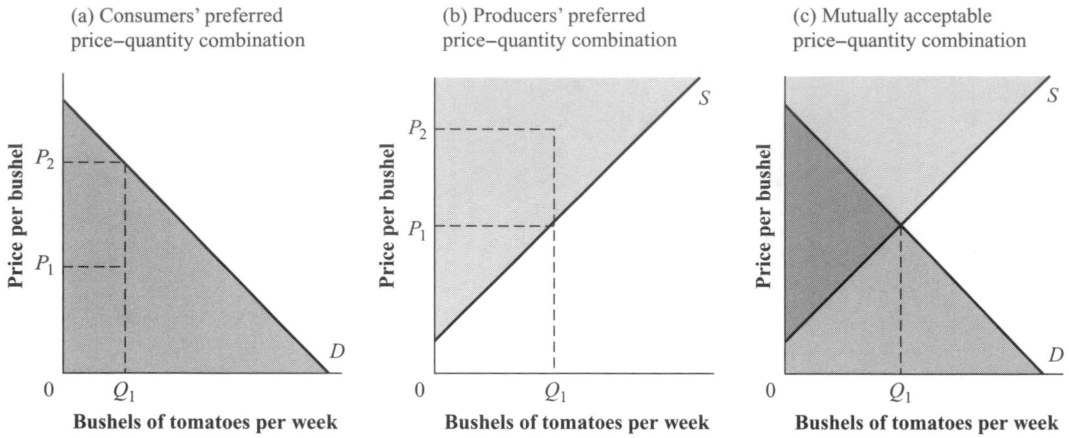

Figure 2.9 The efficiency of the competitive market
Only those price–quantity combinations on or below the demand curve – panel (a) – are acceptable to buyers. Only those price–quantity combinations on or above the supply curve – panel (b) – are acceptable to producers. Those price–quantity combinations that are acceptable to both buyers and producers are shown in the darkest shaded area of panel (c). The competitive market is "efficient" in the sense that it results in output Q_1, the maximum output level acceptable to both buyers and producers.

move the market for produce toward equilibrium. The information provided by the orders, reorders, and cancellations from stores such as Lieberman's eventually reaches the suppliers of goods and then the suppliers of resources. Similarly, wholesale prices give Fred Lieberman information on suppliers' costs of production and the relative scarcity and productivity of resources.

The use of the competitive market system to determine what and how much to produce has two advantages. First, it coordinates the decisions of consumers and producers very effectively. Most of the time the amount produced in a competitive market system is very close to the amount consumers want at the prevailing price – no more, no less. Second, the market system maximizes the amount of output that is acceptable to both buyer and seller. In figure 2.9(a), note that all the price–quantity combinations acceptable to consumers lie either on or below the market demand curve, in the shaded area. (If consumers are willing to pay P_2 for Q_1, then they should also be willing to pay less for that quantity – for example, P_1.) Furthermore, all the price–quantity combinations acceptable to producers lie either on or above the supply curve, in the shaded area shown in figure 2.9(b). (If producers are willing to accept P_1 for quantity Q_1, then they should also be willing to accept a higher price – for example, P_2). When supply and demand curves are combined in figure 2.9(c), we see

Efficiency is the maximization of output through careful allocation of resources, given the constraints of supply (producers' costs) and demand (consumers' preferences).

that all the price–quantity combinations acceptable to both consumers and producers lie in the darkest shaded triangular area. From all those acceptable output levels, the competitive market produces Q_1, the maximum output level that can be produced given what producers and consumers are willing and able to do. In this respect, the competitive market can be said to be *efficient*, or to allocate resources with **efficiency**. The achievement of efficiency means that consumers' or producers' welfare will be reduced by an expansion or contraction of output.

The market system exploits all the possible trades between buyers and sellers. Up to the equilibrium quantity, buyers will pay more than suppliers require (those points on the demand curve lie above the supply curve). Beyond Q_1, buyers will not pay as much as suppliers need to produce more (those points on the supply curve lie above the demand curve). Again, in this regard the market can be called efficient.

Nonprice competition

Markets in which suppliers compete solely in terms of price are relatively rare.[4] In fact, price competition is not always the best method of competition, not only because price reductions mean lower average revenues, but also because the reductions can be costly to communicate to consumers. Advertising is expensive, and consumers may not notice price reductions as readily as they do improvements in quality. Quality changes, furthermore, are not as readily duplicated as are price changes. Consumers' preferences for quality over price should be reflected in the profitability of making such improvements. If consumers prefer a top-of-the-line MP3 player (iPod) to a cheaper basic model, then producing the more sophisticated model could, depending on the cost of the extra features, be more profitable than producing the basic model and communicating its lower price to consumers.

If all consumers had exactly the same preferences – size, color, and so on – producers would presumably make uniform products and compete through price alone. For most products, however, people's preferences differ. To keep the analysis manageable, we will explore nonprice competition in terms of

[4] Table salt is a relatively uniform commodity sold in a market in which price is an important competitive tool. Even producers of salt, however, compete in terms of real or imagined quality differences and the reputation and recognition of brand names. In most industries, competition is through a wide range of product features, such as quality or appearance, design, and durability. In general, competitors can be expected to choose the mix of features that gives them the greatest profit.

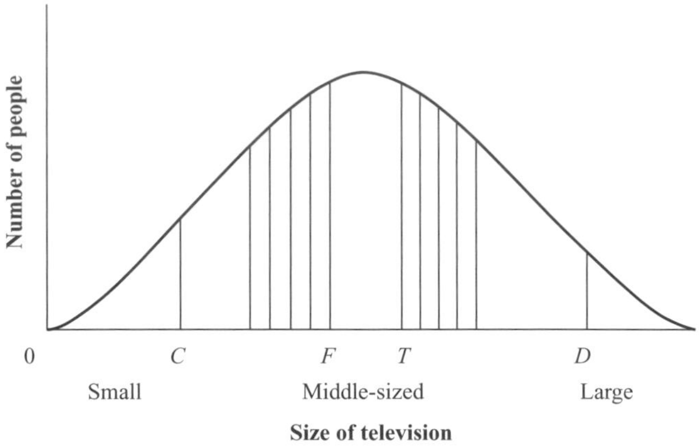

Figure 2.10 Consumer preference in television size
Consumers differ in their wants, but most desire a medium-sized television. Only a few want a very small or a large television.

just one feature – product size. Suppose that in the market for plasma television sets consumer preferences are distributed along the continuum shown in figure 2.10. The curve is bell shaped, indicating that most consumers are clustered in the middle of the distribution and want a medium-sized television. Fewer consumers want a giant screen or a mini-television.

Everything else being equal, the first producer to enter the market, Terrific TV, will probably offer a product that falls somewhere in the middle of the distribution – for example, at the "hump" in figure 2.10. In this way, Terrific TV offers a product that reflects the preferences of the largest number of people. Furthermore, as long as there are no competitors, the firm can expect to pick up customers to the left and right of center. (Terrific TV's product may not come very close to satisfying the wants of consumers who prefer a very large or very small television, but it is the only one available.) The more that Terrific TV can meet the preferences of the greatest number of consumers, everything else being equal, the higher the price it can charge and the greater the profit it can make. (Because consumers value the product more highly, they will pay a higher price for it.)

The first few competitors that enter the market may also locate close to the center – in fact, several may virtually duplicate Terrific TV's product. These firms may conclude that they will enjoy a larger market by sharing the center with several competitors than by moving out into the "wings" of the distribution. They are probably right. Although they may be able to charge more (relative to production cost) for a giant screen or a mini-television that closely reflects some consumers' preferences, there are fewer potential customers for those products

To illustrate, assume that competitor Fabulous Focus locates at *F*, close to *T*. It can then appeal to consumers on the left side of the curve because its product will reflect those consumers' preferences more closely than does Terrific TV's. Terrific TV can still appeal to consumers on the right half of the curve. If Fabulous Focus had located at *C*, however, it would have direct appeal only to consumers to the left of *C*, as well as those between *C* and *T* who are closer to *C*. Terrific TV would have appealed to more of the consumers on the left, between *C* and *T*, than in the first case. In short, Fabulous Focus has a larger potential market at *F* than at *C*.

However, as more competitors move into the market, the center will become so crowded that new competitors will find it advantageous to move away from the center, to *C* or *D*. At those points, the market will not be as large as it is in the center, but competition will be less intense. If producers do not have to compete directly with as many competitors, they can charge higher prices. How far out into the "wings" they move will depend on the trade offs they must make between the number of customers they can appeal to and the price they can charge.

As with price reductions, the movement of competitors into the "wings" of the distribution benefits consumers whose tastes differ from those of the people in the middle. These atypical consumers now have a product that comes closer to, or even directly reflects, their preferences.

Our discussion has assumed free entry into the market. If entry is restricted by monopoly of a strategic resource or by government regulation, the variety of products offered will not be as great as in an open, competitive market. If there are only two or three competitors in a market, everything else being equal, we would expect them to cluster in the middle of a bell shaped distribution. That tendency has been seen in the past in the broadcasting industry, when the number of television stations permitted in a given geographical area was strictly regulated by the Federal Communications Commission (FCC). Not surprisingly, stations carried programs that appealed predominantly to a mass audience – that is, to the middle of the distribution of television watchers. The Public Broadcasting System (PBS) was organized by the government partly to provide programs with less than mass appeal to satisfy viewers on the outer sections of the curve. When cable television emerged and programs became more varied, the prior justification for PBS subsidies became more debatable (with the future survival of PBS in jeopardy at the time of writing).

Even with free market entry, product variety depends on the cost of production and the prices people will pay for variations. Magazine and newsstand operators would behave very much like past television managers if they could carry only two or three magazines. They would choose *Newsweek* or some other magazine that appealed to the largest number of people. Most motel operators, for instance, have room for only a very small newsstand, and so they tend to carry the mass-circulation weeklies and monthlies.

For their own reasons, consumers may also prefer such a compromise. Although they may desire a product that perfectly reflects their tastes, they may buy a product that is not perfectly suitable if they can get it at a lower price. Producers can offer such a product at a lower price because of the economies (of cost savings) gained from selling to a large market (a topic to be taken up in greater detail in chapter 9). For example, instead of private tutorials, most students take predesigned classes in large lecture halls. They do so largely because the mass lecture, although perhaps less suitable for their particular preferences, is substantially cheaper than tutorials. In a market that is open to entry, producers will take advantage of such opportunities.

If producers in one part of a distribution attempt to charge a higher price than necessary, other producers can move into that segment of the market and push the price down; or consumers can switch to other products. In this way, competition in markets can press buyers and sellers to move toward an optimal mix of products. Without freedom of entry, we cannot tell whether it is possible to improve on the existing combination of products. A free, competitive market gives rival firms a chance to better that combination. The case for the free market becomes even stronger when we recognize that market conditions – and therefore the *optimal product mix* – are constantly changing.

Competition in the short run and the long run

One of the best examples of the workings of both price and nonprice competition is the market for calculators. Since the first model was introduced in the United States in 1969, the growth in sales, the advancement in technology and design, and the decline in prices in this market have been spectacular. The first calculator, which Hewlett-Packard sold for $395, had an eight-digit display and performed only four basic functions – addition, subtraction, division, and multiplication. By December 1971, Bowmar was offering an eight-digit, four-function model for $240. The next year, in an attempt to maintain its high prices, Hewlett-Packard introduced a sophisticated model that could perform many more functions, still for $395. By the end of the year, Bowmar, Sears, and other firms had broken the $100 barrier, and firms were offering built-in memories, AC adapters, and 1,500-hour batteries to shore up prices. At the year's end, Casio announced a basic model for $59.95.

In 1973, prices continued to fall. By the end of the year, National Semiconductor was offering a six-digit, four-function model for $29.95, and Hewlett-Packard had lowered the price of its special model by $100 and added extra features. In 1974, six-digit, four-function models sold for as little as $16.95. Eight-digit models that would have sold for more than $300 three or four years earlier carried price tags of $19.95. By 1976, consumers could buy a six-digit model for just $6.95. All this happened during a period when prices in general rose at a rate unprecedented in the United States during peacetime. The relative prices of calculators thus fell by even more than their dramatic price reductions suggest.

Short-run equilibrium is the price–quantity combination that will exist as long as producers do not have time to change their production facilities (or some resource that is fixed in the short run).

Yet the drop in the price of calculators was to be expected. Although the high prices of the first models partly reflected high production costs, they also brought high profits and tempted many other firms into the industry. These new firms duplicated and then improved the existing technology and increased their productivity in order to beat the competition or avoid being beaten themselves. Firms unwilling to move with the competition quickly lost their share of the market.

The increase in competition in the calculator market can be represented visually with supply and demand curves. Such an analysis permits us to observe long-run changes in market equilibrium. Given the limited technology and the small number of firms producing calculators in 1969, as well as restricted demand for this new product, let us assume that the supply and demand curves were initially S_1 and D_1 in figure 2.11. The initial equilibrium price would then be P_2 and Q_1. This is the **short-run equilibrium**.

Long-run equilibrium is the price–quantity combination that will exist after firms have had time to change their production facilities (or some other resource that is fixed in the short run).

Short-run equilibrium did not last long. In the years following 1969, firms expanded production, building new plants and converting facilities that had been producing other small electronic devices. *Economies of scale resulted*, and technological breakthrough lowered the cost of production still further. Several $150 circuits were reduced to very small $2 chips. The increased supply shifted the supply curve to the right, from S_1 to S_2 (see figure 2.11). Meanwhile, because of advertising and word of mouth, people became familiar with the product. Market demand increased, shifting the demand curve from D_1 to D_2. Because supply increased more than demand, the price fell from P_2 to P_1, and quantity rose from Q_1 to Q_2. The new equilibrium price and quantity, P_1 and Q_2, marked the new **long-run equilibrium**.

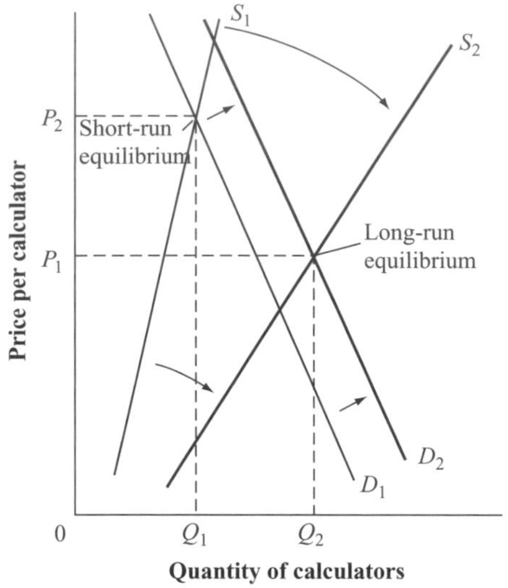

Figure 2.11 Long-run market for calculators
With supply and demand for calculators at D_1 and S_1, the short-run equilibrium price and quantity will be P_2 and Q_1. As existing firms expand production and new firms enter the industry, the supply curve shifts to S_2. Simultaneously, an increase in consumer awareness of the product shifts the demand curve to D_2. The resulting long-run equilibrium price and quantity are P_1 and Q_2, respectively.

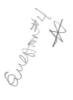

The market does not always move smoothly from the short run to the long run. Because firms do not know exactly what other firms are doing, or exactly what consumer demand will be, they may produce a product that cannot be sold at a price that will cover production costs. In fact, in the mid-1970s, prices fell so far that several companies were losing money. Long-run improvements sometimes come at the expense of short-run losses.

In this example, a long-run market adjustment causes a drop in price (because supply has increased more than demand). The opposite can occur: Demand can increase more than supply, causing a rise in the price and the quantity produced. As shown in figure 2.12(a), when the supply curve shifts to S_2 and the demand curve shifts to D_2, price increases from P_1 to P_2 and quantity produced rises from Q_1 to Q_2. As shown in figure 2.12(b), supply and demand may also adjust so that price remains constant while quantity increases.

Shortcomings of competitive markets

Although the competitive markets may promote long-run improvements in product prices, quality, and output levels, it has deficiencies, and we need to

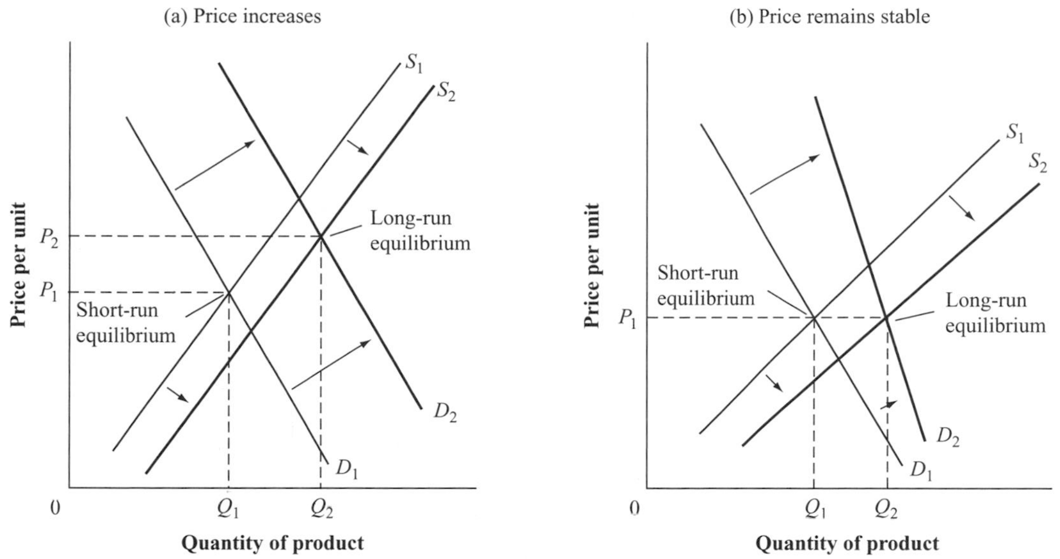

Figure 2.12 Prices in the long run
If demand increases more than supply, the price will rise along with the quantity sold – panel (a). If supply keeps up with demand, however, the price will remain the same even though the quantity sold increases – panel (b).

note several before closing. (Market deficiencies are discussed further in later chapters, especially chapters 5 and 11.)

First, the competitive market process can be quite efficient because production is expanded only as long as any additional unit produced is worth more than it costs. Consumer demand, however, depends on the way *income is distributed.* If market forces or government programs distort income distribution, the demand for goods and services will also be distorted. If, for example, income is concentrated in the hands of a few, the demand for luxury items will be high, but the demand for household appliances and new housing will be low. In such a situation, the results of competition may be "efficient" in a strict economic sense, but it may reflect an unfortunate distribution of income.

Second, the outcome of competition will not be efficient to the extent that production costs are imposed on people who do not consume a product. People whose house paint peels because of industrial pollution bear a portion of the offending firm's production cost, whether or not they buy its product. At the same time, the price that consumers pay for the product is lower than it would be if the producer incurred all costs, including pollution costs. Because of the low price, consumers will buy more than the efficient quantity. In a sense, this is an example of *overproduction.* Because all the costs of production have not been included in the producer's cost calculations, the price is artificially low.

Third, in a free market, competition can promote *socially undesirable* products or services. A competitive market in alcohol, heroin, or contract murders can lead to lower prices and greater quantities consumed – and thus an increase in social problems associated with addiction and murder. Competition is commonly considered undesirable unless it promotes the production of things people consider beneficial, but what is "beneficial" is a matter of values. Many people enjoy products that may be harmful, but are harmful only to those using them. In this case, the disapproval of others is less important than when people harm others with the products they consume.

Fourth, opponents of the market system contend that competition sometimes leads to "product proliferation" – too many versions of essentially the same product, such as aspirin – and to waste in production and advertisement. Because so many types of the same product are available, production of each takes place on a very small scale, and no plant is fully utilized. This may be true. The validity of this objection, however, hinges on whether the range of choice in products compensates for the inefficiencies in production. The question is whether firms should be forced to *standardize* their products and to compete solely in terms of price. What about people who want something different from the standard product?

Fifth, unscrupulous competitors can take advantage of customers' ignorance. A competitor may employ unethical techniques, such as circulating false information about rivals or using bait-and-switch promotional tactics (advertising very low-priced, low-quality products to attract customers and to switch them to higher-priced products when they get into the store). Competition can control some of these abuses. For instance, competitors will generally let consumers know when their rivals are misrepresenting their products. Still, fraudulent sellers can move from one market to another, keeping one step ahead of their reputations.

Perspective Why Queues?

In the supply and demand models covered in this chapter, one observation stands out: *The markets clear.* That is, price adjusts up or down until the quantity demanded exactly equals the quantity supplied.

Why, then, are queues so often seen at concerts, in grocery stores, and at theme parks – indeed, everywhere, suggesting that market shortages abound? Does the existence of queues mean that supply and demand models of markets are defective or irrelevant?

Not really. If nothing else, such models facilitate discussions of how prices can be expected to adjust *toward* (but not necessarily) *to* the equilibrium price. Such models allow us to predict the directional changes in prices, given changes in a variety of market forces, including technological and government policy changes.

There are also several ways of explaining the existence of queues.

First, given how many products are sold in markets, businesses are bound to make mistakes. They will simply choose from time to time a price that they believe to be the market clearing price but is, as they learn from real-world experience, below equilibrium, the result of which being that the quantity demanded exceeds the quantity supplied. Many such "mistakes," which means they do not charge as much as they could have, can be seen as the calculated costs of doing business. Managers can reason that as they raise their prices, they run a growing risk of charging too high a price, the result of which is that they are left with unsold goods (or unfilled seats in theaters and airplanes, the revenue on which is lost forever).

Second, there are solid business reasons for businesses maintaining inventories of the products they sell. They can never predict sales during any time period or a sequence of time periods with complete accuracy. Inventories allow firms to limit the costs of constantly replenishing their inventory stocks and missing sales. Similarly, businesses can understandably seek a "stock" or "inventory" of customers because such stocks, in the form of queues, enable businesses to have some customers in reserve to bring on line, so to speak, if demand varies. In short, businesses might be said to seek optimal stocks of both goods to sell and customers to sell to. Of course, a firm has to consider the strong possibility that if their customers don't receive as much of the firm's product as they want, they will simply go elsewhere.

Third, in some cases queues can be devices for screening out less-desired customers. Consider the challenge faced by promoters of rock concerts. The promoters for Metallica, a rock band, know that some potential (mainly young) attendees are more rabid about seeing the band than others. They can also surmise that the more rabid fans once in the concert hall (or stadium) will be more inclined to buy Metallica albums and concert memorabilia (T-shirts and hats) than other fans with a less intense interest in seeing the band. Queues can be a way of discouraging the less enthusiastic (perhaps older and more highly paid) potential attendees from going to the concert because of their relatively higher opportunity costs of standing in the ticket line.

Fourth (which is an explanation related to the first three), lines can be mutually beneficial to both buyers and sellers with the market clearing by way of shortage-creating prices. Consider grocery stores where lines at checkout counters are common at almost all times of the day (but especially in late afternoon when many people get off work). All they would have to do to eliminate the lines is add checkout counters and hire more clerks. Such added costs are an explanation for why the grocery store managers and their customers would prefer to have lines.

One grocery store might figure that it could reduce its checkout/clerking costs (and hence its prices) by reducing its checkout counters and clerks and allowing lines to form at each of the remaining counters. In short, lines can be profitable. The store's customers might not like incurring the added cost of the time spent standing in line. However, if the efficiency gains to the store are greater than the customers' wait costs, then the store can lower its grocery prices by more than the customer's wait costs, making the customers better off and causing customers to flock to the store with the checkout queues.

Other stores would have to follow suit, and would want to do so, just to protect their market position, if not to add to their profits (which they could if their costs savings are greater than any price reduction they would have to take to compensate consumers for their added wait costs). The result would be an increase in market supply and a decrease in market demand. If stores don't take opportunities to increase the lines when their cost savings are greater than the wait costs customers have to incur, their stock prices will suffer. Some savvy investors could be expected to buy up the stores' stocks at low prices, only then to adjust their lines, realizing cost savings and hiking profits, and selling out at higher stock prices that reflect the stores' expected future profits.

We explained how queues can be profitable to firms who allow them to emerge and beneficial to customers who have to stand in them. If queues were not mutually beneficial, we would have to wonder how they could be so prevalent in competitive markets – for example, in the grocery store industry. If queues created losses for firms, then firms should be expected to eliminate them. If customers did not gain *on balance* from standing in line, then we would expect firms to enter their market and serve such customers without lines forming.

The analysis of queues to this point has side-stepped an important question: How long should stores allow their lines to extend backward from their checkout counters? Obviously, there is some limit to most queues, given that grocery stores rarely have lines stretching to the backs of their stores and beyond. We can't give an answer of how long lines should be in so many feet, but we can give an answer in conceptual terms: To consider allowing even a short queue to form, the cost savings to the store must be greater than the cost customers spend waiting in the queues. Given that starting condition, rational (profit maximizing) store managers should be expected to allow their lines to grow (foot by foot) so long as their additional cost savings for each (foot of) extension of the queues is greater than the added wait costs their customers have to incur. Under this operating rule, with each extension of the lines both customers and stores can be better off. The total value (in profit terms for the stores and lower prices for customers) increases with the length of the line.

However, as the lines are extended, the costs incurred by customers is likely to grow as they have to forgo more and more valuable opportunities for doing other things as the count of minutes in line grows.[5] At the same time, with each extension the cost savings for the stores should begin to contract. As the checkout lines grow with each checkout counter taken out, less and less profitable other goods will be put in the space once occupied by the checkout counters. In addition, as the queues at the counters grow, the people standing in line can obstruct more and more shoppers trying to pull items from shelves.

If the cost savings for queues for the stores are initially greater than the costs incurred by customers, the two costs will move toward equality as the queues lengthen. When the added cost savings of the stores equals the added cost incurred by customers, there are no further mutual gains from extending the line. Hence, there is some "optimum" length line, which is where the stores' added cost savings from the last extension equals the added costs incurred by the customers. If the queues are extended beyond the optimum, then both store owners/managers and customers are worse off than they

[5] To spend the first minute standing in line, the customer will forgo the least-valuable other opportunity he or she has. The next minute in line means that the next-least-valuable opportunity has to be given up. The growing value of the opportunities given up as the time spent standing in line grows translates into an increase in the cost of standing in line.

could be. This means that both "too short" and "too long" lines can give rise to underperformance of firms and a potential change in management.

The optimum length line is likely to differ for different products and services and different markets. As might be imagined, the optimum will depend critically on the *opportunity cost* of their customers' time. Customers with higher wage rates (or more valuable opportunities for use of their time) will incur higher wait **opportunity costs** than customers with lower wage rates. Therefore, as a general rule, we should expect that lines in grocery stores in low-wage-rate neighborhoods (for example, in the South Central area of Los Angeles) will tend to be longer than the lines in high-wage-rate neighborhoods (for example, Newport Beach, California). If wage rates in a given neighborhood rise, we should expect the length of the lines to contract. It follows that high-end grocery stores (for example, Gelson's or Whole Foods Markets) in any given area catering to high-wage-rate customers should be expected to have shorter lines than low-end grocery stores (for example, Albertsons) catering to lower-wage-rate customers. We should not be surprised that the grocery industry is made up of holding companies that hold various "levels" (from low- to high-end) of grocery stores in part to offer a different array of products for their different customer bases, but also in part to optimize the lengths of their lines for different customer bases with different wait costs.

Opportunity cost is the value of the opportunity that someone does not take when anything is done.

PART II ORGANIZATIONAL ECONOMICS AND MANAGEMENT

Overpaying and underpaying workers

This chapter has been about how "markets" do things such as set product prices and production levels through the forces of competition. However, markets don't operate by themselves. Real, live people are involved who sometimes seem to do things that defy conventional market explanation.

Henry Ford's "overpayment"

Take, for example, Henry Ford, who is remembered for his organizational inventiveness (the assembly line) and for his presumption that he could ignore the wishes of his customers (as in his claim that he was willing to give buyers any color car they wanted as long as it was black!). However, he outdid himself when it came to workers: He *seemed* to want to deny the control of the market when it came to setting his workers' wages. But did he?

In 1914, he stunned his board of directors by proposing to raise his workers' wages to $3 a day, a third higher than the going wage ($2.20 a day) in the Detroit automobile industry at the time. When one of his board members wondered out loud why he was not considering giving workers even more, a wage of $4 or $5 a day, Ford quickly agreed to go to $5, more than twice the prevailing market wage. Why?

In the competitive framework illustrated with supply and demand curves, the "market wage" will settle where the market clears, or where the number of workers who are demanded by employers exactly equals the number of workers who are willing to work. And, once more, no profit-hungry employer (at least in the textbook discussions) would ever pay above (or below) the market wage. For that matter, in standard textbooks, employers in competitive markets are *unable* to pay anything other than the market wage, given competition. If employers ever tried to pay more, they could be underpriced and competed out of business by other producers who paid the lower market wage for their labor. If employers paid below the market wage, they would not be able to hire employees and would be left without products to sell.

An answer to why Ford paid more than the prevailing wage won't be found on the pages of standard economics textbooks (Meyer 1981). In those texts, wages are determined by *market conditions* – namely, the forces of supply and demand, as just discussed. The supply of labor is determined by what workers are willing to do, whereas the demand for labor is determined by the combined forces of worker productivity and the prices that can be charged for what the workers produce. The curves are more or less stationary (at least, in the way they are presented), and are certainly not subject to manipulation by employers and their policies.

There are two problems with that perspective from the point of view of this book. First, we don't wish to assume away the problem of business strategy and policy choices. On the contrary, we want to discuss how policies might affect worker productivity, or how employers might achieve maximum productivity from workers. We seek a rationale for Ford's dramatic wage move, if there is one to be found. In doing so, we don't deny that productivity affects worker wages, which is a well-established theoretical proposition in economics. What we insist on is that the reverse is also true – worker wages affect productivity – for very good economic reasons.

Second, a problem with standard market theory is that there is a lot of real-world experience that does not seem to fit the simple supply and demand model. Granted, the standard model is highly useful for discussing how wages might change with movements in the forces of supply and demand. From that framework, we can appreciate, for example, why wages move up when the labor demand increases (which can be attributable to productivity and/or price increases). At the same time, many employers have followed Ford's lead and have paid more than so-called "market wages." All one has to do to check out that claim is to watch how many workers put in applications when a plant announces that it is hiring. Sometimes, the lines stretch for blocks from the plant door. When the departments of history or English in our universities have an open professorship, the departments can expect a hundred or more qualified applicants. The US Postal Service regularly receives far more applications for its carrier jobs than it has jobs available. When Dell Computer announced its intention to hire workers at a new computer assembly plant in Winston-Salem, North Carolina in 2005, the line-up at the work fair stretched for blocks down the street; the end, in fact, could not be seen from the door. These queues cannot be explained by market clearing wages.

Consider the persistence of unemployment. The traditional view of labor markets would predict that the wage should be expected to fall until the market clears and the only evident unemployment should be transitory, encompassing people who are not working because they are between jobs or are looking for jobs. But "involuntary unemployment" abounds and persists, which must be attributable, albeit partially, to employers paying workers "too much" (or above the market clearing wage rate).

We don't pretend to provide a complete explanation for "overpaying" workers here. It may be that employers overpay their workers for some psychological reasons. Overpaying workers might make the employers feel good about themselves and their employees, which can show up in greater loyalty, longer job tenure, and harder and more dedicated work. The above-market wages may also remove workers' financial strains, leaving them with fewer problems at home and more energy to devote themselves to their jobs. Although we think that these can be relevant considerations, we prefer to look for other reasons, mainly as a means of improving incentives for workers to do as the employer wants.

As it turns out, Henry Ford was not offering his workers something extra for nothing in return (Halberstam 1986). He "overpaid" his workers primarily because he could then demand more of them. He could work them harder and longer, and he did. He could also expect to lower his training costs and could be more selective in the people he hired, which could be a boon to all Ford workers. Workers could reason that they would be working with more highly qualified cohorts, all of whom would be forced to devote themselves to their jobs more energetically and productively, creating a more viable firm and greater job security. But there were other benefits for Ford as well.

When workers are paid exactly their market wage, there is little cost to quitting. A worker making his market (or opportunity) wage can simply drop his job and move on to the next job with little loss in income. And, as was the case, Ford's workers were quitting with great frequency. In 1913, Ford had an employee turnover rate of 370 percent! That year, the company had to hire 52,000 workers to maintain a workforce of 13,600 workers.

The company estimated that hiring a worker costs from $35 to $70, and even then they were hard to control (with the costs of hiring workers today, even in the pizza business, being far higher than in Ford's time[6]). For example, before the pay raise, the absentee rate at Ford was 10 percent. Workers could stay home from work, more or less when they wanted, with virtually no threat of penalty. Given that they were being paid the market wage, the cost of their absenteeism was low to the workers. In effect, workers were buying a lot of absent days from work. It was a bargain. They could reason that if they were only receiving the "market wage rate," then that wage rate could be replaced elsewhere if they were ever fired for misbehaving on the job.

At any one time, most workers were new at their jobs. Shirking was rampant. Ford complained that "the undirected worker spends more time walking about for tools and material than he does working; he gets small pay because pedestrianism is not a highly paid line" (Halberstam 1986, 94). In order to control workers, the company figured that the firm had to create some buffer between itself and the fluidity of a "perfectly" functioning labor market.

The nearly $3 Ford paid above the market was, in effect, a premium paid to enforce the strict rules for employment eligibility that he imposed. Ford's so-called Sociology Department was staffed by investigators who, after the pay hike, made frequent home visits and checked into workers' savings plan, marital happiness, alcohol use, and moral conduct, as well as their work habits on the job. He was effectively paying for the right to make those checks, and he made the checks because he thought they would lead to more productive workers.

Ford was also paying for obedience. He is quoted as saying after the pay hike, "I have a thousand men who if I say 'Be at the northeast corner of the building at 4 a.m.' will be there at 4 a.m. That's what we want – obedience" (Halberstam 1986, 94). How much obedience or allegiance he got may be disputed. What

[6] According to a news report, in 2005 Domino's Pizza incurred a hiring cost of $2,500 for every hourly worker it hires. The cost of replacing a Domino's store manager was $20,000 (White 2005).

is not disputable is that he got dramatic results. In 1915, the turnover rate was 16 percent – down from 370 percent – and productivity increased about 50 percent.

It should be pointed out that control over workers is only part of the problem. Even if a boss has total control, there must be some way of knowing what employees should be doing to maximize their contribution to the firm. That wasn't a difficult problem for Ford. On the assembly line, it was obvious what Ford wanted his workers to do, and it was relatively easy to spot shirkers. According to David Halberstam, there was small chance for the shirker to prosper in the Ford plant. After the plant was mechanized and the $5-a-day policy was implemented, foremen were chosen largely for physical strength. According to Halberstam, "If a worker seemed to be loitering, the foreman simply knocked him down" (1986, 94). Given that the high wage attracted many applicants, Ford's workers simply put up with the abuse and threat of abuse because they didn't want to be replaced. The lines outside the employment office were a strong signal to workers. Of course, this type of heavy-handed control wasn't that prevalent in the Ford plants because workers quickly shaped up and responded to the new incentives. And it should be emphasized that the threat of physical punishment doesn't work in every work environment, particularly not today. When productivity requires that workers possess a lot of specialized knowledge that they must exercise creatively or in response to changing situations, heavy-handed enforcement tactics can undermine creativity and productivity. How is a manager to know whether a research chemist, a creator of software, or a manager is behaving in ways that make the best use of his or her talents in promoting the objectives of the firm? Do you knock workers down if they gaze out the window? Of course not. Managers typically provide more subtle incentive programs than a high daily salary and a tough foreman. The big problem is controlling employees who have expertise you lack. One way to inspire effort from those who can't be monitored directly on a daily basis is to "overpay" workers, and ensure that they suffer a cost in the event that their performance, as measured over time, is not adequate. The "overpayment" gives workers a reason to avoid being fired or demoted for such reasons as lack of performance and excessive shirking. Even when shirking is hard to detect, the threat of losing a well-paying job can be sufficient to motivate diligent effort (Shapiro and Stiglitz 1984; Bulow and Summers 1986; Roberts 2004).[7]

[7] So-called "equity theory," based in psychology, suggests that worker overpayment can lead to greater performance because the overpaid workers perceive an inequity in pay among their relevant peers. As a consequence, they seek to redress the overpayment by working longer and harder. Of course, the theory also suggests that underpaid workers will respond by working less diligently and putting in less time (Lawler 1968).

Overpayments to prevent misuse of firm resources

Many workers are in positions of responsibility, meaning that they have control over firm resources (real and financial) that they typically use with discretion – and can also misuse, or appropriate for their own uses. Their actions are also difficult to monitor. Misuse of funds may only infrequently be discovered. How should such employees be paid? More than likely, they should be "overpaid." That is, they should be paid more than their market wage as a way of imposing a cost on them if their misuse of funds – especially, their dishonesty – is ever uncovered. The expected loss of "excess wages" must exceed the potential (discounted) value of the misused funds. The less likely the employees are to be found out, the greater the overpayment must be in order for the cost to be controlling.

Why do managers of branch banks make more than bank tellers? One reason is that the managers' talents are scarcer than tellers' are. That is a point frequently drawn from standard labor market theorizing. We add here two additional factors: First, the manager is very likely in a position to misuse, or just steal, more firm resources than is each individual teller. Second, the manager's actions are less likely to be discovered than the teller's. The manager usually has more discretion than each teller does, and the manager has one less level of supervision.

Why does pay escalate with rank within organizations? There are myriad reasons, several of which we cover later. We suggest here that as managers move up the corporate ladder, they typically acquire more and more responsibility, gain more discretion over more firm resources, and have more opportunities to misuse firm resources. In order to deter the misuse of firm resources, the firm needs to increase the threat of penalty for any misuse, which implies a higher and higher wage premium for each step on the corporate ladder.

Workers in the bowels of their corporations often feel that the people in the executive suite are drastically "overpaid," given that their pay appears to be out of line with what they do. To a degree, the workers are right. People in the executive suite are often paid a premium simply to deter them from misusing their powers. The workers should not necessarily resent the overpayments. The overpayments may be the most efficient way available for making sure that firm resources are used efficiently. To the extent that the overpayments work, the jobs of people at the bottom of the corporate ladder can be more productive, better paying, and more secure.

We have not covered all possible reasons that workers are not paid strictly as suggested by simple supply and demand curve analysis. Nevertheless, the

Ford case permits us to make two general points: First, moving decisions away from the impersonal forces of the marketplace and into the more personal forces inside a firm, with long-term relational contracts, can increase efficiency by reducing costs. And, second, the decisions made on how the firms organize their "overpayments" can have important consequences for the efficiency of production because workers can have a greater incentive to invest "sweat equity" in their firms and to become more productive. The firm that gets the "overpayment" right (and exactly what it should be cannot be settled in theory) can gain a competitive advantage over rivals. Apparently, Ford secured an important advantage by going, in a sense, "off market."

When workers should not accept overpayments

Should workers accept "overpayment"? Better yet, is a greater overpayment always better for workers? The natural tendency is to answer with a strong, "Yes!" Well, we think a more cautious answer is in order, as in "Maybe" or, again, "It depends." Workers would be well advised to carefully assess what is expected of them, immediately and down the road. High pay means that employers can make greater demands – in terms of the scope and intensity of work assignments – on their employees. This is because of the cost they will bear if they do not consent to the demands.

Clearly, workers should expect that their employers will demand value equal to, if not above, the wage payments, and workers should consider whether they contribute as much to their firms' coffers as they take. Otherwise, their job tenure may be tenuous. The value of a job is ultimately equal to how much the workers can expect to earn over time, appropriately adjusted for the fact that future payments are not worth as much to workers as current ones are and for the fact that uncertain payments are not worth as much as certain payments. A high-paying job that is lost almost immediately for inadequate performance may be a poor deal for an employee.

To make this point with focus in our classes, we have often told our MBA students that they are unlikely to be offered upon graduation salaries at the high end of the executive level. However, if by some chance they were offered such a salary – say, $400,000 a year – they should seriously consider turning it down. We suggest that most should probably consider jobs with annual salaries more in the range of $80,000–$100,000, something close to whatever is the going market wage for their graduate school cohorts. Our students are generally startled by our brazen suggestion.

Why should any sane person turn down such a lucrative offer, if a sane employer tendered it? An answer is not all that mysterious. Unless a new graduate is able and willing to return $400,000 a year in value, he or she would be unlikely to retain such a high-paying job for very long. The person who quickly fails at a high salary can end up doing far worse than the person who begins his or her career by succeeding at a more modest salary.

The point that emerges from such a discussion and needs to be remembered is that the actual extent of the "overpayment" will not be determined solely by employers, as was true with Ford in 1913. Employees will also have a say. They have an interest in limiting the overpayment in order to limit the demands placed on them and to increase their job security. That is to say, the extent of the "overpayment" is, itself, determined by negotiation, if not market forces, with the wage pressures not always occurring in the expected ways. The pay negotiations can involve having the workers press for a lower overpayment while the employer presses for the opposite.

The overpayment/underpayment connection

Firms might also "overpay" their workers because they have "underpaid" their workers early in their careers. The "overpayments" are not so much "excess payments" as they are "repayments" of wages forgone early in the workers' careers. Of course, the workers would not likely forgo wages unless they expected their delayed overpayments to include interest on the wages forgone. So, the delayed overpayments must exceed underpayments by the applicable market interest rate. In such cases, the firms are effectively using their workers as sources of capital. The workers themselves become "venture capitalists" of an important kind.

Why would firms do that? Some new firms must do it just to get started. They don't have access to all of the capital they need in their early years, given that their product or service has not been proven. They must ask their workers to invest "sweat equity," which is equal to the difference between what the workers could make in their respective labor markets and what they are paid by their firms. The underpayments not only extend the sources of capital to the firm but also give the workers a strong stake in the future of the firm, which can make the workers work all the harder to make the firm's future a prosperous one. The up-front underpayments can make the firm more profitable and increase its odds of survival, which can be a benefit to workers as well as owners. Of course, this is one reason that many young workers are willing to accept employment in firms that are just starting out. Young workers often have a limited financial base from which to make investments; they do, however, have their time and energy to invest.

Underpayments to workers that are coupled with later overpayments can also be seen as a means by which managers can enhance the incentives workers have to become more productive. If workers are underpaid when they start, their rewards can be hiked later by more than otherwise to account for productivity improvements. These hikes can continue – and must continue – until the workers are effectively overpaid later in their careers (or else the workers would not have accepted the underpayments earlier in their careers). However, managers must understand that they must be able to *commit* themselves to the overpayments and that there must be some end to them.

Mandatory retirement

Not too many years ago, firms regularly required their workers to retire at age sixty-five. Retirement was ritualistic for managers. Shortly after a manager had his or her sixty-fifth birthday, someone would organize a dinner at which the manager would be given a gold watch and a plaque for venerable service and then be shown to the door with one last pleasant goodbye.

Why would a firm impose a mandatory retirement age on its workers? Such a policy seems truly bizarre, given that most companies are intent on making as much money as they can. Often the workers forced to retire are some of the more productive in the firm, simply because they have more experience with the firm and its customer and supplier networks.

Although we acknowledge that mandatory retirement may appear to be a mistake, particularly in the case of highly productive employees, we think that for many companies a mandatory retirement policy makes good business sense – when they have been "overpaying" their workers for some time. (Otherwise, we would be hard pressed to explain why such policies would survive and would need to be outlawed.) To lay out that logic, we must take a detour into an analysis of the way that workers who come under mandatory retirement policies are paid throughout their careers.

Paying market wages, or exactly what workers are worth at every stage in their career, does not always maximize worker incomes. That was a central point of the discussion to this point. We extend that discussion here by showing how the manipulation of a worker's *career* wage structure, or earnings path over time, can actually raise worker productivity and lifetime income. However, as will also be shown, when worker wages diverge from their value over the course

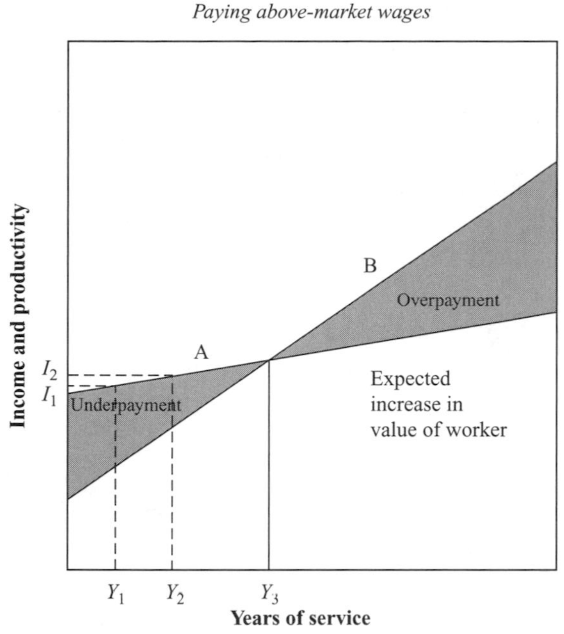

Figure 2.13 Twisted pay scale

The worker expects his productivity to rise along line *A* with years of service. If she starts work with less pay than she could earn elsewhere, then her career pay path could follow line *B*, representing greater increases in pay with time and greater productivity.

of their careers, mandatory retirement is a necessary component of the labor contract (Lazear 1979).

Suppose that a worker goes to work for Apex, Inc. and is paid exactly what she is worth at every point in time. Assume that she can expect to have a modest productivity improvement over the course of a thirty-year career, described by the slightly upward sloping line *A* in figure 2.13. If her income follows her productivity, her salaries will rise in line with the slope of line *A*. In year Y_1, the worker's annual income will be I_1; in year Y_2, it will be I_2, and so forth.

Is there a way by which management can restructure the worker's income path and simultaneously enable both the workers and the firm to gain? No matter what else is done, management must clearly pay the worker an amount equal at least to what he or she is worth *over the course of her career*. Otherwise, the worker would not stay with the company. The worker would exit the firm, moving to secure the available higher career income. However, management need not pay, each year, an amount equal to the income points represented on line *A*. Management could pay the worker less than she is worth for a while, as long as management is willing to compensate by overpaying her later.

For example, suppose that management charts a career pay path given by line *B*, which implies that up until year Y_3, the workers are paid less than they are worth, with the extent of the underpayment equaling the shaded area between the origin and Y_3. However, the workers would be compensated for what amounts to an investment in the firm by an overpayment after year Y_3, with the extent of the overpayment equal to the shaded area above line *A* after Y_3.

Are the firm and worker likely to be better off? Notice that the actual proposed pay line *B* is much steeper than line *A* which, again, represents the worker's income path in the absence of management's intentional twisting of the pay structure. The greatest angle of line *B* means that the worker is less likely to leave the company after she has been with the firm for a while. This increases the expected payoff the firm realizes from investing in the worker with varied assignments and training, investments that would not make sense if the firm thought that the worker was going to take the training and then take her improved skills to another firm. The additional training obviously improves the worker's productivity which shifts up her productive curve in figure 2.13 and her compensation line. This can mean not only more compensation over a worker's entire career, but more compensation at every point in time, even early on when she is being "undercompensated" if her productivity curve shifts up enough.

There is another advantage workers receive from the deferred compensation illustrated in figure 2.13, especially good workers. When interviewing for a job the interviewers would like to know how dedicated and hard working you will be, and how confident you are that you will do what it takes to become a high-productivity worker, the type of person they want to hire. Of course, any one can claim to be a great employee, but the interviewers are likely to discount such claims since they know that they are self-serving, and difficult to check out. If you really are an ambitious, hard-working person who does have confidence that you will be a great employee, it would be to your advantage to be able to convince the firm of those attributes. And one of the most credible ways of doing so is by being willing to accept a pay arrangement in which you work for something less than you might be worth initially, proving your worth before receiving a really significant salary. That is exactly what you are able to do by accepting a job with a steep earning profile (deferred compensation).

There is another reason why good workers may want to work for a firm that intentionally underpays them when they are young or just starting out with the company. The workers can reason that everyone in the firm will have a greater incentive to work harder and smarter. Hence, they can all enjoy higher prospective incomes over the course of their careers. Normally, commentaries on worker pay implicitly assume that the pay structure is what management imposes on workers. Seen from the perspective of the economic realities of what is available for distribution to all workers in a firm, we could just as easily reason that the kind of pay structure represented by line *B* in figure 2.13 is what the workers would encourage management to adopt. Actually, the twisting of the pay structure is nothing more than an innovative way for managers to increase the money they make off their workers while also increasing the money that workers are able to make off their firms. In short, it is a mutually beneficial deal, something of a "free good," in the sense that more is available for everyone.

The role of employers' "credible commitments"

If twisting the pay structure is such a good idea, why isn't it observed more often than it is in industry? Perhaps some variant of twisted pay schedules is more widely used than it is thought to be, primarily because such pay schedules are not identified as such. Public and private universities are notorious for making their assistant professors work harder than full professors who have tenure and far more pay. Large private firms, such as General Motors and IBM, appear to have pay structures that are more like line *B* than line *A* in figure 2.13. However, millions of firms appear to be unwilling or unable to move away from a pay structure such as line *A*.

One of the problems with line *B* is that young workers must accept a cut in pay for a promise of greater pay in the future – and the pay later on must exceed what the workers can get elsewhere *and*, what is crucial to workers, more than what their firm would have to pay if they simply hired replacement workers at the going market wage. Obviously, the workers take the considerable risk that their firm will not live up to its promise and fail to raise their pay later to points above their market wage or, even worse, fire them.

Needless to say, the firm must be able to make a *credible commitment* to its workers that it will live up to its part of the bargain, the *quo* in the *quid pro quo*. Truly credible commitments require that the firm must be able to demonstrate a capacity and inclination to do what it says it will do. The firm must be believable by those who make the early wage concessions. Many firms are not going to be able to twist their pay structures, and thereby gain the productivity improvements, because they are new, maybe small, with a shaky financial base and an uncertain future. New firms have little history by which workers can assess the value of their firms' commitments. Small firms are often short-lived firms. Financially shaky firms, especially those that suffer from problems of insolvency or illiquidity, are not likely to be able to garner the trust of their workers. Firms that are in highly fluid, ever-changing, and competitive markets are also unlikely candidates for having the ability to twist their pay structures. They all will tend to have to pay workers their market worth, or even a premium, to accommodate the risks that workers must accept when the company's existence is in doubt. We have to qualify these comments when considering a new firm with the prospects of a very profitable future (some high-tech firms, for example) even though there is a good chance that it will fail, as will be discussed in a moment.

What firms are most likely to twist their pay structures? Ones that have been established for some time, have a degree of financial and market stability, have some monopoly power – and have proven by their actions that their word is their bond. To prove the latter, firms cannot simply go willy-nilly about dismissing workers or cutting their pay when they find cheaper replacements. To do so would be undermine their credibility with their workers.

We can't be too precise in identifying the types of firms that can twist their pay structures, for the simple reason that there can be extenuating circumstances. For example, we can imagine that some unproved upstart companies would be able to pay their workers below-market wages. As noted, they may have to do so, simply because they do not have the requisite cash flow early in their development. New firms often ask, or demand, that their workers provide "sweat equity" in their firms through the acceptance of below-market wages, but always with the expectation that their investment will pay off. Which new firms are likely to be able to do this?

We suspect that firms with new products that represent a substantial improvement over established products would be good candidates. The likely success of the new product gives a form of baseline credibility to firm owner commitments that they intend to – and can – repay the "sweat equity" later. Indeed, the greater the improvement the new product represents, the more likely it is that the firm can make the repayment, and do so in an expeditious manner, and the more likely the workers will accept below-market wages to start with. The very fact that the product is a substantial improvement increases the likelihood of the firm's eventual success, for two reasons. The first reason is widely recognized: A product that represents a substantial improvement will likely attract considerable consumer attention. The second reason is less obvious: The firm can delay its wage payments, using its scarce cash flow in its initial stages of production for other things, such as quality control, distribution, and promotion. The firm gets capital – sweat equity – from an unheralded source, workers. The workers' investment of their sweat equity can enhance the firms' survival chances and, thereby, even lower the interest rate that the firms must pay on their debt (because the debt is more secure).

Breaking commitments

Of course, there are times when firms must break with their past commitments. For example, if a firm that was once insulated from foreign competition has all of a sudden to confront more cost-effective foreign competitors in domestic markets (because, say, transportation costs have been lowered), then the firm may have to break with its commitments to overpay workers late in their careers. If they don't, the competition will simply pay people the going market wage and erode the markets of those firms who continue to overpay their older workers. Without question, many older American workers – for example, middle managers in the automobile industry – have hard feelings about the advent of the "global marketplace." They may have suffered through years of hard work at below-market wages in the belief that they would be able, later in their careers, to slack off and still see their wages rise further and further above the market rate. The advent of global competition, however, has undercut the capacity of many American firms to fulfill their part of an implied bargain with their workers.

Even though they may have hard feelings, it does not follow that the workers would want their firms to try to hold to their prior agreements. Many workers understand that their wages can be higher *than they otherwise would be* if their firms kept their prior agreement. Without the reneging, the firm might fold. In a sense, the workers made an investment in the firm through their lower wages, and the investment didn't pay off as much as expected. However, we hasten to add that some American workers have probably been burned by firms that have used changing market conditions as an *excuse* to break with their commitments or that have sold their firms to buyers who felt no compulsion to hold to the original owners' prior commitments.[8]

[8] The analysis can really get sticky and convoluted when it is recognized that the *commitments* that firms make are only implicitly made, with no formal contract, often with a host of unstated contingencies. For example, many firms may commit to overpaying their workers *if* the firm is not sold and *if* market conditions do not turn against them. Workers will simply have to consider those contingencies in the wages that they demand early in their careers and later on. All we can say is that the greater the variety and number of contingencies the less the underpayment workers will accept early in their careers, and the less benefits firms and their workers will achieve from twisting the wage structure.

The answer to the question central to this discussion: "Why does mandatory retirement exist?" can now be provided, at least partially. Mandatory retirement at, say, sixty-five or seventy may be instituted for any number of plausible reasons. It might be introduced simply to move out workers who have become mentally or physically impaired. Perhaps, in some ideal world, the policy should not, for this reason, be applied to everyone. After all, many older workers are in the midst of their more productive years, because of their accumulated experience and wisdom, when they are in their sixties and seventies. However, it may still be a reasonable *rule* because its application to *all* workers may mean that *on average*, by applying the policy without exception, the firm is more efficient and profitable than it would be had it incurred the costs of individually scrutinizing workers at retirement time.

However, the *expected* fitness of workers at the time of retirement is simply not the only likely issue at stake. We see mandatory retirement as we see all employment rules, as a part of what is presumed to be a mutually beneficial employment contract, replete with many other rules. It is a contract provision that helps both the firms that adopt it and their workers who must abide by it. Parts of the contract can make the mandatory retirement rule economically sound.

We have spent much of this section exploring the logic of twisting workers' career income paths. If such a twist is productive and profitable, and if workers must be overpaid late in their careers to make the twist doable, then it follows that firms will want, at some point, to cut the overpayments off. What is mandatory retirement? It is – at least at the margin – a means of cutting off at some definite point the stream of overpayments. It is a means of making it possible, and economically practical, for a firm to engage a twisted pay scale and to improve incentives to add to the firm's productivity and profitability. To continue overpayments until workers – even the most productive ones – collapse on the job is nothing short of a policy that courts financial disaster.

Having said that, suppose Congress decides that mandatory retirement is simply an inane employment policy (as it has done)? After all, members of Congress might reason, many of the workers who are forced to retire are still quite productive. What are the consequences?

Clearly, the older workers who are approaching the prior retirement age, who suffered through years of underpayment early in their careers, but who are, at the time of the abolition of mandatory retirement policy, being overpaid, will gain from the passage of the law. They can continue to collect their overpayments until they drop dead or decide that work is something they would prefer not to do. They gain more in overpayments than they could have anticipated (and they get more back from their firms than they paid for in terms of their early underpayments). These employees will, because of the actions of Congress, experience an unexpected wealth gain.

There are, however, clear losers. The owners will suffer a wealth loss; they will have to continue with the overpayments. Knowing that, the owners will likely try to minimize their losses. Assuming that the owners can't lower their older workers' wages to market levels and eliminate the overpayment (because of laws against age discrimination), they will simply seek to capitalize the expected stream of losses from keeping the older workers on and buy them out – that is, pay them some lump-sum amount to induce them to retire.

To buy the workers out, the owners would not have to pay their workers an amount equal to the current value of their expected future wages. The reason is that the worker should be able to collect some lower wage in some other job if he or she is bought out. Presumably, the buyout payments would be no less than the value of the expected stream of *overpayments* (the pay received from the company minus the pay the worker could get elsewhere, appropriately discounted).

In order for the buyout to work, of course, both the owners and workers must be no worse off and, preferably, each group should gain by any deal that is struck. How can that be? Owners and workers could easily make a deal whereby both sides are no worse off. The owners simply pay the workers the current value of the overpayments (adjusted for the timing and uncertainty of the future payments).

But, can both sides *gain* by a buyout deal? That may not always be so easy a result to bring about. The owners would have to be willing to pay workers more than they, the workers, are willing to accept as a minimum. There are several reasons such a deal may be possible in many, but not necessarily all, cases. First, the workers could have a higher discount rate than the owners, and this may often be the case because the owners are more diversified than their workers in their investments. Workers tend to concentrate their capital, a main component of which is *human capital*, in their jobs. By agreeing to a buyout and receiving some form of lump-sum payment in cash (or even in a stream of future cash payments), the workers can diversify their portfolios by scattering the cash among a variety of real and financial assets. Hence, workers might accept less than the current (discounted) value of their overpayments just to gain the greater security of a more diversified investment portfolio. Naturally (and we use that word advisedly), the workers cannot be sure how long they will be around to collect the overpayments. By taking the payments in lump-sum form, they reduce the risk of collection and increase the security of their heirs.

Second, sometimes retirement systems are overfunded – that is, they have greater expected income streams from their investments than are needed for meeting the expected future outflow of retirement payments. This appears to be true (at the time of writing), for example, of the California State Employee Retirement System. Therefore, if the company can tap the retirement funds, as the State of California did in the 1990s, it can pay workers more in the buyout than they would receive in overpayments by continuing to work. In so doing, they can move those salaries "off budget," which is what California has done in order to match its budgeted expenditures with declining funding levels for higher education.

Third, some workers may take the buyout because they expect that their companies will meet with financial difficulty from competition down the road. The higher the probability that the company will fail in the future (especially the near future), the more likely workers would be willing to accept a monetary buyout that is less than the current value of the stream of overpayments

Fourth, some workers might take the buyout simply because they have tired of working for the company or want to walk away from built-up hostilities. To that extent, the buyout can be less than the (discounted) value of the overpayments.

Fifth, of course, older workers have to fear that the employer will not continue to pay workers more than they are worth indefinitely. The owners can, if they choose to do so, lower the amount of the buyout payment simply by making life more difficult for older workers in ways that are not necessarily subject to legal challenge (for example, by changing work and office assignments, secretarial assistance, discretionary budgeted items, flexibility in scheduling, etc.).[9] The owners may never actually have to take such actions to lower the buyout payments. All that is necessary is for the *threat* to be a real consideration. Workers might rightfully expect that the greater their projected overpayments, the more they must fear their owners will use their remaining discretion to make a buyout doable.

[9] Workers also understand that challenging the actions of owners can get expensive, which means that owners might take actions with regard to their older workers that are subject to legal challenge but only in a probabilistic sense. That is to say, owners might simply demote older workers. Even though employers who take such an actions *could* be taken to court, they might not be taken to court, given the expense the worker might have to incur and the likelihood that the challenge will take a long time and might not be successful.

The abolition of mandatory retirement

We should also expect that workers' fears will vary across firms and will be related to a host of factors, not the least of which will be the size of the firm. Workers who work for large firms may not be as fearful as workers for small firms, mainly because large firms are more likely to be sued for any retaliatory use of their discretionary employment practices (and efforts to adjust the work of older workers in response to any law that abolishes mandatory retirement rules). Large firms simply have more to take as a penalty for what are judged to be illegal acts. Moreover, it appears that juries are far more likely to impose much larger penalties on large firms, with lots of equity, than on their smaller counterparts. This unequal treatment before the courts, however, suggests that laws that abolish mandatory retirement rules will give small firms a competitive advantage over their larger market rivals.

However, we hasten to stress that all we have done is to discuss the transitory adjustments firms will make with their older workers, who are near the previous retirement age. We should expect other adjustments for younger workers, not the least of which will be a change in their wage structures. Not being able to overpay their older workers in their later years will probably mean that the owners will have to raise the pay of their younger workers. After all, the only reason the younger workers would accept underpayment for years is the prospect of overpayments later on.

There are three general observations from this line of inquiry that are interesting:

(1) The abolition of mandatory retirement will tend to help those who are about to retire.
(2) Abolition might help some older workers who are years from retirement, who work for large firms, and who can hang on to their overpayments. It can hurt other older workers who are fired, demoted, not given raises, or have their pay actually cut.
(3) It can increase the wages of younger workers by lowering the amount by which they will be underpaid. However, their increase in wages while they are young will come at the expense of smaller overpayments later in their careers. Many, if not all, of these younger workers will not be any better off because of the abolition of mandatory retirement than they would have been with a retirement rule permitted.

Overall, productivity might be expected to suffer, given that owners can no longer twist their career pay structures for their workers. As a consequence, workers will not have as strong an incentive to improve their productivity. They simply cannot gain as much by doing so. This means that the abolition of mandatory retirement rules can lower worker wages from what they otherwise would have been.

The simple point that emerges from this line of discussion is that the level and structure of pay counts for reasons that are not always so obvious. But our point about "overpayment" is fairly general, applying to the purchase of any number of resources other than labor. You may simply want to "overpay" suppliers at times just to ensure that they will provide the agreed-upon level of quality, so that they will not take opportunities to shirk because they can lose, on balance, if they do so (Klein and Leffler 1981).

The moral of the analysis is that most firms have good economic reasons for doing what they do. There are certainly solid economic grounds for overpaying workers, just as there are good reasons for mandatory retirement.[10]

THE BOTTOM LINE

The key takeaways from chapter 2 are the following:

(1) The market is a system that provides producers with incentives to deliver goods and services to others. To respond to those incentives, producers must meet the needs of society. They must compete with other producers to deliver their goods and services in the most cost-effective manner.

(2) A market implies that sellers and buyers can freely respond to incentives and that they have options and can choose among them. It does not mean, however, that behavior is totally unconstrained or that producers can choose from unlimited options. What a competitor can do may be severely limited by what rival firms are willing to do.

(3) Demand curves slope downward (and represent inverse relationships between price and quantity demanded). Supply curves slope upwards (and represent positive relationships between price and quantity produced). The positions of these curves are determined by a number of market forces.

[10] We like to think that members of Congress were well intentioned when they abolished mandatory retirement rules in 1978. Unfortunately, they simply did not think through these complex matters very carefully. (Perhaps the politics of the moment did not allow them to do so.) If they had considered the full complexity of firms' retirement policies, many older workers would not now be suffering through the impaired earnings and employment opportunities that members of Congress are now decrying.

(4) Price and quantity in competitive markets will tend to move toward the intersection of supply and demand, which is the point of maximum efficiency.
(5) Market shortages will lead to price increases. Market surpluses will lead to price decreases.
(6) Equilibrium price and quantity in competitive markets can be expected to change in predictable ways relative to increases and decreases in supply and demand.
(7) Price ceilings give rise to market shortages. Price floors give rise to market surpluses.
(8) Queues occur in competitive markets when they are mutually beneficial to both buyers and suppliers.
(9) The market system is not perfect. Producers may have difficulty acquiring enough information to make reliable production decisions. People take time to respond to incentives, and producers can make high profits while others are gathering their resources to respond to an opportunity.
(10) An uncontrolled market system also carries with it the possibility that one firm will acquire at least some monopoly power, restricting the ability of others to enter into competition, produce more, and push prices and profits down (a topic to which we shall return in chapter 11).
(11) Under certain conditions, firms would be well advised not to match up worker pay with worker "worth" at every moment in time. Current and prospective pay can be used as a means of increasing worker productivity and rewards over time.
(12) Mandatory retirement can also have unheralded benefits for workers as well as their employers. Mandatory retirement can allow for "overpayments" for workers, which can increase workers' incentives to improve their productivity over the course of their careers.

REVIEW QUESTIONS

(1) Why does the demand curve have a negative slope and the supply curve a positive slope?
(2) You overhear someone say, "We know that markets don't always clear in the sense that the quantity supplied and demanded do not always match. Queues can be observed everywhere. Store shelves are often emptied or overstocked. Hence, why pay so much attention to the intersection of supply and demand?" Your task is to answer that question.
(3) Why will the competitive market tend to move toward the price–quantity combination at the intersection of the supply and demand

curves? What might keep the market from moving all the way to that equilibrium point?

(4) Suppose you work for Levi-Strauss and the demand for blue jeans suddenly increases. Discuss possible short-run and long-run movements of the market and the consequences for your company.

(5) Henry Ford more than doubled his workers' wages. Did workers' real income double by Ford's pay policy? Reflecting on the general principles behind Ford's pay action, when should any firm – your firm – stop raising the pay of workers (not in terms of actual dollar amount but in terms of some economic/management principle that you can devise)?

(6) Workers and their employers often talk about how workers "earn" their wages but firms "give" their workers health insurance (or any other fringe benefit). Should these different methods of pay be discussed in different terms?

CHAPTER 3

Principles of rational behavior in society and business

We are not ready to suspect any person of being defective in selfishness. **Adam Smith**

With this chapter, we begin a detailed examination of key issues in microeconomics, namely the study of how prices are determined in individual markets. Prices are important – or, rather, should be important – to managers because of their unavoidable impact on the decisions of managers within individual firms. We have already seen how the forces of supply and demand determine prices (chapter 2). Now we will explore the *determinants* of the supply and demand for goods, services, and resources.

Microeconomics rests on certain assumptions about individual behavior. One is that people are capable of envisioning various ways of improving their position in life. This chapter reviews and extends the discussion begun in chapter 1 of how people – business people included – go about choosing among those alternatives. According to microeconomic theory, consumers and producers make choices rationally, so as to maximize their own welfare. This seemingly innocuous basic premise about human behavior will allow us to deduce an amazing variety of implications for business and many other areas of human endeavor.

> **Utility** is the satisfaction a person receives from the consumption of a good or service or from participation in an activity. Happiness, joy, contentment, or pleasure might all be substituted for satisfaction in the definition of utility.

PART I THEORY AND PUBLIC POLICY APPLICATIONS

Rationality: a basis for exploring human behavior

People's wants are ever-expanding. We can never satisfy all our wants because we will always conceive of new ones. The best we can do is to maximize our satisfaction, or **utility**, in the face of scarcity. Economists attempt to capture in one word – utility – the many contributions made to our wellbeing when we wear, drink, eat, or play something.

The ultimate assumption behind this theory is that *people act with a purpose*. In the words of Ludwig von Mises, they act because they are "dissatisfied with the state of affairs as it prevails" (Mises 1962, 2–3).

The acting individual

If people act in order to satisfy their consciously perceived wants, their behavior must be self-directed rather than externally controlled – at least to some extent. However, there is no way to prove this assertion. Economists simply presume that individuals, as opposed to groups, perform actions. It is the individual who has wants and desires, and looks for the means to fulfill them. It is the individual who attempts to render his or her state less unsatisfactory.

Group action, when it occurs, results from the actions of the individuals in the group. Social values, for instance, draw their meaning from the values held collectively by individuals. Economists would even say that group action cannot be separated from individual action, although economists do not deny that individual actions can lead to outcomes that no member of the group wants. But economists can explain such outcomes as the result of rational individuals responding to incentives that need to be improved.

Of course, individuals in a group affect one another's behavior. In fact, the size and structure of a group can have a dramatic effect on individual behavior (as we shall see in chapter 4). When economists speak of a competitive market, they are actually talking about the influence that other competitors have on the individual consumer or firm.

Rational behavior

Rational behavior is consistent behavior that maximizes an individual's satisfaction.

When individuals act to satisfy their wants, they exhibit **rational behavior**. The notion of rational behavior rests on three assumptions:

- First, that the individual has a preference and can identify, within limits, what he or she wants.
- Second, that the individual is capable of ordering his or her wants consistently, from most preferred to least preferred.
- Third, that the individual will choose consistently from these ordered preferences to maximize his or her satisfaction.

Even though the individual cannot fully satisfy all her wants, when possible she will always choose more of what she wants rather than less. In short, the rational individual always stands ready to further her own interests.

Some readers will find these assertions obvious and acceptable. To others, they may seem narrow and uninspiring. Later in the chapter we examine some possible objections to the concept of rational behavior, but first we must examine its logical consequences.

Rational decisions in a constrained environment

Several important conclusions flow from the economist's presumption of rational behavior. First, the individual makes choices from an array of alternatives. Second, in making each choice, a person must forgo one or more things for something else. All rational behavior involves a cost, which is the value of the most preferred alternative forgone. Third, in striving to maximize his or her welfare, the individual will take those actions whose benefits exceed their costs.

Choice

We assume that the individual can evaluate the available alternatives and select the one that maximizes her utility. Nothing in the economic definition of rational behavior suggests that the individual is completely free to do as she wishes. Whenever we talk about individual choices, we are actually talking about *constrained choices* – choices that are limited by outside forces. For example, you as a student or manager find yourself in a certain social and physical environment and have certain physical and mental abilities. These environmental and personal factors influence the options open to you. You may not have the money, the time, nor the stomach to become a surgeon, and you certainly don't have the time to take all of the courses listed in the schedule for your MBA program.

Although your range of choices may not be wide, choices do exist. At this moment you could be doing any number of things instead of reading this book. You could be studying some other subject, or going out on a date, playing with your son or daughter, or completing a pressing company project. Or you could have chosen to go shopping, to engage in intramural spots, or to jog around the block. In fact, you not only can make choices, you must make them.

Suppose that you have an exam tomorrow in economics and that there are exactly two things you can do within the next twelve hours. You can study economics, or you can play your favorite video game. These two options are represented in figure 3.1. Suppose you spend the entire twelve hours studying economics. In our example, the most you could study is four chapters, or E_1.

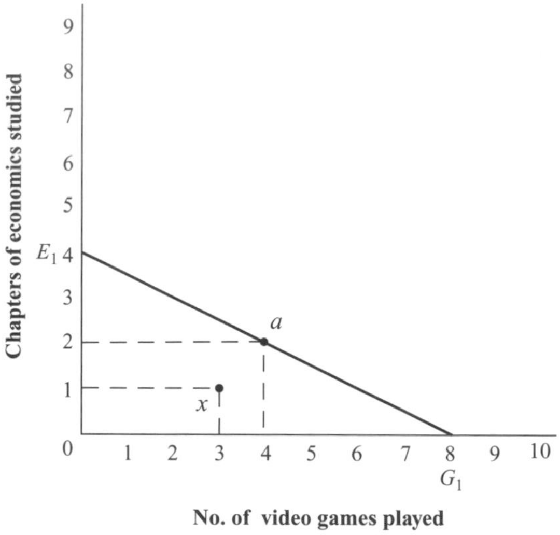

Figure 3.1 Constrained choice

With a given amount of time and other resources, you can produce any combination of study and games along the curve E_1G_1. The particular combination you choose will depend on your personal preferences for those two goods. You will not choose point *x*, because it represents less than you are capable of achieving – and, as a rational person, you will strive to maximize your utility. Because of constraints on your time and resources, you cannot achieve a point above E_1G_1.

At the other extreme, you could do nothing but play games – but again, there is a limit: eight games or G_1.

Neither extreme is likely to be acceptable. Assuming that you aim both to pass your exam and to have fun, what combination of games and study should you choose? The available options are represented by the straight line E_1G_1, the production possibilities curve (PPC) for study and play and the area underneath it. If you want to maximize your production, you will choose some point on E_1G_1, such as *a*: two chapters of economics and four games. You might yearn for five games and the same amount of study, but that point is above the curve and beyond your capabilities. If you settle for less – say one chapter and three games, or point *x* – you will be doing less than you are capable of doing and will not be maximizing your utility. The combination you actually choose will depend on your preference.

Changes in your environment or your physical capabilities can affect your opportunities and consequently the choices you make. For example, if you improve your study skills, your production rate for chapters studied will

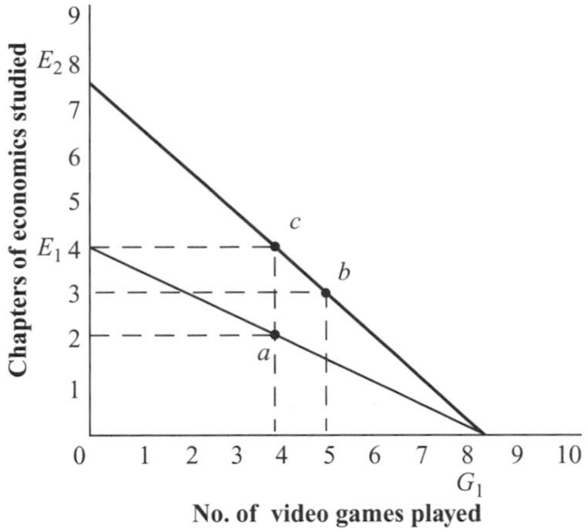

Figure 3.2 Change in constraints

If your study skills improve and your ability at the game remains constant, your production possibilities curve will shift from E_1G_1 to E_2G_1. Both the number of chapters you can study and the number of games you can play will increase. On your old curve, E_1G_1, you could study two chapters and play four games (point *a*). On your new curve E_2G_1, you can study three chapters and play five games (point *b*).

rise. You might then be able to study eight units of economics in twelve hours – in which case your production possibilities curve would expand outward. Even if your ability to play Amazons from Outer Space remained the same, your greater proficiency in studying would enable you to increase the number of games played. Your new set of production possibilities would be E_2G_1 in figure 3.2.

Again, you can choose any point along this curve or in the area below it. You may decide against further games and opt instead for four chapters of economics (point *c*). Or you could move to point *b*, in which case you would still be learning more economics – three chapters instead of two – but would also be playing more games. The important point is that you are able to choose from a range of opportunities. The option you take is not predetermined.

> **Cost** (or more precisely, opportunity cost) is the value of the most highly preferred alternative not taken at the time the choice is made.

Cost

The fact that choices exist implies that some alternative must be forgone when another is taken. For example, suppose that you have decided to spend an hour watching television programs. The two programs you most want to watch are *Oprah* (a US show whose guest list is dominated by celebrities) and *Jerry*

Springer (a show whose guest list is dominated by weirdos). If you choose *Oprah*, the cost is the pleasure you sacrifice by not watching a (staged) brawl among the guests on *Jerry Springer*.

Notice that cost does not require spending money. The cost of watching one TV show instead of another has nothing to do with money. Money can be a useful measure of costs, however, because it reduces to one common denominator. But money is not a cost itself. The shoes you are wearing may have cost you $50 (a **money cost**), but the real cost (the opportunity cost) is the value of what you could have purchased instead. The real cost is the actual benefits given up from the most preferred alternative not taken when a choice is made. When economists use the term "cost," they mean real, or opportunity, cost.

Money cost is a monetary measure of the benefits forgone when a choice is made.

As long as you have alternative uses for your time and other resources, "there is no such thing as a free lunch," a pat phrase economists repeat often. Nothing can be free if other opportunities are available. One goal of economics courses is to help you recognize this very simple principle and to train you to search for hidden costs. There is a cost to writing a poem, to watching a sunset, to extending a common courtesy of opening a door for someone. Although money is not always involved in choices, the opportunity to do other things is. *A cost is incurred in every choice.*

Maximizing satisfaction: cost–benefit analysis

An individual who behaves rationally will choose an option only when its benefits are greater than or equal to its costs. This is equivalent to choosing the most favorable option available. That is, people will produce or consume those goods and services whose benefits exceed the benefits of the most favored opportunity not taken.

This restatement of the *maximizing principle*, as it is called, explains individual choice in terms of cost. In figure 3.1, the choices along curve $E_1 G_1$ represent various cost–benefit trade-offs. If you choose point *a*, we must assume that you prefer *a* to any other combination because it yields the most favorable ratio of benefits to costs.

A change in cost will produce a change in behavior. Suppose you and a friend set a date to play checkers, but at the last moment he receives a lucrative job offer for the day of the match. Most likely the contest will be rescheduled. The job offer will change your friend's opportunities in such a way that what otherwise would have been a rational act (playing checkers) is no longer rational. The cost of playing checkers has risen significantly enough to exceed the benefits of the checkers games.

Cost–benefit analysis is the careful calculation and comparison of all costs and benefits associated with a given course of action.

Economists see **cost–benefit analysis** (CBA) as the basis of much (but certainly not all) of our behavior. Why do you attend classes, for example? The obvious answer is that at the time you decide to attend class, you expect the benefits of attending to exceed the costs. The principle applies even to classes you dislike. A particular course may have no intrinsic value, but you may fear that by cutting class you will miss information that would be useful for the examination. Thus the benefits of attending are a higher grade than you would otherwise expect. Besides, other options open to you on Tuesday evening at 7.00 p.m. may have so little appeal that the cost of going to class is very slight.

Take another example. Americans are known for the amount of waste they pile up. Our gross national garbage (what Americans collectively discard annually) is estimated to be more valuable than the gross national output of many other nations. We throw away many things that people in other parts of the world would be glad to have. However morally reprehensible some people may find such "waste," it can be seen as the result of economically rational behavior. The food wrappings people throw away, for example, adds convenience and freshness to the food, the value of which can exceed the costs. So does it make sense to say that using and disposing of food wrapping is wasteful?

Is life priceless? Not at the margin. People routinely sacrifice a little life expectancy to acquire other things they value. For example, people drive at excessive speeds to arrive at a party a few minutes earlier. The total value of your life may be priceless, but not necessarily at the margin.

The behavior of business people is not materially different from that of drivers, consumers, or students. People in business are constantly concerned with cost–benefit calculations, except that the comparisons are often (but not always) made in dollar terms: for example, will the cost of improving the quality of a product a little be more than matched by the additional (marginal) benefits of the improvement? In other words, will consumers value the added benefits enough to pay for them? In assessing the safety of their products, for example, business people must consider how much consumers are willing to pay for the additional safety, and how much it costs. It doesn't pay to make products as safe as possible because doing so would result in providing additional safety that costs more than it is worth. Automobile manufacturers could build cars like Sherman tanks that would be safe under most driving conditions, but could not sell them at a price necessary to cover the cost of making them.

The effects of time and risk on costs and benefits

When an individual acts, all the costs and benefits are not necessarily incurred immediately. The decision to have a child is a good example. At 2005 prices, a college-educated couple's first child can easily cost more than $500,000, from birth through college, when the cost of parental time involved is considered.[1] Fortunately this high cost is incurred over a relatively long period of time (or people would rarely become parents!).

Benefits received in the future must also be compared with present benefits. If you had a choice between receiving $10,000 now and $10,000 one year from now, you would take $10,000 today. You could put the money in a bank, if nothing else, where it would earn interest, or you could avoid the effects of future inflation by spending the money now. In other words, future benefits must be greater than present benefits to be more attractive than present benefits.

Present value is the value of future costs and benefits in terms of current dollars.

To compare future costs and benefits on an equal footing with costs and benefits realized today, we must adjust them to their **present value** (PV). The usual procedure for calculating present value – a process called *discounting* – involves an adjustment for the interest that could be earned (or would have to be paid) if the money were received (or due) today rather than in the future.[2]

If there is any uncertainty about whether future benefits or costs will actually be received or paid, further adjustments must be made. Without such adjustments, perfectly rational acts may appear to be quite irrational. For example, not all business ventures can be expected to succeed. Some will be less profitable than expected or may collapse altogether. The *average* fast-food franchise may earn a yearly profit of $1 million but only nine out of ten franchises may survive their first year (because the *average* profits is distorted by the considerable earnings of one franchise). Thus the estimated profits for such a franchise must be discounted, or multiplied by 0.90. If 10 percent of such ventures can be expected to fail, on average each will earn $900,000 ($1 million × 0.90).

The entrepreneur who starts a single business venture runs the risk that it may be the one out of ten that fails. In that case, profit will be zero. To avoid putting all their eggs in one basket, many entrepreneurs prefer to initiate several new ventures, thereby spreading the risk of doing business. In the same way,

[1] For rough estimates of the time involved in rearing children across a number of countries, see Craig (2003).

[2] The mathematical formula for computing the present value of future costs or benefits received one year from now is $PV = [1(1 + r)] f$, where PV stands for present value, r for the rate of interest, and f for future costs or benefits. The interest rate used in this formula is the rate at which we discount future costs and benefits.

investors spread their risk by investing in a wide variety of companies, and firms spread their risk by producing a number of products.

To give another example, criminal behavior may appear irrational if only the raw costs and benefits are considered. A burglar who nets $1,500 from the sale of stolen property may have to spend a year in jail if caught, prosecuted, and convicted. He could lose the annual income from his legitimate job, perhaps $10,000. That is a high cost to pay for a $1,500 profit on stolen property, but he pays that cost only if he is caught, prosecuted, convicted, and sentenced. The police cannot be everywhere at all times; prosecutors may be reluctant to prosecute; and suspended sentences are commonplace. All in all, even an inept burglar may have no more than a 10 percent chance of spending a year in jail.[3]

To estimate the actual cost faced by the burglar who is caught, sentenced, and sent to jail for a year, we might multiply the cost if caught, $10,000, by 0.10. That calculation indicates that to a burglar who is sent to jail for an average of one out of ten burglaries, the *expected* cost of any one burglary is only $1,000. Thus the actual *expected* cost of the burglary is less than the benefits received, $1,500. Although it may be morally reprehensible, the criminal act can conceivably be a rational one.[4]

The same logical process of discounting can be applied to your life as a student. When you signed up for your MBA program, you actually had limited information on how it would work out for you. (Admit it: It was a gamble, although a fairly safe one!) Similarly, when you sign up for courses, you usually have only a very rough idea of how difficult and time-consuming they will be, and what benefits you will receive from them. In other words, you are rarely certain of their costs and benefits. To make your decision, you will have to discount the raw costs and benefits by the probability of their being realized. Risks are pervasive in human experience, and rational behavior takes those risks into account.

[3] This is not an unreasonably low figure. Gregory Krohm concluded "that the chance of an 'adult' (seventeen or older) burglar being sent to prison for any single offense is 0.0024 . . . For juveniles . . . the risk was much lower, 0.0015" (1973, 33).

[4] Surveys of criminal activities and their rewards tend to support such a conclusion. A study of burglary and grand larceny cases in Norfolk, Virginia, showed that for the unusual criminal who committed just one crime and was caught in the act, crime did not pay. The typical criminal, however, convicted the average number of times and sentenced to the average number of years in prison, more than tripled the lifetime income he could have earned from a regular salaried job – even allowing for one or more years of unsalaried incarceration (Cobb 1973). When this study was replicated in Minnesota, the results were not quite as dramatic, but the criminal's lifetime income still doubled (Johnson 1974). For criminals who are never caught, crime pays even more handsomely.

What rational behavior does *not* mean

The concept of rational behavior often proves bothersome to the noneconomist. Most of the difficulties surrounding this concept arise from a misunderstanding of what rationality means. Common objections include the following:

(1) *People do many things that do not work out to their benefit* A driver speeds and ends up in the hospital. A student cheats, gets caught, and is expelled from school. Many other examples can be cited. But saying people behave "rationally" does not mean that they never make mistakes. We can calculate our options with some probability, but we do not have perfect knowledge, nor can we fully control the future. We will make mistakes, but we base our choices on what we *expect* to happen, not on what does happen. We speed because we expect not to crash, and we cheat because we expect not to be caught. Both can be rational behaviors from a narrow cost/benefit perspective.

(2) *Rational behavior implies that a person is totally self-centered, doing only things that are of direct personal benefit* Wrong rational behavior need not be selfish or narrowly defined. Most of us get pleasure from seeing others happy, particularly when their happiness is the result of our actions. But whether a person's goal is to improve her own wellbeing or to help others, they have a motivation to act rationally – make decisions that do the most to accomplish her objectives.

(3) *People's behavior is subject to psychological quirks, hang-ups, habits, and impulses* True enough! Can such behavior be considered "rational"? Why not? Human actions are governed by the constraints of our physical and mental makeup. As is true of our intelligence, our inclination toward aberrant or impulsive behavior is one of those constraints. Such constraints make our decision making less precise and contribute to our mistakes, but they do not prevent our acting rationally. Moreover, what looks to be impulsive or habitual behavior may actually be the product of some prior rational choice. The human mind can handle only so much information and make only so many decisions in one day. Consequently, we may attempt to economize on decision making by reducing some behaviors to habit. For example, we might make slightly better decisions if we examined all the information available on the cereal selection at the grocery store every time we bought a box. But such scrutiny could cost more than the benefit of the improved choice. Instead, having found a brand of cereal that we enjoy, we tend to stick with it for a long period of time – buy it out of habit – and use our limited time on making better decisions that yield bigger payoffs.

(4) *People do not necessarily maximize their satisfaction* For instance, many people do not perform to the limit of their abilities. But satisfaction is a question of personal taste. To some individuals, lounging around is an economic good. By consuming leisure, people can increase their welfare. Criticizing the decisions others make is often based on the assumption that others have the same preferences and face the same constraints, including costs, that you do. Anyone who equates rational behavior with what she would do will have no trouble concluding that others are irrational.

Disincentives in poverty relief

Our discussion of rational behavior can be used to understand one of the biggest policy issues of our time: welfare reform. We can do this by assuming that welfare recipients are tolerably rational.

So much of the public discussion about welfare programs, especially cuts in them, assumes that because Congress has the authority to change the programs, it can alter the programs any way it wishes without creating problems. However, as we can easily see, Congress is in something of an economic, if not political, bind on welfare relief, given how incentives change when the program is adjusted. The basic problem is that the practice of reducing welfare benefits as earned income rises creates an implicit marginal tax on additional earned income that discourages the poor from working. Why not lower the implicit marginal tax rate?

Figure 3.3 gives the answer. The 45-degree line that extends out from the origin indicates points of equal distance from each axis – that is, points at which spendable income equals earned income. At point *y*, for example, a poor person earns and can spend $5,000 annually. At points above the line, spendable income exceeds earned income. For instance, at point *x*, a poor person earns $5,000 annually and can spend $7,500. He receives a subsidy equal to $y - x$, or $2,500.

Suppose the government establishes a negative income tax with a guaranteed annual income level of $5,000, or SI_1. The break-even earned income level is $10,000, or EI_1. A person who earns nothing will receive a subsidy of $5,000 a year. As his earned income rises, the subsidy will decline, until it reaches zero at $10,000. Curve $SI_1 a$ shows the spendable income of people in this program at various earned-income levels. They lose $500 in subsidies for every $1,000 of additional earned income. That is, they face an implicit marginal tax rate of 50 percent.

If policy makers want to reduce the implicit marginal tax rate on an earned income of $10,000 to less than 50 percent, they must either reduce the

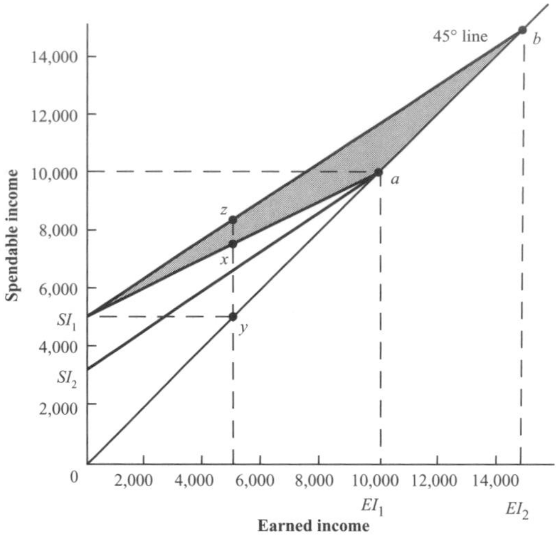

Figure 3.3

Policy trade-offs of a negative income tax

With a guaranteed income of SI_1($5,000) and a break-even earned income level of EI_1($10,000), the implicit marginal tax rate on the poor is 50 percent. If policy makers attempt to reduce the implicit tax rate by raising the break-even income level, however, the government's poverty relief budget will rise by the shaded area SI_1ab. A higher explicit tax burden will fall on a smaller group of taxpaying workers.

guaranteed spendable income level or raise the break-even earned-income level. If they raise the break-even earned-income level – to $15,000, or EI_2, for example – curve SI_1a will shift to SI_1b. But then more people – all those with earned incomes up to $15,000 – will receive benefits. Moreover, all the people covered originally will receive larger subsidies. A person with an income of $5,000 will receive $8,000 instead of $7,000 in spendable income (point *z* instead of point *x*), for example. The total increase in the government's poverty relief expenditures would equal the shaded area in figure 3.3 bounded by SI_1ab.

The increase in expenditures would place a greater tax burden on taxpaying workers. Yet because more workers would be covered by the negative income tax, fewer people would share the increased tax burden. Thus the explicit marginal tax rate on high-income workers rises – lowering their incentive to work and earn additional income.

If the government reduces the guaranteed income level, say from SI_1 to SI_0, a different problem will result. On the new curve SI_0a, the poor will receive less government aid at each earned-income level. They may have more incentive to work under such an arrangement, but they have less to live on.

Policy makers, then, face difficult *trade-offs* between the goal of helping the poor and the goal of minimizing the disincentive to work. To provide adequate aid, they may have to raise the break-even income level high enough that some people benefit who are not strictly poor. Yet to reduce aid to people who are not truly poor, they would have to lower the break-even income level – thus increasing the implicit tax rate on the poor. To keep the implicit marginal tax rate down, they could lower the guaranteed income level – decreasing the benefits that go to the truly poor.

Our graphic analysis suggests that there may be economic as well as altruistic limits to the government's ability to transfer income from the rich to the poor. To transfer more income to the poor, either the guaranteed income or break-even income level must go up. If only the guaranteed income level is raised, the implicit marginal tax rate facing the poor increases. If that problem is avoided by raising the break-even income level, poverty relief will cover more people, and the taxes paid by the remaining workers will go up.

Perspective Maslow's Hierarchy of Needs and Demand

MBA students will rarely make it through their programs without encountering "Maslow's hierarchy of needs" in several of their courses, most notably their marketing courses. Often, Maslow's hierarchy is treated with some reverence, as though it were a form of revealed truth about human behavior.

A. H. Maslow, a psychologist, argued that basic human needs can be specified with reasonable clarity and can be ranked according to their importance in providing motivation and influencing behavior (Maslow 1954, primarily chapter 5). Embedded in Maslow's hierarchy of needs is a theory of human behavior that is to a notable degree foreign to the economist's way of thinking. In this Perspective, Maslow's system will be outlined so that we may be able to use it for comparative purposes and to clarify the nature of the economic way of thinking.

Maslow's hierarchy

Maslow's needs hierarchy is shown in figure 3.4. The importance of needs – in terms of how powerful or demanding they are in affecting human behavior – ascends as one moves downward through the pyramid. That is, the most fundamental or prepotent needs, which are physiological in nature, are at the bottom. This category of needs includes on one level all attempts

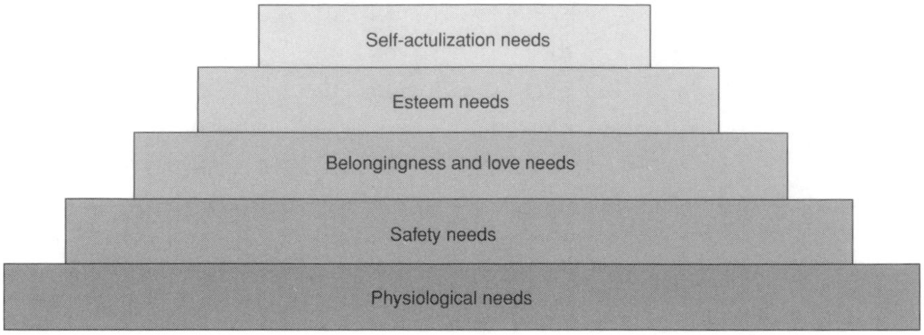

Figure 3.4 Maslow's hierarchy of needs
The pyramid orders human needs by broad categories from the most prepotent needs on the bottom to lesser and lesser prepotent needs as an individual moves up the pyramid. According to Maslow, an individual can be expected to satisfy her needs in the order of their prepotence, or will move from the bottom of the pyramid through the various levels to the top, so long as the individual's resources to satisfy her needs last.

of the body to maintain certain chemical balances (such as water, oxygen, and hydrogen ion levels) within the body. On a higher level, the physiological needs include the individual's desires for food, sex, sleep, sensory pleasures, and sheer activity (meaning the need to be busy).

The need for safety, which is next in prepotence, may include the desires of the individual for security, order, protection, and family stability. The next category, belongingness and love needs, may include, among other things, the desire for companionship, acceptance, and affection; Maslow lists under the heading of esteem needs the individual's desire for achievement, adequacy reputation, dominance, recognition, attention, appreciation, and importance. He argues that the need for self-actualization 'refers to man's desire for self-fulfillment, namely, to the tendency that might be phrased as the desire to become more and more what one is, to become everything that one is capable of becoming" (Maslow 1954, 90–2).

Maslow stresses that such an individual may indicate she (or he) is striving after one need when in fact she is pursuing something else. For example, the individual may say that she is hungry because by doing so and going out to dinner, she can acquire companionship, affection, and attention. This may be the case because the individual may find it useful to deceive another person or because she does not consciously know what her true motivation is. In addition, Maslow argues that certain preconditions, such as the freedom to express oneself, are necessary before basic needs can be satisfied. Consequently, individuals can be motivated to establish the necessary preconditions; they may not appear to be attempting to satisfy basic needs.

Maslow does not hold rigidly to the ordering of needs as indicated in figure 3.4. He specifies this particular ranking because it appeared to him (from surveying a few dozen people in the 1950s) to be descriptive of the people with whom he has associated and because it appears to be a reasonably good generality concerning human motivation. Because of cultural or environmental factors or because, for example, love has been denied in the past, some people may place more emphasis on esteem needs than on the need for love. Maslow also reasons that "There are other apparently innately creative people in whom the drive to creativeness seems to be more important than any other counter-determinant. Their creativeness might appear not as self actualization released by basic satisfaction, but in spite of the lack of basic satisfaction" (Maslow 1954, 98).

Although he qualifies his argument, the core proposition in Maslow's theory of human behavior is the argument that a person will first satisfy her most basic needs (physiological needs) before she attempts to satisfy needs of higher order:

> If all the needs are unsatisfied, the organism is then dominated by the physiological needs, all other needs may become simply nonexistent or be pushed into the background. It is then fair to characterize the whole organism by saying simply it is hungry, for consciousness is almost completely preempted by hunger. All capacities are put into the service of hunger-satisfaction, and the organization of these capacities is almost entirely determined by the one purpose of satisfying hunger . . . Capacities that are not useful for this purpose lie dormant, or are pushed into the background (Maslow 1954, 92).

If the most basic needs are satisfied, "At once other (and higher) needs emerge and these, rather than physiological hungers, dominate the organism. And when these in turn are satisfied, again new (and still higher) needs emerge, and so on" (Maslow 1954, 92). One gets the impression from reading Maslow that the individual will not attempt to satisfy her second most prepotent needs until the most prepotent needs are almost fully satisfied; she will not move to the third tier in the hierarchy until the needs at the second tier are "fairly well gratified" (Maslow 1954, 89).[5] Apparently, the individual will not attempt to effect any self-actualization until she has moved through

[5] Maslow adds, "*If* both the physiological and safety needs are fairly well gratified, there will emerge the love and affection and belongingness needs" (1954, 89). Maslow never explains what will keep the individual from fully satisfying any given need level before moving on to a higher tier.

all the earlier tiers. If any tier in the hierarchy is skipped entirely, it is because of insurmountable environmental or physiological barriers.[6]

Economics and Maslow's hierarchy

Maslow's approach to human motivation and behavior resembles the approach of economists in several respects. First, they are similar in that at the foundation of both theories is an assumption that the individual is able to rank all of her wants (or needs) according to their importance to her. In the Maslow system, anything that is not directly a basic need is ranked according to how close it is to a basic need. Other needs beyond the five categories mentioned, such as the need to know or understand and the need for aesthetic quality, can be handled by adding additional tiers.[7] As pointed out earlier in this chapter, the economist simply starts with an assumption that the individual knows what she wants and is able to rank all possible goods and services that are able to satisfy her wants.

However, the two approaches are dissimilar when it comes to specifying the ranking. Maslow is willing to argue that in general the basic needs and their ranking can also be identified; that is, he can say what the individual's needs are and is willing to venture a statement about their relative importance (again, given his survey of a small number of people). On the other hand, economists would generally take the position that the relative importance of needs varies so much from person to person that a hierarchy of needs, although perhaps insightful for some limited purposes, does not move us very far in our understanding of human behavior.

Economists may specify whether a good or service may add to or subtract from the individual's utility and will argue that more of something that gives positive utility is preferred to less; but they would be unwilling to try to say exactly where the good (or need) may lie on some relative scale. We must presume that the specificity Maslow seeks is to him a useful, if not necessary, basis for predicting human behavior. Economists believe that they can say a great deal about human behavior without actually specifying the relative importance of the things people want. We certainly admit that the economist's inability to specify the relative importance of needs is a limitation to economic theory.

[6] Admittedly, this is an interpretation of Maslow and may be an unfair statement of what his true position is; however, he does tend to write in black and white terms – either the barriers are there or they are not.

[7] Maslow is less certain about the relative positions of the need to know and the need for aesthetic quality because of the limited research that had been done on the subject at the time he wrote the book.

The two systems are similar to the extent that they view the individual as consuming those things that give the greatest satisfaction. Even in the Maslow system, which lacks a direct statement to that effect, there is the implicit assumption that the individual is a *utility maximizer*. Maslow also assumes diminishing marginal utility as more of the need is consumed; if this is not the case, it is difficult to understand how the individual can become fully or almost fully satisfied (or "fairly well gratified") at any need level.

The two systems are different because of their views of the constraints that operate on the ability of the individual to maximize her utility. The constraints in the Maslow hierarchy include environmental and cultural factors and the individual's character, or her beliefs about what is right and wrong. There is no mention in Maslow of the individual's productive ability or income (unless these are implied in the environmental or cultural constraints) or of the costs of the means by which her basic needs can be fulfilled. These considerations are basic constraints in the economist's view of human behavior.

By not considering cost, Maslow appears to assume either that there is no cost to need gratification or that (in spite of an implicit assumption concerning diminishing marginal utility) the demand curve for any need is vertical (or perfectly inelastic). This means that the quantity of the need fulfilled is unaffected by the cost. An implied assumption of the vertical demand curve is that the basic needs are independent of one another. They are not substitutes; for example, a unit of an esteem need fulfilled does not appear in the Maslow system to be able to take the place of even a small fraction of a unit of physiological need.

Maslow recognizes that most people have only partially fulfilled their needs at each level:

> So far, our theoretical discussions may have given the impression that these five sets of needs are somehow in such terms as the following: if one need is satisfied, then another emerges. This statement might give the false impression that a need must be satisfied 100 percent before the next need emerges. In actual *fact*, most members of our society who are normal are partially satisfied in all their basic needs and partially unsatisfied in all their basic needs at the same time. A more realistic description of the hierarchy would be in terms of decreasing percentages of satisfaction as we go up the hierarchy of prepotency. For instance . . . it is as if the average citizen is satisfied 85 percent in his physiological needs, 70 percent in his safety needs, 50 percent in his love needs, 40 percent in his self-esteem needs, and 10 percent in his self-actualization needs. (Maslow 1954, 100–1)

Maslow does not, however, explain why this will be the case, nor does he provide an explanation for why a person will not fully satisfy the higher needs before he moves to the next tier.

The relevance of demand

The economist might concede for purposes of argument, as we do, that the demand for a physiological need is greater (with the quantity bought being relatively unresponsive to price changes) than the demand for a safety need, which in turn is greater than the demand for a love need. However, it does not follow that, as Maslow suggests, the love need will be less fulfilled in percentage terms than the safety or physiological needs. To what extent the different needs are gratified depends on the cost or the price of the means for satisfying a need and exactly how people respond to the price.

To illustrate our point, consider figure 3.5(a). The demand for a means of gratifying a physiological need is depicted as being greater (meaning it is further out to the right) than the other demands. (For the sake of simplicity we consider only three needs.) We assume that any given need is fully satisfied if the quantity of the need purchased is equal to the quantity at the point where the respective demand curves intersect the horizontal axis.

If, as in this example, the cost of satisfying each need is the same, P_1, the individual will consume Qp_1, of the means of satisfying his physiological need. As far as units are concerned, this is greater than the quantity of units consumed for satisfying the other needs; however, the percentage of the need gratified does not have to be greater. If demand for the physiological need were sufficiently inelastic, the percentage of the need gratified could be greater.

It is doubtful, however, that the costs of satisfying the different needs are the same. The availability of the resources needed for satisfying the different needs can easily be different; consequently, the costs of need gratification can be different. If the cost of fulfilling the physiological need were substantially greater, even though the demand for the need were greater, the percentage of the physiological need fulfilled could be less than the percentage of the other needs fulfilled.

In figure 3.5(b), the prices (or cost per unit) of the means by which a physiological need can be satisfied (P_p) are greater than the prices of the means for satisfying the other needs. The price of satisfying the safety need (Ps) is assumed to be greater than the price of satisfying the love need (P_1).

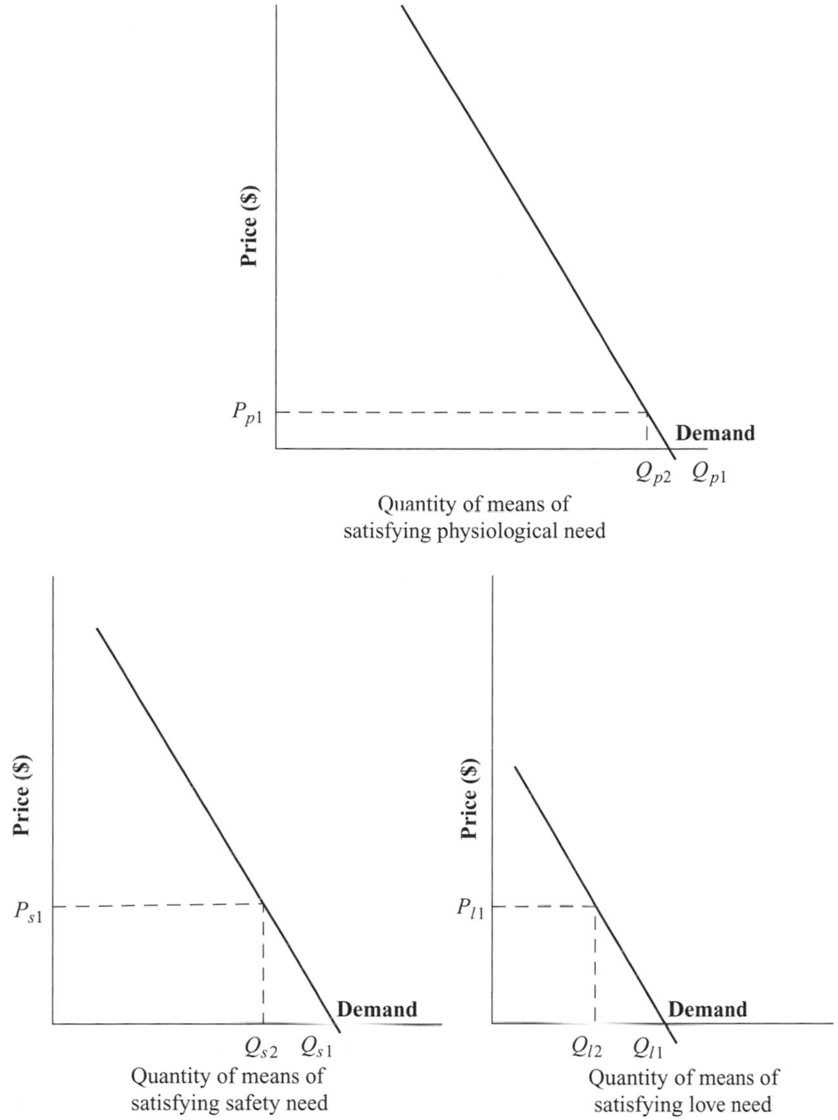

Figure 3.5(a) Demand, price, and need satisfaction

The extent to which needs are satisfied depends, in the economists' view of the world, on the nature of the need's demand and its price. Physiological needs may indeed be more completely satisfied than other needs, but that may only be because physiological needs have relatively low prices (panel (a)). But then, as shown in this figure (panel (b)), the price of the means of satisfying physiological needs might be higher than the prices of the means of satisfying safety and love needs.

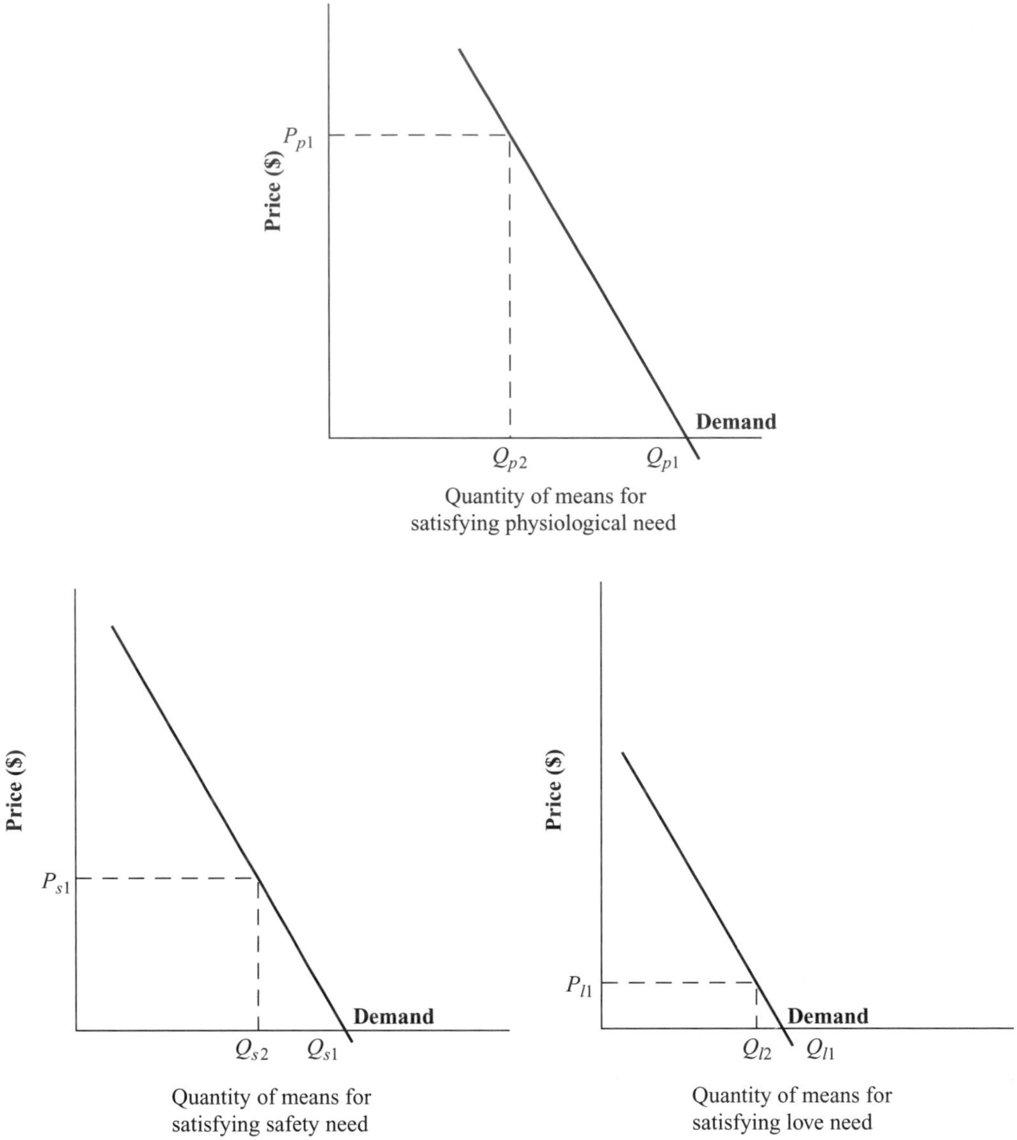
Price ($)
P_{p1}
Demand
Q_{p2}
Q_{p1}
Quantity of means for
satisfying physiological need
Price ($)
P_{s1}
Demand
Q_{s2}
Q_{s1}
Quantity of means for
satisfying safety need
Price ($)
P_{l1}
Demand
Q_{l2}
Q_{l1}
Quantity of means for
satisfying love need

Figure 3.5(b)

The result in this case is what we suggested it *could* be; the individual will fulfill a lower percentage of her physiological needs than she will fulfill of her other needs In fact the order of need fulfillment is reversed from the order suggested by Maslow: the individual fulfills a higher percentage of her love need than of the other needs.

* * *

Maslow has apparently observed that people fulfill a higher percentage of their physiological needs than of other needs. Our line of argument suggests that this may have been the case because the price of physiological need fulfillment is lower than the prices of fulfilling the other needs. The important point we wish to make is that a change in the price (or cost) structure can bring about a change in the extent of need gratification at each level. In such an event, our (and psychologists') definition of what may be considered "normal" as far as need gratification is concerned should be reconsidered. People's behavior need not have changed in any fundamental sense; they may merely be responding to different prices, while their basic preferences and attitudes remain the same.

PART II ORGANIZATIONAL ECONOMICS AND MANAGEMENT

The last-period problem

Much of this chapter has been concerned with how people behave rationally. Here, we introduce "opportunistic behavior" as a form of rational behavior that people in business will want to protect themselves from. We suggest ways in which different parties to business deals can take advantage of other parties and how managers can structure their organizational and pay policies to minimize what we call "opportunistic behavior." More specifically, this section is concerned with how an announced end to a business relationship can inspire opportunistic behavior. Its goal, however, is the constructive one of explaining how business deals can be structured to maximize the durability and profitability of the deals. To do that, business relationships must be ongoing, or have no clearly defined last period. Having a fixed termination date can encourage rational suppliers and creditors to engage in opportunistic behavior, which can reduce firm revenues and profits. That is to say, a reputation for continuing in business has *economic value*, which explains why managers work hard to create such a reputation.

Problems with the end of contracts

A terrific *advantage* of dealing with outside suppliers is that the relationship is constantly up for renewal and can easily be terminated if it is not satisfactory to both parties. But therein lies an important *disadvantage* of dealing with outside suppliers: the relationship lacks the permanence or confidence that any given buyer–supplier relationship will be renewed. The supplier must attribute some probability that the end of the contract will be the end of the relationship, given that he or she might not be the low bidder next time, a conclusion that can have profound effects on the relationship that the astute manager must recognize. When a relationship is known to be coming to an end on a known date, a serious problem arises.

The basic problem is that during the last period of any business relationship, there is little, if any, penalty for cheating, which implies a maximum incentive to cheat. As a consequence, cheating on deals is more likely in the last period than at any other time in the relationship.

Consider a simple business deal. Suppose that you want 1,000 widgets of a given quality delivered every month, starting with January and continuing through December, and that you have agreed to make a fixed payment to the supplier when the delivery is made. If you discover after you have made payment that your supplier sent fewer than 1,000 units or sent the requisite 1,000 units but at inferior quality, you can simply withhold future checks until the supplier makes good on his or her end of the bargain. Indeed, you can terminate the year-long contract, which can impose a substantial penalty for any cheating early in the contract. Knowing that, the supplier will tend to have a strong incentive early on in the contract period to do what he or she has agreed to do.

However, the supplier's incentive to uphold his or her end of the bargain begins to fade as the year unfolds, for the simple reason that there is less of a penalty – in terms of what is lost from your ending the working relationship – that you can impose. The supplier might go so far as to reason that during the last period (December), the penalty for cheating is very low, if not zero. The supplier can cut the quantity or quality of the widgets delivered during December and then can take the check before you know what has been done. The biggest fear the supplier has is that you might inspect the shipment before handing over the final check. You may be able to get the supplier to increase

The **last-period (or end-period) problem,** refers to the costs that can be expected to be incurred from opportunistic behavior when the end of a working relationship approaches.

the quantity or quality somewhat with inspection, but you should expect him or her to be somewhat more difficult to deal with. And you should not *expect* the same level of performance or quality.

The problem is that you have lost a great deal of your bargaining power during that last month, and that is the source of what we call and mean by the **last-period problem**. It is a problem, however, that can be mitigated in several ways.

Solutions to the last-period problem

The simplest and perhaps most common way is by maintaining continuing relationships. If you constantly jump from one supplier to another, you might save a few bucks in terms of the quoted prices, but you might also raise your costs in terms of unfulfilled promises by suppliers during the last period of their association with you. "Working relationships," in other words, have an economic value apart from what the relationship actually involves – for example, the delivery of so many widgets. This is one important reason that businesses spend so much time cultivating and maintaining their relationships and why they may stick with suppliers and customers through temporary difficulties.

Nothing works to solve the last-period problem, however, like success. The more successful a firm is – the greater the rate of growth for the firm and its industry – the more likely others will recognize that the firm will continue in business for some time into the future. The opposite is also true: Failure can feed on itself as suppliers, buyers, and workers begin to think that the last period is near. Firms understand these facts of business life. As a consequence, executives tend to stress their successes and downplay their failures. Their intent may not be totally unethical, given how bad business news can cause the news to get worse. Outsiders understand these tendencies. As a consequence, many investors pay special attention to whether executives are buying or selling their stock in their companies. The executives may have access to (accurate) insider information that is not being distributed to the public.

Another simple way of dealing with the last-period problem in new relationships is to leave open the prospect of future business, in which case the potential penalty is elevated (in a probabilistic sense) in the mind of the supplier. When there is no prospect of future business, the *expected* cost from cheating is what can be lost during the last period. When there is some prospect of future business, the cost to a supplier who underperforms during the last period is greater, and so the rational supplier is more likely to maintain the quality and quantity of his product.

When dealing with remodeling or advertising firms, for instance, you can devise a contract for a specified period, but you can suggest, or intimate, in a variety of creative ways, that if the work is done as promised and there are no problems, you might extend the contract or expand the scope of the relationship. In the case of the remodeling firm, you might point out other repairs in the office that you are thinking of having done. In the case of the advertising firm, you might suggest that there are other ad campaigns for other products and services that you are considering.

You should, therefore, be able to secure somewhat better compliance with your supplier during the last period of the contract, and how much the compliance is improved can be related to just how well you can convince your supplier that you mean business (and a lot of it) for some time into the future. However, we are not suggesting that you should lie outright about uncertain future business. The problem with lying is that it can, when discovered, undercut the value of your suggestions of further business and revive the last-period problem. You need, in other words, to be prepared to extend, from time to time (if not always), working relationships when in fact they work the way you want them to work.

However, if you are not able to develop that impression, the last period can come sooner than you might think (or sooner than December in our earlier example). That is, the contractual relationship can unravel because of the way you and the supplier begin to *think* about what the other is thinking and how the other might act as a consequence.

If both you and your supplier are inclined to cheat on the contract, and you have already figured that your supplier will cheat to the maximum (send nothing) during the last period, then December becomes irrelevant and November becomes the last period. Your incentive then is to cheat on the supplier in November. Well, with November now the last period, you can imagine what your supplier is thinking. He is contemplating cheating in November before you get a chance to cheat. Ah, but you can best the supplier by cheating in October. That thought suggests that when contemplating the contract before it is signed and sealed, you and the supplier can reach the conclusion that January is the (relevant) last period – which means that the deal will never be consummated. In this way, the last-period problem becomes a *first*-period problem, actually one of setting the terms of the contract. This way of thinking about it can make the signing problematic, and more costly than it needs to be, assuming that there are ways around the problem.

This line of argument can be overdone, which reminds us of an old joke about a prisoner condemned to death. As it happened, the prisoner was told on Sunday that he would be hung between Monday and Saturday, *but the day of his hanging would be a total surprise.* He reasoned: "They can't hang me on Saturday because it wouldn't be a surprise. So, Friday is the last day of the relevant period." But then he reasoned, "They can't hang me on Friday because if they wait until then, it won't be a surprise." Continuing this line of reasoning, he soon concluded that they couldn't hang him. When they hanged him on Wednesday, he really was surprised! This joke suggests that the last-period problem doesn't always lead to an unraveling in which the last period becomes the first. But the last-period problem is potentially serious one, as several examples validate.

Firms are collections of departments (and people) who have continuing relationships that are not always up for re-bidding, which means that the parties can figure that they will be continued, with there being no clear last period.

The **corporation** is a legal entity whose existence is independent of the life of the owner or owners; the corporation typically lives on beyond the owners' death.

A reason firms exist

The last-period problem is one reason that **firms** exist. The last-period problem is also a significant reason that the **corporation** is such an important form of doing business. Given that ownership is in shares, the corporation makes for relatively easy and seamless transfer of ownership, which means that the life of the company is, in an expectational sense, longer as a corporation than as a partnership or proprietorship, which are two organizational forms that can die with the current owners. This means that the corporate charter should be prized simply because it adds value to the company by muting (though not always eliminating) the last-period problem.

The FIGMO problem

The last-period problem extends beyond buyer–supplier relationships of the sort we described above involving the purchase of widgets. There is clearly a last-period problem for military personnel. When officers or enlisted men and women are given their transfer orders, they can sit back and relax, given that the penalties that can then be imposed on them have been severely limited by the orders to move on. The problem becomes especially severe when personnel are about to leave the military altogether. Military people have a favorite expression for what we call shirking during the last period. They call it "FIGMO": "F**k you, I've got my orders." We are sure that the military has devised a variety of ways to mute the impact of FIGMO, but it is equally clear that the problem of shirking as military men and women approach the end of their assignment remains a pressing one. Sometimes you just have to accept some costs of shirking (otherwise you might end up concluding that people should be fired the moment they enlist, which can be more costly than the shirking).

Fired workers

The last-period problem can surface with a vengeance when an employee who has access to easily destroyed records and equipment is fired. The firm doing the firing must worry that the employee will use his or her remaining time in the plant or office to impose costs on the firm, to "get back" at the firm. As a consequence, firings are often a surprise, done quickly, with the employee given little more time than to collect her personal things in the office – all to minimize the damage to the firm. The firm may even hand the employee a paycheck for hours of work not done, simply to make the break as quickly as possible and discourage fired workers from imposing even greater costs through damage to records and equipment. Indeed, when the potential for serious damage is present and likely, firms may hire a security guard to be with the fired employee until he or she is escorted to the door for the last time.

Shirking close to retirement

The last-period problem can also show up in the greater incentives people have to shirk as they approach retirement. To prevent workers from shirking, deferred compensation (as discussed in chapter 2) can be used with some of the compensation withdrawn if shirking ever does occur. A variation of this type of solution for executives is to tie their compensation to stock that they cannot sell without penalty until some time after their retirements. If executives shirk toward the end of their career, causing their companies to do poorly, then the executives lose more than any remaining salary they are due for the duration of their tenure: they lose the decline in the value of the stock they own – a decline that could occur at least in part by their preretirement shirking.

Apparently, corporations' executive compensation committees are aware of the last-period problem. Economists Robert Gibbons and Kevin Murphy have found from their econometric studies that as CEOs get closer to retirement age, their compensation tends to become more closely tied to their firm's stock market performance (Gibbons and Murphy 1992).

Another way of solving the last-period problem is through performance payments, which means that payments are made as a project is completed. For example, separate payments (stage payments) can be made for constructing a house when the house is framed, when the roof is on, and when the wiring is in and the interior walls have been finished. However, a significant portion of the total amount due is withheld until after the entire project is completed and the results approved. For example, 20 percent of the entire construction cost is often not paid until after the final inspection.

Underfunded pension plans

Business critics often decry the extent to which many pension plans are not fully "funded" – that is, not enough has been set aside by the firm in investment accounts to meet the retirees' scheduled benefits. Underfunded pension plans can be a way by which firms seek to solve a form of the last-period problem of retired workers, especially unionized workers, whose concern for the financial stability of the firm may stop when they retire.

Unions often negotiate the retirement payments and fringe benefits for unionized retirees at the same time that they negotiate the pay packages for the current workers. Even when retirement benefits are fixed for retirees' lives, the retirees have an interest in the continuation of the firm, but only when the pension plans are not fully funded. When they are fully funded, the retirees don't have as much of a stake in the continuation of the firm. They can reason, "Who cares what the workers get paid; we've got ours!" When the retirement plans are not fully funded, the retirees must worry that excessive wage demands by current workers will decrease the ability of the firm to fund the retirement benefits in the future and thereby meet the scheduled benefit payments. Current workers also have a motivation not to put the firm's future profitability at risk with excessive wage demands. Today's wage demands can reduce the capital investment and research necessary for the firm to remain variable and earn the profits to pay for the retirement of the current workers. Hence, underfunded pension plans can be a way of tempering union wage demands by giving retirees a stake in wage rates that are lower than otherwise.

Business sales by "old" owners

The very fact that an "old" owner of a business can sell to a "young" owner also enhances the incentive of the old owner to maintain the reputation of the firm. However, after the firm is sold, there is an incentive for the old owner to allow the firm's reputation to decline, a prospect that encourages a speedy transfer of a business when the deal is closed. If the new owner can't take over the business in a timely fashion, then he or she might overcome the last-period problem by arranging for the old owner to receive some of the profits in the business after he retires.

If the old owner retains some interest in the firm, then he also has an incentive to work with the new owners, giving them time to develop the required reputation for honest dealing with employees and customers and to take control of one of the more elusive business assets – the network of contacts. The practice of keeping the old owner on after the sale of the business is common among businesses such as medical offices. Doctors first form a firm that looks and operates like a partnership, after which they finalize the sale. In all of these cases, the old owners will want to work with the new owners to make the transfer as "seamless" as possible, simply because the sale price will be higher and the chance will be greater for the new owner to establish a reputation for honest dealing and take charge of the contacts.

Partial sales of companies by founders

In 1983, Scott Cook developed the widely used home-finance software package called "Quicken," the major product of Cook's firm, Intuit, Inc., which was courted for a buyout in the early 1990s by Microsoft. Cook eventually agreed to sell Intuit to Microsoft for $1.5 billion in Microsoft stock, 40 percent above Intuit's market price at the time. Microsoft agreed to pay a premium price, for two reasons. First, Bill Gates, the then CEO of Microsoft, saw a need to have a dominant personal finance program that could be integrated into his Microsoft Office line and that would allow him to pursue his goal of transforming the way people manage their money. The value of Intuit was greater as an integrated part of Microsoft than by itself. Second, and more important for the purposes of this chapter, Cook agreed to become a vice president of Microsoft and to retain an interest in the future development and use of Quicken, if Microsoft bought Intuit. This way, Cook could minimize the impact of the last-period problem, and the sale of Intuit would mean that Quicken might continue to develop. The proposed buyout of Intuit was eventually terminated by the Justice Department, which threatened to sue Microsoft for antitrust violation. However, the example is still a good one, not only because it involves prominent business personalities and their successful firms but also because of the lesson it illuminates: Sometimes, by selling only a part of the company, an owner can increase the value of the part that is sold, enhancing the combined value of the part that is sold and the part that is retained.

Family business

The last-period problem also helps to explain why fathers (or mothers) are so anxious for one of their sons (or daughters) to go into their business as retirement age approaches. This not only extends the life of the business but also increases the amount of business that can be done as the retirement age is approached, given that with the elevation of the son or daughter to partner/owner, the last period is then put off until some time in the future.

Why do signs on business establishments sometimes read, for example, "Sampson & Sons" or "Delilah & Daughters"? The usual answer is that the parent is proud to announce that a daughter (or son) has joined the business. That is probably often the case, but we also think it has a lot to do with the parent seeking to assure customers and suppliers that the original owner, the parent, will not soon begin to take advantage of them.

Economists have found that the rate of occupational following within families with a self-employed proprietor is three times greater than that within other families, which suggests that proprietors have a good reason – measured in continuing the value of their companies – to bring their children into the business that other people don't have (LaBand and Lentz 1990). Caterpillar, the manufacturer of farm equipment and heavy machinery, depends on its dealers to maintain customer trust and goodwill. One way in which Caterpillar has attempted to enhance customer trust has been to set up a school to help children of dealers learn about and pursue careers in Caterpillar dealerships (Davidow and Malone 1992, 234).

Bankruptcy laws

Firms commonly complain that goods delivered in the last days of the supplier's operation are of inferior quality. The problem? It may be one of the incentives, or lack thereof, that people have to deliver goods of waning quality during their last days. Bankruptcy laws can be explained in part as a means of reducing these end-period problems.[8] They extend the potential end of the firm, and can give the firm a new lease on life and set back the last-period problem indefinitely.

Also, a firm in financial trouble can be pressed into liquidation by nervous bondholders, a fact that can exacerbate the last-period problem, given that

[8] Gibbons and Murphy (1992).

suppliers would have to worry that nervous bondholders will encourage firms to deliver shoddy merchandise, which can make customers more nervous about dealing with the financially strapped firm. By allowing firms in financial trouble to continue operating, bankruptcy laws make it more likely that the bankrupt firms will keep up the quality of the products, and provide more motivation for suppliers to keep up honest dealing.

The *keiretsu* as a solution to the last-period problem

Japanese firms are renowned for organizing themselves into groups of firms called *keiretsus*. *Keiretsu* members buy from one another, share information, and organize joint ventures to produce goods and services in concert with one another. The largest and best-known *keiretsu* is Mitsubishi, which has more than two dozen member firms and hundreds of other firms that are loosely tied to the core firms. They integrate their activities in a number of ways, not the least of which is having their headquarters close together, having the CEOs of the various firms meet regularly to exchange information, and organizing social and business clubs that are open to employees of the *keiretsu* member firms. The members often own stock in one another.

In the United States, many of the activities of any *keiretsu* would likely worry the antitrust authorities because the organization would be construed as monopolistic. No doubt, some *keiretsu* activities might indeed restrain competition in some markets, causing prices of Japanese goods to be higher than they otherwise would be (especially in the domestic market, in which competition from other producers from around the world can be impaired by import restrictions). The *keiretsu* might also be seen as a highly efficient means by which Japanese firms are able to make use of new technologies, quickly incorporating them into products. The Japanese have demonstrated a knack for bringing new products to market quickly.

However, we mention the *keiretsu* organizational form here only because of one of its more unheralded benefits: It is a form of business organization that helps solve the last-period problem. The integration of the member firms' purchases and sales and strategic plans for the future is a means by which members can assure one another that their business relationship will be enduring – or that the member employees have a minimum incentive to behave opportunistically in the short run and have a maximum incentive to work with their joint future income stream in mind (see Prestowitz 1988). Being ousted from the *keiretsu* can inflict substantial costs on the opportunistic firms and their employees. Even the social gatherings of *keiretsu* employees can be construed as a means by which the employees can "bond." Here, we are not so much concerned with the "warm and fuzzy" feelings people might have from integrating their lives. Instead, we mean that by integrating their lives at the social level, employees can provide each other with the mutual assurance that they will live up to expectations in their business dealings – that they will not act opportunistically. In leaving the *keiretsu*, the employees can lose the long-term benefits of their social and business relationships.[9]

In short, the *keiretsu* is a clever means by which opportunistic behavior is made more costly. It seeks to reduce some of the shirking and monitoring costs of doing business when business is done at arm's length. Indeed, one of the more unrecognized benefits of the *firm* in general is that it does, under one "roof," what is attempted under a *keiretsu*. The firm seeks to bring people together and have them associate and work together on a continuing basis for the purpose of minimizing the last-period problem. As we noted early in the book, it's quite possible for all departments within a firm and all stages of an assembly line to be operated on a market basis, with every department and every stage of the assembly line buying from one another. However, you can imagine that such an organization of economic activity would give rise to a multitude of last-period problems, especially if there were no attempt to ensure that everyone "worked together" as something approximating to an in-house *keiretsu*.

The relatively greater use of formal and informal long-term buyer–supplier relationships by the Japanese – sometimes cited as "strategic industrial sourcing" combined with so-called "relational contracting" – may be partially explained by the fact that the Japanese, as commonly argued, have the required business culture, one grounded in a long-term, future-oriented business perspective that prescribes long-term contracts. The Japanese may, to a greater degree than Americans and Europeans, have a pervasive sense of duty that ensures that the parties will abide by any contracts that have been consummated, and the Japanese may have a greater aversion than others to the ongoing contentious bargaining relationships that would be required if contracts were always up for grabs by the low-cost bidders (Dore 1987).[10]

[9] As Clyde Prestowitz notes, "Thus the *Keiretsu* system reduces risks for the Nippon Electric Company and the other Japanese companies through the accumulation of relationships that can be counted upon to cushion shock in time and trouble" (Prestowitz 1988, 164).

[10] The long-term business relationships may also be a consequence of the growing affluence in Japan, which has elevated the importance of quality over price that, in turn, has induced

But it seems to us altogether reasonable that long-term contracting must be grounded in factors other than culture and affluence. One economic explanation may start with a recognition of the extent to which firms are integrated in Japan. The fact of the matter is that in some industries, Japanese production is far less integrated into identified "firms" than, say, in the United States and other countries. In the United States and Western Europe, for example, 50–60 percent of the automobile manufacturing costs are incurred "in-house." In Japanese firms, on the other hand, only 25–30 percent of the automobile production costs are typically incurred "in-house," or inside Japanese firms (Nishiguchi and Masayoshi 1996). Because of the lack of integration, Japanese firms may need to develop long-term buyer–supplier relationships to a much greater degree than more highly integrated firms do just to overcome the potential last-period problems.

Put another way, Japanese firms are able to engage in what is called "strategic outsourcing," and do so competitively, *because* they are willing and able to develop long-term working relationships. If they didn't, they would have to endure the added costs associated with the ever-present closing of those relationships. It doesn't surprise us that many buyer–supplier relationships in Japan have the "look and feel" of integrated firms, with buyers and suppliers helping each other and investing in each other (which is what happens, to more or less degree, within unified firms).

The role of markets in solving last-period problems

Should production be rigidly integrated as in American firms or more loosely integrated as in Japanese business consortiums? No one can answer that question with the certitude that many readers will want. Japanese firms obviously gain the benefits of keeping their suppliers in a position that is marginally more tenuous and, maybe, more competitive with other potential suppliers, but they have to deal with the marginally more severe last-period problems. Many factors, which are offsetting and subject to change with the costs associated with contracting and with principal–agency problems we have discussed, are involved. We suspect that different organizational forms will

large Japanese firms to work with their suppliers in an effort to enhance product quality. The long-term contracting can also be explained partially by the encouragement given by the Japanese government to the creation of long-term buyer–supplier relationships in the past (especially during the Second World War) and the existing laws and legal sanctions against abusive treatment of subcontractors by their customers (Dore 1987, 188).

suit different situations and eras (as has obviously been the case in Japan, where relational contracting has not always been prevalent (Nishiguchi. 1994, chapter 2)).

Answers will come from real-world experimentation in the marketplace. We suspect that competition will press firms to adjust their organization forms, and the inherent incentive structures, as some variation of organizational form emerges as being relatively more successful. Many American firms have had to seriously consider and, to a degree, duplicate the added organizational flexibility of Japanese firms. Why? Their management methods have obviously worked in some industries, most notably the automobile industry. It takes seventeen hours to assemble a car in Japan and between twenty-five and thirty-seven hours to assemble a comparable car in the United States and Europe. Japanese firms can develop a new car in forty-three months, whereas it takes American and European firms over sixty months, and Japanese cars come off the production lines with 30 percent fewer defects. The worst American-made air conditioning units have a thousand defects for every defect in the best Japanese-made units (Nishiguchi 1994, 5–6).

Firm integration and relational contracting are hardly the only means of moderating last-period problems. Joint ventures (JVs) which more often than not require up-front investments by the firms involved, can also be seen as extensions of firm efforts to reduce last-period problems, with the potential of enhancing the quality of the goods and services produced and lowering production costs. Joint ventures might lower production costs because they give rise to economies of scale and scope through the application of technology, but they also can lower production costs by lowering the potential costs associated with opportunistic behavior and monitoring. They make the future income streams of each party a function of the continuation of the relationship.

Problems as a source of profits

The "last-period" problem is nothing more than what we have tagged it, a "problem" that businesses must consider and handle. It implies costs. At the same time, firms can make money by coming up with creative ways of making customers and suppliers believe that the "last period" will occur at some reasonable and uncertain future time. Failing firms have a tough time doing that, which is one explanation why the pace of failure quickens when the prospects of failure are recognized, given that customers and suppliers can be expected to withdraw their dealings as a likely end-period approaches.

Firms that want to continue to exist have an obvious interest in making sure there is a resale market for their firm as a whole, not just a market for its separate assets. The owners and workers can then capture the long-run value of their efforts to build the firm. By highlighting the last-period problem, we are suggesting that the firm resale market can boost the long-term value of its assets simply by alerting people to the fact that the firm can continue for some time into the future. This means that those firms – brokers – who make a market for the sale of firms add value in a way not commonly recognized, by giving firms the prospect of longevity. When a firm is expected to remain profitable, it is more likely that rational people will respond in ways that enhance its profitability.

THE BOTTOM LINE

The key takeaways from chapter 3 are the following:

(1) The concept of rational behavior means that the individual has alternatives, can order those alternatives on the basis of preference, and can act consistently on that basis. The rational individual will also choose those alternatives whose expected benefits exceed their expected costs.

(2) Traditionally, economics has focused on the activities of business firms, and much of this book is devoted to exploring human behavior in a market setting. However, the concept of rational behavior can be applied to other activities, from politics and government to family life and leisure pursuits. Any differences in our behavior can be ascribed to differences in our preferences and in the institutional settings, or constraints, within which we operate.

(3) Rational behavior implies that people have choices, and choices imply that there is a cost to anything.

(4) All choices involve cost–benefit calculations.

(5) The timing and riskiness of options will affect their present value. The more distant into the future benefits will be received or costs incurred, the lower their present values. The more risky options are, the greater their cost (or the lower their net value).

(6) From the economist's way of thinking, people don't move up some consumption pyramid in the manner described by Maslow's hierarchy of needs. Rather,

they weigh the relative marginal values of different goods and services. How satiated people are in the consumption of any set of goods depends on their relative prices.

(7) Individual rationality can give rise to a nontrivial problem for managers developed in this chapter, the last-period problem, which can make deals costly. At the same time, we have indicated how thinking in terms of rational precepts can suggest ways by which managers can deal with their last-period problems to lower firm costs and raise firm profitability.

REVIEW QUESTIONS

(1) What are the costs and benefits of taking this course in microeconomics? Develop a theory of how much a student can be expected to study for this course. How might the student's current employment status affect her studying time?

(2) Some psychologists see people's behavior as determined largely by family history and external environmental conditions. How would "cost" fit into their explanations?

(3) Why not base a course on an assumption of widespread "irrational" behavior?

(4) Okay, so no one is totally rational. Does that undermine the use of "rational behavior" as a means of thinking about markets and management problems?

(5) How could drug use and suicide be considered "rational"?

(6) If your firm were consistently dealing with "irrational behavior" among the owners and workers, what would happen to correct the problem? More to the point, what might you do to correct the problem?

(7) Develop an economic explanation for why professors give examinations at the end of their courses. Would you expect final examinations to be more necessary in undergraduate courses or MBA courses? In which classes – undergraduate or MBA – would you expect more cheating?

(8) Queues have been considered in chapter 2 and this chapter as devices for making money. Why don't grocery stores have one or two checkout counters that have signs at their entrance that read, "Anyone who goes through this line will have 10% added to their total bill"?

CHAPTER

4

The logic of group behavior In business and elsewhere

Men journey together with a view to particular advantage and by way of providing some particular thing needed for the purpose of life, and similarly the political association seems to have come together originally . . . for the sake of the general advantage it brings.
Aristotle, *Ethics*

Unless the number of individuals in a group is quite small, or unless there is coercion, . . . rational, self-interested individuals will not act to achieve their common or group interest. In other words, even if all . . . would gain if, as a group, they acted to achieve their common interest or objective, they will still not voluntarily act to achieve that common or group interest. **Olson (1971, 2)**

In earlier chapters, we introduced the usefulness of markets. However, as is evident inside firms, not all human interactions are through "markets." People often act cooperatively in groups or, as the case may be, in "firms." In this chapter our central purpose is to explore how, and under what conditions, people can organize their behavior into voluntary cooperative associations (groups and firms) in which all work together for the attainment of some common objective – say, greater environmental cleanliness, the development of a "club atmosphere," or the maximization of firm profits. The focus of our attention is on the viability of groups such as families, cliques, communes, clubs, unions, and professional associations and societies, as well as firms, in which individual participation is voluntary to cohere and pursue the common interests of the members.

We consider two dominant and conflicting theories of group behavior. They are "the common-interest theory" and "the economic theory" of group behavior. The former is based on the proposition that a group is an organic whole identified by the "common interest" shared by its individual members. Its basic thesis is that all groups, even very large ones, are organized to pursue the common interest of the group members. Taking this theory one step further, it implies that if people share a common interest, they will organize themselves into a group and voluntarily pursue their shared interest.

According to the economic theory of group behavior, the group is a collection of independently motivated individuals who organize voluntarily to pursue their common interest only in small groups, such as families, clubs, or firms in which there are few people. In large groups, the common interest is very often ineffective in motivating group behavior. The logic of this theory seems perverse; as we shall show in later chapters, however, it is the basis for almost all economic discussion of markets and explains why many policy proponents argue that governments must be delegated coercive powers to collect taxes and to pursue the "public interest." It also helps explain why firms are organized the way they are and why managers manage the way they do. This is, therefore, one of the pivotal chapters in this book.

PART I THEORY AND PUBLIC POLICY APPLICATIONS

Common-interest theory of group behavior

There are almost as many theories of group behavior as there are group theorists. However, categorizing theories according to dominant themes or characteristics is sensible in the light of our limited space.

All theories of group behavior begin by recognizing the multiplicity of forces which affect group members and, therefore, groups. This is especially true of what we term the *common-interest theory*. Many present-day sociologists, political scientists, and psychologists generally share this point of view, which has been prominent at least since the time of Aristotle in the 4th century BC. The determinants of group behavior most often singled out are the "leadership quality" of specific group members and the need felt among group members for "affiliation," "security," "recognition," "social status," or money. Groups such as clubs or unions form so that members can achieve or satisfy a want that they could not satisfy as efficiently through individual action. All these considerations are instrumental in affecting "group cohesion," which, in turn, affects the "strength" of the group and its ability to compete with other groups for the same objectives. From the perspective of this theory, when people join firms, they accept the firm's objective and pursue it because everyone else wants the same thing, leading to self-enforcing group cohesion.

The common-interest theory views the "group" as an organic whole, much like an individual, as opposed to a collection of individuals whose separate actions appear to be "group action." According to the theory, the group has a life of its own that is to a degree independent of the individuals who comprise it. Herbert Spencer (1896), a nineteenth-century sociologist, often described the group as a "social organism" or as a "superorganic" entity.[1] It was probably the social-organism view of groups that Karl Marx had in mind when he wrote of the "class struggle" and predicted that the proletariat class would bring down "bourgeois capitalism" and in its place, erect a communist society. Aristotle probably had the same view of groups in mind when he wrote, "Man is by nature a political animal."

Two major reasons are given for viewing groups as a social organism. First, a group consists of a mass of *interdependencies*, which connect the individuals in the group. Without the interdependencies, there would be only isolated individuals, and the term "group" would have no meaning. Individuals in groups are like the nodes of a spider's web. The spider's web is constructed on these nodes, and the movements in one part of the web can be transmitted to all other parts. Similar to the process of synergism in biology,[2] the actions of individuals within a group combine to form a force that is greater than the sum of the forces generated by individuals isolated from one another. The group must, so the argument goes, be thought of as more than the sum total of its individuals. This argument is often used to arouse support for labor unions, for example. Union leaders argue that unions can get higher wage increases for all workers than individual workers can obtain by acting independently. The reason is that union leaders efficiently coordinate the efforts of all. Environmental groups make essentially the same argument: With well-placed lobbyists, the environmental group can have a greater political impact than all the individuals they represent could have by writing independent letters to their representatives at different times.

Second, groups tend to emerge because they satisfy some interest shared by all the group's members. Because all share this "common interest," individuals have an intrinsic incentive to work with others to pursue that interest, sharing the costs as they work together. Aristotle wrote, "Men journey together with a view to particular advantage" (*Ethics*, 1160a) and Arthur Bentley said,

[1] Spencer (1896) was actually somewhat ambivalent on the subject; at times he also wrote of groups as a composite of individuals. This aspect of his writing reflected the influence that David Hume and Adam Smith had had on his thinking.

[2] This is the process whereby two or more substances (gases or pollutants) come together, and combined can have a greater effect than the sum of the effects of each taken separately.

"There is no group without its interest . . . The group and the interest are not separate . . . If we try to take the group without the interest, we simply have nothing at all" (Bentley 1967, 211–13).

Having observed that a common interest can be shared by all of a group's members, the adherents of this theory of group behavior argue that a group can, with slight modification, be treated as an individual. The primary modification is the relative tightness or looseness of the ties that bind the group members together. This usually makes group action and reaction less decisive and precise than those of individuals, but the difference between a group and an individual is still a matter of degree, not kind. For instance, the difficulty of passing information about group goals from person to person can make the group's response to new information somewhat sluggish. Nevertheless, a group can be assumed to maximize the attainment of its common objective. Furthermore, the implicit assumption is made that this will be true of large as well as small groups. It is on this deduction that Mancur Olson and many economists take issue with this approach to analysis of group behavior.

The economic theory of group behavior

Mancur Olson, on whose (1971) work this section rests, agrees that the "common interest" can be influential and is very important in motivating behavior – but only the behavior of members of small groups. However, he, like so many other economists, insists that a group must be looked upon as a composite of individuals as opposed to an anthropomorphic whole, and that the common interest, which can be so effective in motivating members of small groups, can be impotent in motivating members of large groups: "Unless there is coercion in large groups . . . , *rational self-interested individuals will not act to achieve their common or group interest*" (1971, 2, emphasis in the original). Furthermore, he contends, "These points hold true when there is unanimous agreement in a group about the common goal and the methods of achieving it" (Olson 1971, 2). To understand this theory, we first examine the propositions upon which it is founded, and then consider some qualifications.

Basic propositions

Using economic analysis, people are assumed to be as rational in their decision to join a group as they are toward doing anything else; they will join a group if the benefits of doing so are greater than the costs they must bear. As explained in chapter 3, these costs and benefits, like all others relevant to any other act, must be discounted by the going interest on borrowed funds to account for any time delay in the incurrence of the costs and receipt of any benefits and by the probability that the costs and benefits will be realized.[3] There are several direct, private benefits to belonging to groups, such as companionship, security, recognition, and social status. A person may also belong to a group for no other reason than to receive mail from it and, in that small way, to feel important. A group may serve as an outlet for our altruistic or charitable feelings. If by "common interest" we mean a collection of these types of *private benefits*, it is easy to see how they can motivate group behavior. Entrepreneurs can emerge to "sell" these types of private benefits as they do in the case of private golf clubs or Weight Watchers. The group action is then, basically, a market phenomenon – that is, based in straightforward exchange of **private goods**.

A **private good** is any good – or service – the benefits of which are received exclusively by the purchaser.

However, the central concern of this theory is a "common interest" that is separate and detached from the diverse private interests of members of the group. The problem arises because the public, or common, benefits that transcend the entire group cannot be provided by the market, and can be obtained only by some form of *collective action*. That is, a group of people must band together to change things from what they would otherwise be. Examples include the common interest of an environmental group in getting anti-pollution legislation passed; the interest of labor unions to secure higher wages and better fringe benefits than could be obtained by the independent actions of laborers; the interest of students to resist tuition increases, etc. These are examples of the common interest being a **public** (or collective) **good**, as distinguished from a private good.

A **public good** is a good – or service – the benefits of which are shared by all members of the relevant group if the good is provided or consumed by anyone.

Small groups

Small groups are not without their problems in pursuing the "common interest" of their members. They have a problem of becoming organized, holding together, and ensuring that everyone contributes her part to the group's common interest. This point is relevant to Fred and Harry's (or Crusoe's and Friday's) problems of setting up a social contract considered in chapter 1, and it can be understood in terms of all those little things that we can do with friends and neighbors but that will go undone because of the problems associated with having two or three people come together for the "common good." For

[3] This type of cost–benefit analysis has been explicit, if not implicit, in much of the writing of those in support of the "common-interest theory of groups" explained above. There would be little reason for talking about a "common interest" if it did not have something to do with benefits of group participation (Cartwright 1968).

example, it may be in the common interest of three neighbors – Fred, Harry, and now Judy – for all to rid their yards of dandelions. If one person does it, and the other two do not, the person who removes the dandelions may find his yard full of them the next year because of seeds from the other two yards. Why do we so often find such a small number of neighbors failing to join together to do something as simple as eradicating dandelions?

Even though Fred, Harry, and Judy may not ever agree to work out their common problem (or interest) cooperatively, there are several things that make it more likely that a small group will compete than a large group. Everyone can know everyone else. What benefits or costs may arise from an individual's action are spread over just a few people and, therefore, the effect felt by any one person can be significant. (Fred knows that there is a reasonably high probability that what he does to eliminate dandelions from the border of his property affects Harry's and Judy's welfare.) If the individual providing the public good is concerned about the welfare of those within his group and receives personal satisfaction from knowing that he has in some way helped them, he has an incentive to contribute to the common good; and we emphasize that *before the common good can be realized, individuals must have some motivation for contributing to it.* Furthermore, so-called "free-riders" are easily detected in a small group. (Harry can tell with relative ease when Fred is not working on, or has not worked on, the dandelions in his yard.) If one person tries to let the others shoulder his share, the absence of his contribution will be detected with a reasonably high probability. Others can then bring social pressure (accompanied by the sting of a cost) to bear to encourage (if not force) him to live up to his end of the bargain. The enforcement costs are low because the group is small. There are many ways to let a neighbor know you are displeased with some aspect of his behavior.[4]

[4] As Mancur Olson points out, even students of history have noticed a difference in the ability of large and small groups to cohere and survive. Olson provides us with this quote from a book by George Homans (1950):

> At the level of . . . the small group, at the level, that is, of a social unit (no matter by what name we call it) each of whose members can have some first-hand knowledge of each of the others, human society, for many millennia longer than written history, has been able to cohere . . . they have tended to produce a surplus of the goods that make organization successful . . .
>
> ancient Egypt and Mesopotamia were civilizations. So were classical India and China; so was Greco-Roman civilization, and so is our own Eastern civilization that grew out of medieval Christendom.
>
> But at the level of the tribe or group society has always found itself able to cohere. (Homans 1950, 454–6)

Finally, in small groups, an individual shirking her responsibilities can sometimes be excluded from the group if she does not contribute to the common good (although this would be difficult in the dandelion example) and joins the group merely to free-ride on the efforts of others. In larger groups, such as nations, exclusion is usually more difficult (more costly) and, therefore, less likely.

The problem of organizing "group behavior" to serve the common interest has been a problem for almost all groups, even the utopian communities that sprang up during the nineteenth century and in the 1960s. Rosebeth Kanter, in her study of successful nineteenth-century utopian communities, concluded:

> The primary issue with which a utopian community must cope in order to have the strength and solidarity to endure is its human organization: how people arrange to do the work that the community needs to survive as a group, and how the group in turn manages to satisfy and involve its members over a long period of time. The idealized version of communal life must be meshed with the reality of the work to be done in the community, involving difficult problems of social organization. In utopia, for instance, who takes out the garbage? (Kanter 1973, 64)

Kanter found that the most successful communities minimized the free-rider problems by restricting entry into the community. They restricted entry by requiring potential members to make commitments to the group. Six "commitment mechanisms" distinguished the successful from the unsuccessful utopias:

(1) Sacrifice of habits common to the outside world, such as the use of alcohol and tobacco or, in some cases, sex
(2) Assignment of all worldly goods to the community
(3) Adoption of rules that would minimize the disruptive effects of relationships between members and nonmembers and that would (through, for example, the wearing of uniforms) distinguish members from nonmembers
(4) Collective sharing of all property and all communal work
(5) Submission to public confession and criticism
(6) Expressed commitment to an identifiable power structure and tradition. Needless to say, the cost implied in these "commitment mechanisms" would tend to discourage most potential free-riders from joining the society.

By identifying the boundaries to societies, these mechanisms made exclusion possible. As Kanter points out, the importance of these commitment mechanisms is illustrated by the fact that their breakdown foreshadowed the end of the community.

Other means of bringing about collective behavior on the part of group members are suggested by the cattlemen's associations formed during the nineteenth century. At that time, cattle were allowed to run free over the ranges of the West. The cattlemen had a common interest in preventing a tragedy of the commons – i.e. ensuring that the ranges were not overstocked and overgrazed (remember the discussion of the tragedy of the commons in chapter 1) – and in securing cooperation in rounding up the cattle. To provide for these common interests, cattlemen formed associations that sent out patrols to keep out intruders and that were responsible for the roundups. Any cattleman who failed to contribute his share toward these ends could be excluded from the association, which generally meant that his cattle were excluded from the roundup or were confiscated by the association if they were rounded up.[5]

The family is a small group, which by its very nature is designed to promote the common interest of its members. That common interest may be something called "a happy family life," which is, admittedly, difficult to define. The family obviously does not escape difficulties, given the prevalence of divorces and even more common family feuds. At present its validity as a viable institution is being challenged by many sources; however, it does have several redeeming features that we think will cause it to endure as a basic component of the social fabric. Because of the smallness of the group, contributions made toward the common interest of the family can be shared and appreciated directly. Parents usually know when their children are failing to take the interest of the family into account, and children can easily ascertain similar behavior in their parents. Family members are able, at least in most cases, to know personally what others in the group like and dislike; they can set up an interpersonal cost–benefit structure among themselves that can guide all members toward the common interest. Most collective decisions are also made with relative ease.[6] However, even with all the advantages of close personal contact, the family as a small group often fails to achieve the common interest. Given the frequent failure of the family, the failure of much larger groups to achieve their expressed common objectives is not difficult to understand.

Large groups

In a large-group setting, the problems of having individual members contribute toward the development of the common interest are potentially much greater.

[5] For a very interesting historical investigation of the cattle business during the late nineteenth century, see Dennen (1975).

[6] See, for more discussion on the economics of the family, see McKenzie and Tullock (1994, chapter 8).

The direct, personal interface that is present in small groups is usually lacking in larger groups; and because of the size of large groups, the public good they produce is spread over such a large number of people that no one sees his actions as having an insignificant effect on anyone, even themselves. As a result, no one perceives either personal benefits from his contribution, or benefits for others.

Even when an individual can detect benefits from his actions, he must weigh those benefits against the costs he has to incur to achieve them. For a large group, the costs of providing detectable benefits can be substantial. This can occur not only because there are more people to be served by the good but also because large groups are normally organized to provide public goods that are rather expensive to begin with.[7] Police protection, national defense, and schools are examples of very costly public goods provided by large groups. If all people contribute to the public good, the cost to any one person can be slight; but the question confronting the individual is how much he will have to contribute to make his actions detectable, *given what all the others do.*

In the context of a nation, a very large group indeed, suppose there are certain common objectives to which we can all subscribe, such as a specific charitable program. It is, in other words, in our "common interest" to promote this program (by assumption, for purposes of argument). Will people be willing to voluntarily contribute to the federal treasury for the purpose of achieving this goal? Certainly some people will, but many may not. A person may reason that although he agrees with the national objective, or common interest, his contribution will have no detectable effect in achieving it. This explains why compulsory taxes are necessary. As Olson writes:

> Almost any government is economically beneficial to its citizens, in that the law and order it provides is a prerequisite to all civilized economic activity. But despite the force of patriotism, the appeal of the national ideology, the bond of a common culture, and the indispensability of the system of law and order no major state in modern history has been able to support itself through voluntary dues or contributions. Philanthropic contributions are not even a significant source of revenues for most countries. Taxes, compulsory payments by definition, are needed. Indeed, as the old saying indicates, their necessity is as certain as death itself. (Olson 1971, 13)

The general tenor of the argument also applies to contributions that go to organizations such as World Vision, a voluntary charitable organization

[7] For a pure public good, the costs, by definition, do not rise with a few additional members. However, most groups provide services that are less than a *pure* public good. Education is an example of an impure public good; all education does not benefit all members of society simultaneously and to the same degree. Under these circumstances, the costs can rise, as we have suggested, with the membership, although by a lower percentage.

interested mainly in improving the diets of impoverished people around the world. Many readers of these pages will have been disturbed by scenes of undernourished and malnourished children shown in TV commercials for World Vision. All those who are disturbed would probably like to see something done for these children. They have had an opportunity to make a contribution, but how many people ever actually contribute so much as a dollar? Needless to say, many do give. They are like Harry, who is willing to dig, voluntarily, some of the weeds from his yard. On the other hand, we emphasize the point that a very large number of people who have been concerned never make a contribution. There are many reasons for people not giving, and we do not mean to understate the importance of these reasons; we mean only to emphasize that the large-group problem is one significant reason.

True, if all members of a large group make a small contribution toward the common interest, whatever it is, there may be sizable benefits to all within the group. But, again, the problem that must be overcome is the potential lack of *individual* incentives from which the collective behavior must emerge. Through appropriate organization of group members, the common interest *may* be achieved, even if the membership is large. This, however, merely shifts our attention to the problem of developing that organization. The organization of a large group can be construed as a public good, and there are likely to be costs to making the organization workable. This is likely for two reasons.

First, there are a large number of people to organize, which means that even if there is no resistance on the part of the people to be organized, there will be costs associated with getting them together or having them work at the same time for the same objectives.

Second, some individuals may try to free-ride on the efforts of others, which means it will cost more to get people to become members of the group. Further, each free-rider implies a greater burden on the active members of the group. If everyone waits for "the other guy to take the initiative," the group may never be organized. It is because of the organization costs that students complain so often about the instructional quality of the faculty or some other aspect of university life without doing anything about it. This is also why most people who are disgruntled with the two major political parties do not form a party with those who share their views. The probability of getting sufficient support is frequently very low, which is another way of saying the expected costs are high.

Because an organization may appear to be an obvious way to promote the public good, individuals who try to organize people for that purpose may go through a learning experience before they conclude that it is too costly a venture for them. Even if the organization is successful, the success may be temporary. Eventually, the free-rider problem emerges and the group may fall apart.

During the winter of 1973–4, the United States was in the midst of an "energy crisis." Fuel prices were high even with price controls, and the controls made it more difficult for everyone, including truckers, to get fuel. Truckers were not only having a difficult time obtaining adequate supplies of diesel fuel, they felt that they could not adequately pass their higher operating costs through to consumers because of the then regulatory controls on their rates. Independent truckers sensed that it was in their common interest (not the public's, of course,) to halt their deliveries of goods and services and, in that way, put pressure on the authorities to increase rates and to allocate more fuel supplies for the use of truckers. The call for cooperation met with some success; some truckers did terminate operations and some made headlines by blocking traffic on major highways. However, there were many unwilling to go along with the work stoppage – something that (so it was argued) was in their *common* interest. Consequently, the supporters of the work stoppage resorted to violence, and it was the threat of violence, and not the common interest, that kept many truckers off the road. If it had not been for the violence and the initial willingness of state police departments to allow truckers to flout the law by stopping traffic, including other truckers, it is very doubtful that the truckers would have had as much success as they did.

In more contemporary times, we note that shirking can show up in worker absenteeism for a variety of reasons, including sickness (which can be real or feigned[8]). The Office for National Statistics (ONS) in the United Kingdom found that in the month of May 2004 alone, the British economy lost 1.7 million days of work to sickness, which means that during the survey week, nearly 3 percent of workers took at least one day of sick leave. Not surprisingly, the rate of absence for sickness was 10 percent higher in the public sector than in the private sector (perhaps attributable in part to the pressure of private firms to avoid losses and make a profit). Consistent with the "logic of collective action" as developed in this chapter, the study also found that in private firms with 500 workers and over the rate of sickness absences for the survey week was 29 percent higher than the rate in firms with fewer than twenty-five workers (Barham and Begum 2005, 154).[9]

[8] According to a British study reported here, employers estimated that 20 percent of absences for sickness were not genuine (Barham and Begum 2005, 157).

[9] It should be noted that some unknown portion of the greater number of absences in in large companies than small ones could be attributable to factors other than company size – for example, the demographics of the workforces of large and small firms. Interestingly, and

Economist Stephen Levitt and journalist Stephen Dubner (2005) report on their findings from the sales data collected by Paul Feldman, who sold bagels on the "honor plan" for many years in Washington, DC. Feldman would leave bagels early in the morning at gathering places for office workers. The workers were initially asked to leave their payments in open baskets. Because the money often was taken from the baskets, Feldman made wooden boxes with slits in the top for depositing payments. Initially, in the early 1980s, when he started his bagel business, Feldman suffered a 10 percent loss of bagels (that is, received no payment for 10 percent of the bagels he left). After 1992, his losses of bagels began a slight but steady rise. By 2001, he reached 13 percent over all companies, only to go back down to 11 percent during the two years following 9/11. (Levitt and Dubner speculate that the 15 percent decline in the nonpayment rate could possibly be attributed to the fact that many of his DC customers were connected to national security with an heightened sense for doing what was right.) Relevant to the "logic of collective action," Feldman found that honesty measured by payments received for bagels was marginally affected by firm size: "An office with a few dozen employees generally outpays by 3 to 5 percent an office with a few hundred employees" (Levitt and Dubner 2005, 49). We have to suspect that the difference in the payment rate between small and large offices might be greater were the required payment higher than the price of a bagel.

Qualifications to the economic theory

Obviously, there are many cases in which people acting in what may appear to be rather large groups try to accomplish things that are in the common interest of the membership. Early in the civil rights struggle, the League of Women Voters pushed hard for passage of the Equal Rights Amendment to the Constitution. Labor unions work for minimum wage increases, and the American Medical Association lobbies for legislation that is in the common interest of a large number of doctors. Churches, the Blood Mobile, and other charitable groups are able to work fairly effectively for the "public interest," and several of the possible explanations for this observed behavior force us to step outside the standard economic arguments about public goods.

Why might people work for the "public interest"? There are several reasons. First, as Immanuel Kant, an eighteenth-century philosopher said, people can

contrary to expectations, the authors of absences for reason of sickness in the United Kingdom found that sick leave days were not concentrated on Fridays and Mondays, but were fairly evenly distributed among the five days of the workweek (Barham and Begum 2005, 150).

place value on the *act* itself as distinguished from the results or consequences of the act. The *act* of making a charitable contribution, which can be broadly defined to include picking up trash in public areas or holding the door for someone with an armful of packages, may have a value in and of itself. This is true whether the effects of the act are detectable to the individual making the charitable contribution or not. The personal satisfaction (or value) that comes from the act itself is probably the dominant reason that some people give to CARE. To the extent that people behave in this way, the public good theory loses force. Notice, however, that Olson, in formulating his argument, focused on rational, *economic man* (or woman) as opposed to the *moral man* (or woman) envisioned by Kant. We expect that as the group becomes larger, a greater effort will be made to instill people with the belief that the *act* itself is important.

Second, the contribution that a person has to make in group settings is often so slight that even though the private benefits are small, the contribution to the common interest is also small and can be a rational policy course. This may explain, for example, student membership in groups such as a local Chamber of Commerce. All one has to do in many situations such as this one is to show up at an occasional meeting and make a small dues payment. Further, the private benefits of being with others at the meetings and finding out what the plans are for the association can be sufficient incentive to motivate limited action that is in the common interest.

Third, all may not equally share the benefits received by group members from promotion of the common interest. One or more persons may receive a sizable portion of the total benefits and, accordingly, be willing to provide the public good, at least up to some limit. Many businessmen are willing to participate in local politics or to support advertising campaigns to promote their community as a recreational area. Although a restaurant owner may believe that the entire community will benefit economically from an influx of tourists, he is surely aware that a share of these benefits will accrue to him. Businessmen may also support such community efforts because of implied threats of being socially ostracized.

Fourth, large organizations can be broken down into smaller groups. Because of the personal contact with the smaller units, the common interest of the unit can be realized. In promoting the interest of the small unit to which they belong, people can promote the common interest of the large group. The League of Women Voters is broken down into small community clubs that promote interests common to other League clubs around the country. The national Chamber of Commerce has local chapters. The Lions Club collectively promotes programs to prevent blindness and to help the blind; members do this through a highly decentralized organizational structure.

Political parties are structured in such a way that the local precinct units "get out the votes." The surest way for a presidential contender to lose an election is to fail to have a "grass-roots" (meaning small-group) organization. Churches are organized into congregations, and each congregation is decentralized further into circles and fellowship groups. Most of the work in the Congress is done in committees and subcommittees.

Quite often, a multiplicity of small groups is actually responsible for what may appear to be the activity of a large group. Large firms almost always divide their operations into divisions and then smaller departments. The decentralization that is so prevalent among voluntary and business groups tends to support the economic view of groups.[10]

Fifth, large groups may be viable because the group organizers sell their members a service and use the profits from sales to promote projects that are in the common interest of the group. The Sierra Club, which is in the forefront of the environmental movement, is a rather large group that has members in every part of North America. The group receives voluntary contributions from members and nonmembers alike to research and lobby for environmental issues. However, it also sells a number of publications and offers a variety of environmentally related tours for its members. From these activities, it secures substantial resources to promote the common interest of its membership. The American Economic Association (AEA) has several thousand members. However, most economists do not belong to the AEA for what they can do for it; they join primarily to receive its journal and to be able to tell others that they belong – both of which are private benefits. The AEA also provides economists with information on employment opportunities.

Sixth, the basic argument for any group is that people can accomplish more through groups than they can through independent action. This means that there are potential benefits to be reaped (or, some may say, "skimmed off") by anyone who is willing to bear some of the cost of developing and maintaining the organization. A business firm is fundamentally a *group* of workers and stockholders interested in producing a good (a public good, to them). They have a common interest in seeing a good produced that will sell at a profit. The entrepreneur is essentially a person who organizes a group of people into a production unit; she overcomes all the problems associated with trying to get a large number of people to work in their common interest by providing workers with private benefits – that is, she pays them for their contribution

[10] Admittedly, other explanations for decentralization can be made, one of which relates to *diseconomies of scale.* That is, the organization just becomes technically less efficient as its size is expanded. The economic theory of groups rests on the motivational aspect of large organizations, rather than on the technical *capabilities* of the organization.

to the production of the good. The entrepreneur-manager can be viewed as a person who is responsible for reducing any tendency of workers to avoid their responsibilities to the large-group firm.

Because it is in their interest to eliminate shirking, the workers may be just as interested as stockholders in having and paying someone to perform this task. An individual worker may be delighted if he is allowed to remain idle while no one else is, but he will want to avoid the risks of all workers shirking. If all shirk, nothing will be sold, the firm will collapse, and workers will lose their wages. In summary, workers have an interest in having bosses who induce them to work.

Perspective Management Snooping

Technology has given workers a chance to loaf on the job while they appear busy at their desk. All workers have to do is surf the Web for entertainment, shopping, and sex sites on their office computers while giving passersby (including their bosses) the impression that they, the workers, couldn't be more focused on company business. And workers are often good at acting busy and engaged.[11]

At the same time, technology began coming to the rescue of manager/monitors – or bosses who want to crack down on shirkers. Programs such as NetNanny, SurfWatch, and CyberPatrol enable managers to block worker access to Web sites with certain words on the site, for example, "sex." However, with the aid of a program called com.Policy from SilverStone Software, managers now can, from their own desktop computers, go much further and check out what workers have on their computer screens. The software can take a snapshot of the worker's computer screen and send it, via the local area network (LAN), to the boss' screen. If a worker visits an XXX-rated Web site or writes a love note to a coworker or someone across

[11] The peak count of online orders for personal goods and services occurs during the 9-to-5 workday, not in the evening hours when workers presumably should be doing personal chores. Online orders begin to stream into e-tailers around 9.00 a.m. in the morning, peaking around lunchtime, according to the *Wall Street Journal* (Lisser 1999). One leisure-time e-tailer, Gamedealer.com, figures that 65 percent of its games are ordered during the workday. Indeed, its orders fall off substantially over the weekends. Other e-tailers report that only a few of their online orders come with the request that the order confirmations should not be sent to the work email address of the person making the order. Moreover, a third of the visits to pornography Web sites, according to one report, occur during the workday (Ferrell 2000, A1), and some companies apparently now receive deliveries of more UPS packages for personal use than business use (Lisser 1999, A1).

the country, managers can know it and, depending on how tough they want to be, can penalize or dismiss the workers for using company equipment for personal use. Presumably, the managers can, with the aid of the software, increase worker productivity, given that the penalties or threat of penalties can eliminate worker shirking.

The real question is: Should managers use technology that allows them to "snoop" (to use the characterization of the technology's critics)? Would workers want them to use it? Clearly, there are good reasons why managers and workers alike would not want to use the software – it represents an invasion of worker privacy. Many managers and, we suppose, almost all workers, find "snooping" distasteful. But, as in all other business matters, what each individual (worker) considers undesirable may be considered quite desirable by individuals (workers) as a group.

Workers might not want their privacy invaded at the whim of their bosses, but the workers can understand the interesting dilemma they are in – one in which what is seen as rational behavior by each worker is irrational when engaged in by all. In large offices, the workers can reason that everyone else is misusing (at least to some extent) their computers, that their individual misuse will have an inconsequential impact on the firm's profitability or survivability, and that each worker should do what everyone else is doing: take advantage of the opportunity to misuse their computers – even though long-run firm profits and worker wages will suffer as a result of what all the workers end up doing (or not doing).

Accordingly, workers could welcome the invasion of their privacy, primarily because the gain in income and long-term job security is of greater value than the loss of privacy. Managers can use the software simply because they are doing what their stockholders *and* workers want them to do: make mutually beneficial trades with their workers which, in this case, means asking them to give up some privacy in exchange for the prospects of higher wages and security.

At the same time, we should not expect that the above deduction will apply in every worker group. Some worker groups will value their privacy very highly, so highly in fact that in some instances the managers would have to add more to worker wages than the firm could gain in greater productivity from use of the monitoring software. In such cases, use of the software would be nonsensical: It would hurt both the workers and the firm's bottom line. Put another way, some bosses aren't as tough as they might want to be simply because, beyond some point, toughness – added "snooping" – doesn't pay; it can be a net drain on the company.

Critics of the snooping software are prone to characterize it as "intrusive," if not "Orwellian." One such critic was reported to have reacted to the software's introduction with the comment: "It worries me that with the assistance of a variety of tools every moment of a person's workday can be monitored. Workers are not robots that work 24 hours a day without ceasing."[12]

We simply don't see the matter in such black-and-white terms. The old quip "different strokes for different folks" contains much wisdom, especially in business. We see nothing wrong with employers warning their employees: "The computers are the firm's, and we reserve the right to snoop on what you are doing with the firm's equipment as we see fit." To the extent that the (potential) snooping is seen as a threat to workers, the firm would have to pay in higher wages for any snooping bosses might do. If they did not pay a higher wage for the announcement, some workers (usually the most productive ones) could be expected to go elsewhere, to firms that explicitly rule out snooping.

What is understandably objectionable to employees is the presence of snooping when it has not been announced – or, worse yet, when managers profess, or just intimate, that they will not use the available technology, but then snoop anyway. Such managers not only violate the privacy and trust of their workers but also engage in a form of fraud. They effectively ask their workers to take a lower rate of pay than they would otherwise demand, and then don't give their workers what they pay for, privacy. Moreover, such after-the-fact snooping doesn't do what the firm wants, that is, increase *beforehand* the incentive workers have to apply themselves to their work.

Unannounced snooping is just poor management policy on virtually all scores. With announced snooping policies, workers can sort themselves among firms. Those workers who value their privacy or on-the-job entertainment highly can work for firms that don't snoop. Those workers who value their privacy very little can work for firms that announce that they might snoop. "Different strokes for different folks" can be a means of elevating on-the-job satisfaction.

What firms would be most likely to use the monitoring software (or any other technology that permits close scrutiny of worker behavior)?

[12] As quoted in Wirthman (1997).

We can't give a totally satisfactory answer. Workplace conditions and worker preferences vary greatly across industries. But we can say with conviction that there is no "one-size-fits-all" monitoring policy. We can imagine only that different firms will announce different levels of snooping – with some firms ruling it out, other firms adopting close snooping, and still others announcing occasional snooping. And many firms with the same level of snooping can be expected to impose penalties with different levels of severity.

Although we can't say much in theory about what firms should do, we can note that the snooping software, and similar technologies, would more likely be used in "large" firms in which the output of individual workers is hard to detect, measure, and monitor than it is in "small" firms, in which output is relatively easy to detect, measure, and monitor precisely because each worker's contribution to firm output is such a large share of the total. The snooping technology would not likely be used among workers whose incomes are tied strongly to measures of their performance – for example, sales people who are on commission and far removed from the company headquarters. Such workers will suffer a personal cost if they spend their work time surfing the Web or writing love notes. Managers should be little more concerned with such workers' misuse of their company computers than they are concerned about how their workers use their paychecks at the mall. If such workers are not performing (because they are "spending" too much of their pay on Net surfing), then the firm should consider the prospect that they need to increase the cost of wasted time by more strongly tying pay to performance (a subject to which we return in chapter 13).

By implication, managers will not likely use the software to monitor employees who are highly creative. "Creativity" does not always happen when workers diligently apply themselves, and often occurs precisely because workers are relaxed, with the ability to do as they please without fear of being penalized for goofing off. Firms would probably be more inclined to use the software with employees who are paid by the hour and have little or no personal payoff from working hard and smart. It should go without saying that the more workers value their privacy, the less likely that monitoring software will be used. This is because the more workers value their privacy, the more managers would have to pay in higher wages to invade the privacy.

PART II ORGANIZATIONAL ECONOMICS AND MANAGEMENT

The value of tough bosses

What does the "logic of group behavior" have to do with the direct interest of MBA students who seek to run businesses and direct the work of others? In a word, "plenty," as we demonstrate throughout the rest of the book. We show how the "logic" is central to how competitive markets (and cartels) work (or don't work), and we discuss a multitude of ways to apply the "logic" directly to management problems.

For now, we can stress a maxim that emerges from the economic view of group behavior: Being a tough boss is tough, but a boss who isn't tough might not be worth much. And because tough bosses are valuable and lenient bosses are not, there is a reason for believing that existing organizational arrangements impose the discipline on bosses necessary to ensure that they do a good job of imposing discipline on the workforce. Competition will press firms to hire tough bosses, and, as we shall show in this chapter, the owners of the firm, or their manager-agents, not workers, will tend to be the bosses. That is to say, owners or their agents will tend to boss workers, not the other way around, for the simple reason that worker-bosses are not likely to survive in competitive markets. Workers may not like tough-bossed firms but, as we explain, workers can be better off with tough bosses.

Everyone recognizes that firms compete with each other by providing better products at lower prices in a constant effort to capture the consumer dollar. This competition takes place on a number of fronts, including innovative new products, cost-cutting production techniques, clever and informative advertising, and the right pricing policy. But a continuing theme of this and other management books is that none of these competitive efforts can be successful unless a firm backs them up with an organizational structure that motivates its employees to work diligently and cooperatively. This brings us back to the value of tough bosses.

Take this job and . . .

Though probably overstated, common wisdom has it that workers do not like their bosses, much less tough bosses. The sentiment expressed in Johnny Paycheck's well-known country song "Take This Job and Shove It" could be directed only at a boss. Bosses are also the butts of much humor. There is the old quip that boss spelled backward is "Double SOB."

And there is the story about the fellow who went to the president of a major university and offered his services as a full professor. Noticing that the fellow had no advanced degree, the president informed him that he was unqualified. The fellow then offered his services as an associate professor and received the same response. After offering his services as an assistant professor and hearing that he was still unqualified, the fellow muttered. "I'll be a son-of-a-bitch," at which point the president said, "Why didn't you tell me earlier? I'm looking for someone to be dean of the business school."

If it were not for an element of truth contained in them, such jokes would be hopelessly unfunny. Bosses are often unpopular with those they boss. But tough bosses have much in common with foul-tasting medicines for the sick; you don't like them, but you want them anyway because they are good for you. Workers may not like tough bosses, but they willingly put up with them because tough bosses mean higher productivity, more job security, and better wages.

The productivity of workers is an important factor in determining their wages. More productive workers receive higher wages than less productive workers. Firms would soon go bankrupt in competitive markets if they paid workers more than their productivity is worth, but firms would soon lose workers if they paid them less.

Many things, of course, determine how productive workers are. The amount of physical capital they work with, and the amount of experience and education (human capital) they bring to their jobs are two extremely important, and commonly discussed, factors in worker productivity.

But how well the workers in a firm function together *as a team* is also important. An individual worker can have all the training, capital, and diligence needed to be highly productive, but productivity will suffer unless other workers pull their weight by properly performing their duties. The productivity of each worker is crucially dependent upon the efforts of *all* workers in the vast majority of firms.

So *all* workers are better off if they *all* work conscientiously on their *individual* tasks as part of a team. In other words, it is collectively rational for everyone to work diligently and cooperatively. But there is little individual motivation to work hard to promote the collective interest of a group, or a large firm, as noted earlier in the chapter.

Although each worker wants other workers to work hard to maintain the general productivity of the firm, each worker recognizes that (at least in very large firms) her contribution to the general productivity is small. By shirking

Table 4.1 *The inclination to shirk on the job.*

		Other workers		
		None shirk	Some shirk	All shirk
Jane	Don't shirk	100	75	25
	Shirk	125	100	30

some responsibilities, she receives all the benefits from the extra leisure but suffers only a very small portion of the productivity loss, which is spread over everyone in the firm. She suffers, of course, from some of the productivity loss when other workers choose to loaf on the job, but she knows that the decisions others make are independent of whether she shirks or not. And if everyone else shirks, little good will result for her, or for the firm, from diligent effort on her part. So no matter what she believes that other workers will do, the rational thing for her to do is to capture the private benefits from shirking at practically every opportunity. With all other workers facing the same incentives, the strong tendency is for shirking on the job to reduce the productivity, and the wages, of all workers in the firm, and quite possibly to threaten their jobs by threatening the firm's viability. The situation just described is another example of the general problem of the logic of group behavior – or, more precisely, a form of the Prisoner's Dilemma that we considered earlier.

Games workers play

Consider a slightly different form of the Prisoner's Dilemma that is described in the matrix in table 4.1, which shows the payoff to Jane for different combinations of shirking on her part and shirking on the part of her fellow workers.[13] No matter what Jane believes others will do, the biggest payoff to her (in terms of the value of her expected financial compensation and leisure time) comes from shirking. Clearly, she hopes that everyone else works responsibly so that general labor productivity and the firm's profits will be high despite her lack of effort, in which case she receives the highest possible payoff that any one individual can receive, 125. Unfortunately for Jane, all workers face payoff

[13] The payoff can be in dollars, utility, or any other unit of measure. The only important consideration is that higher numbers represent higher payoffs. This is in contrast to the original Prisoner's Dilemma example in which the number in the payoff matrix represented the length of prison sentences, so that the higher number represented lower payoffs.

possibilities similar to the ones she faces (and to simplify the discussion, we assume that everyone faces the same payoffs). So, everyone will shirk, which means that everyone will end up with a payoff of 30, which is the lowest possible collective payoff for workers.[14]

Workers are faced with self-destructive incentives when their work environment is described by the shirking version of the Prisoner's Dilemma. It is clearly desirable for workers to extricate themselves from this Prisoner's Dilemma. But how?

In an abstract sense, the only way to escape this Prisoner's Dilemma is to somehow alter the payoffs for shirking. More concretely, this requires workers to agree to collectively subject themselves to tough penalties that no one individual would unilaterally be willing to accept. Although no one likes being subjected to tough penalties, everyone can benefit from having those penalties imposed on everyone, including themselves.

The situation here is analogous to many other situations we find ourselves in. For example, consider the problem of controlling pollution that was briefly mentioned in chapter 1. Although each person would find it convenient to be able to freely pollute the environment, when everyone is free to do so, we each lose more from the pollution of others than we gain from our own freedom to pollute. So, we accept restrictions on our own polluting behavior in return for having restrictions imposed on the polluting behavior of others. Polluting and shirking may not often be thought of as analogous, but they are. One harms the natural environment and the other harms the work environment.

Another analogy is that between workers and undergraduate college students who are often required to take general education courses because they see no intrinsic or personal career value in them. The "productivity" of a college from the student's perspective depends on its reputation for turning out well-educated graduates with high grades as a reliable indication that a student has worked hard and learned a lot. But undergraduate students are often tempted to take courses from professors who let them spend more time at parties than in the library and still give high grades. But if all professors curried favor with their students with lax grading policies, all students would be harmed as the value of their degrees decreased. Although students may not like the discipline imposed on them by tough professors, they value the result of a tough professor – a college with a good reputation for graduating well-educated students (Lee 1990).

[14] Jane would receive the lower payoff of 25 if she were the only one who did not shirk, but because of her effort the collective payoff would be higher than if she did shirk. This is true because her effort would raise the payoff to the shirkers to something slightly higher than 30.

Table 4.2 *Shirking in large-worker groups*

		Other workers		
		None shirk	Some shirk	All shirk
Jane	Don't shirk	100	75	25
	Shirk	95	70	0

The ideal situation for each student is for the professor to go easy on her alone and to be demanding of all other students, but obviously this is not possible for all students.

This desire for easy treatment is less likely to be true of MBA students, especially those in fully employed and executive programs, who have come back to school for highly focused personal and professional reasons. They understand that their future income and career paths can be significantly affected by what they take from their classes. As a consequence, they are less inclined to cut classes and to yield to the temptation to take professors who offer the chance of earning grades with little effort.

Similarly, workers may not like bosses who carefully monitor their behavior, spot the shirkers, and ruthlessly penalize them, but they want such bosses. We mean penalties sufficiently harsh to change the payoffs in table 4.1 and eliminate the Prisoner's Dilemma. As shown in table 4.1, the representative worker Jane benefits from shirking no matter what other workers do. If she had a boss tough enough to impose 30 units of cost on Jane (and everyone else) if she (they) engaged in shirking, her relevant payoff matrix would be transformed into that shown in table 4.2. Jane may not like her new boss, but she would cease to find advantages in shirking. And with a tough boss monitoring all workers, and unmercifully penalizing those who dare shirk, Jane will find that she is more than compensated because her fellow workers have also quit shirking. Instead of being in an unproductive firm, surrounded by a bunch of other unproductive workers, each receiving a payoff of 30, she will find herself as part of a hard-working, cooperative team of workers, each receiving a payoff of 100.

The common perception is that bosses hire workers, and in most situations this is what appears to happen. Bosses see benefits that can be realized only by having workers, and so they hire them. But because it is also true that workers see benefits that can be realized only from having a boss, it is not unreasonable to think of workers hiring a boss, and preferably a tough one.

Actual tough bosses

The idea of workers hiring a tough boss is illustrated by an interesting, though probably apocryphal, story of a missionary in nineteenth-century China. Soon after arriving in China, the missionary, who was then full of enthusiasm for doing good, came upon a group of men pulling a heavily loaded barge up a river. Each man was pulling on to a rope attached to the barge as he struggled forward against the river's current. A large Chinese man with a long whip on the barge lashed the back of anyone who let his rope go slack. Upon seeing this, the missionary rushed up to the group of Chinamen to inform them that he would put an end to such outrageous abuse. Instead of being appreciative of the missionary's concern, however, the Chinamen told him to butt out, that they owned the barge, they earned more money the faster they got the cargo up the river, and they had hired the brute with the whip to eliminate the temptation each would otherwise have to slack off.

The missionary story may be doubted, but the point shouldn't be. Even highly skilled and disciplined workers can benefit from having a "boss" who helps them overcome the shirking that can be motivated by the Prisoner's Dilemma. Consider the experience related by Gordon E. Moore, a highly regarded scientist and one of the founders of Intel, Inc. Before Intel, Moore and seven other scientists entered a business venture that failed because of what Moore described as "chaos." Because of the inability of the group of scientists to act as an effective team in this initial venture, before embarking on their next, Moore said that "The first thing we had to do was to hire our own boss – essentially hire someone to run the company" (Moore 1994).

Pointing to stories and actual cases where the workers hire their boss is instructive in emphasizing the importance of tough bosses to workers. But the typical situation finds the boss hiring the workers, not the other way around. We will explain later why this is the case, but we can lay the groundwork for such an explanation by recognizing that our discussion of the advantages of having tough bosses has left an important question unanswered. An important job of bosses is to monitor workers and impose penalties on those who shirk, but how do we make sure that the bosses don't shirk themselves? How can you organize a firm to make sure that bosses are tough?

The work of a boss is not easy or pleasant. It requires serious effort to keep close tabs on a group of workers. It is not always easy to know when a worker is really shirking or just taking a justifiable break. A certain amount of what appears to be shirking at the moment has to be allowed for workers to be fully productive over the long run. There is always some tension between reasonable flexibility and credible predictability in enforcing the rules, and it is difficult to strike the best balance. Too much flexibility can lead to an undisciplined workforce, and too much rigidity can destroy worker morale. Also, quite apart from the difficulty of knowing when to impose tough penalties on a worker is the unpleasantness of doing so. Few people enjoy disciplining those they work with by giving them unsatisfactory progress reports, reducing their pay, or dismissing them. The easiest thing for a boss to do is not to be tough on shirkers. But the boss who is not tough on shirkers is also a shirker.

A boss can also be tempted to form an alliance with a group of workers who provide favors in return for letting them shirk more than other workers. Such a group improves its wellbeing at the expense of the firm's productivity, but most of this cost can be shifted to those outside the alliance.

Of course, you could always have someone whose job it is to monitor the boss and penalize him when he shirks his responsibility to penalize workers who are shirking. But two problems with this solution immediately come to mind. One, the second boss will be even more removed from workers than the first boss, and so will have an even more difficult time knowing whether the workers are being properly disciplined. Second, and even more important, who is going to monitor the second boss and penalize him or her for shirking? Who is going to monitor the monitor? This approach leads to an infinite regress, which means it leads nowhere. A solution to the problem lies in the observation that workers should want their bosses to be "incentivized" to remain tough in spite of all the temptations to concede in particular circumstances for particular workers.

Jack Welch, the former chief executive officer (CEO) of General Electric (GE), has played out the central point of this "Organizational economics and management" section because he surely qualifies as a tough boss. Indeed, *Fortune* once named Welch "America's Toughest Boss" (Tichy and Sherman 1993). Welch earned his reputation by cutting payrolls, closing plants, and demanding more from those that remained open. Needless to say, these decisions were not always popular with workers at GE. But today, GE is one of America's most profitable companies, creating far more wealth for the economy and opportunities for its workers than it would have if the tough and unpopular decisions had not been made. In Welch's words: "Now people come to work with a different agenda: They want to win against the competition, because they know that . . . customers are their only source of job security. They don't like weak managers, because they know that the weak managers of the 1970s and 1980s cost millions of people their jobs" (Tichy and Sherman 1993, 92).

Table 4.3 *The Battle of the Sexes*

		Tom	
		Shakespeare in Love	*Saving Private Ryan*
Marsha	*Shakespeare in Love*	100 \ 75	60 \ 60
	Saving Private Ryan	−40 \ −40	75 \ 100

The value of tough leadership and the Battle of the Sexes

In the previous section we pointed out how workers could benefit from tough bosses who help them overcome the Prisoner's Dilemma workers otherwise find themselves in. The Prisoner's Dilemma is an example of the type of situation that is analyzed by *game theory* – the study of how people make decisions when the benefit each person realizes from the decision she makes depends on the decisions others make in response. But there are "games" other than the Prisoner's Dilemmas that workers find themselves in and which explain how managers can be useful as tough bosses, or tough leaders. An interesting game that falls into this category is commonly called the "Battle of the Sexes." The name of this game comes from conflict between the sexes, but it illustrates a more general conflict that is best resolved by managers who can make tough decisions.

Let's consider first the conflict between the sexes. Tom and Marsha have just started dating and enjoy each other's company. Both also like going to the movies, preferably together. But they have different tastes in films – Marsha prefers romantic films while Tom prefers war films. They are planning on going out on Saturday night, but Marsha wants to see *Shakespeare in Love* and Tom wants to see *Saving Private Ryan.* The value each receives from going out on Saturday night depends on what movie he/she sees and whether he/she sees it with Marsha/Tom, or alone. The payoffs for Tom and Marsha are given in table 4.3, which shows the different possible outcomes for Saturday, with the first number in each box representing Marsha's payoff and the second number representing Tom's payoff. As shown, if both go to *Shakespeare in Love*, Marsha will receive a payoff of 100 and Tom gets a payoff of 75. If both go to *Saving Private Ryan*, Marsha receives a payoff of 75 and Tom gets the 100 payoff. If each goes to their choice of movies, but goes alone, then both receive a payoff of 60. And in the highly unlikely event that they each go alone to the other's favorite movies (but in the throes of romance, men and women do strange things) each will receive a payoff of −40.

As opposed to the Prisoner's Dilemma game, in which the best choice for each (makes the noncooperative choice) is the same no matter what the other is expected to do, in the Battle-of-the-Sexes game, the best choice for each varies, depending on what the other person is expected to do. For example, if Marsha can convince Tom that she is definitely going to see *Shakespeare in Love*, then the best choice for Tom is to see the same movie and get a payoff of 75 instead of 60. But it may be difficult for Marsha to convince Tom that she is going to her preferred movie, come what may. Tom knows that if he can convince Marsha that he is definitely going to see *Saving Private Ryan*, then that will be Marsha's best choice. So making a credible commitment may be difficult for both Marsha and Tom.

Further aggravating the problem is that both may decide that it is worth going to a movie alone (reducing their payoff by 15 this time) rather than acquiescing to the stubbornness of the other. By doing so, each can hope to establish a reputation for making credible threats that will improve the chances of getting his/her way in the future. The result can be a lot of time and emotion expended negotiating over which movie to attend when the most important thing is for both to attend the same movie – something that may not happen despite costly negotiation.

Workers routinely confront their own Battle-of-the-Sexes problems on the job, although these problems have nothing to do with gender-based preferences or the movies. Workplace decisions often have to be made about issues for which workers have different preferences, but that will yield the greatest payoff to all workers if they all accept the same decision. For example, some workers will prefer to start working at 6.30 a.m., have a one-hour lunch, and leave at 3.30 p.m. Others will prefer to start at 7.00 a.m., take no lunch, and leave at 3.00 p.m. Others will prefer to start at 10.00 a.m., take a two-hour lunch, and leave at 8.00 p.m. Indeed, there will probably be as many different preferences as there are workers, with these preferences changing from day to day. But it is typically the case that it is best for everyone in a firm to be in at the same time every workday.

Another example is that people will have different preferences with respect to the computers and software they use at work, but for reasons of compatibility and savings from bulk purchases, the best choice is the same choice for everyone. Or everyone in the production engineering department may have a different preference for the type of redesign that should be engineered into their firm's product. But the most important thing is that they all work on the same redesign.

Some might feel that it is best to resolve such individual differences "democratically" in these situations, with everyone being able to make their case until an agreement on a decision emerges, with this consensus decision most likely to be the best one. But agreement may never emerge and even if it did, the cost would probably far exceed the benefit from a better decision. At some point fairly early on in the discussion, the best approach is for a manager to assume leadership and make a decision that everyone has to accept. There are a lot of characteristics that go into making a good leader, and certainly one of the first most people think of is the ability to make good decisions. And obviously it's better to have a leader who makes good decisions than one who doesn't. But keep in mind that often the most important thing in making a good decision is not the decision that is made, but getting everyone to accept it. It is hard to argue that the decision to have everyone drive on the right-hand side of the road is better than having everyone drive on the left-hand side. Either decision is a good one as long as everyone abides by it. And getting everyone to accept a decision can require a tough-minded leader who imposes his/her will on others. Ideally leaders will get the job done through gentle persuasion rather than bull-headed arrogance. But if the former doesn't work, it's nice to have the latter in reserve.

The role of the residual claimant

Every good boss understands that he or she has to be more than just "tough." A boss needs to be a good "leader," a good "coach," and a good "nursemaid," as well as many other things. The good boss inspires allegiance to the firm and the commonly shared corporate goals. Every good boss wants workers to seek the cooperative solutions in the various Prisoner's Dilemmas that invariably arise in the workplace. Having said that, however, a good boss will invariably be called upon to make some pretty tough decisions, mainly because the boss usually stands astride the interests of the owners above and the workers below. The lesson of this section on this point should not be forgotten: "Woe to the boss who simply seeks to be a nice guy." But firms must structure themselves so that bosses will *want* to be tough, but appropriately tough. How can that be done?

Residual claimants are people who have legal claim to any residual (commonly referred to as profits) that remains from the sales revenue after all the expenses have been paid.

In many firms, the boss is also the owner. The owner/boss is someone who owns the physical capital (such as the building, the land, the machinery, and the office furniture), provides the raw materials and other supplies used in the business, and hires and supervises the workers necessary to convert those factors of production into goods and services. In return for assuming the responsibility of paying for all of the productive inputs, including labor, the owner earns the right to all of the revenue generated by those inputs.

Economists refer to the owners as **residual claimants**. As the boss, the owner is responsible for monitoring the workers to see whether each one of them is properly performing her job, and for applying the appropriate penalties (or encouragement) if they aren't. By combining the roles of ownership and boss in the same individual, a boss is created who, as a residual claimant, has a powerful incentive to work hard at being a tough boss.

The employees who have the toughest bosses are likely to be those who work for residual claimants. But the residual claimants probably have the toughest boss of all – themselves. There is a lot of truth to the old saying that when you run your own business, you are the toughest boss you will ever have. Small business owners commonly work long and hard because there is a very direct and immediate connection between their efforts and their income. When they are able to obtain more output from their workers, they increase the residual they are able to claim for themselves. A residual claimant boss may be uncomfortable disciplining those who work for her, or dismissing someone who is not doing the job, and indeed may choose to ignore some shirking. But in this case the cost of the shirking is concentrated on the boss who allows it, rather than diffused over a large number of people who individually have little control over the shirking and little motivation to do anything about it even if they did. So with a boss who is also a residual claimant, there is little danger that shirking on the part of workers will be allowed to get out of hand.

When productive activity is organized by a residual claimant, all resources – not just labor – tend to be employed more productively than when those who make the management decisions are not residual claimants. The contrast between government agencies and private firms managed by owner/bosses, or proprietors, is instructive. Examples abound of the panic that seizes the managers of public agencies at the end of the budget year if their agencies have not spent all of the year's appropriations. The managers of public agencies are not claimants to the difference between the value their agency creates and the cost of creating the value. This does not mean that public agencies have no incentive to economize on resources, only that their incentives to do so are impaired by the absence of direct, close-at-hand residual claimants.[15]

[15] Granted, taxpayers could be viewed as the residual claimants to any efficiency improvement resulting from tough managerial decisions in public enterprises, given that efficiency improvement can result in lower tax bills. However, taxpayers have little incentive to closely monitor the activities of public agencies and, as a matter of fact, do little of it. The reason is simple: Each taxpayer can reason that there is little direct payoff to anyone incurring the costs of monitoring and enforcing greater efficiency in public agencies (Tullock 1972, chapter 7).

If, for example, a public agency managed to perform the same service for $100,000 a year less than in previous years, the agency administrator would not benefit by being able to put the savings in her pocket. In fact, she would likely find herself worse off because she would be in charge of an agency with a smaller budget and therefore one less prestigious in the political pecking order. She would also realize that the money she saved by her diligence would be captured by an overbudgeted agency elsewhere, enhancing the prestige of its less efficient administrator.

The clever public administrator is one who makes sure that every last cent, and more, of the budget is spent by the end of the budget year, regardless of whether it is spent on anything that actually improves productivity. Can you imagine a proprietor of a private firm responding to the news that production costs are less than expected by urging his employees to buy more computers and office furniture, and attend more conferences before the end of the year?

To make the point differently, assume that as a result of your management training you become an expert on maximizing the efficiency of trash pickup services. In one nearby town the trash is picked up by the municipal sanitation department, financed out of tax revenue, and headed by a government official on a fixed salary. In another nearby town the trash is picked up by a private firm, financed by direct consumer charges, and owned by a local businessperson who is proud of her loyal workers and impressive fleet of trash trucks. By applying linear programming techniques to the routing pattern, you discover that each trash service can continue to provide the same pickup with half the number of trucks and personnel currently being used.

Who is going to be most receptive to your consulting proposal to streamline their trash pickup operation – the bureaucratic manager who never misses an opportunity to tell of his devotion to the taxpaying public, or the proprietor who is devoted to her workers and treasures her trash trucks?

On the other hand, the proprietor will hire you as a consultant as soon as she becomes convinced that your ideas will allow her to lay off half of her workers and sell half of her trucks. The manager who is also a residual claimant can be depended on to economize on resources despite her other concerns. The manager who is not a residual claimant can be depended on to waste resources despite her statements to the contrary.[16]

[16] Much of the motivation for privatizing municipal services comes from the cost reductions that take place when residual claimants are in charge of supplying these services. There is plenty of evidence that privatization of some government services does significantly lower the cost, often by 50 percent or more, of basic municipal services such as trash pickup, fire protection, and school buses (Bennett and Johnson 1983).

No matter how cheaply a service is produced, resources have to be employed that could have otherwise been used to produce other things of value. The value of the sacrificed alternative has to be known and taken into account to make sure that the right amount of the service is produced. As a residual claimant, a proprietor not only has a strong motivation to produce a service as cheaply as possible but also has the information and motivation to increase the output of the service only as long as the *additional value generated is greater than the value forgone elsewhere in the economy.*

The prices of labor and other productive inputs are the best indicators of the value of those resources in their best alternative uses. So, the total wage and input expense of a firm reflects quite well the value sacrificed elsewhere in the economy to manufacture that firm's product. Similarly, the revenue obtained from selling the product is a reasonable reflection of the product's value. Therefore, proprietors of businesses receive a constant flow of information on the *net value* their firm is contributing to the economy, and their self-interest motivates a constant effort to produce any given level of output, and produce it in the way that maximizes firms' contributions.

When the one controlling the firm can claim a firm's profits, those profits serve a very useful function in guiding resources into their most valuable uses. If, for example, consumers increase the value they place on musical earrings (if such were ever made) relative to the value they place on other products, the price of musical earrings will increase in response to increased demand, as will the profits of the firms producing them. The increased profit will give the proprietors of these firms the financial ability, and the motivation, to obtain additional inputs to expand output of this dual-purpose fashion accessory of which consumers now want more. Also, some proprietors of firms making other products will now experience declining profits and find advantages in shifting into production of musical earrings. This redirection of labor and other productive resources continues, driving down prices and profits in musical earring production, until the return in this productive activity is no greater than the return in other productive activities. At this point, there is no way to further redirect resources to increase the net value they generate.[17]

The incentives created by residual claimant business arrangements do a reasonable job of lining up the interests of bosses with the interests of their workers, their customers, and the general goal of economic efficiency – using

[17] The profits received by firms that are too large to be managed by single proprietors also serve to direct resources into their highest-valued uses. This is true because these firms are organized in ways that allow the owners (the residual claimants) to exert some control over those who manage the firm (the hired bosses). The problem that owners of large corporations face in controlling managers is discussed in chapters 6 and 9.

scarce resources to create as much wealth as possible. This alignment of interests is a crucial factor in getting large numbers of people with diverse objectives and limited concern for the objectives of others to cooperate with one another in ways that promote their general wellbeing. Having the residual claimant direct resources is, understandably, an organizational arrangement that workers should applaud. The residual claimant can be expected to press all workers to work diligently so that wages, fringes, and job security can be enhanced. Indeed, the workers would be willing to pay the residual claimants to force all workers to apply themselves diligently (which is what workers effectively do); both workers and residual claimants can share in the added productivity from added diligence.

Risk taking, risk aversion, and firm ownership

Certainly this ability to productively harmonize a diversity of interests is a major reason for the emergence and sustainability of residual claimant business arrangements. But there is another reason that firms are commonly owned and managed by the same person, a reason that helps explain why the typical situation involves the boss hiring the workers instead of the workers hiring the boss.

People differ in a host of ways, and many of their differences have important implications for the type of productive efforts for which they are best suited. For example, both of the authors would have liked to have been successful movie stars, but because we have slightly less charisma than baking soda, we became economists instead. (Had we been endowed with even less charm, we would have become accountants.) More relevant to the current discussion, however, is the fact that people differ in their willingness to accept risk. Most people are what economists call *risk averse*: they shy away from activities whose outcomes are not known with reasonable certitude. Such people would, for example, prefer a sure $500 to a 50 percent chance of receiving $1,500 with a 50 percent chance of losing $500 (which has an expected value of $500).[18] But

[18] The prevalence of insurance reflects the risk averseness of most people. Insurance allows people to experience a relatively small loss with 100 percent probability (their insurance premiums) in order to avoid a small chance of a much larger loss, but a loss with an expected value that is less than the insurance premiums. It is interesting to note, however, that the same people who buy fire insurance on their houses may also buy lottery tickets. Buying a lottery ticket reflects risk-loving behavior because you are taking a small loss with 100 percent probability (the price of the lottery ticket) in order to take a chance on a payoff that is smaller in expected value than the loss. Explanations exist for why rational individuals would buy insurance and gamble. Probably the best known of these explanations was given by Friedman and Savage (1948). But the fact remains that in situations that would put a significant amount of their wealth or income at risk, most people are risk averse.

some people are more risk averse than others, as measured by how much less than $500 a sure payoff would have to be before they would no longer prefer it to a gamble with a $500 expected value. And people who are highly risk averse will make very different career choices than those who are not.

Consider the choice between becoming a residual claimant by starting your own business and taking a job offered by a residual claimant. The choice to become a residual claimant is a risky one, requiring the purchase of productive capital and the hiring of workers (thereby obligating yourself to fixed payments) with no guarantee that the revenue generated will cover those costs. The person who starts a firm can lose a tremendous amount of money. Of course, in return for accepting this risk, a residual claimant who combines keen foresight, hard work, and a certain amount of luck may end up claiming a lot of residual and becoming quite wealthy. Clearly, those willing to accept risks will tend to be attracted to a career of owning and managing businesses as residual claimants.

Those people who are more risk averse will tend to avoid the financial perils of entrepreneurship. They will find it more attractive to accept a job with a fixed and *relatively* secure wage, even though the return from such a job is less than the expected return from riskier entrepreneurial activity.

So, business arrangements that put management control in the hands of residual claimants not only create strong incentives for efficient decisions but also allow people to occupationally sort themselves out in accordance with an important difference in their productive attributes and their attitude toward risk. Not only will people who are not very risk averse be more comfortable as residual claimants than most people, they will generally be more competent at dealing with the risks that are inherent in organizing production in order to best respond to the constantly changing preferences of consumers. At the same time, those who are not averse to taking risks are likely to be less reliable at the relatively routine and predictable activity typically associated with earning a fixed wage than are those who are highly averse to risk.

Consider the prospect that more risk averse workers own their firms and hire the less risk averse owners of capital (as well as other resources) who would be paid a fixed return on their investments (with the fixed return having all the guarantees that are usually accorded worker wages).[19] Workers would then, in effect, be the residual claimants, and worker wages would then tend to vary (as do profits in the usual capitalist-owned firm) in less than predictable ways with the shifts in market forces and general economic conditions. Such a firm would not likely be a durable arrangement for even moderately large firms in

[19] In effect, the owners of capital would hold financial assets that would have the look and feel of bonds.

which fixed investments are important. It's not hard to see why (Jensen and Meckling 1979).

The workers *might* be spurred to work harder and smarter because of the sense of ownership, which the proponents of worker ownership argue would be the case. But, then, maybe not. Workers might be more inclined to shirk, given that they are no longer pushed to work harder and smarter by owner-capitalists. Finding themselves back in a Prisoner's Dilemma, each worker can reason that her contribution to profits is very little (especially in large firms), so little that the power of being residual claimants is lost in the dispersion of ownership among workers. For this reason alone, we would expect most worker-owned firms to be relatively small.

Risk averse worker-owners would require a "risk premium" built into their expected incomes, and their risk premium would be greater than the risk premium that the less averse owners of capital would require. Hence, the cost of doing business for the worker-owned firm would be higher than that for the capitalist-owned firm, which means the worker-owned firms would tend to fail in competition with capitalist-owned firms. Instead of outright failure, we might expect many worker-owned firms to be converted to capitalist-owned firms simply because the workers would want to sell their ownership rights to the less risk averse capitalists who, because of their lower risk aversion, can pay a higher price for ownership rights than it is worth to the workers. The worker-owned firms would continue only if the workers were not allowed to sell their supposed ownership rights, which was true in the former Soviet Union.

However, the worker-owned firm would be fraught with other competitive difficulties. Because of their risk aversion, workers would demand higher rates of return on their investments, a fact that would likely restrict their investments and lower their competitiveness and viability over the long run. Moreover, with workers in control of the flow of payments to the capitalists after they, the capitalists, have made the fixed investment, the capitalists would have a serious worry. The capitalists must fear that the workers would tend to use their controlling position to appropriate the capital by paying themselves noncompetitive wages and fringe benefits, a fear that is not so prominent among workers when capitalists own the fixed assets and pay the workers a fixed wage (Klein, Crawford, and Alchian 1978).[20] Therefore, even the

[20] The problem of appropriation by workers is especially acute if the fixed assets are firm-specific, because the assets have no alternative use, which implies a limited resale value. As we have seen in other instances, owners of fixed assets with limited resale values open themselves to opportunistic behavior on the part of the buyer – in this case, the workers who, after the specific investment is made, can appropriate the difference between the purchase

capitalists would require a risk premium before they invested in worker-owned firms.

Of course, the workers could make the requisite investment, but we must wonder where they would obtain the investment funds. Out of their own pockets? Would they not want to put their own funds in secure investments? We must also wonder whether workers would be interested in investing in their own worker-run firms. As can capitalists, workers can understand the threat to their investments from other workers, given the limited competitiveness of their worker-owned firms and the tendency of workers to restrict investment and drain the capital stock through overpayments in wages and fringe benefits. Workers, however, have an additional problem: If they invest their financial resources in their own firms, they will have a very narrow range of personal investments. By their work for their firms, they already plan to invest a great deal of their resources – themselves – in their jobs just by spending time at work. Adding a financial investment means restricting the scope of assets in their personal portfolio of investments. That fact alone will increase their aversion to risky investments by their firms, and the longer the term of the investment, the greater the risk. Accordingly, we would expect the investments of worker-owned firms to be for shorter periods than would be the case in capitalist-owned firms, which implies that worker-owned firms would tend to lag in the development and application of new technologies. Such a tendency would once again make worker-owned firms less competitive, especially over the long run.

We are not suggesting that no firms will be worker-owned and managed. After all, some are. Instead, the analysis explains why there are relatively few such firms, and why they are typically small firms, relying primarily on human capital of the owner/workers rather than physical capital. When large firms, such as Weirton Steel and United Airlines, are worker-owned (which they were for a short time), they are not worker-managed. The worker-owners of such firms immediately hire bosses to make the tough decisions that have to be made to keep a firm viable, but then there are the inevitable tensions that come with worker ownership.

and resale price. Workers hired by their capitalist-owners do not generally have the same worry about their work-related investments with their capitalist-owners. The workers' investments in their job-related skills are typically not firm-specific. If workers need firm-specific skills, the workers can protect themselves from appropriation by having their firm pay for the investment they might make in firm-specific skills. Put another way, when human capital is relatively important on the job, we would expect the workers to also be the owners, which tends to be the case in accounting and law firms, in which the ratio of human to physical capital investments tends to be high.

Optimal shirking

To this point, we have discussed shirking as if it were all "bad," always and everywhere a net drain on corporate profits. Hence, the task of managers is, in such a world, relatively simple: Eliminate any and all shirking by monitoring and "cracking the corporate whip." While our approach has been useful to highlight key points, we need to stress is closing out our discussion of shirking by noting that shirking on the job, at least up to a point, can be viewed as a worker fringe benefit, something that has intrinsic value to workers. To the extent that this is the case, some shirking can actually increase company profits because it leads to a greater supply of good workers willing to work for the firm that allows some shirking and lower wage rates paid by the company. The company's lower productivity can (up to a point) be more than offset by its lower wage bill. Indeed, the workers can be "better off" with some shirking. This is because the intrinsic value of some shirking on the job can afford them more utility than the additional money wages they would receive for not shirking.

Of course, so long as on-the-job shirking has value to workers, firms would not want to eliminate all shirking even if doing so required them to incur zero monitoring costs. The elimination of shirking could raise the company's wage bill by more than it raises the workers' productivity. In short, as in all things, managers have a very complicated problem, one of seeking an *optimum* amount of shirking. That is, they should allow shirking to mount so long as the reduction in the wage bill exceeds the lost productivity.

THE BOTTOM LINE

The key takeaways from chapter 4 are the following:

(1) The importance of the "cause" or the groups' "common interest" can significantly affect the willingness of group members to cohere and pursue the common interest of the membership. However, a "cause" or "common interest" can more effectively motivate a "small" group than a "large" group. This suggests that, given other considerations, an increase in group size beyond some point can have an adverse effect on the motivation that group members have to pursue their group's common interest.[21]

[21] Several studies have revealed that as far as being able to take action, smaller groups, generally with fewer than seven or eight members, are more efficient than larger ones (James 1951; Hare 1952). Studies also show that as group size within industry increases, job satisfaction tends to decrease, and absentee rates, turnover rates, and the incidence of labor disputes tend to increase (Porter and Lawyer 1965).

(2) The logic of collective action can explain the growth in employee shirking and the misuse of resources as firms grow. The logic can also explain why firms divide their operations into small groups, including departments and teams.
(3) A boss who is tough on employees can have supporters among employees as well as owners. There is, however, both an optimal amount of toughness on the part of bosses and an optimal amount of shirking on the part of workers.
(4) A boss who is not tough on shirkers is also a shirker.
(5) Overcoming the logic of collective action can be seen as a Prisoner's Dilemma game in which all – workers and bosses – prefer a cooperative outcome (which may need to be achieved by properly constructed incentives).
(6) Leadership the form of setting a course for all to follow can be productive since it can reduce the haggling over what course of action all should take.
(7) Residual claimants have powerful incentives to encourage firms to minimize costs and maximize profits since such claimants have claims to any firm resources after all other claims have been fulfilled.
(8) Companies are typically controlled by the owners of capital because they would otherwise have to fear that their capital, once deployed in companies, would be subject to appropriation by workers.

With a reasonable degree of clarity, both the theory and the evidence suggest that if society wishes to pursue some interest that is common to people on a very broad scale, some means other than voluntary group cooperation must be found. It is for this reason that we begin again a study of the markets after we have looked inside the "firm" to see how the "logic of group behavior" can help explain incentive structures within groups, most notably firms.

REVIEW QUESTIONS

(1) Explain why the "free-rider" problem is likely to be greater in a "large" group than in a "small" group.
(2) The common interest of people who are in a burning theater is to walk out in an orderly fashion and avoid a panic. If that is the case, why do people so frequently panic in such situations? Use rational behavior and the logic of collective action in your answer.
(3) Discuss the costs of making collective decisions in large and small groups. What do these costs have to do with the viability of large and small groups?

(4) Intelligent collective decisions can be a common interest shared by members of a large group. Does the analysis of in this chapter suggest anything about the incentive that individuals have to obtain information or about the intelligence of decisions that a large group will make?

(5) In what ways do firms overcome the problems discussed in this chapter relating to large groups? How do market pressures affect firm incentives to overcome these problems?

(6) Would you expect private firms or government bureaucracies to be more efficient in pursuing the stated "common objectives" of the organization? Explain in terms of the logic of collective action and market forces.

(7) You may have a class in which the professor grades according to a curve, whereby the professor adjusts the grading scale to fit the test results. This may also be a class in which all the students in it would prefer not to learn as much as they can. If you are in such a situation (or can imagine one like it), the "common interest" of the class members can be for everyone to study less. The same grading distribution can be obtained, and everyone can receive the same relative grade for less effort. Why do class members not collude and restrict the amount of studying they do? Would you expect collusion to not study to be more likely in undergraduate general education courses, core classes in your MBA program, or elective classes in your MBA program?

CHAPTER

5

Government controls: how management incentives are affected

Without bandying jargon or exhibiting formulae, without being superficial or condescending, the scientist should be able to communicate to the public the nature and variety of consequences that can reasonably be expected to flow from a given action or sequence of actions. In the case of the economist, he can often reveal in an informal way, if not the detailed chain of reasoning by which he reaches his conclusions, at least the broad contours of the argument.
E. J. Mishan

Chapters 1–4 showed how the models of competitive markets illuminate the economic effects of market changes, such as an increase in the price of oil. This chapter examines the use of government controls to soften the impact of such changes. We consider four types of government control: excise taxes, gasoline price controls, minimum-wage laws, and pollution controls. As you will see, government controls can inspire management reactions that negate some of the expected effects of the controls.

PART I THEORY AND PUBLIC POLICY APPLICATIONS

Who pays the tax?

Most people are convinced that consumers bear the burden of excise (or sales) taxes. They believe that producers simply pass the tax on to consumers at higher prices. Yet every time a new (or increased) excise tax is proposed, producers lobby against it. If excise taxes could be passed on to consumers, firms would have little reason to spend hundreds of thousands of dollars opposing them. In fact, excise taxes do hurt producers.

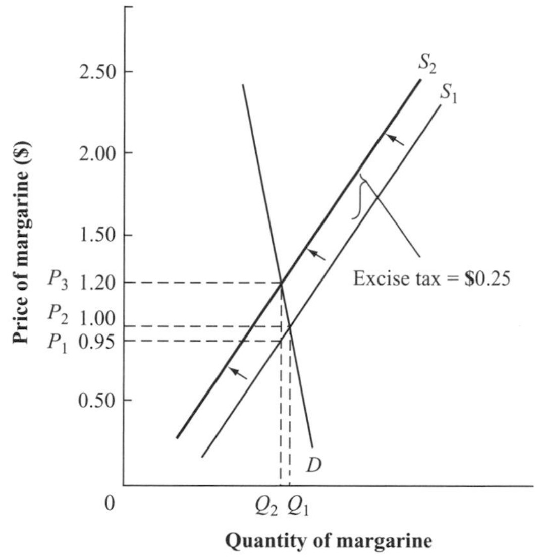

Figure 5.1 The economic effect of an excise tax
An excise tax of $0.25 will shift the supply curve for margarine to the left, from S_1 to S_2. The quantity produced will fall from Q_3 to Q_2; the price will rise from P_2 to P_3. The increase, $0.20, however, will not cover the added cost to the producer, $0.25.

Figure 5.1 shows the margarine industry's supply and demand curves, S_1 and *D*. In a competitive market, the price will tend toward P_2 and the quantity sold toward Q_1. If the state imposes a $0.25 tax on each pound of margarine sold and collects the tax from producers, it effectively raises the cost of production. The producer must now pay a price not just for the right to use resources, such as equipment and raw materials, but for the right to continue production legally. The supply curve, reflecting this cost increase, shifts to S_2. The vertical difference between the two curves, P_1 and P_3, represents the extra $0.25 cost added by the tax.

Given the shift in supply, the quantity of margarine produced falls to Q_2 and the price rises to P_3. Note, however, that the equilibrium price increase (P_2 to P_3) is less than the vertical distance between the two supply curves (P_2 to P_1). That is, the price increases by less than the amount of the tax that caused the shift in supply. Clearly, the producer's net, after-tax price has fallen. If the tax is $0.25, but the price paid by consumers rises only $0.20 ($1.20 – $1.00), the producer loses $0.05 per unit sold. It now nets only $0.20 per unit on a product that used to bring $0.25. In other words, the tax not only reduces the quantity of margarine producers can sell but also lowers the after-tax price to

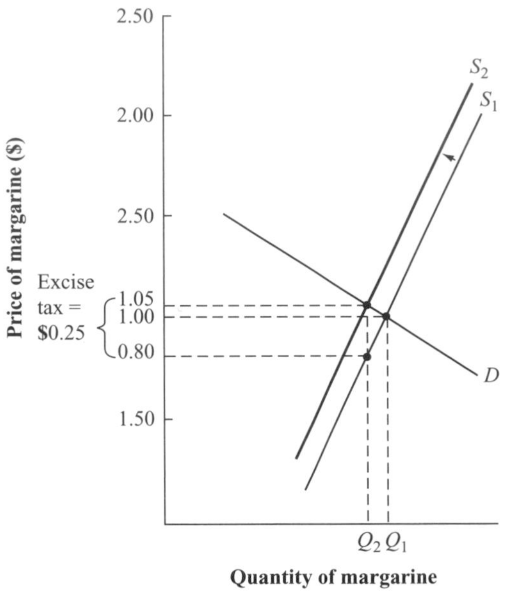

Figure 5.2 The effect of an excise tax when demand is more elastic than supply
If demand is much more elastic than supply, the quantity purchased declines significantly when supply decreases from S_1 to S_2 in response to the added cost of the excise tax. Producers will lose $0.20; consumers will pay only $0.05 more.

the margarine producers, which is reason enough for them to be against such excise taxes.

Incidentally, butter producers have a clear incentive to support a tax on margarine. When the price of margarine increases, consumers will seek substitutes. The demand for butter will rise, and producers will be able to sell more butter and charge more for each pound.

The $0.25 tax in our example is divided between consumers and producers, although most of it ($0.20) is paid by consumers. Why do consumers pay most of the tax? Consumers bear most of the tax burden because consumers are relatively unresponsive to the price change. The result, as depicted in figure 5.1, is that consumers bear most of the tax burden while producers pay only a small part (20 percent) of the tax. If consumers were more responsive to the price change, then a greater share of the tax burden would fall on producers, who would then have more incentive to oppose the tax politically.

As can be seen in figure 5.2, with the consumers more responsive to a price change than is the case in figure 5.1, the price consumers pay rises from $1 to $1.05. The after-tax price received by producers falls from $1 to $.80, meaning that the producers pay 80 percent of the tax in this case. This suggests, we should point out, that the amount of money producers would be willing to spend to oppose taxes on their products (through campaign contributions or lobbying) would depend critically on the responsiveness of consumers to a price change. The more responsive consumers are, the more producers should be willing to spend to oppose the tax.

Price and rent controls

Price controls are by no means a modern invention. The first recorded legal code, the four-thousand-year-old Code of Hammurabi, included regulations governing the maximum wage, housing prices, and rents on property such as boats, animals, and tools. In AD 301, the Roman Emperor Diocletian issued an edict specifying maximum prices for everything from poultry to gold, and maximum wages for everyone from lawyers to the cleaners of sewer systems. The penalty for violating the edict was death. More recently in the United States, wage and price controls have been used both in wartime (during the Second World War and the Korean War) and in peacetime. President Richard Nixon imposed an across-the-board wage–price freeze in 1971. President Jimmy Carter controlled energy prices in 1977 and later proposed the control of natural gas. As is true of attempts to control expenditures, wage and price controls often create more problems than they solve, as they did in the 1970s: when gasoline prices were controlled in the 1970s long lines at gas pumps were seen everywhere, an outcome completely consistent with economic theory.

In a competitive market, any restriction on the upward movement of prices will lead to shortages. Consider figure 5.3, which shows supply and demand curves for gasoline. Initially, the supply and demand curves are S_1 and D, and the equilibrium price is P_1. Now suppose that the supply of gasoline shifts to S_2, and government officials, believing that the new equilibrium price is unjust, freeze the price at P_1. What will happen to the market for gasoline?

At price P_1, which is now below the equilibrium, the number of gallons demanded by consumers is Q_2, but the number of gallons supplied is much lower, Q_1. A shortage of $Q_2 - Q_1$ gallons has developed. As a result, some consumers will not get all the gasoline they want. Some may be unable to get any.

Because of the shortage, consumers will have to wait in line to get whatever gasoline they can. To avoid a long line, they may try to get to the service station early – but others may do the same. To assure themselves a prime position, consumers may have to sit at the pumps before the station opens. In winter, waiting in line may mean wasting gas to keep warm. The moral of the story:

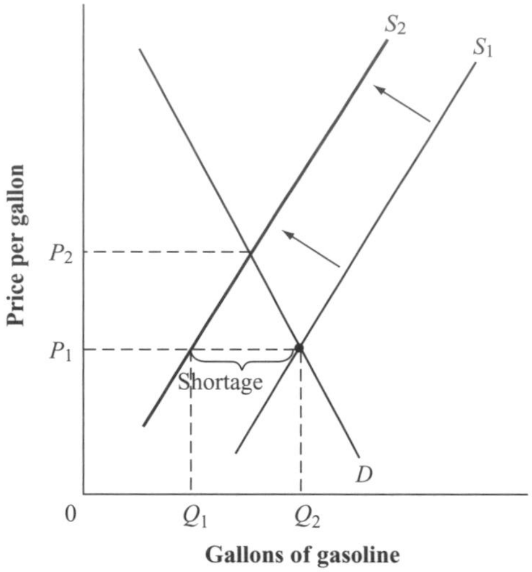

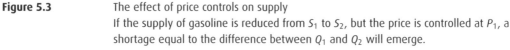

Figure 5.3 The effect of price controls on supply
If the supply of gasoline is reduced from S_1 to S_2, but the price is controlled at P_1, a shortage equal to the difference between Q_1 and Q_2 will emerge.

Although the pump price of gasoline may be held constant at P_1, the effective price – the sum of the pump price and the values of time lost waiting in line – will rise.

Shortages can raise the effective price of a product in other ways. With a long line of customers waiting to buy, a service station owner can afford to lower the quality of services provided and allow their stations to become less clean. As a result, the effective price of gasoline rises still higher. Again, during the energy crises of the 1970s, the last time controls were used (the country learned a valuable economic lesson), some service station owners started closing on weekends and at night. A few required customers to sign long-term contracts and pay in advance for their gasoline. The added interest cost of advance payment raised the price of gasoline even higher.

Besides such legal maneuvers to evade price controls, some businesses may engage in fraud or black marketeering. They can tie in the sale of the controlled good with the sale of the uncontrolled good, thus raising the price of the controlled good by increasing the price of the uncontrolled good. Indeed, the ways of circumventing price controls are limited only by the creativity of firms.

During the 1970s, many gasoline station owners filled their premium tanks with regular gasoline and sold it at premium prices. At the same time, a greater-than-expected shortage of heating oil developed. Truckers, unable to get all the diesel fuel they wanted at the controlled price, had found they could use home

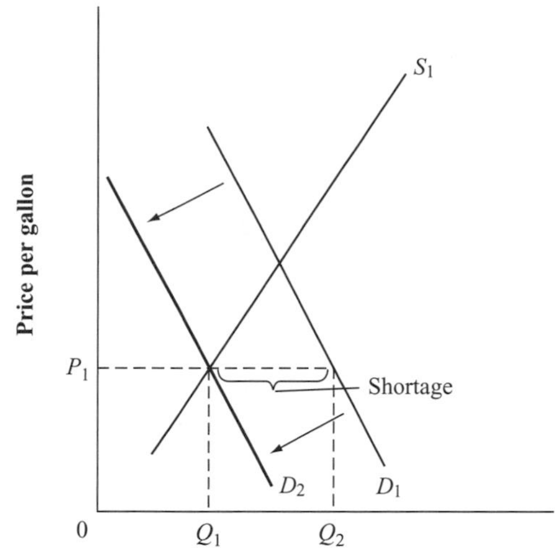

Figure 5.4 The effect of rationing on demand

Price controls can create a shortage. For instance, at the controlled price P_1, a shortage of $Q_2 - Q_1$ gallons will develop. By issuing a limited number of coupons that must be used to purchase a product, the government can reduce demand and eliminate the shortage. Here, rationing reduces demand from D_1 to D_2, where demand intersects the supply curve at the controlled price.

heating oil in their trucks. They paid home heating oil dealers a black market price for fuel oil, thus reducing the supply available to home owners. As always, government controls bring enforcement problems.

To assure fair and equitable distribution of goods in short supply, some means of *rationing* is needed. If no formal system is adopted, supplies will be distributed on a first-come, first-served basis – in effect, rationing by congestion. A more efficient method is to issue coupons that entitle people to buy specific quantities of the rationed good at the prevailing price. By limiting the number of coupons, the government reduces the demand for the product to match the available supply, thereby eliminating the shortage and relieving the congestion in the marketplace. In figure 5.4, for example, demand is reduced from D_1 to D_2.

The coupon system may appear to be fair and simple, but how are the coupons to be distributed? Clearly the government will not want to auction off the coupons, for that would amount to letting consumers bid up the price. Should coupons be distributed equally among all consumers? Not everyone lives the same distance from work or school. Some, such as salespeople, must travel much more than others. Should a commuter receive more gas than a retired person? If so, how much more? Should the distribution of coupons be based on the distance traveled? (And if such a system is adopted, will people lie about their needs?) These are formidable questions that must be answered if a coupon system is to be truly equitable. By comparison, the pricing system inherently allows people to reflect the intensity of their needs in their purchases.

After the coupons have been distributed, should the recipients be allowed to sell them to others? That is, should legal markets for coupons be permitted to spring up? If the deals made in such a market are voluntary, both parties to the exchange will benefit. The person who buys coupons values gasoline more than money. The person who sells coupons may have to cut back on driving but values the additional money more than enough to compensate for the inconvenience. The positive (and often high) market value of coupons that will inevitably occur shows that price controls have not really eliminated the shortage.

Furthermore, if the coupons have a value, the price of a gallon of gasoline has not really been held constant. If the price of an extra coupon for one gallon of gasoline is $0.50 and the pump price of that gallon is $2.00, the total price to the consumer is $2.50. The existence of a coupon market means that the price of gasoline has risen. In fact, the price to the consumer will be greater under a rationing system than under a pricing system. This added price increase will occur because the quantity supplied by refineries will be reduced.

Perhaps the most damaging aspect of a rationing system is that the benefits of such a price increase are not received by producers – oil companies, refineries, and service stations – but rather by those fortunate enough to get coupons. Thus the price increase does not provide producers with an incentive to supply more gasoline. (If the increase went to producers, their higher profits would encourage them to search for new sources of oil and step up their production plans.)

Controls on apartment rents have been tried throughout the ages in the name of fairness, in the main, to low-income tenants. They can be expected to have, and have had, the same effect as gasoline price controls (Tucker 1997). As long as the rent is controlled below the equilibrium price, the result should be a market shortage as the quantity of available apartments is reduced and the number of people wanting to rent the available units increases. Faced with more prospective tenants wanting their apartments than they have apartments available at the controlled rent, landlords can be expected to respond to the rent controls in any number of ways:

- If the rent controls apply to "low-income housing," some landlords can be expected to upgrade their apartments and escape the controls. Otherwise, they can sell their apartments as condominiums.

- Landlords can rent to higher-income tenants who are more likely to pay their rent and pay it on time, thus shifting the benefits of the rent controls away from the targeted low-income tenant group.
- Landlords can reduce their costs by lowering the quality of their units, shifting the maintenance costs to the tenants. In this case, the tenants' demand may fall (indicating a reduction in the rent tenants are willing to pay for lower-quality units), but the reduced demand is of no consequence to the landlords since they still have more anxious tenants than they can accommodate. The point is that the landlords can offset some (but not all) of the effect of the suppressed rent with lower costs. Presumably, the higher quality of the rental units was provided in the first place because the tenants were willing to pay more for the quality enhancement than the quality enhancement cost the landlords. Hence, when the quality of the apartments is reduced, the tenants can be made worse off by the quality reductions.

Minimum wages

In any future debate, much will likely be made of how the federal minimum wage of $5.15 (as of mid-2005) an hour has no more purchasing power than did the minimum wage of the early 1950s. The minimum wage in current dollars has been raised in a series of nineteen steps from 25 cents an hour when the first federal minimum wage took effect in October 1938 to where it is today, $5.15 an hour. However, in constant, (June) 2004 dollars, the minimum wage rose irregularly from $3.40 an hour in October 1938 to $8.96 an hour in 1968, only to fall irregularly from the 1968 peak to its 2005 level of $5.15, which is more than 40 percent below the 1968 peak. This means that the mid-2005 minimum wage was significantly below the real minimum wage when it was raised at the start of 1950 (at which time it was about $6.00 an hour in mid-2005 dollars).[1]

What effect does the minimum wage have on the covered labor markets? In this section, we offer two perspectives, the conventional and unconventional. Under the conventional perspective, employers don't alter the way in which workers are paid and how much workers are asked to work. Under the unconventional perspective, employers alter both the form of compensation and work demands.

[1] At the time this chapter was being finalized (mid-2005), both the Republicans and Democrats in the US Senate had introduced bills to hike the minimum wage. The democratic champion of a minimum wage increase, Senator Edward Kennedy (MA), proposed to raise the minimum wage in three stages to $7.25 over twenty-six months, an increase of 41 percent. The Republican champion, Senator Rick Santorum (PA), proposed to raise the minimum wage in two increments to $6.25 over eighteen months (Associated Press 2005c).

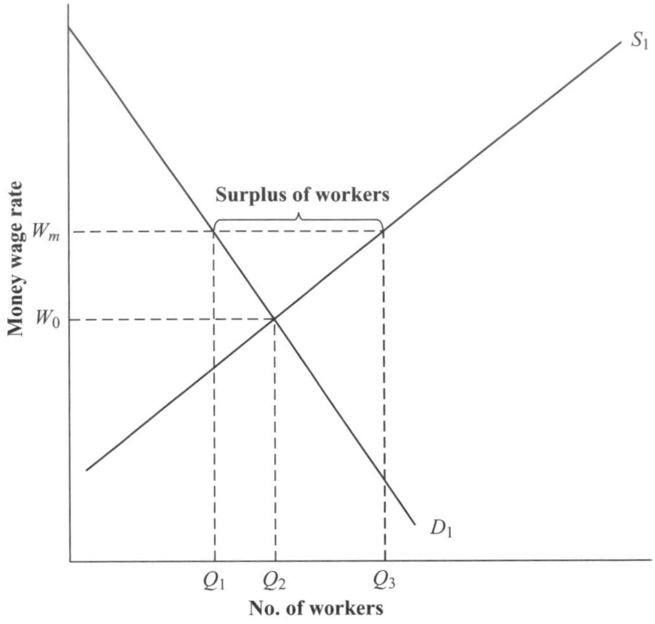

Figure 5.5 The conventional view of the impact of the minimum wage
When the minimum wage is set at W_m (and the market clearing wage is W_o), employment will fall from Q_2 to Q_1; simultaneously, the number of workers who are willing to work in this labor market will expand from Q_2 to Q_3. The market surplus is then $Q_3 - Q_1$.

The conventional view

Economists traditionally have argued that minimum-wage increases reduce employment in competitive markets, thereby increasing the welfare of those low-skilled workers who remain employed but decreasing the welfare of others who lose their jobs (who may remain unemployed or accept less gainful employment in areas of the economy in which minimum-wage regulations are not applied). Also, economists point out that the minimum wage can increase the crime rate. The following discussion examines how economists reach such conclusions.

Labor-market effects

Consider figure 5.5, which depicts a downward sloping demand curve for, and an upward sloping supply curve of, low-skilled labor. The downward sloping demand curve implies that employers will hire more workers (everything else remaining constant) at a lower rather than higher wage. There are several reasons for this:

- First, profit maximizing employers will tend to expand production until the marginal contribution of additional workers begins to diminish, which implies that within the relevant range of production, additional workers will be worth (in terms of the market value of the product they can produce) progressively less as more are hired. When the wage rate falls, employers can hire workers who are worth less at the margin.
- Second, lower wages can inspire a substitution of low-skilled workers for other resources used in production, such as higher-skilled workers and expensive equipment.
- Third, a decline in the wage rate implies lower costs and prices for the product produced by the firms, which can inspire more sales and lead, in turn, to a greater need for workers to satisfy the additional quantity demanded of the product.

The upward sloping curve that represents the supply of labor implies that the wage must be raised in order to attract additional workers. The main reason for this upward slope is that some workers have higher-valued opportunities than others. Any given wage will attract workers into the market whose alternative opportunities are lower than that wage rate. The wage offered in a low-skilled (or any other) labor market must be progressively raised in order to offset the progressively higher-valued opportunities the additional workers must forgo.

If the market is competitive and free of government intervention, the wage rate will settle, as shown in figure 5.5, at the intersection of the supply and demand curves, or at W_0. A wage above W_0 would indicate that more workers are seeking jobs than there are jobs available and that competitive pressure would push the wage down. A wage below W_0 would imply that more workers are demanded than there are workers willing to work at the going wage which causes upward competitive pressure on the wage.

Suppose, however, that politicians consider that market wage, W_0, too low to provide a decent living and pass a law requiring employers to pay no less than W_m. The law reduces employment because in the face of worker productivity and reduced sales, employers cannot afford to employ as many people and the quantity of labor demanded falls from Q_2 to Q_1.

As the argument is normally developed by economists, those who manage to keep their jobs at the minimum wage will be better off (their take-home pay will increase from W_0 to W_m). Others, however, will no longer have jobs.

These workers will either become permanently unemployed or settle for work in different, lower-paying, and/or less desirable labor markets. If the minimum wage displaces them from their preferred employment, their full-wage rate – that is, their money wage plus the nonmonetary benefits of their jobs – is reduced. For those who become permanently unemployed, their money wage will drop from a level that minimum-wage supporters judge to be unacceptable to a level of zero.

To make matters worse, when a minimum wage is introduced, greater numbers of workers are willing to work (see figure 5.5). Workers with jobs paying W_0, and who have fewer opportunities at W_m, must now compete with an influx of other workers. Almost all of the empirical studies done since the 1970s support the gloomy predictions of the model.[2]

Economists have probably understated the adverse consequences of the minimum wage for the targeted worker groups by making the common presumption that low-skilled workers who retain their jobs are "better off." Economists also commonly presume that the workers who have the Q_1 jobs, after the minimum wage is imposed, represent a subgroup of the workers who had the Q_2 jobs when the wage was determined strictly by the forces of supply and demand. But this is unlikely because the minimum wage will attract additional workers, $Q_3 - Q_2$, into the market. Some, perhaps most, of these additional workers will be more productive than the workers who were in the market when the wage was W_0, as evidenced by the fact that they have been positioned further up the supply curve and have had higher-valued opportunities elsewhere. In short, many if not all of the workers who have jobs at W_0 can be expected either to withdraw from the market or to be supplanted by new arrivals who have been induced by the higher wage to enter the market.

[2] For a review of the economic literature on the minimum wage through the early 1980s, see Brown, Gilroy, and Kohen (1982). In the late 1960s, two other scholars concluded: "The impression created in most government studies that federal minimum wage policy has produced no adverse effects is erroneous . . . Minimum wage rates produce gains for some groups of workers at the expense of those that are the least favored in terms of marketable skills or location" (Peterson and Stewart 1969, 151–5). Other researchers observed that minimum-wage laws have tended to destabilize employment among the workers covered by such laws, particularly nonwhites and young people (Kosters and Welch 1972). When the demand for goods and services falls, employers cannot lower prices to boost sales, because their wages cannot drop below the minimum. Instead, the employers are forced to adjust to changing market conditions by reducing employment. A study from the early 1970s corroborates these findings. Minimum-wage legislation was found to hurt teenagers – especially nonwhite teenage males. Specifically, with the boost in the minimum wage from $1.25 in 1966 to $1.60 in 1972, employment among teenagers fell by 3.8 percent (Ragan 1977).

Social effects

Economists maintain that minimum-wage laws also have several social effects that often are overlooked. By increasing unemployment, minimum-wage laws increase the number of people receiving public assistance and unemployment compensation. (Proponents of the minimum wage argue the opposite – that is, that the minimum wage reduces the need for welfare by raising the income of low-skilled workers above the poverty level.) The laws may also account for increases in some criminal activity, because the unemployed who lack opportunities in the legitimate labor market may see crime as an alternative to employment (indeed, crime is a form of employment). With the larger labor pool that develops when the minimum-wage increases, competition for jobs is likely to harbor potential for increased discrimination on the basis of sex, race, religion, and so on (Williams 2005).

Political support

Why do minimum-wage laws attract so much political support? Part of the reason may be that the general public is largely unaware of their negative effects. Many forces operate on the labor market, making it almost impossible for the average person to single out the effects of one law. Few give enough thought to the idea of a minimum wage adversely affecting employment opportunities. Those on whom the burden of these laws falls hardest – that is, young, relatively unproductive workers, many of whom cannot vote – are least likely to understand the negative effects. The people who retain their jobs at the higher wage are also visible members of the work force; those who lose their jobs are often far less visible, many of whom are concentrated in urban ghettos.

Following the standard minimum-wage argument, another reason that minimum-wage laws attract political support is that many people may benefit from the laws – mainly, those who retain their jobs and receive higher paychecks. Many college students may favor the minimum wage, perhaps because they are generally more productive than less-educated members of their generation and are less likely to lose their entry-level jobs because of the minimum wage. Labor unions, too, have an incentive to support minimum-wage laws: Unions are in a better bargaining position when the government raises wages in nonunion sectors of the economy. Under such circumstances, union wage demands are not as likely to prompt employers to move into nonunionized sectors of the economy.[3]

[3] In fact, as was argued by the editors of the *New York Times* in 1937 when the federal minimum wage was originally proposed, the first minimum wage retarded the exodus of firms and jobs to the nonunionized South from the unionized North. The introduction of the minimum wage reduced the net benefit of moving south, slowing the exodus (McKenzie 1994).

The nonconventional view

The conventional line of analysis and policy proposals relating to the market consequences of the minimum wage misses several important but relatively simple points. The most important of these is that the minimum wage does not necessarily make a significant share of the targeted workers better off. Moreover, the analysis leads to the conclusion that minimum-wage increases should not be expected to have substantial adverse employment effects in most low-skilled labor markets, primarily because employers can be expected to adjust to the added labor costs of the minimum wage by lowering the nonwage benefits of employment or increasing the work demands imposed on covered workers. The analysis that follows helps to explain why studies have generally found that a 10 percent increase in the minimum wage can be expected to reduce employment among teenagers (the group of workers most likely to be affected by the minimum wage) by as little as 0.5–3 percent (Brown, Gilroy, and Kohen (1982). Economists David Card and Alan Krueger have found, in their study of the impact of a minimum-wage hike in the fast-food restaurant industry, that employment actually increases with the hike. Although these researchers do not appear to believe the positive relationship between the wage increase and employment, they do deduce that the wage increase probably has had a close to zero, if not zero, employment effect (Card and Krueger 1995). However, a new line of analysis, which lends theoretical support to such findings, fortifies the case against the minimum wage.

Payment effects

Minimum-wage laws establish a legal floor for *money wages*; they do not, however, suppress competitive pressures. These restrictions cap the pressures in only one of the multitude of competitive outlets, namely money wages. More to the point, they do not set a legal minimum for the *effective wage* (including the money and nonmoney benefits of employment) that is paid to workers.

The impact of mandating minimum wages depends on the ability of the employer to adjust the nonmoney conditions of work, or fringe benefits, in response to a required pay change. Conventional analysis of minimum-wage laws, embedded in many economics textbooks, implicitly assumes that money wages are the only form of labor compensation. Hence, when the money wage is set at a legal minimum, employment falls by some amount given by the demand for labor.

The conventional line of analysis already presented may still be fully applicable to those few labor markets in which money is the only form of compensation and in which employers can do little or nothing to change the skill and production demands imposed on workers. In such cases, minimum-wage laws may still have the predicted effect, a labor-market surplus of unemployed menial workers caused by an above-market level of compensation.

However, the standard line of analysis does not consider the possibility that profit-maximizing competitive employers will adjust to the labor-market surplus created by the minimum-wage law. But employers are quite capable of adjusting other conditions of work in response to the labor market surplus. Indeed, to remain cost competitive, employers in competitive labor markets must adjust to the labor surplus by cutting labor costs in nonwage ways – for example, eliminating workplace outings, reducing fringe benefits, or increasing production demands.[4] Employers in such labor markets can be expected to reduce their labor costs in nonmoney ways until they are no longer confronted by a worker surplus – that is, until their labor markets clear once again.[5] That being said, the labor market effects of employers' nonmoney adjustments made in response to a wage minimum can be discussed briefly in terms of two general cases.

Employers can be expected to respond to a minimum-wage law by cutting or eliminating those fringe benefits and conditions of work, such as workplace outings, that increase the supply of labor but do not materially affect labor productivity. By reducing such nonmoney benefits of employment, the labor costs are reduced from what they would otherwise have been and nothing is lost in the way of reduced labor productivity.

Continuation of such nonmoney benefits is made uneconomical by the money-wage minimum; they no longer pay for themselves in terms of lower wage rates. Furthermore, employers in highly competitive final products markets must adjust such work conditions to remain competitive and to survive. Otherwise, other firms will lower their labor costs (by contracting or by eliminating fringe benefits) and force out of business the employers who

[4] Clearly, many minimum-wage jobs do not carry standard fringe benefits, such as life and medical insurance and retirement plans. However, most do offer fringe benefits in the form of conditions in the work environment, attitudes of the bosses, breaks, frequency and promptness of pay, variety of work, uniforms, use of company tools and supplies, meals and drinks, flexible hours, and precautions against accidents. These fringe benefits are subject to withdrawal when minimum wages are mandated.

[5] More precisely, the labor markets should, after adjustments, clear more or less to the same extent as they did before the minimum-wage law was imposed. Of course, employers are not directly concerned with ensuring that their labor market clears. They are, however, interested in minimizing their labor costs, a motivation that drives them to adjust the conditions of work until the market clears. The point is that if the employer is confronted by more workers than it needs, it can offer less compensation, broadly defined, until the surplus is eliminated.

retain their fringe benefits and continue to pay the higher minimum-wage rate.

Because of the changes in work conditions, the supply curve of labor (the position of which is partially determined by working conditions and fringe benefits) can be expected to shift upward. The effects of such a supply shift are shown in figure 5.6, which incorporates the supply and demand curves of figure 5.5 The vertical shift in the supply curve will be equal to labor's dollar valuation, on the margin, of what they lost because of the decline in employment conditions. The demand curve for labor will shift upward to the right, reflecting the reduced expenditure per unit of labor on fringe benefits.[6]

As before, fringe benefits are provided as long as their cost to the firm per unit of labor is less than the reduced wage rate – and as long as labor's evaluation of the fringe benefits lost is greater than the firms' costs. Therefore, when the fringe benefits are taken away, the vertical, upward shift in the supply curve will be greater than the vertical, upward shift in the demand curve. In figure 5.6, the vertical shift in the supply curve is *ac*, and the vertical shift in the demand curve is less, *ab*.[7] It is important to note that the market clears, however, at the minimum wage because of secondary market adjustments in fringe benefits. But it is equally important to see that the market clears at an employment level, Q_c, which is lower than the employment level before the minimum wage is imposed, Q_2. In other words, the surplus of labor that conventional analysis suggests exists in face of a minimum-wage law is eliminated by the shifts in the curves. However, labor is worse off because of the wage floor and adjustments in fringe benefits. After the vertical distance between the two supply curves, *ac* (which, again, is labor's dollar evaluation of the fringe benefits lost because of the minimum wage) is subtracted from the minimum wage W_m, the effective wage paid to labor is reduced to W_1, or by $W_m - W_1$. In short, when labor is paid in many forms, a minimum wage *reduces*, not increases, the effective payment going to affected workers, even those who keep their jobs.

Conventional analysis suggests that a minimum wage of W_m will cause employment opportunities for labor to fall to Q_1. The adjustments that

[6] Remember that the demand for labor curve is net of fringe benefits. A reduction in fringe benefits will thereby increase an employer's willingness to pay higher wages, which explains the increase in (or shift outward of) the demand for labor.

[7] If the vertical distance of the shift in the supply curve were not greater than the vertical distance of the shift in the demand curve, then the change in fringe benefits would have been made even in the absence of the minimum wage.

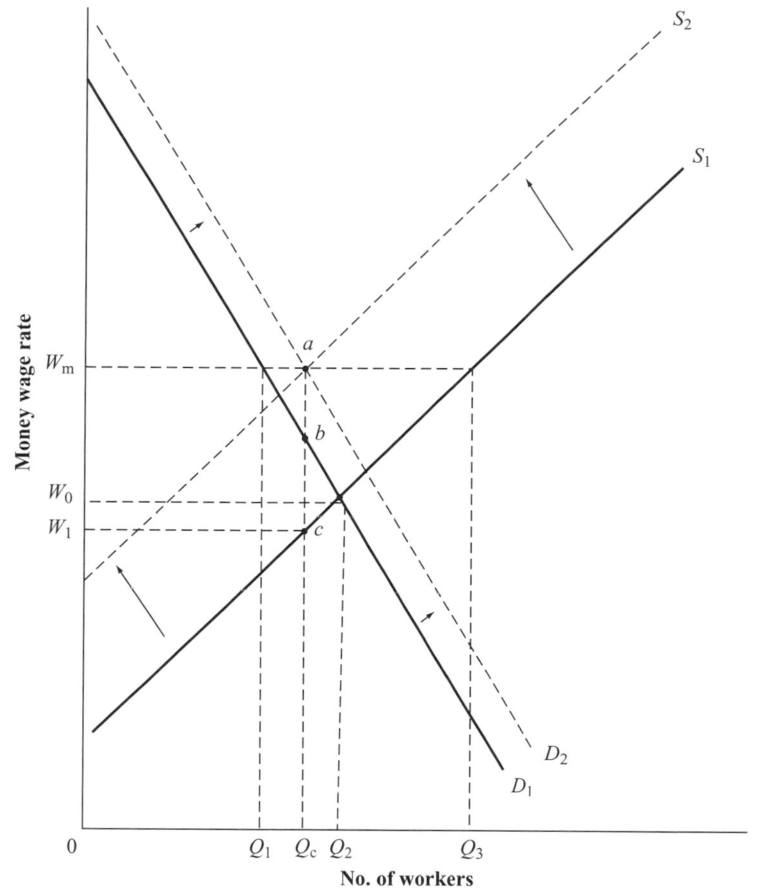

Figure 5.6 An unconventional view of the impact of the minimum wage
When the minimum wage is raised to W_m, a surplus is created equal to $Q_3 - Q_1$. As a consequence, employers can be expected to respond to the surplus by reducing fringe benefits or increasing work demands on workers. The supply curve of labor contracts, reflecting the greater wage the workers will demand to compensate for the reduction in fringe benefits or increase in work demands. The employers' demand for labor increases, reflecting the higher wage they are *willing to* pay workers in terms of money wages who get fewer fringe benefits or work harder and produce more.

employers make to nonmoney conditions of work cause employment opportunities to fall by less, to only Q_c in figure 5.6.[8]

[8] Indeed, if employers had an infinite number of ways to adjust nonmoney conditions of work, and the market money wage were a small part of total labor payment, the minimum wage would not significantly affect employment opportunities. When employers have an infinite or

If employers increase work demands without (or even with) fringe benefit reductions, the analysis is much the same. The demand for labor will rise, given that workers' productivity per hour worked goes up, making employers willing to pay workers more per hour. Nevertheless, the vertical shift in the supply curve will be greater than the vertical shift in the demand curve. Again, this is because employers would initially have relaxed work demands in the absence of the minimum wage only if workers would then have been willing to give up more in pay than employers lost in productivity.

Differences in perspective

This analysis conflicts with the conventional textbook treatment of minimum wages in several important respects. Conventional analysis holds that the effective wage rate increases for some workers and declines for others. As noted, this is because of the implicit assumption that an increase in the minimum-wage rate is equivalent to an increase in the effective wage rate. Our analysis, however, leads to the conclusion that the effective wage rate of *all* workers, including those who retain their jobs in spite of minimum wages, decreases; they are worse off to the extent that employers have the opportunity to adjust working conditions and fringe benefits. For that reason, minimum wages appear patently unfair to those who are covered by them (even by the standards of many of those who promote legislated minimum wages). Although still not a mainstream perspective, this new perspective on the adverse effects of minimum-wage laws is supported by a growing body of research.[9]

The case of Wal-Mart

Because US-based Wal-Mart is the largest retailer in the world, earning some $10 billion in profits on $288 billion in sales in 2004, the company is continually under attack for paying its full-time workers an average of $9.68 an hour and for skimping on its annual average payments for employees' medical care ($3,500 per employee versus $5,600 per employee paid by other American corporations) (Greenhouse 2005). Of course, the critics argue that Wal-Mart *should* treat its workers better. We can hardly settle this emerging debate over what a company should or should not do, but this section does direct attention to important questions that need to be addressed by both Wal-Mart's critics

even a very large number of ways to pay labor, a change in the money wage by law will not significantly affect the payment options open to employers and the ability of the employers to pay the effective market wage.

[9] The key econometric findings are listed in the appendix (p. 217).

and supporters: If Wal-Mart does gets far more qualified applicants to fill its positions when it opens new stores, as news reports suggest is the case (Greenhouse 2005), is Wal-Mart still "underpaying" its workers? If Wal-Mart pays its workers more than it now does, what might happen to its employment? What about its work demands? Its fringe benefits? How might its stockholders react? What might happen to the wages and fringe benefits paid by Wal-Mart's competitors?

Pollution controls: external costs and benefits

A **market failure** occurs when maximum efficiency is not achieved by trades (which means that part of the excess benefits shown by the shaded area in figure 5.7 are not be realized by either buyers or sellers).

In a competitive market, producers must minimize their production costs at each level of production and quality in order to lower their prices, increase their production levels, and improve the quality of their products, with the success of their efforts being shown by the *supply curve*. Consumers demonstrate how much they value another unit of the product by their willingness to pay for it, a willingness shown by the *demand curve*. In a competitive market, production will move toward the intersection of the market supply and demand curves – Q_1 in figure 5.7. At that point, the marginal cost of the last unit produced will equal its marginal benefit to consumers.

To the extent that the market moves toward equilibrium in supply and demand, it is *efficient* in a very special sense. As long as the marginal benefit of anything people do is greater than the marginal cost, people are presumed to be better off if quantity increases. As shown in figure 5.7, for each loaf of bread up to Q_1, the marginal benefit of consumption (as shown by the height of the demand curve) exceeds the marginal cost of production (as shown by the height of the supply curve). Because the marginal cost of a loaf of bread is the value of the most attractive alternative forgone, people must be getting more value out of each of those loaves than they could from any alternative good. By producing exactly Q_1 loaves – no more and no less – the market extracts the possible surplus or excess benefits from production (see the shaded area on figure 5.7) and divides them among buyers and sellers. In this sense, production and distribution of economic resources can be said to be efficient.

Externalities are the positive or negative effects that exchanges may have on people who are not in the market. They are sometimes called third-party effects.

These results cannot be achieved unless competition is intense, buyers receive all the product's benefits, and producers pay all the costs of production. If such optimum conditions are not achieved, the market fails, or there is a so-called **market failure**.

One potential for such failure occurs when exchanges between buyers and sellers affect people who are not directly involved in the trades; they are said to have external effects, or to generate **externalities**. When such effects are pleasurable they are called *external benefits*. When they are unpleasant,

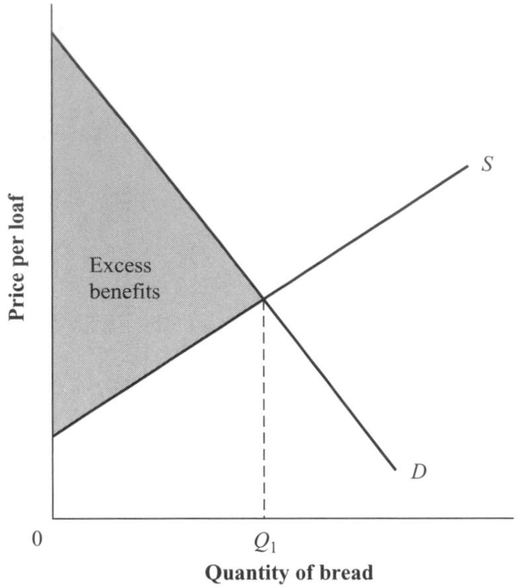

Figure 5.7 Marginal benefit versus marginal cost
The demand curve reflects the marginal benefits of each loaf of bread produced. The supply curve reflects the marginal cost of producing each loaf. For each loaf of bread up to Q_1, the marginal benefits exceed the marginal cost. The shaded area shows the maximum welfare that can be gained from the production of bread. When the market is at equilibrium (when supply equals demand), all those benefits will be realized.

or impose a cost on people other than the buyers or sellers, they are called *external costs*. The effects of external costs and benefits on production and market efficiency can be seen with the aid of supply and demand curves.

External costs

Figure 5.8 represents the market for a paper product. The market demand curve, *D*, indicates the benefits consumers receive from the product. To make paper, the producers must pay the costs of labor, chemicals, and pulpwood. The industry supply curve, S_1, shows the cost on which paper manufacturers must base their production decisions. In a highly competitive market, the quantity of the paper product that is bought will be Q_2, and the price paid by consumers will be P_1.

Producers may not bear all the costs associated with production, however. A by-product of the production process may be waste dumped into rivers or

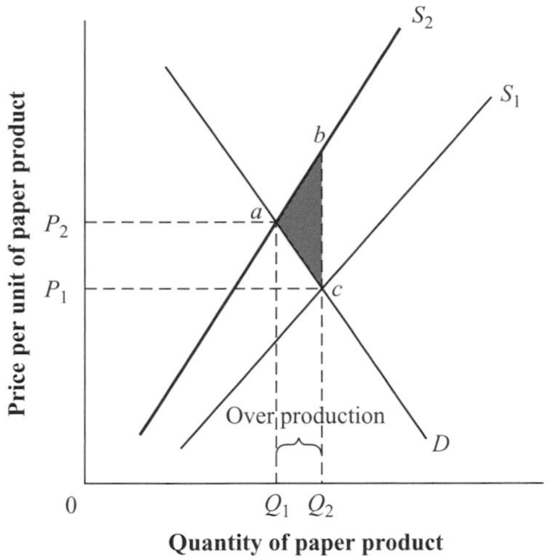

Figure 5.8 External costs

Ignoring the external costs associated with the manufacture of paper products, firms will base their production and pricing decisions on the supply curve S_1. If they consider external costs, such as the cost of pollution, they will operate on the basis of the supply curve S_2, producing Q_1 instead of Q_2 units. The shaded area *abc* shows the amount by which the marginal cost of production of $Q_2 - Q_1$ units exceeds the marginal benefits to consumers. It indicates the inefficiency of the private market when external costs are not borne by producers.

emitted into the atmosphere. The stench of production may pervade the surrounding community. Towns located downstream may have to clean up the water. People may have to paint their houses more frequently or seek medical attention for eye irritation. Home owners may have to accept lower prices than usual for their property. All these costs are imposed on people not directly involved in the production, consumption, or exchange of the paper product. Nonetheless, these external costs are part of the *total cost of production to society.*

In a highly competitive market, in which all participants act independently, survival may require that a producer impose external costs on others. An individual producer who voluntarily installs equipment to clean up pollution will incur costs higher than those of its competitors. It will not be able to match price cuts, and so in the long run may be out of business – and some producers may not care whether they cause harm to others by polluting the environment. Even socially concerned producers may not be able to care a great deal about the environment.

The supply curve S_2 incorporates both the external production costs of pollution and the private costs borne by producers. If producers have to bear all those costs, the price of the product will be higher (P_2 rather than P_1), and consumers will buy a small quantity (Q_1 rather than Q_2). Thus the true marginal cost of each unit of paper between $Q_1$and Q_2 is greater than the marginal benefit to consumers. If consumers have to pay for external costs, they will value other goods more highly than those units. In a sense, then, the paper manufacturers are *overproducing*, by $Q_2 - Q_1$ units. The marginal cost of those units exceeds their marginal benefit by the shaded triangular area in figure 5.8.

It might be thought that the culprits in the pollution problem are the producers, but they are trapped in a competitive (Prisoner's) Dilemma. They can not organize themselves to curb production and pollution. But then consumers could also be seen as culprits, since they are buying "too much" at "too low" prices. They could solve the pollution problem, but they are also in a competitive (Prisoner's) Dilemma and can't organize themselves to curb their excessive purchases.

Other examples of external costs that encourage overproduction are the highway congestion created by automobiles and the noise created by airplanes in and around airports. The argument can also be extended to include other examples, such as the death and destruction caused by speeding and reckless driving. If government does not penalize such behaviors, people will overproduce them, at a potentially high external costs to others. In the same way, adult bookstores, street drugs, and brothels can impose costs on neighboring businesses. Their often sordid appearance may drive away many people who might otherwise patronize more reputable businesses in the area.

External benefits

Sometimes market inefficiencies are created by external benefits. Market demand does not always reflect all the benefits received from a good. Instead, people not directly involved in the production, consumption, or exchange of the good receive some of its benefits.

To see the effects of external benefits on the allocation of resources, consider the market for flu shots. The cost of producing a vaccine includes labor, research and production equipment, materials, and transportation. Assuming that all those costs are borne by the producers, the market supply curve will be S in figure 5.9.

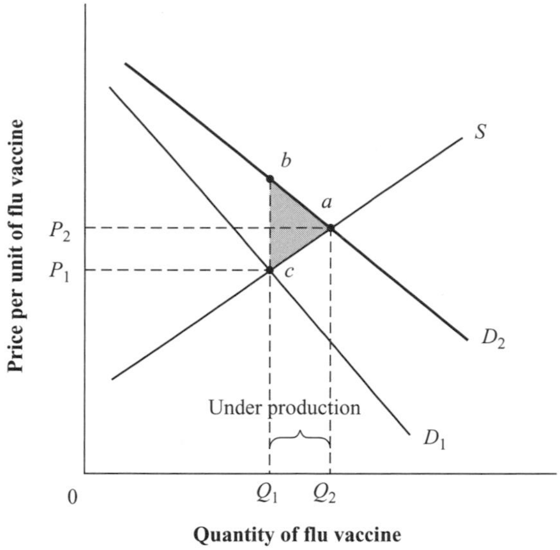

Figure 5.9 External benefits
Ignoring the external benefits of getting flu shots, consumers will base their purchases on the demand curve D_1 instead of D_2. Fewer shots will be purchased than could be justified economically – Q_1 instead of Q_2. Because the marginal benefit of each shot between Q_1 and Q_2 (as shown by demand curve D_2) exceeds its marginal cost of production, external benefits are not being realized. The shaded area *abc* indicates market inefficiency.

Individuals receive important personal benefits from flu shots. The fact that many millions of people pay for them every year shows that there is a demand, illustrated by curve D_1 in figure 5.9. In getting shots for themselves, however, people also provide external benefits for others. By protecting themselves, they reduce the probability that the flu will spread to others. When others escape the medical expenses and lost work time associated with flu, those benefits are not captured in the market demand curve, D_1. Only in the higher societal demand curve, labeled D_2, are those benefits realized.

Left to itself, a highly competitive market will produce at the intersection of the market supply and market demand curves (S and D_1), or at point *c*. At that point, the equilibrium price will be P_1 and the quantity produced will be Q_1. If external benefits are considered in the production decision, however, the marginal benefit of flu shots between Q_1 and Q_2 (shown by the demand curve D_2) will exceed their marginal cost of production (shown by the supply curve).

In other words, if all benefits, both private and external, were considered, Q_2 shots would be produced and purchased at a price of P_2. At Q_2, the marginal cost of the last shot would equal its marginal benefit. Social welfare would rise by an amount equal to the triangular shaded area *abc* in figure 5.9. The problem of this external benefit is even worse when, as was the case in the fall of 2004, production problems reduce the quantity of flu shots available in the United States below the quantity people want at prices that normally cover the marginal cost of production. Long lines for the shots formed all across the country.

Because a free market can fail to capture such external benefits, government action to subsidize flu shots may be justified. On such grounds governments all over the world have mounted programs to inoculate people against diseases such as smallpox. The external benefits argument has also been used to justify government support of medical research. It can also be extended to services such as public transportation: City buses provide direct benefits to the general population. Education that leads to an informed and articulate citizenry raises both the level of public discourse and the general standard of living.[10] Public parks and environmental programs can also provide external benefits that are not likely to be realized by private efforts alone because of the high cost to individuals to achieve them. Again, government action may be required to supplement private efforts.

The pros and cons of government action

Perhaps more often than not, exchanges between buyers and sellers affect others. People buy clothes partly to keep warm in the winter and dry in the rain, but most people value the appearance of clothing at least as much as its comfort. We choose clothing because we want others to be pleased or impressed (or perhaps irritated). The same can be said about the cars we purchase, the places we go to eat, the DVDs we buy, the haircuts and styling we get, and even the MBA programs we select. We impose the external effects of our actions deliberately as well as accidentally.

The presence of externalities in economic transactions does not necessarily mean that government should intervene. First, the economic distortions created by externalities are often quite small, if not inconsequential. So far, our

[10] The ratio of public to private benefits varies by educational level. Elementary school education develops crucial social and communication skills; its private benefits (or those benefits received by the people who are educated) are largely side-effects. At the college level, however, the private benefits to students may dominate the public benefits. Thus elementary education is supported almost entirely by public sources, whereas college education is only partially subsidized.

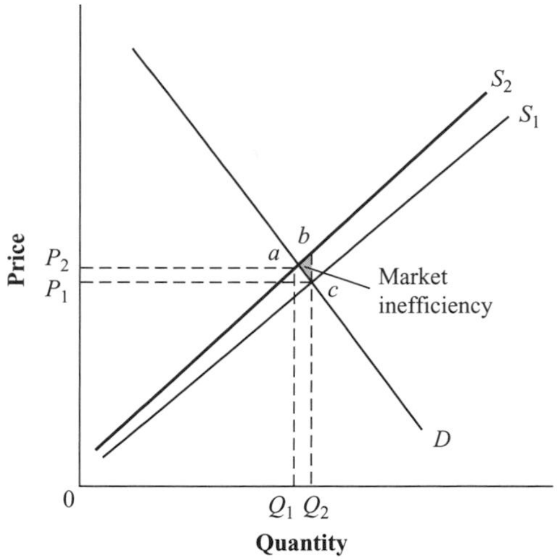

Figure 5.10 Is government action justified?
Because of external costs, the market illustrated produces more than the efficient output. Market inefficiency, represented by the shaded triangular area *abc*, is quite small – so small that government intervention may not be justified on economic grounds alone.

main examples of external costs and benefits have involved possibly significant distortions of market forces. In figure 5.10, however, the supply curve S_2, which incorporates both private and external costs, lies only slightly to the left of the market supply curve, S_1. The difference between the market output level, Q_2, and the optimum output level, Q_1, is small, as is the market inefficiency, shown by the shaded triangular area in figure 5.10. Little can therefore be gained by government intervention.

This limited benefit must be weighed against the cost of government action. Whenever government intervenes in any situation, agencies are set up, employees are hired, papers are shuffled, and reports are filed. Almost invariably, suits are brought against firms and individuals who have violated government rules, often obscure and sometimes silly. In short, significant costs can be incurred in trying to correct small market inefficiencies. If the cost of government intervention exceeds the cost of the market's inefficiencies, government action will actually increase inefficiency, even if the market inefficiencies are corrected by the government action.

A second reason for limiting government action is that it generates external costs of its own. If government dictates the construction methods to be used in building homes, the way firms should reduce pollution, and who has the qualifications to cut hair, the people who impose the regulations create costs – which are usually external to them – borne by those who are prevented from providing services at lower costs than the regulations permit, and their customers. We may agree with some government rules but strenuously object to others.

In certain markets, government action may not be necessary. Over the long run, some of the external costs and benefits that cause market distortions may be *internalized.* That is, they may become private costs and benefits. Suppose the development of a park would generate external benefits for all businesses in a shopping district. More customers would be attracted to the district, and more sales would be made. An alert entrepreneur could internalize those benefits by building a shopping mall with a park in the middle. Because the mall would attract more customers than other shopping areas would, the owner could benefit from higher rents. When shopping centers can internalize such externalities, economic efficiency will be enhanced – without government intervention.

When Walt Disney built Disneyland on a small plot of land in Orange County, California, he conferred benefits on merchants in the Anaheim area. Other businesses quickly moved in to take advantage of the external benefits – the crowds of visitors – spilling over from the amusement park. Disney did not make the same mistake twice. When he built Disney World in Orlando, Florida, he bought enough land so that most of the benefits of the amusement park would stay within the Disney domain. Inside the more than 6,000 acres of Disney-owned land in Florida, development has been controlled and profits captured by the Disney Corporation. Although other businesses have established themselves on the perimeters of Disney World, their distance from its center makes it more difficult for them to capture the benefits spilling over from the Disney amusement park.

Methods of reducing externalities

Government action can undoubtedly guarantee that certain goods and services will be produced more efficiently. The benefits of such action may be substantial, even when compared with the costs. In such cases, only the form of government intervention remains to be determined. Government action can take several forms: persuasion; assignment of communal property rights to individuals; government production of goods and services; regulation of production through published standards; and control of product prices through taxes, fines, and subsidies. Economists generally argue that if government is going to intervene, it should choose the least costly means sufficient for the task at hand.

Persuasion

External costs arise partly because we do not consider the welfare of others in our decisions. Indeed, if we fully recognized the adverse effects of our actions on others, external cost would not exist. Our production decisions would be based as much as possible on the total costs of production to society.

Government can thus alleviate market distortions by persuading citizens to consider how their behavior affects others. Forest Service advertisements urge people not to drop litter or risk forest fires when camping. Other government campaigns encourage people not to drive if they drink, to cultivate their land so as to minimize erosion, and to conserve water and gas. Although such efforts are limited in their effect, they may be more acceptable than other approaches, given political constraints.

Persuasion can take the form of publicity. The government can publish studies demonstrating that particular products or activities have external costs or benefits. The resultant publicity may in turn encourage those activities with external benefits and discourage those activities with external costs. The government has, for example, used this method in the case of cigarettes, publishing studies showing the external costs of smoking.

Assignment of property rights

As discussed in chapter 1, when property rights are held communally or left unassigned, property tends to be overused. As long as no one else is already using the property, anyone can use it without paying for its use. Costs that are not borne by users are, of course, passed on to others as external costs. When public land was open to grazing in the West in the 1850s, for instance, ranchers allowed their herds to overgraze. The external cost of their indiscriminate use of the land has been borne by later generations, who have inherited a barren, wasted environment.

The assignment of property rights can thus eliminate some externalities. If land rights are assigned to individuals, they will bear the cost of their own neglect. If owners allow their cattle to strip a range of its grass, they will no longer be able to raise their cattle there – and the price of the land will decline with its productivity.

Some resources, such as air and water, cannot always be divided into parcels. In those cases, the property rights solution will work poorly, if at all.

Government production

Through nationalization of some industries, government can attempt to internalize external costs. The argument is that because government is concerned with social consequences, it will consider the total costs of production, both internal and external. On the basis of that argument, governments in the United States operate schools, public health services, national and state parks, transportation systems, harbors, and electric power plants. In other nations, government also operates major industries, such as the steel and automobile industries.

Government production can be a mixed blessing. When other producers remain in the market, government participation may increase competition. Sometimes, however, it means the elimination of competition. Consider the US Postal Service, which has exclusive rights to the delivery of first-class mail. As a government agency, the Post Office is not permitted to make a profit that can be turned over to shareholders. Because of its market position with little competition for home delivery of mail, however, it may tolerate higher costs and lower work standards than competitive firms could.

Some government production, such as the provision of public goods such as national defense, is unavoidable. In most cases, however, direct ownership and production may not be necessary. Instead of producing goods with which externalities are associated, government could simply contract with private firms for the business. That is precisely how most states handle road construction, how several states handle the penal system, and how a few city governments provide ambulance, police, and firefighting services.

Taxes and subsidies

Government can deal with some external costs by taxing producers. Pollution can be discouraged by a tax on either the pollution itself or the final product. Taxing the pollution emitted by firms internalizes external costs, increasing the total costs to the producer. Imposing such taxes should have a twofold effect in reducing pollution:

- First, many producers would find the cost of pollution control cheaper than the pollution tax.
- Second, the tax would raise the prices of final products, reducing the number of units consumed – and hence reducing the level of pollution.

The size of the tax can be adjusted to achieve whatever level of pollution is judged acceptable. If a tax of $1 per unit produced does not reduce pollution sufficiently, the tax can be raised to $2. In terms of figure 5.1, the ideal tax would be just enough to encourage producers to view their supply curve as

S_2 instead of S_1. The resulting cutback in production from Q_1 to Q_2 would eliminate market inefficiency, represented by the shaded area *abc*.

Theoretically, the government could achieve the same result by subsidizing firms in their efforts to eliminate pollution. It could give tax credits for the installation of pollution controls or pay firms outright to install the equipment. In fact, until 1985, the federal government used tax credits to encourage the installation of fuel-saving devices, which indirectly reduced pollution.

Production standards

Alternatively, the government could simply impose standards on all producers. It could rule, for example, that polluters may not emit more than a certain amount of pollutants during a given period. Offenders would either have to pay for a cleanup or risk a fine. A firm that flagrantly violated the standard might be forced to shut down.

Choosing the most efficient remedy for externalities

Selecting the most efficient method of minimizing externalities can be a complicated process. To illustrate, we compare the costs of two approaches to controlling pollution, government standards versus property rights

Suppose five firms are emitting sulfur dioxide, a pollutant that causes acid rain. The reduction of the unwanted emissions can be thought of as an *economic good* whose production involves a cost. We can assume that the marginal cost of reducing sulfur dioxide emissions will rise as more and more units are eliminated. We can also assume that such costs will differ from firm to firm. Table 5.1 incorporates these assumptions. Firm *A*, for example, must pay $100 to eliminate the first unit of sulfur dioxide and $200 to eliminate the second. Firm *B* must pay $200 for the first unit and $600 for the second. Although the information in table 5.1 is hypothetical, it reflects the structure of real-world pollution cleanup costs. Firms face increasing marginal costs when they clean up the air as well as when they produce goods and services.

Suppose the Environmental Protection Agency (EPA) decides that the maximum acceptable level of sulfur dioxide is 10 units. To achieve that level, the EPA prohibits firms from emitting more than 2 units of sulfur dioxide each. If each firm were emitting 5 units, each would have to reduce its emissions by 3 units. The total cost of meeting the limit of two units is shown in the lower half of table 5.1. Firm *A* incurs the relatively modest cost of

Table 5.1 *Costs of reducing sulfur dioxide emissions*

	Firms				
	A	*B*	*C*	*D*	*E*
Marginal cost of eliminating each unit of pollution:	($)	($)	($)	($)	($)
First unit	100	200	200	600	1,000
Second unit	200	600	400	1,000	2,000
Third unit	400	1,800	600	1,400	3,000
Fourth unit	800	5,400	800	1,800	4,000
Fifth unit	1,600	16,200	1,000	2,200	5,000

Cost of reducing pollution by establishment of government standards		*Cost of reducing pollution by sale of pollution rights*	
Cost to *A* of eliminating 3 units	700	Cost to *A* of eliminating 4 units	1,500
Cost to *B* of eliminating 3 units	2,600	Cost to *B* of eliminating 2 units	800
Cost to *C* of eliminating 3 units	1,200	Cost to *C* of eliminating 5 units	3,000
Cost to *D* of eliminating 3 units	3,000	Cost to *D* of eliminating 3 units	3,000
Cost to *E* of eliminating 3 units	6,000	Cost to *E* of eliminating 1 unit	1,000
Total cost for all five firms units	**13,500**	**Total cost for all five firms units**	**9,300**

$700 ($100 + $200 + $400). But firm *B* must pay $2,600 ($200 + $600 + $1,800). The total cost to all firms is $13,500.

What if the EPA adopts a different strategy and sells the rights to pollute? Such rights can be thought of as tickets that authorize firms to dump a unit of waste into the atmosphere. The more tickets a firm purchases, the more waste it can dump, and the more cleanup costs it can avoid.

Remember that the EPA can control the number of tickets it sells. To limit pollution to the maximum acceptable level of 10 units, all it needs to do is sell no more than 10 tickets. Either way, whether by pollution standards or rights, the level of pollution is kept down to 10 units, but the pollution rights method allows firms that want to avoid the cost of a cleanup to bid for tickets.

The potential market for such rights can be illustrated by conventional supply and demand curves, as in figure 5.11. The supply curve is determined by EPA policy makers, who limit the number of tickets to 10. Because in this example the supply is fixed, the supply curve must be vertical (perfectly inelastic). Whatever the price, the number of pollution rights remains the same. The demand curve is derived from the costs firms must bear to clean up their emissions. The higher the cost of the cleanup, the more attractive pollution rights will be. As with all

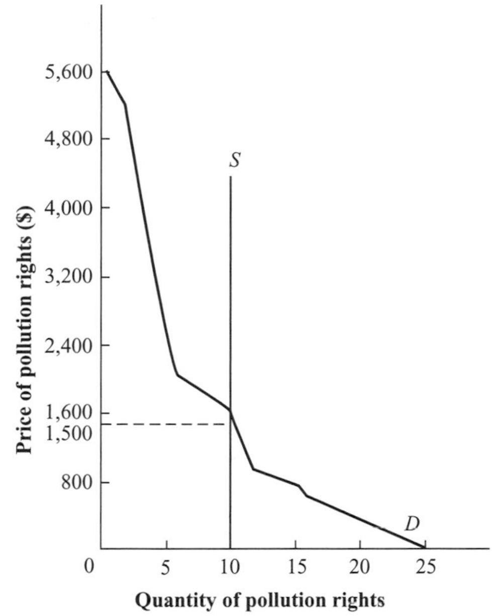

Figure 5.11 Market for pollution rights
Reducing pollution is costly (see table 5.1). It adds to the costs of production, increasing product prices and reducing the quantities of products demanded. Therefore firms have a demand for the right to avoid pollution abatement costs. The lower the price of such rights, the greater the quantity of rights that firms will demand. If the government fixes the supply of pollution rights at ten and sells those ten rights to the highest bidder, the price of the rights will settle at the intersection of the supply and demand curves – here, about $1,500.

demand curves, price and quantity are inversely related. The lower the price of pollution rights, thc higher the quantity demanded.

Table 5.2 shows the total quantity demanded by the firms at various prices. At a price of zero, the firms want 25 rights (5 each). At a price of $201, they demand only 21. Firm *A* wants only 3, because the cost to clean up its first 2 units (at costs of $100 and $200) is less than to buy rights to emit them at a price of $201. Firm *B* wants 4 rights, for its cleanup costs are higher.

Given that the information in table 5.2, the market clearing price (the price at which the quantity of property rights demanded exactly equals the number of rights for sale) will be something over $1,400 (say $1,500), who will buy those rights, and what will the cost of the program be?

At a price of $1,500 per ticket, firm *A* will buy 1 and only 1 ticket. At that price, it is cheaper for the firm to clean up its first 4 units (the cost of the

Table 5.2 *Demand for property rights*

Price ($)	Quantity	Price ($)	Quantity
0	25	1,601	9
101	24	1,801	7
201	21	2,001	6
401	19	2,201	5
601	16	3,001	4
801	14	4,001	3
1,001	11	5,001	2
1,401	10	5,601	0

cleanup is $100 + $200 + $400 + $800). Only the fifth unit, which would cost $1,600 to clean up, makes the purchase of a $1,500 ticket worthwhile. Similarly, firm *B* will buy 3 tickets, firm *C* none, firm *D* 2, and firm *E* 4. The cost of any cleanup must be measured by the value of the resources that go into it. The value of the resources is approximated by the firms' expenditures on the cleanup – not by their expenditures on pollution tickets. (The tickets do not represent real resources, but a transfer of purchasing power from the firms to the government.) Accordingly, the economic cost of reducing pollution to 10 units is $9,300: $1,500 for firm *A*; $800 for *B*; $3,000 each for *C* and *D*; and $1,000 for *E*. This figure is significantly less than the $13,500 cost of the cleanup when each firm is required to eliminate 3 units of pollution. Yet in each case, 15 units are eliminated. In short, the pricing system is more economical – more cost-effective or efficient – than setting standards. Because it is more efficient, it is also the more economical way of producing goods and services. More resources go into production and fewer into cleanup.

The idea of selling rights to pollute may not sound attractive, but it makes sense economically. When the government sets standards, it is giving away rights to pollute. In our example, telling each firm that it must reduce its sulfur dioxide emissions by 3 units is effectively giving each one permission to dump 2 units into the atmosphere. One might ask whether the government should be giving away rights to the atmosphere, which has many other uses besides the absorption of pollution. Though some pollution may be necessary to continued production, that is no argument for giving away pollution rights. Land is needed in many production processes, but the Forest Service does not give away the rights to public lands. When pollution rights are sold, on the other hand, potential users can express the relative values they place on the right to pollute.[11] In that way, rights can be assigned to their most valuable and productive uses.

Perspective The Problem of Spam: for Spammers As Well As Spammees

Spam is an Internet scourge that, ironically, many spammers will learn to hate, if they don't already, as much as their victims – all spammees who are greeted daily with dozens of unwanted emails in their inboxes pitching anything from herbal enhancements for body parts to jokes for every occasion to obvious scams from exiled foreign princes who will share any returned fortune with those who send checks to help defray their legal fees. What we shall see in this Perspective is that in the spammers' own dislike of spam lies the seed of solutions.

In his seminal article in *Science*, biologist Garrett Hardin (1968) coined the phrase, the "tragedy of the commons," a concept considered in chapter 1. With that phrase, Hardin made a general point with an example relevant to the spam plague: If a pasture is left as common property – meaning that the surrounding ranchers don't have private rights to the property, most notably, the right of exclusion – the ranchers will put cattle on the pasture until the grass is eaten to the nub, resulting in the cattle being sent off to market thin to the bone. As economics students now learn, the tragedy occurs because the ranchers impose a portion of their costs on each other: The grass that one rancher's steer eats makes eating more costly for other ranchers' steers and, hence, each rancher's costs for putting steers on the pasture are understated. The solution to the commons tragedy? Privatize the pasture – that is, give someone the right of exclusion, meaning the right to curb the count of steers by entry charges.

Think of people's email boxes (or their attention spans) as a "commons." Think of spammees as the grass. Think of the spammers as the ranchers (or cows). Seen in this light, the tragedy of the spam commons is as much a tragedy for many spammers as it is for us spammees.

Spammees experience the tragedy since, like grass in the commons, their time is overused as they waste so much of it deleting unwanted emails. The

[11] Note that the system allows environmental groups as well as producers to express the value they place on property rights. If environmental groups think that 10 units of sulfur dioxide is too much pollution, they can buy some of the tickets themselves and then not exercise their right to pollute.

tragedy faced by many spammers is that their emails are largely ignored because of the overwhelming flow of spam. Only gullible people pay attention to spam – and because they do, they share blame for the spam scourge. (If no spammees responded to spam, then surely spammers would not waste their time concocting their scams.)

And the spam problem has, no doubt, gotten worse for the *spammers* as they have escalated their "spam arms race," with each spammer trying to compensate for their own spam's growing ineffectiveness by hiking their volume, a process that has undermined, and will continue to undermine, the credibility of all broadcast email messages.

A partial solution for the escalating tragedy may come from a legislated or court-ordained assertion that email box "owners" have rights of exclusion and the right to charge for entry – a solution that many spammers can be expected to press politically (see p. 205 below). Barring such an imposed solution, private solutions remain: Have someone – anyone, or lots of people – develop an anti-spam program that is so effective that spammers can be excluded from the spam commons and, accordingly, can be charged for the right to spam targeted audiences – all to the benefit of the spammers as well as the spammees.

The benefits of the antispam software to the software's developers and spammees are obvious. The software developers can turn a profit by charging spammers for the right to spam people who, in turn, have been paid for the right of "safe passage" to their email boxes. Alternatively, the software developers can sell their software to email boxholders who can then charge spammers directly for *not* blocking their spam (as several firms were trying to do when this chapter was being completed). With the charges, spammers can benefit from the greater effectiveness of the reduced flow of spam through the "owners'" antispam gates. With a reduced spam flow, and the prospects of more spam being opened and acted upon, spammers could possibly charge higher prices for their services – that is, when they have a real service to provide.

A part of the spam problem has already been solved by SpamNet (and many other software programs) that provides spam-blocking programs (which automatically deleted over 18,000 spam messages to one of the authors over the twelve months prior to when this chapter was being written). Internet service providers have good reason to seek improved solutions to their customers' spam tragedy: There's money to be made in antispam. Similarly, Microsoft has reason to seek a solution to spam because much spam is targeted at Outlook users, which means that spam obviously impacts the value of Outlook – and undercuts Bill Gates' and Bill Balmer's considerable wealth.[12]

Unfortunately, many of the worst spammers are workplace colleagues who can't resist clicking the "everyone" email list and distributing daily their banal jokes or invectives against political leaders and other colleagues. Firms will soon realize that they have a partial solution at hand: Assert their control over their internal "email commons" by allocating employees an email (or discretionary) budget and then charging a per-recipient fee (perhaps equal to a first-class stamp) for each email distributed. The price placed on emails would cause workers to think twice about how many emails to write and whom should receive them. Without this kind of arrangement, the value a worker places on sending an email to additional colleagues is zero. With a price charged, the worker would have to view the value of the email being sent to an additional person more than the price that is charged. Hence, fewer emails sent to fewer people could be expected.

In short, the spam tragedy could become less tragic in the not-too-distant future with the privatization of the spam commons. Indeed, the antispam solutions developed might be so effective that the policy problem of the future could well be one that has already been raised in academic circles, the "tragedy of the anticommons," or too much control over the use of a resource (as discussed in the Perspective in chapter 1).

PART II ORGANIZATIONAL ECONOMICS AND MANAGEMENT

How honesty pays in business

There exists the popular perception that markets fail because business is full of dishonest scoundrels – especially high-ranking executives – who cheat, lie,

[12] At the time this chapter was being finalized, Microsoft was developing a sender verification program that would admit email into recipients' email boxes so long as it came from an authorized source. Microsoft anticipated that its verification program would reduce spam by increasing radically the time spammers' computers would take to distribute their millions of email transmissions. Other software firms – for example, IronPort and Habeas – are emerging with an interesting business model: Make money by charging spammers for the right to have their spam authenticated and sent through their controlled distribution networks of firms and organizations that allow spam through their spam gates for a fee. Spammees can be expected to open more of the controlled spam because of the restricted volume and because the spammers, by virtue of the fees paid, attest that their spam has some potential, albeit it slight, value.

steal, and worse to increase their profits. This perception is reflected in and reinforced by the way business people are depicted in the media.[13] No one can deny that people in business have done all kinds of nasty things for a buck. But the impression of pervasively dishonest business people is surely greatly exaggerated. Business people are no more likely to behave dishonestly than are other people. In fact, business people might behave more honestly than the typical American on the street because they find it advantageous to commit themselves to incentive arrangements that motivate honest behavior.

The role of honesty in business

The case to be made for honesty in business is not based on any claim that business people are particularly virtuous or ethical compared to people in many other walks of life. We can make no claim to keen insights into the virtue of business people or anyone else. We might even be persuaded that business people have less virtue on average than do those who choose more caring occupations, such as teachers, social workers, missionaries, and nurses. But we do claim to know one simple fact about human behavior: People respond to incentives in predictable ways. In particular, the lower the personal cost of dishonesty, the more dishonesty we shall observe. If business people act honestly to an unusual degree, it must be in part because they expect to pay a high price for behaving dishonestly. This is, in fact, the case because business people have found, somewhat paradoxically, that they can increase profits by accepting institutional and contractual arrangements that impose large losses on them if they are dishonest.

Though this fact is seldom mentioned in nightly news reports of business scandals, most business activity requires a high degree of honest behavior. If business is to be conducted at any but the simplest level, products must be represented honestly, promises must be kept, costly commitments must be made, and business people must cooperate with each other to take the interests of others, particularly consumers, into consideration. Indeed, if the proverbial man from Mars came down and observed business activity, he might very well conclude that business people are extraordinarily honest, trusting, and cooperative. They sell precious gems that really are precious to customers who cannot tell the difference between a diamond and cut glass. They promise not to raise the price of a product once customers make investments that make switching to another product costly, and they typically keep the promise. They

[13] According to one study, during the 1980s almost 90 percent of all business characters on television were portrayed as corrupt (Lichter, Lichter, and Rothman 1990).

make good-faith pledges that the businesses they own, but are about to sell, will continue to give their customers good service. They commit themselves to costly investments to serve customers, knowing that the investments will become worthless if customers shift their business elsewhere.

Business people behave in the marketplace in ways that suggests a level of morality, even though economists typically assume that self-interest is the dominant motivation in business decisions. Some argue that the economist's assumption of self-interest is extreme, and we recognize that many people, including many business people, behave honestly simply because they feel it is the right thing to do. But few would recommend that we blindly trust in the honesty of others when engaged in business activity. People who are foolish enough to assume that all business people are honest and trustworthy have only to encounter a few who are not to find themselves separated quickly from their wealth.

Again, we want to emphasize that dishonest behavior of the above type does occur. But such dishonest behavior is the exception, not the rule, despite the storytelling talents of Hollywood writers. The reason is that in addition to being a virtue from a strictly moral perspective, honesty is important for materialistic reasons. An economy in which people deal with each other honestly can produce more wealth than one in which people are chronically dishonest. So there are gains to be realized from honesty, and when there are gains to be captured there are people who, given the opportunities available in market economies, will devise ways to capture them.

A business person who attempts to profit from dishonest dealing faces the fact that few people are naïvely trusting, certainly not of those who have taken advantage of that trust. It may be possible to profit from dishonesty in the short run, but those who do so find it increasingly difficult to get people to deal with them in the long run. And in some businesses it is extremely difficult to profit from dishonesty even in the short run. How many people, for example, would pay full price for a "genuine" Rolex watch, or diamond necklace, from someone selling them out of a Volkswagen van at the curb of a busy street? Without being able to provide some assurance of honesty, the opportunities to profit in business are very limited.

Business people therefore have a strong motivation to put themselves in situations in which their own dishonest behavior is penalized. Only by doing so can they provide potential customers, workers, and investors with the assurance of the honest dealing required for those people to become *actual* customers, workers, and investors.

The advantage of honesty in business can be illustrated by considering the problem facing Mary, who has a well-maintained older-model Honda Accord that she is willing to sell for as little as $4,000. If interested buyers know how well maintained the car is, they will be willing to pay as much as $5,000 for it. Therefore, a wealth-increasing exchange appears to be possible because any price between $4,000 and $5,000 will result in the car being transferred to someone who values it more than the existing owner. But there is a problem. Many owners of same-year Honda Accords who are selling their cars are doing so because their cars have not been well maintained and are about to experience serious mechanical problems. More precisely, assume that that 75 percent of the used Honda Accords being sold are in such poor condition that the most a fully informed buyer would be willing to pay for them is $3,000. The remaining 25 percent of these cars on the market are worth $5,000. This means that a buyer with no information on the condition of a car for sale would expect a same-year Honda Accord to be worth, on average, only $3,500. But if buyers are willing to pay only $3,500 for an Accord as old as Mary's, many of the sellers whose cars are in good condition will refuse to sell, as is the case with Mary, who is unwilling to sell for less than $4,000.

So, the mix of such Accords for sale will tilt more in the direction of poorly maintained cars, their expected value will decline, and even fewer well-maintained Accords will be sold. This situation is often described as a market for "lemons," and illustrates the value of sellers being able to commit themselves to honesty (Akerlof 1970). If Mary could somehow convince potential buyers of her honesty when she claims that her Accord is in good condition, she would be better off, and so would those who are looking for a good used car. The advantage of being able to commit to honesty in business extends to any situation in which it is difficult for buyers to determine the quality of products they are buying.

Games of trust

The advantages of honesty in business and the problem of trying to provide credible assurances of that honesty can also be illustrated as a game. In table 5.3, we present a payoff matrix for a buyer and a seller giving the consequences from different choice combinations. The first number in the brackets gives the payoff to the seller; the second number gives the payoff to the buyer. If the seller is honest (the quality of the product is as high as he claims) and the buyer trusts the seller (she pays the high-quality price), then both realize a payoff of 100. On the other hand, if the seller is honest but the buyer does not trust him, then no exchange takes place and both receive a payoff of zero. If the seller is dishonest while the buyer is trusting, then the seller captures a payoff

Table 5.3 *The problem of trust in business*

		BUYER	
		Trust	Doesn't Trust
SELLER	Honest	(100, 100)	(0, 0)
	Dishonest	(150, –50)	(25, 25)

of 150, while the buyer gets the sucker's payoff of – 50. Finally, if the seller is dishonest and the buyer does not trust him, then an exchange takes place with the buyer paying a price that reflects the presumed low quality of the product and getting a lower-quality product than she would be willing to pay for. Both the seller and buyer receive a payoff of 25. From a joint perspective, honesty and trust are the best choices, because this combination results in more wealth for the two to share.

But this will not likely be the outcome, given the incentives created by the payoffs in table 5.3. The buyer will not trust the seller. The buyer knows that if her trust of the seller is taken for granted by the seller, he will attempt to capture the largest possible payoff from acting dishonestly. On the other hand, if he believes that she does not trust him, his highest payoff is still realized by acting dishonestly. So she will reasonably expect the seller to act dishonestly. This is a *self-fulfilling expectation* because when the seller doesn't expect to be trusted, his best response is to act dishonestly.

The seller would clearly be better off in this situation (and so would the buyer) if he somehow created an arrangement that reduced the payoff he could realize from acting dishonestly. If, for example, the seller arranged it so that he received a payoff of only 50 from acting dishonestly when the buyer trusted him, as is shown in table 5.4, then the buyer (assuming that she knows of the arrangement) can trust the seller to respond honestly to her commitment to buy. The seller's commitment to honesty allows both seller and buyer to each realize a payoff of 100 rather than the 25 they each receive without the commitment.

But how can a seller commit himself or herself to honesty in a way that is convincing to buyers? What kind of arrangements can sellers establish that penalize them if they attempt to profit through dishonesty at the expense of customers?

There are many business arrangements and practices that can cause sellers to commit to honest dealings, and we briefly consider some of them here. The arrangements are varied, as one would expect, because the ways a seller can profit from dishonest activity are also varied.

Table 5.4 *The problem of trust in business, again*

		BUYER	
		Trust	**Doesn't Trust**
SELLER	**Honest**	(100, 100)	(0, 0)
	Dishonest	(150, –50)	(25, 25)

Notice that our discussion of the situation described in table 5.3 implicitly assumes that the buyer and seller deal with each other only once. This is clearly a situation in which the temptation for the seller to cheat the buyer is the strongest, because the immediate gain from dishonesty will not be offset by a loss of future business from a mistreated buyer. If a significant amount of repeat business is possible, then the temptation to cheat decreases, and may disappear altogether. What the seller gains from dishonest dealing on the first sale can be more than offset by the loss of repeat sales. So, one way for sellers to attempt to move from the situation described in table 5.3 to the one described in table 5.4 is by demonstrating that they are in business for the long run. For example, selling out of a permanent building with the seller's name or logo on it, rather than a Volkswagen van, informs potential customers that the seller has been (or plans on being) around for a long time. Sellers commonly advertise how long they have been in business (for example, "Since 1982" is added under the business name), to inform people that they have a history of honest dealing (or otherwise they would have been out of business long ago) and plan on remaining in business.

As we have shown in our discussion of "the last-period problem" in chapter 3, however, the advantages motivated by repeated encounters tend to break down if it is known that the encounters will come to an end at a specified date. For this reason firms will attempt to maintain continuity beyond what would seem to be a natural end-period. Single proprietorships, for example, would seem to be less trustworthy when the owner is about to retire or sell. But, as discussed earlier, a common way of reducing this problem is for the owner's offspring to join the business ("Samson and Sons" or "Delilah and Daughters") and ensure continuity after their parent's retirement. Indeed, even though large corporations have lives that extend far beyond that of any of their managers, they often depend on single proprietorships to represent and sell their products. As discussed in chapter 3, Caterpillar, the heavy equipment company, has a program to encourage the sons and daughters of these single proprietors to follow in their parents' footsteps.

The role of "hostages" in business

A **hostage** is something of value to the seller that customers can destroy by taking their business elsewhere if the seller does not keep her promises.

The advantage of letting people know that you have been and are planning to be in business a long time is that it informs them that you have something to lose – potential future business – if you engage in dishonest dealing. In effect, you are providing potential customers with a **hostage**. There are numerous other ways that businesses create arrangements to provide hostages that make their commitments to honest dealing credible.

The best hostage is one that the person giving it up values highly and that the person receiving it values not at all. Therefore it serves no purpose other than to motivate the person giving it up to keep his promise. A firm's reputation can be thought of as a hostage that the firm puts in the hands of its customers as assurance that it is committed to honest dealing. A firm's reputation is an ideal hostage because it is valuable to the firm but has no value to customers apart from its ability to ensure honesty. A firm has a motivation to remain honest in order to prevent its reputation from being destroyed by customer dissatisfaction, but customers cannot capture the value of the reputation for themselves. The more a firm can show that it values its reputation, the better hostage its reputation makes.

Firm logos

Consider the value of a logo to a firm. Companies commonly spend what seems an enormous amount of money for logos to identify them to the public. Well-known artists are paid handsomely to produce designs that do not seem any more attractive than those that could be rendered by lesser-known artists (or some unknown artists whose artistic efforts have never gone beyond bathroom walls). Furthermore, companies are seldom shy about publicizing the high costs of their logos.

It may seem wasteful for a company to spend so much for a logo, and silly to let consumers know about the waste (the cost of which ends up in the price of its products). But expensive logos make sense when we recognize that much of the value of a company's logo depends on its cost. The more expensive a company's logo, the more that company has to lose if it engages in business practices that harm its reputation with consumers, a reputation embodied in the company logo. The company that spends a lot on its logo is effectively giving consumers a hostage that is very valuable to the company. Consumers have no interest in the logo except as an indication of the company's commitment to honest dealing, but will not hesitate to destroy the value of the logo (hostage) by no longer buying the company's products if it fails to live up to that commitment.

Storefronts and fixtures

Expensive logos are an example of how businesses make nonsalvageable investments to penalize themselves if they engage in dishonest dealing. Such investments are particularly common when the quality of the product is difficult for consumers to determine. The products sold in jewelry stores, for example, can vary tremendously, and few consumers can judge that value themselves. Those jewelry stores that carry the more expensive products want to be convincing when they tell customers that those products are worth the prices being charged. One way of doing this is by selling jewelry in stores with expensive fixtures that would be difficult to use in other locations: ornate chandeliers, unusually shaped display cases, expensive countertops, and generous floor space. What could the store do with this stuff if it went out of business? Not much, and this tells the customers that the store has a lot to lose by misrepresenting its merchandise to capture short-run profits. Nonsalvageable investments serve as hostages that sellers put into the hands of customers.

Firm profitability

Another rather subtle way that sellers use “hostages” to provide assurances of honesty is by letting consumers know that they (the sellers) are making lots of money. If it is known that a business is making a lot more profit from its existing activity than it could make in alternative activities, consumers will have more confidence that the business won’t risk that profit with misleading claims. The extra profits of the business are a hostage that will be destroyed by consumers’ choices if the business begins employing dishonest practices. Expensive logos and nonsalvageable capital not only are hostages in themselves but also inform consumers that the firm is making enough money to afford such extravagances. Expensive advertising campaigns, often using well-known celebrities, also serve the same purpose. Through expensive advertising, a company is doing more than informing potential customers about the availability of the product; it is letting them know that it has a lot of profits to lose by misrepresenting the quality of the product.

Creation of competition

The importance that business people attach to committing themselves to honesty sometimes leads them to put their profits in a position to be competed away by other firms. Consider the situation of a firm with a patent on a high-quality product that consumers would like to purchase at the advertised price, but the product would be difficult to stop using because its use requires costly commitments. The fear of the potential buyers is that the seller will exploit the long-term patent monopoly on the product by raising the price after the buyer commits to it at the attractive initial price. The seller may promise not to raise the price, but the buyer will be taking an expensive risk to trust the honesty of the promise. A long-term contract is possible, but it is difficult to specify all the contingencies under which a price increase (or decrease) would be justified. Also, such a contract can reduce the flexibility of the buyer as well as the seller, and legal action to enforce the contract is expensive.

Another possibility is for the seller to give up her monopoly position by licensing another firm to sell the product. By doing so, the seller makes credible the promise to charge a reasonable price in the future, because breaking the promise allows the buyer to turn to an alternative seller. Giving up a monopoly position is a costly move, of course, but it is exactly what semiconductor firms that have developed patented chips have done. To make credible their promise of a reliable and competitively priced supply of a new proprietary chip (the use of which requires costly commitments by the user), semiconductor firms have licensed such chips to competitive firms. Such a licensing arrangement is another example of a firm giving up a hostage to encourage honesty.[14]

Joint ownership

The more difficult it is for consumers to determine the quality of a product or service, the more advantage there is in committing to honesty with hostage arrangements. Consider the case of repair work. When people purchase repair work on their cars, for example, they can generally tell whether the work eliminates the problem. The car is running again, the rattle is gone, the front wheels now turn in the same direction as the steering wheel, etc. But few people know whether the repair shop charged them for only the repairs necessary, or whether it charged for lots of parts and hours of labor when tightening a screw was all they did. One way for repair shops to reduce the payoff to dishonest repair charges is through joint ownership with the dealership selling the cars being repaired. In this way the owner of the dealership makes future car sales a hostage to honest repair work. Dealerships depend on repeat sales from satisfied customers, and an important factor in how satisfied people are with their cars is the cost of upkeep and repairs. The gains that a dealership could realize from overcharging for repair work would be quickly offset by reductions in both repair business and car sales.

[14] When Intel developed its 286 microprocessor in the late 1970s, it gave up its monopoly by licensing other firms to produce it (as discussed by Brandenburger and Nalebuff 1996, 105–6).

Guarantees

Automobiles are not the only products in which it is common to find repairs and sales tied together in ways that provide incentives for honest dealing. Many products come with guarantees entitling the buyer to repairs and replacement of defective parts for a specified period of time. These guarantees also serve as hostages against poor quality and high repair costs. Of course, guarantees provide not only assurance of quality but also protection against the failure of that assurance. Sellers often offer extra assurance, and the opportunity to reduce their risk, by selling a warranty with their product that extends the time and often the coverage of the standard guarantee.

Moral hazards and adverse selection

Although guarantees and warranties reduce the incentive of sellers to act dishonestly, they create opportunities for buyers to benefit from less than totally honest behavior. These opportunities are present to one degree or another in all forms of insurance and come as two separate problems, one known as **moral hazard**. The other problem is **adverse selection**. Consider first the problem of moral hazard.

A **moral hazard** is the tendency of behavior to change after contracts are signed, resulting in unfavorable outcomes from the use of a good or service.

Adverse selection is the tendency of people with characteristics undesirable to sellers to buy a good or service from those sellers.

Knowing that a product is under guarantee or warranty can tempt buyers to use the product improperly and carelessly and then blame the seller for the consequences. With this moral hazard in mind, sellers put restrictions on guarantees and warranties that leave buyers responsible for problems that they are in the best position to prevent. For example, refrigerator manufacturers ensure against defects in the motor but not against damage to the shelves or finish. Similarly, automobile manufacturers ensure against problems in the engine and drive train (if the car has been properly serviced) but not against damage to the body and the seat covers. Although such restrictions obviously serve the interests of sellers, they also serve the interests of buyers. When a buyer takes advantage of a guarantee by misrepresenting the cause of a difficulty with a product, all consumers pay because of higher costs to the seller. Buyers are in a Prisoner's Dilemma in which they are better off collectively using the product with care and not exploiting a guarantee for problems they could have avoided. But without restrictions on the guarantee, each individual is tempted to shift the cost of her careless behavior to others.

Adverse selection is a problem associated with distortions arising from the fact that buyers and sellers often have different information that is relevant to a transaction. Most of this chapter has been concerned with the ways in which sellers commit themselves to honestly revealing the quality of products when they have more information about that quality than do buyers. But in the case of warranties it is the buyer who has crucial information that is difficult for the seller to obtain. Some buyers are harder on the product than average and others are easier on the product than average. The use of automobiles is the most obvious example. Some people drive in ways that greatly increase the probability that their cars will need expensive repair work, whereas others drive in ways that reduce that probability. If a car manufacturer offers a warranty at a price equal to the average cost of repairs, only those who know that their driving causes greater-than-average repair costs will purchase the warranty, which is therefore being sold at a loss. If the car manufacturer attempts to increase the price of the warranty to cover the higher-than-expected repair costs, then more people will drop out of the market, leaving only the worst drivers buying the warranty.[15]

Even though people would like to be able to reduce their risks by purchasing warranties at prices that accurately reflect their expected repair bills, the market for these warranties can obviously collapse unless sellers can somehow obtain information on the driving behavior of different drivers. If all buyers were honest in revealing this information, they would be better off collectively. But because individual buyers have a strong motivation to claim that they are easier on their cars than they actually are, sellers of warranties try to find indirect ways of securing honest information on the driving behavior of customers. For example, warranties on "muscle" cars that appeal to young males are either more expensive or provide less coverage than warranties on station wagons.

THE BOTTOM LINE

The key takeaways from chapter 5 are the following:

(1) The market system can perform the very valuable service of rationing scarce resources among those who want them. Markets, however, are not always permitted to operate unobstructed. Government has objectives of its own, objectives that are determined collectively rather than individually. This fact has important implications for the types and the efficiency of policies that are selected (a topic to which we return again and again in this book).

(2) Excise taxes, under normal market conditions, tend to be only partially passed on to consumers, meaning producers often pay a portion of the tax in the form of a

[15] This warranty problem is similar to the lemon problem discussed earlier in the chapter, but in this case it is the buyers who are supplying the lemons, in the form of their behavior.

lower after-tax price. How the tax is shared between buyers and sellers depends upon the elasticity of supply and demand.

(3) Price and rent controls tend to result in shortages. They also tend to result in costs being passed along to buyers in various ways and tend to result in a reduction in the quality of whatever good's price is subject to control.

(4) Minimum-wage laws (as a form of price floors) tend to result in market surpluses. However, such surpluses enable employers to offset at least partially the employment effects of minimum wages by reducing fringe benefits or increasing work demands.

(5) A market economy will overproduce goods and services that impose external costs on society. It will underproduce goods and services that confer external benefits.

(6) Sometimes, but not always, government intervention can be justified to correct for externalities. To be worthwhile, the benefits of action must outweigh the costs.

(7) Some ways of dealing with external costs and benefits are more efficient than others.

(8) Some critics of markets suggest that markets are bound to fail because of the gains to business from being dishonest, which implies a form of "externality." Nevertheless, markets have built-in incentives for people to be more honest than they might otherwise be.

REVIEW QUESTIONS

(1) Is a tax on margarine "efficient" in the economic sense of the term? Why would margarine producers prefer to have an excise tax imposed on both butter and margarine? Would such a tax be more or less efficient than a tax on margarine alone?

(2) If, in a competitive market, prices are held below market equilibrium by government controls, what will be the effect on output? How might managers be expected to react to the laws?

(3) Why might some managers want price controls? Why wouldn't they get together and control prices themselves (if it were legal)?

(4) How could price controls affect a firm's incentive to innovate? Explain.

(5) "If a price ceiling is imposed in only one competitive industry, the resulting shortage in that industry will be greater than if price ceilings were imposed in all industries." Do you agree? Explain.

(6) "Price controls can be more effective in the short run than in the long run." Explain.

(7) The existence of external costs is not in itself a sufficient reason for government intervention in the market. Why not?
(8) Developers frequently buy land and hold it on speculation; in effect, they "bank" land. Should firms be permitted to buy and bank pollution rights in the same say? Would such a practice contribute to overall economic efficiency?
(9) "If allowing firms to trade pollution rights lowers the cost of meeting pollution standards, it should also allow government to tighten standards without increasing costs." Do you agree or disagree? Why?
(10) If businesses are permitted to sell pollution rights, should brokers in pollution rights be expected to emerge? Why or why not? Would such agents increase the efficiency with which pollution is cleaned up?
(11) If pollution rights are traded, should the government impose a price ceiling on them? Would such a system contribute to the efficient allocation of resources? If you were a producer, which method of pollution control would you favor, the setting of government standards or the auction of pollution rights by government? Why?
(12) Explain how a reputation for "honest dealing" on the part of executives can elevate a company's stock.
(13) Why do many consumers pay extra for goods with "brand names"?

Appendix: key econometric findings

We noted in the body of the chapter that there had been a number of econometric studies on how minimum-wage increase have undercut fringe benefits and have increased work demands. Here are the key findings:

- Writing in the *American Economic Review*, Masanori Hashimoto (1982) found that under the 1967 minimum-wage hike, workers gained 32 cents in money income but lost 41 cents per hour in training – a net loss of 9 cents an hour in full-income compensation.
- Linda Leighton and Jacob Mincer (1981) in one study and Belton Fleisher (1981) in another came to a similar conclusion: Increases in the minimum wage reduce on-the-job training – and, as a result, dampen growth in the real long-run income of covered workers.
- Walter Wessels (1987) found that the minimum wages caused retail establishments in New York to increase work demands. In response to a minimum-wage increase, only 714 of the surveyed stores cut back store hours, but 4,827 stores reduced the number of workers and/or their employees' hours worked. Thus, in most stores, fewer workers were given fewer hours to do the same work as before.

- The research of Belton Fleisher (1981), L. F. Dunn (1985), and William Alpert (1986), shows that minimum-wage increases lead to large reductions in fringe benefits and to worsening working conditions.
- More recently, Mindy Marks (2004) found that workers covered by state minimum-wage laws in states with high minimum wage rates, relative to states' average wage rates, were slightly (but to a statistically significant degree) less likely to receive employer-provided health insurance. Workers covered by the federal minimum wage law were also more likely to work part time, given that part-time workers can be excluded from employer-provided health insurance plans. Marks found that the $0.90 per hour increase in the federal minimum wage rate in 1990 reduced the probability of workers receiving employer-provided health insurance from 66.2 percent to 63.1 percent, and gave rise to a 26 percent increase in the likelihood of covered workers working part time.
- If the minimum wage does *not* cause employers to make substantial reductions in nonmoney benefits and increases in work demands, then increases in the minimum wage should cause (1) an increase in the labor-force participation rates of covered workers (because workers would be moving up their supply of labor curves), (2) a reduction in the rate at which covered workers quit their jobs (because their jobs would then be more attractive), and (3) a significant increase in prices of production processes heavily dependent on covered minimum-wage workers. Wessels found little empirical support for such conclusions drawn from conventional theory, however. Indeed, in general, he found that minimum-wage increases had exactly the opposite effect: (1) participation rates went down, (2) quit rates went up, and (3) prices did not rise appreciably – which are findings consistent only with the view that minimum-wage increases make workers worse off. With regard to quit rates, Wessels writes, "I could find no industry which had a significant decrease in their quit rates. Two industries had a significant increase in their quit rates . . . These results are only consistent with a lower full compensation" (1987, 13). Given the findings of his own as well as other researchers' studies, Wessels deduces that every 10 percent increase in the hourly minimum wage will make workers 2 percent worse off. This means that an increase in the minimum of $1.30 (equal to the 1987 congressional proposal) could, on balance, make the covered workers worse off to the tune of 26 cents per hour (1987, 15).

CHAPTER 6

Reasons for firms and incentives

Amazing things happen when people take responsibility for everything themselves. The results are quite different, and at times people are unrecognizable. Work changes and attitudes to it, too. **Mikhail Gorbachev, former Premier of the Soviet Union**

In conventional economic discussions of how firms are managed, incentives are nowhere considered. This is the case because the "firm" is little more than a theoretical "black box" in which things happen somewhat mysteriously. MBA students who have taken an undergraduate course in microeconomics might remember that economics textbooks typically acknowledge that the "firm" is the basic production unit, but little or nothing is said of why the firm ever came into existence or, for that matter, what the firm *is*. As a consequence, we are told little about why firms do what they do (and don't do). There is nothing in conventional discussions that tells us about the role of real people in a firm.

How are firms to be distinguished from the markets they inhabit, especially in terms of the incentives people in firms and markets face? That question is seldom addressed (other than, perhaps, specifying that firms can be one of several legal forms, for example, proprietorships, partnerships, professional associations, or corporations). In conventional discussions of the "theory of the firm," firms maximize their profits, which is their only noted *raison d'être*. But students of conventional theory are never told how firms do what they are supposed to do, or why they do what they do.

The owners, presumably, devise ways to ensure that everyone in the organization follows instructions, all of which exist to squeeze every ounce of profit from every opportunity. Students are never told what the instructions are, or what is done to ensure that workers follow them. The structure of incentives inside the firm never comes up because their purpose is effectively assumed away: People do what they are supposed to do, naturally or by some unspecified mysterious process.

For people in business (and MBA students), the conventional economist's approach to the "firm" must appear strange indeed, given that business people spend much of their working day trying to coax people to do what they are supposed to do. Nothing is more problematic in business than getting employees to consistently devote their efforts to increasing their firms' profits (as opposed to devoting themselves to more personal concerns).

In this chapter, before we delve into the structure of firm costs in chapters 8–9, we address the issue of *why firms exist.* This is not just an interesting academic question. Rather, we are concerned with the reasons firms exist because an explanation can help us understand why the existence of firms and incentives go hand in hand.

PART I THEORY AND PUBLIC POLICY APPLICATIONS

Firms and market efficiency

Why is it that firms add to the efficiency of markets? That is an intriguing question, especially given how standard theories trumpet the superior efficiency of markets. Students of conventional theory might rightfully wonder: If markets are so efficient, why do so many entrepreneurs go to the trouble of organizing firms? Why not just have everything done by way of markets, with little or nothing actually done (in the sense that things are "made") inside firms? All of the firm's inputs could be bought instead by individuals, with each individual adding value to the inputs she purchases and then selling this result to another individual, who adds more value, and so on until a final product is produced and a final market is reached, at which point the completed product is sold to consumers. The various independent suppliers may be at the same general location, even in the same building, but everyone, at all times, could be available for contracting with all other suppliers or some centralized buyer of the inputs. By keeping everything on a market basis, the benefits of competition could be constantly reaped. Entrepreneurs could always look for competitive bids from alternative suppliers for everything used – whether in the form of parts to be assembled, accounting and computer services to be used, or, for that matter, executive talent to be employed.

Individuals, as producers relying exclusively on markets, could always take the least costly bid. They could also keep their options open, including the option of immediately switching to new suppliers who propose better deals. No one would be tied down to internal sources of supply for their production needs. They would not have to incur the considerable costs of organizing themselves into production teams and departments and various levels of management. They would not have to incur the costs of internal management and having to deal with the Prisoner's Dilemma of shirking workers. They could, so to speak, maintain a great deal of freedom!

So why do firms exist? More to the point, if markets are so efficient in getting things done, why do less than 30 percent of all transactions in the United States occur through markets, which means that more than 70 percent of transactions are made through firms (McMillan 2002, 168–9)?

What is the incentive – the driving force – behind firms? For that matter, what is a *firm* in the first place? Law and Economics Professor Ronald Coase, on whose classic work, "The nature of the firm", much of this chapter is based and from which many of the particular arguments are drawn, proposed a substantially new but deceptively simple explanation (see also Coase 1988, chapter 2). Coase reasoned that the *firm* is any organization that supersedes the pricing system, in which hierarchy, and methods of command and control, are substituted for exchanges. To use his exact words: "A firm, therefore, consists of the system of relationships which comes into existence when the direction of resources is dependent on an entrepreneur" (1988, 41–2).[1]

Good alternative answers to the question of why firms exist are more complicated and longer in the making than might be thought, but space limitations in this book require us to be brief. Some economists have speculated that firms exist because of the *economies of specialization* of resources, a key one being labor. Clearly, Adam Smith and many of his followers were correct when they observed that when tasks are divided among a number of workers, the workers become more proficient at what they do. Smith began his economic classic *The Wealth of Nations* by writing about how specialization of labor increased "pin" (really, nail) production (Smith 1937, 4–12). By specializing, workers can become more proficient at what they do, which means they can produce more in their time at work. They also don't have to waste time changing tasks, leaving more time to be spent directly on production.

Although efficiency improvements can certainly result from specialization of any resource, especially labor, Smith was wrong to conclude that firms were

[1] Similarly, Herbert Simon (1951) argued that a firm replaces market bargaining with command and control hierarchies but stressed that management control over subordinates was made necessary because of the inability of anyone to foresee the ever-changing array of tasks that need to be done and the high cost of renegotiating contracts in markets to meet changing conditions.

necessary to coordinate the workers' separate tasks. This error is clear because, as economists have long recognized, workers' separate tasks could be coordinated by the pricing system within markets.

Conceivably, markets can exist even within the stages of production that are held together by, say, assembly lines. Workers at the various stages could simply buy what is produced before them. The person who produces soles in a shoe factory could buy the leather and then sell the completed soles to the shoe assemblers. The bookkeeping services provided to a shoe factory by its accounting department could easily be bought on the market (and many firms do buy their accounting services from accounting firms). Similarly, all the intermediate goods involved in Smith's pin production could be bought and sold until the completed pins were sold to those who want them.

Why, then, do we observe *firms* as such, which organize activities by hierarchies and directions that are not based on charging prices (which distinguishes them from markets)? In terms of our examples, why are there shoe and pin companies? Over the years economists have tendered various answers.[2]

There are probably many reasons people might think firms exist, several of which Coase dismisses for being wrongheaded or unimportant (1988, 41–2).[3]

[2] Writing before Coase, Frank Knight (1971, latest edition of a work first published in 1921) speculated that firms arise because of *uncertainty*. According to Knight, if business were conducted in a totally certain world, there would be no need for firms. Workers would know their pattern of rewards, and no need would exist for anyone to specialize in the acceptance of the costs of dealing with the risks and uncertainties that abound in the real world of business.
As it is, according to Knight, some workers are willing to work for firms because of the type of deal that is struck: The workers accept a reduction in their expected pay in order to reduce the variability and outright uncertainty of that pay. Entrepreneurs are willing to make such a bargain with their workers because they are effectively paid to do so by their workers (who accept a reduction in pay) and because the employers can reduce their exposure to risk and uncertainties faced by individual workers by making similar bargains with a host of workers. As Knight put it:

> With human nature as we know it, it would be impracticable or very unusual for one man to guarantee to another a definite result of the latter's actions without being given power to direct his work. And on the other hand the second party would not place himself under the direction of the first without such a guarantee . . . The result of this manifold specialization of function is the enterprise and wage system of industry. Its existence in the world is the direct result of the fact of uncertainty. (1971, 269–70)

[3] For example, Coase concedes that some people might prefer to be directed in their work. As a consequence, they might accept lower pay just to be told what to do. However, Coase dismisses this explanation as unlikely to be important because "it would rather seem that the opposite tendency is operating if one judges from the stress normally laid on the advantage of 'being one's own master'" (1988, 38). Of course, it might be that some people like to control others, meaning that they would give up a portion of their pay to have other people follow their direction. However, again Coase finds such an explanation lacking, mainly because it could not possibly be true "in the majority of the cases" (1988, 38). People who direct the work of others are frequently paid a premium for their efforts.

What Coase was interested in, however, was not a catalog of "small" explanations for this or that firm, but an explanation for the existence of virtually all firms. And in his 1937 article, he struck upon an unbelievably simple explanation, but one so insightful that it earned him the Nobel Prize in Economics, more than a half-century later!

Reasons for firms

How did Coase explain the existence of firms? Simply put, he observed that there are costs of dealing in markets. He dubbed these *marketing costs*, but most economists now call them *transaction costs*. Whatever they are called, these costs include the time and resources that must be devoted to organizing economic activity through markets. Transaction costs include the real economic costs of discovering the best deals as evaluated in terms of prices and attributes of products, negotiating contracts, and enforcing the terms of the contract. When we were going through our explanation of how work on an assembly line could be viewed as passing through various markets, most readers probably imagined that the whole process would be terribly time-consuming, especially if the suppliers and producers at the various stages were constantly looking for new people to deal with, constantly negotiating new agreements, and constantly subject to replacement by competitors.

Once the costs of market activity are recognized, the reason for the emergence of the firm is transparent: Firms, which substitute internal direction for markets, arise because they *reduce the need for making market transactions*. Firms lower the costs that go with market transactions. If internal direction were not, at times and up to some point, more cost-effective than markets, then no one would have an incentive to go to the trouble of creating a firm. Although firms will never eliminate the need for markets, neither will markets ever eliminate the need for the internal direction of firms.

Entrepreneurs and their hired workers essentially substitute one long-term contract for a series of short-term contracts: The workers agree to accept directions from the entrepreneurs (or their agents, or managers) within certain broad limits (with the exact limits varying from firm to firm) in exchange for security and a level of welfare (including pay) that is higher than the workers would be able to receive in the market without firms. Similarly, the entrepreneurs (or their agents) agree to share with the workers some of the efficiency gains obtained from reducing transaction costs.[4]

[4] Coase recognizes that entrepreneurs could overcome some of the costs of repeatedly negotiating and enforcing short-term contracts by devising one long-term contract. However, as the time period over which a contract is in force is extended, more and more unknowns are

The firm is a viable economic institution because *both sides to the contract* – owners and workers – gain. Firms can be expected to proliferate in markets simply because of the mutually beneficial deals that can be made. Those entrepreneurs who refuse to operate within firms and stick solely to market-based contracts, when in fact a firm's hierarchical organization is more cost-effective than are market-based organizations, will simply be out-competed for resources by the firms that do form and achieve the efficiency-improving deals with workers (and owners of other resources).

If firms reduce transaction costs, does it follow that one giant firm should span the entire economy, as, say, Lenin and his followers thought was possible for the Soviet Union? Our intuition says, "No!" But aside from mere intuition, sound reasons exist for limiting the size of firms.

Cost limits to firm size

Clearly, by organizing activities under the "umbrella" of firms, entrepreneurs give up some of the benefits of markets, which provide competitively delivered goods and services. Managers suffer from their own limited organizational skills, and skilled managers are scarce, as evidenced by the relatively high salaries they command. Communication problems within firms expand as firms grow, encompassing more activities, more levels of production, and more diverse products. Because many people may not like to take direction, the firm, as it expands to include more people, may have to pay progressively higher prices to workers and other resource owners in order to draw them into the firm and then direct them.

There are, in short, limits to what can be done through organizations. These limits can not always be overcome, except at costs that exceed the benefits of doing so. Even with the application of the best organizational techniques, whether through the establishment of teams, through the empowerment of employees, or through the creation of new business and departmental structures (for example, relying on top-down, bottom-up, or participatory decision making), firms are limited in their ability to reduce organizational costs.

covered, which implies that the contract must allow for progressively greater flexibility for the parties to the contract. The firm is, in essence, a substitute for such a long-term contract in that it covers an indefinite future and provides for flexibility. That is to say, the firm as a legal institution permits workers to exit more or less at will and gives managers the authority, within bounds, to change the directives given to workers.

The agency problem

Firms are restricted in their size because they suffer from what is called the *agency problem* (or, alternatively, the *principal–agent problem*) which will be considered and reconsidered often in this book. This problem is easily understood as a conflict of interests between identifiable individuals and groups within firms. The entrepreneurs or owners of firms (the *principals*) organize firms to pursue their (the principals') own interest, which is often (but, admittedly, not always) seeking greater profits. To pursue profits, however, the entrepreneurs (or shareholders) must hire managers who then hire workers (all of whom are *agents*). However, the interests of the worker/agents are not always compatible with the interests of the owner/principals. Indeed, they are often in direct conflict.

The problem the principals face is getting the agents to work diligently to serve their (the principal's) interests (which is the business problem that Adam Smith recognized in the 1770s.[5] Needless to say, agents often resist doing the principals' bidding, a fact that makes it difficult – i.e. costly – for the principals to achieve their goals.

It might be thought that most, if not all, of these conflicts can be resolved through contracts, and many can. However, as with all business arrangements, contracts have serious limitations, not the least of which is that they can't be all-inclusive, covering all aspects of even "simple" business relationships. Contracts simply cannot anticipate and cover all possible ways that the parties to the contract can, if they are so inclined, get around specific provisions. The cost of enforcing the contracts is a problem, and represents an added cost, even when both parties know that provisions have been violated. Each party will recognize these enforcement costs and may be tempted to exploit them, assuming that the other is equally tempted. Ideally, contracts will be *self-enforcing* – that is, the provisions of the contracts encourage each party to live up to the letter and spirit of the contract because it is in the interest of each party to do so. This is where incentives will come in, helping to make contracts as self-enforcing as possible, though they can seldom be perfectly self-enforcing. Incentives can encourage the parties to more faithfully follow the intent and letter of contracts.

[5] In his classic *The Wealth of Nations* (1776) Adam Smith wrote : "The directors of such companies, however, being the managers rather of other people's money than of their own, it cannot be well expected, that they should watch over it with the same anxious vigilance with which the partners in a private copartnery frequently watch over their own themselves a dispensation from having it" (1937, 700).

Competition serves as a powerful force in minimizing agency costs. Firms in competitive markets that are not able to control agency costs are firms that are not likely to survive for long, mainly because of what has been dubbed the "market for corporate control" (Manne 1963). Firms that allow agency costs to get out of hand risk either failure or takeover (by way of proxy fights, tender offers, or mergers). In chapters 9, 10, and 12, we discuss at length how managers can solve their own agency problems, including controlling their own behavior as agents for shareholders. At the same time, we would be remiss if we didn't repeatedly point out the market pressures on managers to solve such problems, even if they are not naturally inclined to do so. If corporations are not able to adequately solve their agency problems, we can imagine that the corporate form of doing business will be "eclipsed" as new forms of business emerge (according to Jensen 1989). Of course, this means that obstruction in the market for corporate control (for example, legal impediments to takeovers) can translate into greater agency costs and less efficient corporate governance. This also suggests why both firms and markets are needed if we are to fully benefit from either one.

Why are firms the sizes they are? When economists in or out of business address that question, the usual answer relates in one way or another to **economies of scale**. In some industries, it is indeed true that as more and more of all resources are added to production within a given firm, output expands in percentage terms by more than the use of resources. That is to say, if resource use expands by 10 percent and output expands by 15 percent, then the firm experiences economies of scale. Its (long-run) average cost of production declines. Why does that happen? The answer that is almost always given is "technology," which is another way of saying that it "just happens," given what is known about combining inputs and getting output. This is not the most satisfying explanation, but it is nonetheless true that economies of scale are available in some industries (steel and automobile) but not so much in others (beauty shops and music composition).

Economies of scale are the cost savings that emerge when all resource inputs – labor, land, and capital – are increased together.

We agree that the standard approach toward explaining firm size is instructive. We have spent long hours at our classroom overhead projectors with markers in hand developing and describing scale economies in the typical fashion of professors, using (long-run) average cost curves and pointing out when firms should contemplate starting a new plant. We think the standard approach (which we take up in some detail in chapter 9) is useful, but we also believe it leaves out a lot of interesting forces at work on managers within firms. This is understandable, given that standard economic theory assumes away the roles of managers, which we intend to discuss at length.

Coase and his followers have taken a dramatically different tack in explaining why firms are the sizes they are in terms of scale of operations and scope of products delivered to market. The new breed of theorists pays special attention to the difficulties managers face as they seek to expand the scale and scope of the firm. They posit that as a firm expands, *agency costs* increase. This happens primarily because workers (including managers) have more and more opportunities to engage in what we have considered before and have tagged *opportunistic behavior* – or taking advantage of their position for personal gain at the expense of the firm's profits (and therefore at the expense of the firm's owners). *Shirking*, or not working with due diligence, is one form of opportunistic behavior that is known to all employees. Theft of firm resources is another form. Employees politicking their bosses for advancement or choice assignments and their selectively using firm and market information to make the case for their advancement or reassignment are other common forms of opportunistic behavior that can drive up agency costs (as well as the need for more monitoring costs).[6]

As the firm grows, the contributions of the individual worker become less detectable, which means that workers have progressively fewer incentives to work diligently on behalf of firm objectives or to do what they are told by their superiors. They can more easily hide.

The tendency for larger size to undercut the incentives of participants in any group is not just theoretical speculation. It has been observed in closely monitored experiments. In an experiment conducted more than a half century ago, with the findings still relevant today, a German scientist asked workers to pull on a rope connected to a meter that would measure the effort expended. Total effort for *all* workers *combined* increased as workers were added to the group doing the pulling. Simultaneously, the *individual* efforts of the workers declined. When three workers pulled on the rope, the individual effort averaged 84 percent of the effort expended by one worker. With eight workers pulling, the average individual effort was half the effort of the one worker (Furnham 1993). Hence, group size and individual effort were – as they are in most group circumstances – inversely related.

[6] One way firms have attempted to control employee politicking (or internal "rent seeking") has been to develop well-defined rules and procedures for salary increases and promotions, relying on measures – say, seniority – that may have little connection to workers' relative productivity. Having seniority determining outcome may impair workers' incentive to work harder and smarter for the firm, but seniority can also reduce the incentive for workers to waste resources in internal politicking (Roberts 2004, chapter 3).

The problem is that each worker's incentive to expend effort deteriorates as the group expands. Each person's effort counts for less in the context of the larger group, a point that Mancur Olson (1971) elaborated upon in the 1970s (and that we considered in detail in chapter 4). The "common objectives" of the group become less and less compelling in directing individual efforts. Such a finding means that if each worker added to the group must be paid the same as all others, the cost of additional production obviously rises with the size of the working group. The finding also implies that to get a constant increase in effort with the additional workers, all workers must be given greater incentive to hold to their previous level of effort.[7]

Optimum-size firms

How large should a firm be? Contrary to what might be thought, the answer depends on more than technology-based economies of scale. Technology determines what *might* be done, but not what *is* done. And what is done depends on policies that minimize shirking and maximize the use of the technology by workers. This means that scale economies depend as much or more on what happens within any given firm as they do on what is technologically possible. The size of the firm obviously depends on the extent to which owners must incur greater monitoring costs with increases in the size of the firm and additional layers of hierarchy (a point well developed by Williamson 1967, in a classic article in organizational economics). However, the size of the firm also depends on the cost of using the market.

Management information system theorists Vijay Gurbaxani and Seungjin Whang (1991) have devised a graphical means of illustrating the "optimal firm size" as the consequence of two opposing cost forces: "internal coordinating costs" and "external coordinating costs." As a firm expands, its internal coordinating costs are likely to increase. This is because the firm's hierarchical pyramid will likely become larger with more and more decisions made at the top by managers who are further and further removed from the local information available to workers at the bottom of the pyramid. There is a need to process information up and down the pyramid. When the information goes up, there are unavoidable problems and, hence, costs: costs of communication, costs of miscommunication, and opportunity costs associated with delays in

[7] Workers can also reason that if the residual from their added effort goes to the firm owners, they can possibly garner some of the residual by collusively (by explicit or tacit means) restricting their effort and hiking their rate of pay, which means that the incentive system must seek to undermine such collusive agreements (Fitzroy and Kraft 1987).

communication, all of which can lead to suboptimal decisions. These "decision information costs" become progressively greater as the decision rights are moved up the pyramid.

Attempts to rectify the decision costs by delegating decision making to the lower ranks may help, but this can – and *will* – also introduce another form of costs, those that we previously referred to as *agency costs*. These include the cost of monitoring (managers actually watching employees as they work or checking their production) and bonding (workers providing assurance that the tasks or services will be done as the agreement requires), and the loss of the residual gains (or profits) through worker shirking, which we covered in chapter 4.

The basic problem managers face is one of balancing the decision information costs with agency costs and finding that location for decision rights that minimizes the two forms of costs. From this perspective, where the decision rights are located will depend heavily on the amount of information flow per unit of time. When upward flow of information is high, the decision rights will tend to be located toward the floor of the firm, mainly because the costs of suboptimal decisions by having the decision making done high up the hierarchy can be considerable. The firm, in other words, can afford to tolerate agency costs because the costs of avoiding them, via centralized decisions, can be higher.

Nevertheless, as the firm expands, we should expect the internal coordinating costs (both the decision information cost and the agency cost) along with the cost of operations to increase. The upward sloping line in figure 6.1 depicts this relationship.

But internal costs are not all that matter to a firm contemplating an expansion. It must also consider the cost of the market, or what Gurbaxani and Whang (1991) call "external coordination costs." If the firm remains "small" and buys many of its parts, supplies, and services (such as accounting, legal, and advertising services) from outside venders, then it must consider the resulting "transaction costs." These include the costs of transportation; inventory holding; communication; contract writing, monitoring, and enforcing. However, as the firm expands in size, these transaction costs should be expected to diminish. After all, as a firm becomes larger it will have eliminated those market transactions with the highest transaction costs. The downward sloping line in figure 6.1(a) depicts this inverse relationship between firm size and transaction costs.

Again, how large should a firm be? If a firm vertically integrates, it will engage in fewer market transactions, lowering its transaction costs. It can also

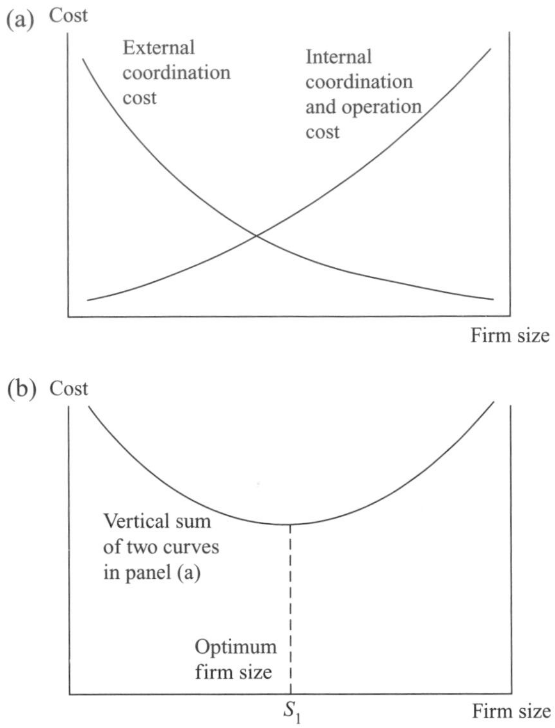

Figure 6.1 External and internal coordinating costs
As the firm expands, the internal coordinating costs increase as the external coordinating costs fall. The optimum firm size is determined by summing these two cost structures, which is done in panel (b) of the figure.

benefit from technical economies of scale (or increases in productivity that lead to costs rising less rapidly than production as all factors of production are increased). However, in the process of expanding, it will confront growing internal coordination costs, or all the problems of trying to move information up the decision making chain, getting the "right" decisions, and then preventing people from exploiting their decision making authority to their own advantage.

The firm should stop expanding in scale and scope when the total of the two types of costs – external and internal coordinating costs – are minimized. This minimum can be shown graphically by summing the two curves in figure 6.1(a) to obtain the "U" shaped curve in figure 6.1(b). The *optimal* (or most efficient/cost-effective) firm size is at the bottom of the "U".

This way of thinking about firm size would have only limited interest if it did not lend itself to additional observations about the location, shape, and changes in the curve. First, the exact location of the bottom will, of course, vary for different firms in different industries. Different firms have different capacities to coordinate activities through markets and hierarchies. Second, firm size will also vary according to the changing abilities of firms to coordinate activities internally and externally.

Of course, knowing that the owners recognize that their manager/agents can exploit their positions to benefit at the expense of the owners, managers will see advantages in "bonding" themselves against exploitation of their positions. (And, as in the past, we don't use the term "bonding" in the modern pop-psychology sense of developing warm and fuzzy relationships; rather, we use it in the same sense that is common when accused criminals post a bond, or give some assurance that they will appear in court if released from jail.) That is to say, managers have an interest in letting the owners know that they, the managers, will suffer some loss when exploitation occurs. Devices such as audits of the company are clearly in the interest of stockholders. But they are also in the interest of managers since reducing the scope for managerial misdeeds increases the market value of the company – and the market value of its managers. By buying their companies' stock, manager/agents can also bond themselves, assuring stockholders that they will incur at least some losses from agency costs. To the extent that manager/agents can bond themselves convincingly, the firm can grow from expanded sources of external investment funds. By bonding themselves, manager/agents can demand higher compensation. Firms can be expected to expand and contract with reductions and increases in the costs of developing effective managerial bonds (Jensen and Meckling 1976).

Changes in organizational costs

The size of the firm can be expected to change with changes in the relative costs of organizing a given set of activities by way of markets and hierarchies. For example, suppose that the costs of engaging in market transactions are lowered, meaning markets become relatively more economical *vis-à-vis* firms. Entrepreneurs should be expected to organize more of their activities through markets, fewer through firms. Then, those firms that more fully exploit markets, and rely less on internal directions, should be able to reduce their cost without sacrificing output by becoming smaller – or by *downsizing*, to use a popular expression.

An old, well-worn, and widely appreciated explanation for downsizing is that modern technology has enabled firms to produce more with less. Personal computers, with their ever-escalating power, have enabled firms to lay off workers (or hire fewer workers). Banks no longer need as many tellers, given the advent of the ATM.

One less widely appreciated explanation is that markets have become cheaper, which means that firms have less incentive to use hierarchical structures and more incentive to use markets. One good reason that firms have found markets relatively more attractive is the rapidly developing computer and communication technology, which has reduced the costs of entrepreneurs operating in markets. The new technology has lowered the costs of locating suitable trading partners and suppliers, as well as negotiating, consummating, and monitoring market-based deals (and the contracts that go with them). In terms of figure 6.1, the downward sloping transaction costs curve has dropped down and to the left, causing the bottom of the "U" to move leftward.

"Outsourcing" became a management buzzword as far back as the 1980s because the growing efficiency of markets, through technology, made it more economical to use markets, often on a global scale. Outsourcing continued apace in the 1990s (Byrne 1996), contributing significantly to the relatively faster pace of manufacturing productivity growth in the 1990s and the first few years of the twenty-first century (Bureau of Labor Statistics 2004).

But modern technology has also improved the monitoring of employees – reducing the costs of providing employee incentives and encouraging cooperation among workers – thereby reducing agency costs and enabling the expansion of firms (Roberts 2004, chapter 3). This is because firms have been able to use technology to garner more of the gains from economies of scale and scope.

The optical scanners at grocery store checkout counters are valuable because they can speed up the flow of customers through the checkout counters, but they can also be used for other purposes, such as inventory control and restocking. Each sale is immediately transmitted to warehouse computers that determine the daily shipments to stores. The scanners can also be used to monitor the work of the clerks, a factor that can diminish agency costs and increase the size of the firm. (Even "Employee of the Month Awards" at large retail stores are often apparently made based on reports from scanners.) Books on Tape, a firm that rents audio versions of books, tracks its production of tapes by way of scanners, not so much to reward and punish workers but to be able to identify problem areas. In terms of figure 6.1, the upward sloping curve moves down and to the right, while the "U" shaped curve in the lower panel moves to the right.

Companies as diverse as FedEx and Frito-Lay have issued their sales people hand scanners that are connected by satellite to their offices, in part to increase the reliability of the flow of information back to company distribution centers, but also to track their work. The company can obtain reports on when each employee starts and stops work, the time spent on trips between stores, and the number of returns. Accordingly, the sales people can be asked to account for more of their time and activities while they are on the job.

Obviously, we have not covered the full spectrum of explanations for the rich variety of sizes of firms that exists in the "real world" of business. We have also left the net impact of technology somewhat up in the air, given that it is pressing some firms to expand and others to downsize. The reason is simple: Technology is having a multitude of impacts that can be exploited in different ways by firms in different situations.

Overcoming the large-numbers, Prisoner's Dilemma problems

The discussion to this point reduces to a relatively simple message: *Firms exist to bring about cost savings, and they generate the cost savings through cooperation.* However, cooperation is not always and everywhere "natural" (at least, not beyond some point as the group of cooperators expands[8]); people often realize personal gains by "cheating," or not doing what they are supposed to do or have agreed to do. This may be the case because of the powerful incentives toward noncooperation that are built into many business environments.

An illustration of the tendency toward noncooperative behavior, despite the general advantage from cooperation, is a classic so-called "conditional-sum game," also known as the Prisoner's Dilemma (which we have already introduced without using the proper game-theoretic name), discussed in

[8] Behavioral biologists, evolutionary psychologists, and economists working in the emerging field of bioeconomics, however, do argue that 10,000 or more years ago, when people were hunter gatherers and when human behavioral patterns were hard-wired in people's growing brains, those people who learned to cooperate in limited-size groups with greater frequency in killing game, defending themselves against human attackers, and predating against others were more likely to survive and, hence, were more likely to pass on their genes, which included a predisposition to cooperate. This does not mean that people did not face the free-rider problem. They did, and had to find ways of suppressing it. It means only that the free-rider problem tended to be curbed somewhat by evolutionary forces, but it remains a central obstacle for managers who seek to expand the sizes of their firms, and do so profitably. (For a survey of the literature and a discussion of how evolutionary forces affect people's economic proclivities, see Rubin 2002.)

earlier chapters.[9] Overcoming a large-number Prisoner's Dilemma by motivating cooperative behavior is obviously difficult, but not impossible. The best hope for those who are in a Prisoner's Dilemma situation *is to agree ahead of time to certain rules, restrictions, or arrangements that will punish those who choose the noncooperative option.* For example, those who are jointly engaging in criminal activity will see advantages in forming gangs whose members are committed to punishing noncooperative behavior. The gang members who are confronted with the Prisoner's Dilemma orchestrated by the police will seriously consider the possibility that the shorter sentence received for confessing will hasten the time when a far more harsh punishment for "squealing" on a fellow gang member is imposed by the gang.

Many areas of business are fertile grounds for the conditional-sum game situations represented by the Prisoner's Dilemma. A number of examples of business-related dilemmas are discussed in some detail in subsequent chapters, because an important task of managers is to identify and resolve these dilemmas as they arise both within the firm and with suppliers and customers of the firm. Indeed, we see the task of "management" as being largely concerned with finding resolutions of Prisoners' Dilemmas. Good managers constantly seek to remind members of the firm of the benefits of cooperation and of the costs that can be imposed on people who insist on taking the noncooperative course.

Consider, for example, the issue of corporate travel, which is a major business expense which can run into the hundreds of billions of dollars each year. If a business were able to economize on travel costs, it would realize significant gains. And much of these gains would be captured by the firms' traveling employees who, if they were able to travel at less cost, would earn higher incomes as their net value to the firm increased. So, all the traveling employees in a firm could be better off if they all cut back on unnecessary travel expenses. But the employees are often in a Prisoner's Dilemma with respect to reducing travel costs, because each recognizes that she is personally better off by flying first class, staying at hotels with multiple stars, and dining at elegant restaurants (behaving noncooperatively) than by making the least expensive travel plans (behaving cooperatively) regardless of what the other employees do. Each individual employee would be best off if all other employees economized, which would allow the individual's salary to be higher as she continued to take luxury trips. But if the others also make the more expensive travel arrangements, an

[9] "Conditional-sum games" are games in which the value available to the participants is dependent on how the game is played.

individual would be foolish not to do so as well because the sacrifice would not noticeably increase her salary. Management of travel is a problem of making cooperative solutions pay for individual workers.

However, airlines have an interest in excessive business travel, have recognized the "games" people play with their bosses and other workers, and have played along by making the travel game more rewarding to business travelers, more costly to the travelers' firms, and more profitable to the airlines – all through their "frequent-flier" programs. Of course, you can bet that managers are more than incidentally concerned about the use of frequent-flier programs by employees.

When American Airlines initiated its AAdvantage frequent-flier program in 1981, the company was intent on staving off the fierce price competition that had broken out among established and new airlines after fares and routes were deregulated in 1978. As other writers have noted, American was seeking to enhance "customer loyalty" by offering its best, most regular customers free or reduced-price flights after they had built up their mileage accounts. Greater customer loyalty can mean that customers are less responsive to price increases, which could translate into actual higher prices than could otherwise be charged.[10]

At the same time, there is more to the issue than "customer loyalty." No doubt, American Airlines figured that it could benefit from the obvious Prisoner's Dilemma its customers, especially business travelers, were in. By setting up the frequent-flier program, American Airlines (and all others that followed suit) increased the individual payoff to business travelers for noncooperative behavior. American Airlines did this under its frequent-flier program by allowing travelers to benefit from more free flights and first-class upgrades by choosing more expensive, and sometimes less direct, flights. They encouraged business people to act opportunistically, to use their discretion for their own benefit at the expense of everyone else in their firms.

The Prisoner's Dilemma problem for workers and their companies has, of course, prompted a host of other non-airline firms – rental car companies, hotels, and restaurants – to begin granting frequent-buyer points, if not frequent-flier miles, with selected airlines for the travel services people buy with them, encouraging once again higher than necessary travel costs. The company incurs the cost of the added miles plus the lost time.

[10] For a discussion of frequent-flier programs as a means of enhancing customer loyalty, see Brandenburger and Nalebuff (1996, 132–58).

Now, use of frequent-flier miles might actually lower worker wages (because of the added cost to their firms, which can reduce the demand for workers, and the benefit of the miles to workers, which can increase worker supply and lower wages). Still, workers have an incentive to exploit the program. Again, they are in a Prisoner's Dilemma under which the cooperative strategy might be best for all, but the noncooperative strategy dominates the choice each individual faces. These problems created by frequent-flier programs are not trivial for many businesses, and we expect that the bigger the firm, the greater the problem (given the greater opportunity for opportunistic behavior in large firms).[11]

Frequent-flier programs put business travelers in a game situation that benefits the airlines at the expense of business travelers and their firms by encouraging noncooperative behavior. Recognizing this game, and the noncooperative incentives, is important for managers who are trying to cut travel costs. And in the effort to cut these costs, managers are also in a game with the airlines, which respond to cost-cutting measures with new wrinkles designed to intensify the Prisoner's Dilemma faced by business travelers (Stephenson and Fox 1992).

The resulting costly airfares, particularly for business travelers, are being countered by the low-cost airlines such as Southwest, Air Tran and Jet Blue, which are capturing an increasing share of the market by offering low-fare, no-frills service.

Make-or-buy decisions

Exactly what should firms make inside their organizations, and what should they buy from some outside vendor? Business commentators have a habit of coming up with rules that don't add very much to the answer. For example, one CEO deduced, "You should only do, in-house, what gives you a competitive advantage" (Dunlap and Andelman 1996, 55). Okay, but why would anyone get a competitive advantage by doing anything inside given that such a move reduces, to one degree or another, the advantage of buying from

[11] Thirty percent of business travelers working for Mitsubishi Electronics America wait until the last few days before booking their flights, according to corporate travel manager John Fazio. Fazio adds, "We have people who need to travel at the last minute, but it's not 30 percent" (Dahl 1994). Corporate travel managers complain that the frequent-flier programs have resulted in excessive air fares (a problem for 87 percent of the surveyed firms), wasted employee time (a problem for 68 percent of the surveyed firms), use of more expensive hotels (a problems for 67 percent of the surveyed firms), and unnecessary travel (a problem for 59 percent of the surveyed firms). The corporate travel managers interviewed felt that the frequent-flier programs resulted in an average "waste" of about 8 percent of all of their travel expenditures (Stephenson and Fox 1992, 41).

the cheapest outside competitor? Answers have varied over time (although the one we intend to stress relates to incentives).

At one time, the answer to the make-or-buy problem would have focused on technological considerations: Firms often produce more than one product because of what economists call **economies of scope**.[12] But even firms with diverse product lines are actually quite specialized in that they purchase most of the inputs they use in the market rather than produce them in-house. General Motors, for example, does not produce its own steel, tires, plastic, or carpeting. Instead, it is cheaper for General Motors, and the other automobile manufacturers, to purchase these products from firms that specialize in them and to concentrate on the assembly of automobiles. Neither do many restaurants grow their own vegetables, raise their own beef, catch their own fish, and none that we know of produce their own toothpicks.

Economies of scope emerge because the skills developed in the production, distribution, and sale of one product lower the cost of producing other products.

Given the advantages of specialization in productive activities and buying most of the necessary inputs in the marketplace, a reasonable question is. Why do firms do as much as they do internally? Why don't firms buy almost all the inputs they need, as they need them, from others and use them to add value in very specialized ways? Instead of having employees in the typical sense, for example, a firm could hire workers on an hourly or daily basis at a market-determined wage reflecting their alternative value at the time. Instead of owning and maintaining a fleet of trucks, a transport company could rent trucks, paying only for the time they were in use. Loading and unloading the trucks could be contracted out to firms that specialized in loading and unloading trucks: the transport firm would specialize in actually transporting products. Similarly, the paperwork required for such things as internal control, payroll, and taxes could be contracted out to those who specialized in providing these services. Indeed, taking this concept to the limit would eliminate firms as we typically think of them.

The problem with total reliance on the market should now be familiar: Significant costs – transaction costs – are associated with making market exchanges. In general, the higher the cost of transacting through markets, the more a firm will make for itself with its own employees rather than buying from other firms. The reason that restaurants don't make their own toothpicks is that the cost of transactions is extremely low. It is hard to imagine the transaction costs of acquiring toothpicks ever getting so high that restaurants would make their own.[13]

[12] For example, a firm that has the equipment necessary to produce one type of electrical appliance may find that this equipment can be fully utilized if it is also used to produce other types of electrical appliances.

[13] One might have thought the same about beef until McDonald's opened an outlet in Moscow before the downfall and break-up of the Soviet Union. Because of the primitive nature of

Pipelines

Negotiating an agreement between two parties can be costly, but the most costly part of a transaction often involves attempts to avoid opportunistic behavior by the parties after the agreement has been reached. Agreements commonly call for one or both parties to make investments in expensive plant and equipment that are highly specific to a particular productive activity. After the investment is made, it has little, if any value in alternative activities. Investments in highly specific capital are often very risky, and therefore unattractive, even though the cost of the capital is less than it is worth. The problem is that once someone commits to an investment in specific capital to provide a service to another party, the other party can take advantage of the investor's inflexibility by paying less than the original agreement called for. There are so-called "quasi-rents" that are appropriable, or that can be taken by another party through unscrupulous, opportunistic dealing.[14] The desire to avoid this risk of opportunistic behavior can be a major factor in a firm's decision to make rather than buy what it needs.

Consider an example of a pipeline to transport natural gas to an electric generating plant. Such a pipeline is very expensive to construct, but assume that it lowers the cost of producing electricity by more than enough to provide an attractive return on the investment. To be more specific, assume that the cost of constructing the pipeline is $1 billion. Assuming an interest rate of 10 percent (which we select only for clarity of calculations), the annual capital cost of the pipeline is $100 million.[15] Further assume that the annual cost of maintaining and operating the pipeline is $25 million. Obviously it would not pay investors to build the pipeline for less than a $125 million annual payment, but it would be attractive to build it for any annual payment greater than that.[16] Finally,

markets in Russia when McDonald's opened its first Moscow outlet, relying on outside suppliers for beef of a specified quality was highly risky. Because of the then high transaction costs embedded in the antiquated and bureaucratic Russian economy, McDonald's raised its own cattle to supply much of its beef requirements for its Moscow restaurant.

14 Appropriable quasi-rents are the differences between the purchase and subsequent selling price of an asset, when the selling price is lower than the purchase price simply because of the limited resale market for the asset (Klein, Crawford, and Alchian, 1978).

15 Technically, this scenario assumes that the pipeline lasts forever. Although this assumption is obviously wrong, it doesn't alter the cost figure much, if the pipeline lasts a long time. The assumption helps us to simplify the example without distorting the main point.

16 The 10 percent interest rate is assumed to be an investor's opportunity cost of capital investment. So any return greater than 10 percent is sufficient to make an investment attractive. It is assumed that the annual $25 million for maintaining and operating the pipeline includes all opportunity costs. (If the payments to compensate the investor for maintenance and operation costs are made as these costs are incurred, then the costs for these items are not affected by the interest rate.)

assume that if the pipeline is constructed, it will lower the cost of producing electricity by $150 million dollars a year. The pipeline costs less than it saves and is clearly a good investment for the economy. But would you invest your money to build it?

Any price between $125 and $150 million a year would be attractive both to investors in the pipeline and to the electric generating plant that would use it. If, for example, the generating plant agrees to pay investors $137.5 million each year to build and operate the pipeline, both parties would realize annual profits of $12.5 million from the project. But the investors would be taking a serious risk because of the lack of flexibility after the pipeline is built. The main problem is that a pipeline is a *dedicated* investment, meaning that there is a big difference in the return needed to make the pipeline worth building and the return needed to make it worth operating after it is built. Although it takes at least $125 million per year to motivate the building of the pipeline, it will pay, after it has been built, to maintain and operate it for anything more than $25 million. Why? Because that is all it takes to operate the line. The pipeline investment itself is a sunk cost, literally and figuratively, not to be recaptured once it has been made. So after investors have made the commitment to construct the pipeline, the generating plant would be in a position to capture almost the entire value of initial pipeline investment by repudiating the original agreement and offering to pay only slightly more than $25 million per year.[17]

Of course, our example is much too extreme. The generating plant is not likely to risk its reputation by blatantly repudiating a contract. And even if it did, the pipeline investors would have legal recourse, with a good chance of recovering much, if not all, of their loss. Furthermore, as the example is constructed, the generating plant has more to lose from opportunistic behavior by the pipeline owners than vice versa. If the pipeline refuses service to the plant, the cost of producing electricity increases by $150 million per year. So the pipeline owners could act opportunistically by threatening to cut off the supply of natural gas unless they receive an annual payment of almost $150 million per year.

[17] Economists refer to this as "capturing all the quasi-rents from the investment". To elaborate on what we have already said about quasi-rents, rent is any amount in excess of what it takes to motivate the supply of a good or service before any investment has been made. In the case of the pipeline, anything in addition to $125 million a year is rent. On the other hand, a quasi-rent is any amount in excess of what it takes to motivate the supply of a good or service after the required investment is made. In the pipeline example, anything in excess of $25 million a year is quasi-rent. So once the investor has committed to the a pipeline, any offer over $25 million a year will motivate the supply of a pipeline service and allow the generating plant to capture almost all of the quasi-rent.

But our main point dare not be overlooked and should be taken seriously by cost minimizing and profit maximizing business people: Any time a transaction requires a large investment in dedicated capital (limited in use to a particular project), there is *the potential for costly problems in negotiating and enforcing agreements.*

True, opportunistic behavior (actions taken as a consequence of an investment that has been made and cannot be recaptured) will seldom be as blatant as in the above example, in which it is clear that a lower price is a violation of the contract. But in actual contracts involving long-term capital commitments, unforeseen changes in circumstances (higher costs, interrupted supplies, stricter government regulations, etc.) can justify changes in prices, or other terms of the contract. Typically, contracts will attempt to anticipate some of these changes and incorporate them into the agreed-upon terms, but it is impossible to anticipate and specify appropriate responses to all possible changes in relevant conditions. Therefore, there will usually be ambiguities in long-term contractual arrangements that open the door for opportunistic behavior of the type just discussed, and that can be resolved only through protracted and expensive legal action.

So, committing to investments in dedicated capital carries great risk of opportunistic behavior without some assurance that such behavior will not pay. One way to obtain this assurance is for the investment to be made by the same firm that will be using the output it produces. Alternatively, the firm that makes the investment in the specific capital can merge with the firm that depends on the output from that investment.

Coal and electricity production

The construction of electric generating plants next to coal mines provides an example of the potential benefits to a firm for producing an input rather than buying it when highly specific capital is involved. There is an obvious advantage in "mine-mouth" arrangements from reducing the cost of transporting coal to the generating plant. But if the mine and the generating plant are separately owned, the potential for opportunistic behavior exists after the costly investments are made. The mine owner could, for example, take advantage of the fact that the generating plant is far removed from a rail line connecting it to other coal supplies by increasing the price of coal. To avoid such risks, common ownership of both the mine and the generating plant is much more likely in the case of "mine-mouth" generating plants than in the case of generating plants that can rely on alternative sources of coal. And, when ownership is separate in a "mine-mouth" arrangement, the terms of exchange between the generating plant and mine are typically spelled out in very detailed and long-term contracts that cover a wide range of future contingencies (Joskow 1985).

Hold-ups and equipment rentals

There are other ways for a firm to benefit from the advantages of buying an input rather than producing it while reducing the risks of being "held-up" by a supplier who uses specialized equipment to produce a crucial input. It can make sense for the firm to buy the specialized equipment and then rent it to the supplier. If the supplier attempts to take advantage of the crucial nature of the input, the firm can move the specialized equipment to another supplier rather than be forced to pay a higher than expected price for the input. This is exactly the arrangement that automobile companies have with some of their suppliers. Ford, for example, buys components from many small and specialized companies, but commonly owns the specialized equipment needed and rents it to the contracting firms (Cooter and Ulen 1988, 245–6).

Firms are also aware that those who supply them with services are reluctant to commit themselves to costly capital investments that, once made, leave them vulnerable to *hold-up* (demands that the terms and conditions of the relationship be changed after an investment that cannot be recaptured has been made). In such a case, the firm that provides the capital equipment and rents it to the supplier can benefit from the fact that less threatened suppliers will charge lower prices. This consideration may also be a motivation for auto manufacturers to own the equipment that some of their suppliers use. It also provides a very good incentive-based explanation, and justification, for a business arrangement that has been widely criticized.

Company towns

An arrangement that reduced the threat of opportunistic behavior on the part of firms against workers has been the much-criticized "company town." In the past, it was common for companies (typically mining companies) to set up operations in what were at the time very remote locations. In the company towns, the company owned the stores in which employees shopped and the houses in which they lived. The popular view of these company towns is that they allowed the companies to exploit their workers with outrageous prices and rents, often charging them more for basic necessities than they earned from backbreaking work in the mines. The late Tennessee Ernie Ford captured this popular view in his famous song "Sixteen Tons."[18]

Without denying that the lives of nineteenth-century miners were tough, company stores and houses can be seen as a way for the companies to reduce (but not totally eliminate) their ability to exploit their workers by behaving opportunistically. Certainly workers would be reluctant to purchase a house in a remote location with only one employer. The worker who committed to such an investment would be far more vulnerable to opportunistic wage reductions by the employer than would the worker who rented company housing. Similarly, few merchants would be willing to establish a store in such a location, knowing that once the investment was made they would be vulnerable to opportunistic demands for price reductions that just covered their variable costs, leaving no return on their capital cost.

Again, in an ideal world without transaction costs – and without opportunistic behavior – mining companies would have specialized in extracting ore and would have let suppliers of labor buy their housing and other provisions through other specialists. But in the real world of transaction costs (including the temptations of opportunistic behavior), it was better for mining companies also to provide basic services for their employees. This is not to say that there was no exploitation. But the exploitation was surely less under the company town arrangement than if, for example, workers had bought their own houses (Fishback 1992, chapters 8, 9). Exploitation of workers on rent and company store prices could restrict the supply of workers and increase the wages company would have to pay.

Farm unions

The threat to one party of a transaction from opportunistic behavior on the part of the other party explains other business and social practices. Consider the fact that, despite valiant efforts, the vast majority of farm workers have never been able to effectively unionize in the United States. No doubt many reasons explain this failure, but one reason is that a union of farm workers would be in a position to harm farmers through opportunistic behavior. A crop is a highly specialized and, before harvested, immobile investment, and one whose value is easy to expropriate at harvest time. In most cases, if a crop is not harvested within a short window of opportunity, its value perishes. Therefore, a labor union could use its control over the supply of farm workers

[18] The lyrics of which went, "Sixteen tons and what do you get? Another day older and deeper in debt. Saint Peter don't you call me 'cause I can't go. I owe my soul to the company store."

to capture most of a crop's value in higher wages by threatening to strike right before the harvest. Although this threat would not necessarily be carried out in every case, it is too serious for those who have made large commitments of capital to agricultural crops to ignore. Not surprisingly, farm owners have strongly resisted the unionization of farm workers.

A good general rule for a manager is to buy the productive inputs the firm needs rather than make them. When inputs are produced in-house, some of the efficiency advantages of specialization provided through market exchange are lost. But as with most general rules, there are lots of exceptions to that of buying rather than making. In many cases, the loss from making rather than buying will be more than offset by the savings in transaction costs. Typically, firms should favor making those things that require capital that is of little value outside the firm and, therefore, will not have a ready resale market.

The value of reputation, again

A theme that runs through this chapter is that when firms make investments to serve very specific purposes, they open themselves to opportunistic behavior – or more to the point, to hold-ups. The threat of hold-ups invariably converts to risk costs, which have to be covered one way or another and can undermine firms' competitive positions in their product markets.

As noted, American auto makers have generally solved the hold-up problem for their suppliers by buying the specialized equipment their suppliers need to provide the auto makers with parts (Roberts 2004, 204–6). Toyota has solved its suppliers' hold-up threat by developing a reputation among its suppliers for not acting opportunistically. To increase its suppliers' confidence in its pledge to not act opportunistically, Toyota encourages its suppliers to talk with one another through an association of suppliers. Each supplier can reason that such ongoing interactions among them can increase the cost that Toyota will incur from taking advantage of any one supplier, thus reducing the probability that Toyota will engage in forms of opportunistic behavior, especially hold-ups. Toyota's formal and informal contracts with suppliers are thus made *self-enforcing* (to a greater degree than they otherwise would be).

As a consequence, Toyota's suppliers have no problem with investing in equipment – for example, dies for Toyota parts – that can be used only for meeting Toyota's orders. Toyota's reputation for fair dealing translates into lower risk costs throughout its supply chain which, in turn, translates into lower production costs for suppliers and lower prices for Toyota's parts. The economies of reputation can reveal themselves to consumers in the relatively lower prices of the company's cars.

The franchise decision

The decision a firm faces over whether to expand through additional outlets owned and operated by the firm or ones that are franchised to outside investors who will operate them has many of the features of the decision to make or buy inputs. Franchising is simply a type of firm expansion – with special contractual features and with all the attendant problems. Franchise contracts between the "franchiser" (franchise seller) and the "franchisee" (franchise buyer) typically have several key features:

- The franchisee generally makes some up-front payment, plus some royalty that is a percentage of monthly sales, for the right to use a brand name and/or trademark – for example, the name "McDonald's" along with the "golden arches."
- The franchisee also agrees to conduct business along the lines specified by the franchise, including the nature and quality of the good or service, operating hours, sources of purchases of key resources in the production process, and the prices that will be charged.
- The franchiser, on the other hand, agrees to provide managerial advice and to undertake national advertising, to provide training, and to ensure that quality standards are maintained across all franchisees.
- The franchiser typically retains the right to terminate a franchise agreement for specified reasons, if not at will.

The own-or-franchise decision is similar to the make-or-buy decision because both types of decisions involve problems of monitoring, risk sharing, and opportunistic behavior. At one time, scholars believed that firms expanded by way of franchising only as a means of raising additional capital through tapping the franchisee's credit worthiness. If the firm owned the additional outlet, it would have to bring in more investors or lenders at higher capital costs. Supposedly, franchisees could raise the money more cheaply than could the franchiser (Thompson 1971).

However, economist Paul Rubin (1978) has argued that franchising does not reduce the overall cost of capital – at least not as directly as previously argued. A firm in the restaurant business, for example, can contemplate expanding through franchising only if it has a successful anchor store. It can establish another outlet through the sale of its own securities, equities, or bonds, in which case the investors will have an interest in both the successful anchor restaurant and the new one. That investment in a proven and new franchised restaurant is likely to be less risky than any single investment in a totally independent restaurant which, because it has the same menu as the anchor restaurant, has a good chance of success. Hence, the cost of capital for the franchisee, everything else held constant, is likely to be higher than it is for the central restaurant firm.

Why franchise at all? Rubin argues (1978) that the reason for franchising is that the agency cost is lowered (but not totally eliminated) by expanding through franchising. The manager of the company-owned restaurant will likely be paid a salary plus some commission on (or bonus related to) the amount of business. The manager's incentive is related, but not strongly, to the interests of the owners. Hence, the manager will have to be closely monitored. The franchisee, on the other hand, becomes the residual claimant on the new restaurant business and, accordingly, has a stronger incentive not to shirk himself and to reduce shirking and other forms of opportunistic behavior by the employees.

As just noted, monitoring costs are *not eliminated* through franchising. The franchisee has some reason to shirk even though he is a residual claimant to the profits generated by his outlet. Customers often go to franchised outlets because they have high confidence in the quality of the goods and services offered. McDonald's customers know that they may not get the best burger in town when they go to a McDonald's, but they do have strong expectations on the size and taste of the burgers and the cleanliness of the restaurant. McDonald's has a strong incentive to build and maintain a desired reputation for its stores, and therein lies the monitoring catch. Each franchisee, especially those that have limited repeat business, can "cheat" (or free-ride on McDonald's overall reputation) by cutting the size of the burgers or letting their restaurants deteriorate. The cost savings for the individual cheating store can translate into a reduced demand for other McDonald's restaurants. This is a Prisoner's Dilemma in which all stores can be worse off if noncooperative behavior becomes a widespread problem. So, McDonald's must set (and has strong incentives to do so) production and cleanliness standards and then back them up with inspections and fines, if not outright termination of the franchise contract.

McDonald's (and any other franchiser) controls quality by requiring the individual restaurants to buy its ingredients – for example, burger patties and buns – from McDonald's itself or from approved suppliers. McDonald's has good reason to want its franchisees to buy the ingredients from McDonald's, not because (contrary to legal opinion) it gives McDonald's some sort of monopoly control, but because McDonald's has a problem in monitoring outside suppliers (Rubin 1978, 254).[19] Outside suppliers have an incentive to shirk on the quality standards with the consent of the franchisees that, individually, have an interest in cutting their individual costs. Moreover, by selling key ingredients,

[19] For a review of legal opinion on the so-called "tie-in sales" of franchise relationships, see Klein and Saft (1985).

the franchiser has an indirect way of determining whether its royalties are being accurately computed. These "tie-in sales" are simply a means of reducing monitoring costs. Of course, the franchisees also have an interest in their franchiser having the lowest possible monitoring cost: it minimizes the chances of free-riding by the franchisees and maintains the value of the franchise.

Similarly, a franchiser such as McDonald's has (as do the franchisees) an interest in holding all franchisees to uniform prices that are higher than each individual might choose. By maintaining uniform retail prices, McDonald's provides consumers with the confidence that they know what to expect, and a slightly higher price encourages its franchisees to maintain desired quality standards.

The chances for opportunistic behavior can be lowered through franchising, but hardly eliminated (Brickley and Dark 1987). If the franchisee buys the rights to the franchise and then invests in the store that has limited resale value, the franchiser can appropriate the rents simply by demanding higher franchise payments or failing to enforce production and quality standards with the franchisees, increasing the take of the franchiser but curbing the resale value of the franchise. On the other hand, if the franchisee pays for the building that has a limited resale value, the franchisee can, after the fact, demand lower franchise fees and special treatment (to the extent that the franchiser must incur a cost in locating another franchisee).

These points help explain the up-front payment and royalty provisions in franchise contracts. The value of the franchise to the franchisee – and what the franchisee will pay, at a maximum, for the franchise – is equal to the expected present value of the difference between two income streams, the income that could be earned with and without the franchise. The greater the difference, the greater the up-front payment the franchisee is willing to make. However, the franchisee is not likely to want to pay the full difference up-front. This is because the franchiser would then have little incentive to live up to the contract (to maintain the flow of business and to police all franchisees). The franchiser could run off with all the gains and no costs. As a consequence, both the franchiser and franchisee will likely agree to an up-front payment that is less than the difference in the two income streams identified above and to add a royalty payment. The royalty payment is something the franchisee, not just the franchiser, will want to include in the contract simply because the franchiser will then have a stake in maintaining the franchisee's business. A combination of some up-front payment and royalty is likely to maximize the gains to both franchisee and franchiser.

Franchising also has risk problems no matter how carefully the contract may be drawn. Typically, franchisees invest heavily in their franchise, which means that the franchisee has a risky investment portfolio because it is not highly diversified. This can make the franchisee reluctant to engage in additional capital investment that could be viewed as risky only because of the lack of spread of the investment. As a consequence, franchisers will tend to favor franchisees that own multiple outlets. A franchisee with multiple outlets can spread the risk of its investments and can more likely internalize the benefits of its investments in maintaining store quality (customers are more likely to patronize, or fail to do so, another of the owner's outlets).

Obviously, both ownership and franchise methods of expansion have costs and benefits for investors. We can't settle the issue here of how a firm such as McDonald's should expand, by ownership of additional outlets or by franchising them. All we can do is point out that franchising should not be as important when markets are "local." It should not, therefore, be a surprise that franchising grew rapidly in the 1950s with the spread of television, which greatly expanded the market potential for many goods and services and then, when transportation costs began declining rapidly (for example with the development of the interstate highway system), allowing people to move among local markets (Mathewson and Winter 1985, 504).

Franchising will tend to be favored when there is a low investment risk for the franchisee and when there are few incentives for free-riding by both franchisee and franchisers. We should expect franchises to grow in favor as the monitoring costs increase (implying that the farther the store location is from the franchiser, the more likely that expansion will take place through franchising, a conclusion that has been supported by empirical studies, Brickley and Dark 1987, 411–16). Also, we would expect that the fewer the repeat customers in a given location, the greater the likelihood that the store will be company-owned. When a store has few repeat customers, the incentive for the franchisee to cheat is strong, which means that the franchiser will have to maintain close monitoring to suppress the incentive for the franchisee to cheat or free-ride – which implies that there may be fewer cost advantages to franchising the location.[20] If monitoring costs go down, we should expect firms to increase their ownership of their outlets.

[20] Unfortunately, the only available study on the relationship between the extent of such business and the likelihood of franchising (Brickley and Dark 1987) does not confirm the theory. These researchers investigated how the location of outlets near freeways affected the likelihood that they would be franchised. They assumed that locations near freeways would have limited repeat business. Hence, they expected that locations near freeways would tend to be company owned, but they found the exact opposite: outlets near freeways tended to be franchised. The inconsistency between the findings and the prediction could be explained by the fact that the theory is missing something. However, it could also be, as the researchers speculate, that the problem is their measure of repeat business; locations near freeways may not be a good measure of such business. Such locations might get more repeat business than was assumed when freeway locations were selected as a proxy.

Perspective Evolutionary Foundations of Cooperation

Much of our analysis in this book is grounded in the *principal–agent problem*, or the tendency of underlings to pursue their own private goals at the expense of the goals of the firm and its owners. We take that approach for a simple reason: by understanding how employees *might* behave, managers can draw up policies and incentives that protect the firm and its owners from agency costs.

We are not suggesting that people are not completely unmotivated by an innate sense of duty or obligation to do what they are supposed to do as a employee or lack totally any predisposition to cooperate with others in acknowledged common interests. On the contrary, people seem to have a built-in tendency to cooperate – at least to a degree. A substantial literature has grown up around the proposition that evolution has left modern humans "hard wired," to one degree or another, to work together for their own survival, if not greater prosperity. In the eons before humans developed agriculture – that is, during the Pleistocene Epoch, which lasted from about 1.6 million until about 10,000 or years ago – humans spent 40,000 years as hunter gatherers (Klein 2000) in groups of 25–150 (with kinship likely playing an important role in groups' coherence, Hamilton, Jay, and Madison 1964; Dawkins 1976) – small enough for group members to monitor each other but large enough for free-riding to emerge (Dunbar 1998; Bowles and Gintis 2001). Hunter gatherers needed to cooperate to bring down game that was generally too large or dangerous for individuals to kill alone, to defend themselves against the predation of other groups of hunter gatherers, and successively to predate against other bands of humans. Evolutionary theorists have maintained that those humans who had a predisposition to cooperate efficiently (by developing the requisite rules and incentives, including penalties, that engendered cooperation, Hirshleifer 1999) survived with greater frequency than those groups that were not so inclined to cooperate efficiently and, hence, saw their genes (and predisposition for cooperation) passed down through the succeeding generations. As Paul Rubin observes, summarizing a mountain of research in evolutionary psychology, behavioral biology, and the newly emerging subdiscipline in economic dubbed "bioeconomics:"

> The groups formed by more cooperative players will do better than groups with less cooperative members, and members of the cooperative group will have more offspring. As a result, the degree of cooperativeness can grow in the population over time. This assortment by cooperativeness has another interesting feature. Everyone

(cooperator or cheater) would prefer to deal with a cooperator. Therefore, individuals will have an incentive to appear to be cooperators even if they are not. (2002, 60–1)

The prospect of people pretending to be cooperators means that people should be expected to evolve skills to detect deception and cheating (Trivers 1971; Frank 1988; Cosmides and Tooby 1992).

Survival economist and criminologist James Q. Wilson (1993) has argued, with reference both to casual observation and a host of psychological experiments, that most people have evolved a "moral sense," which can show up in their willingness to forgo individual advantage (or opportunities to shirk) for the good of the group, which can be a firm. Moreover, a variety of factors – including considerations of equity and fairness – influence people's willingness to cooperate (Ostrom 2000; Fehr and Schmidt 2002). As organizational behaviorists have shown, "culture" has an impact on the extent of cooperation. People from "collectivistic" societies, such as China, may be more inclined to cooperate than will be people from "individualistic" societies, such as the United States (Earley 1989). Training in "group values" can affect the extent of cooperation, although evolutionary forces have left all cultures with admixtures of people who exhibit varying degrees of selfishness and non-selfishness (Sethi and Somanathan 1996; Gintis 2000b; Bowles and Gintis 2001; Henrich *et al.* 2001).

Experiments have shown that people will be more likely cooperative with more equal shares of whatever it is that is being divided, with women more inclined to favor "equal shares" than men (Knauft 1991; Boehm 1993). People are willing to extend favors in cooperative ventures in the knowledge that the favor will be returned (Trivers 1971; Steiner *et al.* 1998; Gintis 2000a, 200b). They will work harder when they believe that they are not underpaid (Fehr and Schmidt 2002). People are more likely to cooperate with close family members and friends than with strangers, and they will be less likely to cooperate with others, whether friends or stranger, when the cost of cooperating is high. Experiments have shown that people are not only willing to cooperate, to a degree, but that some are willing to go a step further, and devote some of their own resources to punish shirkers and cheaters (McCabe and Smith 1999). Cooperation is more likely when people are allowed to communicate with one another and made to feel as though they are members of the relevant group (Thaler 1992; Ledyard 1995; Hoffman, McCabe, and Smith 1998).

Why is it that people are inclined to cooperate more or less naturally? Wilson repeats a favorite example of game theorists to explain why "cooperativeness" might be partially explained as an outcome of natural selection. Consider two people in early times, Trog and Helga, who are subject to attack by saber-toothed tigers. The "game" they must play in the woods is a variant of the Prisoner's Dilemma game. If they both run on spotting the tiger, then the tiger will kill and eat the slower runner. If they both stand their ground – and cooperate in their struggle – then perhaps they can defeat the tiger, or scare him off. However, each has an incentive to run when the other stands his or her ground, leaving the brave soul to be eaten.

What do people do? What *should* they do? Better yet, what do we *expect* them to do? We suspect that different twosomes caught in the woods by saber-toothed tigers over the millennia have tried a number of strategies. However, running is, over the long run, a strategy for possible extinction, given that the tiger can pick off the runners one by one. Societies that have found ways of cooperating have prospered and survived. Those that haven't have languished or retrogressed into economic oblivion, leaving the current generation with a disproportionate number of ancestors who behaved cooperatively. Those who didn't cooperate long ago when confronted with attacks by saber-toothed tigers were eaten; those who did cooperate with greater frequency lived to propagate future generations.

Our point is that human society is complex, driven by a variety of forces – based in both psychology and economics – that vary in intensity with respect to one another and that are at times conflicting. However, there are evolutionary reasons, if nothing else, to expect that people who cooperate will be disproportionately represented in societies that survive. Organizations can exploit – and, given the forces of competition, must exploit – people's limited but inherent desire or tendency to work together, to be a part of something that is bigger and better than they are. Organizations should be expected to try to reap the *synergetic consequences* of their individual and collective efforts.

However, if that were the whole story – if all that mattered were people's tendencies to cooperate – then management would hardly be a discipline worthy of much professional reflection. Little or no need or role for managers, other than that of cheerleader, would exist. The problem is that our cooperative tendencies are not sufficient to overcome the temptation of uncooperative behavior we have been stressing.

It may well be that two people can work together "naturally," fully capturing their synergetic potential. The same may be said of groups of three and four people, maybe ten or even thirty. The point that emerges from the "logic of collective action" is that as the group size – team or firm – gets progressively larger, the consequences of impaired incentives mount, giving rise to the growing prospects that people will shirk or in other ways take advantage of the fact that they and others cannot properly assess what they contribute to the group.[21]

PART II ORGANIZATIONAL ECONOMICS AND MANAGEMENT

Fringe benefits, incentives, and profits

Varying the form of pay is one important way in which firms seek to motivate workers – and overcome the Prisoner's Dilemma/principal–agent problems

[21] Wilson (1993) also stresses that experimental evidence shows that people in small towns are, indeed, more helpful than people in larger cities, and the more densely packed the city population, the less helpful people will be. Presumably, people in smaller cities believe that their assistance is more detectable. People in larger cities are also less inclined to make eye contact with passers by and to walk faster, presumably to reduce their chances of being assaulted by people who are more likely to commit crimes.

In his survey of the literature on the contribution of individuals to team output, Gary Miller (1992) reports that when people think that their contribution to group goals – for example, pulling on a rope – cannot be measured, then individuals will reduce their effort. When members of a team pulling on a rope were blindfolded and then told that others were pulling with them, the individual members exerted 90 percent of their best individual effort when one other person was supposed to be pulling. The effort fell to 85 percent when two – six other players were pulling. The shirking that occurs in large groups is now so well documented that it has a name – "social loafing."

The central point of this discussion is not that managers can never expect workers to cooperate. We have conceded that they will – but only *to a degree, given normal circumstances.* However, there are countervailing incentive forces which, unless attention is given to the details of firm organization, can undercut the power of people's natural tendencies to cooperate and achieve their synergetic potential.

The analysis of this section can be readily interpreted in terms of figure 6.1(a) and 6.1(b). To the extent that modern humans have been "programmed" by evolutionary forces to cooperate and thus now have a "taste for cooperation" (a phrase Rubin 2002 uses), the upward sloping internal coordinating cost curve in Figure 6.1(a) will be shifted to the left (and perhaps will be flatter than otherwise). Nevertheless, that curve should still be upward sloping because of the growing temptation of people to shirk (or in other ways misuse and abuse firm resources) as the size of the firm expands. At the same time, any innate tendency of people to cooperate (possibly because of their built-in "moral sense" (Wilson 1993) should lead to lower monitoring costs and larger size firms (and other nonprofit organizations and political units) and less reliance on market transactions. This implies less need for outsourcing.

that have been at the heart of this chapter. And workers' pay can take many forms, from simple cash to an assortment of fringe benefits. However, it needs to be noted that workers tend to think and talk about their fringe benefits in remarkably different terms than they do about their wages. Workers who recognize that they "earn" their wages will describe their fringe benefits (or "fringes") with reference to what their employers "give" them. "Gee, our bosses *give* us three weeks of vacation, thirty minutes of coffee breaks a day, the right to flexible schedules, and discounts on purchases of company goods. They also give us medical and dental insurance and cover 80 percent of the cost. Would you believe we only have to pay 20 percent!"

Wages are the result of hard work, but fringe benefits, it seems, are a matter of employer generosity. Fringe benefits are assumed to come from a substantially different source, such as the pockets of the stockholders, than wages, which come out of the revenues that workers add to the bottom line.

Employers use some of the same language, and their answers to any question of why fringe benefits are provided are typically equally misleading, though probably more gratuitous. The main difference is that employers inevitably talk in terms of the cost of their fringe benefits. "Would you believe that the annual cost of health insurance to our firm is $4,486 *per employee*? That means that we give away millions, if not tens of millions, each year on all of our employees' health insurance. Our total fringe benefit package costs us an amount equal to 36.4 percent of our total wage bill!" The point that is intended, though often left unstated, is: "Aren't we nice?"

If either the workers or the employers who make such comments are in fact telling the truth, then the company should be a prime candidate for a takeover, that is, a buyout. Someone – a more pragmatic and resourceful business person – should buy the owners out, quit being so generous to workers by giving them fringe benefits, increase profits for the shareholders, and push up the company's stock price.

Our argument here will be a challenge to many readers, because it will develop a radically different way of thinking about fringe benefits. It will require readers to set aside any preconceived view that fringe benefits are a gift. The approach used here employs what we call *marginal* analysis, or the evaluation of fringe benefits in terms of their *marginal (or added) cost* and *marginal (or added) value.* It is grounded in the principle that profits can be increased as long as the marginal value of doing something in business is greater than the marginal cost.

This principle implies that a firm should extend its output for as long as the marginal value of doing so (in terms of additional revenue) exceeds the marginal cost of each successive extension. It should do the same with a fringe benefit: provide it as long as it "pays," meaning as long as the marginal cost of the fringe benefit is less than its marginal value (in terms of the wages that workers are willing to forgo) to workers. This way of looking at firm decision making means that changes in the cost of fringe benefits can have predictable consequences. An increase in the cost of any fringe benefit can give rise to a cut in the amount of the benefit that is provided. An increase in the value of the benefit to workers can lead to more of it being provided.

Workers as profit centers

We don't want to be overly crass in our view of business (although that may appear to be our intention from the words we have to use within the limited space we have in which to develop our arguments). We only want to be realistic when we surmise that the overwhelming majority of firms that provide their workers with fringe benefits do so for the very same reason that they hire their workers in the first place: *To add more to their profits than they could if they didn't.* Like it or not, most firms are in the business of making money off their employees – in all kinds of ways.

The reason many firms don't provide their workers with fringe benefits – with health insurance being the most common missing benefit, in small businesses especially – is that they can't add to profits by doing so. The critical difference between employers who do provide benefits and those who don't is not likely to have anything to do with how nice each group wants to be to its employees. There is no reason to suspect that one group is nicer, or more crass, than the other.

When making decisions on fringe benefits, employers face two unavoidable *economic* realities: First, fringe benefits are costly, and some, such as health insurance, are extraordinarily costly. Second, there are limits to the value that workers place on such benefits. The reason is simply that workers value a lot of things, and what they *buy*, directly from vendors or indirectly via their employers, is largely dependent on who is the lowest-cost provider.

Workers *buy* fringe benefits from employers. They do so when the value they place on the benefits exceeds their cost to the firms. When that condition holds, firms can make money by, effectively, "selling" benefits – for example, health insurance – to their workers. How? Most firms don't send sales people around the office and plant selling health insurance or weeks of vacation to their employees the way they sell fruit in the company cafeteria, but they nevertheless make the sales. If workers truly value a particular benefit, then the firms that provide it will see an increase in the supply of labor available to them. They will be able to hire more workers at a lower wage and/or be able to increase the "quality" (productivity) of the workers that they do hire.

Firms are paid for the cost of providing fringe benefits primarily in two ways: One, their real wage bill goes down with the increased competition for the available jobs that results from the greater number of job seekers (who are attracted by the benefit). This reflects the willingness of workers to *pay* employers for the benefits. Two, employers gain by being more discriminatory in terms of whom they hire, employing more productive workers for the wages paid. (The appendix to this chapter, p. 259, contains a discussion of points made about the effects of fringe benefits on wages and employment with the aid of supply and demand curves.)

Optimum fringe benefits

We expect employers and workers to treat such benefits the way they do everything else, seeking some *optimum* combination of benefits and money wages. Again, this means that employers and workers should be expected to weigh their additional (or marginal) value against their additional (or marginal) cost. An employer will add to a benefit such as health insurance as long as the marginal value (measured in money wage concessions or increased production from workers) is greater than the marginal cost of the added benefit. Similarly, workers will "buy" more of any benefit from their employer as long as its marginal value (in terms of improved health or reduction in the cost of private purchase) is greater than its marginal cost (wage concessions).

Although we can't give specifics, we do know that managers are well advised to search earnestly for the "optimum" combination (which means that some experimentation would likely be in order), even though the process of finding the optimum is never precise. The firms that come closest to the optimum will make the most money from their employees and also provide their employees the greatest compensation for the money spent – and so will have the lowest cost structure and be the most competitive. By trying to make as much money as possible from their employees, firms not only stay more competitive, but also benefit their workers.

So far, we have considered only fringe benefits in which the added cost of the benefit to the firm is less than the value of the benefit to the workers. What if that is not the case? Looking at figure 6A.1 in the appendix (p. 260), suppose that the cost of the benefit to firms were greater than its value to workers (in the graph, the vertical distance *bc* would be greater than the vertical distance *ac*, which means that the increase in demand would have to be greater than the increase in supply). What would happen? The straight answer is: Nothing. The benefit would not be provided. The reason is obvious: Both sides, workers and owners, would lose. The resulting drop in the wage would be less than the cost of the benefit to the employers, and the resulting drop in the wage would be greater than the value of the benefit to the workers. (To see this point, just try drawing a graph with the vertical drop in the demand greater than the outward shift of the supply.) *Such a benefit would not – and should not – be provided, simply because it is a loser for both sides.*

Firms that persisted in providing such a benefit would have difficulty competing, because their cost structure would be higher than other producers. Such firms would be subject to takeovers. The takeover would very likely be friendly because those bidding for the firm in the takeover would be able to pay a higher price for the stock than the going market price, which would be depressed by the fact that one or more benefits provided to workers was not profitable. Those involved in the takeover could, after acquiring control, eliminate the excessively costly benefit(s) (or reduce it (them) to profitable levels), enhance the firm's profitability and competitive position, and then sell the firm's stock at a price higher than the purchase price.[22]

The workers would support such a takeover – and might be the ones managing it – because they could see two advantages: They could have a benefit eliminated that is not worth the cost that they would have to pay in terms of lower wages. They could also gain some employment security, given the improved competitive position of their firm. The workers might even take the firm over for the same reason anyone else might do so: They could improve the firm's profitability and stock price.

Fringe benefits provided by large and small firms

We can now understand why it is that so many large firms provide their employees with health insurance and so many small firms do not. At the most general level, it pays for large firms to provide the insurance, whereas it does not pay for small firms to do so. Large firms can sell a large number of health insurance policies, achieving economies associated with scale and of spreading the risk. That is a widely recognized answer.

[22] Engaging in a takeover can be very expensive, and we recognize that a firm is not likely to be taken over because of the failure of the firm to provide one efficiency-enhancing fringe benefit. But when enough of these types of mistakes are made, the inefficiency mounts, increasing the chance that the firm will be a takeover target.

At another level, the answer is more complicated and obscure. "Small" and "large" firms do not generally hire from the same labor markets. Small firms tend to provide lower-paying jobs. The workers in lower-paying jobs within small firms simply don't have the means to buy a lot of things that workers in larger firms have, and one of the things workers in small firms don't seem to buy in great quantities is insurance. Given their limited income, workers simply don't think that insurance is a good deal, and they would prefer to buy other things with higher monetary compensation. One of the reasons that low-income workers may gravitate to small firms is that if they worked for large firms they would have to give up wages to buy the insurance, because of company policies that apply to all workers.

Of course, the analysis gets even trickier when it takes into account that lower-income workers, many of whom work for small firms, tend to be younger workers – who also tend to be healthier and prefer a different combination of fringe benefits than older workers. The young can appreciate that the price they would have to pay for health insurance through their firms is inflated by a number of factors related to supply and demand. First, the price of health insurance has been inflated by a host of cost factors, not the least of which is the increased liability doctors face for virtually anything that goes wrong with patients when they are under the doctors' care. The radical application of expensive medical technologies to care for older, dying patients has also jacked up the cost of insurance and care for the young.

Second, older workers, many of whom are in large firms and tend to have a strong demand for health insurance, have increased the demand for insurance (and healthcare). The exemption of health insurance from taxable income (which helps higher-income workers in higher tax brackets more than lower-income workers) has also artificially inflated the demand for health insurance (and healthcare). The net result of the cost and demand effects has been to increase health insurance costs, making the insurance an unattractive deal for many young and low-income workers, many of whom work for small firms.

If the analysis of this section has led to any clear conclusion, it is that the workers pay for what they get. They may not hand over a check for the benefits, but they give up the money nonetheless, through a reduction in their pay. If workers didn't give up anything for the fringe benefit, we would have to conclude that it was not worth anything to the workers, the supply curve would not move out, and the wage rate would not fall. That would mean that the employers would have to cover the full cost of the fringe benefit, which would put them in the rather irrational position of adding to their costs without getting anything for it. Workers should not want that to happen, if for no other reason than that their job security would be threatened.

But critics might argue that managers don't know that certain fringe benefits are "good" for business and their workers. That is often the case, and the history of business is strewn with the corpses of firms that failed to serve the interests of their workers and customers and who were forced into bankruptcy by other firms who were better at finding the best way to increase value at lower cost, including providing the right combination of fringe benefits. However, we see the market as a powerful, though imperfect, educational system. If the critics know better than existing firms, they could make lots of money by pointing out to firms why they are wrong and how they could make money from their employees by providing (selling) fringe benefits not now being provided, or adjusting the combination of existing fringe benefits in marginal ways.[23]

We think that workers and owners should talk as frankly about fringe benefits as they do about their wages. Workers earn their wages. The same is true for fringe benefits. No gift is involved. Both wages and fringe benefits represent mutually beneficial exchanges between workers and their firms.

THE BOTTOM LINE

The key takeaways from chapter 6 are the following:

(1) Incentives are important. They are worthy of serious reflection, mainly as an unheralded source of profit enhancement. But that doesn't mean to suggest that incentives are *all* that matter. Surely, many things matter. As noted, leadership, product design, and customer service, as well as company adaptability, culture, and goals, also matter. However, all those good things in business may not matter very much or for long if the incentives are not right.

[23] We must note that we also don't believe that managers are the only ones who should search for the right combination of fringe benefits. Workers should have an interest in joining the search, because they can gain in spite of the fact that their efforts will include a search for how their firms can make more money off them. If workers want more of one benefit, it would seem that all they would have to do is tell their bosses and show them how additional profits can be made *from the workers.* Workers, however, who want benefits without paying for them shouldn't waste their bosses' time. Managers hear from a lot of people who want something for nothing.

(2) Firms exist because they tend to reduce the overall cost of doing business, most prominently external coordinating (or transaction) costs.
(3) Firm size is limited not only by economies of scale but also by agency costs.
(4) Firm size is crucially dependent on balancing internal and external coordinating costs. Firms can be expected to contract in size if market transactions costs are lowered, everything else equal.
(5) Firms are advised to buy as many of their inputs as they can from competitive sources of supply. They often make their inputs because of the potential for opportunistic behavior – or hold-up – in dealing with outside suppliers when investments in firm-specific resources must be made before payment for the produced good are made.
(6) Franchises exist not so much to increase capital available to franchisers, but to increase the incentives of franchise operators to produce cost effectively.
(7) In their effort to get incentives right, it is understandable why firms provide fringe benefits: such benefits can reduce firms' compensation costs while increasing the incentive for better workers to seek employment with firms that provide them.
(8) People will behave opportunistically. However, it is wrong to conclude that *all* people are *always* willing to behave opportunistically, which is also contradicted by everyday experience. The business world is full of both saints and sinners, and most people are some combination of both. Opportunistic behavior has been emphasized because that is the threat managers want to protect themselves against. Business people don't have to worry about the Mother Teresas of the world. They do have to worry about less than saintly people. (And they do have to worry about people who pretend to be like Mother Teresa before any deal is consummated.) They need to understand the consequences of opportunistic behavior in order that they can appropriately structure their contracts and embedded incentives.

REVIEW QUESTIONS

(1) Why are some firms "large" and other firms "small"? Use the concept of "coordinating costs" in your answer
(2) Suppose firms get smaller. Why might that happen?
(3) If worker monitoring costs go down, what will happen to the size of the firm?
(4) What have been the various effects of the computer/telecommunication revolution on the sizes of firms?

(5) Why would a firm hire its own accountants to keep the books but, at the same time, use outside lawyers to do its legal work?
(6) If your firm fears being "held-up" by an outside supplier of a critical part to your production process, what can your firm do to reduce the chance of such a hold-up?

Appendix

The supply of and demand for fringe benefits

To see the points relating to the labor market effects of fringe benefits with greater clarity, we must look to a graph, albeit a simple one, using only the supply and demand curves with which you must now be familiar. Figure 6A.1 shows normal labor supply and demand curves. The downward sloping labor demand curve, D_1, shows that more workers will be demanded by firms at lower wage rates than will be at higher wage rates, and it reflects the circumstance in which no fringe benefit is provided. The upward sloping curve, S_1, shows that more workers will come on the markets at higher wage rates than at lower ones and reflects an initial circumstance in which a given fringe benefit (such as health insurance) is not provided. These embedded assumptions regarding the slopes of the curves are totally reasonable and widely accepted as reflecting market conditions. At any rate, without the fringe benefit, the workers will receive a wage rate of W_1, where the market clears.

Consider the simplest of cases, the one in which the firm's cost in providing a fringe benefit is a uniform amount for each worker and in which the provision of the benefit has no impact on worker productivity, but increases the value of work and increases the supply of workers. The demand curve in figure 6A.1 drops down vertically by the per-worker cost of the benefit, from D_1 to D_2. This happens because the firms are simply not willing to pay as high a wage to their workers as they would be if they didn't have to cover the cost of the benefit. On the other hand, the supply of workers shifts outward, from S_1 to S_2, because work is now more attractive because of the benefit, leading to more workers applying for jobs. Workers are willing to work for a lower money wage *when the fringe benefit is provided* (and, again, for simplicity we assume that each worker values the benefit by the same amount). The vertical difference between S_1 and S_2 represents how much each worker values the benefit and is willing to give up in her wage rate for it; this vertical difference is a money measure of the value of the benefit to workers.

What happens, given these shifts in supply and demand? As can be seen in figure 6A.1, the market clearing wage falls from W_1 to W_2. Are workers and firms better off? A close examination of figure 6A.1 reveals that more workers are employed (Q_2 instead of $Q1$), which suggests that something good must have happened.

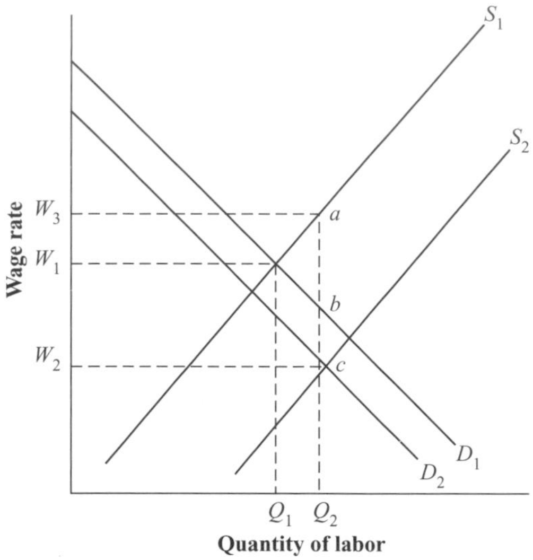

Figure 6.A1 Fringe benefits and the labor market

If fringe benefits are more valuable to workers and impose a cost on the employers, the supply of labor will increase from S_1 to S_2 while the demand curve falls from D_1 to D_2. The wage rate falls from W_1 to W_2, but the workers get fringe benefits that have a value of *ac*, which means that their overall payment goes up from W_1 to W_3.

Otherwise, we must wonder why firms would want to hire more workers, and more workers would be willing to be employed. It just doesn't make much sense to argue that firms and/or workers are not better off when both sides agree to more work (and when the benefit is provided voluntarily).

Notice that the total cost of the benefit, the vertical distance between the two demand curves, or *bc*, is less than the reductions in the wage, $W_1 - W_2$, from which we can draw two implications: First, the firm is clearly making money off its original employees ($W_2 + bc$ is less than W_1). Second, the firm's total cost per worker ($W_2 + bc$) falls, which explains why the firm is willing to expand its hires.

Notice also that while the workers accept a lower wage rate, W_2 instead of W_1, they gain the value of the benefit, which in figure 6A.1 is the vertical distance *ac.* The sum of the new lower wage, W_1, plus the value of the fringe, *ac*, is W_3, which is higher than the wage without the fringe ($W_2 + ac = W_3 > W_1$). Both sides gain.

How much of the fringe benefit should be provided? It would be nice if we could tell each person reading this book exactly what to do. It would be silly to try, given the variation of business and market circumstances. What we can do is look to rules that are generally applicable. The rule the firms should follow is no different from the rule they should follow in any other productive market circumstance: Firms should continue to expand the benefit as long as the *added (marginal) cost from the benefit is less than the marginal reduction in their wage bills, which can be no greater than the workers' evaluation of the marginal increase in the benefit.*

For example, the number of days of paid vacation should be extended as long as the value that workers place on additional vacation days is greater than the marginal cost to the employer of providing the additional days. Given that workers' evaluation of each additional day will fall (at least after a certain number of days) and the cost of the additional day will rise, after a certain number of days off a point will be reached beyond which equality between the additional cost of the next vacation day will exceed its marginal value (or the possible reduction in the wage bill). At that point, employers have maximized their profit from "selling" the benefit to their workers.

Of course, tax rules will affect the exact amount of the benefit, as well as the combination of benefits offered. Certainly, if the value of fringe benefits – for example, health insurance – are not subject to taxation, then employers should, naturally, provide more of them than otherwise, simply because part of the cost of the benefit is covered by a reduction in worker taxes. The result might be that workers actually get more of the benefit than they would buy, *if they were covering all of the cost themselves.* Employers must provide such benefits; otherwise, they will not keep their compensation costs competitive with that of rival employers.

CHAPTER

7

Consumer choice and demand in traditional and network markets

It is not the province of economics to determine the value of life in "hedonic units" or any other units, but to work out, on the basis of the general principles of conduct and the fundamental facts of social situations, the laws which determine prices of commodities and the direction of the social economic process. It is therefore not quantities, not even intensities, of satisfaction with which we are concerned . . . or any other absolute magnitude whatever, but the purely relative judgment of comparative significance of alternatives open to choice.
Frank Knight

People adjust to changes in some economic conditions with a reasonable degree of predictability. When department stores announce lower prices, customers will pour through the doors. The lower the prices go, the larger the crowd will be. When the price of gasoline goes up, drivers will make fewer and shorter trips. If the price stays up, drivers will buy smaller, more economical cars. Even the Defense Department will reduce its planned purchases of tanks and bombers when their prices rise.

Behavior that is not measured in dollars and cents is also predictable in some respects. Students who stray from the sidewalks to dirt paths on sunny days stick to concrete when the weather is damp. Professors who raise their course requirements and grading standards find their classes shrinking in size. Small children shy away from doing things for which they have recently been punished. When lines for movie tickets become long, some people go elsewhere for entertainment.

On an intuitive level, you very likely find these examples of behavior reasonable. Going one step beyond intuition, the economist would say that such responses are governed by the *law of demand*, a concept we first introduced in chapter 3 and now take up in greater detail, with greater precision, and with more varied applications.

PART I THEORY AND PUBLIC POLICY APPLICATIONS

Predicting consumer demand

The assumptions about rational behavior described in chapter 3 provide a useful basis for explaining behavior. People will do things whose expected benefits exceed their expected costs. They will avoid doing things for which the opposite is true. The law of demand, which is a logical consequence of the assumption of rational behavior, allows us to make such general predictions of consumer behavior.

Our ability to predict is always limited. We cannot specify with precision every choice the individual will make. For instance, we cannot say at the conceptual level anything about what a particular person wants or how sensitive her desire for what she values is to changes in prices. But we can predict the general direction of her behavior, given her wants, with the aid of the *law of demand* which we now derive.

Rational consumption: the concept of marginal utility

The essence of the economist's notion of rational consumer behavior is that consumers will allocate their incomes over goods and services so as to maximize their satisfaction, or utility. This implies that consumers compare the value of consuming an additional unit of various goods.

Generally speaking, the value the individual places on any one unit of a good depends on the number of units already consumed. For example, you may be planning to consume two hot dogs and two Cokes for your next meal. Although you may pay the same price for each unit of both goods, the value you place on the second unit of each good will generally be less than the value realized from the first unit of each (at least beyond some point as consumption proceeds).[1] For example, the value of the second hot dog – its marginal utility – depends on the fact that you have already eaten one. We represent marginal utility as *MU*, which equals the change in total utility from consuming one more unit.

[1] We focus on diminishing marginal utility because that is the relevant range of consumption for most people consuming most goods. If people experience increasing marginal utility for goods, then they will continue to consume them and will face choice problems only when diminishing marginal utility sets in.

Achieving consumer equilibrium

Marginal utility determines the variety of a quantity of goods and services you consume. The rule is simple. If the two goods, Cokes and hot dogs, both have the same price (a temporary assumption), you will fully allocate your income so that the marginal utility of the last unit consumed of each will be equal. This rule can be stated as

$$MU_c = MU_h$$

where MU_c equals the marginal utility of a Coke and MU_h equals the marginal utility of a hot dog. This is to say, if the price of a Coke is the same as the price of a hot dog, the last Coke you drink should give you the same amount of enjoyment as the last hot dog you eat. If this is not the case, you could increase your utility with the same amount of money by reducing your consumption of the good with the lowest marginal utility by 1 unit and buying another unit of the one with the highest marginal utility. When the marginal utilities of goods purchased by the consumer are equal, the resulting state is called **consumer equilibrium**. Unless conditions – income, taste, prices, etc. – change, the consumer equilibrium remains the same.

Consumer equilibrium is a state of stability in consumer purchasing patterns in which the individual has maximized her utility.

An example can illustrate how equilibrium is reached. Suppose for the sake of simplicity that you can buy only two goods, Cokes and hot dogs. Suppose further that each costs the same, $1, and you intend to spend your whole income. For purposes of illustrating the point, assume that utility (joy, satisfaction) can be measured. Finally, suppose that the marginal utility of the last Coke you consume is equal to 20 utils (a util being a unit of satisfaction, or utility) and the marginal utility of the hot dog is 12 utils. Obviously you have not maximized your utility, for the marginal utility of your last Coke is greater than (>) the marginal utility of your last hot dog:

$$MU_c > MU_h$$

You could have purchased 1 fewer hot dog and used the dollar saved to buy an additional Coke. In doing so, you would have given up 12 utils of satisfaction (the marginal utility of the last hot dog purchased), but you would have acquired an additional 20 utils from the new Coke. On balance, your total utility would have risen by 8 utils (20–12). You can continue to increase your utility without spending any more by adjusting your purchases of Coke and hot dogs until their marginal utilities are equal. We make the reasonable assumption here that (at least beyond some point) the marginal utility of both

Cokes and hot dogs decrease as more are consumed. This is known as the *law of diminishing marginal utility.*

According to the law of diminishing marginal utility, as more of a good is consumed, its marginal utility (or value relative to the marginal value of the good or goods given up) eventually diminishes. Thus, if $MU_h > MU_c$, and MU_h falls relative to MU_c as more hot dogs and fewer Cokes are consumed, sooner or later the result will be $MU_h = MU_c$. The law of diminishing marginal utility applies to all goods.[2]

Adjusting for differences in price and unit size

Different goods, including Cokes and hot dogs, are seldom sold at exactly the same price, so we now drop the assumption of equal prices. Now the condition for choosing the combination of Coke and hot dogs that maximize utility becomes:

$$\frac{MU_c}{P_c} = \frac{MU_h}{P_h}$$

where MU_c equals the marginal utility of a Coke, MU_h the marginal utility of a hot dog, P_c the price of a Coke, and P_h the price of a hot dog. The consumer must allocate her money so that the last penny spent on each commodity yields the same amount of satisfaction. We leave it to the reader to consider how the consumer can increase her utility without spending more money if the above equality is not satisfied, and how doing so will eventually result in the equality being satisfied.

So far, we have been talking in terms of buying whole units of Cokes and hot dogs, but the same principles apply to other kinds of choices as well. Marginal utility is involved when a consumer chooses a 12-ounce rather than a 16-ounce can of Coke, or a regular-size hot dog rather than a foot-long hot dog. The concept could also be applied to the decision of whether to add cole slaw and chili to the hot dog. The pivotal question the consumer faces in all these situations is whether the marginal utility of the additional quantity consumed

[2] For some goods, as noted, it may very well be the case that as one starts consuming units of a given good (beer, for example), the marginal utility of successive units initially rises. If marginal utility always rose, then we might expect a person to end up devoting her entire income to the consumption of the one good. Since people typically consume combinations of many goods (and illustrations involving only two goods are meant to represent typical behavior), we must assume that diminishing marginal utility sets in within the income constraint of the representative consumers.

is greater or less than the marginal utility of other goods that can be purchased for the same price.

Most consumers do not think in terms of utils when they are buying their lunch, but this does not mean that they are not weighing the alternatives (*as if* they were thinking in terms of the utils obtained from each additional unit). Suppose you walk into a snack bar with only $3 to spend for lunch. Your first reaction may be to look at the menu and weigh the marginal values of the various things you can eat. If you have 20¢ to spare, do you not find yourself mentally asking whether the difference between a large Coke and a small one is worth more to you than lettuce and tomato on your hamburger? (If not, why do you choose a small Coke instead of a large one?) You are probably so accustomed to making decisions of this sort that you are almost unaware of the act of weighing the marginal values of the alternatives.

Consumers do not usually make choices with conscious precision. Nor can they achieve a perfect equilibrium – the prices, unit sizes, and values of the various products available may not permit it. They are trying to come as close to equality as possible. The economist's assumption is that the individual will move toward equilibrium, not that he or she will always achieve it.[3]

Changes in price and the law of demand

If the price of hot dogs goes down relative to the price of Coke, the rational person will buy more hot dogs. If the price of Coke rises relative to the price

[3] Suppose your marginal utility for Coke and hot dogs is as shown in the table below:

Unit consumed	Marginal utility of cokes (at $0.50) (utils)	Marginal utility of hot dogs (at $1) (utils)
First	10	30
Second	9	15
Third	3	12

If a Coke is priced at $0.50 and a hot dog at $1, $3 will buy you 2 hot dogs and 2 Cokes – the best you can do with $3 at those prices. Now suppose the price of Coke rises to $0.75 and the price of hot dogs falls to $0.75. With a budget of $3 you can still buy 2 hot dogs and 2 Cokes, but you will no longer be maximizing your utility. Instead you will be inclined to reduce your consumption of Coke and increase your consumption of hot dogs.

At the old prices, the original combination (2 Cokes and 2 hot dogs) gave you a total utility of only 64 utils (45 from hot dogs and 19 from Cokes). If you cut back to 1 Coke and 3 hot dogs now, your total utility will rise to 67 utils (57 from hot dogs and 10 from Coke). Your new utility maximizing combination – the one that best satisfies your preferences – will therefore be 1 Coke and 3 hot dogs. No other combination of Coke and hot dogs will give you greater satisfaction. (Try to find one.)

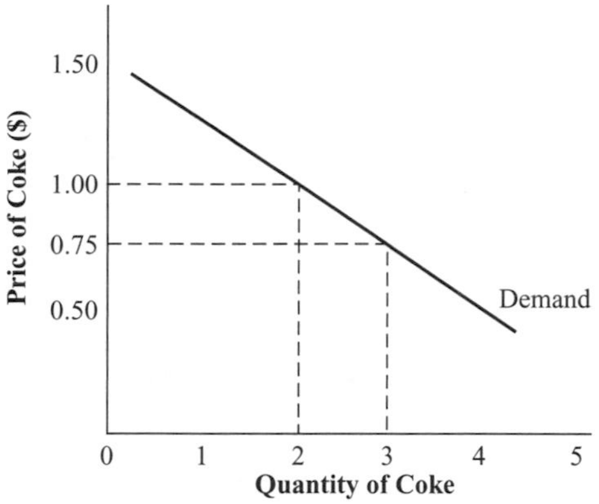

Figure 7.1

The law of demand
Price varies inversely with the quantity consumed, producing a downward sloping curve such as this one. If the price of Coke falls from $1 to $0.75, the consumer will buy three Cokes instead of two.

of hot dogs, the rational person will buy less Coke.[4] If the consumer is in equilibrium to begin with, then

$$\frac{MU_c}{P_c} = \frac{MU_h}{P_h}$$

When the price of Coke rises and the price of hot dogs falls, then there is a disequilibrium, meaning that

$$\frac{MU_c}{P_c} < \frac{MU_h}{P_h}$$

To reestablish equilibrium, the consumer must shift expenditures from Cokes to hot dogs. This principle will hold true for any good or service, and is commonly known as the **law of demand**. If the relative price of a good falls, the individual will buy more of the good. If the relative price rises, the individual will buy less.

The **law of demand** states the assumed inverse relationship between product price and quantity demanded, everything else held constant.

Figure 7.1 shows the demand curve for Coke – that is, the quantity of Coke purchased at different prices. The inverse relationship between price and quantity is reflected in the curve's downward slope. If the price falls from $1 to $0.75, the quantity the consumer will buy increases from two Cokes to three.

[4] In our example, this equality is not always satisfied when the consumer is doing the best he can do because we aren't considering fractional amounts of Cokes and hot dogs. In our examples, a price change creates a situation where a change in the consumption bundles allows the consumer to move closer to the above equality, if not actually to an equality.

The opposite will occur if the price goes up. (The law of demand can also be derived using what economists call "indifference curves," which are graphical devices for structuring consumer preferences based on the simple proposition that consumers prefer more to less of any good. Indifference curve analysis has been relegated to appendix A of this chapter, p. 300.)

Thus the assumption of rational behavior, coupled with the consumer's willingness and ability to substitute less costly goods when prices go up, leads to the law of demand. We cannot say how many Cokes and hot dogs a particular person will buy to maximize his satisfaction. That depends on the individual's income and preferences, which depend in turn on other factors (how much he likes hot dogs, whether he is on a diet, and how much he worries about the nutritional deficiencies of such a lunch). But we can predict the general response, whether positive or negative, to a change in prices.

Price is the value of whatever a person must give up in exchange for a unit of a good or service. It is a rate of exchange and is typically expressed in dollars per unit. Note that price is not necessarily the same as cost. In an exchange between two people – a buyer and a seller – the price at which a good sells can be above or below the cost of producing the good. What the buyer gives up to obtain the good does not have to match what the seller–producer gives up in order to provide the good.

Nor is price always stated in dollars and cents. Some people have a desire to watch sunsets – a desire characterized by the same downward sloping demand curve as the one for Coke. The price of the sunset experience is not necessarily denominated in money. Instead, it may be the lost opportunity to do something else, or the added cost and trouble of finding a home that will offer a view of the sunset. (In that case, price and cost are the same because the buyer and the producer are one and the same.) The law of demand will apply nevertheless. The individual will spend some optimum number of minutes per day watching the sunset and will vary that number of minutes inversely with the price of watching. And the price of pleasant views often takes the form of money when, for example, people pay more for a house with a nice view of the ocean than for one that doesn't.

Market demand is the summation of the quantities demanded by all consumers of a good or service at each and every price during some specified time period.

From individual demand to market demand

Thus far, we have discussed demand solely in terms of the individual's behavior. The concept is most useful, however, when applied to whole markets or segments of the population for goods consumed separately by individuals, with **market demand** interacting with market supply to determine price. To obtain

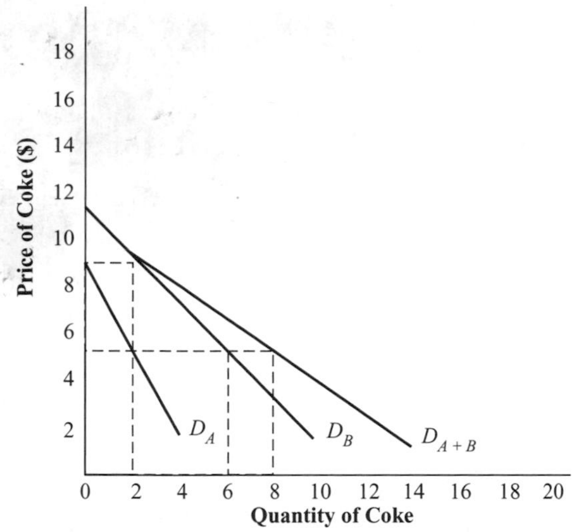

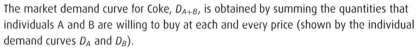

Figure 7.2 Market demand curve

The market demand curve for Coke, D_{A+B}, is obtained by summing the quantities that individuals A and B are willing to buy at each and every price (shown by the individual demand curves D_A and D_B).

the market demand for a product, we need to find some way of *adding up* the wants of the individuals who collectively make up the market.

The market demand can be shown graphically as the horizontal summation of the quantity of a product each individual will buy at each price. Assume that the market for Coke is composed of two individuals, Anna and Betty, who differ in their demand for Coke, as shown in figure 7.2. The demand of Anna is D_A and the demand of Betty is D_B. Then to determine the number of Cokes both of them will demand at any price, we simply add together the quantities each will purchase, at each price (see table 7.1). At a price of $11, neither person is willing to buy any Coke; consequently, the market demand must begin below $11. At $9, Anna is still unwilling to buy any Coke, but Betty will buy two units per unit of time, say a week. The market quantity demanded is therefore two. If the price falls to $5, Anna wants two Cokes and Betty, given her greater demand, wants much more, six. The two quantities combined equal eight. If we continue to drop the price and add the quantities bought at each new price, we will obtain a series of market quantities demanded. When plotted on a graph, they will yield curve D_{A+B}, the market demand for Coke (see figure 7.2). This is, of course, an extremely simple example, because only two individuals are involved. The market demand curves for much larger groups of people, however, are derived in essentially the same way. The demands of Fred, Marsha, Roberta, and others

Table 7.1 *Market demand for Coke*

Price of Coke (1) ($)	Quantity demanded by Anna (D_A) (2)	Quantity demanded by Betty (D_B) (3)	Quantity demanded by both Anna and Betty (D_{A+B}) (4)
11	0	0	0
10	0	1	1.0
9	0	2	2.0
8	0.5	3	3.5
7	1.0	4	5.0
6	1.5	5	6.5
5	2.0	6	8.0
4	2.5	7	9.5
3	3.0	8	11.0
2	3.5	9	12.5
1	4.0	10	14.0

Note: The market demand curve, D_{A+B}, in figure 7.2 is obtained by plotting the quantities in column (4) against their respective prices in column (1).

would be added to those of Anna and Betty. As more people demand more Coke, the market demand extends further to the right.

Price elasticity of demand is a measure of the responsiveness of consumers, in terms of the quantity purchased, to a change in price, everything else held constant.

Elastic demand is a relatively sensitive consumer response to price changes. If the price goes up or down, consumers will respond with a large decrease or increase in the quantity demanded.

Elasticity: consumers' responsiveness to price changes

In the media and in general conversation, we often hear claims that a price change will have no effect on purchases. Someone may predict that an increase in the price of prescription drugs will not affect people's use of them. The same remark is heard in connection with many other goods and services, from gasoline and public parks to medical services and salt. What people usually mean by such statements is that a price change will have only a *slight* effect on consumption. The law of demand states only that a price change will have an inverse effect on the quantity of a good purchased. It does not specify how much of an effect the price change will have.

In other words, we have established only that the market demand curve for a good will slope downward. The actual demand curve for a product may be relatively flat, like curve D_1 in figure 7.3, or relatively steep, like curve D_2. Notice that at a price of P_1, the quantity of the good or service consumed is the same in both markets. If the price is raised to P_2, however, the response is substantially greater in market D_1 than in D_2. In D_1, consumers will reduce their purchases all the way to Q_1. In D_2, consumption will drop only to Q_2.

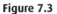

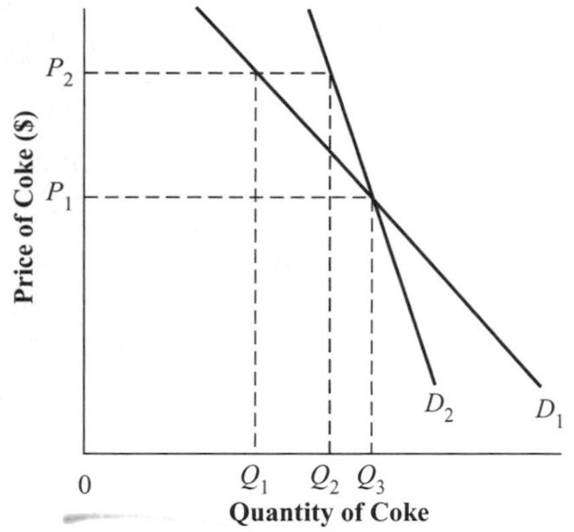

Figure 7.3 Elastic and inelastic demand
Demand curves differ in their relative elasticity. Curve D_1 is more elastic than curve D_2, in the sense that consumers on curve D_1 are more responsive to a given price change (P_2 to P_1) than are consumers on curve D_2.

Question 7.4

Inelastic demand is a relatively insensitive consumer response to price changes. If the price goes up or down, consumers will respond with a small decrease or increase in the quantity demanded.

Economists refer to this relative responsiveness of demand curves as the **price elasticity** of demand. Demand is relatively **elastic** or **inelastic**, depending on the degree of responsiveness to price change.

Demand curve D_1 in figure 7.3 may be characterized as relatively elastic. Demand curve D_2 in figure 7.3 is relatively inelastic.

The elasticity of demand is a useful concept, but our definitions of elastic and inelastic demands are imprecise. What do we mean by "relatively sensitive" or "relatively insensitive"? Under what circumstances is consumer response sensitive or insensitive? There are two ways to add precision to our definition. One is to calculate the effect of a change in price on total consumer expenditures (which must equal producer revenues). The other is to develop a mathematical formula that will yield different values for various levels of elasticity. We next deal with each in turn.

Analyzing total consumer expenditures

An increase in the price of a particular product can cause consumers to buy less. Whether total consumer expenditures (which necessarily equal total business revenues) rise, fall, or stay the same, however, depends on the extent of the consumer response. Many people assume that businesses will maximize profits by charging the highest price possible. But high prices are not always the best policy. For example, if a firm sells 50 units of a product for \$1, its total revenue (consumers' total expenditures) for the product will be \$50 ($50 \times \$1$). If it raises the price to \$1.50 and consumers cut back to 40 units, its total revenue could rise to \$60 ($40 \times \$1.50$). If consumers are highly sensitive to price changes for this particular good, however, the 50¢ increase may lower the quantity sold to 30 units. In that case, total consumer expenditures would fall to \$45 ($\$1.50 \times 30$).

Similarly, lowering price doesn't always lower revenues. If a firm establishes a price of \$1.50 and then lowers it to \$1, the quantity sold may rise enough to increase total revenues. Whether this happens, however, depends on the degree of consumer response. In other words, consumer responsiveness determines whether a firm should raise or lower its price. (Although we shall see later that generally the firm is not interested in maximizing revenues.)

We can define a simple rule of thumb for using total consumer expenditures to analyze the elasticity of demand. Demand is *elastic*:

- if total consumer expenditures rise when the price falls, or
- if total consumer expenditures fall when the price rises.

Demand is *inelastic*:

- if total consumer expenditures rise when the price rises, or
- if total consumer expenditures fall when the price falls.

Determining elasticity coefficients

Although we have refined our definition of elasticity, it still does not allow us to distinguish degrees of elasticity or inelasticity. **Elasticity coefficients** do just that. Expressed as a formula,[5] the elasticity coefficient is

The elasticity coefficient of demand (E_d) is the ratio of the percentage change in the quantity demanded to the percentage change in price.

$$E_d = \frac{\text{Percentage change in quantity}}{\text{Percentage change in price}}$$

[5] There are actually two formulas for elasticity recognized by economists, one for use at specific points on the curve, called *point elasticity*, and one for measuring average elasticity between two points, called *arc elasticity*. The formula for point elasticity, which is used for very small changes in price and quantity, is:

$$E_d = \frac{\text{Change in quantity demanded}}{\text{Initial quantity demanded}} \div \frac{\text{Change in price}}{\text{Initial price}}$$

or

$$E_d = \frac{Q_1 - Q_2}{Q_1} \div \frac{P_1 - P_2}{P_1}$$

The formula for arc elasticity is:

$$E_d = \frac{Q_1 - Q_2}{\frac{1}{2}(Q_1 + Q_2)} \div \frac{P_1 - P_2}{\frac{1}{2}(P_1 + P_2)}$$

where the subscripts 1 and 2 represent two distinct points, or prices, on the demand curve. (Note that although the calculated elasticity is always negative, economists, by convention, speak of it as a positive number. Economists, in effect, use the absolute value of elasticity.) The difference in arc elasticity over different regions of a demand curve can be illustrated by computing the arc elasticity between points, *ab* and then between points *cd* on the demand

Elasticity coefficients can tell us much at a glance. When the percentage change in quantity is greater than the percentage change in price, the elasticity coefficient is greater than 1.0. In these cases, demand is said to be elastic. When the percentage change in quantity is less than the percentage change in price, the elasticity coefficient is less than 1.0 and demand is said to be inelastic. When the percentage change in the price is equal to the percentage change in quantity, the elasticity coefficient is 1.0, and demand is unitary elastic.[6] In short[7]:

Elastic demand	$E_d > 1$
Inelastic demand	$E_d < 1$
Unitary elastic demand	$E_d = 1$

Elasticity coefficients provide useful information on the relationship between price changes and revenue changes, as discussed earlier. For reasons that will become clear, pricing the product of a firm to maximize profits almost always requires that a price on the elastic portion of the demand curve.

curve in figure 7.4. Arc elasticity between points *a* and *b* is:

$$E_d = \tfrac{1}{2}\frac{10-20}{(10+20)} \div \tfrac{1}{2}\frac{10-9}{(10+9)} = -\frac{10}{15} \div \frac{1}{9.5} = -\frac{95}{15} = -6.33$$

or 6.33 in absolute value.

Arc elasticity between points *c* and *d* is:

$$E_d - \tfrac{1}{2}\frac{90-100}{(90+100)} \div \tfrac{1}{2}\frac{2-1}{(2+1)} = -95 \div \frac{10}{1.5} = -\frac{1}{0.16}$$

or 0.16 in absolute value.

6 Remember that all elasticity coefficients are negative and are preceded by a minus sign. (The demand curve has a negative slope.) Economists generally omit the minus sign, as we have seen.

7 To prove this result, let's look at marginal revenue *MR*, or the change in total revenue in response to a change in quantity *Q*. Taking the derivative of $P(Q) \bullet Q$ with respect to *Q*, we obtain

$$MR = \frac{d[P(Q) \bullet Q]}{dQ} = P(Q) + \frac{dP}{dQ} \bullet Q$$

Factoring price out of the right-hand side of this equation gives us

$$MR = P\left[1 + \frac{dP}{dQ} \bullet \frac{Q}{P}\right]$$

which, because $E = -\left(\frac{dQ}{dP}\right) Q/P$, is the same as

$$MR = P\left[1 - \frac{1}{E}\right] \begin{matrix} > 0 \text{ if } E > 1 \\ = 0 \text{ if } E = 1 \\ < 0 \text{ if } E < 1 \end{matrix}$$

From this it follows immediately that an increase in *Q* (a decrease in *P*) increases total revenue if $E > 1$, has no effect on total revenue if $E = 1$, and reduces total revenue if $E < 1$.

Elasticity and slope of the demand curve

Students often confuse the concept of elasticity of demand with the slope of the demand curve. A comparison of their mathematical formulas, however, shows that they are quite different:

$$\text{Slope} = \frac{\text{Rise}}{\text{Run}} = \frac{\text{Change in price}}{\text{Change in quantity}}$$

$$\text{Elasticity} = \frac{\text{Percentage change in quantity}}{\text{Percentage change in price}}$$

The confusion is understandable. The slope of a demand curve does say something about consumers' responsiveness: It shows how much the quantity consumed goes up when the price goes down by a given amount. Slope is an unreliable indicator of consumer responsiveness, however, because it varies with the units of measurement for price and quantity. For example, suppose that when the price rises from \$10 to \$20, quantity demanded decreases from 100 pounds to 60 pounds The slope is $-1/4$:

$$\text{Slope} = \frac{-10}{40} = \frac{-1}{4}$$

If a price is measured in pennies instead of dollars (with quantity still measured in pounds) however, the slope comes out at -25:

$$\text{Slope} = \frac{-1,000}{40} = \frac{-25}{1}$$

No matter what units are used to measure price and quantity, however, the percentage changes in price and quantity remain the same and the elasticity of demand is not affected by changes from one set of units to another.

Elasticity along a straight-line demand curve

Since slope and elasticity are different concepts, it should not surprise anyone that the elasticity coefficient will generally be different at different points on the demand curve. Consider the linear demand curve in figure 7.4. At every point on the curve, a price reduction of \$1 causes quantity demanded by rise by ten units, but a \$1 decrease in price at the top of the curve is a much smaller percentage change than a \$1 decrease at the bottom of the curve. Similarly, an increase of ten units in the quantity demanded is a much larger percentage change when the quantity is low than when it is high. Therefore the elasticity coefficient falls as consumers move down their demand curve. Generally, a

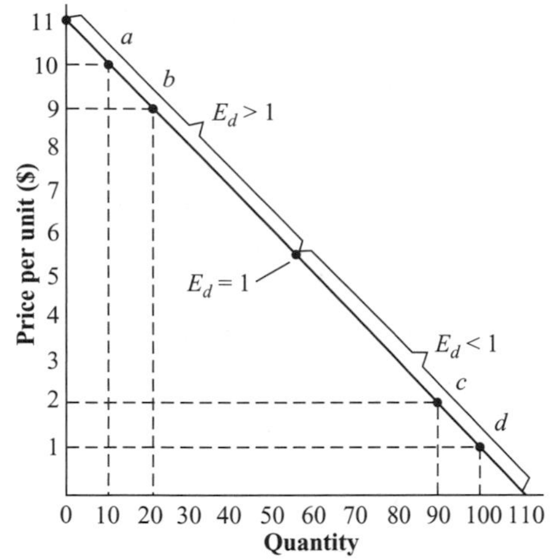

Figure 7.4 Changes in the elasticity coefficient

The elasticity coefficient decreases as a firm moves down the demand curve. The upper half of a linear demand curve is elastic, meaning that the elasticity coefficient is greater than one. The lower half is inelastic, meaning that the elasticity coefficient is less than one. This means that the middle of the linear demand curve has an elasticity coefficient equal to one.

straight-line demand curve has an inelastic range at the bottom, a unitary elastic point in the center, and an elastic range at the top.[8]

[8] To prove this, we recognize that the equation for a linear domain curve can be expressed mathematically as

$$P = A - BQ$$

where P represents price, Q is quantity demanded, and A and B are positive constants. The total revenue associated with this demand curve is given by

$$PQ = AQ - BQ^2$$

The marginal revenue is obtained by taking the derivative of total revenue with respect to Q, or

$$MR = A - 2BQ$$

We know that when marginal revenue is equal to 0, elasticity is equal to 1. This implies that $E = 1$ when

$$A - 2BQ = 0$$

or when

$$Q = \frac{1}{2} \bullet \frac{A}{B}$$

We know that when the demand curve intersects the Q axis, $P = 0$ and

$$Q = \frac{A}{B}$$

Applications of the concept of elasticity

Elasticity of demand is particularly important to producers. Together with the cost of production, it determines the prices firms can charge for their products. We have shown that an increase or decrease in price can cause total consumer expenditures to rise, fall, or remain the same, depending on the elasticity of demand. Thus if a firm lowers its price and incurs greater production costs (because it is producing and selling more units), it may still increase its profits. As long as the demand curve is elastic, revenues can (but will not necessarily) go up more than costs. Cell phone companies have lowered their rates in response to intense competition, but also in part due to the fact that they see their demand as highly elastic.

Producers of concerts and dances estimate the elasticity of demand when they establish the price of admission. If at an admission price of $10 tickets are left unsold, a lower price, say, $7, will allow more tickets to be sold and may increase profits. Even if costs rise (for extra workers and more programs), revenues may still rise more.

Government, too, must consider elasticity of demand, for the consumer's demand for taxable items is not inexhaustible. If a government raises excise taxes on cars or jewelry too much, it may end up with lower tax revenues. The higher tax, added to the final price of the product, may cause a negative consumer response. It is no accident that the heaviest excise taxes are usually imposed on goods for which the demand tends to be inelastic, such as cigarettes and liquor.[9]

Thus, with a linear demand curve, $E = 1$ when Q is one-half the distance between $Q = 0$ and the Q that drives price down to 0. The reader is invited to prove that $E > 1 Q < \frac{1}{2} \bullet A/B$ when and that $E < 1$ when $Q > \frac{1}{2} \bullet A/B$.

[9] The same reasoning applies to property taxes. Many large cities have tended to underestimate the elasticity of demand for living space. Indeed, a major reason for the recent migration from city to suburbs in many metropolitan areas has been the desire of residents to escape rising tax rates. By moving just outside a city's boundaries, people can retain many of the benefits a city provides without actually paying for them. This movement of city dwellers to the suburbs lowers the demand for property within the city, undermining property values, and destroying the city's tax base. Thus, even governments need to pay attention to the elasticity of demand for the services they provide if they want to maintain their tax revenues. We can predict that the elasticity of demand for the services of local governments is greater than the elasticity of demand for services of the national government because people can more easily move from one local government to another (vote with their feet) than they can from one national government to another.

Determinants of the price elasticity of demand

So far, our analysis of elasticity has presumed that consumers are able to respond to a price change. However, consumers' ability to respond can be affected by various factors, such as the number of substitutes and the amount of time consumers have to respond to a change in price by shifting to other products or producers.

Substitutes

Substitutes allow consumers to respond to a price increase by switching to another good. If the price of orange juice goes up, you can substitute a variety of other drinks, including water, wine, and soda.

The elasticity of demand for any good depends very much on what substitutes are available. The existence of a large number and variety of substitutes means that demand is likely to be elastic. That is, if people can switch easily to another product that will yield approximately the same value, many will do so when faced with a price increase. The similarity of substitutes – how well they can satisfy the same basic want – also affects elasticity. The closer substitutes are to a product, the more elastic the demand for the product will be. If there are no close substitutes, demand will tend to be inelastic. What we call "necessities" are often things that lack close substitutes.

Few goods have *no substitutes* at all. Because there are many substitutes for orange juice – soda, wine, prune juice, and so on – we would expect the demand for orange juice to be more elastic than the demand for salt, which has fewer viable alternatives. Yet even salt has synthetic substitutes. Furthermore, though human beings need a certain amount of salt to survive, most of us consume much more than the minimum and can easily cut back if the price of salt rises. The extra flavor that salt adds is a benefit that can be partially recouped by buying other things.

At the other extreme from goods with no substitutes are goods with *perfect substitutes.* Perfect substitutes exist for goods produced by an individual firm engaged in perfect competition. An individual wheat farmer, for example, is only one among thousands of producers of essentially the same product. The wheat produced by others is a perfect substitute for the wheat produced by the single farmer. Perfect substitutability can lead to perfect elasticity of demand.

The demand curve facing the perfect competitor is horizontal, like the one in figure 7.5. If the individual competitor raises her price even a minute

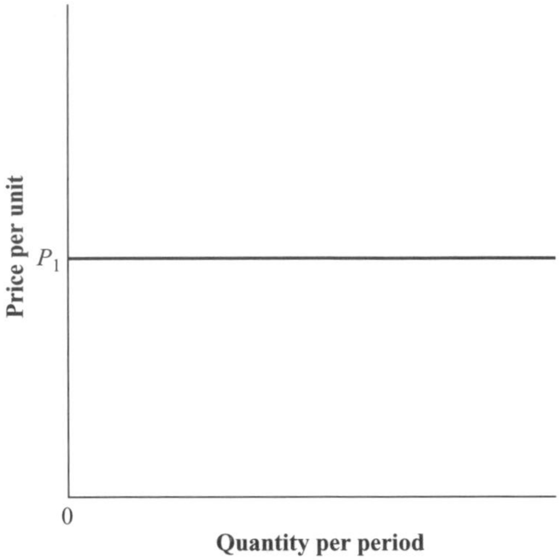

Figure 7.5 Perfectly elastic demand
A firm that has many competitors may lose all its sales if it increases its price even slightly. Its customers can simply move to another producer. In that case, its demand curve is horizontal, with an elasticity coefficient of infinity.

A perfectly elastic demand is a demand that has an elasticity coefficient of infinity. It is expressed graphically as a curve horizontal to the *X*-axis.

percentage above the going market price, consumers will switch to other sellers. The elasticity coefficient of such a horizontal demand curve is infinite. Thus this demand curve is described as **perfectly elastic**.

Time

Consumption requires time. Accordingly, a demand curve must describe some particular time period. Over a very short period of time – say, a day – the demand for a good may not react immediately. It takes time to find substitutes. With enough time, however, consumers will respond to a price increase. Thus a demand curve that covers a long period will be more elastic than one for a short period.[10]

[10] Oil provides a good example of how the elasticity of demand can change over time. When the price of oil, and therefore gasoline, increased sharply in the fall of 2004, consumers were limited in their ability to reduce consumption because of their gas-guzzling SUVs and suburban homes located far from their work places. If those high gas prices remain high for a long time, however, consumers will begin buying smaller cars and some will relocate closer to work and the consumer response to the higher gas prices will become greater. The long-term demand curve for gasoline is much more elastic than the short-term demand curve.

Changes in demand

The determinants of the elasticity of demand are fewer and easier to identify than the determinants of demand itself. As discussed in chapter 2, the demand for almost all goods is affected in one way or another by:

- Consumer incomes
- Prices of other goods
- Number of consumers
- Expectations concerning future prices and incomes
- Consumer tastes and preferences.

Additional variables apply in differing degrees to different goods. The amount of ice cream and the number of golf balls bought both depend on the weather (fewer golf balls in Montana are sold in the winter than the summer). The number of cribs demanded depends on the birthrate. Together, all these variables determine the position of the demand curve. If any variable changes, so will the position of the demand curve.

We showed in chapter 2 that if consumer preference for a product – say, low-rise pants – increases, the change will be reflected in an outward movement of the demand curve (as we show here in figure 7.6). That is what happened during the early 2000s, when people's (mainly women's) tastes changed and wearing pants (at times, at half-moon!) became chic. By definition, such a change in taste means that consumers are willing to buy more of the good at the going market price. If the price is P_1, the quantity demanded will increase from Q_2 to Q_3. A change in tastes can also mean that people are willing to buy more low-rise pants at each and every price. At P_2 they are now willing to buy Q_2 instead of Q_1 low-rise pants. We can infer from this pattern that consumers are willing to pay a higher price for any given quantity. In figure 7.6, the increase in demand means that consumers are willing to pay as much as P_2 for Q_2 pairs of low-rise pants, whereas formerly they would pay only P_1. (If consumers' tastes change in the opposite direction, the demand curve moves downward to the left as a quantity demanded at a given price decreases, see figure 7.7.)

Whether demand increases or decreases, the demand curve will still slope downward. Everything else held constant, people will buy more of the good at a lower price than a higher one. To assume that other variables will remain constant is, of course, unrealistic because markets are generally in a state of flux. In the real world, all variables do not stay put just to allow the price of a good to change by itself. Even if conditions change at the same time that price changes, the law of demand tells us that a decrease in price will lead people to

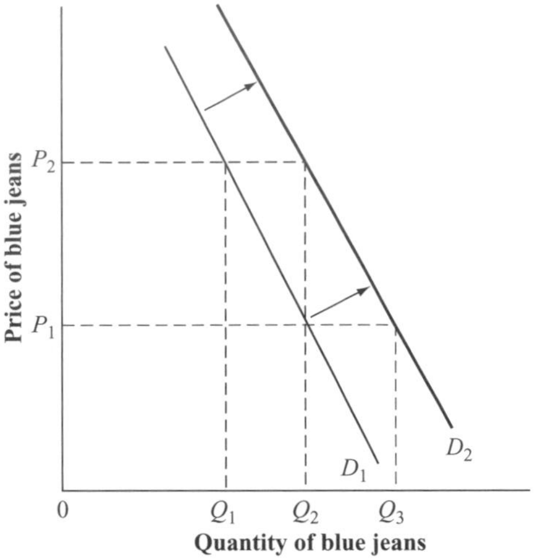

Figure 7.6 Increase in demand
When consumer demand for low-rise pants increases, the demand curve shifts from D_1 to D_2. Consumers are now willing to buy a larger quantity of low-rise pants at the same price, or the same quantity at a higher price. At price P_1, for instance, they will buy Q_3 instead of Q_2. And they are now willing to pay P_2 for Q_2 low-rise pants, whereas before they would pay only P_1.

buy more than they would otherwise, and an increase in price will lead them to buy less.

For example, figure 7.7 shows a situation where the demand for low-rise pants has decreased because consumers are less willing to buy the product as another style becomes fashionable. A price reduction can partially offset the decline in demand. If producers lower their price from P_2 to P_1, quantity demanded will fall only to Q_2 instead of Q_1. Although consumers are buying fewer low-rise pants than they once did (Q_2 as opposed to Q_3) because of changing tastes, the law of demand still holds. Because of the price change, consumers have increased their consumption over what it would otherwise have been.

> A **normal good or service** is any good or service for which demand rises with an increase in income and falls with a decrease in income.

Normal and inferior goods

A change in consumer incomes will affect demand in more complicated ways. The demand for most goods, called **normal goods**, increases with income. Golf lessons are very likely a good example of a normal good (since so many low-income people can be seen taking them, relatively speaking). Beans are an

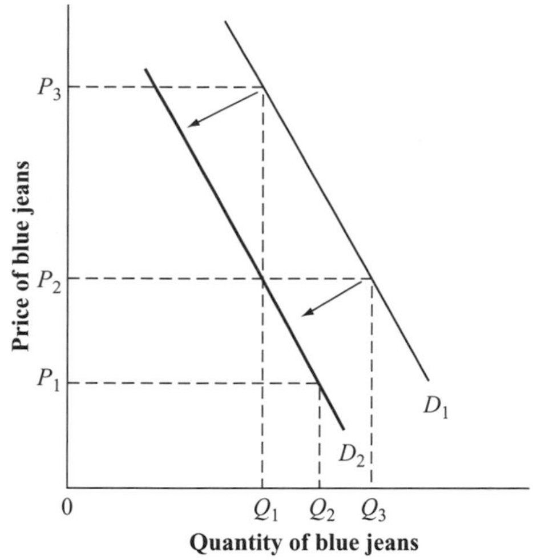

Figure 7.7

Decrease in demand

A downward shift in demand, from D_1 to D_2, represents a decrease in the quantity of low-rise pants consumers are willing to buy at each and every price. It also indicates a decrease in the price they are willing to pay for each and every quantity of low-rise pants. At price P_2, for instance, consumers will now buy only Q_1 low-rise pants (not Q_3, as before); and they will now pay only P_2 for Q_1 low-rise pants – not P_3, as before.

An **inferior good or service** is any good or service for which demand falls with an increase in income and rises with a decrease in income.

example of what a good many people would consider **inferior**. People who rely on beans as a staple or filler food when their incomes are low may substitute meat and other higher-priced foods when their incomes rise.

Thus, whereas economists can confidently predict the directional movement of consumption when prices change, they cannot say what will happen to the demand for a particular good when income changes, because each individual determines whether a particular good is a normal or inferior good. Different people will tend to answer this question differently in different markets. Beans may be an inferior good to most low-income consumers but a normal good to many others.

For example, how do you think a change in income will affect the demand for low-, medium-, and high-quality liquor? You may have some intuitive notion about the effect, but you are probably not as confident about it as you are about the effect of a price decrease. In fact, during past recessions, the demand for both low- and high-quality liquor has increased. Some consumers may have switched to high-quality liquor to impress their friends, and to suggest that they have been unaffected by the economic malaise. Others may have tried to maintain their old level of consumption by switching to a low-quality brand.

Substitutes and complementary goods

The effect of a change in the price of other goods is similarly complicated. Here the important factor is the relationship of one good – say, ice cream – to other commodities. Are the goods in question substitutes for ice cream, such as frozen yogurt? Are they complements, such as cones? Are they used independently of ice cream? Demand for ice cream is unlikely to be affected by a drop in the price of baby rattles, but it may well decline if the price of frozen yogurt drops.

Substitute goods

Two products are generally considered *substitutes* if the demand for one goes up when the price of the other rises. The price of a product does not have to rise above the price of its substitute before the demand for the substitute is affected. Assume that the price of sirloin steak is $6 per pound and the price of hamburger is $2 per pound. The price difference reflects the fact that consumers believe that the two meats are of different quality. If the price of hamburgers rises to $4 per pound while the price of sirloin remains constant at $6, many buyers will increase their demand for steak. The perceived difference in quality now outweighs the difference in price.

Complementary goods

Because *complementary* products – razors and razor blades, oil and oil filters, DVDs and DVD players (and burners) – are consumed *jointly*, a change in the price of one will cause an increase or decrease in the demand for both products simultaneously. An increase in the price of razor blades, for instance, will induce some people to switch to electric razors, causing a decrease in the quantity of razor blades demanded and a decrease in the demand for safety razors. Again, economists cannot predict how many people will decide that the switch is worthwhile; they can merely predict from theory the direction in which demand for the product will move. (Many students often worry about the law of demand on the grounds that people are not always as rational as economists assume and that some goods may have upward sloping demand curves because prices carry messages about goods' relative value and about the relative economic standing of the buyers of the goods. These issues are taken up in Appendix B to this chapter, p. 308.)

Lagged demands and network effects

Almost all microeconomics textbooks do what we have done with demand, which is to provide a lengthy discussion of the demand for "standard" goods. They explain that the quantity of the good purchased will be related to the price of the good in question and a number of other considerations (such as weather, income, and the prices of other goods), as we have stressed. The lower the price of a candy bar, for example, the greater the quantity purchased, and vice versa. This inverse relationship between price and quantity is so revered in economics that it has a special label, the "law of demand." The general rule deduced is that the more scarce the good, the greater the (marginal) value and price.

Little is usually said in most textbooks, however, about how the benefits received by any one candy bar buyer in one time period might affect the benefits received in subsequent time periods – or, rather, how the consumption level today might affect the demand in the future. Also, little or nothing is written about how the benefits (and demand) can depend upon how many other people have bought candy bars. This lack of coverage is understandable. The benefit that one person gets from eating a candy bar in one time period does not materially affect the benefits received from eating another bar later, and is also not materially affected by how many other people are buying and consuming candy bars. People just buy and consume candy bars independently of one another, and couldn't care less about how much other people are enjoying candy bars.

A **lagged-demand** good is one in which consumption today affects consumption tomorrow (or future time periods).

This is not true for two special classes of goods called **lagged-demand** goods and network goods. A lagged-demand good has one defining feature: the greater the quantity purchased today, the greater the demand tomorrow. Good examples of lagged-demand goods include cigarettes, alcohol, and street drugs, given that they tend to be addictive in consumption. As we shall show, the theory of lagged demand is similar to the theory of "rational addiction," or the view that before consumption begins, people can rationally weigh the long-term costs and benefits, or pros and cons, of consuming goods that can be physically compelling in consumption.

A **network good** is a product or service whose value to consumers depends intrinsically on how many other people buy the good.

A **network good** has one defining feature: the greater the number of buyers, the greater the benefits most, if not all, buyers receive. These goods are said to exhibit a "network effect" (or are sometimes called "network externalities"), which has been appropriately described by one economist as "a phenomenon in which the attractiveness of a product to customers increases with the use of that product by others" (Fisher 1998, 15). Good examples of network goods include telephones, fax machines, and computer software. One person's telephone is useless unless someone else owns a phone, and the more people there are who are buying phones, the greater the value of the phone is to everyone, because more people can be called.

As you can see, lagged-demand goods and network goods have much in common – the interconnectedness of consumption. This commonality has important implications for pricing strategy.

Lagged demands

One of the authors of this book (Lee) was involved in the development of the theory of lagged demands (Lee and Kreutzer 1982). He and economist David Kreutzer have argued that the future demands for some goods can be, and often are, dependent on the current demand. From this perspective, a lagged-demand good is one in which the future good is a complement to the current good; they go together. According to Lee and Kreutzer,

> The crucial assumption behind our analysis is that lags exist in the demand for the resource; future demands are influenced by current availability. The demand for petroleum is clearly an example of such a lagged demand structure, with future demand for petroleum significantly influenced by investment decisions made in response to current availability. (1982, 580)

Hence, it follows that as with all complements, the future demand for a product depends upon the current price for the same good. Behind such an obvious point lie important insights that might otherwise go unrecognized when seen from the usual view of demand.

As a consequence of the complementarity in consumption over time, firms faced with lagged demand have an incentive to lower their current price in order to stimulate future sales. They might even charge a price in (or marginally lower their price toward) the inelastic range of their current demand curves, despite losing current revenues (and profits) from doing so, just so that they can stimulate a greater future demand, which will permit them to raise their future prices and can lead to greater profits in the future. This is only true, of course, as long as the producers' rights to exploit future profits are not threatened.

What makes this perspective interesting is that under conditions of lagged demand, a cartel of firms (considered in detail in chapter 12) may form, not with the intent of raising the group's current price but rather with the intent of lowering the current price (below) and expanding current output (above) levels that would exist under competition. The standard view is that firms form cartels to increase their prices above the level that would be possible under competition, and that cartels tend to break down because individual firms will cheat on the cartel agreement by lowering price to gain customers at the expense of the other cartel firms.[11]

Also, we should note that the conventional treatment of demand, under which demand tomorrow is unrelated to consumption level today, predicts that threats to the future stability of property rights will lead to "overproduction" during the current time period. This is the case because if a firm – for example, an oil company – fears losing its property rights to its reserves, then it has an incentive to increase production and expand sales today. Never mind that the added supply of oil might depress the current price. The oil firm can reason that if it doesn't pump the oil out of the ground in the short term, it will not have rights to the oil in the future.

For goods subject to the lagged-demand phenomenon, any looming threat to property rights can cause some firms to do the opposite: reduce the production of oil (or the exploitation of any other resource), hike the current price, and extract whatever profits remain. When its property rights are threatened, the firm no longer has an incentive to artificially suppress its current price in order to cultivate future demand.

Rational addiction

Gary Becker and Kevin Murphy (1988) have developed a similar line of argument. The major difference is that their purpose was primarily to develop an economic theory of "addiction," which is a general concept also intended to suggest a tie-in between current and future consumption of a good or activity. The tie-in is, however, physical (or maybe chemical), as in the case of cigarettes. People's future demand for smokes can be tied to their current consumption simply because of the body's chemical dependency on the intake of nicotine. As in the case of lagged-demand goods, producers of addictive goods have an incentive to suppress the current price of their good – cigarettes – in order to stimulate the future demand for it. The lower the current price, the greater the future demand and the greater the future consumption.

This complementarity in consumption for an addictive (and lagged demand) good is illustrated in figure 7.8. At price P_3 in the current time period, the

[11] Such a cartel may also dissolve because of rampant cheating involving price increases, with all firms seeking to benefit from the greater demand stimulated by lower prices charged by other cartel members.

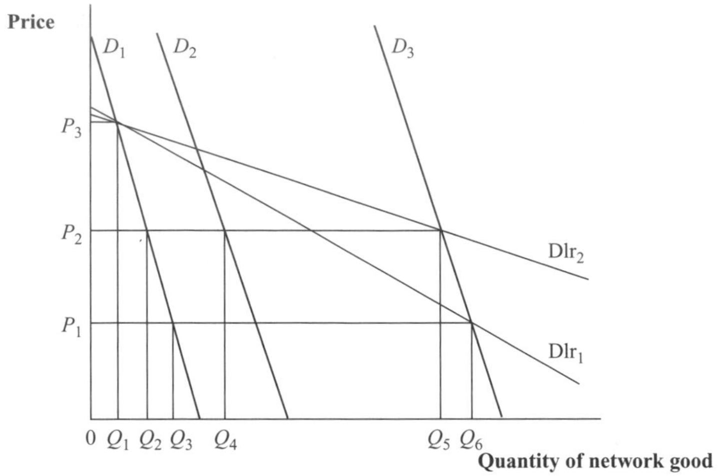

Figure 7.8 Network effects and demand

As the price falls from P_3 to P_2, the quantity demanded in the short run rises from Q_1 to Q_2. However, sales build on sales, causing the demand in the future to expand outward to, say, D_2. The lower the price in the current time period, the greater the expansion of demand in the future. The more the demand expands over time in response to greater sales in the current time period, the more elastic is the long-run demand.

consumption will be Q_1 in the current time period. However, because of that current consumption level, the demand in the future rises to D_2. At a price of P_2, current consumption rises to Q_2, but the future demand rises to D_3. You can imagine that at even lower prices, P_1, there will be some even higher demand curve, D_3, in the future time period. You can see from figure 7.8 why firms have an incentive to lower the current price: the future demand rises. With other complementary goods, if the price of one complement goes down and more of it is sold, then the demand for the other complement goes up, with its price rising. The same thing happens in this case. The only difference is that the complements are the same good but are consumed in different time periods.

The current demand for one addictive good, cigarettes, might be highly inelastic, as is commonly presumed in microeconomics, but this does not mean that the long-run demand is necessarily inelastic. As illustrated in figure 7.8, the short-term demand curves (the thin lines) are each very inelastic, but the long-term demand curve (the thicker dark line Dlr_1) is rather elastic.

Indeed, Becker and Murphy (1988, 695) maintain that the more addictive the good, the more elastic will be the long-term demand. This is the case because a reduction in the *current* time period might not stimulate *current* sales very much. However, for highly addictive goods, current consumption can give an even greater increase in the future demand because the buyers "have to have more of it," thus resulting in even more future consumption than would be the case for less addictive goods. Hence, it is altogether understandable why in the 1960s cigarette firms would often have "cigarette girls" parading around campus in short skirts giving away small packs of cigarettes, and why many drug dealers to this day eagerly give away the first "hits" to their potential customers. Indeed, it seems reasonable to conclude from the Becker–Murphy line of argument that the more addictive the good, the lower the current price for first-time users. We might not even be surprised that for some highly addictive goods, the producers would "sell" their goods at below-zero prices (or would pay their customers to take the good).

In contrast to the theory of lagged demand, this theory of rational addiction suggests explanations for a variety of behaviors, most notably the observed differences in the consumption behavior of young and old, the tendency of overweight people to go on "crash diets" even when they may want to lose only a modest amount of weight, or alcoholics who become "teetotalers" when they decide to curtail their drinking. Old people may be less concerned about addictive behavior, everything else held constant, than the young. Old people simply have less to lose over time from addictions than do younger people (given older people's shorter remaining life expectancies). People who are addicted to food may rationally choose to drastically reduce their intake of food even though they may need to lose only a few pounds because their intake of food compels them to "overconsume." Similarly, alcoholics may "get on the wagon" in order to temper their future demands for booze because even a modest consumption level can have a snowballing effect, with a little consumption leading to more drinks, which can lead to even more.

Standard excise tax theory suggests that producers' opposition to excise taxes should be tempered by the fact that the tax can be extensively passed on to the consumers in the form of a price increase (that must always be less than the tax itself). The theory of lagged demand suggests otherwise: Producers of such goods have a substantial incentive to oppose the tax because of the elastic nature of their long-run demands. Although they may be able to pass along a major share of the tax in the short run, they will not be able to do so in the long run.

Network effects

The theory of "network effects" shares one key construct with the theory of lagged demand: the interconnectedness of demands (see Arthur 1996; Farrell and Klemperer 2005). The interconnectedness in the theory of lagged demand is formed through time. The interconnectedness in the theory of network effects is formed across people and markets. The theory of network effects is best understood in terms of telephone systems that actually form "networks"– that is, are tied together with telephone lines (as well as microwave disks and satellites). No one would want to own a phone or buy a telephone service if he or she were the only phone owner. There would be no one to call. However, if two people – *A* and *B* – buy phones, then each person has someone to call, and there are two pair-wise calls that can be made: *A* can call *B*, and *B* can also call *A*. As more and more people buy phones, the benefits of phone ownership escalate geometrically, given that there are progressively more people to call and even more possible pair-wise calls.[12] It is important to remember that the benefits that buyers garner from others who are joining the network can rise just from the *potential* to call others; they need not ever call all the additional joiners. Neither of this book's authors ever expects to call every business in the country, but each author still gains from being able to call any of the businesses that have phones.

Accordingly, the demand for phones can be expected to rise with phone ownership. That is to say, the benefits from ownership go up as more people join the network. Hence, people should be willing to pay more for phones as phone ownership increases. Some of the benefits of phone ownership are said to be "external" to the buyers of phones because people other than those who buy phones gain by the purchases (as was true in our study of public goods and external benefits in chapter 6). In more concrete terms, when one of the authors, Lee, buys a phone, then the other author, McKenzie, gains from Lee's purchase – and McKenzie pays nothing for Lee's phone. For that matter, everyone who has a phone gains more opportunities to call as other people buy phones, or as the network expands (at least up to some point). The gains that others receive from Lee's or anyone else's purchase are "external" to Lee,

[12] If there are three phone owners – *A*, *B*, and *C* – then calls can be made in six pair-wise ways: *A* can call *B* or *C*, *B* can call *A* or *C*, and *C* can call *A* or *B*. If there are four phone owners, then there are twelve potential pair-wise calls; five phone owners, twenty potential pair-wise calls; twenty phone owners, 380; and so forth. If the network allows for conference calls, the count of the ways in which calls can be made will quickly go through the roof with the rise in the number of phone owners.

hence are dubbed "external benefits" or, more to the point of this discussion, "network externalities."

Objections to demand theory

From years of teaching the theory of demand, we have learned that MBA students are especially skeptical of aspects of demand theory. They are all too often prone to think, if not speak in class, about how:

- Consumers are not as rational as is presumed in the development of the law of demand
- Consumers exhibit some randomness in their buying decisions
- Consumers often buy goods because the price rises, because higher prices convey a message to others whom the consumers want to impress.

We are mindful of these objections, but we have decided to treat such issues in an appendix B to this chapter (p. 308), partially as a way to keep the length of the body of this chapter within reasonable bounds but also because our discussions in appendix B end up reinforcing the basic point of the foregoing sections: Demand curves slope downward.

Scarcity, abundance, and economic value

Notice that networks and network goods tend to turn one basic economic proposition on its head. There is a canon in economic theory that we have stressed from the start: As any good becomes scarcer, it becomes more valuable. In the case of network goods, just the opposite is true: as a good becomes more abundant, its value goes up (Kelly 1998, chapter 3). This does not mean, however, that the demand curve for a network good slopes upward. Given the number of phones that others have, people can be expected to buy more phones at a low price than a high price.

There are two basic problems that a phone company faces in building its network. First, the company has the initial problem of getting people to buy phones, given that at the start the benefits will be low. Second, if some of the benefits of buying a phone are "external" to the buyer, then each buyer's willingness to buy a phone can be impaired. How does the phone company build the network? One obvious solution is for the phone company to do what the producers in the theory of lagged demand do: "underprice" (or subsidize) their products – phones – or, at the extreme, give them away (or even pay people to install phones in their houses and offices).

Perspective Software Networks

The network effects in the software industry – for example, operating systems – are similar but, of course, differ in detail from the network effects in the telephone industry. Indeed, the software developer may face more difficult problems, given that the software development must somehow get the computer users on one side of the market and application developers on the other side to join the network more or less together.

Few people, other than "geeks," are likely to buy an operating system without applications (for example, word processing programs or games) being available. If a producer of an operating system is able to get only a few consumers to buy and use its product, the demand for the operating system can be highly restricted. A major problem is that few firms producing applications will write for an operating system with a very limited number of users, given the prospects of few sales for their applications, which in turn keeps demand for the operating system low. However, if the firm producing the operating system can motivate more consumers to purchase it, a cycle of increased demand can result as the number of applications written for the operating system can be expected to grow – which stimulates yet more demand for the system, more applications written for the operating system, etc. resulting in a possible snowball effect.

As in the case of telephones, some of the benefits of purchases of the operating system (and applications) are "external" to the people who buy them. People who join the operating system network increase the benefits to all previous joiners, given that they have more people with whom they can share computers or share files. All joiners have the additional benefit of knowing that a greater number of operating system users can increase the likelihood of more applications from which they can choose. However, as in phone purchases, when the benefits are "external," potential users have an impaired demand for buying into the network. The greater the "external benefits," the greater the buying resistance (or willingness to cover the operating system cost).

The network may grow slowly at the start, because people (both computer users and programmers) may be initially skeptical that any given operating system will be able to become a sizable network (and provide the "external benefits" that a large network can provide). But if the network for a given operating system continues to grow, more and more people will begin to believe that the operating system will become sizable, if not "dominant," which means that the network can grow at an escalating pace.

In short, such network growth can reach a "tipping point," beyond which the growth in the market for the operating system will take on a life of its own – grow at an ever-faster pace *because* it has grown at an ever-faster pace (see Gladwell 2000). People will buy the operating system because everyone else is using it (which can mean that the accelerating growth of one operating system causes a contraction in the market share for other operating systems). After the "tipping point" has been reached, the firm's eventual market dominance – and (according to the US Department of Justice, Klein *et al.* 1998) monopoly power is practically assured.

This discussion has relevance to the history of the dominance of the Apple and Microsoft operating systems. Before the introduction of the IBM personal computer, Apple was the dominant personal computer (PC), running the CP/M operating system. However, IBM and Microsoft jointly developed their respective operating systems, PC-DOS and MS-DOS, in 1981. At that time, 90 percent of programs ran under some version of CP/M. CP/M's market dominance was likely undermined by two important factors: First, CP/M was selling at the time for $240 a copy; DOS was introduced at $40. Second, the dominance of IBM in the mainframe computer market no doubt convinced many buyers that some version of DOS would eventually be the dominant operating system. In addition, Apple refused to "unbundle" its computer system: It insisted on selling its own operating system with the Macintosh (and later-generation models), and at a price inflated by the restricted availability of Apple machines and operating systems (Evans, Nichols, and Reddy 1999, 4).

Microsoft took a radically different approach: It got IBM to agree to allow it to license MS-DOS to other computer manufacturers, and then did just that to all comers, in the expectation that competition among nonApple computer manufacturers would spread the use of their computers – and, not incidentally, Microsoft's operating system. This expectation was realized and the "abundance" of MS-DOS systems led to an even greater demand for such systems, and to a lower demand for Apple systems. Many people started joining the Microsoft network, not necessarily because they thought that MS-DOS or Windows was a superior operating system to that of Apple but because of the benefits of the larger network. There was a "tipping point" for Microsoft sometime in the late 1980s or early 1990s (possibly with the release of Windows 3.1) that caused Windows to take off, sending Apple into a market-share tailspin.

In 1998, the Justice Department took Microsoft to court for violation of US antitrust laws. Among other charges, the Justice Department maintained that Microsoft was a monopolist, as evidenced by its dominant (90+ percent) market share in the operating system market, and that Microsoft was engaging in "predatory" pricing of its browser Internet Explorer. Microsoft had been giving away Internet Explorer with Windows 95 and had integrated Internet Explorer into Windows 98. The Justice Department claimed that the only reason Microsoft could possibly have had to offer Internet Explorer was to eliminate Netscape Navigator from the market. We can't settle these issues here (see McKenzie 2000). But we can point out that the Justice Department starts its case against Microsoft with the claim that the operating system market software markets are full of "network effects." Although it might be true that Microsoft engaged in pricing designed to eliminate competition, it may also be true that Microsoft was responding to the dictates of "network effects," underpricing its product in order to build its network and future demand. It had another reason to lower its price to levels that Netscape might not consider reasonable. If Microsoft lowered its price on Internet Explorer (or lowered its *effective* price for Windows by including Internet Explorer in Windows), then more computers could be sold, which means that more copies of Windows would be sold *and* more copies of Microsoft's applications – Word, Excel, etc. – would be sold. This means that a lower price for Internet Explorer or Windows could give rise to higher sales, prices, and profits on the other applications.

PART II ORGANIZATIONAL ECONOMICS AND MANAGEMENT

Covering relocation costs of new hires

Major corporations are constantly relocating the workers they hire from one part of the country to another, often more expensive, part. Few question whether corporations should pay the cost of the moving van and travel. The trickier issue is whether they should fully cover the difference in the cost of living. Our answer is, "it depends." Based on the analysis of consumer choice earlier in this chapter, we can show that if the cost-of-living difference is spread across all goods bought by the relocating workers, the entire living cost difference will likely have to be covered. However, if the cost difference is concentrated in any one good (for example, housing), the firm can get by with increasing the relocating workers' salaries by less than the full cost-of-living difference.

Covering the added housing costs of new hires

Suppose that your company's headquarters is in La Jolla, California, where the cost of housing is much higher than in many other parts of the country. Suppose also that you want to hire an engineer from Six Mile, South Carolina, where the cost of housing is relatively low. In fact, suppose you learn that the cost of housing in La Jolla is exactly five times the cost of housing in Six Mile. A modestly equipped, 2,000 ft^2 house in La Jolla on a one-tenth-of-an-acre lot, for example, sells for about \$1 million. Approximately the same house can be bought in Six Mile (with much more land) for \$135,000.

The engineer you are interested in hiring is earning \$100,000 a year in Six Mile. In your interviews with the engineer, she tells you, quite honestly, that she likes the job you have for her. However, she also informs you that she is concerned with the difference in the cost of housing between La Jolla and her home town, which is the only significant cost difference. There are minor cost differences for things such as food, clothing, and medical care, but those differences wash out, especially after considering quality differences. The two areas are substantially different, she admits, but she values the amenities in the two locations more or less the same. La Jolla has the ocean close by, but Six Mile has the mountains just a short distance to the west.

However, the engineer stresses that at an interest rate of 6 percent, the \$865,000 additional mortgage she will have to take out to buy a house in La Jolla that is comparable to the one she has back in Six Mile means an added annual housing expenditure for her of nearly \$52,000. Therefore, she wants you to compensate her for the difference in the cost of housing, which implies an annual salary of \$152,000 (plus, she expects all moving and adjustment costs to be covered by your firm).

Do you have to concede to her demands? Many managers do succumb to the temptation. But, assuming that she is being truthful when she says that the amenities of the areas and the other costs of living balance out, the answer is emphatically "No". You can fully compensate her for the increased cost of living in La Jolla by paying less than \$152,000 a year. There are two ways of explaining why. First, you should recognize that the engineer is getting a lot of purchasing power back in Six Mile in one good, housing. If you gave her the demanded \$52,000 in additional salary, she would be able to replace her

Six Mile house in La Jolla. However, the money payment you provide is fungible, which means that she could buy any number of other things with the added income, including a nicer car, more clothing, or more meals out (and there are far more restaurants in La Jolla). And given the price of housing in La Jolla, relative to these other goods, compared to Six Mile, she would surely buy a smaller house in La Jolla than she has in Six Mile and spend more on other goods and services.

Hence, the engineer would actually prefer the $152,000 annual income in La Jolla to the $100,000 income in Six Mile. Or she would be happier in La Jolla with something less than $152,000 in salary than she is in Six Mile. To get her to take your job, all you need to do is make her slightly better off at your company's location than she is in Six Mile. Doing that does not require full compensation in the housing cost.

We can make the point with greater clarity through the use of figure 7.9, which contains a representation of the engineer's income constraints in the two locations. To make the analysis as simple as possible and stay within the constraints of the two-dimensional graph, we consider two categories of goods: housing, which is on the horizontal axis, and a representative bundle of all other goods on the vertical axis.

Figure 7.9 shows that with her $100,000 salary in Six Mile, the engineer could buy H_1 units of housing if she spent all of her income on housing (which, admittedly, would never be practical), or she could buy A_1 bundles of all other goods if she bought no housing (which is also not practical). More than likely, the engineer will buy some combination of housing and all other goods – say, combination H_2 of housing and A_2 of all other goods.

If the engineer were to get only the same $100,000 in income in La Jolla, she would have to choose from combinations along the inside curve, which extends from A_1 (meaning that she could still buy, at the limit, the same number of bundles of all other goods) to H_3 (much less housing if only housing were bought). Clearly, the engineer would be unlikely to take an offer of $100,000, simply because there is no combination along A_1H_3 that is superior to combination *a* in Six Mile.

If you conceded to her demand of $152,000 in annual income, her income constraint would be the thin line that is parallel to A_1H_3 and goes through *a*.[13]

[13] By receiving $152,000, the engineer can buy the exact combination of goods, A_2 and H_2, that she had back in Six Mile. The extra $52,000 in salary would go totally to housing, leaving her with the same amount of after-housing income that she had in Six Mile. Her new income constraint line is parallel with A_1H_3 simply because the prices of the bundles and housing are the same as those under A_1H_3, and the relative prices of those goods determine the slope of the income constraint.

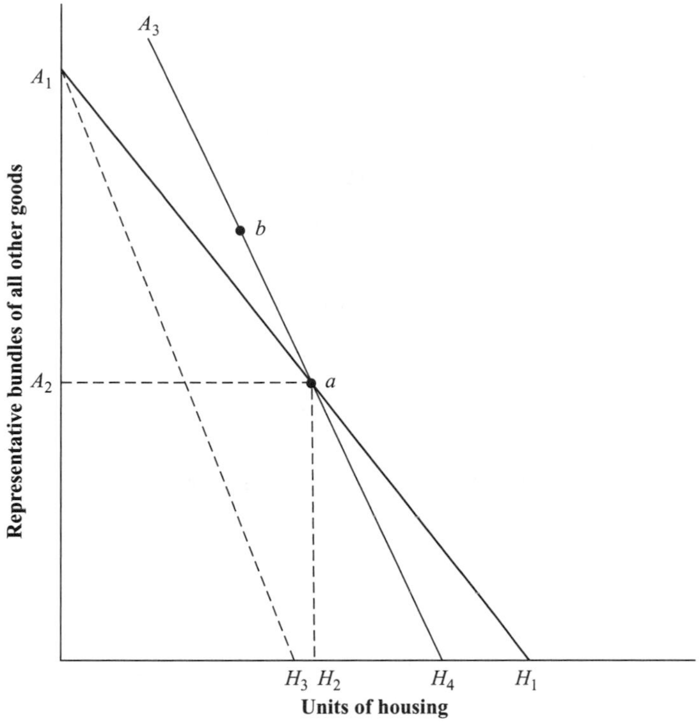

Figure 7.9 Choosing between housing and bundles of other goods
The budget line in Six Mile is A_1H_1 with an income of \$100,000. The budget line in La Jolla is A_1H_3 with the same income. If the employer were to offer the engineer a salary of \$152,000, which covers the additional cost of housing, the engineer's budget line would be the thin line cutting A_1H_1 at a. Hence, the engineer could choose combination b and be better off than in Six Mile. This means that the employer can offer the engineer less than \$152,000.

Clearly, she could be as well off in La Jolla at such a salary because she could still take combination *a*. But is that what she is likely to do?

The answer is "No", because of the changes in relative prices. The price of housing in La Jolla is much higher than the price of housing in Six Mile, which is why the engineer's dashed income constraint (A_3H_4) is much steeper than her old income constraint (A_1H_1). The law of demand (the economist's analytical pride and joy) applies to housing in our example. Hence, the engineer will buy less housing and more of other goods, which implies a movement toward the vertical axis. She will choose a combination such as *b*. She will obviously be better off there because, were she not, she would have remained with consumption bundle *a*. If she is better off, then you can cut her income below $152,000, taking part of the gains she would otherwise get.[14]

The logic of not fully compensating new hires for their added housing costs

We can't say, theoretically, exactly how little you can pay the engineer. All we can say is that, given the conditions of this problem, you don't have to pay her $152,000. You might be able to pay her $145,000 or $135,000 – something between $100,000 and $152,000. You will have to negotiate with the engineer to get a better estimate of how much she will accept, but it will be helpful in those negotiations to know that she will accept less than $152,000, given the assumptions we have made.

The only time a $52,000 raise would be required is when the added costs of living in La Jolla are distributed more or less evenly among all goods, not just concentrated in housing (which is where a sizable share of the cost differential actually is). This leads us to the conclusion that the more concentrated the cost differential between two areas, the less of the overall cost differential that must be made up in the form of salary, or money income, and vice versa.

This leads to another useful insight. If you are looking for an employee who is living in an area where the cost of living is lower than yours, then you can save on salary by looking where the lower cost of living is concentrated in a single good, such as housing. Conversely, if you are thinking about moving your plant to a "low-cost area" such as Six Mile, then don't expect to save in salaries an amount that is equal to the difference in the cost of living. You will be able to lower your salaries, but not by the entire cost-of-living differential.

We understand that our problem has been relatively simple, given that we have assumed away many of the differences between the two locations. Candidates appraise locations differently. Some people like urban life and the Pacific coastal areas, and other people like rural areas and the mountains of the Appalachian region. Those "comparative likes" will be important in determining the salary that you will have to pay. You may want someone who is competent to do the job you have, but that is not all you will be concerned

[14] We suggest that you consider the extended discussion of indifference curves that are considered in the appendix A and then add indifference curves to the diagram in figure 7.9. You will see with the addition of indifference curves that the engineer will have an indifference curve tangent to the budget line A_1H_1 at point *a*. However, that necessarily means that she can reach an even higher indifference curve that is tangent to the steeper budget line that cuts through A_1H_1 at *a* in figure 7.9. This means that the engineer can move to a point such as *b*.

about. You might take someone who is less competent than someone else simply because that person appreciates the amenities of your area more than other more competent candidates do, which means that you can get the targeted, less competent person for less and she will be happier than the more competent worker. And even if that person does not produce as much, she can still be more cost effective.

When talking about their hiring processes, business people almost always talk about getting the "best" person. This is true if they are careful about what they mean by "best". A more accurate statement is that business people want the most *cost-effective* person, and that person is not necessarily, or even often, the most competent.

Our way of looking at the complicated process of business hiring is obviously not fully descriptive of what actually goes on. We can't deal with all the complications here, and would not want to waste your time if we could. We are suggesting, perhaps, some new thoughts, drawn from the economic way of thinking – a way of thinking that provides real guidance in the search for, and bargaining with, job candidates.

A few qualifications

Returning to our original question: Should relocating workers be compensated for housing cost differences? The answer is a qualified "No". If housing makes up the main cost difference, then workers moving to a higher-housing-cost location would be too well compensated if the full cost-of-living difference were paid. She would take less. How much less is a problem that can be solved only by way of interviews and negotiations.

We caution, however, that our analysis flows from an unstated but important assumption, that the housing-cost difference in the two locations reflects actual *cost* differences that are not offset by benefit differences. That is often a questionable assumption. Property near the coast in Southern California is much more expensive than in most other parts of the country, for a reason. Property is much higher-cost in La Jolla than in Six Mile because most people must see some added benefits for being in La Jolla. This implies that, for a lot of people, La Jolla may be more attractive than Six Mile even with the higher housing costs. And for an even larger number of people, at least some of the difference in living cost is covered by the "nonmoney income" associated with the additional amenities in La Jolla that are not available in Six Mile.

The first rule of management (and other disciplines) has sometimes been stated as "Different Strokes for Different Folks." In our foregoing discussion, we do not mean to suggest that everyone would want to live in La Jolla. If that were the case, the price of land in La Jolla would be far higher than it already is. We mean only to point out that "cost-of-living" differences cited by business people are not always relevant cost differences because of benefit differences.

To make our point in more concrete terms, it may be true that the measured "cost of living" in La Jolla is 30 percent higher than the cost of living in Six Mile and, for that matter, 30 percent higher than the average for the rest of the country. However, no one should conclude that the cost of *doing business* in La Jolla (or any other "high-cost" area) is 30 percent higher than other parts of the country. The so-called "cost of living" can be offset in part by amenities and in part by more productive people who are attracted to the high-cost area. Many people with limited productivity will simply not be able to compete with their more productive counterparts in their search for property.[15] In making their employment decisions, firms need to keep these considerations in focus. They need to look carefully at what is implied by "cost of living."

THE BOTTOM LINE

The key takeaways from chapter 7 are the following:

(1) Rational consumers will equate at the margins. That is to say, they will so allocate their expenditures that the marginal utility of the last unit of every good is equal to every other.
(2) The law of demand is a natural consequence of rational behavior.
(3) Demand does not consist of what people would like to have or are willing to buy at a given price. Rather it represents the inverse relationship between price and quantity, a relationship described by a downward sloping curve.
(4) Although economists do not have complete confidence in all applications of the law of demand, they consider the relationship between price and quantity to be

[15] We should, therefore, expect people in high-cost areas such as La Jolla to have relatively high incomes. One reason is obvious: People need a high income to cover the high cost of living. Another reason can go unnoticed: People who can afford to live in high-cost-of-living areas are likely to be, on average, more productive than those who cannot. We aren't claiming that this is a big consideration in the higher pay people in high-cost-of-living areas earn – there are very productive people in every area of the country – but it is a consideration that shouldn't be completely ignored.

so firmly established, both theoretically and empirically, that they call it a law. (For a discussion of how people's preferences can be given graphical structure with "indifference curves," and indifference curves can be used to provide even more theoretical support for the downward sloping demand curve, see appendix A to this chapter, p. 300.)

(5) In the real world, when the price of a good goes down, the quantity purchased may fall rather than rise. In such cases, economists normally assume (until strong evidence is presented to the contrary) that some other variable has changed, offsetting the positive effects of the reduction in price.

(6) The market demand curve for a private good is obtained by horizontally summing individuals' demand curves for the good.

(7) Total revenue will rise when demand is elastic and the price is reduced, and vice versa. Total revenue will fall when demand is inelastic and the price is reduced, and vice versa.

(8) The slope and elasticity of a demand curve are not the same. The slope of a straight-line demand curve is the same at all points along the demand curve. The elasticity of demand, as measured by the elasticity coefficient, increases with movements up a straight-lined demand curve.

(9) When the price of a network good is lowered, the demand for the good can (eventually) rise as the value of the good rises with the increase in the number of consumers. Producers of the network good can (depending on the extent of the network effects) have an incentive to charge zero and negative prices.

(10) When a new hire is brought from a low-cost housing area to work in a high-housing area, the new hire's salary need not be increased by the amount of the greater housing cost.

(11) Not all downward sloping demand curves are alike. They differ radically in terms of the elasticity of demand, or the responsiveness of consumers to a price change. The elasticity of demand can heavily influence business pricing strategies.

REVIEW QUESTIONS

(1) What role does the law of demand play in economic analysis?

(2) If the price of jeans rises and the quantity sold goes up, does this mean that the demand curve slopes upward? Why or why not?

(3) If the prices of most goods are rising by an average of 15 percent per year, but the price of gasoline rises just 10 percent per year, what is happening to the real, or relative, price of gasoline? How do you expect consumers to react?

(4) Suppose that a producer raises the price of a good from $4 to $7, and the quantity sold drops from 250 to 200 units. Is demand for the good elastic or inelastic?

(5) If the campus police force is expanded and officers are instructed to increase the number of parking tickets they give out, why might the initial effect of this policy increase revenues from fines more than the long-run effect? What does your answer have to do with the elasticity of demand for illegal parking?

(6) If the government subsidizes flood insurance, what will happen to the price of that insurance? What will happen to the value of the property that is lost during floods? Why?

(7) Many computer programs – for example, operating systems and word processors – are said to be "network goods." Software piracy is often relatively easy because of the digital nature of software. Should software developers be against all piracy?

(8) Consider two markets, one in which the market "tips" and another in which it does not. Compare the incentives of firms in the two markets to lower their prices initially before the market tips.

(9) Assume network effects in two markets. In one market, there are no "switching costs." In the other, there are substantial switching costs. How will the switching costs (or the absence thereof) affect the initial price competition in the two markets?

Appendix A: Indifference curves and budget lines

Our discussion in chapter 7 has been based on the assumption that individuals know what they want – what their *preferences* are. "Preference," however, is a nebulous concept. In this appendix, we can add a little more concreteness to the concept of preference by developing the concept of *indifference curves*, which can be used to derive in a different way the law of demand and to consider policy applications.

Derivation of the indifference curve

Consider a student who wants only two goods, pens and books. Figure 7A.1 shows all the possible combinations of pens and books she may choose. The student will prefer a combination far from the origin to one closer in. At point *b*, for instance, she will have more books and more pens than at point *a*. For the same reason, she will prefer

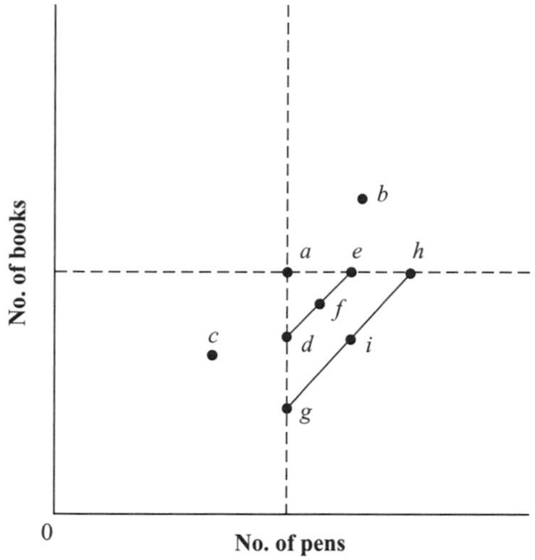

Figure 7A.1

Derivation of an indifference curve

Because the consumer prefers more of a good to less, point *a* is preferable to point *c*, and point *b* is preferable to point *a*. If *a* is preferable to *d* but *e* is preferable to *a*, then when we move from point *d* to *e*, we must move from a combination that is less preferred to the one that is more preferred. In doing so, we must cross a point – for example, *f* – that is equal in value to *a*. Indifference curves are composed by connecting all those points – *a*, *f*, *i*, and so on – that are of equal value to the consumer.

a to *c*. In fact the student will prefer *a* to any point in the lower-left quadrant of the graph and will prefer any point in the upper-right quadrant to *a*.

We can also reason that the student would prefer *a* to *d*, where she gets the same number of pens but fewer books than at *a*. Likewise, she will prefer *e* to *a* because it yields the same number of books and more pens than *a*. If *a* is preferred to *d* and *e* is preferred to *a*, then as the student moves diagonally from *d* to *e*, she must move from a less preferable to a more preferable position with respect to *a*. At some point along that path, the student will reach a combination of books and pens that equals the value of point *a*. Assuming that combination to be *f* (it can be any point between *d* and *e*), we can say that the individual is indifferent between *a* and *f*.

> An **indifference curve** shows the various combinations of two goods that yield the same level of total utility.

Using a similar line of logic, we can locate another point along the line *gih* that will be equal in value to *a* and therefore to *f*. In fact, any number of points in the lower-right and upper-left quadrants of the graph are of equal value to *a*. Taken together, these points form what is called an **indifference curve** (see curve I_1 in figure 7A.2).

Using the same line of reasoning, we can construct a second indifference curve through point *b*. Because *b* is preferable to *a*, and all points on the new indifference curve will be equal in value to point *b*, we can conclude that any point along the new

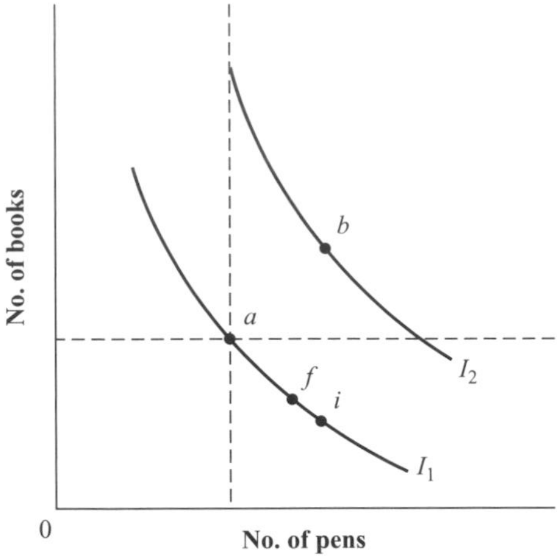

Figure 7A.2 Indifference curves for pens and books
Any combination of pens and books that falls along curve I_1 will yield the same level of utility as any other combination on that curve. The consumer is indifferent among them. By extension, any combination on curve I_2 will be preferable to any combination on curve I_1.

curve I_2 is preferable to any point on I_1. Using this same procedure, we can continue to derive any number of curves, each one higher than, and preferable to, the previous one.

From this line of reasoning, an economist can draw several conclusions about the student's preference structure (called an "indifference map"):

(1) A person's total utility level rises as she moves up and to the right, from one indifference curve to the next.
(2) Indifference curves slope downward to the right.
(3) Indifference curves cannot bend backwards, or take on an "S" shape. (This is because such a shape for an indifference curve would mean that all combinations on the curves were of equal value. However, with the backward or *S* shape to the curves, there would be combinations of the two goods that contain more of both goods, which should suggest that the value of the combinations on the curve were unequal in value, given our basic proposition underlying indifference curves that "more is preferred to less."[16])

[16] As Becker (1971, 25–9) has shown, indifference curves do not have to be strictly convex to the origin throughout their lengths. They can be wavy downward sloping curves (so long as they do not bend backwards). That is, they can have convex and concave ranges. However, the reason textbooks such as this one draw indifference curves convex throughout is that even when the indifference curves are wavy downward sloping curves, consumer equilibrium, to be taken up in the next section, will always occur in a convex range of an indifference curve.

(4) Indifference curves cannot intersect. (An intersection would imply that all points on all the intersecting curves are of equal value, contradicting the conclusion that higher indifference curves represent higher levels of utility).

(5) As a consumer has more of one good relative to the other, she has to receive a larger amount of the relatively abundant good to compensate for the loss of a unit of the relatively scarce good. This assumption causes each indifference curve to be convex to the origin – that is, become less negatively sloped as we move farther to the right and down along the indifference curve.[17]

Budget lines and consumer equilibrium

The **budget line** depicts the income constraint and shows graphically all the combinations of two goods that a consumer can buy with a given amount of income.

From indifference curves we can derive the law of demand. First we need to construct the individual's **budget line**, a special form of the production possibilities curve (PPC). Assume that our student earns an income of $150, which she uses to buy books and pens. Books cost $3 each and pens cost $5 a package. The student can spend all $150 on fifty books or thirty pen packs, or she can divide her expenditures in any number of ways to yield various combinations of books and pens. By plotting all the possible combinations, we obtain the student's budget line, B_1P_1 in figure 7A.3.

All combinations on the budget line can be purchased by the student. She can choose point *a*, twenty-five books and fifteen pen packs, or point *b*, forty-five books and three pen packs. Either combination exhausts her $150 budget. The rational individual will choose that point where the budget line just touches (is tangent to) an indifference curve – point *a* in this case.[18] Points further up or down the budget line will put the student on a lower indifference curve and are therefore less preferable. (If, for instance, the student moves to *c* on the budget line, she will be on a lower indifference curve, I_2 instead of I_1.) At point *a*, the individual is said to be in equilibrium. As long as her

That is to say, within the relevant range of consumer equilibrium, indifference curves will be convex.

[17] The indifference curves can also be shown to be convex to the origin because that is the only shape of indifference curves that leads in a two-good world to a combination of goods being bought in our two-good model. We want such an internal equilibrium solution because our two goods in the graphs are intended to represent all goods, and we observe all consumers buying combinations of goods, not just one good. If indifference curves were downward sloping straight lines, then the consumer would end up buying all of one good or the other (books or pens), because such a purchase would put the consumer on her highest indifference curve. If the indifference curve were concave to the origins (that is, bowed out), the same thing would result: the consumer would consume all of one good and none of the other, because, again, such a consumption combination would put the consumer on her highest indifference curve.

[18] This tangency condition can be derived mathematically by maximizing the consumer's utility subject to the budget constraint, or by maximizing $U(X,Y)$ with respect to X and Y, subject to $P_x X + P_y Y = I$. This constrained maximization problem can be carried out by forming the Lagrangian function

$$L = U(X_1 Y) + \lambda(I - P_X X - P_Y Y) \quad (7.1)$$

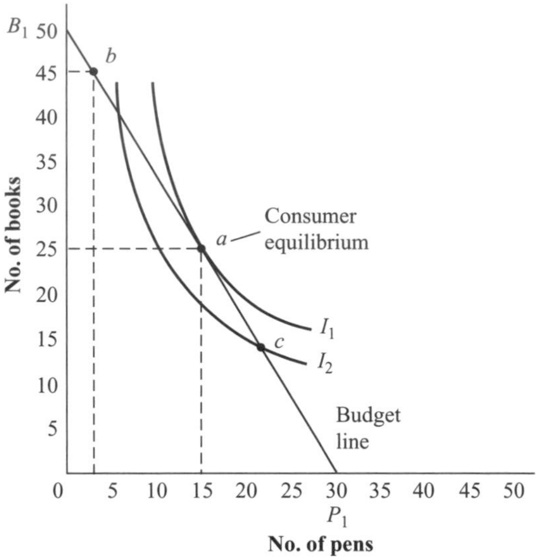

Figure 7A.3 The budget line and consumer equilibrium

Constrained by her budget, the consumer will seek to maximize her utility by consuming at the point where her budget line is tangent to an indifference curve. Here the consumer chooses point *a*, where her budget line just touches indifference curve I_1. All other combinations on the consumer's budget line will fall on a lower indifference curve, providing less utility. Point *c*, for instance, falls on indifference curve I_2.

where λ is known as a *Lagrangian multiplier*, and maximizing it with respect to *X* and *Y* and minimizing it with respect to λ. The necessary conditions are:

$$\frac{\partial L}{\partial X} = \frac{\partial U}{\partial X} - \lambda P_X = 0 \tag{7.2}$$

$$\frac{\partial L}{\partial Y} = \frac{\partial U}{\partial Y} - \lambda P_Y = 0$$

$$\frac{\partial L}{\partial \lambda} = I - P_X X - P_Y Y = 0$$

Equation (7.1) can be divided by (7.2) which, after simple algebraic manipulation, yields

$$-\frac{\partial U/\partial X}{\partial U/\partial Y} = -\frac{P_X}{P_y}$$

The left-hand side of this equation is −1 multiplied by the ratio of the marginal utility of good *X* to the marginal utility of good *Y*, or the slope of the indifference curve. The right-hand side is −1 multiplied by the ratio of the price of good *X* to the price of good *Y*, or the slope of the budget constraint. The equality of these two slopes is dependent on the assumption that the consumer will consume positive quantities of both goods. Later in this chapter, we shall consider the possibility that the consumer may maximize utility subject to the budget constraint by deciding to consume none of one of the goods.

income and preferences and the prices of books and pens remain the same, she has no reason to move from that point.[19]

What happens if prices change? Suppose the individual's wants are in equilibrium at point *a* in figure 7A.3 when the price of pens falls from $5 a pack to $3 a pack. (The price of books stays the same.) The budget line will pivot to $B_1 P_2$ in figure 7A.4, reflecting the greater buying power of the student's income. (She can now buy fifty pen packs with $150.) The new budget line gives the student a chance to move to a higher indifference curve – for instance, to point *c*, twenty-two pens and twenty-eight books.

The law of demand, again

The result of the price reduction is that the student buys more pens. Thus we derive the law of demand, that quantity demanded is inversely related to price. The downward sloping demand curve for pens shown in figure 7A.5 is obtained by plotting the quantities of pen packs bought from figure 7A.4 against the price paid per pack. When the price of pens falls from $5 to $3 a pack in figure 7A.4, the consumer increases the quantity purchased from fifteen to twenty-two packages.[20]

[19] We can provide another intuitive rationale for the required condition for consumer equilibrium. Starting with the tangency requirement

$$\frac{MU_X}{MU_Y} = \frac{P_X}{P_Y}$$

we can obtain the equivalent condition

$$\frac{MU_X}{P_X} = \frac{MU_Y}{P_Y}$$

by simple algebraic manipulation. In words, this means that the consumer receives the same increase in utility from spending $1 more on good *X* as would be received from spending more on good *Y*. We can see that this condition is necessary if utility is being maximized subject to the budget constraint by assuming that the condition is not satisfied. Assume, for example, that

$$\frac{MU_X}{P_X} > \frac{MU_Y}{P_Y}$$

This tells us that if $1 less is spent on good *Y*, utility will not decline as much as it will increase if $1 more is spent on good *X*. Therefore, the consumer can increase total utility without increasing expenditures by reducing the consumption of good *Y* and increasing the consumption of good *X*. This will continue to be true until the equality is restored, which will happen eventually as MU_Y increases relative to MU_X. In a similar manner, we can argue that the consumer will move toward the equilibrium condition if we assume that

$$\frac{MU_X}{P_X} < \frac{MU_Y}{P_Y}$$

[20] There exists a possibility that the analysis can find a price decrease (increase) for a good leading to a decrease (increase) in the amount of the good purchased. But this possibility is so unlikely that it is of only of theoretical interest.

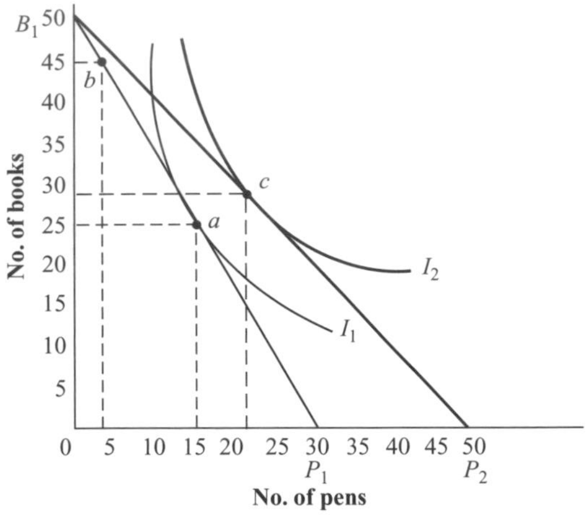

Figure 7A.4 Effect of a change in price on consumer equilibrium

If the price of pens falls, the consumer's budget line will pivot outward, from B_1P_1 to B_1P_2. As a result, the consumers can move to a higher indifference curve, I_2 instead of I_1. At the new price, the consumer buys more pens, twenty-two packs as opposed to fifteen.

Application: cash vs. in-kind transfers

A cash grant will raise the welfare of the poor more than an in-kind transfer of equal value will. Figure 7A.6 illustrates a poor family's budget line for housing and higher education, H_3E_3. Without subsidies, this family can buy as much as E_3 units of education (and no housing) or H_3 units of housing (and no education). Because the family wants both housing and higher education, it will probably divide its income between the two, choosing some combination such as point *a* – that is, E_1 education and H_1 housing.

Suppose that the government decides to subsidize the family's higher education purchases through reduced university tuition. Its action lowers the total price of education, pivoting the family's budget line out to H_3E_5. The result is that the family can now consume more of both items, education and housing. The family will probably move to some combination such as point *b*, H_2 housing and E_2 education. Its education consumption has gone up, and the additional housing purchased represents an increase in income equal to the vertical distance between *b* and *c*.

Suppose the family were given the cash equivalent of *bc* instead. The additional money would not change the relative prices of higher education and housing, as the reduced tuition program did. Instead it would shift the budget line from H_3E_3 to a parallel position, H_4E_4 (dashed line). The relative price of housing is lower on H_4E_4 than on H_3E_5. Thus the family would tend to prefer *d* to *b*, both of which are available on line H_4E_4, so we must presume that it would prefer cash to an in-kind subsidy.

This point can be seen even more clearly with the help of indifference curves. Imagine an indifference curve tangent to H_3E_3 in the absence of government relief, causing the

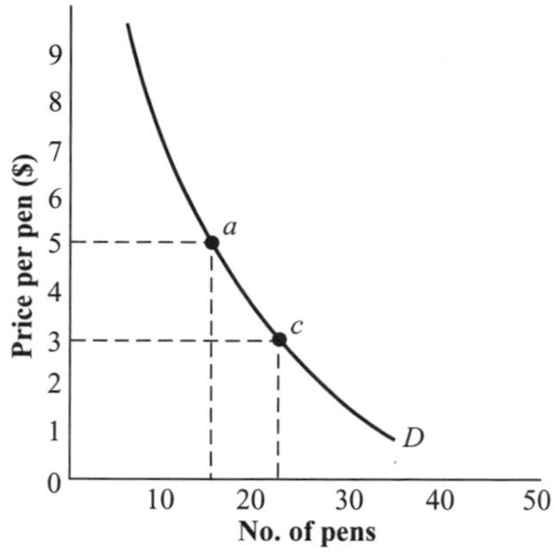

Figure 7A.5 Derivation of the demand curve for pens

When the price of pens changes, shifting the consumer's budget line from B_1P_1 to B_1P_2 in figure 7A.4, the consumer equilibrium point changes with it, from *a* to *c*. The consumer's demand curve for pens is obtained by plotting her equilibrium quantity of pens at various prices. At \$5 a pack, the consumer buys fifteen packs of pens (point *a*). At \$3 a pack, she buys twenty-two packages (point *c*).

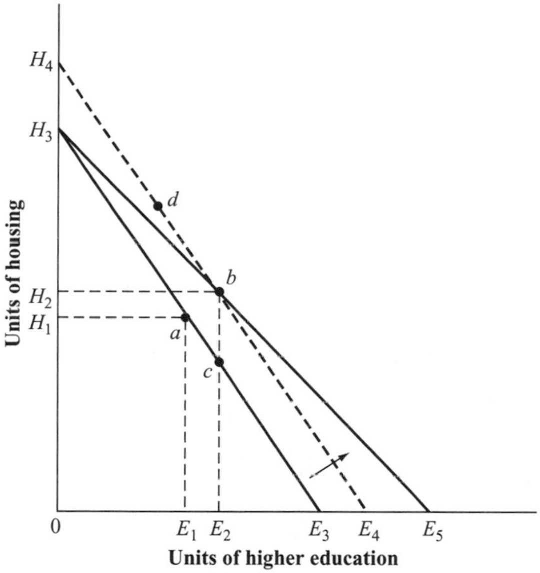

Figure 7A.6 Budget line: cash grants vs. education subsidies

If the price of education is reduced by an in-kind subsidy, a family's budget line will pivot from H_3E_3 to H_3E_5. The family will move from point *a* to point *b*, where it can consume more food and housing. If the family is given the same subsidy in cash, its budget line will move from H_3E_3 to H_4E_4. Because the relative price of housing is lower on H_4E_4 than on H_3E_5, the family will choose a point such as *d* over *b*. Because *b* was the family's preferred point on H_3E_5, but it prefers *d* to *b* on H_4E_4 which allows the purchase of *b*, we must presume that it also prefers cash to a food subsidy.

family to choose point *a*. Imagine a higher indifference curve that is tangent to H_3E_5 at point *b*. Now, imagine an even higher indifference curve tangent to H_4E_4 at point *d*.

This analysis is important to managers who are considering substituting more fringe benefits for money in compensating workers. As we saw in chapter 5, providing fringe benefits to workers at the cost of reducing their salaries by enough to pay for them can increase the value of the compensation to workers while reducing the cost of that compensation to the firm. But it should always be kept in mind that unless there is a clear preference by workers in favor of the fringe benefits (in-kind payments), adding more fringe benefits are a bad idea since, everything else equal, workers prefer more money that they can spend on what they want to more fringe benefits.

Appendix B: common concerns relating to the law of demand

Many MBA students being introduced to the law of demand harbor understandable concerns over the claim of economists that all demand curves slope downward, or that price and quantity are always and everywhere inversely related. We readily concede that such a claim seems too absolute. With the billions of goods and services in the world, there might well be some goods that violate the law of demand. Nevertheless, given the frequency with which the law of demand appears to apply, it still can be a pretty good rule for firms to adopt, until they are given strong reasons to assume otherwise.

From our classroom experience, we have found that MBAs still worry that many consumers will buy more of some good when their prices rise *because their prices rise.* A good's price may indicate something about a good's relative value. Hence, an increase in the price leads to greater consumption. Alternatively, many consumers are thought to be "irrational" (or "nonrational"), which means they cannot be expected to respond to price changes in the same way as rational consumers. Indeed, irrational consumers might not even consider price in their purchases and, hence, might not be expected to respond at all to a price change. We consider each of these concerns in turn.

Conspicuous consumption and the law of demand

Sociologist Thorstein Veblen (1902, 68–101) argued in his well-known book *The Theory of the Leisure Class* that many high-income and "high-bred" people engage in "conspicuous consumption." That is, they often buy high-price goods in order to put their income and wealth on display. This often means that high-price goods have value, apart from their intrinsic worth, because of the not-so-hidden messages such purchases convey to others. An all-too-easy deduction is that the demand curves for

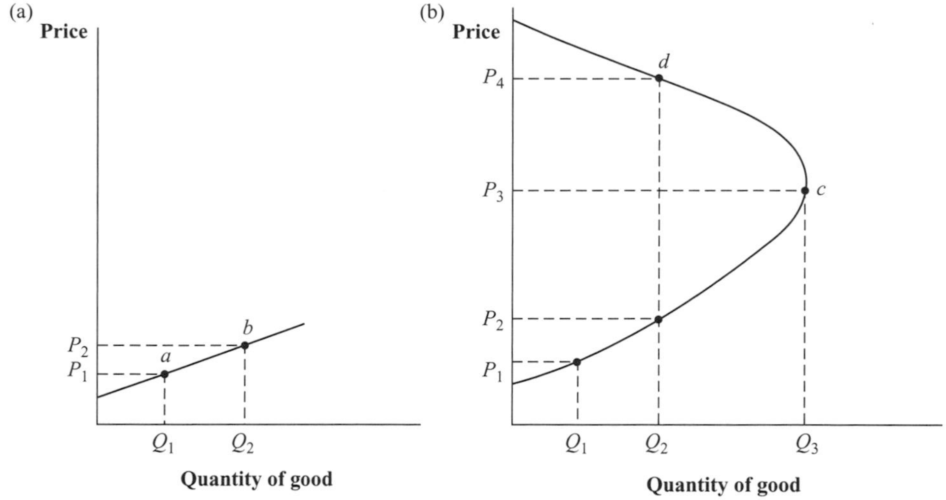

Figure 7B.1 Upward sloping demand?
A good might have an upward sloping range, as described in panel (a), given that a price increase might convey greater value to consumers. However, there must be some higher price that will cause sales to contract, since many consumers will no longer be able to buy the good. This means that the demand curve must go beyond some price, P_3 in panel (b), must bend backwards and, thus, must have a downward sloping range. The downward sloping range of the curve in panel (b) is the relevant range. If the seller is at combination *b*, then there is some combination such as *d* in the downward sloping range of the entire demand curve that is more profitable than combination *b*.

"conspicuous consumption goods" are upward sloping, supposedly clear violations of the law of demand.

For purposes of argument, we might agree that prices can convey messages and that they can, to a degree and at times, indicate goods' relative worth.[21] Higher-price goods can indicate greater value, which can mean that some increase in price from an initial low price can lead to greater purchases. In terms of figure 7B.1(a), an increase in price from P_1 to P_2 can lead to an increase in quantity from Q_1 to Q_2. A higher price can lead to an even higher quantity consumed. Why? People deduce that with the higher price, the value of the good is greater (and may be greater because its purchase conveys

[21] After all, if a high-priced good were consistently found by buyers not to be worth the price sellers command, then buyers would move to lower-priced goods. Hence, to the extent that markets work efficiently, prices can, to a degree, carry valuable information to consumers – so long as some consumers judge the good on grounds other than price. If *all* consumers judged the worth of goods based solely on price, then prices would carry no information on the goods' relative intrinsic worth.

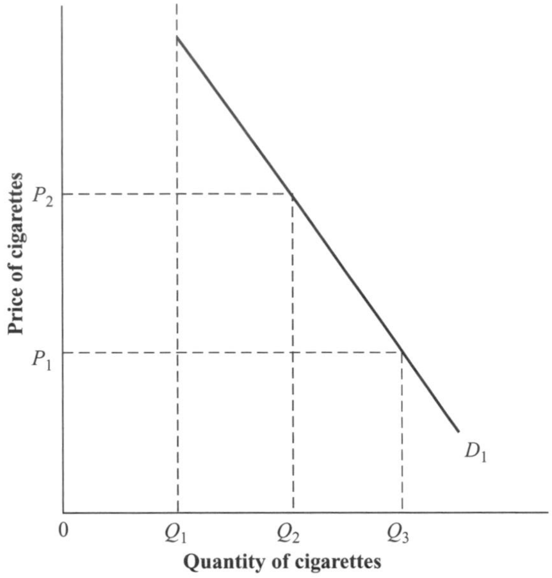

Figure 7B.2 Demand including irrational behavior
If irrational consumers demand Q_1 cigarettes no matter what the price, but rational consumers take price into consideration, market demand will be D_1. The quantity purchased will still vary inversely with the price.

to relevant others that the buyers have done well in life). By raising its price on its S500 model cars from an initial low price to a higher price, Mercedes Benz might be able to sell more cars.

However, after making such a concession on how consumers react to price increases at low prices, we have to insist that there will be some high price after which sales of the good (Mercedes Benz S500s or any other supposedly conspicuous consumption good) will contract. This is because, beyond some very high price, many buyers will not be able to afford the good, resulting in a backward bending demand curve, as illustrated in figure 7B.1(b). In that figure, beyond a price of P_3, sales contract, and continue to contract with higher prices. Very likely, the seller will raise the price above P_3, given that the demand curve above P_3 will for some distance likely be inelastic (which means that revenues can rise with a higher price) and production costs can be expected to fall with the cutback in sales, leading to greater profits. Also, we note that if the seller is selling initially in the upward sloping portion of the demand curve, say, at price–quantity combination *b*, there is some higher combination, *d*, that would be preferred to *b*. This is because the same quantity Q_2 can be sold at a higher price, P_4, which necessarily means that combination *d* is more profitable than combination *b*. Hence, the relevant portion of the demand curve is the downward portion, because that is where sellers can maximize profits.

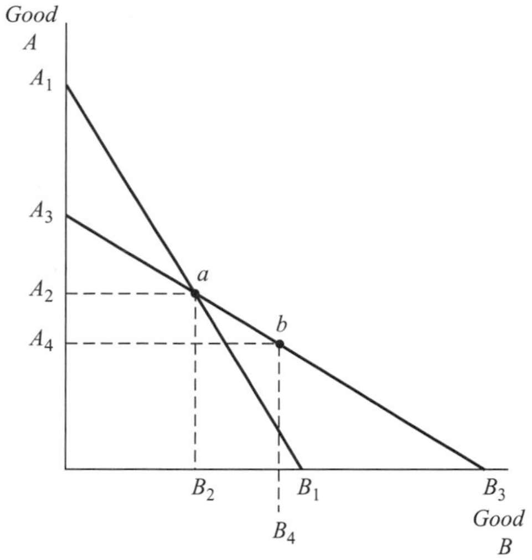

Figure 7B.3 Random behavior, budget lines, and downward sloping demand curves
If a number of buyers are faced initially with budget line A_1B_1 and behave randomly, they will buy an average quantity of A_2B_2. If the price of A increases while the price of B decreases, the budget line pivots on a, causing buyers to purchase on average more of B (B_4) and less of A (A_4). Thus, quantity changes in the direction predicted by the law of demand (in spite of the absence of rational behavior).

Our point here is that even *if* there were an upward sloping range for a demand curve for some "conspicuous consumption good" (over which we have serious doubts), the upward sloping portion of the entire demand curve would not be the relevant range, or the portion of the complete demand curve in figure 7B.1(b). The relevant portion or range would be the downward sloping portion, because that is where profit maximizing sellers would operate, if given a choice in the matter.

Irrationality and the law of demand

So far, we have been discussing demand in terms of rational behavior. Suppose there were some people who did not act rationally and, therefore, were not inclined to respond to price. Even if some consumers behave irrationally, the law of demand will apply. As long as some people in the market respond rationally, the amount demanded will decrease (increase) with an increase (decrease) in price.

For instance, many people buy cigarettes because they are addicted to them. At times, habitual smokers may not consider price in making their purchases. Therefore the quantity they buy may not always vary with price (except to the extent that it affects their total purchasing power). If occasional smokers take price into consideration when they buy, however, their demand for cigarettes will produce the normal downward sloping curve. If we add the quantity bought by smokers who are addicted to the quantity bought by those who are not, the total market demand curve will slope downward (see figure 7B.2). At a price of P_1, Q_1 cigarettes will be bought by addicted consumers, and $Q_3 - Q_1$ cigarettes will be bought by occasional consumers. If the price then rises to P_2, the total quantity bought will fall to Q_2, reflecting a predictable drop in the quantity purchased by occasional consumers.

This kind of reasoning can be extended to impulse buying. Some people respond more to the packaging and display of products than to their price. Their demand *may* not slope downward. As long as some people check prices and resist advertising, however, the total demand for any good will slope downward. Store managers must therefore assume that changes in price will affect the quantity demanded. The fact that some people may behave irrationally reduces the elasticity of demand but does not invalidate the concept of demand.

Random behavior and demand

Critics of demand curve theory might still complain: "The demand *curve* [drawn as a thin line on the graphs throughout this chapter] presumes that buyers know exactly how much they want to buy at any given price. Buyers are not always that well informed of their own preferences for particular goods. There is certainly a degree of randomness in how much people are willing and able to buy at various prices."

This concern can be dealt with in two ways. First, Gary Becker (1971, 29–31) has pointed out that even if buyers behaved totally randomly in their purchases, scarcity would ensure downward sloping demand curves when relative prices change. Consider figure 7B.3 in which there are many buyers with identical budget lines, A_1B_1, for two goods *A* and *B*. (See appendix A to this chapter for a discussion of the construction of budget lines.) If buyers are faced with such a budget constraint and if they randomly buy combinations of *A* and *B* along A_1B_1, then buyers will be spread out along A_1B_1 in a normal, bell shaped distribution. The *mean* quantities of *A* and *B* purchased along A_1B_1 will be in the middle of that line, combination *a*, or A_2B_2. If the price of *A* is raised and the price of *B* is lowered such that consumers can still buy combination *a*, then the buyers' budget line will pivot on *a* to A_3B_3. Buying randomly along the new budget line means that buyers on average will then buy combination *b*, or A_4B_4. That means that the drop in the price of *B* leads to more *B* being bought on average – and more being bought in total. Similarly, the increase in the price of *A* leads to less of *A* being bought on average – and in total. Hence, the overall market demand curves for *A* and *B* are downward sloping even though individuals are acting randomly.

Second, suppose that buyers' market demand curve is not a thin downward sloping line, but a downward sloping "band," like the one drawn in figure 7B.4. The "band" indicates some randomness in the quantity buyers will purchase at any given price. At

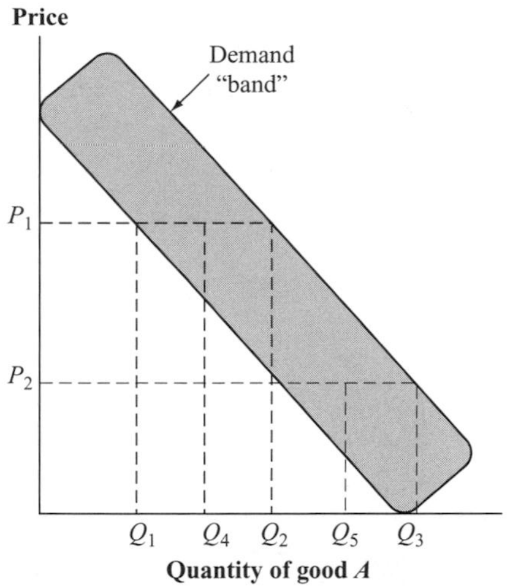

Figure 7B.4 Random behavior and the demand curve as a "band"
If buyers randomly purchase anywhere from Q_1 to Q_2 when the price is P_1 and anywhere from Q_2 to Q_3 when the price is P_2, then they will tend to increase their average quantity purchased from Q_4 to Q_5 when the price falls from P_1 to P_2.

P_1, buyers can be expected to buy anywhere from Q_1 to Q_2 of good A. At P_2, they will buy anywhere from Q_2 to Q_3. Exactly how much individual buyers consume is uncertain, but if the "band" indicates true randomness among buyer purchases, then we know that when faced with a price of P_1, buyers can be expected to buy on average Q_4 (the middle quantity between Q_1 and Q_2). When the price falls to P_2, they can be expected to buy on average Q_5 (or the middle of Q_2 and Q_3. This means that even in markets where individuals' preferences exhibit a degree of randomness (or uncertainty) – the demand is a band – price and total quantity purchased in the market will tend to be inversely related, or follow the law of demand.

CHAPTER

8

Production costs and business decisions

The economist's stock in trade – his tools – lies in his ability to and proclivity to think about all questions in terms of alternatives. The truth judgment of the moralist, which says that something is either wholly right or wholly wrong, is foreign to him. The win-list, yes–no discussion of politics is not within his purview. He does not recognize the either-or, the all-or-nothing situation as his own. His is not the world of the mutually exclusive. Instead, his is the world of adjustment, of coordinated conflict, of mutual gain.
James M. Buchanan

Cost is pervasive in human action. Managers (as well as everyone else) are constantly forced to make choices, to do one thing and not another. Cost – or more precisely, opportunity cost – is the most highly valued opportunity not chosen. Although money is the most frequently used measure of cost, it is not cost itself.

Although we may not recognize it as such, cost also pervades our everyday thought and conversation. When we say "that course is difficult" or "the sermon seemed endless" or "changes to the product design at this stage can't be made," we are really indicating something about the cost involved. If the preacher's extended commentary delayed the church picnic, the sermon was costly. Although complaints about excessive costs sometimes indicate an absolute limitation, more often they merely mean that the benefits of the activity are too small to justify the cost. Many people who "can't afford" a vacation actually have the money but do not wish to spend it on travel, and most students who find writing research papers "impossible" are simply not willing to put forth the necessary effort.

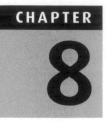

This chapter explores the meaning of cost in business, specifically, and human behavior, generally. We begin by showing how seemingly irrational behavior can often be explained by the hidden costs of a choice. We then develop further the concept of marginal cost which, together with the related concepts of demand and supply, defines the limits of rational behavior, from personal activities such as painting and fishing to business decisions such as how much to produce.

Unavoidably, points made earlier in this book are reviewed and extended in this chapter. There is a cost in this repetition, but there is also some benefit in a few varied reiterations.

We use the cost analysis to make points that seem to defy common sense in business. For example, we show that a firm should not necessarily seek to produce at the level at which the average cost of production is minimized or the average revenue is maximized.

Explicit cost is the money expenditure required to obtain a resource, product, or service.

PART I THEORY AND PUBLIC POLICY APPLICATIONS

Various cost conceptions

For purposes of effective communication, if nothing else, economists have identified a number of key cost concepts.

Explicit and implicit costs

An **implicit cost** is the forgone opportunity to do or acquire something else or to put one's resources to another use that doesn't require a monetary payment.

Not all costs are obvious. It is not difficult to recognize an out-of-pocket expenditure – the monthly price you pay for a product or service. This is called an **explicit cost**. For example, the price of your book is an explicit cost of taking a course in economics. Other costs are less immediately apparent. Such costs of the course might include the time spent going to class and studying, the risk of receiving a failing grade, and the discomfort of being confronted with material that may challenge some of your beliefs. These are **implicit costs**; together they add up to the value of what you could have done instead. Although implicit costs may not be recognized, they are often much larger than the more obvious explicit costs of an action.

A **sunk cost** is a past cost. It is a cost that has already been incurred, which means it cannot be changed and, hence, is irrelevant to current decisions.

"Sunk costs": why they don't matter

Then, there are some "costs" that are recognized on accounting statements that should not be considered in making business decisions. These costs are called "**sunk costs**." Accordingly, sunk costs should be ignored in decision making.

This is because current decisions cannot alter costs that have already been incurred. Such costs are beyond the realm of choice.

An example can help illustrate the irrelevance of sunk, or fixed, costs. Suppose an oil exploration firm purchases the mineral rights to a particular piece of property for $1 million which, for purposes of clarity in argument, we assume initially has no resale market. After several months of drilling, the firm concludes that the land contains no oil (or other valuable mineral resources). Will the firm reason that, having spent $1 million for the mineral rights, it should continue to look for oil on the land? If the chances of finding oil are nonexistent, the rational firm will cease drilling on the land and try somewhere else. The $1 million is a sunk cost that should not influence the decision to continue or cease exploration. Indeed, the firm may begin drilling on land for which it paid far less for the mineral rights, if management believes that the chances of finding oil are higher there than on the $1 million property.

The underlying reason that sunk costs do not matter to current production decisions is that the term "sunk costs" itself is misleading and something of a misnomer, since "sunk costs" are not really "costs" at all. The opportunity cost of an activity is the value of the best alternative not chosen. In the case of an historical cost, however, there are no longer any alternatives. Although the oil exploration firm at one time could have chosen an alternative way to spend the $1 million, after the money was spent the alternative ceased to be available. Nor can the firm resell the mineral rights for $1 million; those rights are now worth far less because of accumulated evidence that the land contains little or no valuable minerals. Sunk costs, however painful the memory of them might be, are gone and best forgotten by the firm. Profits are made by looking forward, not backward.

If the land can be sold, then there is a cost of using or just holding onto it. However, the cost that should be considered is not the $1 million purpose price, but rather its resale price, which could be far lower than the purchase price.

The cost of an education

A good illustration of the magnitude of implicit costs is the cost of an education. Suppose an executive or fully employed MBA student takes a course and pays $2,000 for tuition and $300 for books and other class materials. The money cost of the course is $2,300, but that figure does not include the implicit costs to the student. To take a course, the student must attend class for about thirty hours (on the quarter system) and may have to spend three times that much time traveling to and from class, completing class assignments, and studying

Table 8.1 *Total cost of an MBA course*

Explicit costs	($)
Tuition	2,000
Books	300
Total explicit cost	2,300
Implicit costs	
Time	4,800
Anxiety	500
Total implicit cost	5,300
Total costs of course	**7,600**

for examinations. The total number of hours spent on any one course, then, might be 120.

The MBA student could have spent that time doing other things, including working for a money wage. If the student's time is valued at $40 per hour (the wage she might have received if working), the time cost of the course is $4,800 (120 hours × $40/hour). Moreover, if she experiences some anxiety because of taking the course, that psychic or risk cost must be added to the total as well. If she would be willing to pay $500 to avoid the anxiety, the total implicit cost of taking the course climbs to $5,300 (table 8.1).

The implicit cost of the student's time represents the largest component of the total cost of the course. The value of one's time varies from person to person.[1] The time cost also explains the popularity of executive MBA programs, which allow the students to do more of their work online and on weekends. By the same token, few CEOs of major corporations can be found in MBA programs of any type. Their explicit costs of the programs are much the same as everyone else, but their implicit (time) costs are far higher, so much so that they have no hope of recovering their MBA investments. This is especially true since many CEOs are in their fifties and sixties and have only a few years left in their careers.

The cost of bargains

Every week, most supermarkets run large newspaper ads listing their weekly specials. Generally only a few items are offered at especially low prices, for store

[1] For students who are unable to find work or have few productive skills, the time costs of taking a course may be quite small. That is why most college students are young. Their time cost is generally lower than that of experienced workers who must give up the opportunity to earn a good wage in order to attend classes full time.

Normal profits are the opportunity and risk costs of doing business not reported on firms' P&L statements that must be covered in order that the owners will not redeploy firm resources.

Book profits are the profits reported on firms' "bottom lines" of their P&L statements.

An economic loss occurs when firms' *total costs,* including their unrecorded opportunity and risk costs, exceed their total revenues.

Economic profits are realized when firms' *total costs* are less than their total revenues.

managers know that most bargain seekers can be attracted to the store with just a few carefully selected specials. After the customer has gone to the store that is offering a special on, say, steak, he would have to incur a travel cost in order to buy other items in a different store. Even though peanut butter may be on sale elsewhere, the sum of the sale price and the travel cost exceed the regular price in the first store. Through attractive displays and packaging, customers can be persuaded to buy many other goods not on sale, particularly toiletries, which tend to bear high markups. So the stores manage to recoup some of the revenues lost on sale items by charging higher prices on other goods. In other words, the cost of a bargain on sirloin steak may be a high price for toothpaste.

Some shoppers make the rounds of the grocery stores when sales are announced. For such people, time and transportation are cheap. A person who values his or her time at $40 an hour is not going to spend an hour trying to save a dollar or two. The cost of gas alone can make it prohibitively expensive to visit several stores. Because of the costs of acquiring information, many shoppers do not even bother to look for sales. The expected benefits are simply not great enough to justify the information cost. These shoppers enter the market "rationally ignorant."

Normal profit as a cost

In accounting, profit is what is on the "bottom line" on profit and loss (P&L) (or income) statements, or the difference between recorded revenues and recorded expenses. However, some costs of doing business are never reported on a company's books. Three such frequently-unrecorded costs are:

(1) The opportunity cost of the firm's owner/manager (equal to the salary the owner/manager could have gotten working for someone else)
(2) the opportunity cost of capital (the earnings that could have been received had the firm owner invested his finance in some risk-free investment (say, a government bond)
(3) The risk cost of doing business (or the expected losses from firm failure).

Even though these costs may not be recognized on a firm's books, they must be recovered in order for the firm to continue in business. These costs are called **normal profits** by economists. The "profit" reported by a firm on its P&L statement is called **book profits** by economists. Book profits can be more or less than normal profits.

If book profits are less than normal profits, the firm is said to have incurred an **economic loss**. If book profits are greater than normal profits, the firm is said to make **economic profits**. The amount by which book profits exceed normal profits is economic profit. Economic profit is a return that is more than necessary to keep resources employed where they are.

Peter Drucker (2001), a widely cited and respected management professor, once quipped that, "Few US businesses have been profitable since World War II" (2001, 117). Most readers may find such a statement hard to accept, and those who do believe it may interpret Drucker as talking about business failure. But Drucker was commenting about *economic profits* and, once that is understood, his statement can be seen as a comment on the success of the US economy. As Drucker wrote, "Until a business returns a profit that is greater than its cost of capital [opportunity cost], it operates at a loss . . . The enterprise . . . returns less to the economy than it uses up in resources" (2001, 117). On the other hand, if a lot of firms made large economic profits, it would also be a sign of failure of the economy – failure to reallocate resources to the profitable endeavors where the resources add more to the economy than they are adding where currently employed.

The special significance of marginal cost

So far, we have been considering cost as the determining factor in the decision to undertake a particular course of action. Obviously benefits are important as well. The rational person weighs the cost of an action against its benefits and comes to a decision: whether to invest in an education, to shop around for a bargain, or to learn how to fly. The question is, how much of a given good or service will an individual choose to produce or consume? How does cost limit a behavior after a person has decided to engage in it? The answer relies partially on the concepts of **marginal cost**. We emphasize marginal cost in this chapter, but *marginal benefits* are just as critical to our production and consumption decisions, as shown in chapter 7 and as will be discussed more fully in chapter 10.

Marginal cost is the additional cost incurred by producing one additional unit of a good, activity, or service.

Rational behavior and marginal cost

Marginal cost is the cost incurred by reading one additional page, making one additional friend, giving one additional gift, or going one additional mile. Depending on the good, activity, or service in question, marginal cost may stay the same or vary as additional units are produced. For example, imagine that Jan Smith wants to give Halloween candy to ten of her friends. In a sense, Jan is producing gifts by procuring bags of candy. If she can buy as many bags as she wants at a unit price of 50¢, the marginal cost of each additional unit she buys is the same, 50¢. The marginal cost is constant over the range of production.

However, marginal cost can vary with the level of output, for two reasons. The first has to do with the opportunity cost of time. Suppose Jan wants to give each friend a miniature watercolor, which she will paint herself over the course of the day. To make time for painting, Jan can forgo any of the various activities that usually make up her day. She may choose to give up recreational activities, gardening chores, or time spent at work or study.

If she behaves rationally, she will give up the activities she values least. To do the first painting, she may forgo laying soil on a bare spot in her lawn – an activity that is low on most people's lists of preferences and can be postponed without much inconvenience. The marginal cost of her first watercolor is therefore a lawn eyesore. To paint the second watercolor, Jan will give up the next more valuable item on her list of activities. As she produces more and more paintings, Jan will forgo more and more valuable alternatives. Hence, the marginal cost of her paintings will rise with her output.

If the marginal cost of each new painting is plotted against the quantity of paintings produced, a curve like that in figure 8.1 will result. Because the marginal cost of each additional painting is higher than the marginal cost of the last one, the curve slopes upward to the right.

Although the marginal cost curve is generally assumed to slope upward, as that in figure 8.1 does, that need not be the case, as in the case of giving gifts of candy. In that example, Jan's marginal cost was constant and the marginal cost curve is horizontal.

The law of diminishing marginal returns states that as more and more units of one resource – labor, fertilizer, or any other resource – are applied to a fixed quantity of another resource – land, for instance – the increase in total added output gained from each additional unit of the variable resource will eventually begin to diminish.

The law of diminishing returns

The second reason that marginal cost may vary with output involves a technological relationship known as the **law of diminishing marginal returns**. Under this "law," beyond some point, less output is received for each added unit of a resource. Alternatively stated, more of the resource will be required to produce the same amount of output as before. Beyond some point, the marginal cost of additional units of output rises.

Although the law of diminishing returns applies to any production process, its meaning can be easily grasped in the context of agricultural production. Assume that you are producing tomatoes. You have a fixed amount of land (an acre) but can vary the quantity of labor you apply to it. If you try to do planting all by yourself – dig the holes, pour the water, insert the plants, and cover up the roots – you will waste time changing tools. If a friend helps you,

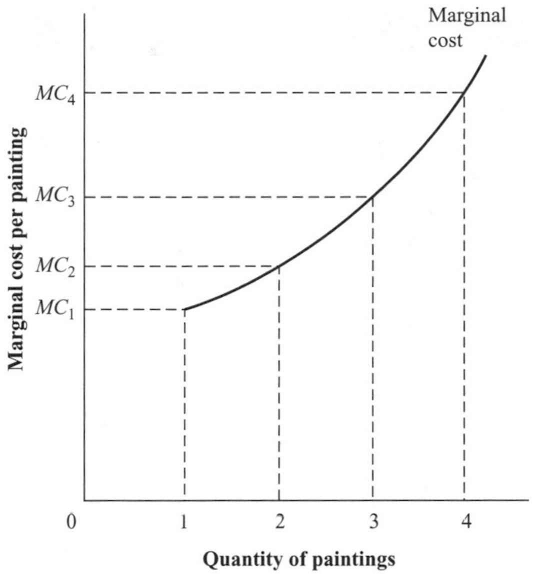

Figure 8.1

Rising marginal cost
To produce each new watercolor, Jan must give up an opportunity more valuable than the last. Thus the marginal cost of her paintings rises with each new work.

you can divide the tasks and specialize. Less time will be wasted in changing tools.

The time you would have spent changing tools can be spent planting more tomatoes, thus increasing the harvest. At first, output may expand faster than the labor force. That is, one laborer may be able to plant 100 tomatoes an hour; two working together may be able to plant 250 an hour. Thus the marginal cost of planting the additional 150 plants is lower than the cost of the first 100. Up to a point, the more workers, the greater their efficiency and the lower the marginal cost – all because of the economies of specialization. At some point, however, the addition of another laborer will not contribute as much to production as did adding the previous one, if only because workers begin bumping into one another. The point of diminishing marginal returns has been reached and the marginal cost of putting plants into the ground will begin to rise.

Diminishing marginal returns are an inescapable fact of life. If marginal returns did not diminish at some point, and eventually become negative (adding another laborer actually reduces output) output would expand indefinitely and the world's food supply could be grown on just one acre of land. (For that matter, it could be grown in a flower box.) If more labor can be added to a fixed quantity of land, then the labor/land ratio goes up, giving rise to

Table 8.2 *Marginal costs of producing tomatoes*

No. of workers employed (1)	Total no. of bushels (2)	Contribution of each worker to production (marginal product) (3)	No. of workers required to produce each additional bushel (4)	Marginal cost of each bushel, at $5 per worker (5)
1	0.25	0.25 } (1st bushel)		
2	1.00	0.75 }	2	$10
3	2.00	1.00 (2nd bushel)	1	$5
Point at which diminishing marginal returns emerge				
4	2.60	0.60 } (3rd bushel)		
5	3.00	0.40 }	2	$10
6	3.30	0.30		
7	3.55	0.25		
8	3.75	0.20 (4th bushel)	5	
9	3.90	0.15		
10	4.00	0.10		$25

an increase in total output. The thinking can be reversed: The output can be increased by increasing the labor/land ratio, which can be accomplished with a reduction in land.

Since we know that the world's food supply can't be grown on an acre of land (or in a flower pot), diminishing marginal returns must be observed eventually as more labor is added to the fixed resource, in this case, land. However, we need to note that the point at which output begins to diminish varies from one production process to the next, but eventually all marginal cost curves will slope upward to the right, as in figure 8.1.

Marginal product is the increase in total output that results when one additional unit of a resource – for example, labor, fertilizer, and land – is added to the production process, everything else held constant.

Table 8.2 shows the marginal cost of producing tomatoes with various numbers of workers, assuming that each worker is paid $5 and that production is limited to 1 acre. Working alone, one worker can produce a quarter of a bushel; two can produce a full bushel, and so on (columns (1) and (2)). Column (3) shows the amount that each additional worker adds to total production, called the **marginal product**. The first worker contributed 0.25 (one quarter) of a bushel; the second worker, an additional 0.75 of a bushel, and so on. These are the marginal products of successive units of labor.

The important information is shown in columns (4) and (5) of table 8.1. Although two workers are needed to produce the first bushel (column (4)), the efficiencies of specialization require only one additional worker to produce the second bushel. Beyond that point, however, marginal returns diminish. Each additional worker contributes less, so two more workers are needed to produce

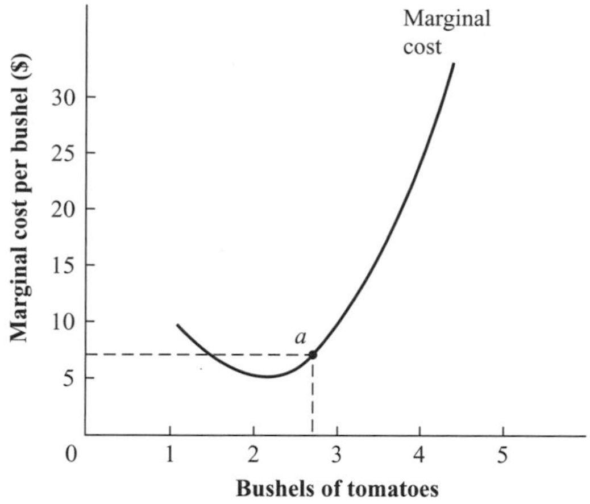

Figure 8.2 The law of diminishing marginal returns
As production expands with the addition of new workers, efficiencies of specialization initially cause marginal cost to fall. At some point, however – here, just beyond two bushels – marginal cost will begin to rise again. At that point, marginal returns will begin to diminish and marginal costs will begin to rise.

the third bushel and five more to produce the fourth. If table 8.1 were extended, each bushel beyond the fourth would require a progressively larger number of workers and eventually additional workers would begin reducing output.

Column (5) shows that if all workers are paid the same wage, $5, the marginal cost of a bushel of tomatoes will decline from $10 for the first bushel to $5 for the second before rising to $10 again for the third bushel. That is, increasing marginal costs (or diminishing returns) emerge with the addition of the third worker, and continue to increase, going to $25 for the fourth bushel.

If the marginal cost of each bushel (column (5)) is plotted against the number of bushels harvested, a curve such as that in figure 8.2 will result. Although the curve slopes downward at first, for most purposes the relevant segment of the curve is a major part of the upward sloping portion of what will be, for most industries, a U shaped marginal cost curve (as is explained in detail later).

The cost–benefit trade-off

Just as a producer's marginal cost schedule shows the increasing marginal cost of supplying more goods, so does the demand curve (as explained earlier) show the decreasing marginal value or marginal benefit of those goods to the people consuming them. Together, marginal costs and benefits determine the amount

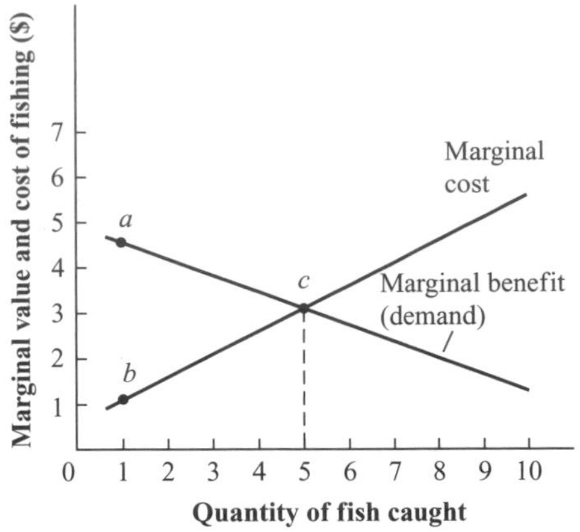

Figure 8.3 Costs and benefits of fishing

For each fish up to the fifth one, Gary receives more in benefits than he pays in costs. The first fish gives him $4.67 in benefits (point *a*) and costs him only $1 (point *b*). The fifth yields equal costs and benefits (point *c*), but the sixth costs more than it is worth. Therefore Gary will catch no more than five fish.

of production and consumption that creates the greatest net value. Producers and consumers gain from both producing and consuming more of a good as long as the marginal cost of producing it is less than the marginal value of consuming it. That is, there are additional gains to be had from increasing production and consumption until the marginal cost curve intersects the marginal benefit curve for the good. The intersection of the two curves represents the point where welfare is maximized. To demonstrate this point, we consider the costs and benefits of an activity such as fishing.

The costs and benefits of fishing

Assume that Gary likes to fish. What he does with the fish he catches is of no consequence to our discussion; he can make them into trophies, give them away, or store them in the freezer. Even if Gary places no money value on the fish, we can use dollars to illustrate the marginal costs and benefits of fishing to Gary. (Money figures are not values but rather a means of indicating relative value.)

What is important is that Gary wants to fish. How many fish will he catch? From our earlier analysis of Jan's desire to paint, we know that the cost of catching each additional fish will be higher than the cost of the one before. Gary will confront an upward sloping marginal cost curve like that in figure 8.3.

Gary's demand curve for fishing will slope downward (see figure 8.3) because as he catches more fish over some period of time (say, a day) the marginal value he receives from catching fish will eventually start declining.

From the positions of the two curves, we can see that Gary will catch up to five fish before he packs up his rod and heads for home. He places a relatively high value of $4.67 on the first fish (point *a* in figure 8.3) and figures that the first fish caught has a relatively low marginal cost of $1 (point *b*) – the value of the forgone opportunities. In other words, he gets $3.67 more value from using his time, energy, and other resources to catch the first fish than he would receive from his next best alternative. The marginal benefit of the second fish also exceeds its marginal cost, although by a small amount ($4.25 – $2.75 = $1.50). Gary continues to gain with the third and fourth fishes, but the fifth fish is a matter of indifference to him. Its marginal value equals its marginal cost (point *c*). Although we cannot say that Gary will actually bother to catch a fifth fish, we do know that five is the limit toward which he will aim. He will not catch a sixth – at least during the period of time offered by the graph – because it would cost him more than he would receive in benefits.

The costs and benefits of preventing accidents

All of us would prefer to avoid accidents. In that sense, we have a demand for accident prevention, whose curve should slope downward as do all other demand curves. We benefit more from trying to prevent the most likely and harmful accidents before trying to prevent those that are less likely and harmful. Preventing accidents also entails costs, however – whether in time, forgone opportunities, or money. Should we attempt to prevent all accidents? No. Eventually the cost of preventing an accident is greater than the expected benefit from doing so. Would you spend $10,000 to prevent an occasional paper cut from opening the mail?

As with the question of how long to fish, marginal cost and benefit curves can help illustrate the point at which preventing accidents ceases to be cost-effective. Suppose that Al Rosa's experience indicates that he can expect to have ten accidents over the course of the year. If he tries to prevent all of them, the value of preventing the last one, as indicated by the demand curve in figure 8.4, will be only $1 (point *a*). The marginal cost of preventing it will be much greater: approximately $6 (point *b*). If Al is rational, he will not try to prevent the last accident. As a matter of fact, he will try to prevent only five accidents (point *c*). As with the tenth accident, it will cost more than it is worth to Al to prevent the sixth through ninth accidents. He would try to prevent all ten

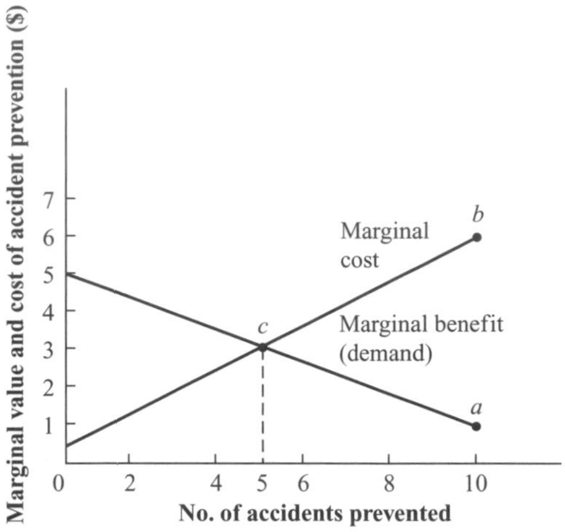

Figure 8.4 Accident prevention
Given the increasing marginal cost of preventing accidents and the decreasing marginal value of preventing the accidents, *c* or 5 accidents will be prevented.

accidents only if his demand for accident prevention were so great that his demand curve intersected, or passed over, the marginal cost curve at point *b*.

Some accidents may be unavoidable. In that case, the marginal cost curve will eventually become vertical. Other accidents may be "avoidable" in the sense that it is physically possible to take measures to prevent them – although the rational course may be to allow them to happen.

The production function

Business firms combine various factors of production in order to produce various goods and services. Although there are thousands of different factors of production, or inputs, for simplicity's sake we often use a model with only two factors, labor and capital. We can then study how the two inputs can be combined to produce an output, according to a known **production function**. The general equation for the production function is

> The **production function** is the relationship between inputs and outputs with a given technology.

$$Q = f(L, K)$$

where Q is output, L is labor, K is capital, and f is the functional relationship between inputs and output. In the short run, we assume that capital cannot be varied; labor is therefore the only variable factor. To increase output, then, a firm must increase the amount of labor.

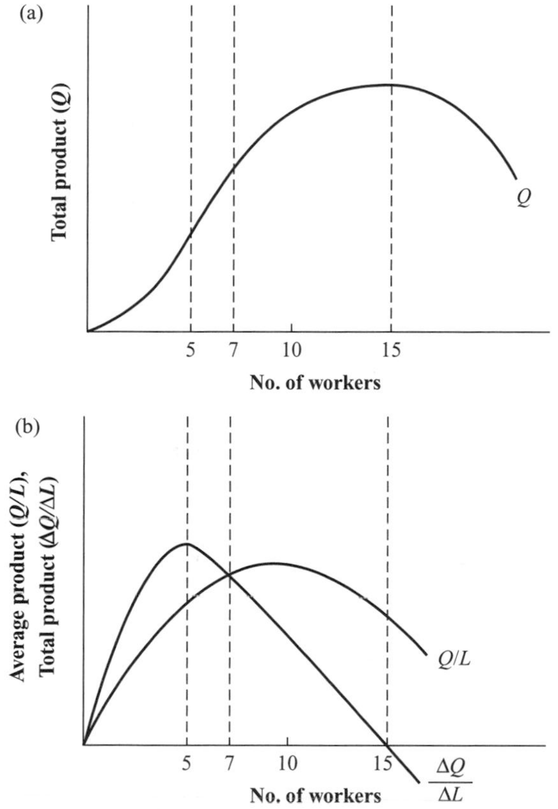

Figure 8.5 Total, average, and marginal product curves

The total product curve shows how output changes when the amount of the variable input, labor, changes. Total product rises first at an increasing rate (0–five workers), then at a decreasing rate (five–fifteen workers), before declining (beyond fifteen workers). The marginal and average product curves reflect what is happening to total product. Marginal product rises when total product is rising at an increasing rate and falls when total product is rising at a decreasing rate. Marginal product is positive when total product is rising and negative when total product is falling.

The relationship between the amount of the variable input (labor) and output can be illustrated with a total product curve such as that in figure 8.5(a). Suppose that the curve is that of a commercial fishing firm. The firm's capital – the boat and equipment – is fixed in the short run. Only the number of workers can vary. As the amount of labor increases from zero, the fish catch (output) increases. Between zero and five workers, output increases at an increasing rate. As more workers are hired, total output continues to increase, although at a decreasing rate, until fifteen workers are hired. Beyond that point, hiring more workers *reduces* output.

The reason the total product curve has that particular shape can be seen more clearly in figure 8.5(b), which shows the average and marginal product curves. The average product of labor is total output divided by the amount of labor, or *Q/L*. The marginal product of labor is the change in total output brought about by changing the amount of labor by one unit. Because at least some workers are needed to operate the boat and the equipment, the first few workers hired greatly increase total output; marginal product is rising. Between five and fifteen workers, the marginal product of labor falls, although the average product continues to rise (because it is less than marginal product). Total product continues to rise, but no longer at an increasing rate. The law of diminishing marginal returns has taken effect. At seven workers, marginal product equals average product, and average product is maximized. As more workers are hired, average product falls. Note that as long as marginal product is positive, more labor means more output and the total product curve will have a positive slope. Beyond fifteen workers, marginal product becomes negative and total product falls. The boat may be so crowded that workers bump into each other and reduce the amount of work that each does. To catch more fish after this stage has been reached, the firm must buy a larger boat.

Some economists divide the production function of figure 8.5 into three stages. In stage one, from zero to five workers, total product and average product of labor both rise. In stage two, between five and fifteen workers, total product rises while marginal product falls. In stage three, beyond fifteen workers, total product and average product both fall (and marginal product is negative).

Price and marginal cost: producing to maximize profits

Production is not generally an end in itself in business. Most firms seek to make a profit. We can usefully consider how firms go about the task of trying to maximize profits by converting the total and marginal product curves into *cost curves*. By doing so we can engage in familiar marginal cost/marginal benefit analyses.

Granted, many business people derive intrinsic reward from their work. They may value the satisfaction of producing a product that meets a human need just as much as they value the profits that they earn. Some business people may even accept lower profits so that their products can sell at lower prices and serve more people. For most business people, however, the profit generated by sales is the major motivation for doing business. So it is useful as a first approximation to assume that firms maximize profits. And if firms don't maximize profits, they will be subject to takeover by entrepreneurs who will see a chance to buy the firms at prices depressed by the managers not trying to maximize profits and to sell the firm at a higher price, after the firms' profit making policies have been changed.

How much will a profit maximizing firm produce? Assume that its marginal cost curve is like that in figure 8.6(a), and that the owners can sell as many units as they want at a price of P_1. The price of its product, P_1, can be thought of as the marginal benefit the firm receives for each unit sold, or P_1 is the firm's **marginal revenue**. Each time the firm sells one additional unit, its revenues rise by P_1.

Marginal revenue is the additional revenue that a firm acquires by selling another unit of output.

Clearly, a profit maximizing firm will produce and sell any unit for which the marginal revenue (*MR*) exceeds the marginal cost (*MC*). (Profits are the difference between total costs and total revenues. Therefore a firm's profits rise whenever an increase in revenues exceeds the increase in its costs.) At a price of P_1, then, this firm will produce up to, and no more than, Q_1 units of its product. For every unit up to Q_1, price (or marginal revenue) is greater than marginal cost and for every unit beyond Q_1, the marginal revenue is less than marginal cost.

The vertical distance between P_1 and the marginal cost of each unit, as shown by the marginal cost curve, is the additional profit obtained from each additional unit produced. By taking the difference between the vertical distance P_1 and vertical distance on the marginal cost curve for all units up to Q_1, we can obtain the firm's total profits from producing a_1 (see the dark shaded area in figure 8.6(a). Total profits can also be represented as a curve, as in the line TP_1 in figure 8.6(b). Notice that the curve peaks at Q_1, the point at which the firm chooses to stop producing. Since beyond Q_1, marginal cost is greater than marginal revenue, total profits fall, as shown by the downward slope of the total profits curve.

What will the firm do if the price of its product rises from P_1 to P_2? For the firm that can sell all it wants at a constant price, a rise in price means a rise in marginal revenue. After the price rises to P_2, the marginal revenue of an additional $Q_2 - Q_1$ units exceeds their marginal cost. At the higher price, a larger number of units can be profitably produced and sold. The firm will seek to produce up to the point at which marginal cost equals the new, higher marginal revenue, P_2, or output, Q_2, in figure 8.6(a). As before, profit is equal

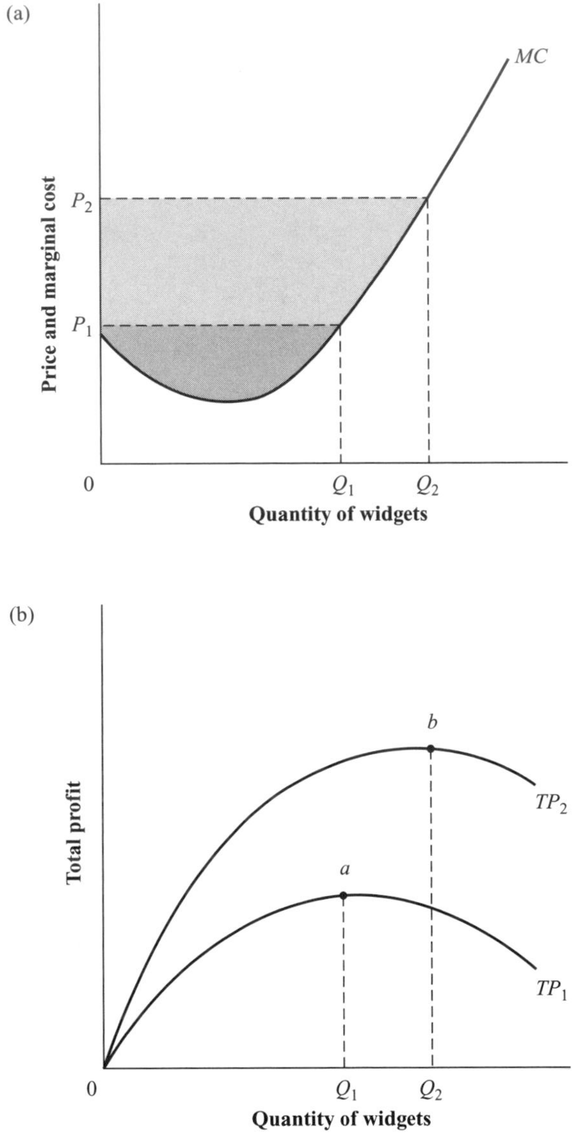

Figure 8.6 Marginal costs and maximization of profit

At price P_1 (panel (a)), this firm's marginal revenue, represented by the area under P_1 up to Q_1, exceeds its marginal cost up to the output level of Q_1. At that point total profit, shown in panel (b), peaks (point *a*). At price P_2, marginal revenue exceeds marginal cost up to an output level of Q_2. The increase in price shifts the profit curve in panel (*b*) upward, from TP_1 to TP_2, and profits peak at *b*.

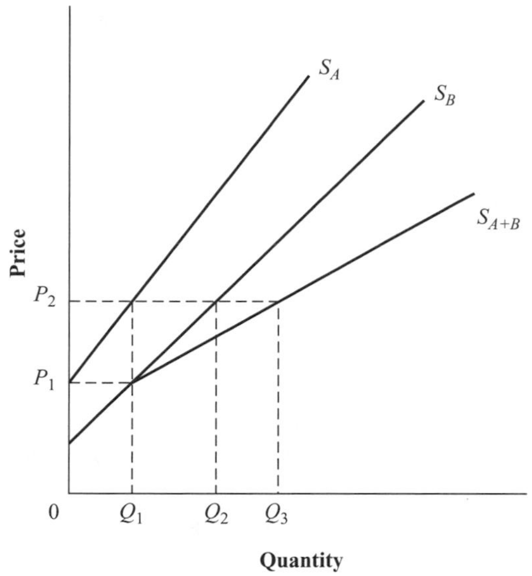

Figure 8.7

Market supply curve

The market supply curve (S_{A+B}) is obtained by adding together the amount producers *A* and *B* are willing to offer at each and every price, as shown by the individual supply curves S_A and S_B. (The individual supply curves are obtained from the upward sloping portions of the firms' marginal cost curve.)

to the vertical distance between the price line, P_2, and the marginal cost curve, or the dark-shaded area plus the light-shaded area in figure 8.6(a). The total profit curve shifts to the position of the line TP_2 in figure 8.6(b).

From individual supply to market supply

The upward sloping portion of the firm's marginal cost curve is its supply curve – for each price, the amount the firm will supply is given by the firm's marginal cost at that price (and more will be said about this in chapter 10). If the market supply is the amount all producers are willing to produce at various prices, we can obtain the market supply curve by adding together the upward sloping portions of the individual firms' marginal cost curves. (This procedure resembles the one followed in determining the market demand curve in chapter 7.)

Figure 8.7 shows the supply curves S_A and S_B, derived from the marginal cost curves of two producers, *A* and *B*. At a price of P_1, only producer *B* is willing to produce anything, and it is willing to offer only Q_1. The total quantity supplied to the market at P_1 is therefore Q_1. At the higher prices of P_2, however, both producers are willing to compete. Producer A offers Q_1, whereas producer *B* offers more, Q_2. The total quantity supplied is therefore Q_3, the sum of Q_1 and Q_2.

The market supply curve, S_{A+B}, is obtained by adding the amounts that *A* and *B* are willing to sell at each price and splitting the totals. Note that the market supply curve lies further from the origin and is flatter than the individual producers' supply curves. The entry of more producers will shift the market supply curve further out and lower its slope even more. (More will be said about cost and supply in later chapters.)

Perspective A Reason for Corporations: Cost Savings

Competition determines which business arrangements will survive and which will not. The prevalence of single proprietorships is explained by the advantage of this business form in producing those products the consumers want as inexpensively as possible. But changing circumstances can reduce the competitive advantage of a business arrangement as new ways are found to do a better job of organizing productive activity. Technological advances that took place during the latter part of the nineteenth century made it possible to realize huge economies from large-scale production in many manufacturing industries. These technological advances shifted the advantage to business organizations that were far too large to be owned and managed by one proprietor, or even by a few. But the advantage of large business firms is reduced by the fact that they make it impossible to concentrate the motivation created by ownership entirely in the hands of those making management decisions.

Those manufacturing firms that developed organizational arrangements that did the best job of reducing the disconnection between the owners' incentives and the managers' control were best able to take advantage of economies from large-scale production. The result was a competition that resulted in the development of the modern corporation, the business form that today accounts for most of the value produced in the US economy, even though small owner-managed firms still make up by far the largest number of firms in the economy.

However, it must be remembered that (contrary to what is often taught in business books) the corporation, an organization under which investors have limited liability, was not a creation of the state (Hesson 1979). The corporation, which is a legal entity that affords owners limited liability protection, emerged before states got into the incorporating business. Groups of private investors formed corporations, through contracts among themselves, because they believed that there were economies (cost savings) to be had if they all agreed to create a business in which outside parties could not hold the individual investors liable for more than their investment in the corporation (that is, the investors' personal fortunes would not be at risk from the operation of the firm, as was and remains true of proprietorships and most partnerships).

Clearly, such a public announcement of limited liability – made publicly evident with "Inc." in corporate names – might make lenders wary and cause them to demand higher interest rates on loans. However, the firm would have the offsetting advantage of being able to attract more funds from more investors, increasing firm equity, a force that not only could increase the firm's ability to achieve scale economies in production grounded in technology but could also lower the risk to lenders, since the survivability and profitability of the firm could be increased. This is especially true since investors would, with limited liability protection, be willing to accept a lower rate of return on their investment.

Of course, the outside investors could be hard taskmasters, given that they could shift their investment away from firms not maximizing profitably. But this doesn't mean that the workers would find the corporate form unattractive: not necessarily. Given the potential scale economies and risk reductions to owners, corporations can provide more secure, and higher-paying, employment than do small proprietorships, which are subject to higher risk costs for owners and more constricted sources of financial capital.

PART II ORGANIZATIONAL ECONOMICS AND MANAGEMENT

Cutting health insurance costs

The cost curves that we have developed in this chapter and shall develop in chapter 9 are often presented in textbooks as if they appear as a part of nature or are magically given to businesses. Nothing could be more misleading. As MBAs know, or should know, the cost of doing business is a constant worry for all firms. Finding ways of minimizing costs (and getting the firm's cost curves as low as possible) absorbs much of the time of many managers, especially when firm costs are largely determined by market and political forces outside of firms, with costs rising and falling with the ebb and flow of major policy debates in the nation's capital.

The national "healthcare crisis" and market forces

A current example of how market and political forces can interact can influence a firm's cost structure is the so-dubbed "healthcare crisis" in the United States as reflected in the high cost of healthcare. Firms' cost structures, and competitive positions, are affected by the cost of healthcare because healthcare costs affect health insurance costs and because of the importance of health insurance as a fringe benefit in compensation packages for workers.

The cost of healthcare, like almost everything else, is largely determined by the market forces of supply and demand. Unfortunately, market forces have been distorted by legal and political factors that have distorted the incentives for healthcare providers and users. In our view, the "crisis" is more a matter of political policy and rhetoric than economics. Political grandstanding alone will hardly solve whatever healthcare problem exists. Careful reflection by policy makers and managers on the exact sources of the problem might, however. The current situation presents a possibility for managers to benefit both their firms and its workers by decisions that they can make, to a large degree (though not entirely) independently of political policy.

Granted, healthcare costs, as well as the insurance premiums that finance a major share of healthcare expenditures, have risen faster than the prices of almost all other goods since the 1970s. Indeed, the cost of health insurance provided by firms was escalating at double-digit rates in the late 1980s and the early 1990s when increases in the consumer price index (CPI), a broad measure of the cost-of-living, were in the low single digits. In the mid-1990s, the increase in healthcare costs slowed, only to pick up momentum in the late 1990s and the early 2000s.

To understand the problem of insurance cost increases, we need first to consider the market forces that have been at work to drive up healthcare costs. What are those forces? Consider the following list of factors affecting the supply and demand of healthcare:

(1) Doctors have been subject to a rising degree of litigation. They have been sued with growing frequency partly because they have made mistakes, but also because they are now being held responsible for problems over which

in the past they were assumed to have no control. Patients have found that they can make money by blaming doctors for an increasing number of problems that emerge when they are being treated. Fearful that they will be sued for problems that might have conceivably been avoided with enough precaution, doctors have been covering their financial and professional backsides by ordering tests that might be only marginally valuable from a medical perspective but can help them defend themselves if they are sued when problems emerge.

(2) Federal expenditures on Medicare for older patients and Medicaid for low-income patients have increased the demand for healthcare services since the late 1960s, a trend that has tended to boost prices and forced many younger and lower-income patients out of the health insurance market.

(3) Medical care has become technologically more sophisticated, and doctors have applied the new technology as an offensive strategy (to keep patients alive longer) and as a defensive one (to avoid accusations of negligence for failing to employ the latest life-saving technology). The extensive use of the latest and best technology may have saved and prolonged lives, but medical care costs have been driven up in the process.

(4) The healthcare industry has always been plagued by the problem of "asymmetric information" – that is, doctors knowing more about many patients' medical conditions and their remedies than do the patients themselves. As a consequence, doctors have always been in a position to induce patients to buy more medical care than the patients might buy if they had the doctors' information and knowledge at their own disposal. Patients are now more likely to go along with a doctor's recommendation for more extensive and costly care today because they are paying less of the bill directly than they did in the past.

(5) Medical technology has drastically lowered the cost of many medical procedures and has, as a consequence, lowered the cost of extending the lives of patients by some varying and uncertain number of months and years. For example, not many decades ago, heart and kidney transplants and heart bypass operations were impossible – the costs of those procedures were infinite. The lower cost and price of these, and other life-saving procedures today (though still high), mean that an increased number of patients (especially with the help of insurers and government) are willing and able to pay for them. Although the issue has not been statistically evaluated to our knowledge, the lower prices for many medical procedures have probably increased total medical expenditures as a percentage of national income, given that demand for years of life can be highly elastic. Hence, some of

the so-called healthcare "crisis" probably mirrors, to a degree, the success of the healthcare industry in lowering the cost of prolonging life.

(6) The cost of employer-provided medical insurance is tax-deductible, which means that its price has been artificially lowered, causing more consumers to buy more complete insurance coverage and to demand more medical services than they otherwise would. The greater demand has enabled medical professionals to boost their prices. As tax rates rose in the 1960s and 1970s and again in the 1990s, workers naturally had a growing incentive to take more of their income in tax-deductible fringe benefits and less of an incentive to take their income in taxable money wages. The higher tax rates spurred demand for health insurance and healthcare – and added to the pressure on healthcare costs.

(7) Employers have typically bought insurance policies with very low deductibles, for example, $200 a year. This means that after the first $200 of medical care expenditures in any one year, the cost of additional medical services to the insured patient is only a small fraction of the actual cost. This feature of insurance policies has encouraged excessive use of healthcare services which, in turn, has driven up employees' insurance premiums and caused some workers to forgo health insurance altogether.[2] We are in a Prisoner's Dilemma with respect to our healthcare decisions. We would be better off collectively if we all moderated the amount of healthcare we demanded, as we would if we were paying the full cost of that care, but because of insurance and government subsidies it is in the interest of each of use to ignore most of the cost when choosing how much healthcare to demand.

(8) The growth in social problems – crimes involving bodily injury, the use of street drugs, and teenage pregnancy – has also contributed to the demand for medical services, which has driven up their prices as well as the price of insurance. The unwillingness or inability of medical professionals to legally or morally deny services to people who cannot pay for the services has also increased the number of people seeking services. Social attitudes favoring

[2] As you may recall from our study of consumer behavior in chapter 7, a working rule of consumer maximizing behavior is that the consumer will continue to buy units of any good or service until the point at which the marginal cost of the last unit consumed just equals the marginal value of the last unit. If the person consumes more than that amount, the additional cost of any additional units will exceed their additional value. By "excessive" consumption, we mean that patients are induced to go beyond the point at which the marginal value is, while still positive, less than the marginal cost. This excessive consumption occurs because the individual consumer isn't paying the entire cost of additional medical care.

universal medical care coverage have reduced the cost of irresponsible behavior (a form of moral hazard), increasing the demand on the healthcare industry and inflating costs.

Without question, if the grocery industry were operated over the past decades the way the healthcare industry has operated, then the nation would likely have a "crisis" in the grocery business. The reason is simple: People would pay a fixed sum each month (their grocery premium) through their employer that would entitle them to virtually unlimited access to the grocery store shelves (after they have covered the $200 annual deductible) at a small fraction of the actual cost. Under such an arrangement, we should not be surprised if people consumed significantly more and better food, some of which would have limited value. We should also not be surprised if the shoppers' grocery price premiums went through the roof as few consumers would have much incentive to moderate their purchases by considering the full cost of the food they are buying.

Business solutions for the healthcare crisis

How can the so-called "crisis" be solved, at least partially? We do not intend to offer a detailed set of public policy solutions here. Other specialists in the field have done that (Goodman and Musgrave 1992; Goodman, Musgrave, and Herrick 2004). We point out here only that many of the supply and demand forces listed above are beyond the control of individual businesses. There is no way that individual businesses can offset completely the broad sweep of social attitudes and government tax and expenditure policies.

Barring changes in public policies, what can businesses themselves do to ameliorate their own healthcare costs? Many businesses have done what has come naturally: tried to select workers who are not likely to have medical problems and therefore drive up the firms' insurance costs. This is a solution that can benefit both owners *and* many workers, given that healthier workers can mean lower labor costs for firms and lower health insurance premiums. Although people might object to this solution on fairness grounds, we stress that it is the type of discriminatory hiring policy that is likely to emerge when health insurance costs have been distorted by political factors, such as those included in the list above.

Another private policy solution can emerge if employers and employees recognize that low deductibles on health insurance policies are very expensive because they encourage workers to spend someone else's money, which motivates excessive demand for healthcare and high insurance premiums. With a deductible of $5,000, the price of an additional dollar of insurance coverage for a forty-year-old male is measured as a tiny fraction of a cent (actually, 0.06 of a cent). However, when the deductible is $500, the price escalates to 55 cents. When the deductible is as low as $100, the price of an additional dollar of coverage rises to $2.14, a poor bargain for owners and their employees (Goodman and Musgrave 1992; Goodman, Musgrave, and Herrick 2004).

There is an obvious solution to the health insurance problem that has the potential not only of introducing greater efficiency into the healthcare business but also of improving the fairness of the system, without any policy change in Washington. This solution seeks to lower the private demand for healthcare by changing the incentives that workers have to consume healthcare services.

As discussed previously, many, if not most, firms that offer their workers health insurance provide "Cadillac policies," ones with small deductibles and broad coverage for just about everything that can go wrong with a person, regardless if she is partly responsible, through risky and unhealthy behavior, for the problems encountered. Each worker has an incentive to use healthcare services for the slightest problem, and she has less (though certainly not no) incentive to alter an unhealthy lifestyle.

Again, each worker can reason that if she were to cut back on personal usage of this or that healthcare service, the company's health insurance costs would not be materially affected. Certainly, the individual's health insurance premiums would not fall by the full value of the healthcare services not utilized. The savings from nonuse by any one individual, if the savings are detectable at all, will be spread over the entire group of workers through slightly lower premiums for everyone. Hence, the individual has little incentive to curb consumption.[3]

Granted, if everyone in a firm were to cut back on healthcare usage, then everyone could possibly gain in terms of reduced insurance premiums. The amount of savings could be substantial, and everyone would share in the savings of everyone else. However, as is so often true in business – and, for that matter, all group settings – getting everyone to do what is in their best collective interest comes up against the Prisoner's Dilemma discussed repeatedly. If everyone else cuts back, there is still no necessary and compelling reason for any one person to cut back. The one person's reduction is, again, inconsequential – regardless of what all others do. And, we must add, as we have throughout the book, the

[3] Of course, the extent to which the individual's actions can be detected depends on the size of the employment group. In small groups of workers, it would be easier to detect the impact of what one individual does or does not do.

larger the group, the more difficult the problem in bringing about collective cohesiveness of purpose.[4]

The basic problem for the firm should be seen as one of finding a means of giving all workers an incentive to cut their consumption. This can be done by raising the price of healthcare usage for employers, without making them worse off. But how can this be done by a firm?

Economist John Goodman and his colleagues recommend a practical solution, one that firms can (some already have) institute on their own – to the benefit of the workers *and* the firm.

To see how Goodman's proposal might work, we can start with a few observations and assumptions. Large employers spend $6,181 annually per worker on low-deductible health insurance, partially because workers under such systems have little incentive to consider the cost of most of the healthcare they consume. A basic *catastrophic* health insurance policy, one with a very large deductible of about $3,000 (meaning that the insurance covers only major medical problems), greatly increases the incentive to consider the cost of rather routine healthcare, and for this reason it can be purchased for each employee for a premium of about $1,200 per year, according to new reports (Alonzo-Zaldivar 2005).

Suppose that the employer agrees to provide this catastrophic insurance policy and, at the same time, also agrees to place in a bank reserve account (what Goodman prefers to call a "Medical Savings Account," or MSA) a sum of $3,000 each year per employee. The employer tells the employees that they can draw on that account for any medical "need" (with "need" being defined broadly). The workers can use the account, for example, to pay for routine visits to doctors, to cover the cost of hospital stays not covered by insurance, or to pay for a membership in a fitness center (given that exercise can prevent the need for some medical care). Finally, suppose that the workers are also told that the balance remaining in the account at the end of the year can be carried over to future years and applied to their individual retirement accounts, or even withdrawn at the end of the year for any purpose that the workers choose.[5]

[4] One of the more serious problems in having government provide health insurance is that the relevant *group* is really large, extending to the boundaries of the country, which means that people may have absolutely no incentives to curb their consumption of healthcare services. The benefits of doing so are spread ever so thinly over too many people.

[5] The particulars of the MSAs are not important here. The important characteristic is broad discretion on the part of the worker, which will likely mean that the worker has a sum of money that is set aside to cover the large deductible under a catastrophic medical insurance policy and that can be used by the employee when it is not spent for medical purposes.

This proposal has a chance of lowering the employees' healthcare consumption because it requires that people pay for most routine medical care with their own money (or money that will be theirs if they do not draw down their MSA accounts). Under common insurance arrangements, the additional cost of medical procedures (other than the patients' time) to the individual is much lower than the actual cost (after the low deductible is met). Under the MSA proposal, the cost to the employee of the first $3,000 of medical care is exactly equal to the cost of the service. This is because the employee is made the *residual claimant* on the balance at the end of the year. Hence, we should expect that workers will more carefully evaluate their usage of medical services and cut back. After all, under the old system, the workers were probably consuming "too much," given the low cost (or close to zero) that they incurred.

We would expect that the gains from this new MSA system could be shared by both the workers and their firm. We have already developed the example in a way that obviously benefits the firm. The firm was paying $6,181 a year for the insurance of each worker. Now, it must pay $1,200 for the insurance and $3,000 for the MSA, for a total of $4,200. The firm saves nearly $1,981 per worker.

The workers can also gain. Under the old arrangement, the workers were getting "paid" with insurance, not money. Under the MSA system, they are given a pot of money, $3,000, that they can use, if they choose, to buy low-deductible health insurance. But few are likely to do that. They can self-insure just by holding onto the money and paying the first $3,000 in medical bills. However, they can, conceivably, also buy a variety of other things, from new televisions to education programs to additional days of vacation.[6] Accordingly, the additional money should enable workers to be better off by allocating the sum to higher-valued uses.

Both workers and their employers can also gain because the new insurance arrangement can be expected to lower the amount of healthcare workers demand. Many workers will want to be careful not to use up their $3,000 account so they become more careful "shoppers" of medical care. Workers will make use of the catastrophic insurance only in those situations when they have serious problems and little choice but to make use of medical care, which explains why the premiums for catastrophic insurance are so low.

[6] Any actual MSA program might for political reasons have restrictions on the range of goods and services that the workers can buy with any MSA balance remaining at the end of the year. For example, one MSA-type proposal would require that the balance go into a worker's retirement account.

By providing catastrophic health insurance coupled with a MSA, a firm can attract better workers by providing them with a more valuable compensation package at lower cost. In other words, firms can be expected to scrutinize its workers for health problems. The MSA is a way also that employers can induce workers to self-select. Those with few anticipated medical problems can be expected to gravitate toward those firms that use MSAs. Those workers with substantial health needs can be expected to go to firms with more generous policies and few penalties for obtaining healthcare. Overall, we would expect the firms that adopt this type of insurance system to be more productive and competitive.

However, we hasten to add that our simple example does not reflect the full complexity of the employment conditions most firms face. The problem managers will have in developing acceptance of the MSA relates to the cross-subsidies that are embedded in current insurance programs. Low-risk workers typically subsidize high-risk workers. Hence, we doubt that the firm's deposit into workers' MSA accounts would equal the insurance deductible, as we have assumed in our example. The reason is that many healthy (typically younger) workers are fortunate in that they often don't go to the doctor or hospital in any given year, and other workers have only modest medical expenditures in most years. They are subsidizing the unhealthy (typically older) workers who make extensive use of medical care. If the MSA deposit equaled the deductible, this cross-subsidy would be wiped out, and the insurance company would very likely be hit with high bills from the high-risk workers without the payments from the low-risk workers. To make the MSA system work, the deposit would have to be limited, with the workers themselves sharing in some of the gains in the event they have limited expenses but also sharing in some of the risks if their expenses exceed their MSA deposits. Therein lies the rub, which will rule out many firms' desire to institute the deal. However, some firms will still be able to find a reasonable compromise.

Problems with MSAs

Managers must also be mindful of the possibility that MSAs can set up perverse incentives for some workers, for some types of healthcare. Knowing that they will have to draw down their MSA account in order to cover annual physical examinations, for example (and other preventive healthcare measures), workers can reason that MSAs will increase the immediate cost of physical examinations. Some employees will still get physicals because they will value them more than the cost. These employees will be motivated by a combination of health and financial concerns, wanting to increase the probability of catching a harmful medical problem early to increase the chances of being cured, and also reasoning that catching a health problem early can lower future health-related expenditures.

However, we suspect that some employees will not be able, or willing, to make such careful calculations or properly assess the current and future benefits of physicals. Other workers may reason that most of their later healthcare expenditures for "major" problems that go undetected will be covered as the catastrophic health insurance kicks in. To accommodate these potential problems, employers can consider covering a portion of the current cost of physicals and other preventive measures. The employers can cover the added cost of subsidizing physicals and some preventive care with any reduction in their (employers') insurance premiums they get from encouraging preventive care. If there are no insurance savings from the subsidy, then it seems reasonable to conclude that either the "problem" of employees skipping preventive care is not a problem or is such a minor one that the insurance companies see no need to reduce the insurance premiums of firms that encourage preventive care.

The main point is that managers must tread carefully in trying to accommodate problems with "preventive care." The problem is that "preventive care" can include not only physicals but also an array of tests that have little useful medical value. If "preventive care" is defined too broadly and the subsidies are high, managers can be back in the Prisoner's Dilemma trap that results in excessive healthcare and health care insurance expenditures, the net effect of which is that healthcare benefits that are not worth the costs to the workers.

Finally, managers must be mindful that if they allow their employees to choose to switch between health insurance in the form of a high-deductible policy (combined with a medical savings account) and low premiums and the standard low-deductible policy, then they can encourage workers to take the high-deductible policy when they think they will be healthy, only to switch to the low-deductible policy when they think they will be getting sick. The ability to switch back and forth can give rise to an erosion of medical care savings. If employers don't allow their workers to switch between the policies, then healthy workers can be expected to crowd into the high-deductible policies, leaving the workers who have health problems behind in the low-deductible policy – the payments on which for both workers and employers should be expected to rise (Alonzo-Zaldivar 2005).

Business experience with MSAs

Has the MSA concept been tried, and has it worked? "Yes," on both counts, although the trials to date do not correspond exactly with our example above. Nevertheless, several firms have already tried the system with beneficial effects (with these observations being pertinent at the time this book was written):

- After Quaker Oats put $300 in each worker's MSA per month, the company's healthcare costs grew 6.3 percent a year. However, this occurred during a period when the healthcare costs of the rest of the country were growing at double-digit rates.
- *Forbes* magazine encouraged its employees to curb medical care expenditures with a variation of the MSA, by paying workers $2 for every $1 of medical costs not incurred up to $1,000. This means that if a *Forbes* employee incurred medical costs of only $300 in a given year, the employee was rewarded with a check of $1,400 at the end of the year [2 × ($1,000 – $300)]. The magazine's healthcare costs fell 17 and 12 percent in successive years after medical savings accounts were offered, years during which other firms' insurance costs were rising.
- The utility holding company Dominion Resources gave each worker who chose a $3,000 deductible on the company's health insurance policy a deposit of $1,650 a year. Its insurance premiums have not risen since 1989, whereas the insurance premiums of other companies have risen by an average of 13 percent a year.
- Golden Rule Insurance Company gave each worker a $2,000 annual deposit if he or she selected a deductible of $3,000. The company's health insurance costs dropped (from what they would otherwise have been) the first year by 40 percent (National Center for Policy Analysis 1994, 1; Cannon 2003).

We don't propose to tell firms what to do in their own particular circumstances, for a very good reason: We obviously don't know the details of the individual circumstances. We can use our incentive-based approach to explore the *types* of business policies that managers should consider and then adjust to fit the particulars of their circumstances. Moreover, our focus on health insurance is illustrative of insights that are relevant across a firm's entire fringe benefit package.

The important point of this discussion is by now an old one in this book: Incentives matter. One of the several important reasons that many workers pay high health insurance premiums is that they don't have much of an incentive to carefully evaluate their health care purchases. The best way of ensuring that workers get the most out of their health care benefits is one that is as old as business itself: Make the buyer pay a price that reflects the true cost of his or her decision.

MSAs are simply a means (perhaps one of many that have not yet been devised) of making workers potentially better off with incentives that result from requiring people to pay, as near as possible, the full cost of what they consume. This solution may not work for all businesses. Some worker groups may not want to be bothered with considering the costs of their behaviors. However, it appears that many firms and their workers have not considered policies such as MSAs because they have not realized that they harbor the potential of making everyone better off. These are the types of policies all managers should examine. Such policies can raise their workers' welfare, their firm's stock prices, and the compensation of managers. Again we return to what is by now an old point in the book: Firms can make money not only by selling more of their product or service but also by creatively restructuring incentives in mutually beneficial ways.

THE BOTTOM LINE

The key takeaways from chapter 8 are the following:

(1) Cost plays a pivotal role in a producer's choices. Costs change with the quantity produced. The pattern of those changes determines the limit of a producer's activity – from the production of saleable goods and services to the employment of leisure time.

(2) The maximizing individual will produce a good or service, or engage in an activity, until marginal cost equals marginal benefit (marginal revenue). Graphically, this is the point at which the supply and demand curves for the individual's behavior intersect. At this point, although additional benefits might be obtained by producing additional units of the good, service, or activity, the additional costs that would be incurred discourage further production.

(3) Costs will not affect an individual's behavior unless she perceives them as costs. For this reason, managers can often improve incentives – increasing firm profits and employees' benefits – by looking for hidden, or implicit costs, in the choices being made, and making the changes necessary to insure that they, and their workers, confront those choices.

(4) All costs – explicit and implicit – must be considered when deciding whether to produce anything and when deciding how much of anything should be produced if profits are to be maximized.
(5) Sunk costs, which are costs that cannot be recouped, don't matter in production decisions.
(6) Normal profit is a cost of doing business.
(7) Marginal cost is a key cost concept.
(8) The market supply curve in a competitive goods market is the horizontal summation of individual firms' supply curves (or their marginal cost curves above the minimum of the average variable cost curve).
(9) One way that firms can cut their health insurance costs is to impose some of the cost of care on workers. One means of imposing costs on workers is to offer them MSAs, along with health insurance policies that cover major health problems.

REVIEW QUESTIONS

(1) Evaluate the old adages "haste makes waste" and "a stitch in time saves nine" from an economic point of view.
(2) If executives' time is as valuable as they claim, why are they frequently found reading the advertisements in airline magazines en route to a business meeting?
(3) When cell phones were first introduced, the price of a one-minute long-distance call on a cell phone was several times the cost of a call on a land-line phone. Does that mean that at the time of their introduction, cell phones increased the cost of long-distance calling?
(4) In discussing accident prevention, we assumed an increasing marginal cost. Suppose, instead, that the marginal cost of preventing accidents remains constant. How will that assumption affect the analysis?
(5) Using the analysis of accident prevention, develop an analysis of pollution control. Using demand and supply curves for clean air, determine the efficient level of pollution control.
(6) People take some measures to avoid becoming victims of crime. Can the probability of becoming a victim be reduced to (virtually) zero? If so, why don't people eliminate that probability? What does the underlying logic of your answer suggest about the cost of committing crimes and the crime rate?
(7) If the money price of a good rises from $5 to $10, the economist can confidently predict that less will be purchased. One cannot be equally

confident that denying a child a dessert for bad behavior will improve his behavior, however. Explain why.

(8) Consider the information in the production schedule that follows. (a) At what output level do diminishing returns set in? (b) Assume that each worker receives $8. Fill in the marginal product column, and develop a marginal cost schedule and a marginal cost curve for the production process.

No. of workers	Total product of all workers per day	Marginal product of each worker
1	0.10	
2	0.30	
3	0.60	
4	1.00	
5	1.45	
6	2.00	
7	2.50	
8	2.80	
9	3.00	
10	3.19	
11	3.37	
12	3.54	
13	3.70	
14	3.85	
15	4.00	
16	3.90	
17	3.70	

CHAPTER

9

Production costs in the short run and long run

In economics, the cost of an event is the highest-valued opportunity necessarily forsaken. The usefulness of the concept of cost is a logical implication of choice among available options. Only if no alternatives were possible or if amounts of all resources were available beyond everyone's desires, so that all goods were free, would the concepts of cost and of choice be irrelevant. **Armen Alchian**

The individual firm plays a critical role both in theory and in the real world. It straddles two basic economic institutions: the markets for resources (labor, capital, and land) and the markets for goods and services (everything from trucks to truffles). The firm must be able to identify what people want to buy, at what price, and to organize the great variety of available resources into an efficient production process. It must sell its product at a price that covers the cost of its resources, yet allows it to compete with other firms. Moreover, it must accomplish those objectives while competing firms are seeking to meet the same goals.

How does the firm do all this? Clearly, firms do not all operate in exactly the same way. They differ in organizational structure and in management style, in the resources they use and in the products they sell. This chapter cannot possibly cover the great diversity of business management techniques. Rather, our purpose is to develop the broad principles that guide the production decisions of most firms.

As with individuals, firms are beset by the necessity of choice which, as Armen Alchian reminds us in the chapter epigraph, implies a cost. Costs are both the result of having to make choices, and obstacles to those choices; they restrict us in what we do. Thus a firm's cost structure (the way cost varies with production) reflects how firms deal with the obstacles of making a profitable production decision, in both the short run and in the long run. There is a very good reason why MBA students should know something about a firm's

The **short run** is the period during which one or more resources (and thus one or more costs of production) cannot be changed – either increased or decreased.

A **fixed cost** is any cost that does not vary with the level of output. Fixed costs include overhead expenditures that extend over a period of months or years: insurance premiums, leasing and rental payments, land and equipment purchases, and interest on loans.

A **variable cost** is any cost that changes with the level of output.

cost structure. "Firms" don't do anything on their own. Managers are the forces behind the activities and the decisions of firms that ultimately determine whether they are profitable or not.

Our analysis of a firm's "cost structure" is different from the costs on accounting statements. Accounting statements indicate the costs that were incurred when the firm produced the output that it did. They provide only a snapshot of what costs the firm has incurred in a given period of time and for a given output level.

In this chapter, we want to devise a cost structure that relates production costs to many different output levels. The reason is simple: We want to use this structure to help us think through the question of which among many output levels will enable the firm to maximize profits.

You will also notice that our cost structure is *abstract*, meaning that it is independent of the experience of any given real-world firm in any given real-world industry. We develop the cost structure in abstract terms for another good reason: MBA students plan to work in a variety of industries and in a variety of firms within those different industries. We want to devise a cost structure that is potentially useful in many different business contexts. To do this, we need to construct costs in several different ways for different time periods, because production costs depend critically on the amount of time over which production takes place.

PART I THEORY AND PUBLIC POLICY APPLICATIONS

Fixed, variable, and total costs in the short run

Time is required to produce any good or service. Therefore, any output level must be founded on some recognized period of time. Even more important, the costs a firm incurs vary over time. To think about costs clearly, we must identify the period of time over which they apply. For reasons that will become apparent as we progress, economists speak of costs in terms of the extent to which they can be varied, rather than the number of months or years required to pay them off. Although in the long run all costs can be varied, in the **short run** firms face some costs that cannot be varied. Short-run costs can be either **fixed** or **variable**. Total fixed costs (*TFC*) remain the same whether the firm's factories are standing idle or producing at capacity. As long as the firm faces

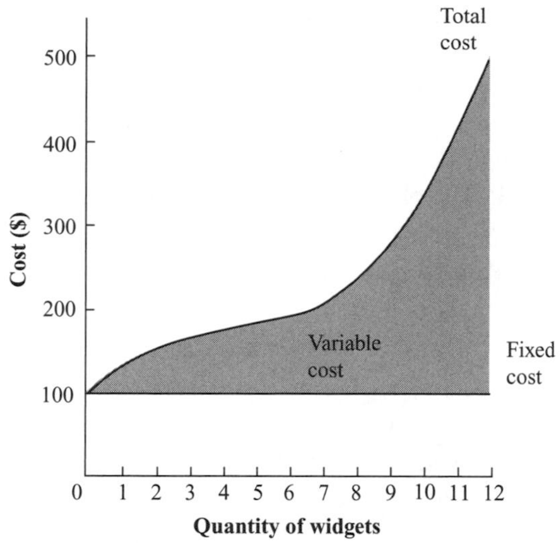

Figure 9.1 Total fixed costs, total variable costs, and total costs in the short run
Total fixed cost does not vary with production; therefore, it is drawn as a horizontal line. Total variable cost does rise with production. Here it is represented by the shaded area between the total cost and total fixed cost curves.

even one fixed cost, it is operating in the short run. Variable costs include wages (workers can be hired or laid off on relatively short notice), material, utilities, and office supplies. Total variable costs (*TVC*) increase with the level of output.

Together, total fixed and total variable costs equal total cost. Total cost (*TC*) is the sum of fixed costs and variable costs at each output level.

$$TC = TFC + TVC$$

Columns (1)–(4) of table 9.1 show fixed, variable, and total costs at various production levels. Total fixed costs are constant at $100 for all output levels (see column (2). Total variable costs increase gradually, from $30 to $395, as output expands from 1 to 12 widgets. Total cost, the sum of all fixed and variable costs at each output level (obtained by adding columns (2) and (3) horizontally), increases gradually as well.

Graphically, total fixed cost can be represented by a horizontal line, as in figure 9.1. The total cost curve starts at the same point as the total fixed cost curve (because total cost must at least equal fixed cost) and rises from that point. The vertical distance between the total cost and the total fixed cost curves shows the total variable cost at each level of production.

Marginal and average costs in the short run

The central issue of this chapter, and chapters 10 and 11, is how to determine the profit maximizing level of production. In other words, we want to know what output the firm that is interested in maximizing profits will choose to produce. Although fixed, variable, and total costs are important measures, they are not very useful in determining the firm's profit maximizing (or loss minimizing) output. To arrive at that figure, as well as to estimate profits or losses, we need four additional measures of cost: (1) marginal, (2) average fixed, (3) average variable, and (4) average total. When graphed, those four measures represent the firm's cost structure. A cost structure is the way in which various measures of cost (total cost, total variable cost, and so forth) vary with the production level. These four cost measures cover all costs associated with production, including risk cost and opportunity cost.

Marginal cost

We have defined marginal cost (*MC*) as the additional cost of producing one additional unit. By extension, marginal cost can also be defined as the change in total cost. Because the change in total cost is due solely to the change in variable cost, marginal cost can also be defined as the change in total variable cost per unit:

$$\text{MC} = \frac{\text{Change in TC}}{\text{Change in quantity}} = \frac{\text{Change in TVC}}{\text{Change in quantity}}$$

As you can see from table 9.1, marginal cost declines as output expands from 1 to 4 widgets and then rises, as predicted by the law of diminishing marginal returns. This increasing marginal cost reflects the diminishing marginal productivity of extra workers and other variable resources that the firm must employ in order to expand output beyond four widgets.

The marginal cost curve is shown in figure 9.2. The bottom of the curve (four units) is the point at which marginal returns begin to diminish.

Average fixed cost

Average fixed cost (*AFC*) is total fixed cost divided by the number of units produced (*Q*):

$$AFC = \frac{TFC}{Q}$$

Table 9.1 *Total, marginal, and average cost of production*

Production level (no. of widgets) (1)	Total fixed costs (2) ($)	Total variable costs (3) ($)	Total costs (2) + (3) (4) ($)	Marginal cost (change in (3) or (4)) (5) ($)	Average fixed cost ((2)/ (1)) (6) ($)	Average variable cost ((3)/ (1)) (7) ($)	Average total cost ((4)/ (1)) or ((6) + (7)) (8) ($)
1	100	30	130	30	100.00	30.00	130.00
2	100	50	150	20	50.00	25.00	75.00
3	100	60	160	10	33.33	20.00	53.33
4	100	65	165	5	25.00	16.25	41.25
5	100	75	175	10	20.00	15.00	35.00
6	100	90	190	15	16.67	15.00	31.67
7	100	110	210	20	14.29	15.71	30.00
8	100	140	240	30	12.50	17.50	30.00
9	100	180	280	40	11.11	20.00	31.11
10	100	230	330	50	10.00	23.00	33.00
11	100	300	400	70	9.09	27.27	36.36
12	100	395	495	95	8.33	32.92	41.25

In table 9.1, total fixed costs are constant at \$100. As output expands, therefore, the average fixed cost per unit must decline. (That is what business people mean when they talk about "spreading the overhead." As production expands, the average fixed cost declines.)

In figure 9.2, the average fixed cost curve slopes downward to the right approaching, but never touching, the horizontal axis. That is because average fixed cost is a ratio, *TFC/Q*, and a ratio can never be reduced to zero, no matter how large the denominator (*Q*). (Note that this is a principle of arithmetic, not economics.)

Average variable cost

Average variable cost is total variable cost divided by the number of units produced, or

$$AVC = \frac{TVC}{Q}$$

At an output level of 1 unit, average variable cost necessarily equals marginal cost. Beyond the first unit, marginal and average variable costs diverge, although they are mathematically related. Whenever marginal cost declines, as it does initially in figure 9.2, average variable cost must also decline: the lower marginal value pulls the average value down. A basketball player who scores progressively

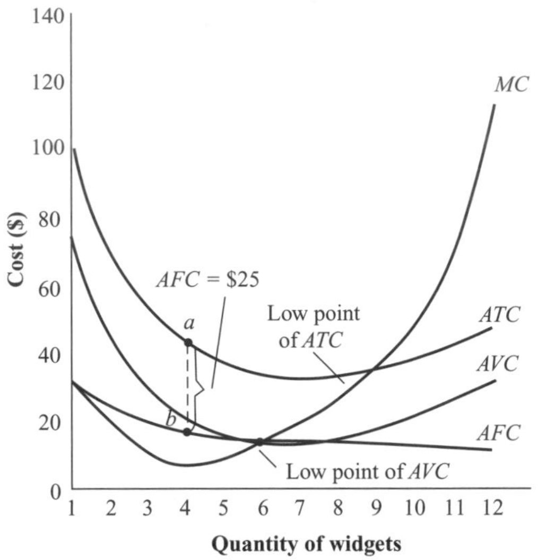

Figure 9.2 Marginal and average costs in the short run
The average fixed cost curve (*AFC*) slopes downward and approaches, but never touches, the horizontal axis. The average variable cost curve (*AVC*) and the total variable cost curve are mathematically related to the marginal cost curve and both intersect with the marginal cost curve (*MC*) at its lowest point. The vertical distance between the average total cost curve (*ATC*) and the average variable cost curve equals the average fixed cost at any given output level. There is no relationship between the *MC* and *AFC* curves.

fewer points in each successive game, for instance, will find her average score falling, although not as rapidly as her marginal score.

Beyond the point of diminishing marginal returns, marginal cost rises, but average variable cost continues to fall for a time (see figure 9.2). As long as marginal cost is below the average variable cost, average variable cost must continue to decline. The two curves meet at an output level of 6 widgets. Beyond that point, the average variable cost curve must rise because the average value will be pulled up by the greater marginal value. (After a game in which she scores more points than her previous average, for instance, the basketball player's average score must rise.) The point at which the marginal cost and average variable cost curves intersect is therefore the low point of the average variable cost curve. Before that intersection, average variable cost must fall. After it, average variable cost must rise. For the same reason, the intersection of the marginal cost curve and the average total cost curve must be the low point of the average total cost curve (see figure 9.2).

Average total cost

Average total cost (ATC) is the total of all fixed and variable costs divided by the number of units produced (Q), or

$$ATC = \frac{TFC + TVC}{Q} = \frac{TC}{Q}$$

Average total cost can also be found by summing the average fixed and average variable costs, if they are known ($ATC = AFC + AVC$). Graphically, the average total cost curve is the vertical summation of the average fixed and average variable cost curves (see figure 9.2).

Because average total cost is the sum of average fixed and variable costs, the average fixed cost can be obtained by subtracting average variable from average total cost: $AFC = ATC - AVC$. On a graph, average fixed cost is the vertical distance between the average total cost curve and the average variable cost curve. For instance, in figure 9.2 at an output level of 4 widgets, the average fixed cost is the vertical distance *ab*, or $25 ($41.25 – $16.25, or column (8) minus column (7) in table 9.1).

From this point on, we do not show the average fixed cost curve on a graph, because doing so complicates the presentation without adding new information. Average fixed cost is hereafter indicated by the vertical distance between the average total and average variable cost curves at any given output.

Exactly how firms go about choosing the appropriate (optimum) mix of resources – land, labor, capital, and technology – to minimize the cost curves developed in this section is the subject of the appendix to this chapter, (p. 377).

Marginal and average costs in the long run

> The **long run** is the period during which all resources (and thus all costs of production) can be changed – either increased or decreased.

So far, our discussion has been restricted to time periods during which at least one resource is fixed. That assumption underlies the concept of fixed cost. Fortunately, all resources that are used in production can be changed over the **long run**. By definition, there are no fixed costs in the long run. All long-run costs are variable.

The foregoing short-run analysis is still useful in analyzing a firm's long-run cost structure. In the long run, the average total cost curve (*ATC* in figure 9.2) represents one possible scale of operation, with one given quantity of plant and equipment (in table 9.1, $100 worth). A change in plant and equipment will change the firm's cost structure, increasing or decreasing its productive capacity.

Economies of scale

Economies of scale are cost savings that technology allows when all resource inputs are increased together.

Figure 9.3 illustrates the long-run production choices facing a typical firm. The curve labeled ATC_1 is the average total cost curve developed in figure 9.2. Additional plant and equipment will add to total fixed costs, and results in an average total cost curve such as ATC_2 in figure 9.3. Because of the additional fixed cost, at low output levels (up to q_1) the average total costs will be higher – curve ATC_2 will lie above ATC_1. But the additional plant and equipment allow **economies of scale** to be realized beyond output q_1, resulting in lower average total costs than is possible with the plant and equipment associated with ATC_1.

Economies of scale can occur for several reasons. Expanded operation generally permits greater specialization of resources. Technologically advanced equipment, such as super computers and management information systems (MIS) combined with telecommunication systems, can be used, and more highly skilled workers can be employed. Expansion may also permit improvements in organization, such as with assembly-line production. Also, by expanding production the firm can spread the higher cost of additional plant and equipment over a larger output level, reducing its average cost of production.

The advantages of economies of scale are always limited, with average costs eventually going up as output increases with more plant and equipment the firm added. When this occurs, we have the point where diseconomies of scale become operative. For example, as more people are hired to work with the additional plant and equipment, the problem of free-riders becomes increasingly troublesome and this can lead to **diseconomies of scale.**[1]

Diseconomies of scale are added costs that, beyond some point, accompany the expansion of production through the use of more of all inputs.

And in some lines of production, diseconomies of scale are encountered at very small output levels independently of free-rider problems. For example, such things as the production of original works of art, cutting hair, repairing shoes, and writing books are typically done by individuals working alone or by firms with very little capital and very few workers.

However, as long as economies of scale remain in force, the average cost curve can be reduced over larger output levels by increasing plant and equipment. Just as curve ATC_2 in figure 9.3 cuts curve ATC_1 and then dips down to a lower minimum average total cost at a higher output level, so does curve ATC_3 with

[1] For a while, a firm may be able to avoid diseconomies of scale by increasing the number of its plants. Management's ability to supervise a growing number of plants is limited, however, and eventually, diseconomies of scale will emerge at the level of the firm, if not the plant. If diseconomies of scale did not exist, in the long run each industry would have only one firm.

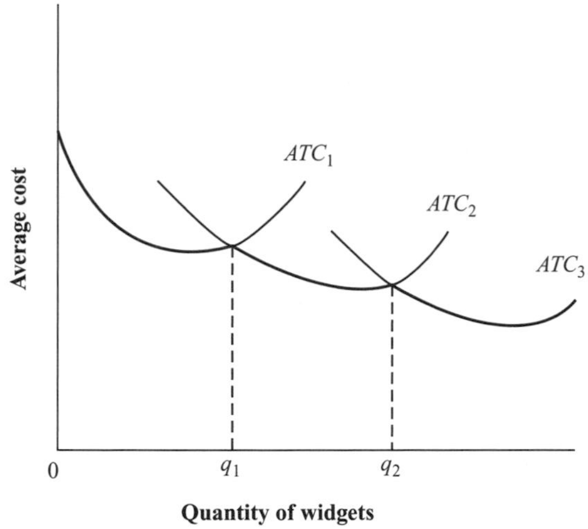

Figure 9.3 Economies of scale

Economies of scale are cost savings associated with the expanded use of resources. To realize such savings, however, a firm must expand its output. Here the firm can lower its costs by expanding production from q_1 to q_2 – a scale of operation that places it on a lower short-run average total cost curve (ATC_2 instead of ATC_1).

respect to the curve ATC_2, indicating that economies of scale haven't been exhausted with the plant and equipment associated with curve ATC_2. But at some point, diseconomies of scale will be encountered.

It is possible, of course, that economies of scale will still be operating when a firm is producing more than it can sell at a profit. In this case, the firm will limit its output below the point where diseconomies of scale are limiting it (a topic that will be considered again and with the addition of the market demand curve in chapter 12).

Long-run average and marginal cost curves

When a firm has enough time to change the amount of all the inputs it is using – to change its scale of operation – it is interested in its long-run cost curves. Therefore the firm can minimize its overall cost of operation by expanding along the envelope portion of the curve ATC_2, and it can push its average costs down to the lowest point by expanding its scale to ATC_4 and output to q_1.

Assuming that there are a very large number of possible scales of operation, the firm's expansion path can be seen as a single overall curve that envelops

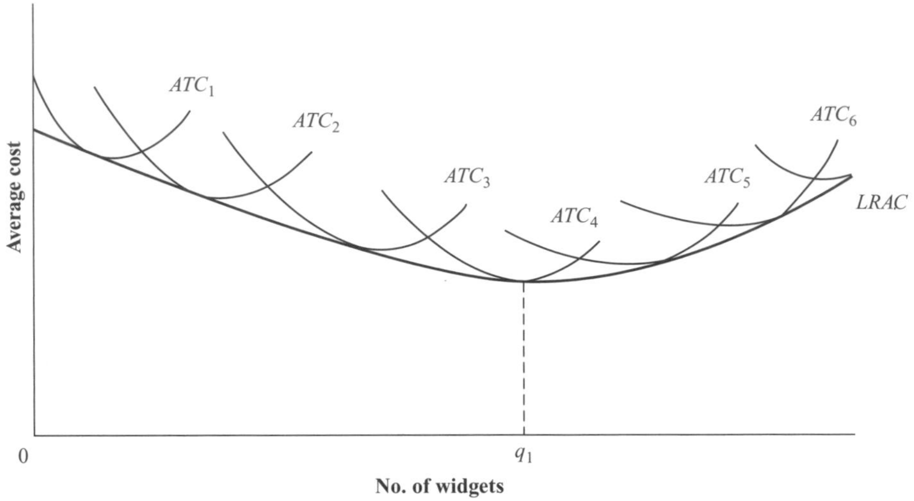

Figure 9.4 Diseconomies of scale

Diseconomies of scale may occur because of the communication problems of larger firms. Here the firm realizes economies of scale through its first short-run average total cost curves. The long-run average cost curve begins to turn up at an output level of q_1, beyond which diseconomies of scale set in.

all of its short-run average cost curves. Such a curve is shown in figure 9.4 and reproduced in figure 9.5 as the long-run average cost curve (*LRAC*).

As do short-run average cost curves, the long-run average cost curve has an accompanying long-run marginal cost curve. If long-run average cost is falling, as it does initially in figure 9.5, it must be because long-run marginal cost is pulling it down. If long-run cost is rising, as it does eventually in figure 9.5, then long-run marginal cost must be pulling it up. Hence at some point, long-run marginal cost must turn upward, intersecting the long-run average cost curve at its lowest point, q_1.

Industry differences in average cost

Not all firms experience economies and diseconomies of scale to the same degree, or at the same levels of production. Their long-run average cost curves, in other words, look very different. Figure 9.6 shows several possible shapes for long-run average cost curves. The curve in figure 9.6(a) belongs to a firm in an industry with few economies of scale and significant diseconomies at relatively low output levels. (This curve might belong to a firm in a service industry, such

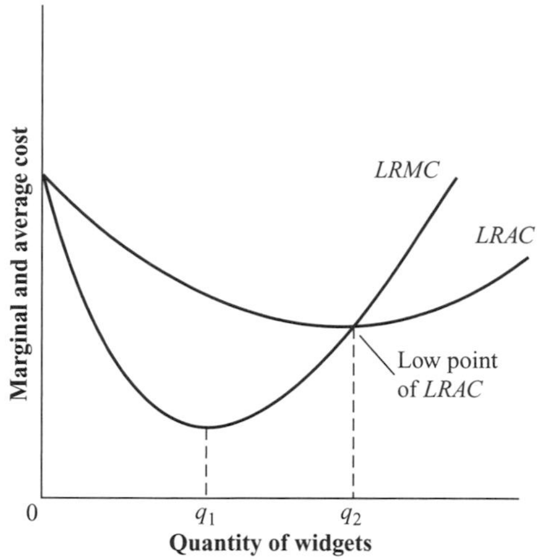

Figure 9.5 Marginal and average cost in the long run
The long-run marginal and average cost curves are mathematically related. The long-run average cost curve slopes downward as long as it is above the long-run marginal cost curve. The two curves intersect at the low point of the long-run average cost curve.

as a shoe repair business.) We would not expect firms in this industry to be very large, because firms with an output level beyond q_1 can easily be underpriced by smaller, lower-cost firms.

Figure 9.6(b) shows the long-run average cost curve for a firm in an industry with modest economies of scale at low output levels and no diseconomies of scale until the firm reaches a fairly high output level. In such an industry – perhaps apparel manufacturing – we would expect to find firms of various sizes, some small and some large. As long as firms are producing between q_1 and q_2, larger firms do not have a cost advantage over smaller firms.

A **natural monopoly** is an industry in which long-run marginal and average costs generally decline with increases in production within the relevant range of the market demand for a good or service.

Figure 9.6(c) illustrates the average costs for a firm in an industry that enjoys extensive economies of scale – for example, an electric power company. No matter how far this firm extends its scale, the long-run average cost curve continues to fall. Diseconomies of scale may exist but, if so, they occur at output levels beyond the effective market for the firm's product. This type of industry tends toward a single seller – a **natural monopoly**. Given the industry's cost structure, that is, one firm can expand its scale, lower its cost of operation, and underprice other firms that attempt to produce on a smaller, higher-cost scale. Electric utilities have been thought for a long time to be natural monopolies (which has supposedly justified their regulation, a subject to which we return in chapter 12).

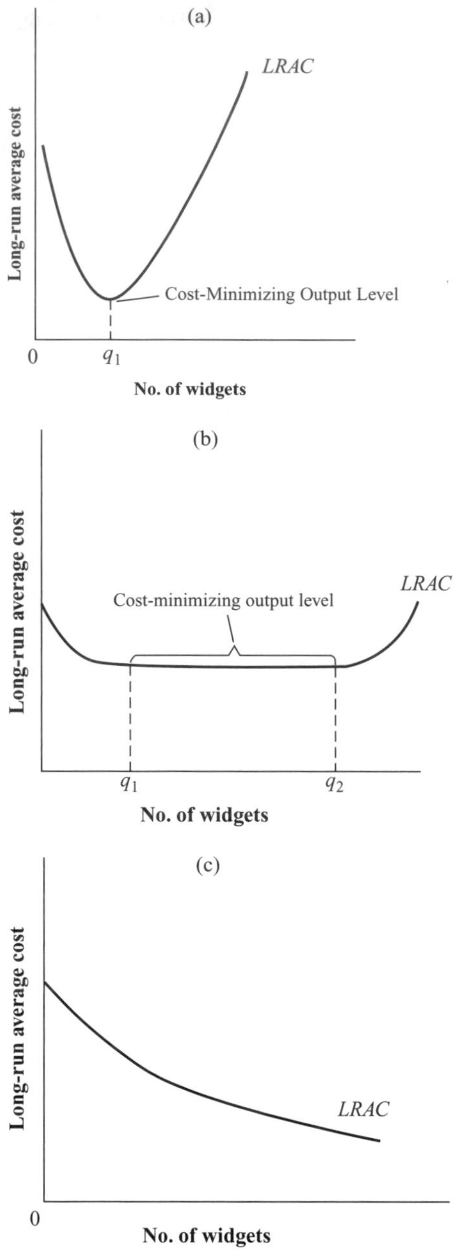

Figure 9.6 Individual differences in long-run average cost curves

The shape of the long-run average cost curve varies according to the extent and persistence of economies and diseconomies of scale. Firms in industries with few economies of scale will have a long-run average cost curve like the one in panel (a). Firms in industries with persistent economies of scale will have a long-run average cost curve like the one in panel (b), and firms in industries with extensive economies of scale may find that their long-run average cost curve slopes continually downward, as in panel (c).

Shifts in the average and marginal cost curves

The average cost curves we have just described all assumed that the prices for resources remain constant. This is a critical assumption. If those prices change, so will the average cost curves. The marginal cost curve may shift as well, depending on the type of average cost – variable or fixed – that changes.

Thus if the price of a variable input – such as the wage rate of labor – rises, the firm's average total cost will rise along with its average variable cost ($AFC + AVC = ATC$), shifting the average total cost curve upward. The firm's marginal cost curve will shift as well, because the additional cost of producing an additional unit must rise with the higher labor cost (see figure 9.7(a)). If a fixed cost, such as insurance premiums, rises, average total cost will also rise, shifting the average total cost curve upward, as in figure 9.7(b). The short-run marginal cost curve will not shift, however, because marginal cost is unaffected by fixed cost. The marginal cost curve is derived only from variable costs.

Because changes in variable cost affect a firm's marginal cost, they influence its production decisions. As first noted in chapter 8, the profit maximizing firm selling at a constant price will produce up to the point at which marginal cost equals price ($MC = P$). At a price of P_1 in figure 9.7(a), then, the firm will produce q_2 widgets. After an increase in variable costs and an upward shift in the marginal cost curve, however, the firm will cut back to q_1 widgets. At q_1 widgets, price again equals marginal cost. The cutback in output has occurred because the marginal cost of producing widgets from q_1 to q_2 now exceeds the price. In other words, an increase in variable cost results in a reduction in a firm's output.

Because a shift in average fixed cost leaves marginal cost unaffected, the firm's profit maximizing output level in figure 9.7 (b) remains at q_1. The firm may make lower profits because of its higher fixed cost, but it cannot increase profits by either expanding or reducing output.

This analysis applies to the short run only. In the long run, all costs are variable, and changes in the price of any resource will affect a firm's production decisions. Long-run changes in the output levels of firms, of course, change the market price of the final product as well as consumer purchases. More will be said on all these points later.

The very long run

Economic analysis tends to be restricted to either the short or the long run, for one major reason. For both periods, costs are known with reasonable precision.

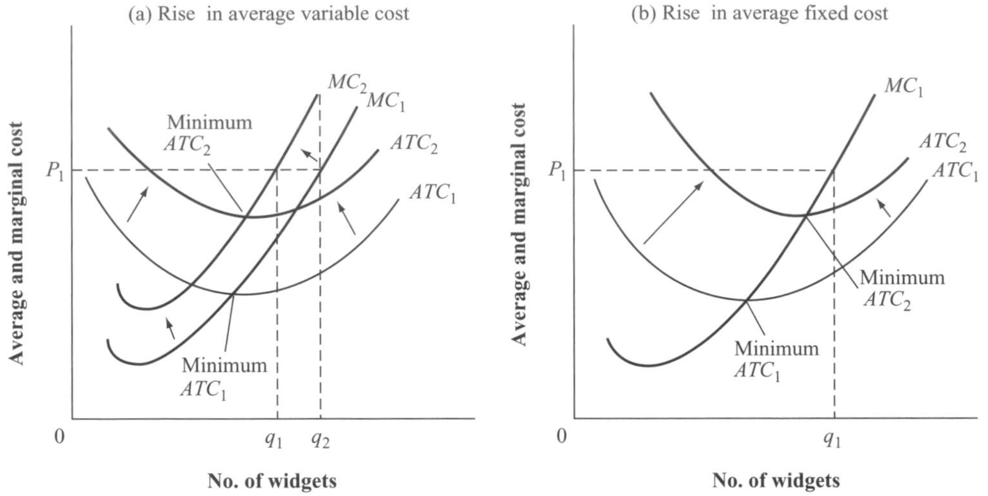

Figure 9.7 Shifts in average and marginal cost curves

An increase in a firm's variable cost (panel (a)) will shift the firm's average total cost curve up, from ATC_1 to ATC_2. It will also shift the marginal cost curve, from MC_1 to MC_2. Production will fall because of the increase in marginal cost. By contrast, an increase in a firm's fixed cost (panel (b)) will shift the average total cost curve upward from ATC_1 to ATC_2, but will not affect the marginal cost curve. (Marginal cost is unaffected by fixed cost.) Thus the firm's level of production will not change.

In the short run, firms know that, beyond some point, increases in the use of a resource (for example, fertilizer) will bring diminishing marginal returns and rising marginal costs. They also know that with increased use of all resources, certain economies and diseconomies of scale can be expected over the long run. Given what is known about the technology of production and the availability of resources, economists can draw certain conclusions about a firm's behavior and the consequences of its actions.

> The **very long run** is the time period during which the technology of production and the availability of resources can change because of invention, innovation, and discovery of new technologies and resources.

As economists look further and further into the future, however, they can predict less about a firm's behavior and its consequences in the marketplace. Less is known about the technology and resources of the distant future. In the **very long run**, everything is subject to change – resources themselves, their availability, and the technology for using them.

By definition, the very long run is, to a significant degree, unpredictable. Firms cannot know today how to make use of unspecified future advances in technology. A hundred years ago firms had little idea how important lasers, satellites, airplanes, and computers would be to today's economy. Indeed, many products taken for granted today were invented or discovered quite by accident.

Edison developed the phonograph while attempting to invent the light bulb. John Rock developed the birth control pill while studying penicillin, Charles Goodyear's development of vulcanization, and Wilhelm Roentgen's invention of the X-ray – all were accidents. And even if these inventions could have been predicted, they all had economic consequences that could not have been predicted.

Not all inventions or innovations are accidental, and we can know something about the very long run. Firms have some idea of the value of investments in research and development (R&D). Research on substitute resources can yield improvements in productivity that translate into cost reductions. Research on new product designs will yield more attractive and useful products. There will be failures as well – research projects that accomplish little or nothing – but, over time, the rewards of research and development can exceed the costs.

Because of the risks involved in research and development, some firms may be expected to fail. In the very long run, they will not be able to keep up with the competition in product design and productivity. They will not adjust sufficiently to changes in the market and will suffer losses. The computer industry provides many examples of firms that have tried to build a better machine but could not keep pace with the rapid technological advances of competitors.

Proponents of a planned economy see the uncertainty of the very long run as an argument for government direction of the nation's development. They stress that competitors often do not know what other firms are doing. They therefore need guidance in the form of government subsidies and tax penalties to ensure that the nation's long-term goals are achieved.

Proponents of the market system agree that it is difficult to look ahead to the very long run, but they see the uncertainties as an argument for keeping production decisions in the hands of firms. Private firms have the economic incentive of profit to stay alert to changes in market conditions, and they can respond quickly to changes in technology and resources. Government control might slow the adjustment process.

Perspective The Myth of the First-Mover Advantage

One of the most widely believed tenets in management theory and practice is the so-called "first-mover advantage." That is, the first firm to market with a product will not only have the market to itself, but will be able to fend off all latecomers and dominate the market for some time to come.

Why? Theory holds that the first mover will achieve name recognition, realize some cost advantage from economies of scale (thus lowering its long-term cost curves), develop brand loyalty (hence, increasing its demand and/or lowering its elasticity of demand), and garner the benefits of "network effects" (meaning that its demand will build with expanded consumption). Beyond some ill-defined point, the first mover can expect its market expansion to reach the "tipping point," beyond which consumers will move to the dominant first mover simply because everyone else is moving in that direction (Gladwell 2000).

The first mover, according to recent theory, can expect to have its market locked up because consumers will be locked in, since consumers will face a high switching cost to move to second and later comers (all concepts discussed in earlier chapters). Hence, investors should flock to first movers because they will achieve a long-term stream of monopoly prices and profits (to be discussed in detail in chapters 11 and 12).

Telling examples

This is a nice theory, but it appears to be dead wrong as a generality – according to extensive research reported by management professors Gerald Tellis and Peter Golder in their important book: *Will and Vision: How Late Comers Grow to Dominate Markets* (Tellis and Golder 2002). They offer many telling examples, but consider this short list of firms that now dominate their markets but who were hardly first movers:

- Gillette is widely believed to have pioneered safety razors because it has dominated the safety razor market for so long. But the concept of safety razors was proposed a century before Gillette introduced its first razor. Moreover, several firms introduced safety razors two decades before Gillette did.
- Hewlett-Packard (HP) is assumed to have created the first laser printer, since it has a commanding share of laser printer sales. However, both Xerox and IBM commercialized laser printers years before HP's laser printers were built, using engines developed by Canon, not HP.
- Many people think that Netscape produced the first Internet browser and a few remember that Mosaic hit the browser market years before Netscape. However, computer geeks remember that Web browsers such as Viola, Erwise, and Midas inspired the development of Mosaic at the University of Illinois.

- Pampers now dominates the disposable diaper market, which is the reason many people think Procter & Gamble was the first mover in that market in the mid-1960s. They have forgotten that Chux diapers, produced by Johnson & Johnson, were on the market as early as 1932.
- Apple Computer hardly dominates the PC market today, but there remains the presumption that Apple initially dominated the early market because it created the product category. However, Micro Instrumentation & Telemetry Systems pioneered personal computing with its Altair machine in 1975.
- The first-mover advantage was hardly an advantage for the CPM personal computer operating system, or for the Mac operating system, both of which in their time dominated the operating system market before Microsoft took over with MS-DOS and later Windows (ten years after the advent of CPM).

The case against the first-mover advantage that Tellis and Golder make goes beyond a mountain of case histories that lead them to their central conclusion, which is that the first-mover advantage has never been the advantage it has been cracked up to be in any but six of the 66 industry groups they studied during the 1990s.

Moreover, the failure rates of pioneers as of the start of the twenty-first century is quite high – 64 percent for all industries studied. For the forty-two traditional industries studied, the failure rate was 71 percent; for high-tech industries, 50 percent. And almost all pioneers dominated their markets when sales were well below mass-market proportions. In 2000, the first movers in the sixty-six industries had an average market share of only 6 percent.

Secret of market leadership

How did the first-mover advantage become the myth that it is? The answer is relatively simple. Many researchers didn't do their historical homework. They often assumed that market leaders today developed their product's category because the dominant firms themselves now claim to be the pioneers and because the first-mover failures have been lost to a history that is all too rarely studied with the care that Tellis and Golder have taken.

What is the secret of market leadership if first-mover advantage is not it? Tellis and Golder (2002) draw an unsurprising old lesson that managers would be well advised to remember:

- Market pioneers rarely endure as leaders. Most of them have low market shares or fail completely. Actually, market pioneering is neither necessary nor sufficient for enduring success.

- The real causes of enduring market leadership are vision and will. Enduring market leaders have a revolutionary and inspiring vision of the mass market, and they exhibit an indomitable will to realize that vision. They persist under adversity, innovate relentlessly, commit financial resources and leverage assets to realize their vision (2002, 41).

PART II ORGANIZATIONAL ECONOMICS AND MANAGEMENT

Firms' debt/equity structures and executive incentives

The cost structure that a firm faces is not *given* to the firm by some divine being. It emerges from the decisions made by managers, and these decisions depend critically upon the incentives they face, along with a number of other factors. Here, we stress the importance of a firm's financial structure in shaping managers' incentives and their firms' cost structure.

The ideal firm is one with a single owner who produces a lot of stuff with no resources, including labor. Such a firm would be infinitely productive. It would totally avoid agency costs, or those costs that are associated with shirking of duties and the misuse, abuse, and overuse of firm resources for the personal benefit of the managers and workers who have control of firm resources. However, such an ideal firm cannot possibly exist. Resources are always required in the productive process, and any time more than a very few people are involved, agency costs will result in lost output and a smaller bottom line for the firm.

The world we all do business in is one in which firms often need more funds for investment than one person can generate from his or her own savings or would want to commit to a single enterprise. Any single owner, if the business is even moderately successful, has typically to find ways of encouraging others to join the firm as owners or lenders (including bondholders, banks, and trade creditors).

Therein lies the source of many firms' problems, not the least of which is that a firm's expansion can give rise to the *agency costs* that a single-person firm would avoid. Managers and workers can use the expanding size of the firm as a screen for their shirking. The addition of equity owners (partners or stockholders) can dilute the incentive of any one owner to monitor what the agents do. Hence, as the firm expands, the agency costs of doing business can erode, if not totally negate, any economies of scale achieved through firm expansion (Jensen and Meckling 1976).

One of the more important questions any single owner of a growing firm must face is: "How will the method of financing growth – debt or equity – affect the extent of the agency cost?" Given that agency costs will always occur with expanding firms, how can the combination of debt and equity be varied to minimize the amount of costs from shirking and opportunism? That question is really one dimension of a more fundamental one: "How can the financial structure affect the firm's costs and competitiveness? That is, how can a firm's financial structure affect its short-run and long-run cost structure (considered in Part I of this chapter)?"

In this chapter, our focus is on debt, but that is only a matter of convenience of exposition, given that any discussion of debt must be juxtaposed with some discussion of equity as a matter of comparison, if nothing else. We could just as easily draw initial attention to equity as a means of financing growth. In fact, debt and equity are simply two alternative categories of finance (subject to much greater variation in form than we are able to consider here) available to owners. Owners need to search for an "optimum combination," given the advantages and disadvantages of both with regard to reducing the production costs considered earlier in this chapter.

Debt and equity as alternative investment vehicles

By debt, of course, we mean the borrowed funds that must be repaid fully at some agreed-upon point in the future and on which regular interest payments must be made in the interim. The interest rate is simply the annual interest payment divided by the principal. Also, we must note that in the event the firm gets into financial problems, the lenders have first claim on the firm's remaining assets (after due worker claims have been paid).

By equity, or stock, we mean the funds provided by people in return for ultimate control over the disposition of firm resources and who accept the status of residual claimants, which means that a return on investment (which is subject to variation) will be paid only after all other claims on the firm have been satisfied. That is to say, the owners (stockholders) will not receive dividends until all required interest payments have been met; the owners are guaranteed nothing in the form of repayment of their initial investments. Obviously, owners (stockholders) accept more risk on their investment than do lenders (or bondholders).[2]

[2] We recognize that debt and equity come in a variety of forms. Common and preferred stock are the two major divisions of equity. Debt can take a form that has the "look and feel" of

Bearing in mind our intentions for this chapter, does it matter whether a firm finances its investments by debt or equity? You bet it does (otherwise, we must wonder why the two broad categories of finance would ever exist). The most important feature of debt is that the payments – both the payoff sum and the interest payments – are fixed. This is important for two reasons. One reason is the obvious one – it enables firms to attract funds from people who want security and certainty in their investments. The modern aphorism, "Different Strokes for Different Folks," if followed in the structuring of financial instruments, can mean lower costs of investment funds, and therefore production cost, which means more growth and greater competitiveness. Debt attracts funds from people who get their "strokes" from added security.

Fixed payments on debt are important for our purposes for another reason: If the firm earns more than the required interest payments on any given investment project, the residual goes to the equity owners. If the company fails because of investments gone sour, and it has to be liquidated for less than the amount owed to lenders, then stockholders (those who bought equity in the firm) will get nothing. Stockholders can claim only what is left after all expenses and the lenders have been paid. That's it.

Clearly, the nature of debt biases, to a degree, the decision making of the owners, or their agent/managers, toward seeking risky investments, ones that will likely carry high rates of return. But these high rates can tempt equity owners to take unduly high risks, given that they get what is left after the fixed interest payments are deducted from high returns and the lenders will suffer most of the cost if the investment fails. If a firm borrows funds at a 10 percent interest rate, for example, and invests those funds in projects that have an expected rate of return of 12 percent, the residual left for the equity owners will be the difference, 2 percent. If, on the other hand, the funds are invested in a much riskier project that has a rate of return of 18 percent, then the residual that can be claimed by the equity owners is 8 percent, four times as great as that of the first case.

Granted, the project with the higher rate has a risk premium built into it (or else everyone investing in the 12 percent projects would direct their funds to the 18 percent projects, causing the rate of returns in the latter to fall and in the

equity. For example, the much-maligned "junk bonds" often carry with them rights of control over firm decisions and may also be about as risky as common stock. In order to contain the length of this chapter, we consider only the two broad categories, and we encourage readers to consult finance texts for more details on financial instruments. However, readers should recognize that variations in the type of debt and equity could help overcome some of the problems that are discussed in this chapter.

former to rise). However, notice that much of that additional risk is imposed on the lenders. They are the ones who must fear that the risk incurred will translate into failed investments (which is what risk implies). But they are not the ones who are compensated for the assumed risk they bear. Indeed, after a lender has made a loan for a specified rate of interest, the managers can increase the risk imposed on the original lenders by pursuing much riskier projects than those lenders anticipated, or by increasing the firm's indebtedness by more borrowing.

As a general rule, the greater the indebtedness, the greater incentive that managers have to engage in risky investments. Again, this is because much of the risk is imposed on the lenders and the benefits, if they materialize, are garnered by the equity owners.

It should surprise no one that as a firm takes on more debt, lenders will become progressively more concerned about losing some or all of their investments. As a consequence, lenders will demand compensation in the form of higher interest payments, which reflect a risk premium. Those lenders who fear that the firm will continue to expand its indebtedness after they make the initial loans will also seek compensation prior to the rise in indebtedness by way of a higher interest rate. To keep interest costs under control, firm managers will want to find ways of making commitments as to how much indebtedness the firm will incur, and they must make the commitments believable, or else higher interest rates will be in the making. Again, we return to a recurring theme in this book: Managers' reputations for credibility have an economic value. In this case, the value emerges in lower interest payments.

Lenders, of course, will seek to protect themselves from risky managerial decisions in other ways. They may, as they often do, seek to obtain rights to monitor and even constrain the indebtedness of the firms to whom they make loans. Managers also have an interest in making such concessions because, although their freedom of action is restricted in one sense, they can be compensated for the accepted restrictions in the form of interest rates that are lower than otherwise. Firm managers are granted greater freedom of action in another respect; they are given a greater residual with which they can work (to add to their salary and perks, if they have the discretion to do so; extend the investments of the firm; or increase the dividends for stockholders).

Lenders may also specify the collateral the firm must commit. Lenders will not be interested in just any form of collateral. They will be most interested in having the firm pledge "general capital," or assets that are resaleable, which means that the lenders can potentially recover their invested funds. Lenders will not be interested in having "firm-specific capital," or assets that are designed only for their given use inside a particular firm as collateral, since they have little, if any, resale market.

Of course, firm assets are often more or less "general" or "firm-specific," which means they can be better or worse forms of collateral. A firm can pledge assets with "firm-specific capital" attributes. However, managers must understand that the more firm-specific the asset (the narrower the resale market), the greater the risk premium that will be tacked onto the firm's interest rate, and the lower the potential residual for the equity owners.

Lenders will also have a preference for lending to those firms that have a stable future income stream and that can be easily monitored. The more stable the future income, the lower the risk of nonpayments of interest. The more easily the firm can be monitored, the less likely managers will be able to leave creditors with uncompensated risks. The more willing lenders are to lend to firms, the greater the likely indebtedness.

Electric utility companies have been good candidates for heavy indebtedness, because their markets have been protected from entry by government controls and regulations, what they do is relatively easily measured, and their future income stream can be assumed to be relatively stable. Accordingly, their interest rates should be relatively low, which should encourage managers to take on additional debt just so that equity owners can claim the residual for themselves. (At the time of writing, the deregulation of electric power production was under way in a few US states, allowing open entry into the generation of electricity. We should expect deregulation to lead to a higher risk premium in interest rates, although the price of electricity can be expected to fall for consumers with increased competition for power sales.)

Past failed incentives in the S&L industry

The incentives of indebtedness are dramatically illustrated by one of the biggest financial debacles of modern times, the dramatic rise in savings and loan (S&L) bank failures of the 1980s. The S&L industry was established in the 1930s to ensure that the savings of individuals, who effectively loaned their funds to the S&Ls, could be channeled to the housing industry (a concentrated focus of S&L investment portfolios that in itself added an element of risk, especially because housing starts vary radically with the business cycle). S&Ls were in a position to loan money for housing, deriving up to 97 percent of the funding from their depositors and only 3 percent from the S&L owners (given reserve and equity requirements). Such a division, of course, made the owners eager to go after high-risk but high-return projects. They could claim the residuals from what was then interest payment on deposits that were kept low by a federal ceiling on the interest rates S&Ls could pay depositors. Of course, the risks S&L owners could take with funds created depositor concerns that they could lose their deposits. But since in the 1970s the deposits were insured by the federal government up to $10,000, depositors' incentives to be concerned about and to monitor S&L risk taking were muted.

The emergence of the crisis

When interest rates began to rise radically with the rising inflation rates of the late 1970s, alternative market-based forms of saving became available – not the least of which were money market and mutual funds, which were unrestricted in the rates of return they could offer savers. As a consequence, savings started flowing out of S&Ls, which greatly increased the pressure on them to hike the interest rates paid on their deposits (which they were free to do in the early 1980s), and to offset the higher interest rates by searching out investments that were riskier but carried higher rates of returns.

The S&Ls' incentive for risky investment was heightened by the fact that depositors' incentives to monitor the loans became much less a restraint on S&L owners when the amount covered by federal deposit insurance was increased to $100,000 in the early 1980s, which effectively assured the overwhelming majority of all depositors that they would lose nothing if their S&L loans lost all their deposits on risky loans.

To compensate for these perverse incentives, the federal government closely monitored and regulated the investments of the S&Ls through 1982. But in that year, S&Ls were given greater freedom to pursue high-risk investments at the same time that the protection to depositors was increased. The hope was that the S&Ls' greater investment freedom would stave off the looming S&L financial crisis (which amounted to hoping that the S&Ls would win a national financial lottery!). The result should have been predictable, based on the simple idea that people respond to incentives. S&Ls went after the high-risk/high-return – and high-residual – investments. The S&Ls that made the risky investments were in a position to pay high interest rates, drawing funds from other more conservative S&Ls. The incentives that had been created for them was "heads they won, tails the taxpayer lost." To protect their deposit base, conservative S&Ls had to raise their interest rates, which meant that they had also to seek riskier investment, all of which led to a shock wave of risky investment spreading through the S&L/development industry.

Unfortunately, many of those investments did what should have been expected given their risky nature: they failed. The government (taxpayers) had to absorb the losses and then return to doing what it had done before 1982 – closely monitoring the industry and severely restricting the riskiness of the investments (given that it was unwilling to give depositors greater incentives to monitor their S&Ls by lowering the size of deposits covered by the federal deposit insurance).

Clearly, fraud was a part of the S&L debacle. Crooks were attracted to the industry (Black, Calavita, and Pontell 1995; Wauzzinski 2003). However, the debacle is a grand illustration of how debt can, and did, affect management decisions. It also enables us to draw out a financial/management principle: If owners want to control the riskiness of their firms' investments, they had better look to how much debt their firms accumulate. Debt can encourage risk taking, which can be "good" or "bad," depending on whether the costs are considered and evaluated against the expected return.

Why then would the original equity owners ever be in favor of issuing more shares of stock and bringing in more equity owners with whom the original owners would have to share the residual? Sometimes, of course, the original owners are unable to provide the additional funds in order for the firm to pursue what are known (in an expectation sense) to be profitable investment projects. The original owners can figure that although their *share* of firm profits will go down, the *absolute level* of the residual they claim will go up. A 60 percent share of $100,000 in profits beats 100 percent of $50,000 in profits any day.

Also, in situations where the firm is involved in new ventures in which the risks are high, and bondholders (lenders) have no protection against losses as S&L depositors did, the firm will have to pay very high interest rates to borrow money. This doesn't mean that firms in high-risk businesses will not borrow any money, but most of their financing will come from equity holders. Only when most of the financing comes from equity will lenders see their risks low enough (even if the firm fails, bondholders can be fully paid from the sale of assets) to loan money at reasonable rates. So additional equity investment means that the equity owners can claim a greater residual (if the firm is successful) because the firm's interest payments fall with the reduction in the risk premium to bondholders.

Investment projects often require a combination of firm-specific and general capital to be used. Consider, for example, the predicament of a remodeling firm that uses specially designed pieces of floor equipment (which may have little or no market value outside the firm) as well as trucks that can easily be sold in well-established used truck markets. The investment projects can be divided according to the interests of the two types of investors. The equity owners can be called upon to take the risk associated with the floor equipment while the lenders are called upon to provide the funds for the trucks. Of course, it is better for the lenders if the trucks, and other general equipment, are profitably used by the firm, and don't have to be sold. So lenders might not even make the loan for the general part of the investment without equity owners taking the firm-specific part precisely because the general investment is less valuable to the firm without the firm-specific capital investment. (The trucks will not be useful to the firm without the output produced by the floor equipment.)

Spreading risks

The original owners can also have an interest in selling a portion of their ownership share because, by doing so, they can reduce the overall risk of their full portfolio of investments by reinvesting among a number of firms. If the original owners held their full investments in the firm and refused to sell off a portion, then they might be "too cautious" in the choice of investments – not making risky investments that yield a higher expected profit than more conservative investments. Once the original owners have spread their ownership over a number of firms, they will find the riskier investments more attractive, since diversification has made them collectively less risky. Again, the financial structure of the firm is important – and it can matter to both management policies and the bottom line.

Free cash flow problem

Former Harvard finance Professor Michael Jensen argues for another reason for some firms to stay in debt: Debt avoids the problems executives may have in dealing with the so-called "free cash flow problem." The interest payments on the debt can tie the hands – or reduce the discretionary authority – of managers who might otherwise engage in opportunism with their firms' residual (Jensen 1989, 65–5). If a firm has little debt, then the managers can have a great deal of funds, or residual, to do with as they please. They can use the residual to provide themselves with higher salaries and more perks. They can also use the funds to contribute to local charities that may have little impact on their firm's business (they may have a warm heart for the cause they support or they may want simply to take credit for being charitable with their firms' funds).

They may also use the funds to expand (without the usual degree of scrutiny) the scope and scale of their firms, thereby justifying their higher salaries and greater perks (because firm size and executive compensation tend to go together).

Even if the investment projects that the managers choose are profitable, if the funds were distributed to the stockholders, they might find even more profitable investments (and even more worthy charitable causes).

Industry maturity and funds misuse

As industries mature (or reach the limits of profitable expansion), the risk of managers "misusing" firm funds increases. Few opportunities may be available for managers to reinvest the earnings in their own industry. They may then be tempted to use the "excess residual" to fulfill some of their own personal flights of managerial fancy (more expensive perks, and greater "generosity"), or reinvest the funds in other industries that may or may not have a solid connection to the original firm's core activities.

How can the firm be made to disgorge the residual? Jensen suggests that indebtedness is a good way to accomplish this: the greater the indebtedness, the smaller the residual and the less waste that can go up in the smoke of managerial opportunism. Jensen argues that one of the reasons for firm takeovers by way of "leveraged buyouts," which means heavy indebtedness, is that the firm that is taken over is forced to give up the residual through higher interest payments. Again, the hands of the agent/managers are tied; their ability to misuse firm funds is curbed. The value of the firm is enhanced by the indebtedness, mainly because it reduces the discretion of managers who have been misusing the funds. And managers can misuse their discretion in counterproductive ways, not the least of which is by diversifying the array of products and services provided on the grounds that diversity can smooth out the company's cash flows over the various cycles that go with the products and services. But shareholders are able to do that for themselves very easily with the large number of mutual funds now available.

Experience teaches that indebtedness is not necessarily the only or easiest way that firms can disgorge such cash: they can pay dividends. Moreover, experience also teaches that what a firm should do with "free cash flow" is not always obvious and can be the subject of strong disagreements among board members and top executives, mainly because of the limitations of available information on the riskiness and rates of returns on alternative corporate strategies.

The thorny issue of what to do with free cash emerged in 2005 when Karl Icahn, renowned for "raiding" (or taking over) faltering corporations, became the biggest stockholder in Blockbuster, the largest bricks-and-mortar video rental retailer in the United States. According to reports, Icahn believed that Blockbuster's management had gone on a "spending spree" and, in the process, had begun to "gamble" away "shareholders' money" on risky investments (Peers 2005). As a new board member, Icahn began insisting that management disgorge its accumulating cash with large dividend payments to stockholders, a strategy that would restrict the ability of top management to engage in investment misadventures, including the company's then ongoing efforts to "reinvent" the company by moving away from rentals at retail stores and toward rentals over the Internet. Seeing that the retail rental business was dying, Icahn wanted management to use its retail outlets as "cash cows," continuing to operate them for as long as the growing competition from mail-order video rental companies would allow. On the other hand, John Antico, chairman of Blockbuster, believed that the company had to reinvent itself, and use its cash flow to undertake a "corporate makeover" to fend off erosion of Blockbuster's market from Internet-based movie rental companies such as Netflix and Wal-Mart (Peers 2005)

Who is right? At the time of writing the answer is unclear, dependent upon information on rates of return and risk on alternative investment strategies that can be known only to corporate insiders. However, there is at least one strong argument to think that Icahn's strategy of paying dividends could be most persuasive. At least having disgorged its free cash flow, Blockbuster's top executives would be required to convince outside investors and Blockbuster's own shareholders that Antico's proposed strategy of reinventing the company could provide them with a greater rate of return than they could achieve by sticking with its bricks-and-mortar rental model, but could also offer investors a greater return than they could achieve in other companies.

Blockbuster's very act of paying out the dividends could be a sign of considerable confidence on the part of management that they had a solid case for reinventing the company and, hence could easily fund their new investment plans. Of course, critics could argue that dividend payouts, along with the issue of new investment instruments, could impose crippling time delays on management's efforts to reposition the company in a highly competitive market. In some matters (this one included) only time will tell who – Icahn and the other board members or Antico and the other top executives – is right and who will control the future of the company.

Firm maturity and indebtedness

This all leads us to an interesting proposition. We should expect firm indebtedness to increase with the maturity of its industry. Firms in a mature industry have more stable future income streams than do those in fledgling industries, and can be monitored more easily, given people's experience in working with the firms and knowing how such firms operate and are inclined to misappropriate funds when they do. Also, by taking on more debt, firms in mature industries can alert the market to their intentions to rid themselves of their residual, conveying the message to the market that managers' discretion to use and misuse firm financial resources will be constricted, all of which can increase the price of the firm's stock.

Of course, if firms in mature industries don't take on relatively more debt and managers continue to misuse the funds by reinvesting the residual in the mature industry or other industries, then the firm can be ripe for a takeover. An outside "raider" may see an opportunity to buy the stock at a depressed price, paying for the stock with debt. The increase in indebtedness can, by itself, raise the price of the stock, making the takeover a profitable venture. However, if the takeover target is, because of past management indiscretions in investment, a disparate collection of production units that do not fit well together, the profit potential for the raiders is even greater: the firm should be worth more in pieces than as a single firm. The raiders can buy the stock at a depressed price, take charge, and break the company apart, selling off the parts for more than the purchase price. In the process, the market value of the "core business" can be enhanced.

The bottom-line consequences of firms' financial structures

The moral of this section should now be self-evident: *The financial structure of firms matters, and it matters a great deal.* By choosing the best combination of debt and equity in financing the firm's productive activities, managers can do a lot to keep the cost curves discussed earlier in this chapter as low as possible. Keeping those cost curves low is a crucial factor determining how effective a firm is at producing wealth and remaining viable in a competitive market. This also means that choice on debt and equity financing can also determine whether the firm will be the subject of a takeover. The one great antidote for a takeover should be obvious to managers, but it is not always (as evidenced by the fact that takeovers are not uncommon): Firms should be structured, in terms of both their financial *and* other policies, *to create incentives to use their resources to produce as much wealth as possible, which will maximize the stock price.* In that case, potential raiders will have nothing to gain by trying to take the firm over. One of the primary functions of a board of directors is to monitor the executives and the policies that are implemented with an eye toward maximizing stockholder value. As we will show in a later chapter, those executives and their boards that do not maximize the price of their stocks do have something to fear from corporate raiders.

THE BOTTOM LINE

The key takeaways for chapter 9 are the following:

(1) Cost structures for firms (made up of average fixed, average variable, average total, and marginal cost curves) are a graphical device designed to draw out insights on how much a firm should produce in order to maximize profits over a range of output level. Such structures help managers go beyond the limitations on thinking presented by a firm's accounting statements, which report the costs incurred for a given output level.
(2) The law of diminishing marginal returns is a fact of nature that shapes a firm's short-run marginal cost curve and ultimately imposes a constraint on how much a firm can produce in the short run if it intends to maximize profits.
(3) A firm in the short run (or long run) should not seek to produce where its average cost is at a minimum. It should produce where marginal costs and marginal revenue (price in the case of a perfect competitor) are equal.
(4) Fixed costs should be ignored in short-run production decisions.
(5) A firm's long-run cost structure will be shaped by economies of scale and diseconomies of scale.
(6) The so-called "first-mover advantage" has not been substantiated by research.
(7) The build-up of equity in a firm can lower the firm's interest rates on borrowed funds, for two reasons. First, firm's lenders stand to lose less in the case of default on interest payments. Second, firms with a lot of equity and few borrowed funds will be inclined to restrain the riskiness of their business ventures.
(8) Indebtedness can inhibit executives' inclination to waste firm resources by reducing the available cash that can be misused.
(9) The maturing of a firm can lead to more indebtedness because mature firms have proven records and tend to have more stable earnings prospects.

In chapters 10 and 11, we extend our analysis of firms' production decisions by combining the average and marginal cost curves described in this chapter with the demand curves described in previous chapters. Within that theoretical framework, we can compare the relative efficiency of competitive and monopolistic markets, as well as the role of profits in directing the production decisions of private firms.

REVIEW QUESTIONS

(1) Complete the cost schedule shown below and develop a graph that shows marginal, average fixed, average variable, and average total cost curves.

Output level	Total fixed costs ($)	Total variable costs ($)	Total cost ($)	Marginal cost ($)	Average fixed cost ($)	Average variable cost ($)	Average total cost ($)
1	200	60					
2	200	110					
3	200	150					
4	200	180					
5	200	200					
6	200	230					
7	200	280					
8	200	350					
9	200	440					
10	200	550					

(2) Explain why the intersection of the average variable cost curve and the marginal cost curve is the point of minimum average variable cost.

(3) Suppose that no economies or diseconomies of scale exist in a given industry. What will the firm's long-run average and marginal cost curves look like? Would you expect firms of different sizes to be able to compete successfully in such an industry?

(4) Why would you expect that all firms would eventually encounter diseconomies of scale? Why might it be irrelevant that some firms will eventually encounter diseconomies of scale?

(5) Suppose that the government imposes a $100 tax on all businesses, regardless of how much they produce. How will the tax affect a firm's short-run cost curves? Its short-run production?

(6) Suppose that the government imposes a $1 tax on every unit of a good sold. How will the tax affect a firm's short-run cost curves? Its short-run output?

(7) Suppose that interest rates fall. How will managers' incentives be affected, and how will the firm's cost structure be affected?

Appendix: choosing the most efficient resource combination: isoquant and isocost curves

The cost curves developed in this and previous chapters were based on the assumption that the producer had chosen the most *technically efficient, cost-effective combination* of resources possible at each output level. That is, resources were fully employed, were producing as much as possible, and were used in the lowest-cost combination. The short-run average total cost curve, for example, was as low as it could be, given the availability and prices of resources.

How does the firm find the most efficient combination of resources? Most products and output levels can be produced with various combinations of resources. A given quantity of blue jeans can be produced with a lot of labor and little capital (equipment) or a lot of capital and little labor. As indicated in Figure 9A.1, a firm can produce 100 pairs of jeans a day with five different combinations of labor and machines. Combination *a* requires seven workers and ten machines; combination *b*, five workers and fifteen machines. (To keep output constant, the use of labor must be reduced when the use of machines is increased. If the use of both were increased, output would rise.)

Curves like that in figure 9A.1 are called *isoquants*. An isoquant curve (from the Greek and Latin words for "same quantity") is a curve that shows the various technically efficient combinations of resources that can be used to produce a given level of output. Different output levels have different isoquants. The higher the output level, the higher the isoquant curve, as shown in figure 9A.2. For example, an output level of 100 pairs of jeans can be produced with the resource combinations shown on curve IQ_1. An output level of 150 pairs of jeans requires larger resource combinations, shown on curve IQ_2.

To understand how the firm determines its most efficient resource combination, we must remember that it operates under conditions of diminishing marginal returns. The firm will always produce in the upward sloping range of its marginal cost curve, and marginal cost increases because marginal returns decline. Therefore, given a fixed quantity of one resource as more of another resource is used, the additional output marginal product of that resource must diminish.

Then, as each additional worker is eliminated in figure 9A.1, the number of machines added to keep output constant at 100 pairs of jeans must rise – and that is just what happens. Notice that as the firm moves down curve *abcde* in figure 9A.1, using fewer

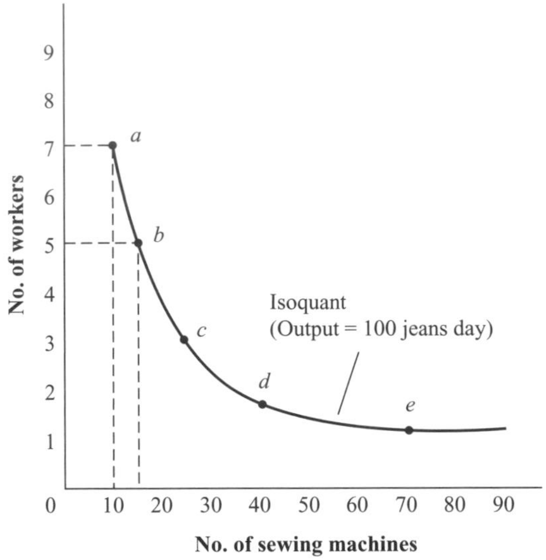

Figure 9A.1 Single isoquant

A firm can produce 100 pairs of jeans a day using any of the various combinations of labor and machinery shown on this curve. Because of diminishing marginal returns, more and more machines must be substituted for each worker who is dropped.

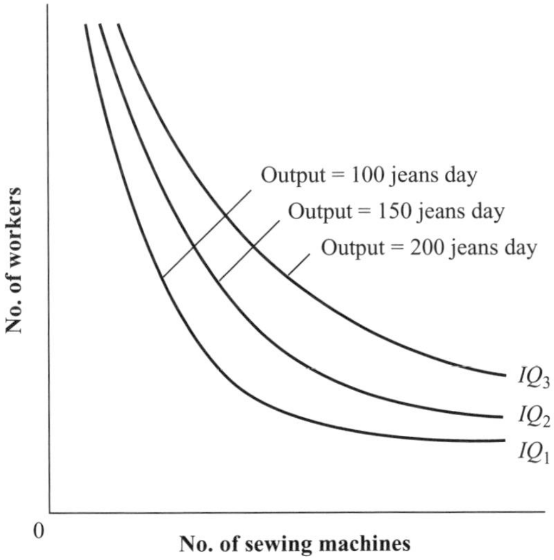

Figure 9A.2 Several isoquants

Different output levels will have different isoquants. The higher the output level, the higher the isoquant.

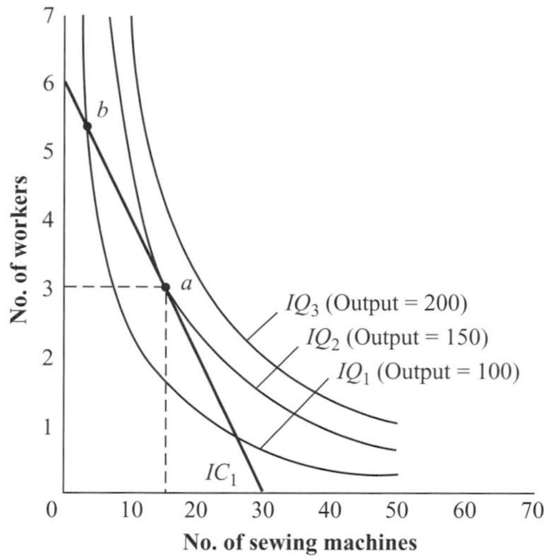

Figure 9A.3 Finding the most efficient combination of resources

Assuming that the daily wage of each worker is $100, and the daily rental on each sewing machine is $20, an expenditure of $600 per day will buy any combination of resources on isocost curve IC_1. The most cost-effective combination of labor and capital is point *a*, three workers and fifteen machines. At that point, the isocost curve is just tangent to isoquant IQ_2, meaning that the firm can product 150 pairs of jeans a day. If the firm chooses any other combination, it will move to a lower isoquant and a lower output level. At point *b* (on isoquant IQ_1), it will be able to produce only 100 pairs of jeans a day.

> An **isocost** (meaning "same cost") **curve** is a curve that shows the various combinations of resources that can be employed at a given total expenditure (cost) level and given resource prices.

and fewer workers, the curve flattens out indicating that larger and larger increases in machines are needed to make up for one fewer worker – or that the marginal product of machines diminishes and the marginal product of the remaining workers rises.

Suppose, for instance, that the daily wage of labor is $100 and the daily rental for a sewing machine is $20. With a daily budget of $600, a firm can employ six workers and no machines or thirty machines and no workers. Or it can combine labor and machinery in various ways. It can employ four workers at a total expenditure of $400 and add ten machines at a total expenditure of $200. Curve IC_1 in figure 9A.3 shows the various combinations of workers and machines the firm could choose. This kind of curve is called an **isocost curve.**

We know, then, that the marginal product of resources differs with their level of use. To determine exactly which combination of resources should be employed to produce any given output level, however, we need to know not only the marginal product but also the prices of labor and capital. The absolute prices of these resources will determine how much can be produced with any given expenditure. The relative prices will determine the most efficient combination.

There are different isocost curves for different output levels. The higher the output, the higher the isocost curve. As long as the prices of labor and capital stay the same,

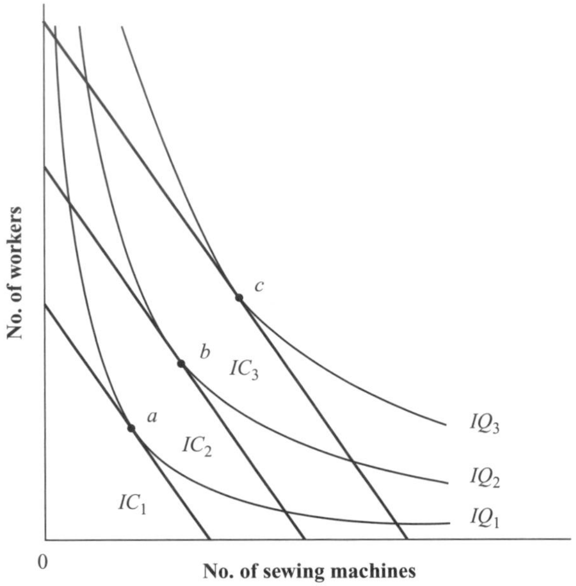

Figure 9A.4 The effect of increased expenditures on resources
An increase in the level of expenditures on resources shifts the isocost curve outward from IC_1 to IC_2. The firm's most efficient combination of resources shifts from point *a* to point *c*.

however, the various isocost curves for different output levels will be parallel to one another and will have the same downward slope.

Using both isoquant and isocost curves, we can determine the most efficient resource combination for a given expenditure level. Assuming that a firm is on isocost curve IC_1 in figure 9A.3 (which represents an expenditure of $600 per day), the most technically efficient and cost-effective combination of labor and capital will be point *a*, three workers and fifteen machines. At point *a*, isocost curve IC_2 is tangent to isoquant curve IQ_2. The firm is producing as much as it can – 150 pairs of jeans a day – with an expenditure of $600. If it spent the same amount but used more labor and less capital, it would move to a lower isoquant and a lower output level. At point *b* on curve IC_1, for instance, the firm would still spend $600 but its production level would fall from 150 to 100 pairs of jeans per day.

Of course, with increased expenditures, the firm can move to a higher isocost curve. In figure 9A.4, as the firm's budget expands, its isocost curve shifts outward from IC_1 to IC_2 to IC_3. At the same time, the firm's most efficient combination of resources increases from *a* to *b* and then to *c*. As expenditures on resources rise, we can anticipate that, beyond some point, the increase in output will not keep pace with the increase in expenditure; at that point, the marginal cost of a pair of jeans will start to rise.

CHAPTER

10

Firm production under idealized competitive conditions

Economists understand by the term market, not any particular market place in which things are bought and sold, but the whole of any region in which buyers and sellers are in such free intercourse with one another that the prices of the same goods tend to equality, easily and quickly. **Augustin Cournot**

Chapters 7–9 largely dealt separately with the two sides of markets – consumers and producers. We devised graphic means of representing consumer preferences (the demand curve) and producer costs (the average and marginal cost curves). This chapter brings demand and cost analysis together in a way that allows us to examine how individual firms react to consumer demand in competitive markets. Our focus is on a highly competitive market structure. We investigate an intriguing question: At the maximum, how much can competitive markets contribute to consumer welfare?

We do not attempt to give a full description of a real-world competitive market setting. Because markets are so diverse, such a description would probably not be very useful. Our aim is rather to devise a theoretical framework that can enable us to *think* about how competitive markets work in general, as a constructive behavioral force. Although our model cannot tell much that is specific about real-world markets, it provides a basis for predicting the general direction of changes in market prices and output. Through its analysis, we should gain a deeper understanding of the meaning of the market forces of supply and demand and of market efficiency.

The competitive market structure considered in this chapter is only one of four basic market structures. The other three, and the detrimental effects of their restrictions on competition, are the subjects of following chapters.

PART I THEORY AND PUBLIC POLICY APPLICATIONS

The four market structures

Markets can be divided into four basic categories, based on the degree of competition that prevails within them – that is, on how strenuously participants attempt to outdo, and avoid being outdone by, their rivals. The most competitive of the four market structures is perfect competition.

Perfect competition

Perfect competition is a market structure in which price competition is so intense that maximum efficiency in the allocation of resources is obtained.

As we stressed much earlier in the book, **perfect competition** represents an ideal degree of competition. Perfect competition can be recognized by the following characteristics:

(1) There are *many producers* in the market, no one of which is large enough to affect the going market price for the product. All producers are price takers, as opposed to price searchers or price makers (see the Perspective below).
(2) All producers sell a *homogeneous product*, meaning that the goods of one producer are indistinguishable from those of all others. Consumers are fully knowledgeable about the prices charged by different producers and are totally indifferent as to which producer they buy from.
(3) Producers enjoy complete *freedom of entry into and exit from* the market – that is, entry and exit costs are minimal, although not completely absent.
(4) There are *many consumers* in the market, no one of whom is powerful enough to affect the market price of the product. As with producers, consumers are price takers.

As we have shown previously in chapter 7, the demand curve facing the individual perfect competitor is not the same as the demand curve faced by all producers. The *market* demand curve slopes downward, as shown in figure 10.1(a). The demand curve facing an *individual* producer – price taker – is horizontal, as in figure 10.1(b). This horizontal demand curve is *perfectly elastic*. That is, the individual firm cannot raise its price even slightly above the going market price without losing all its customers to the numerous other producers in the market or to other producers waiting for an opportunity to enter the market. On the other hand, the individual firm can sell all it wishes at the going market price. Hence it has no reason to offer its output at a lower price. The

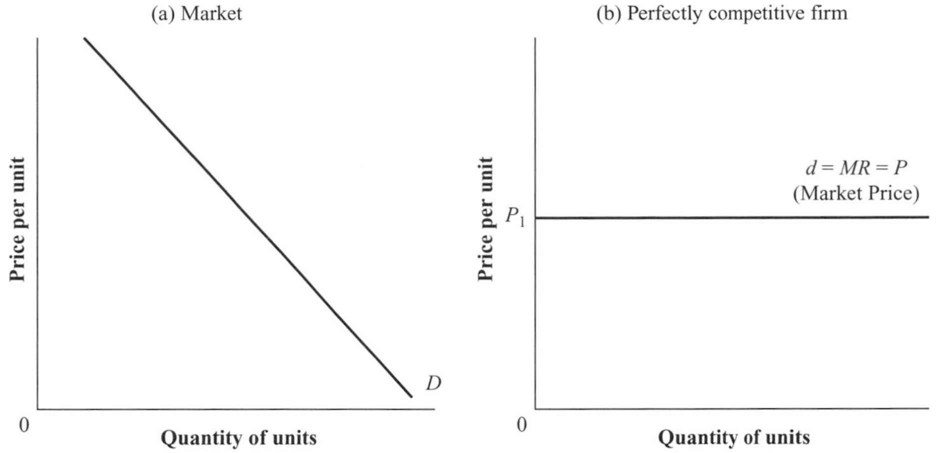

Figure 10.1 Demand curve faced by perfect competitors
The market demand for a product (panel (a)) is always downward sloping. The perfect competitor is on a horizontal, or perfectly elastic, demand curve (panel (b)). It cannot raise its price above the market price even slightly without losing its customers to other producers.

markets for wheat and for integrated computer circuits, or computer chips, are both good (but hardly perfect) examples of real-world markets that come close to perfect competition.

Pure monopoly

> **A pure monopoly** consists of a single seller of a product for which there are no close substitutes and which is protected from competition by barriers to entry into the market.

Pure monopoly is a market structure that is the polar opposite of perfect competition in terms of the intensity of competition. Under a **pure monopoly** there is no price competition because the only producer in the market is protected by prohibitively costly market entry barriers. The barriers to entry into the monopolist's market are described in chapter 11. For now, we simply note that because the monopolistic firm does not have to worry about competitors undercutting its price, it can raise its price without fear that customers will move to other producers of the same product or similar products. All the pure monopolist has to worry about is losing some customers to producers of distantly related products.

Because the monopolist is the only producer of a particular good, the downward sloping market demand curve (figure 10.1(a)) is its individual demand curve. In contrast to the perfect competitor, the monopolist can raise its price and sell less, or lower its price and sell more.

As will be discussed in chapter 11, the critical task of the pure monopolist is to determine the one price–quantity combination of all price–quantity combinations on its demand curve that maximizes its economic profits. In this sense, the pure monopolist is a price searcher. The best (but not perfect) real-world examples of a pure monopoly are regulated electric-power companies, which dominate in given geographical areas, and the government's first-class postal system (which is losing more of its monopoly power every year as technology reduces the costs of alternative ways for people to communicate – for example, by e-mail).

Monopolistic competition

Monopolistic competition is a market composed of a number of producers whose products are differentiated and who face highly elastic, but not perfectly elastic, demand curves.

Monopolistic competition is a market structure that is more descriptive of more real-world markets than perfect competition and pure monopoly. A monopolistically competitive market can be recognized by the following characteristics:

(1) It has a number of competitors that are producing slightly different products.
(2) Advertising and other forms of nonprice competition are prevalent.
(3) Entry into the market is not barred but is restricted by modest entry costs, mainly overhead.
(4) Because of the existence of close substitutes, customers can turn to other producers if a monopolistically competitive firm raises its price. Because of brand loyalty, the monopolistic competitor's demand curve still slopes downward but is fairly elastic (see figure 10.2).

The market for textbooks is a good example of monopolistic competition. Most subjects are covered by two or three dozen textbooks, differing from one another in content, style of presentation, and design. We take up monopolistic competition in chapter 12.

Oligopoly

An **oligopoly** is a market composed of only a handful of dominant producers – as few as two and generally no more than a dozen – whose pricing decisions are interdependent.

Oligopoly is another real-world market structure that has monopoly and competitive characteristics, given the fewness of competitors. Oligopolists may produce either an identical product (such as steel) or highly differentiated products (such as automobiles). Generally the barriers to entry into the market are considerable, but the critical characteristic of oligopolistic firms is that their pricing decisions are *interdependent*: That is, the pricing decisions of any one firm can substantially affect the sales of the others. Therefore, each firm

Table 10.1 *Characteristics of the four market structures*

	No. firms	Freedom of entry	Type of product	Example
Perfect competition	Many	Very easy (or costless)	Homogeneous	Wheat, computers, gold
Pure monopoly	One	Barred (or prohibitively costly)	Single-product	Public utilities, Postal service
Monopolistic competition	Many	Relatively easy	Differentiated	Pens, books, paper, clothing
Oligopoly	Few	Difficult	Either standardized or differentiated	Steel, light bulbs, cereals, autos

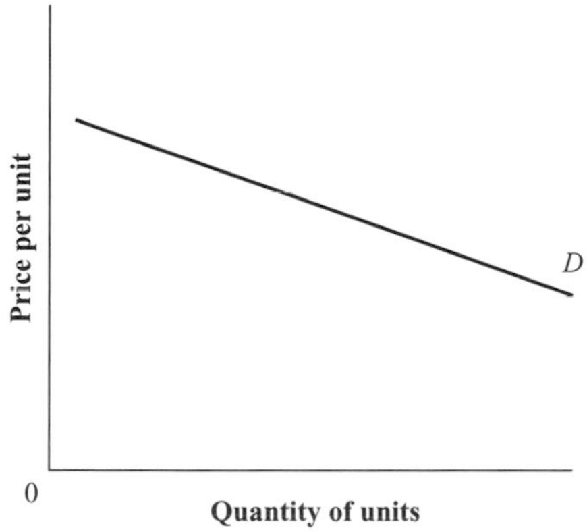

Figure 10.2 Demand curve faced by a monopolistic competitor
Because the product sold by the monopolistically competitive firm is slightly different from the products sold by competing producers, the firm faces a highly elastic, but not perfectly elastic, demand curve.

must monitor and respond to the pricing and production decisions of the other firms in the industry. The importance of this characteristic will become clear in chapter 12.

Table 10.1 summarizes the characteristics of the four market structures.

The perfect competitor's production decision

As discussed in chapter 2, the market price in a perfectly competitive market is determined by the intersection of the supply and demand curves. If the price is above the equilibrium price level, a *surplus* will develop, forcing competitors to lower their prices. If the price is below equilibrium, a *shortage* will emerge, pushing the price upward (see figure 10.3(a)). Given a market price over which it has no control, how much will the individual perfect competitor produce?

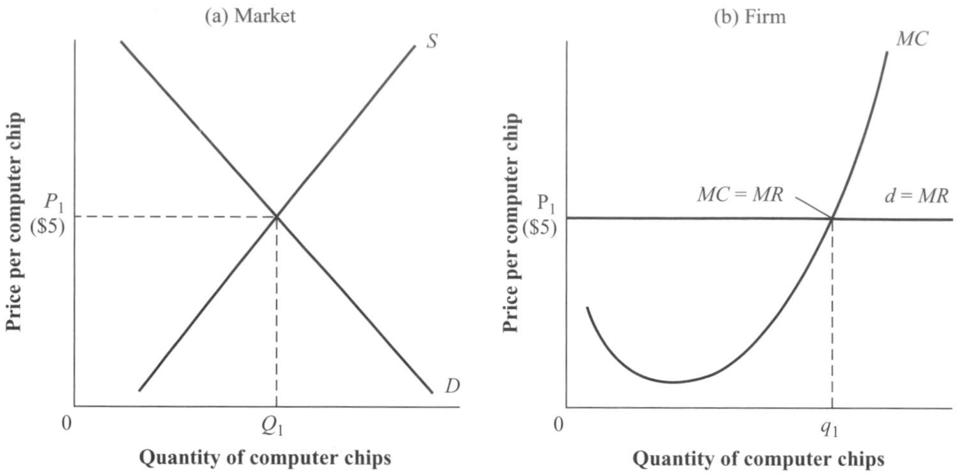

Figure 10.3 The perfect competitor's production decision

The perfect competitor's price is determined by market supply and demand (panel (a)). As long as marginal revenue (*MR*), which equals market price, exceeds marginal cost (*MC*), the perfect competitor will expand production (panel (b)). The profit maximizing production level is the point at which marginal cost equals marginal revenue (price).

The production rule: $MC = MR$

Suppose the price in the perfectly competitive market for computer chips is $5 ($P_1$ in figure 10.3). For each individual competitor, the market price is given – that is, cannot be changed. It must be either accepted or rejected. If the firm rejects the price, however, it must shut down. If it raises its price even slightly above the market level, its customers will move to other competitors. Demand, then, is horizontal at $5.

The firm's perfectly elastic horizontal demand curve is illustrated in figure 10.3(b). This horizontal demand curve is also the firm's marginal revenue curve. As noted, marginal revenue is defined as the additional revenue acquired from selling one additional unit. Because each computer chip can be sold at a constant price of $5, the additional, or marginal, revenue acquired from selling an additional unit must be constant at $5.

The profit maximizing firm will produce any unit for which marginal revenue exceeds marginal cost. Thus the profit maximizing firm in figure 10.3(b) will produce and sell q_1 *units, the quantity at which marginal revenue equals marginal cost* ($MR = MC$). Up to q_1, marginal revenue is greater than marginal cost. Beyond q_1, all additional computer chips are unprofitable: The additional cost of producing them is greater than the additional revenue acquired (with the small "q" being used to remind you that the output of the individual producer in figure 10.3(b) is a small fraction of the output for the market, designated by a capital "Q" in figure 10.3(a)).

Changes in market price

The perfectly competitive firm produces where $MC = MR$, where MR is equal to the price at which the firm can sell its product. Thus the amount the firm produces depends on market price. As long as market demand and supply remain constant, the individual firm's demand, and its price, will also remain constant – assuming, of course, that the costs of production remain constant and the cost curves don't shift. For example, if market demand and price increase, however, the individual firm's demand and price will also increase.

Figure 10.4 (below) shows how the shift occurs. The original market demand of D_1 leads to a market price of P_1 (panel (a)), which is translated into the individual firm's demand, d_1 (panel (b)). Again, the firm maximizes profit by equating marginal cost with marginal revenue, which is equal to d_1, at an output level of q_1.[1]

An increase in market demand to D_2 leads to the higher price P_2 and a higher individual firm demand curve, d_2. At this higher price, which, again, equals marginal revenue, the perfect competitor can support a higher marginal cost. The firm will expand production from q_1 to q_2. In the same way, an even

[1] To prove this statement, first we note that

$$TR = \overline{P}Q$$

Then we define short-run total cost to be a function of output:

$$SRTC = C(Q)$$

Next, we define profits π to be

$$\pi = TR - SRTC = \overline{P}Q - C(Q)$$

Differentiating with respect to Q and equating with 0, we then obtain

$$\frac{d\pi}{dQ} = \overline{P} - \frac{dC(Q)}{dQ} = 0$$

$$\overline{P} = \frac{dC(Q)}{dQ}$$

Because

$$\frac{dC(Q)}{dQ} = SRMC,$$

profits are maximized when

$$SRMC = \overline{P}$$

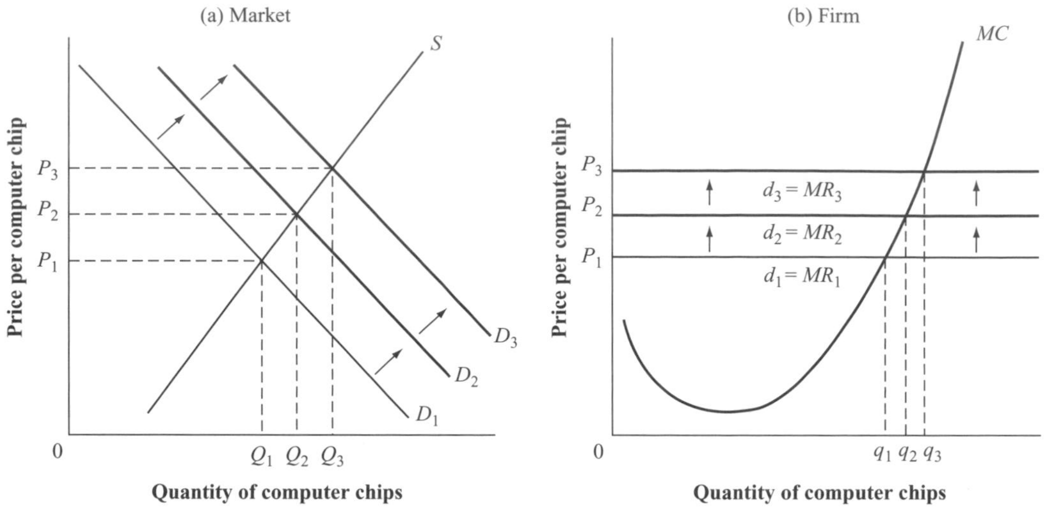

Figure 10.4 Change in the perfect competitor's market price

If the market demand rises from D_1 to D_3 (panel (a)), the price will rise with it, from P_1 to P_3. As a result, the perfectly competitive firm's demand curve will rise, from d_1 to d_3 (panel (b)).

greater market demand, D_3, will lead to even higher output, q_3, by the individual competitor.

Why does the market supply curve slope upward and to the right? The answer lies in the upward sloping marginal cost curves on which each individual firm operates. The firm will never operate where the marginal cost curve is sloping downward. If $MC =$ Price and the marginal cost is getting smaller, the firm could increase profits by increasing output which would reduce MC below Price, and would continue increasing output until MC started increasing and eventually equaled price again. Since the upward sloping portion of the MC curve shows us how much output each firm will produce at every price, the market supply curve is obtained by horizontally adding the firms' upward sloping marginal cost curves (as done in chapter 8).

Maximizing short-run profits

Can perfect competitors make an economic profit? One might think the answer is obviously "Yes," but it is only "Yes" in the (very) short run. To see this, we must incorporate the average and marginal cost curves developed in chapters 8

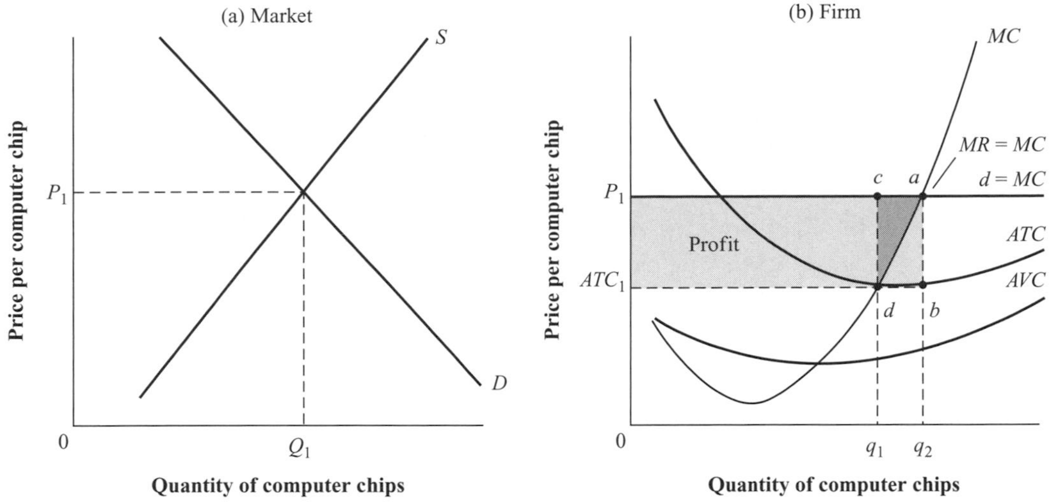

Figure 10.5 The profit maximizing perfect competitor

The perfect competitor's demand curve is established by the market clearing price (panel (a)). The profit maximizing perfect competitor will extend production up to the point at which marginal cost equals marginal revenue (price), or point *a* in panel (b). At that output level – q_2 – the firm will earn a short-run economic profit equal to the shaded area ATC_1P_1ab. If the perfect competitor were to minimize average total cost, it would produce only q_1, losing profits equal to the darker shaded area *dca* in the process.

and 9 into our graph of the perfect competitor's demand curve, as in figure 10.5(b). (Figure 10.5(a) shows the market supply and demand curves.)

As before, the producer maximizes profits by equating marginal cost with price, rather than by looking at average cost. That is exactly what the perfect competitor does. The firm produces q_2 computer chips because that is the point at which the marginal revenue curve (which equals the firm's demand curve) crosses the marginal cost curve. At that intersection, the marginal revenue of the last unit sold equals its marginal cost. If less were produced than q_1, the marginal cost would be less than the marginal revenue, and profits would be lost. Similarly, by producing anything more than q_2 the firm incurs more additional costs (as indicated by the marginal cost curve) than it receives in additional revenue (as indicated by the demand curve, which beyond q_2 is below the *MC* curve).

At q_2, the firm's profit equals total revenue minus total cost ($TR - TC$). To find total revenue at q_2, we multiply the price, P_1 (which also equals average revenue) by the quantity produced, q_2 ($TR = P_1q_2$). Graphically, total revenue is therefore equal to the area of the rectangle bounded by the price and quantity, or $0P_1aq_2$.[2]

Similarly, total cost can be found by multiplying the average total cost of production (*ATC*) by the quantity produced. The *ATC* curve shows that the average total cost of producing q_2 computer chips is ATC_1. Therefore total cost is ATC_1q_2, or the rectangular area bounded by $0ATC_1bq_2$. The profits of the company are therefore $P_1q_2 - ATC_1q_2$, which is the same, mathematically, as $q_2(P_1 - ATC_1)$. This quantity corresponds to the area representing total revenue, $0P_1aq_2$, minus the area representing total cost, $0ATC_1bq_2$. Profit is the shaded rectangle bounded by ATC_1P_1ab. This profit is *economic profit*, since all costs of production (including opportunity and risk costs) are captured in the *ATC* cost curve. This means that the firm is earning more off its deployment of resources in the production of this good than could be earned on any other good.

The perfect competitor does not seek to produce the quantity that results in the lowest average total cost. That quantity, q_1, is defined by the intersection of the marginal cost curve and the average total cost curve. If it produced only q_1, the firm would lose out on some of its profits, shown by the darker triangular shaded area *dca*. This area is the summation of the profit that can be generated by producing units between q_1 and q_2.

Naturally, profit maximizing firms will attempt to minimize their costs of production. That does not mean they will produce at the point of the minimum average total cost curve. Instead, they will try to employ the most efficient technology available and to minimize their payments for resources. That is, they will attempt to keep their cost curves as low as possible. But given those curves, the firm will produce where $MC = MR$, not where the *ATC* curve is at its lowest level. Managers who cannot distinguish between those two objectives will probably operate their businesses on a less profitable basis than they could – and will risk being run out of business.

Minimizing short-run losses

In the foregoing analysis the market-determined price was higher than the firm's average total cost, allowing it to make a profit. Perfect competitors are not guaranteed profits, however. The market price may not be high enough for

[2] The area of any rectangle is one side times the other side. In this graphical illustration, one side is the price ($0P_1$), and the other side is the quantity ($0Q_2$), which means that the area of the rectangle ($P_1 \times Q_2$) represents total revenue at Q_2.

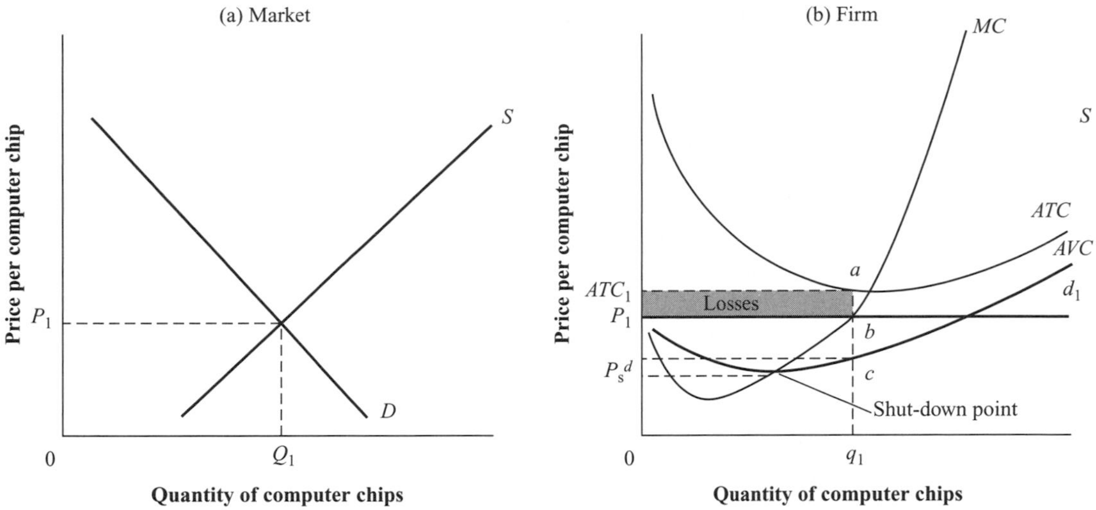

Figure 10.6 The loss minimizing perfect competitor
The market clearing price (panel (a)) establishes the perfect competitor's demand curve (panel (b)). Because the price is below the average total cost curve, this firm is losing money. As long as the price is above the low point of the average variable cost curve, however, the firm should minimize its short-run losses by continuing to produce where marginal cost equals marginal revenue (price or point *b* in panel (b)). This perfect competitor should produce q_1 units; incurring losses equal to the shaded area P_1ATC_1ab. (The alternative would be to shut down, in which case the firm would lose all its fixed costs.)

the firm to make a profit. Suppose, for example, that the market price is P_1, below the firm's average total cost curve (see figure 10.6). Should the firm still produce where marginal cost equals marginal revenue (price)? The answer, for the short run, is "Yes". As long as the firm can cover its variable cost, it should produce q_1 computer chips.

It is true that the firm will lose money. Its total revenues are only P_1q_1, or the area bounded by $0P_1bq_1$, whereas its total costs are ATC_1q_1, or the area $0ATC_1aq_1$. On the graph, its total (economic) losses equal the difference between those two rectangular areas, or the shaded area bounded by P_1ATC_1ab. Whether the firm incurs losses is not the relevant question, however. The real issue is whether the firm loses more money by shutting down or by operating and producing q_1 chips.

In the short run, the firm will continue to incur fixed costs even if it shuts down. If it is not earning any revenues, its losses will equal its total fixed costs. In chapter 9, we showed that the average fixed cost of production is the vertical distance between the average variable cost and average total cost, and that the vertical distance, *ac*, is greater than the average loss, *ab*. Hence, the firm's total fixed cost, or loss on shut down, is greater than the loss from operating.

In short, as long as the price is higher than average variable cost – if the price more than covers the cost associated directly with production – the firm minimizes its short-run losses by producing where marginal cost equals marginal revenue. By earning revenue in excess of its variable costs, the firm loses less than its fixed cost. Only if the price dips below the low point of the average variable cost curve – where the marginal and average variable cost curves intersect – will the firm add to its losses by operating. The firm will shut down when price is at or below that point, P_s in figure 10.6. At prices above that point, the firm simply follows its marginal cost curve to determine its production level. Above the average variable cost curve, then, the marginal cost curve is in effect the firm's supply curve. Therefore, if a perfect competitor produces in the short run at all, it produces in a range of increasing marginal cost – and diminishing marginal returns.

Our analysis has shown why, in the short run, fixed costs should be ignored. The relevant question is whether a given productive activity will add more to the firm's revenues than to its relevant costs – those that are affected by its current decisions. Understanding this principle, businesses may undertake activities that superficially appear to be quite unprofitable. Some grocery stores stay open all night, even though the owners know they will attract few customers. If all costs, including fixed costs, are considered, the decision to operate in the early hours may seem misguided. The only relevant question facing the store manager is, however, whether the additional sales generated are greater than the additional cost of light, goods sold, and labor. Similarly, many businesses that are obviously failing continue to operate, for by operating they can at least cover a portion of their fixed costs – such as rent – that would still be due if they shut down. They stay open until their leases expire or until they can sell out.

Producing over the long run

In the long run, businesses have an opportunity to change their total fixed costs. If the market price remains too low to permit profitable operation, a firm can eliminate its fixed costs, sell its plant and equipment, or terminate its contracts for insurance and office space. If the market price is above average total cost, new firms can enter the market, and existing firms can expand their scale of operation. Such long-run adjustments in turn affect market supply, which

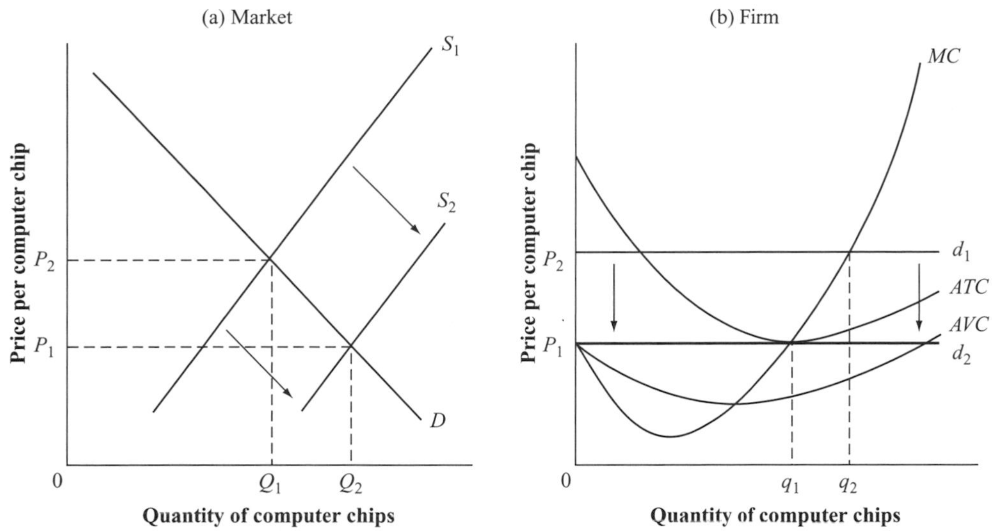

Figure 10.7 The long-run effects of short-run profits
If perfect competitors are making short-run profits, other producers will enter the market, increasing the market supply from S_1 to S_2 and lowering the market price from P_2 to P_1 (panel (a)). The individual firm's demand curve, which is determined by market price, will shift down, from d_1 to d_2 (panel (b)). The firm will reduce its output from q_2 to q_1, the new intersection of marginal revenue (price) and marginal cost. Long-run equilibrium will be achieved when the price falls to the low point of the firm's average total cost curve, eliminating economic profit (price P_1 in panel (b)).

affects price and short-run production decisions. To facilitate the discussion, we will discuss a long-run adjustments in two stages. First, we discuss the effects of market entry and exit, assuming a constant scale of operation. Second, we add adjustments made in response to scale economies.

The long-run effect of short-run profits and losses

When profits encourage new firms to enter an industry and existing firms to expand, the result is an increase in market supply (the supply curve shifts out to the right), a decrease in market price, and a decrease in the profitability of individual firms. For example, in figure 10.7(a), the existence of economic profits (which equal revenues minus *opportunity* costs) in the computer chip market means that investors can earn more in that industry than in the most profitable alternative industry. Some investors will move their resources to the computer chip industry. Because the number of producers increases, the

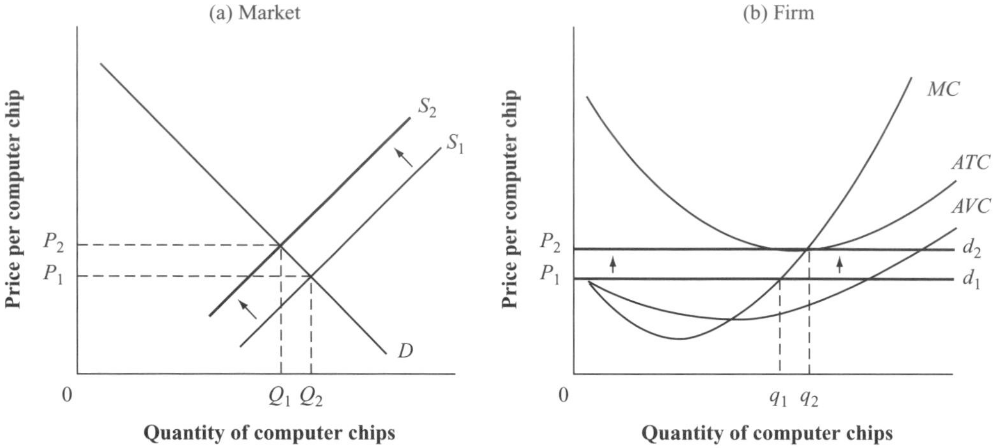

Figure 10.8 The long-run effects of short-run losses

If perfect competitors are suffering short-run losses, some firms will leave the industry, causing the market supply to shift back from S_1 to S_2 and the price to rise, from P_1 to P_2 (panel (a)). The individual firm's demand curve will shift up with price, from d_1 to d_2 (panel (b)). The firm will expand from q_1 to q_2, and equilibrium will be reached when price equals the low point of average total cost P_2, eliminating the firm's short-run losses.

market supply curve shifts outward, expanding total production from Q_1 to Q_2 and depressing the market price from P_2 to P_1.

The expansion of industry supply and the resulting reduction in market price make the computer chip business less profitable for individual firms. The lower market price is reflected in a downward shift of the firm's horizontal demand curve, from d_1 to d_2 (see figure 10.7(b)). The individual firm reduces its output from q_2 to q_1, the intersection of the new marginal revenue (price/demand) curve with the marginal cost curve. Note that q_1 is also the low point of the average total cost curve. Here price equals average total cost, meaning that the economic profit is zero. The firm is making just enough to cover its opportunity and risk costs, but no more. If there were still profits being made in the computer chip industry, firms would continue to move into this industry until the price is equal to the low point on the average cost curve and economic profits are zero.

Losses have the opposite effect on long-run industry supply. In the long run, firms that are losing money will move out of the industry, because their resources can be employed more profitably elsewhere. When firms drop out of the industry, supply contracts and total production falls, from Q_2 to Q_1 in figure 10.8(a). As a result, the price of the product rises, permitting some firms to break even and stay in the business. Long-run equilibrium occurs when the price reaches P_2, where the individual firm's demand curve is tangent to the low point of the average total cost curve (figure 10.8(b)). The output of each remaining individual firm expands (from q_1 to q_2) to take up some of the slack left by the firms that have withdrawn, but the expansion of the remaining firms is not enough to completely offset the reduction in output caused by the firms that leave the industry. Again price and average total cost are equal, and economic profit is zero.

The effect of economies of scale

In the long run, competition forces firms to take advantage of economies of scale and do so as quickly as possible, *if they exist.*

If expanding the use of resources reduces costs, the perfect competitor has two reasons for taking advantage of scale economies. First, if the firm expands before other firms, its lower average total cost will allow it to make greater economic profits (for a short period of time). Second, the firm *must* expand its scale for self-preservation. Otherwise, other firms will expand their scales of operation, lowering their cost structures, increasing market supply, and forcing the market price down below the minimum average cost of any firm that doesn't expand its scale.

We can see this by considering the logic the individual firm might use on perceiving the prospects of scale economies. Consider figure 10.9, for instance. Initially the market is in short-run equilibrium at a price of P_2 (figure 10.9(a)). The individual firm is on cost scale ATC_1, producing q_1 chips and breaking even (figure 10.9(b)). If the firm expands its scale of operation and produces where its demand curve d_1 intersects the long-run marginal cost curve, it will make a profit equal graphically to the shaded area $ATC_1 P_2 ab$. That is the firm's incentive for expansion.

If the firm does not expand and take advantage of these economies, some other firm surely will. Then, any firm still producing on scale ATC_1 will lose money. That's because when the market supply expands, the price will tumble toward P_1, the point at which the long-run average total cost curve (and the short-run curve ATC_m) are at a minimum, and both industry and firm economic profits are zero. Because of rising diseconomies of scale, firms will not be able to expand further. Any firm that tries to produce on a smaller or larger scale – for example, ATC_2 or ATC_3 – will incur average total costs higher than the market price and will lose money. Ultimately it will be driven out of the market or forced to expand or contract its scale. Hence, each individual

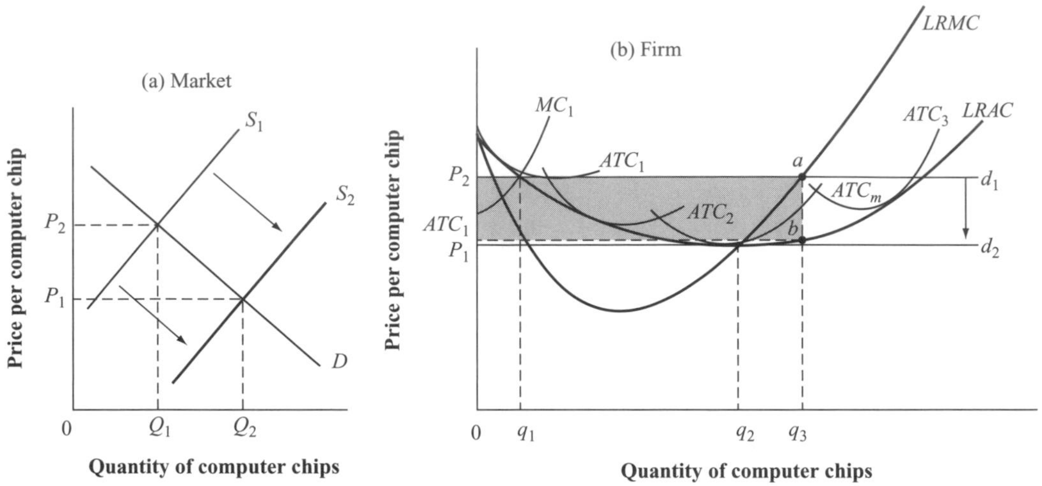

Figure 10.9 The long-run effects of economies of scale
If the market is in equilibrium at price P_1 in panel (a) and the individual firm is producing q_1 units on short-run average total cost curve ATC_1 (panel (b)), firms will be just breaking even. Because of the profit potential represented by the shaded area ATC_1P_2ab, firms can be expected to expand production to q_3, where the long-run marginal cost curve intersects the demand curve (d_1). As they expand production to take advantage of economies of scale, however, supply will expand from S_1 to S_2 in panel (a), pushing the market price down toward P_1, the low point of the long-run average total cost curve (*LRATC* in panel (b)). Economic profit will fall to zero. Because of rising diseconomies of scale, firms will not expand further.

firm will look to the long-run average and marginal costs curves and expand as quickly as it can (and each firm must respond immediately under the idealized conditions of perfect competition).

Marginal benefit vs. marginal cost

Time lags, surpluses, and shortages notwithstanding, the competitive market can produce efficient results in one important sense – the marginal benefit of the last unit produced equals its marginal cost ($MB = MC$). In figure 10.10(a), for every computer chip up to Q_1, consumers are willing to pay a price (as indicated by the demand curve, *D*) greater than its marginal cost (as indicated by the industry supply curve, *S*). The difference between the price that consumers are willing to pay – an objective indication of the product's marginal benefits – and the marginal cost of production is a kind of surplus, or net gain, received from the production of each unit. The net gain is composed of two surpluses,

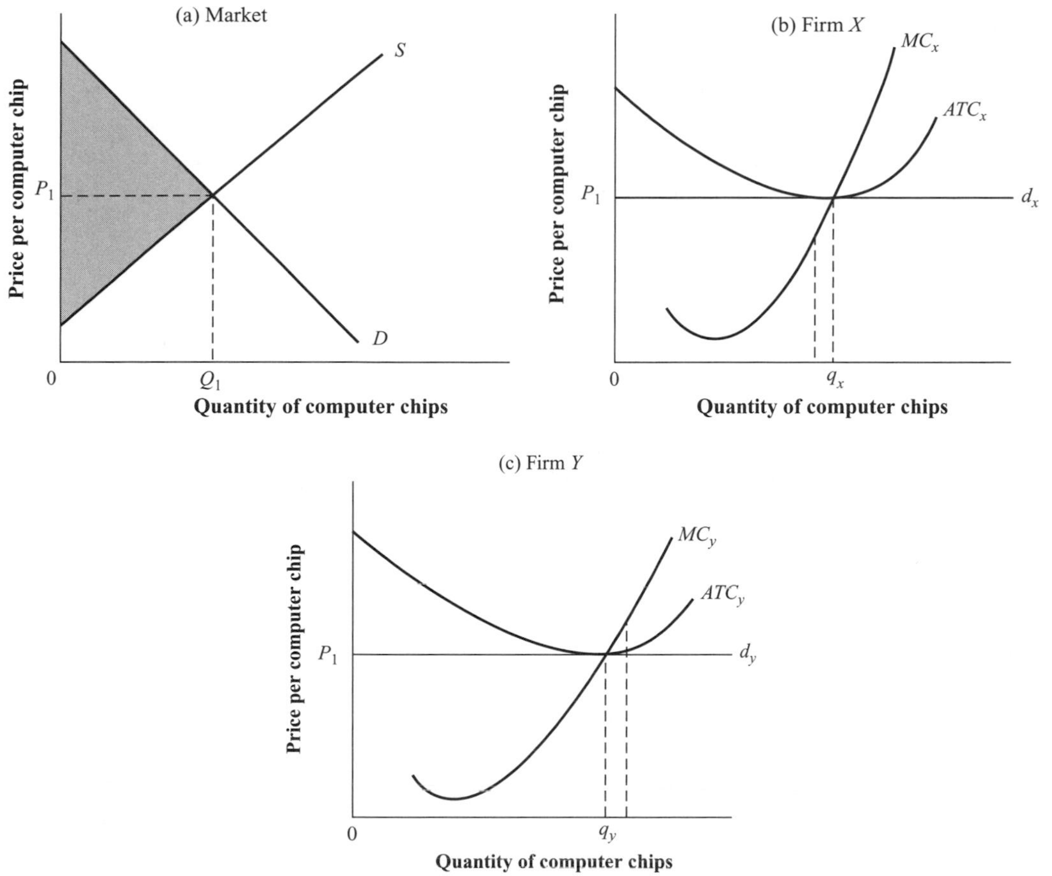

Figure 10.10 The efficiency of the competitive market

Perfectly competitive markets are efficient in the sense that they equate marginal benefit (shown by the demand curve in panel (a)) with marginal cost (shown by the supply curve in panel (a). At the market output level, Q_1, the marginal benefit of the last unit produced equals the marginal cost of production. The gains generated by the production of Q_1 units – that is, the difference between cost and benefits – are shown by the shaded area in panel (a). The perfectly competitive market is also efficient in the sense that the marginal cost of production, P_1, is the same for all firms (panels (b) and (c)). If firm *X* were to produce fewer than its efficient number of units, q_x, firm *Y* would have to produce more than its efficient number, q_y, to meet market demand. Firm *Y* would be pushed up its marginal cost curve, to the point at which the cost of the last unit would exceed its benefits. But competition forces the two firms to produce to exactly the point at which marginal cost equals marginal benefit, thus minimizing the cost of production.

Consumer surplus is the difference between the total willingness of consumers to pay for a good and the total amount actually spent.

Producer surplus is the difference between the minimum total revenue necessary to induce producers to supply any given quantity of output and the actual total revenue received from selling that quantity.

consumer surplus and **producer surplus**. In figure 10.10(a), consumer surplus is the triangular area below the demand curve and above the dotted price line, P_1. In figure 10.10(a), producer surplus is the triangular area above the supply curve and below the dotted price line, P_1. By producing Q_1 units, the industry exploits all potential gains from production, shown graphically by the shaded triangular area in figure 10.10(a). That net gain is brought about by the price that is charged, P_1 – a price that induces individual firms to produce where the marginal cost of production equals the price, which is also equal to consumers' marginal benefit.

The marginal cost of production for each individual firm is also P_1, a fact that results in the production of Q_1 units at the minimum total cost. Figure 10.10(b) and (c) show the cost curves of two firms, *X* and *Y*. In competitive equilibrium, firm *X* produces q_x units.

Suppose that the market output were distributed between the firms differently. Suppose, for example, that firm *X* produced one computer chip fewer than q_x. To maintain a constant market output of Q_1, firm *Y* (or some other firm) would then have to expand production by one unit. The additional chip would force firm *Y* up its marginal cost curve. To *Y*, the marginal cost of the additional chip is greater than P_1, greater than *X*'s marginal cost to produce it. Competition forces firms to produce at a cost-effective output level and therefore minimizes the cost of producing at any given level of output.

Perfectly competitive markets are attractive for another reason. In the long run, competition forces each firm to produce at the low point of its average total cost curve. Firms must either produce at that point, achieving whatever economies of scale are available, or get out of the market, leaving production to some other firm that will minimize average total cost.

The efficiency of perfect competition: a critique

Our discussion of perfect competition has been highly theoretical. In real life, the competitive market system is not as efficient as the analysis may suggest. From this perspective, several aspects of the competitive market deserve further comment.

The tendency toward equilibrium

Market forces are stabilizing: they tend to push the market toward one central point of equilibrium. To that extent, the market is predictable, and it contributes to economic and social stability. In the real world, price does not always move as smoothly toward equilibrium as it appears to do in supply and demand

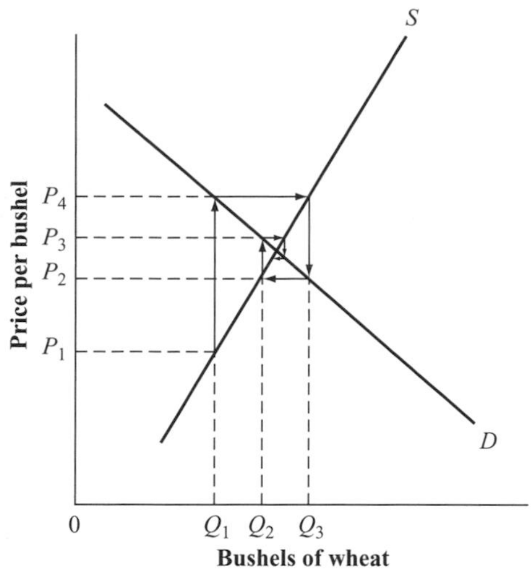

Figure 10.11 Supply and demand cobweb

Markets do not always move smoothly toward equilibrium. If current production decisions are based on past prices, price may adjust to supply in the "cobweb pattern" shown here. Having received price P_1 in the past, farmers will plan to supply only Q_1 bushels of wheat. That amount will not meet market demand, so the price will rise to P_4 – inducing farmers to plan for a harvest of Q_3 bushels. At price P_4, however, Q_3 bushels will not clear the market. The price will fall to P_2, encouraging farmers to cut production back to Q_2. Only after several tries do many farmers find the equilibrium price–quantity combination.

models. The smooth, direct move to equilibrium may happen in markets in which all participants, both buyers and sellers, know exactly what everyone else is doing. Often, however, market participants have only imperfect knowledge of what others intend to do. Indeed, an important function of the market is to generate the pricing and output information that people need to coordinate their actions with one another.

In a world of imperfect information, then, prices may not, and probably will not, move directly toward equilibrium. Those who compete in the market will continually grope for the "best" price, from their own individual perspectives. At times, sellers will produce too little and reap unusually high profits, and at other times they will produce too much and suffer losses. But the advantage of markets is that when mistakes are made, market prices (and profits and losses) provide information on those mistakes and on what has to happen to correct them.

This process of groping toward equilibrium can be represented graphically by a supply and demand "cobweb" (see figure 10.11). Most producers must plan their production at least several months ahead on the basis of prices received today or during the past production period.

Farmers, for instance, may plant for summer harvest on the basis of the previous summer's prices. Suppose farmers received price P_1 for a bushel of wheat last year. Their planning supply curve, S, will encourage them to work for a harvest of only Q_1 bushels this year. Given that limited output and the rather high demand at price P_1, however, the price farmers actually receive is P_4. The price of P_4 in turn induces farmers to plan for a much larger production level, Q_3, the following year. The market will not clear for Q_3 bushels, however, until the price falls to P_2. The next year, farmers plan for a price of P_2 and reduce their production to Q_2 – which causes the price to rise to P_3. As you can see from the graph, instead of moving in a straight line, the market moves toward the intersection of supply and demand in a web-like pattern.

At the same time, we hasten to add that while the "cobweb" is helpful in explaining gyrations in price, actual gyrations will likely be dampened over time with *learning* on the part of market participants. Farmers will learn that high prices one year can lead to "oversupply" the following year and can, accordingly, temper their planting response to high prices in any given year, thereby dampening the drop in prices the following year.

Surpluses and shortages

Some critics complain that the market system creates wasteful surpluses and shortages. Although all resources are limited in quantity, a true market shortage can exist only if the going price is below equilibrium. Thus shortages can be eliminated by a price increase. How much of an increase, theory alone cannot say; we do know, however, that market forces, if allowed free play, will work to boost the price and eliminate the shortage. That means, if course, that people of limited financial resources will be more adversely affected than those with larger incomes – a concern that is used as a justification for many government efforts to legislate market restrictions (not all of which actually help the poor, as we saw in our discussion of rent controls and minimum wages in chapter 5).

Similarly, all surpluses exist because the going price is above equilibrium. Competition will reduce the price, eliminating the surplus. In the process, of course, some firms will be driven out of the market and into other activities where they can now produce more value. In the transition, of course, this can result in unemployed workers. A frequent criticism of the market system is that, when this happens, workers have difficulty finding new employment. Part of the problem, however, is that labor contracts, community custom, or minimum-wage laws prevent wages from adjusting downward. If government controls prices – that is, if prices are not permitted to respond to market conditions – surpluses and shortages will persist.

Externalities, again

Critics stress, however, that supply is based only on the costs that firms bear privately. As discussed in chapter 5, external costs such as air, noise, and water pollution are not counted as part of the cost of production. If the external costs of pollution were counted, the firm's supply curve would be lower (S_2 instead of S_1 in figure 5.8). If producers and consumers had to pay all the costs of production, fewer units would be bought. In this sense, competition leads to an overproduction and a market inefficiency, or *welfare loss* (equal to the shaded triangular area *abc* in figure 5.8). Indeed, perfect competition will maximize the externalization of costs, given that if firms don't externalize all costs that can be externalized, they can be driven from business by firms that do externalize costs and thereby have lower cost structures.

Wealth differences

Critics of the market system also stress that its cost efficiencies are achieved within a specific distribution of resources of wealth, one that depends on the existing distribution of property rights. The distribution of economic power inherent in these property rights, they argue, has no particular ethical or moral significance.

The unreal nature of perfect competition

Finally, critics of the market system argue that most real-world markets are not perfectly competitive. Actual markets are not inhabited by numerous firms producing standard commodities that can be easily duplicated by anyone who would like to enter the market. Indeed, many markets are inhabited by a few large, powerful firms that do not take price as a given. Many firms are either monopolies or possess a high degree of monopoly power. Demanders and suppliers are rarely as well informed as the model suggests. The model of perfect competition was never meant to represent all, or even most, markets. It is merely one of several means economists use to think about markets and the consequences of changes in market conditions and government policy.

We know from the perfectly competitive model that the predicted outcomes of the model hold if there are numerous producers and consumers. However, it does not follow that if there are fewer – even far fewer – than "numerous" producers and consumers, the predicted outcomes of the perfectly competitive model do not hold. So long as the number of producers and consumers is sufficiently large that no one believes they have control over the price and acts accordingly, the perfectly competitive model can be useful in analyzing and predicting market behavior. Hence, the perfectly competitive outcomes could hold with no more than a couple of dozen producers and consumers in the market.

Price takers and price searchers

Perfect competition is an extreme degree of competition, so much so that many students are understandably concerned about its relevance. They often ask: "If there are few market structures that even closely approximate perfect competition, why bother to study it?"

The question is a good one, and not altogether easy to answer. There are few markets that come close to having numerous producers of an identical product with complete freedom of entry and exit. Markets for gold, for some computer chips and agricultural commodities, and for stocks and bonds are probably the closest markets we have to perfect competition, but still the products are not always *completely* identical, and entry and exit costs abound in most markets. Even wheat sold by a Kansas wheat farmer is not always viewed the same as wheat sold by a Texas wheat farmer.

How can sense be made of perfect competition? We know that under the conditions of competition specified, certain results follow. We can logically (with the use of graphs and mathematics) derive these results, as we have in this chapter. One conclusion drawn is that in perfect competition each firm will extend production until the marginal cost of producing the last unit equals the price paid by the consumer. That conclusion *necessarily* follows from the assumptions made. Granted, the demanding conditions for perfect competition are rarely met. We nevertheless cannot conclude *that under less demanding conditions, competitive results would not be observed.* For example, it may be that the number of producers is not "numerous," that the products sold by all producers are not completely "identical," and that there are costs to moving in and out of markets. Nonetheless, individual producers may act *as if* the conditions of perfect competition are met. Individual producers may still act as if they have no control over market price or that there are so many other actual or potential producers that it is best to think in terms of the other producers being "numerous" – in which case many of the predicted results of perfect competition may still be observed in the less than perfect markets. (More real-world markets, called "contestable markets," are taken up in the appendix to this chapter.)

For these reasons, many economists often talk not about *perfect competitors* but about **price takers** (who may or may not fit exactly the description of perfect competitors). They simply observe the market price and either accept it (and accordingly produce to the point at which marginal cost and price are equal) or reject it (and go into some other business). Hence, the price taker is someone who acts *as if* her demand curve is horizontal (perfectly elastic, more or less). She is therefore someone who assumes that the marginal revenue on each unit sold is constant (and equal to the price) – and that the marginal revenue curve is horizontal and the same as the firm's demand curve.

Price takers are sellers who do not believe they can influence the market price significantly by varying their own production levels.

The *price searcher* stands in contrast to the price taker. *Price searchers* are sellers who have some control over the market price. Price searchers have monopoly power because they can alter production and thereby market supply sufficiently to change the price. The individual price searcher's task is not simply to accept or reject the current market price, but (like the monopolist) to "search" through the various price–quantity combinations on her downward sloping demand curve with the intent of maximizing profits. As we demonstrate in chapter 11, the marginal revenue and demand curves of the price searcher are no longer the same. (Exactly where the monopolist's marginal revenue curve lies in relation to the demand curve is discussed in detail in chapter 11).

Perspective The Innovator's Dilemma

In our discussion of perfect competition, the product is given, or assumed into existence, along with the firm's cost structure. In such a model, much of what firms do is assumed away for the purposes of highlighting how price and profits can be influential in settling on how much firms should produce, and on what scale of operation.

When markets are far removed from being perfectly competitive – when products are not given and the potential for innovation in product development abounds (as is true of most real-world market) firm strategy in reacting to competitors and in product development are central management problems. Managers must think through the kind of act-and-react play in the kind of "games" that have been central to our discussions in several chapters. In such "games," expectations of what others might do and what will pay off count a great deal. In effect, this Perspective introduces another reality check, stressing that entrepreneurs often face perplexing dilemmas when considering their options on how to innovate – and, for that matter, whether to innovate. Contrary to many business commentaries, being an innovative company is not always synonymous with profit maximization.

As noted in chapter 9, many business scholars and business people in the 1990s accepted the often-repeated but untested article of business faith that so-called "first movers" (or the first persons or companies to develop product lines) in any market had strong, strategic market advantages over later rivals. However, as also noted earlier, business professors Gerald Tellis and Peter Golder (2002) found that in sixty of the sixty-six manufacturing industries they studied, the first movers had, at the time of their study, long been eclipsed by second, third, and later movers. Moreover, the first movers generally did not then hold minor shares of their markets.

How could it be that first movers so often lose their market leadership? A complete listing of the answers to that question is probably quite long. Economists might point to the fact that markets are constantly being revolutionized and that dominant market positions cannot be held for long, given the rapidity of the ongoing technological advances in products and production processes – and especially if the first movers behave like monopolies, hiking their prices and profits and encouraging new entrants, or not concerning themselves with their costs because of their economic profit cushions. It could well be that although first movers have certain advantages, second movers (or followers) have perhaps greater ones, not the least of which is not having to identify and prove the economic viability of the market for a product category.

We have no quibble with all these explanations, but we hasten to add another, often-overlooked, line of argument – namely, that the retrenchment or demise of firms, especially ones making monopoly profits, is often (but is not always) built into their success (Christensen, 1997; McKenzie and Roman Galar, 2004). This explanation has to do with what business professor Clayton Christensen (1997) calls the "innovator's dilemma."

To see the market predicament of innovators, suppose that decades ago you were the first firm to market with a revolutionary new product – say, a mainframe computer – that was instantly very profitable because the product had considerable (cost-saving) value to buyers and because you could charge (within the constraints of limit pricing) monopoly prices. To maximize profits from the new technology, you would have then needed to develop a corporate culture and incentive system that directs the energies of line workers and managers toward gradually refining, upgrading, and exploiting the known technology.[3] In defining your firm's internal control and development system, you determine not only what will be done in the firm, but also what will not be done. In the case of your research and development work, you will likely limit the range of researchers' investigations, which can preclude research on revolutionary new product categories, ones that do not rely directly on your firm's known technologies.

Of course, you could leave your business and research and development systems unconstrained, which means that employee energies can and will be directed in any number of ways. Your problem is that you have a known product and production technology that are generating profits. If you leave your firm's research and development unfocused on your known product line, your employees can discover or invent the next big product breakthrough – what will be seen in retrospect as a "disruptive technology." However, you may have no more idea where the disruptive technology is coming from than anyone else does, and you can waste a lot of firm resources trying to find it. Furthermore, you can, in the process, divert resources from the exploitation of your known technology. The point of this discussion is that, for many firms, the best option will be keeping the firm's focus on the known technology and having its workers refine and upgrade the known product with the intent of "mining" a fairly predictable research and development strategy. In the process of making that strategic decision (focusing the firm's resources on its "core competencies" – a widely repeated pat phrase), the firm can intentionally leave the discovery and development of new, disruptive technologies to other firms.

Now, it might be thought that the firm in an initial dominant market position can sit back and wait for the new technology to come onto the market and then either buy the firm that develops the product or simply copy it. However, when disruptive technologies first appear, it is not always clear that they are indeed disruptive, or that they will cause the market retreat

[3] Organizational economist John Roberts carefully defines a firm's culture:

> It involves the fundamental shared values of the people in the firm, as well as their shared beliefs about why the firm exists, about what they are collectively and individually doing, and to what end . . . More significantly, it involves the norms of behavior that prevail in dealing with other members of the firm and with outsiders. (Roberts 2004, 18)

or demise of the established firm and its products. After all, new products and technologies are what they are, *new*. This necessarily means they are untested in terms of initial profitability and long-run survivability. No one can initially be sure that the new products and technologies will ever be able to achieve long-run monopoly profits.

The established firm is also constrained in moving off into new markets and adopting new production technologies by its own internal culture and incentive systems. Although the corporate culture and incentive systems might efficiently exploit the known product and technology, those same systems might not work so effectively in the development and exploitation of the new products and technology. Of course, the established firm might frequently test its corporate flexibility, but such tests can be costly and, in themselves, disruptive in the sense that profits from known products and technologies can be lost in the process.[4]

A good example of the type of innovator's dilemma we have in mind is the predicament of IBM in the 1970s with its known mainframe computer technology. IBM was by far the most established mainframe computer producer in the world. When the PC emerged in the 1970s, no one – not Steve Jobs, founder of Apple, nor the people at Big Blue – knew for sure whether the PC would actually challenge to any significant degree the market hegemony of the mainframe computer and IBM's total dominance of the mainframe market. IBM also had a tightly directed corporate culture and incentive system, all directed toward further enhancing and selling mainframe computers and related services. IBM could have chosen early in the 1970s to explore the PC market, but it could also figure that the diversion of corporate talent could be a waste, given that the PC might remain (as it was initially) a sophisticated toy, and might never be a significant challenge to mainframes. IBM could also have reasoned, rightfully (given the best but limited available information at the time) that it could sit back and wait for others to prove (or disprove) the viability of the PC market. Then, using its established market position and brand name, it could quickly take over the then budding market. Needless to say, because of its wait-and-see strategy

[4] John Roberts (2004, 72) explains the cultural dilemma firms face, and draws out a nontrivial paradox relating to how a firm operating at less than known maximum efficiency at every point in time might do better than other "more efficient" firms over time:

> A company that mandates operating strictly according to currently defined best practices and has operations manuals that are always followed will have a very hard time generating the potential improvements in best practices. One that allows more variation will rarely be using best practice at any given point in time in all its operations, but may do better on average.

and because it made several crucial, mistaken, market assessments, IBM was a fairly late mover in PCs and never achieved the prominence and profitability in that computer market that it had in 1970s and earlier in the mainframe market. In 2005, IBM finally gave up pursuit of making its PC division pay off and sold it to Lenovo, a Chinese computer manufacturer.

This is not to say that IBM made the wrong decision in the 1970s to hold its corporate focus on mainframe computers. Clearly, in hindsight, one can say that *if* IBM had become a player in the PC market early on and *if* it had not, concomitantly, taken up any number of other lines of new product development that could have proven to be financial "dry holes" (which a less focused corporate culture could have allowed), then it could have been a much stronger company in PCs in the 1980s and 1990s than it was. However, those are two big "ifs." Who is to say that IBM didn't, from the perspective of the 1970s, make decisions that maximized the then current present value of the company's wealth, even if, by not initially responding to the PC technology, its decisions had wound up causing it to exit the market in 2005? Established companies that try new technologies are often unsuccessful.

Retail giant Wal-Mart entered the online video rental business in mid-2003, challenging Netflix, which had pioneered online video rentals in 1999. Market analysts were understandably concerned for Netflix's future, given Wal-Mart's market savvy in "big box" stores. However, in mid-2005, after investing tens of millions of dollars in promoting its online video rental business and after waging a rental price war with Netflix (as well as Blockbuster), Wal-Mart pulled out of the online video rental business having been able in two years to build a customer base only 10 percent of Netflix's. Wal-Mart set a new, presumably more profitable online course, referring its online customers to Netflix (Hansell 2005).

The innovator's dilemma can manifest itself in brand maintenance, as well as in the adoption of new technologies. The Ford Motor Company's Taurus was the top-selling automobile model in the United States for several years in the late 1980s and early 1990s. However, Ford allowed the Taurus brand name to grow stale by not materially changing the car's appearance and features, perhaps thinking, "Why run the risk associated with redesigning a winning (and top selling) design?" By 2005, Ford had a line-up of largely uninspired model designs that, according to one industry observer, was responsible for the company's loss of market share and for its corporate debt being downgraded to "junk" status by Standard & Poor's (Ingrassia 2005).

Of course, companies have been known to reinvent themselves, as has IBM (from a mainframe and PC manufacturer into a business services firm), Nokia (from a conglomerate into a telecommunication firm), and Nissan (from a failing car company with uninspired car designs in the late 1990s into a profitable company with inspired car designs by 2005); but our point remains that many attempted conversions are failures, as are product development diversions that sometimes are the pet projects of top executives (Roberts 2004, 274–80; Ghosn 2005; Ingrassia 2005). To fortify our point, we can note of the fact that Intel, with its corporate culture largely focused on exploiting and enhancing microprocessor technology, decided that it should develop cameras that could spur the development of teleconferencing that, by the way, would need to be driven by computers – with Intel microprocessors inside. The camera digression proved to be a "dry hole," much to former Intel CEO Andy Grove's chagrin (Burgelman 2002). Similarly, former Apple CEO John Sculley was certain that its Newton personal electronic assistant would be worth the millions Apple devoted to its development, but while the concept was a good one (as the Palm Pilot later proved), the project was a disaster for Sculley and Apple (Roberts 2004, 273).

In other words, contrary to advice often given that the "reinvention" of a failing company is the way to go in business, a company's ultimate market retreat, if not demise, can be – and should be – at times part and parcel of a company's strategy for maximizing the wealth of the company's shareholders.[5] That is, instead of always seeking to maximize the life of a company with innovations in technology or market positioning, executives should at times use their failing companies as "cash cows" and drain the company of its technology and brand capital through lack of investments in reinvention strategies.

[5] Roberts (2004, 67–73) suggests that the innovator's dilemma can be faced by nations. Consider Japan. Before the 1990s, Japan had a business and government policy culture that was well set up to exploit known technologies that Japanese businesses could import and exploit to pursue a national goal of maximizing growth (with profits taking a secondary role). Business practices of providing permanent employment, which resulted in employee loyalty to their companies, as well as a financial system that limited stockholder control over firm growth goals enabled the country recover from the Second World War with remarkable rapidity. However, as Roberts (2004) suggests, the country's business and government policy culture was ill-suited to cope with intensifying global competition. The country had to endure a prolonged lull in economic progress since the early 1990s because of the reluctance of business managers, workers, and policy makers to accept the required changes in business practices and policies: "Indeed, it has taken a long time for the leaders there to begin to realize that the problems are not simple macroeconomic ones, but fundamental structural ones. Japan is still struggling to find a new way (Roberts 2004, 70).

PART II ORGANIZATIONAL ECONOMICS AND MANAGEMENT

The value of teams

Perfectly competitive, or even just highly competitive, market conditions put intense pressure on producers to produce cost-effectively. Those producers who don't find the most cost-effective means of production are doomed. This means that producers must form firms when such organizational structures are more efficient than market exchanges and that they must break down their organization into cohesive and effective working groups. Otherwise, competitive pressures on prices (via the lower-cost curves employed in Part I of this chapter) in the product markets will cause the demise of firms that do not organize themselves so as to constantly find and implement lower-cost ways to produce their output.

As noted in chapter 6, the central reason firms exist is that people are often more productive when they work together – in "teams" – than when they work in isolation from one another but are tied together by markets. Teams are no passing and facile management fad; firms have always utilized them. Indeed, in a broad sense, a firm is a team (or can be viewed as a collection of teams). What seems to be new is the emphasis within management circles on the economies that can be garnered from assigning complex sets of tasks to relatively small teams of workers – those within departments and, for larger projects, across departments, that when used can result in substantial productivity improvements.[6] However, teams also present problems in the form of opportunities for shirking (which should be self-evident to many MBA students who form their own study and project groups to complete class assignments). A central problem that managers face is constructing teams so that they minimize the amount of shirking and maximize production, which is made all the more urgent when competition in product markets is intense.

Team production

What do we mean by "team production"? If Mary and Jim could each produce 100 widgets independently of one another and could together produce

[6] Dell Computer is convinced that its team-based production has improved quality in its made-to-order mail-order sales. Within twelve months of switching to teams in its battery production, a different company, Electrosource, found that its output per worker doubled. Accordingly, the company was able to reduce its workforce (Thomas 1996).

only 200 widgets, there would be no basis for team production, and no basis for the two to form a firm with all of the trappings of a hierarchy. The added cost of their organization would, no doubt, make them uncompetitive *vis-à-vis* other producers such as themselves who worked independently of one another. However, if Mary and Jim could produce 250 widgets when working together, then team production might be profitable (depending on the exact costs associated with operating their two-person organization).

Hence, we would define "team production" as those forms of work in which results are highly interactive: The output of any one member of the group is dependent on what the other group members do. The simplest and clearest form of team work is that which occurs when Mary and Jim (and any number of other people) move objects that neither can handle alone from one place to another. The work of people on an assembly line or on a television advertising project is a more complicated form of teamwork.

Granted, finding business endeavors that have the *potential* for expanding output by more than the growth in the number of employees is a major problem businesses face. But finding such potential opportunities leads to another significant problem, which is making sure that the synergetic potential of the workers who are brought together into a team is actually realized.

We often think of firms failing for purely financial reasons – they incur financial losses. Firms are said to be illiquid and insolvent when they fail. That view of failure is instructive, but the matter can also be seen in a different light, as an organizational problem *and* a failure in organizational incentives. A poorly run organization can mean that all of the 50 "extra" widgets that Mary and Jim can produce together are lost in unnecessary expenditures and impaired productivity because of problems inherent in team production. If the organizational costs exceed the equivalent of 50 widgets, then we can say that Mary and Jim have incurred a loss which would force them to adjust their practices as a firm or to go their own ways.

Many firms do fail and break apart, not because the *potential* for expanded output does not exist, but because their collective potential is not realized when it could be. Why can't people in a team always realize their collective potential? There is a multitude of answers to that question. Firms may not have the requisite product design or a well-thought-out business strategy to promote the products. Some people just can't get along; they rub each other up the wrong way when they try to cooperate. Personal conflicts, which deflect people's energies at work into interpersonal defensive and predatory actions, can be so frequent that the production potentials are missed.

While recognizing many non-economic explanations for organizational problems, we would, however, like to stay with our recurring theme: Managers are unable to find ways to properly align the interests of the workers with the interests of other workers and the owners. People in firms don't cooperate as cost-effectively as they as they can, and should. This is a problem that exists only in teams. For obvious reasons, it doesn't exist in a one-person firm.

In our simple example, involving only two people (Mary and Jim), each party has a strong *personal* incentive (quite apart from an altruistic motivation) to work with the other. After all, each can readily tell when the other person is not contributing what is expected (or agreed upon). Accordingly, when Mary shirks, Jim can "punish" Mary by shirking also, and vice versa, ensuring that they both will be worse off than they would have been had they never sought to cooperate at all. The agreement Mary and Jim have to work together productively can be, in this way, *self-enforcing*, with each checking the other – and each effectively threatening the other with reprisal in kind. The threat of added cost is especially powerful when Mary and Jim are also the owners of the firm. The cost of the shirking and any "tit-for-tat" consequences are fully borne by the two of them. There is no prospect for cost-shifting to a third party.

Two-person firms are, conceptually, the easiest business ventures to organize and manage (with the exception of one-person firms) because the incentives are so obvious and strong and well aligned. Organizational and management problems can begin to mount, however, as the number of people in the firm or "team" begins to mount. As discussed under the "logic of group behavior" in chapter 4, incentives begin to change with the growth in the size of groups. Each individual's contribution to the totality of firm output becomes less and less obvious as the number of people grows. This is especially true when the firm is organized to take advantage of people's specialties. Employees often don't know what their colleagues do and, therefore, are not able to assess their work.

When Mary is one of two people in a firm, then she is responsible for half of the output (assuming equal contributions, of course), but when she is one of a thousand people, her contribution is down to one-tenth of one percent of firm output. If she is a clerk in the advertising department assigned to mailing checks for ads, she might not even be able to tell that she is responsible for one-tenth of a percent of output, income, and profits.

Admittedly, if no one else contributes anything to production (there are no other drops in the bucket), the contribution of any one person is material – in fact, everything. The point is that in large groups, and as output expands, each worker has an *impaired* incentive to do that which is in all of their interests to do – that is, to make their small contribution to the sum total of what the firm does. A central lesson of this discussion is, as stressed before, not that managers can never expect workers to cooperate. There are countervailing incentive forces embedded in the way that groups – or teams – of people work, and these forces can undercut the power of people's natural tendencies to cooperate and achieve their synergetic potential unless attention is given to the details of firm organization.

If all people were angels, always inclined to do as they are told or as they said they would do, then the role of managers would be much less important than it is. Even if almost everyone were inclined to do as they were told or committed to doing, managers would still want to have in place policies and an organizational structure that created incentives for people to behave in the best interest of the firm. Without such incentives rewarding cooperative behavior and punishing uncooperative behavior, a few "bad" people can do serious damage to the firm. Even if most employees are initially willing to pass up opportunities to realize personal benefits at the expense of the firm by shirking on their responsibility, some will soon cease to do so if they see their efforts being undermined by the shirking of others. And as more employees shift from responsible to irresponsible behavior, the greater the incentive for the remaining employees to shift as well, and the culture of cooperation can unravel.

Why are large firms broken into departments? Although it might be thought that the administrative overhead of department structures, which requires that each department have a manager and an office with all the trappings of departmental power, is "unnecessary," departments are a means that firms use to reduce the size of the relevant group within the firm. The purpose is not only to make sure that the actions of individuals can be monitored more closely by bosses, but also that the individuals in any given department can more easily recognize their own and others' contributions to output.

Why is there so much current interest in teams? One good reason is that departments are often too large, meaning that people's individual contributions within departments are too small to detect and monitor. Teams can be ways of reducing the size of the relevant group of workers. Managers have now begun to realize that they can increase worker productivity by reducing the size of the relevant group, as well as to ensure that workers, who know most about what needs to be done in their specialty, can monitor each other. This reduces the need of managers to "micromanage" the work of employees, leaving them more latitude to make the best use of their knowledge for themselves and for the firm.

Team size

One question that is bound to puzzle business managers interested in maximizing firm output is: How large should teams be? How many members should they have? We obviously can't say exactly, given the many factors that explain the great variety of firms in the country. (If we could formulate a pat answer, this book would surely sell zillions!) However, we can make several general observations, the most important of which is that managers must acknowledge that shirking (or "social loafing") will *tend to rise along with the size of the group*, everything else held constant.

In addition, we suggest that because people who have more knowledge of what each other are doing tend to cooperate, the more alike the members, the larger the team can be. The more training team members are given in cooperation, the larger the teams can be. Training, in other words, can pay not only because it makes workers more productive by increasing the value of their direct contribution, but also because it can reduce the added overhead of a larger number of smaller departments.[7]

The more that workers are imbued with a corporate culture and accept the firm's goals, the larger the team can be. The expenditures by corporate leaders trying to define the firm's purpose can be self-financing, given that the resulting larger departments can release financial and real resources.

The more detectable or measurable the outputs of individual team members by other team members are, the larger the team can be. Firms, therefore, have an economic interest in developing ways to make work – or what is

[7] However, a lot depends on the type of training given to workers. Apparently economists, using their maximizing models (and the firmly held belief that everyone will shirk when they can), are inclined to play whatever margins are available to their own personal advantage, or to shirk when feasible, to a degree not true of other professionals. Researchers have found that in single-play experimental games designed to test the tendency of people to free-ride on the group's efforts, not everyone contributed to the group's output. However, they also found that the average group produced 40–60 percent of the "optimal output" of the public good, with the exception of groups made up of graduate students in economics. These graduate students provided only 20 percent of the optimal output (Marwell and Ames 1981). Perhaps that is to be expected, given that economic students are more aware than are most people of how to capture private benefits in such games. But other researchers found that the explanation is less in what economics students learn, and more in the tendency for students who are less prone to cooperate (more "corrupt" in the terminology of the experimenters) to be more likely to major in economics (Frank, Gligorich, and Regan 1996). As a consequence, it probably follows that teams of economists (and other people with similar conceptual leanings) should be smaller than teams of people from other disciplines. Although we may never have intended it, we must fear that the people who read this book may be less disposed to cooperate than they were before they picked it up.

produced – objective. Finally, the greater the importance of quality, the more important team production should be, and the smaller teams will tend to be.

No matter how it is done, the size of the teams within a firm can affect the overall size of the firm. Firms with teams that are "too large" or "too small" can have unnecessarily high cost structures that can restrict the firms' market shares and overall size, as well as the incomes of the workers and owners.

Paying teams

Recognizing that teams can add to firm output is only half the struggle to achieve greater output by getting workers to perform as they should. A question that all too often undercuts the value of teams is: "How are the workers on the team to be motivated and paid?" If workers are rewarded only for the output of the team, then individual workers again have incentives to free-ride on the work of others (to the extent that they can get away with it, given the size of the team), which can be realized not only in slack work but also in absenteeism. If team members are rewarded exclusively for their own individual contributions, then the incentive for actual teamwork is reduced.

Generally, managers effectively "punt" on compensation issues, not knowing exactly how to structure rewards, by offering compensation that is based partly on team output and partly on individual contributions to the team. Team output is generally the easier of the two compensation variables to measure, given that the teams are organized along functional lines, with some measurable objective in mind. Individual contributions are often determined partially by peer evaluation, given that team members are the ones who have localized knowledge of who is contributing how much to team output. But, here again, the compensation problem is not completely solved. Team members can reason that how they work and how they and their cohorts are evaluated can affect their slice of the "compensation pie." Each can figure that the more highly other members of team are evaluated, the lower their own relative evaluation, a consideration that can lead team members to underrate the work of other team members. The result can be team discord, as has been experienced at jeans maker Levi-Strauss, where supervisors reportedly spend a nontrivial amount of time refereeing team member conflicts. To ameliorate (but not totally quell) the discord, Levi-Strauss has resorted to giving employees training in group dynamics and methods of getting along (Mitchell 1994).

One of the questions that our conceptual discussion cannot answer totally satisfactorily is: "How can managers best motivate workers through pay to contribute to team output?" There are four identifiable pay methods worth considering:

(1) The workers can simply share in the revenues generated by the team (or firm). We can call this reward system *revenue sharing*. The gain to each worker is the added revenue received minus the cost to the worker of the added effort expended. Under this method of reward, each worker has the maximum incentive to free-ride, especially when the "team" is large.
(2) The workers can be assigned target production or revenue levels and be given what are called *forcing contracts*, or a guarantee of one high wage level (significantly above their market wage) if the target is achieved and another, lower (penalty) wage if the target is not achieved. Under this system, each worker suffers a personal income loss from the failure of the team to work effectively to meet the target.
(3) The workers can also be given an opportunity to share in the team or firm profits. *Profit sharing* (sometimes called "gain sharing") is, basically, another form of a forcing contract, because the worker will get one income if the firm makes a profit (above some target level) and a lower income if the profit (above a target level) is zero.
(4) The workers within different teams can also be rewarded according to how well they do relative to other teams. They can be asked to participate in *tournaments*, in which the members of the "winning team" are given higher incomes – and, very likely, higher rates of pay by the hour or month – than the members of other teams. We say "very likely" because the winning team members may work harder, longer, and smarter in order to win the tournament "prize." Hence, the "winners'" pay per hour (or any other unit of time) could be lower than the "losers'."

All the pay systems just outlined may have a positive impact on worker input and, as a consequence, on worker output. For example, a number of studies reveal that profit sharing and worker stock ownership plans do seem to have an positive impact on worker productivity (Howard and Dietz 1969; Metzger 1975; Metzger and Colletti 1975; FitzRoy and Kraft 1986; Wagner, Rubin, and Callahan 1988; Weisman and Kruse 1990; US Department of Labor 1993). One study of fifty-two firms in the engineering industry in the United Kingdom (40 percent of which had some form of profit sharing plans and the rest did not) found that profit sharing could add between 3 and 8 percent to firm productivity (Cable and Wilson 1989). It has also been shown that the more "participatory" the decision making process – the more information is shared, the more flexible the job assignment, and the greater the extent of profit sharing – the greater worker performance relative to more traditional organizational structures (Husled 1995; Ichniowski, Shaw, and Prennushi 1996).

Experimental evidence on the effectiveness of team pay

The question that has all too infrequently been addressed is which method of rewarding workers and their teams is *more* effective in overcoming shirking and causing workers to apply themselves? One of the more interesting studies that addresses that question uses an experimental/laboratory approach to develop a tentative assessment of the absolute and relative value of the different pay methods on worker effort. Experimental economists Haig Nalbantian and Andrew Schotter (1997) used two groups of six university economics students in a highly stylized experiment in which the students' pay for their participation in the experiment would be determined by how "profitable" their respective teams were in achieving maximum "output" (Nalbantian and Schotter 1997).

The students did their "work" on computers that were isolated from one another. The students indicated how much "work" they would do in the twenty-five rounds of the experiment by selecting a number from 0 to 100 that had a cost tied to it, and each higher number had a higher cost to the student, just as rising effort tends to impose an escalating cost on workers. The students in each of the two teams always knew two pieces of important information: how much they "worked" (or the number they submitted) in each round and how much the "team" as a total "worked." They did not know the individual "effort levels" of the other students.[8]

Nonetheless, the researchers were able to draw conclusions that generally confirmed expectations from the theory at the heart of this textbook. They found that when the revenue sharing method of pay was employed, the median "effort level" for each of the two teams started at a mere 30 (with a maximum effort level of 100), but because the students were then told how little effort other team members were expending in total, the students began to cut their own effort in each of the successive rounds. The median effort level in both teams trended downward until the twenty-fifth round, when the median effort level was under 13. That finding caused the researchers to assert: "Shirking happens" (Nalbantian and Schotter 1997, 315). They were also able to deduce that the *history of the team performance* matters: The higher the team performance at

[8] Granted, the experiment leaves much to be desired, which the authors fully concede. The experimental setting did not reflect the full complexity of the typical workplace: direct communication among workers, for example, can have an important impact on the effort levels of individual workers. The complexity of the workplace is why it is so difficult to determine how pay systems affect worker performance, especially relative to alternative compensation schemes.

the start, the greater the team performance thereafter (although the effort level might be declining over the rounds, it would still be higher at identified rounds, the higher the starting effort level).

Nalbantian and Schotter (1997) found that forcing contracts and profit sharing could increase the initial level of effort to 40 or above, a third higher than the initial effort level under revenue sharing, but still the effort level under forcing contracts and profit sharing trended downward with succeeding rounds of the experiment. Nalbantian and Schotter (1997) also found that the tournaments that were tried, which forced the team members to think competitively, had median initial effort levels on a par with the initial effort levels observed under forcing contracts. However, the effort level tended to increase in the first few rounds and then held more or less constant through the rest of the twenty-five rounds. At the end of the twenty-five rounds, the teams had a median effort level of 40 to 50, or up to four times the final effort level under the revenue sharing incentive system. Understandably, the authors concluded that "a little competition goes a very long, long way" (Nalbantian and Schotter 1997, 315).

Finally, the authors concluded that monitoring works, which is no surprise, but the extent to which monitoring hiked the effort level grabs attention. No monitoring system works perfectly, so the authors evaluated how the teams would perform with a competitive team pay system under two experimental conditions, one in which the probability of team members being caught shirking was 70 percent of the time and one in which teams members being caught shirking was 30 percent of the time, with the penalty being stiff: loss of their "jobs." The median effort for one 70 percent team level started at about 75 (the predicted effort level from theory) and stayed there until the last round, at which point the effort level fell markedly (a finding that should be understandable from our discussion of the "last-period problem" in chapter 3). The median effort level for the other 70 percent team started at about 50, rose quickly to 70, and stayed there through the rest of the rounds (with one very large drop in effort in the middle of the rounds).

When the probability of being caught shirking dropped to 30 percent, the effort level of one team started at 70 and went up and down wildly between zero and 80 for the next twenty rounds, only to approach zero during the last five rounds. The effort level of the other team started close to zero and stayed very close to zero for most of the following rounds (reaching above 10 only twice).

Obviously, monitoring of team members can have a dramatic impact on team performance but, as in all matters, the cost of the monitoring system can be high. The researchers have not yet been able to say, from the experimental evidence, whether the improvement in team performance is worth the cost of the monitoring system that is required. However, managers can't wait for the experimental findings. They must find ways of minimizing the monitoring costs. One of the great cost-saving advantages of teams, which is not reflected in the way the experiments were run, is that teamwork tends to be self-monitoring, with team members monitoring one another. In the experiment, the team members could not monitor and penalize each other. When the experimental work is extended, we would not be surprised if the effort level increases when the team members are able to monitor and penalize each other.

Should all firms adopt the competitive team approach? The evidence suggests a strong "Yes." But we hasten to add a caveat that managers of some firms must keep in mind. Greater effort to produce more output is desirable as long as it does not come with a sacrifice in "quality" (or some other important dimension of production). Competitive team production may be shunned in firms in industries such as pharmaceuticals and banking that (because of the importance of reputation and also liability concerns, for example) can't tolerate concessions in their quality standards. The competition in the tournaments drives up "output" but can drive down "quality." Such firms would want to use reward systems that keep competition under control and quality standards up. They would also want to rely on close monitoring, despite the cost because of the higher costs that they might suffer with defects. This leads to the obvious conclusion that the greater the cost of mistakes, the greater the cost that can be endured from relaxed competition and from monitoring.

THE BOTTOM LINE

The key takeaways from chapter 10 are the following:

(1) The demand curve facing a perfect competitor is horizontal (or perfectly elastic), meaning the firm is a price taker – that is, it cannot affect market price by any change in its output.
(2) Marginal revenue for a perfect competitor is equal to market price.
(3) A perfect competitor maximizes profits by producing where marginal cost equals marginal revenue, which equals market price.

(4) If the price is below the perfect competitor's average total cost but above its average variable cost curve, the firm will not shut down in the long run. It is still more than covering its fixed costs and therefore is minimizing its losses (over what they would be if the firm ceased to operate). Such a firm will shut down once it is able to get out from under its fixed costs.

(5) In perfectly competitive markets, any economic profits will be reduced to zero in the long run due to entry and the resulting increase in market supply and decrease in market price.

(6) Firms often face an "innovator's dilemma," which is one of continuing to seek additional profits from a known technology or seeking additional profits by venturing into the development of new technologies and products that are necessarily untried when investments must be made.

(7) Perfect competition is an idealized market structure that can never be fully attained in the real world. Nonetheless, the model helps to illuminate the influence of competition in the marketplace, just as the idealized concepts of the physical sciences help to illustrate the workings of the natural world. Physicists, for example, deal with the concept of gravity by talking of the acceleration of a falling body in a vacuum. Vacuums do not exist naturally in the world, but as theoretical constructs they are useful in isolating and emphasizing the directional power of gravitational pull. In a similar fashion, the theoretical construct of perfect competition helps to highlight the directional influence and consequences of competition.

(8) The model of perfect competition also provides a benchmark for comparing the relative efficiency of real-world markets. The perfectly competitive model clarifies the rules of efficient production and suggests that free movement of resources is essential to achieving efficient production levels. Without a free flow of resources, new firms cannot move into profitable production lines, increase market supply, push prices down, and force other firms to minimize their production costs.

(9) Team production in this chapter has been introduced to stress that firms' cost structures are not determined solely by the prices they pay for labor and other resources. The costs of production are largely influenced by firms' organizational structures, including how they make use of teams as a means of tapping into the specialized knowledge known by workers and as a means of increasing the incentives of workers to do what they are hired to do.

(10) Cost-effective team work can be in the interest not only of principals/owners, but also of all team members, since team work can reduce shirking, lower the firm's cost structure, and increase the pay and job security of team members. The more competitive the product markets, the more important it is that managers organize teams and structure their pay in the most cost-effective way.

REVIEW QUESTIONS

(1) Draw the short-run average and marginal cost curves, plus the demand curve, for a perfect competitor. Give the firm's demand, and identify the short-run production level for a profit-maximizing firm. Identify the profits.

(2) On your graph for question 1, indicate with a *Pm* the minimum price the firm requires in order to continue short-run operations.

(3) On your graph for question 1, darken the firm's marginal cost curve above its intersection with the average variable supply cost curve. Explain why that portion of the marginal cost curve is the firm's supply curve.

(4) Why does a perfectly competitive firm seek to equate marginal cost with marginal revenue rather than to produce where average total cost is at a minimum?

(5) If perfectly competitive firms are making a profit in the short run, what will happen to the industry's equilibrium price and quantity in the long run?

(6) Suppose the market demand for a product rises. In the short run, how will a perfect competitor react to the higher market price? Draw a graph to illustrate your answer. What will happen to the market price in the long run? Why?

(7) Suppose that you know absolutely nothing about price and cost in a particular competitive industry. How could you nevertheless determine whether the typical firm in the industry was making economic profits or losses?

(8) Suppose a manager were to refuse to provide a fringe benefit that could lower the wages of their workers, but which on balance benefited workers. Why has this manager prevented the firm's average cost curves from being as low as possible?

(9) When should a firm eliminate fringe benefits?

(10) What points made in the discussion of teams in the chapter are applicable to your study teams? Does your university allow students to move among teams? Why or why not? How might the prospects of switching teams affect team performances? Should students be able to make monetary side-payments to students in other teams to switch teams?

(11) In MBA study teams, in most programs, all team members are typically given the same grade for team projects. How does such a grading rule

affect team member behavior? What would be the consequences of allowing teams to give different members different grades?

(12) Shony's, Coco's, and Hof's Hut are restaurant brands that began to lose market share in Southern California and elsewhere in the 1990s to Outback Steakhouse, Penera Bread café, and Claim Jumper. What are the benefits and problems of having a well-established restaurant brand? Should restaurants try to rebrand themselves when they start losing market share?

Appendix: contestable markets

One of the most important developments in the study of markets is the theory of contestable markets.[9] The contestable market model stresses the importance of *potential* rather than actual competitors in a market. A market is deemed to be "contestable" if entry and exit are relatively easy. A market is "perfectly contestable" if entry is absolutely free and exit is costless. Free entry has a particular meaning in the theory of contestable markets; it means that new firms entering an industry are not at any cost disadvantage compared to existing firms in the industry. In other words, latecomers suffer no cost handicaps. Costless exit means that firms can leave the industry at any time and can recoup all costs incurred by entry.

A contestable market, then, is marked by ease of entry and exit, and in that respect can approximate a perfectly competitive market. As with a perfectly competitive market, a contestable market is characterized by zero economic profits in the long run. For a contestable market, however, we do not need a large number of firms and a homogeneous product. Indeed, multi-product firms are possible in contestable markets. A contestable market may have only two or three firms operating in it. Moreover, those firms produce at rates of output at which price is equal (or approximately equal) to marginal cost.

What brings about this result? Why do firms in contestable markets not produce and price at the monopoly equilibrium? The reason is entry and exit. If price is not equal to marginal cost, profit opportunities exist and new firms will quickly enter the market, causing existing firms to incur losses. The potential competitors force the existing firms to produce where price equals marginal cost. A firm in a contestable market is always open to hit-and-run attacks from its potential competitors. They will therefore be forced to produce and sell at an output at which price will come close to equaling, if it does not actually equal, marginal cost, and economic profits are zero. Any attempt to exploit market power will bring about entry into the market and the dissipation of all profits.

[9] The basic model of a contestable market is presented by Baumol (1982). For a critical analysis of the model, see Shepherd (1984).

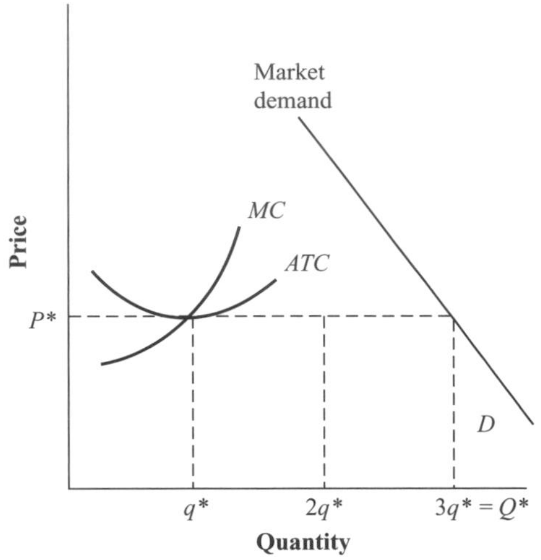

Figure 10A.1 A contestable market

The market is composed of three firms, each producing output q^*, which minimizes average costs. Total industry output is $Q^* = 3q^*$. Any attempt by the three firms to reduce output and increase market price will lead to entry by new firms and the dissipation of profits.

The firms in the contestable market can be forced to operate *as if* they were in perfectly competitive markets.

A contestable market is depicted in figure 10A.1. Note that although only three firms are in the industry, they all produce where price equals marginal and average cost. For the industry as a whole, price is equal to the minimum on the long-run average total cost curve. Each firm produces one-third (q) of total industry output ($3q$). Production at an efficient rate of output and marginal cost pricing, then, does not require the atomistic markets of the perfectly competitive model. A perfectly contestable market will do.

What industries might this model fit? The air travel industry is one candidate. Many major markets are served by only two or three airlines. Yet if an airline with a dominant position in a particular regional market attempted to set price well above costs, entry would quickly follow. Airplanes can be shifted from one market or use to another with ease. New entrants do not appear to be at a cost disadvantage relative to existing firms. If the conditions for a contestable market were indeed met, then we would expect the air travel industry to be characterized by marginal cost pricing and zero economic profits. It is always difficult to determine whether or not price is equal to marginal cost; one indication that contestability characterizes the air travel industry is that prices do not appear to be higher in markets with fewer actual competitors. The zero-profit outcome also describes the air travel industry reasonably well.

CHAPTER 11

Monopoly power and firm pricing decisions

If monopoly persists, monopoly will always sit at the helm of government . . . its bigness is an unwholesome inflation created by privileges and exemptions which it ought not to enjoy. If there are men in this country big enough to own the government of the United States, they are going to own it. **Woodrow Wilson**

That competition is a virtue, at least as far as enterprises are concerned, has been a basic article of faith in the American Tradition, and a vigorous antitrust policy has long been regarded as both beneficial and necessary, not only to extend competitive forces into new regions but also to preserve them where they may be flourishing at the moment. **G. Warren Nutter** and **Henry Alder Einhorn**

At the bottom of almost all arguments against the free market is a deep-seated concern about the distorting (some would say corrupting) influence of monopolies. People who are suspicious of the free market fear that too many producers are not controlled by the forces of competition, but instead hold considerable monopoly power, or control over market outcomes. Unless the government intervenes, these firms are likely to exploit their power for their own selfish benefit. This theme has been fundamental to the writings of economist John Kenneth Galbraith:

The initiative in deciding what is produced comes not from the sovereign consumer who, through the market, issues instructions that bend the productive mechanism to his or her ultimate will. Rather it comes from the great producing organization that reaches forward to control the markets that it is presumed to serve and, beyond, to bend the customers to its needs. (Galbraith 1967, 6)

This chapter is really a continuation of our earlier discussion of "market failures," for *monopoly* is often seen as one of the gravest of all forms of failure in markets. Accordingly, we examine the dynamics of monopoly power and attempt to place the consequences of those dynamics in proper perspective. We also consider the usefulness of antitrust laws in controlling monopoly and promoting competition. In chapter 12, we extend the model of monopoly developed here to two forms of partial monopoly market structures – monopolistic competition and oligopoly.

PART I THEORY AND POLICY APPLICATIONS

The origins of monopoly

We have defined the competitive market as the process by which market rivals, each pursuing their own private interests, strive to outdo one another. This competitive process has many benefits. It enables producers to obtain information about what consumers and other producers are willing to do. It promotes higher production levels, lower prices, and a greater variety of goods and services than would be achieved otherwise.

Monopoly power is the conceptual opposite of competition. Monopoly power is the ability of a firm to raise profitably the market price of its good or service by reducing production and, hence, market supply. Whereas the demand curve of the competitive firm is horizontal (see chapter 10), a firm with monopoly power faces a downward sloping demand curve. By restricting production, the monopoly can raise its market price. To maximize its profits (or minimize its losses), such a firm need only search through the various price–quantity combinations on its demand curve. In very general terms, then, a firm with monopoly power is a *price searcher*. It can control the price it charges because other firms are to some extent unable or unwilling to compete. As a result, a monopolized market produces fewer benefits than perfect competition does.

Businesses vary considerably in the extent of their monopoly power. The Postal Service and your local telephone company both, at least until overnight delivery, email and wireless telephones came along, had significant monopoly power. They confronted few competitors, given that entry into their markets was barred by law (the technology of email and cell phones eventually rendered those legal barriers largely irrelevant). IBM has had since the 1960s far less monopoly power in mainframe computing. Although it can affect the price it charges for its computers by expanding or contracting its sales, IBM is restrained by the possibility that other firms will enter its market. On a smaller scale, grocery stores face the same threat. They may have many competitors already, and they must be concerned about additional stores entering the market. Nevertheless, a grocery store still retains *some* power to restrict sales and raise its prices by virtue of its location, or other features that appeal to some consumers.

How does monopoly arise? To answer that question clearly, we must reflect once again on the basis for competition. Competition occurs where market rivals can enter markets in which profits exist and production technology allows many firms to produce at low costs (economies of scale are not significant for any firm). In the extreme case of perfect competition, there are no barriers to entry, and competitors are numerous. Entrepreneurs are always on the lookout for any opportunity to enter such a market in pursuit of profit. Individual competitors cannot raise their price – for, if they do, their rivals may move in, cut prices, and take away all their customers. If a wheat farmer, for example, asks more than the market price, customers can buy from others at the market price. For this reason, perfect competitors are called *price takers.* They have no real control over the price they charge.

The essential condition for competition is freedom of market entry. In perfect competition, entry is assumed to be completely free (meaning that it is costless). Conversely, the essential condition for monopoly is the presence of *barriers to entry.* Monopolists can manipulate price because such barriers protect them from being undercut by rivals.

Various economists have suggested over the years that barriers to entry can arise from several standard sources:

- First, the monopolist may have sole (or dominant) ownership of a strategic resource, such as bauxite (from which aluminum is extracted).
- Second, the monopolist may have a patent or copyright on the product, which prevents other producers from duplicating it. For years, Polaroid had a patent monopoly on the instant-photograph market. Now, any remaining Polaroid monopoly in instant pictures has been eclipsed by digital photography.
- Third, the monopolist may have an exclusive franchise to sell a given product in a specific geographical area. Consider the exclusive franchise enjoyed by your local bus company, or the franchise that was enjoyed everywhere in the country, until very recently, by your local electric utility.
- Fourth, the monopolist may own the rights to a well-known brand name with a highly loyal group of customers. In that case, the barrier to entry is the costly process of trying to get customers to try a new product.
- Finally, in a monopolized industry, production may be conducted on a very large scale, requiring huge plants and large amounts of equipment. The

enormous financial resources needed to take advantage of large economies of scale can act as a barrier to entry, because a new entrant operating on a small scale would have costs that were too high to compete effectively with the dominant firm.

All in all, these external barriers to entry can be thought of as costs that must be borne by potential competitors before they can compete. Such barriers may be "low," which means that a sole producer's monopoly power may be very limited, but such barriers could, theoretically, also be prohibitively high.

The limits of monopoly power

Even the pure monopolist's market power is not completely unchecked, however. It is restricted in two important ways. First, without government assistance, the monopolist's control over the market for a product is never complete. Even if a producer has a true monopoly of a good, the consumer can still choose a *substitute good* whose production is not monopolized. For instance, until recently in most parts of the United States, only one firm has been permitted to provide a local telephone service. Yet people can always communicate in other ways. They can talk directly with one another; they can write letters or send telegrams; they can use their children as messengers. Obviously none of these alternatives are close substitutes for a telephone, but people can also choose to communicate less and use more of their income on rugs, bicycles, or any number of other things, and use less of the income on telephone services. The consumer's demand curves for all goods are downward sloping, reflecting the fact that not even a monopolist can force consumers to buy its product. As Friedrich Hayek has written:

> If, for instance, I would very much like to be painted by a famous artist [one who has monopoly power] and if he refuses to paint me for less than a very high fee, it would clearly be absurd to say that I am coerced. The same is true of any other commodity or service that I can do without. So long as the services of a particular person are not crucial to my existence or the preservation of what I most value, the conditions he exacts for rendering these services cannot be called "coercion." (Hayek 1960, 136)

This is not to say that the effects of monopoly are not harmful. If monopoly means that one firm has few if any rivals providing the same product, it can be viewed as a force that reduces consumer choice.

But monopoly power can reflect beneficial considerations for consumers. A firm may gain monopoly power because it has built a better mousetrap or developed a good that was previously unavailable. In other words, a firm may be the only producer because it is the first producer, and no one has been able to figure out how to duplicate its product. In this instance, although monopolized, a new product results in an expansion of consumer choice. Furthermore, the monopoly may be only temporary, for other competitors are likely to break into the market eventually.

As Micklethwait and Wooldridge (2003) observed, when Henry Ford started his car company, he "was devoted to handcrafting toys for the super-rich," (2003, 77), but it wasn't long before more than a million Americans were driving Model Ts. George Eastman bought his first (very difficult to use) camera in 1877 for $49.58 (which would be equal to about $500 in today's prices). By 1900, Eastman was selling Brownies for $1 under the slogan "You push the button and we do the rest" (Micklethwait and Wooldridge 2003, 77). The point here is that innovation and competition resulted in large companies, with what many would say had monopoly power, but those companies "improved the living standards of ordinary people, putting the luxuries of the rich within reach of the man in the street" (2003, 77).

The monopolist is also restricted by market conditions – that is, by the cost of production and the downward sloping demand curve for the good. If the monopolistic firm raises its price, it must be prepared to sell less. How much less depends on what substitutes are available. The monopolist must also consider the costs of expanding production and of trying to prevent competitors from entering the market.

In an open market, monopoly power is typically dissolved in the long run. With time, competitors can discover weakly protected avenues through which to invade the monopolist's domain. The Reynolds International Pen Company had a patent monopoly on the first ballpoint pen that it introduced in 1945. Two years later other pen companies had found ways of circumventing the patent and producing a similar but not identical product. The price of ballpoint pens fell from an initial $12.50 (or about $125 in 2005 purchasing power) to the low prices of today. Many other products that are competitively produced today – calculators, video games, cell phones, and cellophane tape, to name a few–were first sold by companies that enjoyed temporary monopolies. Thus the limits on monopoly power are crucial: in the long run, excessively high prices, restricted supply, and high profits give potential competitors the incentive to find ways to benefit consumers by circumventing the monopolist's power.

The most effective way for a monopoly to retain its market power is to enlist the coercive power of government to prevent competition. This strategy has been used effectively for decades in the electric utilities industry and the cable television market. The insurance industry and the medical profession, both of which are protected from competition through licensing procedures, are also good examples. However, even the power of the state may not be enough to shield an industry from competition forever. Consumer tastes and the technology of production and delivery can change dramatically over the very long run. The railroad industry's market, which was protected from price competition by the state for almost a century, has been gradually eroded by the emergence of new competitors, principally airlines, buses, and trucks. Even the first-class mail monopoly of the US Postal Service continues to be eroded by FedEx and a host of other overnight delivery firms, as well as by email and fax machines.

Today, one of the best examples of government-protected monopoly power is in the distribution of alcoholic beverages at the state level. A number of states require that all out-of-state alcoholic beverages be distributed by in-state wholesale distributors. Moreover, the distributors must charge all retailers the same price. In Ohio, beer wholesalers are guaranteed a markup of 25 percent, while wine distributors are guaranteed a markup of 33 percent. Such market restrictions have been supported by the Spirits Wholesalers of America on the grounds that "Alcohol has to be treated as a special product because when it is misused it causes devastating social consequences" (Hirsch 2005). However, because of the protected monopoly the distributors are granted by the state, "Two-Buck Chuck" – the nickname given to Charles Shaw wine, which sells for $1.99 at Trader Joe's grocery stores in California – sells for $3.99 in Columbus, Ohio (Hirsch 2005).[1]

Should government attempt to break up monopolies? Without state protection, monopoly may eventually dissipate, so the relevant public policy questions are how long the monopoly power is likely to persist if left alone, and how costly it will be while it lasts, in terms of lost efficiency and unequal distribution of income. The machinery of government needed to dissolve monopoly power is costly in itself. Thus the decision whether to prosecute antitrust violations

[1] It needs to be noted that advocates of the restrictions on alcohol sales could argue that the *net* welfare loss from the restrictions on distribution in Ohio is not as great as might be suggested by considering the reduction in sales and the increase in the price of Charles Shaw wine. This is because the reduced consumption of Two-Buck Chuck could lead to less drunk driving and fewer highways deaths (as well as a reduction in other social problems associated with alcohol consumption). In addition, it needs to be noted that, as this chapter was being finalized, state bans on interstate sales of alcoholic beverages through the Internet, for example, were being reviewed by the Supreme Court. If that ban is lifted, so the prices of spirits should be expected to fall. The drop in price can be expected to lead to greater consumption – and more social (or external cost) problems associated with drinking.

depends in part on the costs and benefits of such an action. Sometimes the rise of a monopoly does warrant government action, but in some cases the benefits of action cannot justify the costs. As described in chapter 2, the first seller of hand calculators enjoyed a temporary monopoly of the US market in 1969. Subsequently the industry developed very rapidly, however, and in retrospect it is clear that a long, drawn-out antitrust action would have been inappropriate.

To give another example, in 1969 the Justice Department decided that IBM enjoyed an unwarranted monopoly of the domestic computer market, which was dominated by large mainframe computers. It concluded that an antitrust suit against IBM was justified. Prosecution of the case took more than a decade, with the Justice Department dropping the case in January 1982. The accumulated documentation from the proceedings filled a warehouse, and the Justice Department and IBM devoted an untold number of lawyer-hours to the case. In the meantime, IBM's alleged monopoly was seriously eroded by new firms producing minicomputers and microcomputers, a trend that has continued (and accelerated) since 1982. Thus the net benefits to society from the antitrust action against IBM were at best debatable, and probably negative – that is, the costs most likely exceeded the benefits. The cost the US government has incurred to prosecute Microsoft for antitrust violation (starting in 1998) may also, in the long run, outweigh the achieved benefits. The courts did indeed rule that Microsoft is a "monopoly" in the operating system market, but the consumer benefits coming from that ruling in terms of lower prices and greater availability of Microsoft products are, at the time of writing, not obvious.[2]

Equating marginal cost with marginal revenue

In deciding how often to play tennis, people weigh the estimated benefits of each game against its costs. Producers of goods follow a similar procedure, although the benefits of production are measured in terms of *revenue acquired* rather than personal utility. A producer will produce another unit of a good if the additional (or marginal) revenue it brings is greater than the additional cost of its production – in other words, if it increases the firm's profits. The firm will therefore expand production to the point where marginal cost equals marginal revenue ($MC = MR$). This is a fundamental rule that all profit maximizing firms follow, and monopolies are no exception.

[2] For details on the government's antitrust case against Microsoft with counter-arguments, see McKenzie (2000).

Table 11.1 *The monopolist's declining marginal revenue*

Quantity of yo-yos sold (1)	Price of yo-yos (2) ($)	Total revenue (1 × (2)) (3) ($)	Marginal revenue (change in (3)) (4) ($)
0	11	0	0
1	10	10	10
2	9	18	8
3	8	24	6
4	7	28	4
5	6	30	2

Suppose you are in the yo-yo business. You have a patent on edible yo-yos, which come in three flavors – vanilla, chocolate, and strawberry. (We will assume there is a demand for these products – you can work up quite an appetite yo-yoing!) The cost of producing the first yo-yo is $0.50, but you can sell it for $0.75. Your profit on that unit is therefore $0.25 ($0.75–$0.50). If the second unit costs you $0.60 to make (assuming increasing marginal cost) and you can sell it for $0.75, your profit for two yo-yos is $0.40 ($0.25 profit on the first plus $0.15 profit on the second). If you intend to maximize your profits, you – like the perfect competitor – will continue to expand production until the gap between the constant marginal revenue and the increasing marginal cost disappears. As a monopolist, however, you will find that your marginal revenue does not remain constant. Instead, it decreases over the range of production.

The monopolist's marginal revenue declines as output rises because its price must be reduced to entice consumers to buy more. Consider the price schedule in table 11.1. Price and quantity are inversely related, reflecting the assumption that a monopolist faces a downward sloping demand curve. As the price falls from $10 to $6 (column (2)), the number sold rises from one to five (column (1)). If the firm wishes to sell only one yo-yo, it can charge as much as $10. Total revenue at that level of production is then $10. To sell more – say, two yo-yos – the monopolist must reduce the price for each to $9. Total revenue then rises to $18 (column (3)).

By multiplying columns (1) and (2), we can fill in the rest of column (3). As the price is lowered and the quantity sold rises, total revenue rises from $10 for one unit to $30 for five units. With each unit increase in quantity sold, however, total revenue does not rise by an equal amount. Instead, it rises in declining amounts – first by $10, then $8, $6, $4, and $2. These amounts are the marginal revenue from the sale of each unit (column (4)), which the monopolist must compare with the marginal cost of each unit.

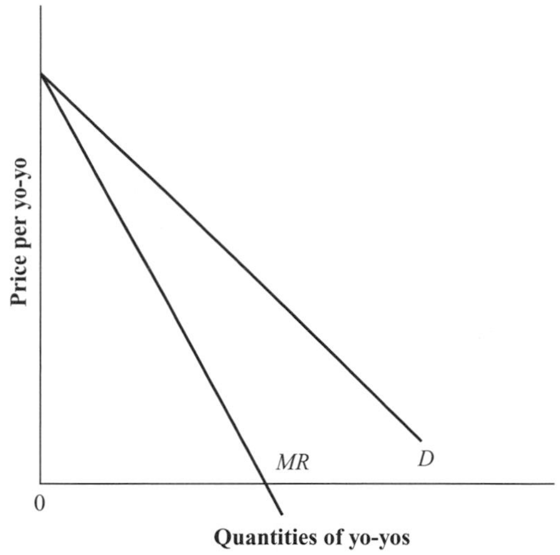

Figure 11.1 The monopolist's demand and marginal revenue curves
The demand curve facing a monopolist slopes downward, for it is the same as market demand. The monopolist's marginal revenue curve is constructed from the information contained in the demand curve (see table 11.1).

At an output level of one yo-yo, marginal revenue equals price, but at every other output level marginal revenue is less than price. Because of the monopolist's downward sloping demand curve, the second yo-yo cannot be sold unless the price of both one and two units is reduced from \$10 to \$9. If we account for the \$1 in revenue lost on the first yo-yo in order to sell the second, the net revenue from the second yo-yo is \$8 (the selling price of \$9 minus the \$1 lost on the first yo-yo). For the third yo-yo to be sold, the price on the first two must be reduced by another dollar each. The loss in revenue on them is therefore \$2. And the marginal revenue for the third yo-yo is its \$8 selling price less the \$2 loss on the first two units, or \$6.

Thus the monopolist's marginal revenue curve (columns (1) and (4)) is derived directly from the market demand curve (columns (1) and (2)). Graphically, the marginal revenue curve lies below the demand curve, and its distance from the demand curve increases as the price falls (see figure 11.1).[3] (More

[3] Prove this to yourself by plotting the figures in columns (1) and (2) vs. the figures in columns (1) and (4) on a sheet of graph paper. (Another simple way of drawing the *MR* curve is to extend the demand curve until it intersects both the vertical and horizontal axes. Then draw the *MR* curve starting from the demand curve's point of intersection with the vertical axis to a point midway between the original and the intersection of the demand curve with the horizontal axis. This method can be used for any linear demand curve.)

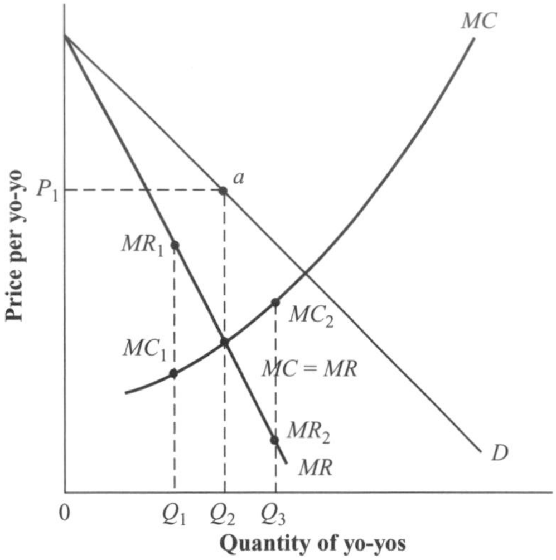

Figure 11.2 Equating marginal cost with marginal revenue
The monopolist will move toward production level Q_2, the level at which marginal cost equals marginal revenue. At production levels below Q_2, marginal revenue will exceed marginal cost; the monopolist will miss the chance to increase profits. At production levels greater than Q_2, marginal cost will exceed marginal revenue; the monopolist will lose money on the extra units.

details on the derivation of the marginal revenue curve can be found in the appendix to this chapter, p. 472.)

Figure 11.2 adds the monopolist's marginal cost curve to the demand and marginal revenue curves from figure 11.1. Because the profit maximizing monopolist will produce to the point where marginal cost equals marginal revenue, our yo-yo maker will produce Q_2 units. At that quantity, the marginal cost and marginal revenue curves intersect. If the yo-yo maker produces fewer than Q_2 yo-yos – say, Q_1 – profits are lost unnecessarily. The marginal revenue acquired from selling the last yo-yo up to Q_1, MR_1, is greater than the marginal cost of producing it, MC_1. Furthermore, for all units between Q_1 and Q_2, marginal revenue exceeds marginal cost. In other words, by expanding production from Q_1 to Q_2, the monopolist can add more to total revenue than to total cost. Up to an output level of Q_2, the firm's profits will rise.

Why does the monopolist produce no more than Q_2 ? Because the marginal cost of all additional units beyond Q_2 is greater than the marginal revenue they bring. Beyond Q_2 units, profits will fall. If it produces Q_3 yo-yos, for

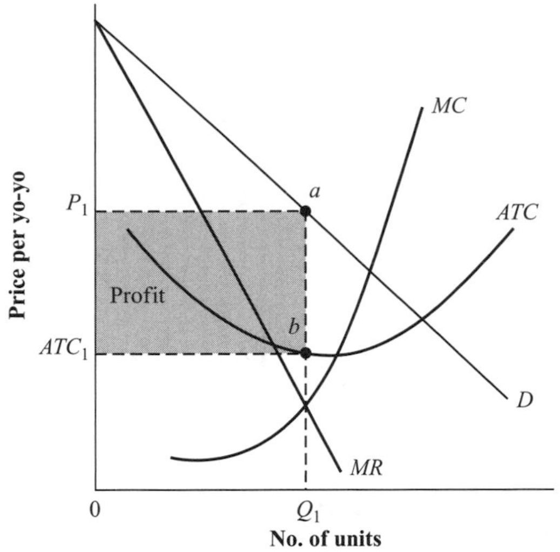

Figure 11.3 The monopolist's profits

The profit maximizing monopoly will produce at the level defined by the intersection of the marginal cost and marginal revenue curves: Q_1. It will charge a price of P_1 – as high as market demand will bear – for that quantity. Because the average total cost of producing Q_1 units is ATC_1, the firm's profit is the shaded area ATC_1P_1ab.

instance, the firm may still make a profit, but not the greatest profit possible. The marginal cost of the last yo-yo up to Q_3 (MC_2) is greater than the marginal revenue received from its sale (MR_2). By producing Q_3 units, the monopolist adds more to cost than to revenues. The result is lower profits.

After the monopolistic firm selects the output at which to produce, the market price of the good is determined. In Figure 11.2, the price that can be charged for Q_2 yo-yos is P_1. (Remember, the demand curve indicates the price that can be charged for any quantity.) Of all the possible price–quantity combinations on the demand curve, therefore, the monopolist will choose combination *a*.

Short-run profits and losses

How much profit will a monopolist make by producing at the point where marginal cost equals marginal revenue? The answer can be found by adding the average total cost curve developed in chapter 10 to the monopolist's demand and marginal revenue curves (see figure 11.3). As we have shown, the monopolist

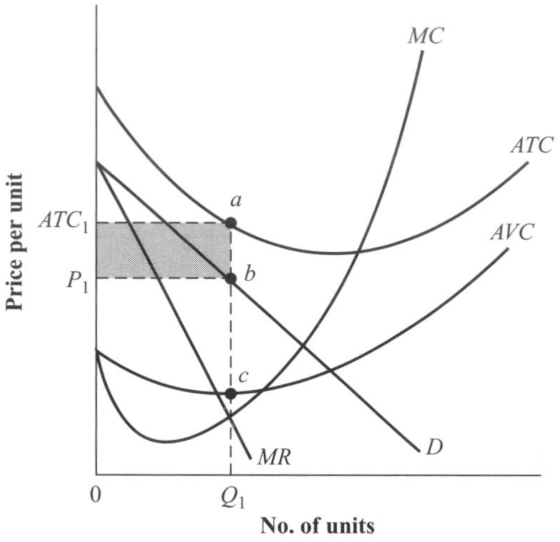

Figure 11.4 The monopolist's short-run Losses
Not all monopolists make a profit. With a demand curve that lies below its average total cost curve, this monopoly will minimize its short-run losses by continuing to produce at the point where marginal cost equals marginal revenue (Q_1 units). It will charge P_1, a price that covers its fixed costs, and will sustain short-run losses equal to the shaded area P_1ATC_1ab.

will produce at the point where the marginal cost and revenue curves intersect, Q_1, and will charge what the market will bear for the quantity, P_1. We know also that profit equals total revenue minus total cost ($Profit = TR - TC$). Total revenue of P_1 times Q_1 is the rectangular area bounded by $0P_1aQ_1$. Total cost is the average total cost, ATC_1, times quantity, Q_1, or the rectangular area bounded by $0ATC_1bQ_1$. Subtracting total cost from total revenue, we find that the monopolist's profit is equal to the shaded rectangular area ATC_1P_1ab (mathematically, the expression $Profit = P_1Q_1 - ATC_1Q_1$ can be converted to the simpler form, $Profit = Q_1(P_1 - ATC_1)$.

As with perfectly competitive firms, monopolies are not guaranteed a profit. If market demand does not allow them to charge a price that covers the cost of production, they will lose money. Figure 11.4 shows the situation of a monopoly that is losing money. Because losses are negative profits, the monopolist's losses are obtained in the same way as that of profits, by subtracting total cost from total revenue. The maximum price the monopolist can charge for its profit maximizing (or, in this case, loss minimizing) output level is P_1, which yields total revenues of P_1Q_1 or $0P_1bQ_1$. Total cost is higher: $0ATC_1aQ_1$.

Thus the monopolist's loss is equal to the shaded rectangular area bounded by $P_1 ATC_1 ab$.

Of course, in the long run, when the monopoly firm is able to extricate itself from its fixed costs, it will shut down.

Why does the monopolist not shut down? Because it follows the same rule as the perfect competitor. Both will continue to produce as long as price exceeds average variable cost – that is, as long as production will help to defray fixed costs. In figure 11.4, average fixed cost is equal to the difference between average total cost, ATC_1, and average variable cost, AVC_1 – or the vertical distance *ac*. Total fixed cost is therefore *ac* times Q_1, or the area bounded by $AVC_1\ ATC_1\ ac$. Because the firm will suffer a greater loss if it shuts down ($AVC_1 ATC_1 ac$) than if it operates ($P_1 ATC_1 ab$), it chooses to operate and minimize its losses.

Production over the long run

In the long run the profitable monopolistic firm follows the same production rule as in the short run: it equates long-run revenue with long-run marginal cost. In figure 11.5(a), for instance, the firm produces quantity Q_a and sells it for price P_a. (As always, profits are found by comparing the price with the long-run average cost. As an exercise, shade in the profit areas in figure 11.5.) Unlike the perfect competitor, the monopoly firm does not end up producing at the lowest point on the long-run average cost curve. With no competition, the monopolistic firm has no need to minimize average total cost. By restricting output, it can charge a higher price and earn greater profits than it can by taking full advantage of economies of scale.

Monopolists *may* produce at the low point of the long-run average cost curve, but only when the marginal revenue curve happens to intersect the long-run marginal and average cost curves at the exact same point (see figure 11.5(b)). In this case the monopolist produces quantity Q_b and sells it at a price of P_b, earning substantial monopoly profits in the process.

If the demand is great enough, the monopolist will actually produce in the range of diseconomies of scale (see figure 11.5(c)). How can the monopolist continue to exist when its price and costs of production are so high? Because barriers to entry protect it from competition. If barriers did not exist, other firms would certainly enter the market and force the monopolistic firm to lower its price. The net effect of competition would be to induce the monopolist to cut back on production, reducing average production costs in the process.

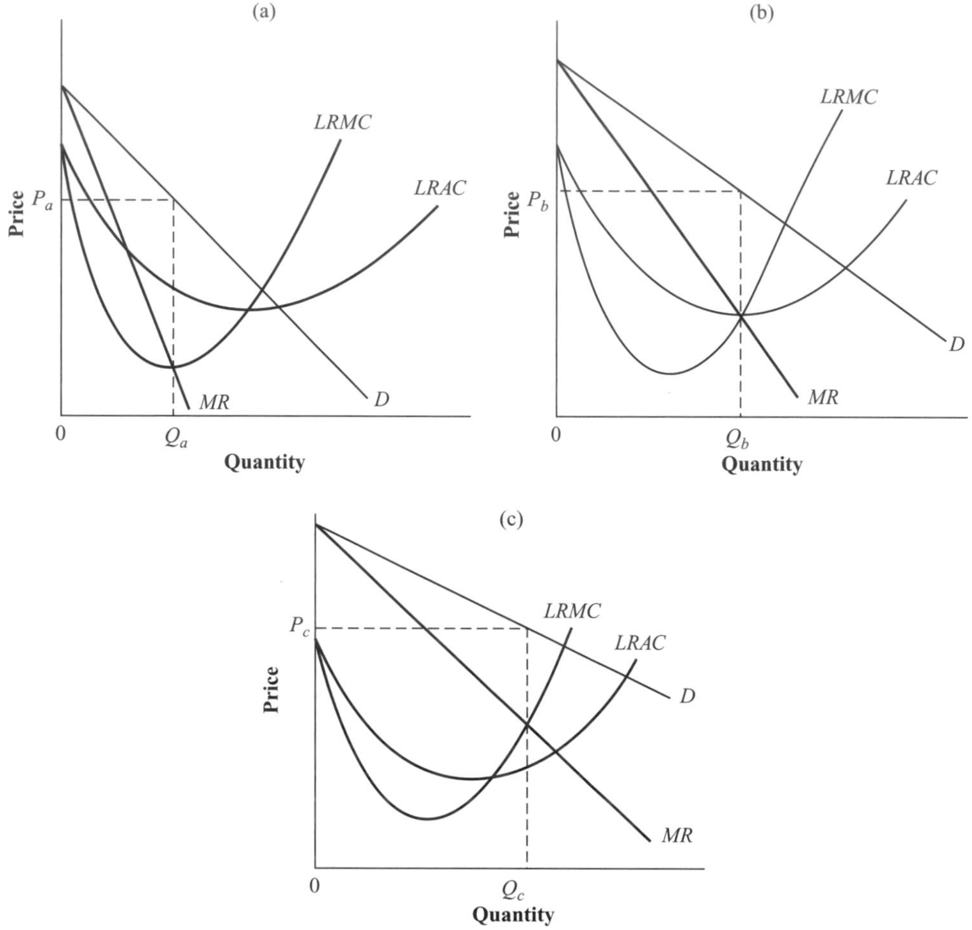

Figure 11.5 Monopolistic production over the long run

In the long run, the monopolist will produce at the intersection of the marginal revenue and long-run marginal cost curves (panel (a)). In contrast to the perfect competitor, the monopolist does not have to minimize long-run average cost by expanding its scale of operation. It can make more profit by restricting production to Q_a and charging price P_a. In panel (b), the monopolist produces at the low point of the long-run average cost curve only because that happens to be the point at which marginal cost and marginal revenue curves intersect. In panel (c), the monopolist produces on a scale beyond the low point of its long-run average cost curve because demand is high enough to justify the cost. In each case, the monopolist charges a price higher than its long-run marginal cost.

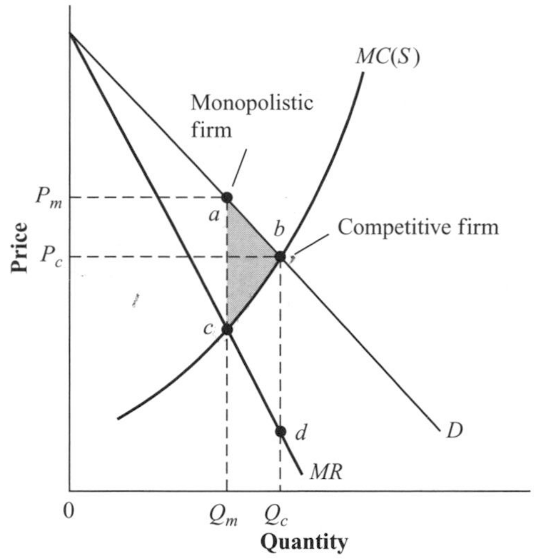

Figure 11.6 The comparative efficiency of monopoly and competition
Firms in a competitive market will tend to produce at point *b*, the intersection of the marginal cost and demand curves (with the price, or marginal benefit given by the height of the demand curve). Monopolists will tend to produce at point *c*, the intersection of marginal cost and marginal revenue, and to charge the highest price the market will bear: P_m. In a competitive market, therefore, the price will tend to be lower (P_c) and the quantity produced greater (Q_c) than in a monopolistic market. The inefficiency of monopoly is shown by the shaded triangular area *abc*, the amount by which the benefits of producing $Q_c - Q_m$ units (shown by the demand curve) exceed their marginal cost of production.

Monopolists cannot exist without barriers to market entry. If other firms had access to the market, the monopolist's profit would be its own undoing – for that profit will be competed away if others can enter the market.

The comparative inefficiency of monopoly

Chapter 10 concluded that in a perfectly competitive market, firms tend to produce at the intersection of the market supply and demand curves. That point (*b* in figure 11.6) is the most efficient production level, in the sense that the marginal benefit to the consumer of the last unit produced equals its marginal cost to the producer. All units whose marginal benefits exceed their marginal costs are produced. All possible net benefits to the consumer have been extracted from production.

For each unit between Q_m and Q_c, the marginal benefits to the consumer, as illustrated by the market demand curve, are greater than the marginal costs of production. These are net benefits that consumers would like to have, but that are not delivered by the monopolistic firm interested in maximizing profits rather than consumer welfare. The resources that are not used in the production of the monopoly good must either remain idle or be used in a less valuable line of production. (Remember, the cost of doing anything is the value of the next-best alternative forgone.) In this sense, economists say that resources are *misallocated by monopoly.* Too few resources are used in the monopolistic industry, and too many elsewhere.

On balance, then, the inefficiency of monopoly consists of the benefits lost minus the cost not incurred when output is restricted. When compared to the outcome under perfect competition, monopoly price is too high and output too low. In figure 11.6, the gross benefit to consumers of $Q_c - Q_m$ units is equal to the area under the demand curve, or $Q_m abQ_c$. The cost of those additional units is equal to the area under the marginal cost curve, or $Q_m cbQ_c$. Therefore the net benefit of the units not produced is equal to the shaded triangular area *abc.* This area represents the inefficiency of monopoly, sometimes called the "dead-weight welfare loss" of monopoly. To put it another way, area *abc* represents the gain in consumer welfare that could be achieved by dissolving the monopoly and expanding production from Q_m to Q_c. This area helps explain why consumers prefer Q_c and producers prefer Q_m. Figure 11.7(a) shows the additional benefits that consumers would receive from $Q_c - Q_m$ units, the area under the demand curve, $Q_m abQ_c$. The additional money that consumers must pay producers for $Q_c - Q_m$ units, shown by the area under the marginal revenue curve, is a much smaller amount: only $Q_m cdQ_c$. That is, the additional benefits of $Q_c - Q_m$ units exceed the cost to consumers by the area *abdc.* Consumers obviously gain from an increase in production.

Yet for virtually the same reason, the monopolistic firm is not interested in providing $Q_c - Q_m$ units. It must incur an additional cost equal to the area $Q_m cbQ_c$ (figure 11.7(b)), while it can expect to receive only $Q_m cbQ_c$ in additional revenues. The extra cost incurred by expanding production from Q_m to Q_c exceeds the additional revenue acquired by the shaded area *cbd.* Thus, an increase in production will reduce the monopolistic firm's profits (or increase its losses). Notice that consumers would gain more from an increase in production than the monopolist would lose. The shaded area in figure 11.7(a) is larger than the shaded area in figure 11.7(b). The difference is the triangular area *abc.* It is worth pointing out that if transactions costs were zero, or low enough, consumers would benefit by getting together and agreeing to "bribe"

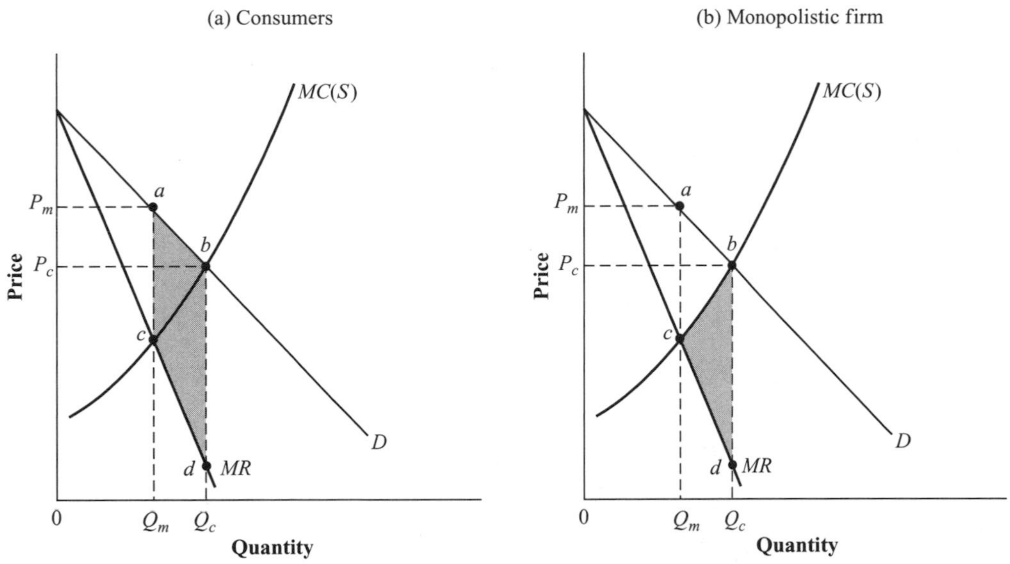

Figure 11.7 The costs and benefits of expanded production
If the monopolist expands production from Q_m to Q_c in panel (a), consumers will receive additional benefits equal to the area bounded by $Q_m abQ_c$. They will pay an amount equal to the area $Q_m cdQ_c$ for those benefits, leaving a net benefit equal to the shaded area *abdc*. To expand production, the monopoly must incur additional production costs equal to the area $Q_m cbQ_c$ in panel (b). It gains additional revenues equal to the area $Q_m cdQ_c$, leaving a net loss equal to the shaded area *cbd*. Thus, expanded production helps the consumer but hurts the monopolist.

the monopolist to expand output to the competitive level. But the cost of this type of collective action by consumers is too high to make it an attractive option for consumers.

Price discrimination

A grocery store may advertise that it will sell one can of beans for \$0.30, but two cans for \$0.55. Is the store trying to give customers a break? Sometimes, this kind of pricing may simply mean that the cost of producing additional cans decreases as more are sold. At other times, it may indicate that customer's demand curves for beans are downward sloping and the store can make more profits by offering customers a volume discount than by selling beans at a constant price. In other words, the store may be exploiting its *limited monopoly power*.

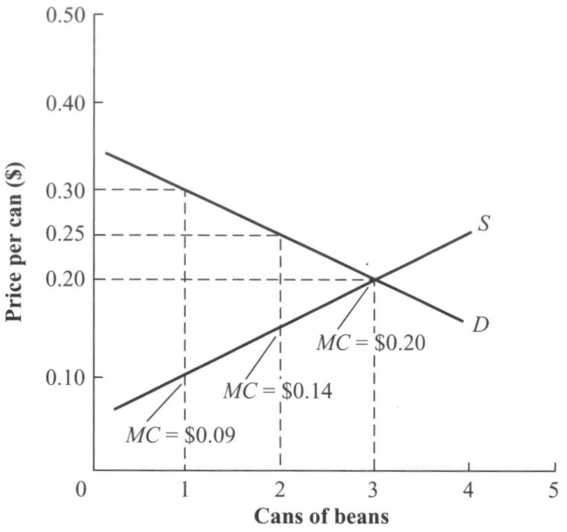

Figure 11.8 Price discrimination

By offering customers one can of beans for $0.30, two cans for $0.55, and three cans for $0.75, a grocery store collects more revenues than if it offers three cans for $0.20 each. In either case, the consumer buys three cans. But by making the special offer, the store earns $0.15 more in revenues per customer.

Consider figure 11.8. Suppose the demand curve represents your demand for beans and the supply curve represents the store's marginal cost of producing and offering the beans for sale. If the store charges the same price for each can of beans, it will have to offer them at $0.25 each to induce you to buy two. Its total revenues will be $0.50. As figure 11.8 shows, however, you are actually willing to pay more for the first can – $0.30 – than for the second. If the store offers one can for $0.30 and two cans for $0.55, you will still buy two cans, but its revenues from the sale will be $0.55 instead of $0.50.[4] Similarly, to entice you to buy three cans, the store need only offer to sell one for $0.30, two for $0.55, and three for $0.75, and its profits will rise further.[5] The deal does not change the marginal cost of providing each can, which is below the selling price for the first two units and equal to the selling price for the third. The marginal cost of the first can is $0.09; the second, $0.14; and the third, $0.20. The total

[4] Notice that if the store had tried to sell all its beans at $0.30, you would have bought only one can, and the store would have forgone the opportunity to make a profit on the second can. Why?

[5] Notice that if the cans had been priced at $0.25 apiece, you would have purchased only two cans.

cost of the three cans to the store is $0.43, regardless of how the cans are priced.

A firm can discriminate in this way only as long as its customers do not resell what they buy for a higher price – and as long as other firms are unable to move into the market and challenge its monopoly power by lowering the price. In the case of canned beans, resale is not very practical. The person who buys three cans has little incentive to seek out someone who is willing to pay $0.25 instead of $0.20 for one can. The profit potential – $0.54 – is just not great enough to bother with. Suppose a car dealer has two identical automobiles carrying a book price of $5,000 each, however. If the dealer offered one car for $5,000 and two cars for $9,000, many people would be willing to buy the two cars selling for $9,000 and spend the time needed to find a buyer for one of them at $4,500. The $500 gain they stand to make would compensate them for their time and effort in searching out a resale. In Part II of this chapter on Management applications, we shall discuss creative ways in which firms can prevent consumers in the low-price market segment from reselling to consumers in the high-price market segment.

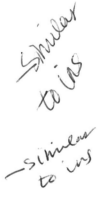

Price discrimination is the practice of varying the price of a given good or service according to how much is bought and who buys it, supposing that marginal costs do not differ across buyers.

Thus, advertised **price discrimination** is much more frequently found in grocery stores than in car dealerships. Car dealers also discriminate with regard to price, however. The salesperson who in casual conversation asks a customer's age, income, place of work, and so forth is actually trying to figure out the customer's demand curve, so as to get as high a price as possible. Similarly, many doctors and lawyers quietly adjust their fees to fit their clients' incomes, using information they obtain from client questionnaires. Whether price discrimination is unadvertised and based on income, as in the case of doctors and car dealers, or advertised and based on volume sold, as in the case of utilities and long-distance phone companies, the important point is that the products or services involved are typically difficult, if not impossible, to resell.

Some monopolies' products are not difficult to resell, and so they cannot engage in price discrimination. For example, copyright law gives the publishers of economics textbooks some monopoly power, but textbooks are easily resold, both through a network of used-book dealers and among students. Thus, although textbook publishers can alter their sales by changing the price, they infrequently engage in price discrimination. Nor do they encourage college bookstores to price-discriminate in their sales to students. The discounts that publishers give bookstores on large sales reflect the cost differences in handling large and small orders, not students' or professors' downward sloping demand curves for books. The same can be said about a host of other products protected by patents and copyrights.

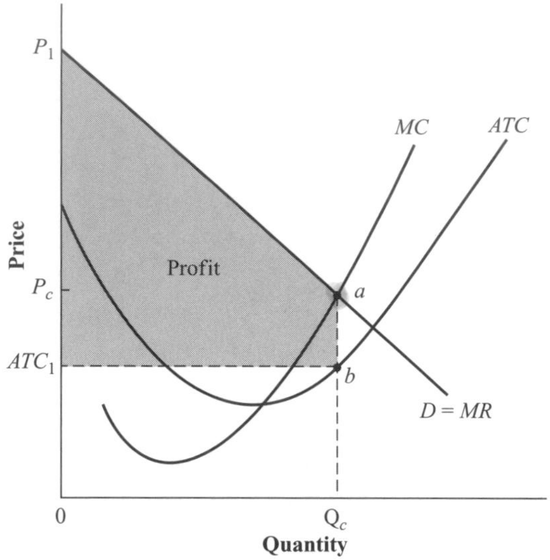

Figure 11.9

Perfect price discrimination

The perfect price-discriminating monopolist will produce at the point where marginal cost and marginal revenue are equal (point *a*). Its output level, Q_c is therefore the same as that achieved under perfect competition. But because the monopolist charges as much as the market will bear for each unit, its profits – the shaded area ATC_1P_1ab – are higher than the competitive firm's.

The monopolist whose production level was shown in figure 11.6 is unable to discriminate among buyers or units bought by each buyer. A monopolist who is able to do so can produce at a higher output level than Q_m and earn greater profits. Just how much greater depends on how free, or "perfect," the monopolist's power to discriminate is.

Perfect price discrimination

> **Perfect price discrimination** is the practice of selling each unit of a given good or service for the maximum possible price.

The monopolist represented in figure 11.9 can charge a different price for each and every unit sold. Theoretically, this firm has the power of **perfect price discrimination** ("perfect" from the standpoint of the *producer*, not the consumer). Under perfect price discrimination, the seller's marginal revenue curve is identical to the seller's demand curve (because the marginal revenue of each unit sold equals the price). This is shown in figure 11.9, where the firm's marginal revenue curve is not separate and distinct from its demand curve, as in figure 11.7. Its demand curve is its marginal revenue curve. If the first unit can be sold for a price of, say, \$20, the marginal revenue from that unit is equal to the price, \$20. If the next unit can be sold for \$19.95, the marginal revenue from that unit is again the same as the price, since selling the second unit doesn't require lowering the price on the first unit; and so on. In short, the seller extracts the *entire consumer surplus.*

As in figure 11.3, the perfect price-discriminating monopolist equates marginal revenue with marginal cost. Equality occurs this time at point *a*, the intersection of the demand curve (now the monopolist's marginal revenue curve) with the marginal cost curve (see figure 11.9). Thus the perfect price discriminating monopolist achieves the same output level as that of the industry involved in perfect competition. In this sense the perfect-price-discriminating firm is an efficient producer. As before, profit is found by subtracting total cost from total revenue. Total revenue here is the area under the demand curve up to the monopolist's output level, or the area bounded by $0P_1aQ_c$. Total cost is the area bounded by $0ATC_1bQ_c$ (found, you may recall, by multiplying average total cost times quantity). Profit is therefore the shaded area above the average total cost line and below the demand curve, bounded by ATC_1P_1ab.

Through price discrimination the monopolist increases profits (compare figure 11.3 with figure 11.9). Consumers also get more of what they want, although not necessarily at the price they want. In the strict economic sense, perfect price discrimination increases the efficiency of a monopolized industry. Consumers would be still better off if they could pay one constant price, P_c, for the quantity Q_c, as they would under perfect competition. This, however, is a choice the price-discriminating monopolist does not allow.

Imperfect price discrimination is the practice of charging a few different prices for different consumption levels or different market segments (based on location, age, income, or some other identifiable characteristic that is unrelated to cost differences).

Discrimination by market segment

Charging a different price for each and every unit sold to each and every buyer is of course improbable, if not impossible. The best that most producers can do is to engage in **imperfect price discrimination** – that is, to charge a few different prices, as did the grocery store that sold beans at different rates. The practice is fairly common. Electric power and telephone companies engage in imperfect price discrimination when they charge different rates for different levels of use, measured in watts or minutes. Universities try to do the same when they charge more for the first course taken than for any additional course. Both practices are examples of multi-part price discrimination. Drugstores price discriminate when they give discounts to senior citizens and students, and theaters price discriminate by charging children less than adults (other than senior citizens). In those cases, discrimination is based on

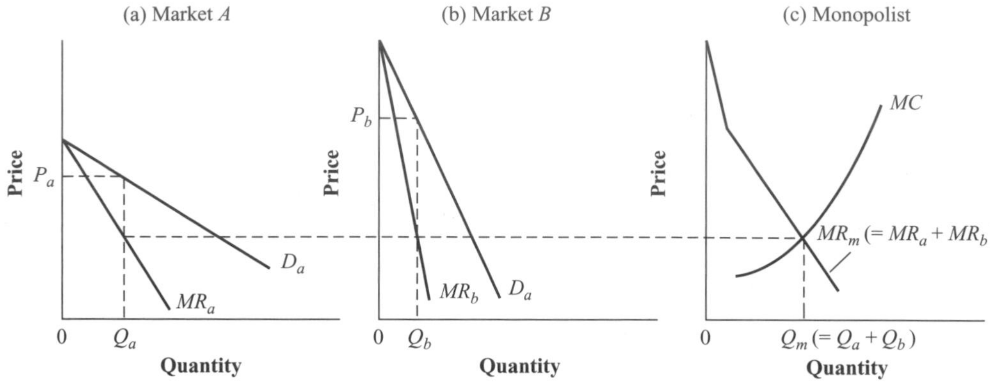

Figure 11.10 Imperfect price discrimination

The monopolist that cannot perfectly price-discriminate may elect to charge a few different prices by segmenting its market. To do so, it divides its market by income, location, or some other factor and finds the demand and marginal revenue curves in each (panels (a) and (b)). Then it adds those marginal revenue curves horizontally to obtain its combined marginal revenue curve for all market segments, MR_m (panel (c)). By equating marginal revenue with marginal cost, it selects its output level, Q_m. Then it divides that quantity between the two market segments by equating the marginal cost of the last unit produced (panel (c)) with marginal revenue in each market (panels (a) and (b)). It sells Q_a in market A and Q_b in market B, and charges different prices in each segment. Generally, the price will be higher in the market segment with the less elastic demand (panel (b)).

market segment – namely, age group. By treating different market segments as having distinctly different demand curves, the firm with monopoly power can charge different prices in each market. (More examples of creative price discrimination will be discussed in Part II of this chapter.)

Figure 11.10 shows how discrimination by market segment works. Two submarkets, each with its own demand curve, are represented in figure 11.10 (a) and (b). Each also has its own marginal revenue curve. To price its product, the firm must first decide on its output level. To do so, it adds its two marginal revenue curves horizontally. The combined marginal revenue curve it obtains is shown in figure 11.10 (c). The firm must then equate this aggregate marginal revenue curve with its marginal cost of production, which is accomplished at the output level Q_m in figure 11.10 (c).

Finally, the firm must divide the resulting output, Q_m, between markets A and B. The division that maximizes the firm's profits is found by equating the marginal revenue in each market (shown in figure 11.10 (a) and (b)) with the marginal cost of the last unit produced (figure 11.10 (c)). That is, the firm equates the marginal cost of producing the last unit of Q_m, (figure 11.10 (c)) with the marginal revenue from the last unit sold in each market segment ($MC = MR_a + MR_b$). For maximum profits, then, output Q_m must be divided into Q_a for market A and Q_b for market B.

Why does selling where $MC = MR_a + MR_b$ result in maximum profit? Suppose that MR_a were greater than MR_b. Then by selling one more unit in market A and one fewer unit in market B, the firm could increase its revenues. Thus the profit maximizing firm can be expected to shift sales to market A from market B until the marginal revenue of the last unit sold in A exactly equals the marginal revenue of the last unit sold in B. And unless the common marginal revenue is equal to the marginal cost, the firm can increase its profit by adjusting output until it is.

Having established the output level for each market segment, the firm will charge whatever price each segment will bear. In market A, quantity Q_a will bring a price of P_a. In market B, quantity Q_b will bring a price of P_b. (Note that the price-discriminating monopolist charges a higher price in a market with the less elastic demand – market B.) To find total profit, add the revenue collected in each market segment (figure 11.10 (a) and (b)) and subtract the total variable cost of production (the area under the marginal cost curve in figure 11.10 (c)) and the fixed cost.

Applications of monopoly theory

Economics is a fascinating course of study because it often leads to counterintuitive conclusions. This is clearly the case with monopoly theory, as we can show by considering several policy issues.

Price controls under monopoly

Market theory suggests that price controls can cause monopolistic firms to increase their output. Figure 11.11 shows the pricing and production of a monopolistic electric utility that is not engaged in price discrimination. Without price controls, the utility will produce Q_m kilowatts and sell them at P_m. If the government declares that price to be too high, it can force the firm to sell at a lower price – for example, P_1. At that price, the firm can sell as many as Q_1 kilowatts. With the price controlled at P_1, the firm's marginal revenue curve for Q_1 units becomes horizontal at $P_1 a$. Every time it sells an additional kilowatt, its total revenues rise by since it doesn't have to lower the price on the previous kilowatts sold. If the price P_1 is set at the point where the demand curve and the

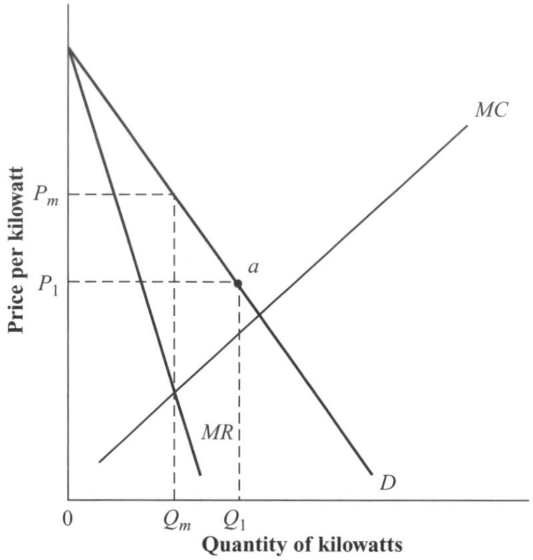

Figure 11.11 The effect of price controls on the monopolistic production decision
In an unregulated market, a monopolistic utility will produce Q_m kilowatts and sell them for P_m. If the firm's price is controlled at P_1, however, its marginal revenue curve will become horizontal at P_1. The firm will produce Q_1 – more than the amount it would normally produce.

MC curve intersect (as it is in figure 11.11) then the profit maximizing monopolist will increase output to the efficient level – where the value consumers place on another unit of output equals the marginal cost of production.

Taxing monopoly profits

Some people claim that the economic profits of monopoly can be taxed with no loss in economic efficiency. By definition, economic profit represents a reward to the resources in a monopolized industry that is greater than is necessary to keep those resources employed where they are. It also represents *a transfer of income*, from consumers to the owners of the monopoly. Therefore a tax extracted solely from the economic profits of monopoly should not affect the distribution of resources and should fall exclusively on monopoly owners – so the argument goes.

The reasoning behind this position is straightforward. This monopoly produces Q_m2, charges P_m1, in figure 11.12, and makes an economic profit equal to the shaded area $ATC_1P_{m1}ab$. Because marginal cost and marginal revenue

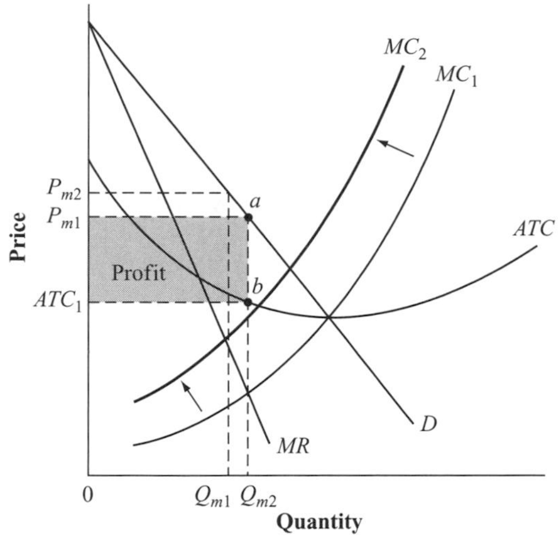

Figure 11.12 Taxing monopoly profits
Theoretically, a tax on the economic profit of monopoly will not be passed on to the consumer – but taxes are levied on book profit, not economic profit. As a result, a tax shifts the first marginal cost curve up, from MC_1 to MC_2, raising the price to the consumer and lowering the production level.

are equal at Q_{m2}, the firm is earning its maximum possible profit. Expansion or contraction of production will not increase its profit. Even if the government were to take away 25, 50, or 90 percent of its economic profit, the firm would not change its production plans or its price (90 percent of the maximum profit is more than 90 percent of a smaller profit). Nor would it raise prices to pass the profits tax on to consumers. The monopolist price–quantity combination, P_{m1} and Q_{m2}, leaves the monopolist with the largest after-tax profit – regardless of the tax rate. There is a practical problem with this, however.

The economic profit shown in figure 11.12 is not the same as the firm's book (or accounting) profit. Book profit tends to exceed economic profit by the sum of the owners' opportunity cost and risk cost. For practical reasons, government must impose its tax on book profit, not economic profit. As a result, the tax falls partly on the legitimate costs of doing business, shifting the firm's marginal cost curve upward, from MC_1 to MC_2 in figure 11.12. The monopolist, in turn, will reduce the quantity produced from Q_{m2} to Q_{m1}, and raise the price from P_{m1} to P_{m2}. Thus, part of the government tax on profits is passed along to consumers as a price increase. Consumers are doubly penalized – first through the monopoly price, which exceeds the competitive price, and second through the surcharge, $P_{m2} - P_{m1}$, added by the profits tax.

Monopolies in "goods" and "bads"

Because monopolies restrict output, raise prices, and misallocate resources, students and policy makers tend to view them as market failures that should be corrected by antitrust action. If a monopolized product or service represents an economic good – something that gives consumers positive utility – restricted sales will necessarily mean a loss in welfare.

Some products and services may, however, be viewed as "bads" by large portions of the citizenry. Drugs, prostitution, contract murder, and pornography may be goods to their buyers, but they represent negative utility to others in the community. Thus monopolies in the production of such goods may be socially desirable. If a drug monopoly attempted to increase its profits by holding the supply of drugs below competitive levels, most citizens would probably consider themselves better off.

The question is not quite that simple, however. A heroin monopoly may restrict the sale of heroin in a given market. Yet because the demand for heroin is highly inelastic (because of drug addiction), higher prices may only increase buyers' expenditures, raising the number of crimes they must commit to support their habit. Paradoxically, then, reducing heroin supplies (for example, because drug enforcement agents in Colombia wipe out a number of producers) could lead to more burglaries, muggings, and bank hold-ups by addicts across the world as the world price of heroin rises and the expenditure of addicts rises (assuming that the demand for heroin is inelastic).

Of course, drugs and other underground services are not normally subject to antitrust action; they are illegal. The analogy may be applied to legal goods and services, such as liquor, however. Given the negative consequences of drinking, as well as religious prohibitions, many people might consider alcoholic beverages an economic "bad". In that case a state long-run liquor monopoly could provide a social service. By restricting liquor sales through monopoly pricing, it would reduce drunk driving, thus limiting the external costs associated with drinking. (The same objective – fewer liquor sales and less drunk driving – could also be accomplished through higher taxes.)

The total cost of monopoly

High prices and restricted production are not the only costs of monopoly. The total social cost of monopoly power is actually greater than is shown by the supply and demand model in figure 11.6. Many firms attempt to achieve the benefits of monopoly power by erecting barriers to entry in their markets.

The resources invested in building barriers are diverted from the production of other goods, which could benefit consumers. The total social cost of monopoly should also include the time and effort that the antitrust Division of the Department of Justice, the Federal Trade Commission (FTC), state attorneys-general, and various harmed private parties devote to thwarting attempts to gain monopoly power and to breaking it up when it is acquired.

Another, more subtle, social cost of monopoly is its *redistributional effect.* Because of monopoly power, consumers pay higher prices than under perfect competition (P_m instead of P_c in figure 11.6). The real purchasing power of consumer incomes is thus decreased, while the incomes of monopoly owners go up. To the extent that monopoly increases the price of a good to consumers and the profits to producers, then, it may redistribute income from lower-income consumers to higher-income entrepreneurs. Many consider this redistributional effect a socially undesirable one.

In addition, when we measure the inefficiency of monopoly by the triangular area *abc* in figure 11.6, we are assuming that demand for the monopolized product and all other goods is unaffected by the redistribution of income from consumers to monopoly owners. This may be a reasonable assumption if the monopolist is a maker of musical toothpicks. It is less reasonable for other monopolies, such as the postal, local telephone, and electric power services. Those firms, which are quite large in relation to the entire economy, can shift the demand for a large number of products, causing further misallocation of resources.

Finally, our analysis has assumed that a monopoly will seek to minimize its cost structure, just as perfect competitors do. That may not be a realistic assumption because the monopolist does not, by definition, face competitive pressure. In addition, if a market is moved from being divided among many producers to one totally controlled by one producer, principal – agent problems (and added costs) can begin to emerge. This is because former principals (owners) in a small competitive firm can be moved to be agents (managers) in a large corporation, a change in function that can cause costs to rise. In the larger firm, as we saw in chapter 10, all agents can have less incentive to work diligently because monitoring can become more difficult. If a monopoly relaxes its attentiveness to costs, the result can be the inefficient employment of resources that is over and above the triangular dead-weight loss area.[6]

[6] There are far more problems with monopoly theory that cannot be covered here, partially because of space limitations and partially because this book is designed to present microeconomic theory as it is taught. For readers interested in a summary of the authors' objections to standard monopoly theory, see (McKenzie 2004).

Durable goods monopoly

If prohibitive barriers to entry protect it, can a monopolist always charge the monopoly price indicated? Ronald Coase wrote a famous article in the 1970s in which he pointed out that even a monopolistic producer of a durable good would charge a competitive price for its product (Coase 1972).

Why? Because no sane person would buy all or any portion of the durable good at a price above the competitive level. He used the example of a monopoly owner of a plot of land. If the owner tried to sell the land all at one time, he would have to lower the price on each parcel until all the land was bought – where the downward sloping demand for land crossed the fixed vertical supply of land – which means that the owner would have to charge the competitive price (where the demand for the land and the supply of the land came together).

You might think that the sole/monopoly owner of land would be able to restrict sales and get more than the competitive price. However, buyers would reason that the monopoly owner would eventually want to sell the remaining land, but that land could be sold only at less than the price the owner is trying to charge for the first few parcels. This means that the buyers would rationally wait to buy until the price came down. This means that the owner would sell nothing at the monopoly price, and would be able to sell the land only at the competitive price.

This analysis works out this way only because the land is *durable*. Monopolies can charge monopoly prices for nondurable goods, and they can do so because they have control over production. This means that one way a monopoly can elevate its price above the competitive level is by somehow making its product less durable, needing replacement. This may explain why many software producers are constantly bringing out new, updated, and upgraded versions of their programs – to make their programs less than durable in the minds of consumers.

The problem firms with monopoly power in a durable good face is that of yielding to the temptation to attract more buyers. It can overcome its own desire (and impatience) to achieve market share by negotiating contracts with buyers that include "most-favored-customer clauses." Such clauses would require the seller to extend to the buyer signing the contract any price concessions given in the future to other buyers. The customer signing the contract can reason that other customers will less likely then get a cost advantage by waiting to buy. The most-favored-customer clause hikes the cost of price concessions to the seller. Hence, buyers can be expected to be more willing to buy at the higher price the seller charges.

The monopoly seller can also rent (or lease) the good for short periods of time. If the rent is lowered to future customers, then the lower rent will shortly have to be extended to other customers renewing their rental contracts, increasing the cost of the price/rent concession and increasing the confidence of buyers that the rent will not be lowered to others.

Still, computer programs must remain, to some degree and for some time, "durable," which ultimately imposes a competitive check on dominant software producers, for example, Microsoft. The Justice Department seems to believe that Microsoft doesn't have competitors. Well, one of Microsoft's biggest competitors is none other than Microsoft itself. Any new version of, say, Windows, must compete head-to-head with the existing stock of old versions, which computer users can continue using at zero price. That very low price on old versions of Windows imposes a check on the prices that Microsoft can charge on any new version.

The Microsoft monopoly

Economists have added to the conditions under which monopoly might be expected to emerge and prosper in recent years with the development of the theory of *networks*, which we have already introduced. As already noted, in 1998 the Justice Department filed an antitrust suit against Microsoft for, among other things, engaging in "predatory" pricing in the Internet browser market. The Justice Department argued that by giving away Internet Explorer, Microsoft was attempting to snuff out a serious market rival in the browser market and a potential competitive threat in the operating system market. The Justice Department also argued that the market dominance Microsoft now enjoys in the operating system market could be equated with monopoly power because of the presumed existence of "high switching costs" and "lock-ins."[7]

Switching costs and lock ins

After people have adopted the operating system, along with the relevant computer hardware, and have learned how to use the accompanying applications, there are presumed costs of switching to other operating systems. To switch, people have to buy a different operating system, and maybe different computer equipment, as well as learn new applications that might require different

[7] One of the authors has written a book on the Microsoft antitrust case in the United States. See McKenzie (2000).

instructions and have a different "look and feel." They might also have to retool and retrain their computer service providers, or switch providers altogether.

Assistant Attorney-General Joel Klein introduced "switching costs" into his argument by first repeating his position that Microsoft was convinced that it could not win the browser war based on the relative merits of Internet Explorer. He then quoted Microsoft's executives, who wrote in an email message that the way to increase Internet Explorer's share of the browser market was by "leveraging our strong share of the desktop": "[I]f they get our technology by default on every desk, then they'll be less inclined to purchase a competitive solution . . ." (Klein *et al* 1998, 38). The Justice Department's chief economist, Franklin Fisher, gave more details in his testimony for the government: "Where network effects are present, a firm that gains a large share of the market, whether through innovation, marketing skill, historical accident, or any other means, *may* thereby gain monopoly power. This is because it will prove increasingly difficult for other firms to persuade customers to buy their products in the presence of a product that is widely used. The firm with a large market share may then be able to charge high prices or slow down innovation without having its business bid away" (Fisher 1998, 15–16), emphasis in the original. Fisher added later, "As a result of scale and network effects, Microsoft's high market share leads to more applications being written for its operating system, which reinforces and increases Microsoft's market share, which in turn leads to still more applications being written for Windows than for other operating systems, and so on" (Fisher 1998, 27).

The government's position on the role of switching costs has been widely adopted in the media. For example, the editors at *The Economist* have summed up the network effects/switching costs/lock-in line of argument very neatly in their retort to Microsoft's supporters:

> The arguments [that suggest that antitrust laws have no relevance for today's information age], plausible as they may seem, are wrong. "Network" effects, in which the value of a product depends on the number of users, occur in many high-tech markets – just as they did in earlier industries such as railways and telephones. These effects hugely increase the risk that one firm may dominate a particular market, probably not forever but certainly for a significant amount of time. True, the products may change, often substantially. But such are the barriers to entry, arising from large installed bases that are locked into a particular technology and from control over distribution, that a dominant firm can still remain entrenched. (*The Economist* 1999)

By suggesting that the operating system market is characterized by network effects that can cause a firm's market share to build on itself, the Justice

Department effectively argued that Microsoft's current market dominance has been a consequence of economic forces outside the company's influence. If Microsoft's market position can be viewed as a product of forces of "nature" – or "technology" – then it might rightfully be deduced that Microsoft has itself achieved virtually nothing, which can mean that the Justice Department, by threatening to force Microsoft to put Netscape's icon on the desktop, is not violating any property rights Microsoft may have justly earned.

One of the real problems with the Justice Department's case is that, contrary to the impression left by all the talk about how network effects build on themselves, network effects don't just happen. They are not a part of "nature" or "technology" in the sense that they exist independently of someone (or some firm) causing them to exist (at least not completely). Network effects are truly brought into existence, or are created, as someone (or some firm) works to build the network, and this is necessarily the case. Someone must think of ways to overcome the initial so-called "chicken-and-egg dilemma" faced by network developers: How does a network firm get customers to buy the product (operating system) when there are no programs, or how does a firm get program developers to write programs when there are no buyers of the product?

Indeed, the operating system buyers and applications must emerge more or less together, and the emergence process must be coordinated, encouraged, and directed by someone (or some firm). And it should be understood that creating the network is likely to be very expensive, because of buyer and developer resistance, and to require a substantial up-front investment on the part of someone (or some firm) – Microsoft, for example – to overcome the resistance.

By arguing that networks are characterized by "high switching costs," the Justice Department is effectively saying that Microsoft's market dominance is protected by an *internal* barrier to entry, which acts like all barriers and restricts entry. Switching costs reduce competition, lower consumer choice, and enable the dominant producer to raise its prices. With high switching costs, the dominant producer doesn't have to worry about its customers switching in response to a higher price, or so the Justice Department argues. Frederick Warren-Bolton, the lead economist for the nineteen state attorneys-general, reasons that computer "users become 'locked in' to a particular operating system," which implies a barrier to entry and expansion for existing competitors. He adds, "The software 'lock-in' phenomenon creates barriers to entry for new PC operating systems to the extent that consumers' estimate of the switching costs are large relative to the perceived incremental value of the new operating system" (Warren-Bolton n.d., 21).

The higher the switching costs, the more the dominant producer can raise its price without fear of the customers switching to existing or new competitors. Indeed, it might be deduced that if switching costs were the only barrier to entry, then a firm's monopoly power – or its ability to raise its price – is limited to the extent of the switching costs. A firm that tries to charge a higher price than that allowed by the switching costs would find that it has left its market open to entry by rivals who would find the consumers perfectly willing to incur the switching costs, because those costs would then be less than the "staying costs" associated with remaining with the established firm that has monopoly power.

By introducing the specter of "lock-ins," the Justice Department sought to suggest that the switching costs are so high that switching is extremely difficult, if not impossible, thus presumably fortifying its argument that Microsoft has substantial monopoly power. Fisher concedes that "market forces and developments can erode monopoly power based solely on network effects," but that is precisely why, according to Fisher, Microsoft felt compelled to engage in "predatory pricing": to wipe out Netscape as a potential alternative software platform for running personal computers (Fisher 1998, 16).

Is that the case? Before people accept the Justice Department's arguments, they need, at least, to pause and ask whether Microsoft's pricing strategy is consistent with the dictate of a market entrenched in network effects. If the economics of networks dictate zero or below-zero prices, then Microsoft's price for its browser is not necessarily "predatory," contrary to what the Justice Department claims.

Perspective The QWERTY Keyboard: A Case of Lock In?

The lock in theory (which suggests that markets are "path dependent," or evolve based on how the initial product was developed) has gained wide support among many academics and policy makers, partially because economic theoreticians and historians have been able to point to two concrete examples of the supposed wrongs of path dependency and lock ins. The classic, widely cited example of path dependency and lock in is the "QWERTY"-style keyboard (the one almost everyone gets with their PCs), which takes its name from the way the keys on the first row of the alphabet keys of most keyboards line up.

According to economic historian Paul David (1985), the arrangement for the keys on this keyboard was first developed in the 1860s for what were then newly invented typewriters, and this arrangement was developed and adopted only because it minimized the prospect for the keys on manual typewriters jamming as their arms moved toward the paper. The original keyboard was, supposedly, adopted by one typewriter manufacturer after the other, not because it was potentially the most productive arrangement of keys, but because it was established as the "standard." Manufacturers became further "locked in" to the QWERTY keyboard when touch-typing was developed in the 1880s and then widely taught thereafter. David writes, "The occurrence of this 'lock in' as early as the mid-1890s does appear to have owed something also to the high costs of software 'conversion' and the resulting *quasi-irreversibility of investments* in specific touch-typing skills" (1985, 335–6, emphasis in the original).

Because of the "lock in" on the key arrangement that was thought to be a "historical accident," the QWERTY key arrangement is now widely used on computer keyboards, but not because QWERTY is better than all potential alternatives. Indeed, according to this view of keyboard history, "competition in the absence of perfect future markets drove the industry permanently into standardization *on the wrong system* – where decentralized decision making subsequently has sufficed to hold it" (1985, 336, emphasis in the original).

According to what has now become (and proven to be) legend, August Dvorak and W. L. Dealey developed a keyboard (referred to as the Dvorak or DSK keyboard) in 1932 that has, according to David, "long held most of the world's records for speed typing" (1985, 332). Moreover, the Navy supposedly showed in experiments that the greater productivity from the Dvorak keyboard could more than cover the cost of the required retraining (1985, 332).

However, the Dvorak keyboard has never gained a toehold in the keyboard market. Why? The advocates of lock ins argue that there are high switching costs for typists who are used to the QWERTY keyboard; they would have to learn another key arrangement. Typewriter manufacturers have never switched to Dvorak because it did not make good business sense, given that they must appeal to the existing typists. Computer keyboard manufacturers adopted the QWERTY key arrangement because they had no other choice, given that all (typewriter) typists, who were potential computer customers, would not buy keyboards with the new key arrangement, in spite of its supposed superiority. The authors of the QWERTY story have imagined that "there are many more QWERTY worlds [in which an inferior standard is adopted by historical accident] lying out there in the past, on the very edges of the modern economic analyst's tidy universe; worlds we do not yet fully perceive or understand, but whose influence, like that of dark stars, extends nonetheless to shape the visible orbits of our contemporary economic affairs" (David 1975, 336).

The implication for the Microsoft case is obvious. If the QWERTY story is true, then it is plausible that the operating systems market might be one of those "dark stars" that has become visible, because tens of millions of computer users are similarly locked into Windows, even though there might be a superior operating system (such as Linux or some combination of Netscape's Navigator and Sun's Java programming language) waiting in the wings to be adopted. However, the superior system doesn't have a chance of making it in the market because each Windows user does not, by herself, have the requisite incentive to make the switch. Unless large numbers of people make the switch more or less together, then any new user may have a technically superior system that has few applications written for it.

Fortunately for consumers and unfortunately for the Justice Department's case, built partially on the theory of path dependency, the QWERTY story is what we have called it, a legend – a good story that has taken on a life of its own but is not grounded in the facts of keyboard history. Economists Stan Liebowitz and Stephen Margolis did what a lot of QWERTY storytellers should have done long ago: They went back and researched the history of keyboards and found that much of the evidence on the supposed superiority of the Dvorak keyboard was from Dvorak's own poorly designed evaluations. Even then, Dvorak's own "evidence was mixed as to whether students, as they progress, retain an advantage when using the Dvorak keyboard because the differences seem to diminish as typing speed increases" (Liebowitz and Margolis 1999, II-30). The claimed benefits from the Navy study are similarly disputable, and other studies found substantial retraining costs, leading Liebowitz and Margolis to conclude that "the claims for the superiority of the Dvorak keyboard are suspect" (1999, II-45).

Even if it were proven that the Dvorak keyboard were superior to the QWERTY keyboard, the future gains from making the switch (in present discounted value terms) must be greater than the current costs incurred before it can be said that the "wrong" keyboard continued in use. If the cost of switching were greater than the gains to be obtained from the switch, switching would constitute a net societal loss (as well as a loss for employers and/or typists). Liebowitz and Margolis argue that although David made provocative claims, he never proved his point.

The Liebowitz/Margolis finding is a plausible one. If a keyboard were substantially more efficient than the established keyboard, it would be hard to see why the new keyboard wouldn't be adopted. Granted, some individual typists might be resistant to making the switch without some outside help. But if the keyboard were substantially superior then, as we pointed out earlier in this chapter, it follows that the manufacturer should have an ample incentive to cover some of the typist's switching costs – through, perhaps, the provision of retraining courses. Companies that hire large numbers of typists, or computer users, would also have an ample incentive to buy the new keyboard. They could prorate the retraining costs over a large number of employees from whom they could garner substantial productivity improvements. Their investment in retraining could be expected to have an immediate upward impact on their company's stock price, given that observant investors would expect the productivity improvement to improve the company's long-term profit stream.[8]

Markets for a variety of goods and services have switching costs, and new entrants have to find ways of overcoming them. New hamburger restaurants have to overcome customer inertia that might be related to the new restaurant's lack of reputation for good food (and clean restrooms) and the small number of convenient locations when getting started. Banks that wish to operate online have the problem of overcoming people's resistance to doing their banking on a computer. But businesses have been creative in finding new ways to cover the switching costs. New restaurants will often cut their prices below cost, or give out coupons that have the same effect. A variety of businesses have offered cash payments or discounts for each online transaction made. In the late 1990s, Chase Bank advertised that it would pay online customers $25 for each of the first five online transactions they made. If there are efficiency improvements to a switch to another product that mean greater profits for new firms, "network externalities" (which

[8] Another similar legend has grown up around how the VHS format for videocassettes tapes and recorders came to dominate the Betamax format, which was supposedly the markedly superior format of the two. The Betamax format may actually be technically superior to the VHS format (we are unwilling to judge), but the VHS format has always had one big advantage over Betamax that counts for more than greater technical attributes: An entire movie could be recorded on a VHS tape, which was not possible on the Betamax. VHS became the adopted format because it better met the needs of the growing home movie rental and sales business (Liebowitz and Margolis 1995).

network effects are sometimes called) may be "external" to buyers, but those network externalities can be "internalized" by entrepreneurial firms. These firms can have ample motivation to make it easy for consumers to switch when a better product is available.

PART II ORGANIZATIONAL ECONOMICS AND MANAGEMENT

Profits from creative pricing

For a monopoly firm to be successful, it has to choose the "right" price, given the demand (or specifics of the inverse relationship between price and quantity) for its products. Saying that a firm with monopoly power must choose the "right" price is easier than actually choosing it. The maxim offers little practical guidance to managers confronting the complex problem of keeping the firm as profitable as possible. For example, managers can never be completely sure what the demand for their company's product is. Moreover, a company's demand is not given from on high; it can be influenced by management decisions. Good managers can increase the demand for their products by improving their quality, increasing the credibility with which they are advertised and their quality is ensured, and establishing a reputation for honesty and fair dealing. But demands are also affected by other factors, and many of them are beyond managers' abilities to control or predict.

So managers, no matter how good they are, will always have to make guesses about the demands for their products – about how much they can sell of their products at different qualities and prices. There are statistical techniques for estimating product demand (a discussion of which goes beyond the purpose of this book) and, though these techniques are never perfect, they can help managers move from making *mere* guesses to making *educated* guesses about their demands.

In the real world, however, there is plenty of scope for creative pricing. And such creativity can be very profitable. We have discussed throughout this book how firms compete on many margins. It is common to think of firms competing by producing better products and charging lower prices. And certainly the long-run consequence of firms struggling against each other for more consumer dollars is better products at lower prices. But in this chapter we concentrate on how managers can increase the profitability of their firms by producing more creative pricing strategies. Managers can often do as much or more for their firms, and their careers, by coming up with better pricing approaches as by coming up with better products. Of course, as is true of everything else in business, managers must have the proper incentives to be creative in their pricing strategies.

Price discrimination in practice

Real-world managers are not limited to charging only one price for a product. As those business people who fly frequently know, there are several different prices being charged for a coach seat (or a first-class seat) on most flights. For example, passengers who book their flights weeks in advance often pay less (often several hundred dollars less) than passengers who book their flights days before their departure. By charging different prices for the same product, firms are able to earn higher profits than are possible with only one price. Some creativity can be exercised by carefully announcing prices.

There is a joke based on the pricing creativity of optometrists. When a customer inquires about the price of a pair of glasses, the optometrist answers, "Seventy five dollars," and then pays close attention to the customer's expression. If he doesn't cringe, the optometrist quickly adds, "for the lenses." If the customer still doesn't cringe, the optometrist adds, "for each one" (Friedman 1996, 134).

Hardback and paperback books

There are better – perhaps less devious – ways of charging different prices than suggested by the above joke. Book publishers cannot differentiate between every potential buyer of a book and charge each a different price. But they can separate the market into two broad categories of buyers – those who are most impatient to read the latest novel by, say, John Grisham, and those who want to read it but do not mind waiting a while. If publishers can separate (or *segment*) these groups, they can charge a different price to each group. But how can they do that? One method is to sell hardback and paperback editions of the same book. Hardback books are issued first and are sold at a significantly higher price than the paperback edition ("significantly" meaning higher than the cost difference in producing a hardback and paperback edition) that will not be made available until six months or more later. In this way, the seller charges those customers who are less sensitive to price (or who have an *inelastic* demand) a higher price than those who are sensitive to price (or who have an *elastic* demand). Those customers with inelastic demands reveal their impatience by their willingness to pay the high hardback price. There is no problem with arbitrage in this case because those who pay the low price do so long after the high-price customers have made their purchases.

Price discrimination through time

Sellers don't always have to package their products differently, as publishers do, to distinguish between buyers who have inelastic demands and those who have elastic demands. Just after new electronic gadgets (USB disks, for example) are introduced, their prices can be quite high, only to fall later. Many chalk up their falling prices to reductions in production costs, which may very well be true. However, we suggest an additional explanation for why computer prices fall with the age of the models: the sellers are using *time* to segment their markets, charging those who are eager to get the new models a high price and charging those who are less eager, as evidenced by their willingness to wait, a lower price.

After-Christmas sales

Department stores almost always have storewide sales after Christmas. Commonly, the after-Christmas sales are explained by the stores' wanting to get rid of excess inventories. There is a measure of truth to that explanation; stores cannot always judge correctly what will sell in December. However, it is also clear that shoppers have more inelastic demands before Christmas than they have after Christmas. Hence, the stores are often doing nothing more than segmenting their markets. They plan to hold after-Christmas sales and order accordingly. They are not making less money by the sales. They are, in truth, making more money because they can charge different prices in the two time periods, attracting customers they otherwise would have lost without lowering the price charged to the consumers who are less price sensitive.

Coupons

Grocery stores and the suppliers of the products that grocery stores sell have also found a way of getting customers to reveal how sensitive they are to price, which allows those who are less price sensitive to be charged more than those who are more price sensitive. In almost every daily newspaper you can find coupons (in the Sunday paper, pages of coupons) that, if you cut them out and take them to the designated store, allow you to save 25¢s, 50¢s, and sometimes more, on a host of different products. No coupons, no savings.

Those who go to the trouble of cutting out these coupons and carrying them to the store are revealing themselves as being relatively price sensitive. So when you fail to present coupons as you go through the checkout line at your local supermarket, you are telling the cashier that you are not very sensitive to price, that your demand is relatively inelastic. The cashier responds by charging you more for the same products than he or she charged the coupon-laden customer ahead of you. The problem of arbitrage is handled by limiting the amount a customer can buy of a product. Moreover, not many people are tempted by the opportunity to buy one bottle of shampoo for 50¢ off and then trying to sell it for 25¢ off to someone in the parking lot who doesn't have a shampoo coupon. The cost of creating the secondary market for something as cheap as shampoo is surely greater than the price differential, especially when few units can be bought at the favorable price and sold at a higher price.

Theater pricing

Sometimes a firm can profit by charging different prices to different customers without appearing to do so. This can be accomplished by putting the same price on two products that are consumed together by some customers but not by others. Consider the owner of a theater who realizes that some customers are willing to pay more to go to the movies than others are. Obviously, the owner would like to charge these customers more. But the owner has no way of determining who the price insensitive customers are when they are paying for their tickets. So how does the manager charge the price insensitive customers more without losing the remaining customers?

There is a way that we have all observed but probably didn't think of as an example of price discrimination. Assume that the theater owner believes that those customers who are willing to pay the most to watch a movie are generally (not always, but generally) the ones who most enjoy snacking while watching. If this assumption is correct (and we will argue in a moment that it probably is), the theater owner can take advantage of the inelastic demand of the enthusiastic movie watchers by charging a moderate price for the tickets to the movie and high prices for the snacks sold in the theater lobby. By keeping the ticket prices moderate, the customers with a high demand elasticity for the movie will still buy a ticket because they are not going to do much snacking anyway. Although the low-elasticity demanders will surely complain about the high prices on all the snacks they eat, they still consider the total cost of their movie experience acceptable because they were willing to pay more for their ticket than they were charged.

If it were not generally true that those who are willing to pay the most to watch a movie also enjoy snacking the most, then it is unlikely that we would observe such high prices for snacks at the movies.[9] For example, assume that the opposite were true, that those who were not willing to pay much to watch a movie were the ones who enjoy snacking the most when watching the movie. If this were the case, the owner of the theater would find that charging moderate prices for the tickets and high prices for the snacks was not a very profitable strategy. Because the avid movie watchers are not snacking much, they would be willing to pay more than the moderate price to get into the theater. And because the other customers care more about snacking than seeing the movie, they would see little advantage in paying the moderate price for the movie when the snacks are so expensive. In this case, the most profitable pricing strategy would be high ticket prices and low snack prices. The enthusiastic movie watchers would still come despite the high ticket price.. And the snackers would now be willing to pay the high ticket prices for the opportunity to eat lots of cheap snacks.[10] The fact that we do not see such pricing in theaters suggests that, at least for most consumers, our assumption is correct.

Prices and functionality

Any time a firm can identify consumers on the basis of their sensitivity to price, it is in a position to vary its price for different groups in ways that increase the incentive for consumers to purchase its product. The advantage of being able to separate customers willing to pay high prices (again, who have relatively inelastic demands) from those who are more price sensitive (who have relatively elastic demands) is so great in some cases that it explains why

[9] It should be noted that some economists have argued that the high price for snacks at the movie theaters reflect the higher cost of supplying them in movie theaters than in food stores. As opposed to food stores, the snack shop in a movie theater is open for only a limited amount of time during the day. So, as the argument goes, the overhead cost is spread over less time and fewer sales (Lott and Roberts 1991). We do not quarrel with this reasoning, but we also believe that creative price discrimination provides at least part of the explanation for the high price of movie snacks.

[10] Determining the exact combination of prices that maximizes profits depends on the relative differences in demand for the two types of customers. If, for example, the avid movie fans were willing to pay a tremendously high price to see the movie, and snackers couldn't care less about the movie but went into frenzies of delight at the mere thought of a Snickers bar, then the best pricing policy would be an extremely high ticket price with extremely low-priced (maybe free) snacks. In this case, the theater owner would probably stipulate that snack customers would have to eat the snacks in the theater to prevent them from filling large take-away sacks with popcorn and candy bars. This would be no different than the policy of all-you-can-eat restaurants.

some firms will incur costs to reduce the quality of their products so that they can sell them for less.

For example, soon after Intel introduced the 486 microprocessor, it renamed it the 486DX and introduced a modified version, which it named the 486SX. The modification was done by disabling the internal math coprocessor in the original 486, a modification that was costly and reduced the performance of the 486SX. Intel then, in 1991, sold the 486SX for less – $333 as compared to $588 for the 486DX. Why would Intel spend money to damage a microprocessor and then sell it for less?[11] The answer is to separate out those customers who are willing to pay a lot for a microprocessor from those whose demand is more sensitive to price. Intel could sell the 486DX to the former at a price that would have driven the latter to competitive firms. Yet it managed to keep the business of the latter customers by lowering the price to them without worrying that this would drive the price down for the high-end customers. There was no way for the lower-price consumers to buy the lower-price product and sell it to the high-end consumers, because its performance had been reduced.

Similarly, when IBM introduced its LaserPrinter E at the start of the 1990s, it set the price lower than the price for its earlier model, the LaserPrinter. The LaserPrinter E was almost exactly the same as the LaserPrinter except that the former printed at a rate of five pages per minute whereas the latter printed at a rate of ten pages per minute. Why was the LaserPrinter E slower? Because IBM went to the expense of adding chips that had no purpose other than to cause the printer to pause so that it printed slower. Why did IBM go to extra expense to produce a lower-performance printer? Again, to separate its market between consumers with inelastic demand from those with elastic demand so that less could be charged to the latter without having to reduce the high price to the former.

Golf balls

One of the authors, Lee, enjoys playing golf. He buys brand-name golf balls that have been labeled with XXX to indicate that they have some flaw and are sold at a discount. Many good golfers are willing to pay the extra money for regular brand-name balls, which supposedly travel farther than the XXX balls. Lee, on the other hand, sees no advantage in hitting his balls further into the woods.

[11] It was cheaper to make the 486DX and then reduce its quality than it was to produce the lower-quality 486SX directly. This example, the following one, and several other cases of firms intentionally reducing the quality of their products are found in Deneckere and McAfee (1996).

And anyway, he is not convinced that there really is any difference between the regular high-priced balls and the XXX balls, except that the manufacturer went to the extra expense of adding the XXXs. Although we have no documentation, we suspect that golf manufacturers simply put XXXs on a certain percentage of their balls so that they can separate their market between golfers like Lee, who are quite sensitive to price, and golfers who, because they have a reasonable idea where their balls are going, are not very sensitive to price.

Unadvertised prices

Another technique firms can use to separate price sensitive consumers from those who are less sensitive is to make unadvertised price discounts available, but only to those who search them out and ask for them. Obviously, those who go to the trouble to find out about a discount, and then ask for it, are more concerned over price than those who do not. This approach to identifying customers for discounts on long-distance calls was used by AT&T in the 1990s. According to an article in the *Wall Street Journal*, AT&T responded to Sprint Corporation's 10 cents a minute for calls during weekends and evening hours by offering a flat rate of 15 cents anytime, a plan they called One Rate (Keller 1997). But AT&T really had two rates, one of which they did not advertise. The unadvertised rate, available only to those who asked for it, allowed AT&T customers to call around the clock for 10¢ a minute. As reported in the article, "AT&T customers can get dime-a-minute calling 24 hours a day, seven days a week – if they know to ask for it. That is the hardest part, for AT&T has been uncharacteristically quiet about the new offer. The company hasn't advertised the 10-cent rate; it hasn't sent out press releases heralding the latest effort to one-up the folks at Sprint" (Keller 1997, B1). The old adage about oiling only what squeaks certainly applies in this case. (We suspect that AT&T was not all that pleased with the *Wall Street Journal* simply because the publicity reduced AT&T's ability to segment its market by reducing the "search costs" that would otherwise have faced AT&T customers who read the *Wall Street Journal*.)

The more competition and price rivalry in an industry, the smaller the gain a firm in that industry can realize from charging different customers different prices. Even relatively price insensitive customers will be bid away by rival firms when price competition is intense, if one firm tries to charge those customers much more than it does its more price sensitive customers. Nevertheless, the more the firms in an industry can segment their market so as to buffer the price competition between them, the greater the scope for creative pricing strategies that can increase profits, a point to which we can now turn.

Cartel cheating

Firms in an industry can simply get together and agree not to compete consumers away from each other by reducing prices. This will allow them to keep prices, and their collective profits, higher than will be possible if all firms make a futile attempt to increase their market shares by charging lower prices. But there are two problems with this approach to reducing price competition. The first problem is that any agreement to restrict competition *can be* illegal, and firms and their managers who enter into such an agreement risk harsh antitrust penalties.

As discussed in Part I of this chapter, the second problem is that even if agreements to restrict price competition were not illegal, they would still be almost impossible to maintain. Members of industry cartels that have agreed to set prices above competitive levels are in another Prisoner's Dilemma. Although they are collectively better off when everyone abides by the agreement, each individual sees the advantage in reducing price below the agreed-upon amount. If other firms maintain the high price, then the firm that cheats on the agreement can capture lots of additional business with a relatively small decrease in its price. On the other hand, if the other firms are expected to cheat on the agreement, it would be foolish for a firm to continue with the high price because that firm would find most of its customers competed away. Only if all firms ignore Prisoner's Dilemma temptations, and take the risk of making the cooperative choice, can cartel price agreements be maintained. Not surprisingly, such agreements tend to break down.

Meet-the-competition pricing policy

There are pricing policies that can, however, moderate price competition between rival firms without the need for a cooperative agreement. Ironically, these strategies reduce competition, when competition motivates most firms in an industry to implement them when the first firm does.

Consider a pricing policy that would seem to favor your customers with protection against high prices but which is a smart policy because it makes higher prices possible. The strategy is quite simple, involving an unqualified pledge: "We will meet or beat any competitor's price." A so-called "meet-the-competition" pricing policy tells your customers that if a competitor offers them a lower price, you will match it. This policy is commonly advertised as "guaranteed lowest prices," by retail stores such as Circuit City and many others. To implement such a policy, you inform your customers that if they can find a lower price on a product within thirty days of purchasing it from you, they will receive a rebate equal to the difference. While such price guarantees appear to benefit customers, if they are offered by all, or most, competitors they allow all firms to charge higher prices. How can this be?

One straightforward explanation is that the price assurance gives customers some insurance and, because of that added attribute, increases their demand. The greater demand leads to higher prices.

But there is another explanation based on an equally simple proposition: If you want to charge higher prices, there is an obvious advantage in discouraging competitors from reducing their prices to compete your customers away. This is exactly what a meet-the-competition policy does. Your competitors are probably not all that anxious, in any event, to initiate a price-cutting campaign. Attempting to compete customers away from another firm through lower prices is always costly. If successful, the new business is likely to be worth less to the price-cutting firm than to the firm that loses it because the price is now lower. Also, existing customers will want to receive a lower price as well, which can eat deeper into any profits that might have otherwise been possible. Of course, if a price-cutting campaign aimed at capturing new customers fails to do so, the campaign is all cost and no benefit. So if your competitors know that you have a meet-the-competition agreement with your customers, they will have less, and likely nothing, to gain from trying to attract those customers by cutting their prices.

A meet-the-competition pricing policy can be good not only for your profits but also for your competitors. By allowing you to keep your prices higher than otherwise, your meet-the-competition policy gives your competitors more room to keep their prices high. This suggests that, as opposed to most competitive strategies that become less effective when mimicked by the competition, your meet-the-competition policy becomes more profitable when other firms in the industry implement the same policy. Just as your competitors are better off when you do not have to worry about the competitive consequences of keeping your prices high, so are you better off when your competitors are relieved of the same worry (Brandenburger and Nalebuff 1996, chapter 6).

Most-favored-customer pricing policy

A related pricing policy is to offer some of your customers the status of most-favored-customer, which entitles them to the best price offered to anyone else. (Again, this policy must be checked with lawyers, given that some such policies in some circumstances might be construed as illegal.) If you lower your price to any customer under this policy you are obligated to lower it for all of your most-favored customers. As with the meet-the-competition policy, what at first glance appears to favor your customers can actually give the advantage to you. A most-favored customer policy increases the cost of trying to compete customers away from rival firms by reducing price. And when one firm has such a policy, its reluctance to engage in price competition makes it easy for other firms to keep their prices high. So, as with meet-the-competition policy, the advantage that firms realize from a most-favored-customer policy is greater when all the firms in an industry have such a policy (Brandenburger and Nalebuff 1996).

If the idea that a policy of being quick to reduce prices for your customers can result in higher prices seems counterproductive, you are in good company. In their book *Coopetition*, Brandenburger and Nalebuff (1996) relate how Congress, in an effort to control the cost of campaigning, required television broadcasters to make candidates for Congress most-favored customers. In the 1971 Federal Election Campaign Act, Congress made it against the law for television broadcasters to lower their rates for an ad to any commercial customer without also lowering their rates to candidates. The result was that television broadcasters found it extremely costly to reduce rates for anyone, and the networks made more money than ever before. Politicians had the satisfaction of knowing that they did not pay more for airtime than anyone else, but they likely ended up paying more (as commercial advertisers did also) than they would have without forcing the broadcasters to implement a most-favored-customer pricing policy.

Congress made a similar mistake in 1990, when it attempted to reduce government reimbursements for drugs by stipulating that Medicaid would pay only 88 percent of the average wholesale price for branded drugs – or, if lower, the lowest price granted anyone in the retail trade drug business. But instead of lowering prices, the law actually raised them. By making itself a most-favored customer, the federal government gave the drug companies a strong incentive to raise prices for everyone. And indeed that is exactly what happened, according to a study cited by Brandenburger and Nalebuff (1996, 104–5) that found that prices on branded drugs increased from 5 to 9 percent because of the 1990 rule changes. The advantage the government may have realized by keeping its price down to 88 percent of the average wholesale price was probably more than offset (it was often receiving a discount anyway) by the higher average prices. And certainly nonMedicare patients ended up paying higher drug prices.

Advantages of frequent-flyer programs

Another pricing strategy that allows the firms in an industry to reduce price competition has become increasingly common since the 1980s. This strategy involves a creative way of identifying those customers who are most likely to buy from your firm anyway and then lowering the price they pay. At first glance, such a strategy would appear counterproductive. Why would you lower the price for those who are likely to buy from you? The answer is that by making what appear to be price concessions to your most loyal customers, you can end up charging them higher prices.

A good way of explaining this seemingly paradoxical possibility is by considering the frequent-flyer programs that almost all airlines now have. These programs are commonly thought of as motivated by each airline's desire to compete business away from other airlines by effectively lowering ticket prices. No doubt this was the primary motivation when, in 1981, American Airlines introduced its AAdvantage program. The rapidity with which other airlines countered with their own frequent-flyer programs suggests intense competition between the airlines. But intended or not, the proliferation of these programs has had the effect of reducing the direct price competition between airlines and, as a result, may be allowing them to maintain higher prices than would otherwise have been possible. An airline's frequent-flyer program reduces the effective, if not the explicit, price it charges its most loyal customers, and reinforces their loyalty.[12] By increasing the motivation of an airline's frequent flyers to concentrate their flying on that airline, it decreases the payoff other airlines can expect from trying to compete those customers away with fare reductions. This allows the airline with the frequent-flyer program to keep its explicit fares higher than if other airlines were aggressively reducing theirs.[13] This decreased motivation to engage in price competition becomes mutually reinforcing as more airlines implement frequent-flyer programs.

From the perspective of each airline, it would be nice to be able to compete away customers from other airlines with lower fares, but collectively the airlines are better off by reducing this ability. And this is exactly what the spread of frequent-flyer programs has done, to some degree, by segmenting the airline

[12] Even when a person is a member of more than one frequent-flyer program, there is an advantage in concentrating patronage on one airline because the programs are designed to increase benefits more than proportionally with accumulated mileage.

[13] You may be thinking that keeping the explicit fares higher does not mean much if, because of the frequent-flyer programs, the actual fares to customers are lower because of the value of their mileage awards. But one of the big advantages of frequent-flyer programs is that they do not cost the airlines as much as they benefit the customer. Flights are seldom completely sold out, so most of the free flights awarded end up filling seats that are unsold. Of course, frequent flyers do use their mileage for flights they would have otherwise paid for. But by allowing frequent flyers to transfer their mileage awards to others, say a spouse or child, the airlines increase the probability that those who would not have otherwise bought a ticket will use those awards.

market. There is now less competitive advantage in reducing airfares, and less competitive disadvantage in raising them. The effect has been to *reduce the elasticity of demand* facing each airline, which allows all airlines to charge higher prices than would otherwise be sustainable.[14]

A pricing strategy similar to frequent-flyer programs has begun to spread in the automobile industry. In 1992, General Motors joined with MasterCard and issued the GM credit card. By using the GM card a consumer earns a credit equal to 5 percent of their charges that can be applied to the purchase or lease of any new GM vehicle (with a limit of $500 per year up to $3,500 for any one purchase). Although not all major auto makers have followed the GM lead, several have. And the more auto makers that join in, the better for the car industry in general. Just like frequent-flyer programs, automobile credit cards allow a car company to focus implicit price reductions on its most loyal customers. An individual is not likely to be using a GM credit card unless she is planning on buying a GM car or truck. As the number of car companies that issue their own credit card increases, the more the auto market will become segmented and the less the advantage from price competition. Again, a pricing policy that allows a firm to target its more loyal customers and favor them with price cuts can have the effect of increasing the prices being charged.

THE BOTTOM LINE

The key takeaways from chapter 11 are the following:

(1) A monopolist maximizes its profits where its marginal cost equals its marginal revenue.
(2) The monopolist faces a downward sloping demand curve, which means that its marginal revenue curve is also downward sloping but underneath its demand curve.
(3) The consequences of monopoly are higher prices and lower production levels than are possible under perfect competition.

[14] Another way of seeing the advantage of segmenting the market is by recognizing that reducing the elasticity of demand facing each airline also reduces the marginal revenue of each airline and brings it more in line with the marginal revenue for the industry. The closer each firm's marginal revenue is to the industry's marginal revenue, the closer the independent pricing decisions of each firm in the industry will come to maximizing the firms' collective profits.

(4) Monopoly power can also result in inefficiency in production, for the monopolistic firm does not produce to the point at which its marginal cost equals the consumer's marginal benefit – the product's price. Consumers might prefer that more resources be used in the production of a monopolized good and might be willing to pay a price that exceeds the cost of production for additional units of the good. However, the profit maximizing monopolist stops short of that point.

(5) In order for a monopolist to be able to garner monopoly profits, it must be protected, to one extent or another, with costly entry barriers.

(6) The source of a monopolist's ability to charge an above-competitive price comes from its ability to materially change market supply through its own production decisions.

(7) A monopolist's ability to hike its price and profits is restricted by the elasticity of its demand, which is influenced by the closeness of substitutes and the costs of entry facing other producers.

(8) A monopolist can increase its profit and increase market efficiency through various and creative forms of price discrimination. However, its ability to price-discriminate is constrained by the potential consumers have for reselling the good.

(9) The new "network economy" often turns much economic analysis on its head. This is especially true when it comes to discussions of "monopoly power." A market for a network good might tend toward a single seller. At the same time, that single seller may have no, or very little, ability to profit from charging a high price, mainly because of the network effect.

(10) A firm selling a network good will have to charge a very low (possibly a zero, or negative price) initially to attract enough market share to achieve a critical level of network value. And once a firm producing a network good achieves a significant market share, it runs the risk of providing an opening for new firms if it attempts to profit by following the textbook monopoly practice of reducing output (which would reduce its network value) and charging a high price.

REVIEW QUESTIONS

(1) Many magazines offer multi-year subscriptions at a lower rate than one-year subscriptions. Explain the logic of such a scheme. Why might it be considered evidence of monopoly power on the part of the magazines?

(2) Explain why a monopolized industry will tend to produce less than a competitive industry.

(3) "If a monopoly retains its market power over the long run, it must be protected by barriers to entry." Explain. List some restrictions on the mobility of resources that might help a firm retain monopoly power.

(4) Why, from an economic point of view, should antitrust action not be taken against all monopolies?

(5) Given the information in the table below, complete the monopolist's marginal cost and marginal revenue schedules. Graph the demand, marginal cost, and marginal revenue curves, and find the profit maximizing point of production. Assuming that this monopolistic firm faces fixed costs of $10 and must charge the same price for all units sold, how much profit does it make?

Quantity produced and sold	Price ($)	Total variable cost ($)	Marginal cost ($)	Marginal revenue ($)
1	12	5		
2	11	9		
3	10	14		
4	9	20		
5	8	28		
6	7	38		

(6) On the graph developed for question 5, identify the output and profits of a monopolist capable of perfect price discrimination.

(7) Suppose a monopoly (not the one in question 5 – make up your own numbers) that is capable of imperfect price discrimination divides its market into two segments. Graph the demands for these two market segments ((a) and (b)). In a third graph (c), draw the monopolist's combined marginal revenue curve. Then, using the monopolist's marginal cost curve that you draw into (c), determine the monopolist's profit maximizing output level. Indicate the quantity and price of the product sold in each market segment.

(8) If buyers of the "network firm's" product fear that a "network firm" will become a true monopolist in the future, what does that fear do to the firm's current pricing policies?

(9) How can antitrust enforcement in a market for a network good harm consumers?

Appendix: marginal revenue curve: a graphical derivation

In chapter 11, we drew the relationship between a monopolist demand and marginal revenues curves. In this appendix, we develop more of the details of how that relationship can be derived. Demand curves can be *linear* or *nonlinear*. After we have learned how to derive the *MR* curve for the linear demand curve, we can readily adapt the procedure to derive the *MR* curve for the nonlinear demand curve.

Linear demand

The graphic derivation of the *MR* curve corresponding to a linear demand curve is easy to present. From our examination of marginal revenue in an earlier chapter, we know that

$$MR = P\left(1 - \frac{1}{E}\right)$$

where P is the price and E is the absolute value of the price elasticity of demand. Because the price elasticity of demand is infinite at the point of intersection of the demand curve and the vertical price axis, we know that $1/E = 0$ at the vertical intercept and $MR = P$.

We have now established one point on the *MR* curve. Because the *MR* curve for a linear demand curve is also linear,[15] we need to determine only one additional point to construct the *MR* curve. The second point can easily be determined by setting the above equation equal to 0 and solving for E, which gives us

$$P\left(1 - \frac{1}{E}\right) = 0$$

$$1 - \frac{1}{E} = 0$$

$$E = 1$$

Thus, when $MR = 0$, $E = 1$. Recall from chapter 7 that the price elasticity of demand is equal to 1 at the midpoint of a linear demand curve. The point on the horizontal axis corresponding to $E = 1$ on the demand curve will be one-half the distance between the origin and the horizontal intersection of the demand curve. Because $MR = 0$ when

[15] This result can be shown with the aid of calculus. Given the linear demand curve

$$P = a - bQ$$

Total revenue is

$$TR = PQ = (a - bQ)Q = aQ - bQ^2$$

And marginal revenue is

$$\frac{dTR}{dQ} = a - 2bQ$$

Thus, the *MR* curve is linear, intersects the vertical axis at a (the demand curve's intercept), and has an absolute slope two times that of the demand curve.

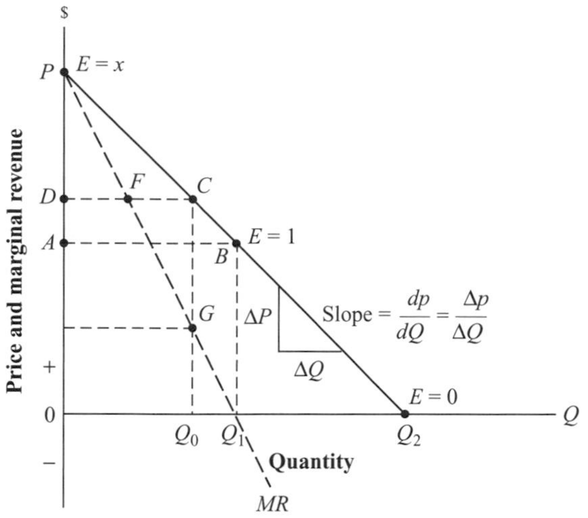

Figure 11A.1 Construction of the linear marginal revenue curve
The marginal revenue curve always starts at the intersection of the vertical axis and any demand curve. However, for a linear demand curve, the marginal revenue curve must slope downward under the demand curve, splitting the horizontal distance between the vertical axis and every point on the demand curve. The marginal revenue curve must cut the horizontal axis at the point below the middle of the linear demand curve, or where the elasticity coefficient equals one.

$E = 1$, the second point on the *MR* curve will lie half the distance between the origin and the horizontal intercept of the demand curve.

Our conclusions concerning the shape and the location of the *MR* curve are illustrated in figure 11.12 (p. 447) The linear demand curve intersects the vertical price axis at point *P*, and this point is also the vertical intercept of the *MR* curve, halfway down the demand curve, $E = 1$ at point *B*, which corresponds to Q_1 on the horizontal axis. Point Q_1, in turn, is midway between the origin and Q_2, which is the horizontal intercept of the demand curve. The *MR* curve is the dashed line connecting point *P* and Q_1 in figure 11A.1.

Since the *MR* curve and the demand curve have the same vertical intercept and the horizontal intercept of the *MR* curve is half that of the demand curve, it follows that the slope of the *MR* curve will be twice the slope of the demand curve.[16]

The fact that the slope of the *MR* curve is twice the slope of the demand curve provides us with an alternative method for graphically determining the marginal revenue at any level of output. To illustrate this method, suppose that we wish to determine *MR* at

[16] From figure 11 A.1, we know that the slope of the demand curve is P/Q_2 and the slope of the *MR* curve is P/Q_1. Because $Q_1 = 1/2\ Q_2$, the slope of the *MR* curve is therefore $P/1/2\ Q_2$ or $2P/Q_2$, which is twice the slope of the demand curve. See also n. 15.

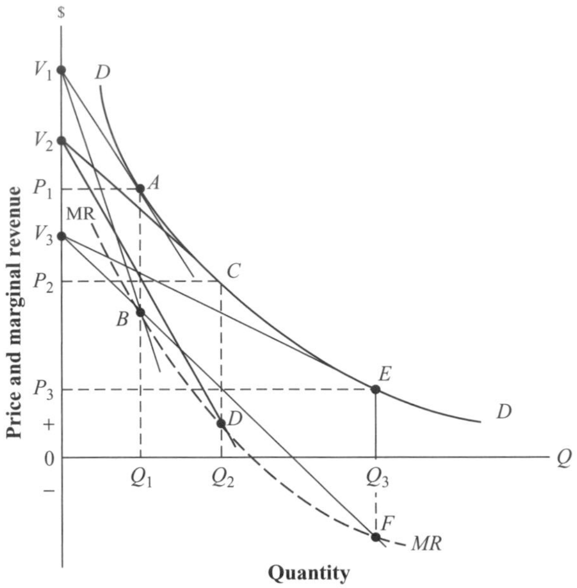

Figure 11A.2 Construction of the nonlinear marginal revenue curve

The marginal revenue curve for a nonlinear demand curve is obtained by imagining linear demand curves tangent to every point on the nonlinear demand curve and finding the midpoint between the vertical axis and the imagined linear demand curves.

output Q_0, which corresponds to point *C* on the demand curve in figure 11A.1. We accomplish this simply by drawing a horizontal line from point *C* to point *D* on the vertical axis. Bisecting the line *DC* gives us point *F*. A straight line drawn from the vertical intercept through point *F* has exactly twice the slope of the demand curve and is therefore the *MR* curve. The intersection of the *MR* curve with the dashed line CQ_0 at point *G* gives us the value of the marginal revenue (read off the horizontal axis) corresponding to point *C*. Although this technique is somewhat laborious, it is useful in graphing the *MR* curve corresponding to a nonlinear demand curve.

Nonlinear demand

When the demand curve is nonlinear, such as curve *DD* in figure 11A.2, the *MR* curve is constructed using a variation of the technique we have just demonstrated. Essentially, we determine the marginal revenues corresponding to several points on the demand curve and then connect these points with a smooth curve to obtain the *MR* curve.

A line originating on the vertical axis at point V_1 is drawn tangent to point *A* on the demand curve in figure 11A.2. If we assume that this tangent line represents a linear demand curve, then the marginal revenue of this demand curve at point *A* is identical to the marginal revenue of the nonlinear demand curve at point *A*, because the slopes of the two demand curves are equal at point *A* and have the same corresponding price P_1 and quantity Q_1. Therefore, to determine the marginal revenue graphically, we simply draw a straight line from V_1 that bisects line P_1A. This line intersects line AQ_1 at point *B*, giving us the marginal revenue that corresponds to point *A* on the demand curve.

Point *B* is the only point on the *MR* curve associated with the nonlinear demand curve *DD*. To construct this *MR* curve, we must determine the marginal revenues that correspond to additional points on curve *DD*. Points *D* and *F* on the *MR* curve are determined for points *C* and *E* on curve *DD* by repeating the steps we followed to locate point *B*. The construction lines required to obtain points *D* and *F* are drawn in figure 11A.2, and you should verify that these points have been correctly determined.

After a sufficient number of points on the *MR* curve have been located, a smooth curve drawn through these points is the graphically constructed *MR* curve associated with the nonlinear demand curve. Figure 11A.2 shows that this *MR* curve is also non-linear and lies below the demand curve.

CHAPTER

12

Firm strategy under imperfectly competitive market conditions

Differences in tastes, desires, incomes and locations of buyers, and differences in the use which they wish to make of commodities all indicate the need for variety and the necessity of substituting for the concept of a "competitive ideal," an ideal involving both monopoly and competition. **Edward Chamberlin**

We have so far considered two distinctly different market structures: *perfect competition* (characterized by producers that cannot influence price at all because of extreme competition) and *pure monopoly* (in which there is only one producer of a product with no close substitutes and whose market is protected by prohibitively high barriers to entry).

Needless to say, most markets are not well described by either of those theoretical structures. Even in the short run, producers typically compete with several or many other producers of similar, but not identical, products. General Motors Corporation competes with Ford Motor Company and a number of foreign producers. McDonald's Corporation competes with Burger King Corporation, Carl's Jr., and any number of other burger franchises, as well as with Pizza Hut, Popeye's Fried Chicken, and Taco Bell.

In the long run, all these firms must compete with new companies that surmount the imperfect barriers to entry into their markets. In short, most companies competing in the imperfect markets can cause producers to be more efficient in their use of resources than under pure monopoly, although less efficient than in perfect competition.

One word of caution, however: The study of so-called "real-world" market structures can be frustrating. Although models may incorporate more or less realistic assumptions about the behavior of real-world firms, the theories developed from them are sometimes conjectural. Real-world markets are imperfect, complex phenomena that often do not lend themselves to hard-and-fast conclusions. This is because decision makers' decisions are so often *mutually interdependent.* That is, each decision maker's decisions depend on what other market participants do, or can be expected to do. Their behavior becomes something of a series of strategic games they play with one another, with each person's moves dependent upon how competitors can be expected to react.

Accordingly, the imperfect, real-world market structures of monopolistic competition and oligopoly developed in this chapter require that we view market movements often as a series of interdependent actions and reactions as is so often the case in games, in which outcomes are sometimes difficult to predict. Nevertheless, key insights can be developed, especially when considering how corporate takeover forces can make imperfect markets less imperfect, or more efficient.

PART I THEORY AND PUBLIC POLICY APPLICATIONS

Monopolistic competition

As we have noted in our study of demand, the greater the number and variety of substitutes for a good, the greater the elasticity of demand for that good – that is, the more consumers will respond to a change in price. By definition, a monopolistically competitive market such as the fast-food industry produces a number of different products, most of which can substitute for each other. If Burger Bippy raises its prices, consumers can move to another restaurant that offers similar food and service. Because of some combination of consumer ignorance, preference for Big Bippy burgers, and the power of habit, however, Burger Bippy is unlikely to lose all its customers by raising its prices. It has some *monopoly power.* Therefore, it can charge slightly more than the ideal competitive price, determined by the intersection of the marginal cost and demand curves. Burger Bippy cannot raise its prices very much, however, without substantially reducing its sales.

The degree to which monopolistically competitive prices can stray from the competitive ideal depends on:

- the number of other competitors
- the ease with which existing competitors can expand their businesses to accommodate new customers (the cost of expansion)
- the ease with which new firms can enter the market (the cost of entry)

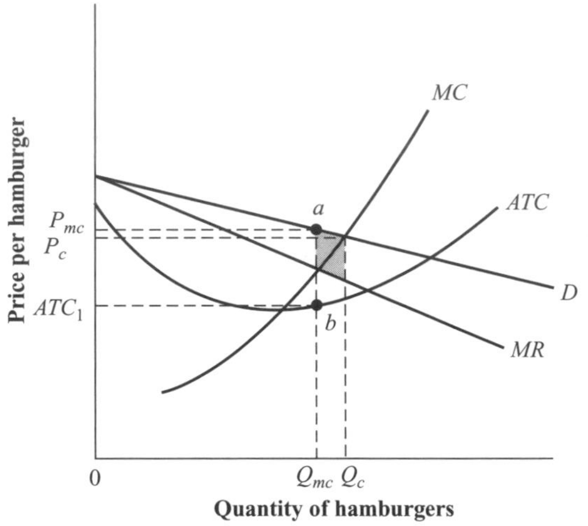

Figure 12.1 Monopolistic competition in the short run
As do all profit maximizing firms, the monopolistic competitor will equate marginal revenue with marginal cost. It will produce Q_{mc} units and charge price P_{mc}, only slightly higher than the price under perfect competition. The monopolistic competitor makes a short-run economic profit equal to the area $ATC_1P_{mc}ab$. The inefficiency of its slightly restricted production level is represented by the shaded area.

- the ability of firms to differentiate their products, by location or by either real or imagined characteristics (the cost differentiation)
- public awareness of price differences (the cost of gaining information on price differences).

Given even limited competition, the firm should face a relatively elastic demand curve – certainly more elastic than the monopolist's.

Monopolistic competition in the short run

In the short run, a monopolistically competitive firm may deviate little from the price–quantity combination produced under perfect competition. The demand curve for fast-food hamburgers in figure 12.1 is highly, although not perfectly, elastic. Following the same rule as the perfect competitor and the pure monopolist, the monopolistically competitive burger maker produces where $MC = MR$. Because the firm's demand curve slopes downward, its marginal revenue curve slopes downward, too, like the pure monopolist's. The firm maximizes profits at Q_{mc} and charges P_{mc}, a price only slightly higher than the price that would be achieved under perfect competition (P_c).[1] The quantity sold with monopolistic competition is also only slightly below the quantity that would be sold under perfect competition, Q_c. Market inefficiency, indicated by the shaded area, is not excessive.

The firm's short-run profits may be slight or substantial, depending on demand for its product and the number of producers in the market. In our example, profit is the area bounded by $ATC_1 P_{mc}ab$, found by subtracting total cost ($0ATC_1 bQ_{mc}$) from total revenues ($0P_{mc}aQ_{mc}$), as with monopolies.

Monopolistic competition in the long run

Because surmounting the barriers to entry into monopolistic competition is not costly, short-run profits will attract other producers into the market. When the market is divided up among more competitors, the individual firm's demand curve will shift downward, reflecting each competitor's smaller market share. As a result, the marginal revenue curve will shift downward as well. The demand curve will also become more elastic, reflecting the greater number of potential substitutes in the market. (These changes are shown in figure 12.2.) The results of the increased competition are as follows:

- The quantity produced falls from Q_{mc2} to Q_{mc1}
- The price falls from P_{mc2} to P_{mc1}.

Profits are eliminated when the price no longer exceeds the firm's average total cost. (As long as economic profit exists, new firms will continue to enter the market. Eventually the price will fall enough to eliminate economic profit.)[2]

Notice that the firm is not producing and pricing its product at the minimum of its average total cost curve, as the perfect competitor would (nor did it in the short run).[3] In this sense, the firm is producing below capacity, by $Q_m - Q_{mc2}$ units.

In terms of price and quantity produced, monopolistic competition can never be as efficient as perfect competition. Perfectly competitive firms obtain

[1] Remember, the perfect competitor faces a horizontal, or perfectly elastic, demand curve, which is also its price and marginal revenue curve. It produces at the intersection of the marginal cost and marginal revenue curves, which is where marginal cost equals price.

[2] The monopolistic competitor will still have an incentive to stay in business, however. It is economic profit, not book profit, that falls to zero. Book profit will still be large enough to cover the opportunity cost of capital plus the risk cost of doing business.

[3] The perfect competitor produces at the minimum of the average total cost curve because its demand curve is horizontal – and therefore the demand curve's point of tangency with the average total cost curve is the low point of that curve.

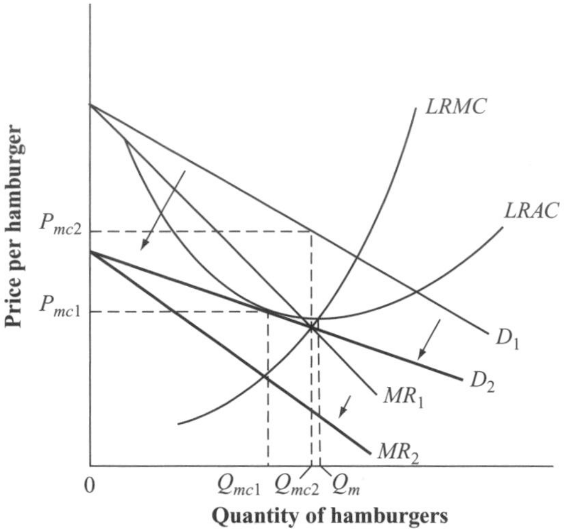

Figure 12.2 Monopolistic competition in the long run

In the long run, firms seeking profits will enter the monopolistically competitive market, shifting the monopolistic competitor's demand curve down from D_1 to D_2 and making it more elastic. Equilibrium will be achieved when the firm's demand curve becomes tangent to the downward sloping portion of the firm's long-run average cost curve Q_m. At that point, price (shown by the demand curve) no longer exceeds average total cost; the firm is making zero economic profit. Unlike the perfect competitor, this firm is not producing at the minimum of the long-run average total cost curve Q_m. In that sense, it is underproducing, by $Q_m - Q_{mc2}$ units. This underproduction is also reflected in the fact that the price is greater than the marginal revenue.

their results partly because all producers are producing the same product. Consumers can choose from a great many suppliers, but they have no product options. In a monopolistically competitive market, on the other hand, consumers must buy from a limited number of producers, but they can choose from a variety of slightly different products. For example, the pen market offers consumers a choice between felt-tipped, fountain, and ballpoint pens of many different styles. This variety in goods comes at a price – the long-run price is above the minimum of the average total cost curve, as illustrated in figure 12.2.

Oligopoly

In a market dominated by a few producers, into which entry is difficult – that is, in an oligopoly – the demand curve facing an individual competitor will be less elastic than the monopolistic competitor's demand curve (see figure 12.3). If General Electric Company raises its price for light bulbs, consumers will have

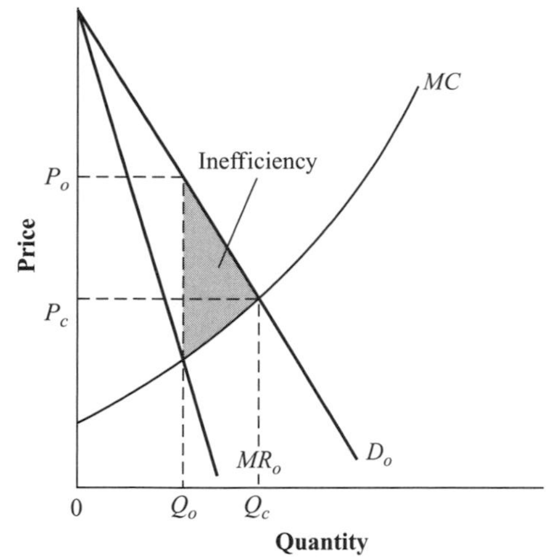

Figure 12.3 The oligopolist as monopolist
With fewer competitors than the monopolistic competitor deals with, the oligopolist faces a less elastic demand curve, D_o. Each oligopolist can afford to produce significantly less (Q_o) and to charge significantly more P_o than the perfect competitor, who produces Q_c, at a price of P_c. The shaded area representing inefficiency is larger than that of a monopolistic competitor.

few alternative sources of supply. A price increase is less likely to drive away customers than it would under monopolistic competition, and the price–quantity combination achieved by the company will probably be further removed from the competitive ideal. In figure 12.3, the oligopolist produces only Q_o units for a relatively high price of P_o, compared with the perfect competitor's price–quantity combination of Q_cP_c. The shaded area representing inefficiency is fairly large.

Exactly how the oligopolist chooses a price is not completely clear. We will examine a few of the major theories proposed. Because each oligopolist is a major factor in the market, oligopolists' pricing decisions are *mutually interdependent.* The price one producer asks significantly affects the others' sales. Hence when one oligopolistic firm lowers its price, all the others can be expected to lower theirs, to prevent erosion of their market shares. The oligopolist may have to second-guess other producers' pricing policies – how they will react to a change in price, and what that might mean for its own policy. In fact, oligopolistic pricing decisions resemble moves in a chess game. The thinking may be so complicated that no one can predict what will happen. Thus, theories of oligopolistic price determination tend to be confined almost exclusively to the short run. (In the long run, virtually anything can happen.)

The oligopolist as monopolist

Given the complexity of the pricing problem, the oligopolistic firm – particularly if it is the dominant firm in the market – may simply decide to behave like a monopolist (because it does have some monopoly power). As does a monopolist, Burger Bippy may simply equate marginal cost with marginal revenue (see figure 12.3) and produce Q_o units for price P_c. Here the oligopolist's price is significantly above the competitive price level, P_c, but not as high as the price charged by a pure monopolist. (If the oligopolist were a pure monopoly, it would not have to fear a loss of business to other producers because of a change in price.) Inefficiency in this market is slightly greater than in a monopolistically competitive market – see the shaded triangular area of figure 12.3.

The oligopolist as price leader

Alternatively, oligopolists may look to others for leadership in determining prices. One producer may assume price leadership because it has the lowest costs of production; the others will have to follow its lead or be underpriced and run out of the market. The producer that dominates industry sales may assume leadership. Figure 12.4 depicts a situation in which all the firms are relatively small and of equal size, except for one large producer. The small firms' collective marginal cost curve (minus the large producer's) is shown in figure 12.4(a), along with the market demand curve, D_m. The dominant producer's marginal cost curve, MC_d, is shown in figure 12.4(b).

The dominant producer can see from figure 12.4(a) that at a price of P_1, the smaller producers will supply the entire market for the product, say, steel. At P_1, the quantity demanded, Q_2, is exactly what the smaller producers are willing to offer. At P_1 or above, therefore, the dominant producer will sell nothing. At prices below P_1, however, the total quantity demanded exceeds the total quantity supplied by the smaller producers. For example, at a price of P_d, the total quantity demanded in figure 12.4(a) is Q_3, whereas the total quantity supplied is Q_1. Therefore the dominant producer will conclude that at price P_d, it can sell the difference, $Q_3 - Q_1$. For that matter, at every price below P_1, it can sell the difference between the quantity supplied by the smaller producers and the quantity demanded by the market.

As the price falls below P_1, the gap between supply and demand expands, so the dominant producer can sell larger and larger quantities. If these gaps between quantity demanded and supplied are plotted on another graph, they will form the dominant producer's demand curve, D_d (figure 12.4(b)). After it has devised its demand curve, the dominant producer can develop its

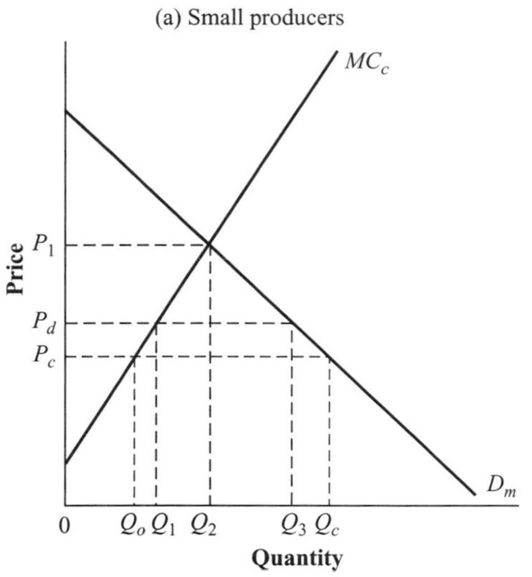

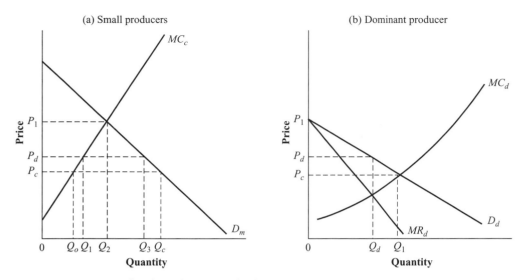

Figure 12.4 The oligopolist as price leader

The dominant producer who acts as a price leader will attempt to undercut the market price established by small producers (panel (a)). At price P_1 the small producers will supply the demand of the entire market, Q_2. At a lower price – P_d or P_c – the market will demand more than the small producers can supply. In panel (b), the dominant firm determines its demand curve by plotting the quantity it can sell at each price in panel (a). Then it determines its profit maximizing output level, Q_d, by equating marginal cost with marginal revenue. It charges the highest price the market will bear for that quantity, P_d, forcing the market price down to P_d in panel (a). The dominant producer sells $Q_3 - Q_1$ units, and the smaller producers supply the rest.

accompanying marginal revenue curve, MR_d, also shown in figure 12.4(b). Using its marginal cost curve, MC_d, and its marginal revenue curve, it establishes its profit maximizing output level and price, Q_d and P_d.

The dominant producer knows that it can charge price P_d for quantity Q_d, because that price–quantity combination (and all others on curve D_d) represents a shortage not supplied by small producers at a particular price in figure 12.4(a). Q_d, as noted earlier, is the difference between the quantity demanded and the quantity supplied at price P_d. So, the dominant producer picks its price, P_d, and the smaller producers must follow.[4] If they try to charge a higher price, they will not sell all they want to sell.

[4] Consider market equilibrium with and without the dominant producer. In the absence of the dominant producer, the market price will be P_1, the equilibrium price for a market composed of only the smaller producers. The dominant producer adds quantity Q_d, which causes the price to fall, forcing the smaller producers to cut back production to Q_1 in figure 12.4(a).

The oligopolist in the long run

In an oligopolistic market, new competitors face significant barriers to entry. Firms in oligopolistic industries can therefore retain their short-run positions much longer than can monopolistically competitive firms.

Oligopoly is normally associated with such industries as the automobile, cigarette, and steel markets, which include some extremely large corporations. In those industries, the financial resources required to establish production on a competitive scale may comprise a formidable barrier to entry. One cannot conclude that all new competition is blocked in an oligopoly, however. Many of the best examples of oligopolies are found in local markets – for instance, drugstores, stereo shops, and lumber stores – in which one, two, or at most a few competitors exist, even though the financial barriers to entry can easily be overcome. Even in the national market, where the financial requirements for entry may be substantial, some large firms have the financial capacity to overcome barriers to entry. If firms in the electric light bulb market exploit their short-run profit opportunities by restricting production and raising prices, outside firms such as General Motors Corporation can move into the light bulb market and make a profit. In recent years, General Motors has in fact moved into the market for electronics and robotics.

While oligopoly power is a cause for concern, the basis for competition is the relative ability of firms to enter a market where profits can be made – not the absolute size of the firms in the industry. The small regional markets of a century ago, isolated by lack of transportation and communication, were perhaps less competitive than today's markets, even if today's firms are larger in an absolute sense. In the nineteenth century, the cost of moving into a faraway market effectively protected many local businesses from the threat of new competition.

A **cartel** is an organization of independent producers intent on thwarting competition among themselves through the joint regulation of market shares, production levels, and prices.

Cartels: incentives to collude and to cheat

In either a monopolistically competitive market or an oligopolistic market, firms may attempt to improve their profits by restricting output and raising their market price. In other words, they may agree to behave as though they were a *unified monopoly*, an arrangement called a **cartel**. The principal purpose of these producers' anticompetitive efforts is to raise their prices and profits above competitive levels. In fact, however, a cartel is not a single, unified monopoly, and cartel members can find it very costly to behave as though they were.

The size of monopoly profits provides a real incentive for competitors to collude – to conspire secretly to fix prices, production levels, and market shares. After they have reduced market supply and raised the price, however, each has an incentive to chisel on the agreement. The individual competitor will be tempted to cut prices in order to expand sales and profits. After all, if competitors are willing to collude for the purpose of improving their own welfare, they will probably also be willing to chisel on cartel rules to enhance their welfare further. The incentive to chisel can eventually cause the cartel to collapse. If a cartel works for long, it is usually because some form of external cost, such as the threat of violence, is imposed on chiselers.[5]

A **duopoly** is an oligopolistic market shared by only two firms.

Although a small cartel is usually a more workable proposition than a large one is, even small groups may not be able to maintain an effective cartel. Consider an oligopoly of only two producers, called a **duopoly**. To keep the analysis simple, we assume here that each duopolist has the same cost structure and demand curve. We also assume a constant marginal cost, which means that marginal cost and average costs are equal and can be represented by one horizontal curve. Figure 12.5 shows the duopolists' combined marginal cost curve, *MC*, along with the market demand curve for the good, *D*. The two producers can maximize monopoly profits if they restrict the total quantity they produce to Q_m and sell it for price P_m. Dividing the total quantity sold between them, each will sell Q_1 at the monopoly price ($2 \times Q_1 = Q_m$). Each will receive an economic profit equal to the area bounded by ATC_1P_mab, which is equal to total revenues ($P_m \times Q_1$) minus total cost ($ATC_1 \times Q_1$).

Once each firm has curbed production, each firm may reason that by reducing the price slightly – to, say, P_1 – and perhaps disguising the price cut through customer rebates or more attractive credit terms, it can capture the entire market and even raise production to Q_2. Each firm may imagine that its own profits can grow from the area bounded by ATC_1P_mab to the much larger area bounded by ATC_1P_1cd. This tempting scenario presumes, of course, that the other firm does not follow suit and lower its price. Each firm must also worry that if it doesn't cheat, the other will by cutting price and capturing most of the market share.

Thus each duopolist has two incentives to chisel on the cartel. The first is offensive, to garner a larger share of the market and more profits. The second

[5] A cartel may provide members with some private benefit that can be denied nonmembers. For example, local medical associations can deny nonmembers the right to practice in local hospitals. In that case, the cost of chiseling is exclusion from membership in the group.

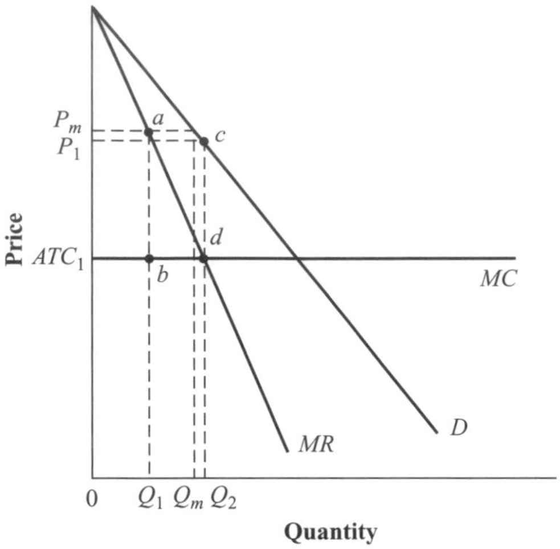

Figure 12.5 A duopoly (two-member cartel)
In an industry composed of two firms of equal size, firms may collude to restrict total output to Q_m and sell at a price of P_m. Having established that price–quantity combination, however, each has an incentive to chisel on the collusive agreement by lowering the price slightly. For example, if one firm charges P_1, it can take the entire market, increasing its sales from Q_1 to Q_2. If the other firm follows suit to protect its market share, each will get a lower price, and the cartel may collapse.

is defensive, to avoid a loss of its market share and profits. Generally, firms that seek higher profits by forming a cartel will also have difficulty holding the cartel together because of these dual incentives. As each firm responds to the incentives to chisel, the two firms undercut each other and the price falls back toward (but not necessarily to) the competitive equilibrium price, at the intersection of the marginal cost and demand curves. Just how far price will decline depends on the firms' ability to impose penalties on each other for chiseling.

The strength and viability of a cartel depend on the number of firms in an industry and the freedom with which other firms can enter. The larger the number of actual or potential competitors, the greater the cost of operating the cartel, of detecting chiselers, and of enforcing the rules. If firms differ in their production capabilities, the task of establishing each firm's share of the market is more difficult. If a cartel member believes it is receiving a smaller market share than it could achieve on its own, it has a greater incentive to chisel. Because of the built-in incentives first to collude and then to chisel, the history of cartels tends to be cyclical. Periods in which output and prices are successfully

Table 12.1 *Cartel incentives*

		Firm *B*	
		High price ($)	Low price ($)
Firm *A*	High price	1,000/1000	400/1,200
	Low price	1,200/400	500/500

controlled are followed by periods of chiseling, which lead eventually to the destruction of the cartel.

Cartels and the Nash equilibrium

The temptation to cheat on a cartel agreement can be usefully illustrated with a simple Prisoner's Dilemma payoff matrix, which allows us to introduce the so-called "Nash equilibrium," an economic/game theoretic construct popularized by *A Beautiful Mind*, a movie on the life of mathematician John Nash, based on the book with the same name by Sylvia Nasar (1998). Assume that we are dealing with two firms (a duopoly), Firm *A* and Firm *B*, each providing jungle cruises in a remote tourist resort. The profits that can be earned by each firm depends on (1) the price it charges and (2) the price the other firm charges. We restrict each firm's pricing to two possibilities, a high (monopoly) price and a low (competitive) price, with the four possible pricing combinations shown in the four cells of the payoff matrix in table 12.1. In each cell, the profits of *A* are shown on the left and the profits of *B* are shown on the right. The two firm maximize their joint profits when each charges the high price for jungle cruises, which yields $1,000 for each one. In negotiations with each other, the only price strategy that both firms could agree on is for both to charge the high price. But notice that if Firm *A* charges the high price, Firm *B* will be able to earn $1,200 by charging the low price. And if Firm *A* charges the low price, Firm *B* will make $400 charging the high price, but $500 charging the low price. So no matter which price *B* thinks *A* will charge, it pays *B* to charge the low price. Exactly the same situation holds for *A*. As is easily seen, no matter what price *B* charges, *A* will do better charging the low price. The temptation then is for both of them to cheat on the agreement for both to charge the high price. The dilemma is, of course, that while cheating by charging the low price is the best pricing strategy for both, it leads to the worse possible collective outcome for the two firms – total profits of $1,000 as opposed to total profits of $2,000 when no one cheats.

It is of interest to note that the outcome in which both firms charge the low price is referred to as a *Nash equilibrium*, after John Nash, the mathematician whose work has been known by economists since the 1950s and who won the Nobel prize for economics in 1994 for his contributions to game theory. Game theory is the study of how decisions are made by people when the payoff they receive depends not only on their decisions, but also on the decisions of others. The Prisoner's Dilemma is just one of many possible games which are analyzed by game theory.

A Nash equilibrium occurs when each decision maker has made the best decision for herself given the decisions that others have made – any unilateral change by a decision maker would make her worse off. For example, in the above cartel–Prisoner's Dilemma, when each firm is charging the low price, if either one of the firms shifted to a high price its profits would fall by $100. So, as indicated, the low-price/low-price outcome is a Nash equilibrium. The low-price decision is also what game theorists called a "dominant strategy," meaning the one that yields the largest payoff to a decision maker regardless of what other decisions others make. Not every Nash equilibrium is the result of a dominant strategy. There are games such as the Battle of the Sexes game in which the Nash equilibrium is not the result of a dominant strategy. Even when everyone is doing the best they can do, given what others are doing, if someone changed their decision, it would pay others to change theirs as well.

As good as the movie *A Beautiful Mind* is, it misrepresents the Nash equilibrium and the implications of game theory for economics in a key scene, one of the most interesting in the movie and where Nash supposedly got the idea for the Nash equilibrium. The scene finds Nash in a bar with some male friends. Three good-looking women come in, but Nash and his friends all agreed that the blonde was the best looking of the three. In discussing the best strategy for meeting these women, and possibly getting dates, it was decided that if they all made a play for the blond none of them would likely be successful, so their best chance would be to concentrate their attention on the other two. While that may have been the best strategy, it wasn't one that would lead to a Nash equilibrium. With Nash and his friends ignoring the blonde, the chance of getting a date with her goes up, and so the best payoff for each of them is now to switch strategies and make a play for the blonde.[6]

[6] In another scene from the movie, Nash is talking to his professor about his paper on game theory and his then newly formulated Nash equilibrium, and his professor tells him that his theory discredits almost 200 years of economic theory. This comment is also in Nasar's book, in which she explains that the Nash equilibrium in Prisoner's Dilemma "contradicts

Government regulation of cartels

Government can either encourage or discourage a cartel. Through regulatory agencies that fix prices, determine market shares, and enforce cartel rules, government can keep competitors or cartel members from doing what comes naturally – chiseling. In doing so, government may be providing an important service to the industry. Perhaps that is why, in most states, insurance companies oppose deregulation of their rate structures. In seeking or welcoming regulation, an industry may calculate that it is easier to control one regulatory agency than a whole group of firms plus potential competitors.

In 1975, the airline industry opposed President Ford's proposal that Congress curtail the power of the Civil Aeronautics Board to set rates and determine airline routes. As the *Wall Street Journal* reported when airline deregulation was being debated in Congress:

> The administration bill quickly drew a sharp blast from the Air Transport Association, which was speaking for the airline industry. The proposed legislation "would tear apart a national transportation system recognized as the finest in the world," the trade group said, urging Congress to reject it because it would cause "a major reduction or elimination of scheduled air service to many communities and would lead inevitably to increased costs to consumers". (*Wall Street Journal* 1975)

The real reason the airlines opposed deregulation became clear in the early 1980s, when several airlines filed for bankruptcy. Partial deregulation, begun in 1979, had increased competition, depressing fares and profits. Fares began to rise again in 1980, mainly because of rapidly escalating fuel costs. Real fares have nonetheless fallen significantly since deregulation and the big airlines are being forced to operate more efficiently in response to the competitive pressures coming from small innovative airlines that are capturing a larger share of the airline market with lower cost and prices (*The Economist* 2004b).

Government can suppress competition in many other ways that have nothing to do with price. Prohibiting the sale of hard liquor on Sunday, for example, can benefit liquor dealers, who might otherwise be forced to stay open on

Adam Smith's metaphor of the Invisible Hand in economics" (Nasar 2001, 119) The suggestion here is that Smith was wrong in arguing that when each person pursues his (or her) own interest, he/she is also serving the collective interest of others in game. Exactly the opposite is true in a Prisoner's Dilemma where the result of each person trying to do as well as possible is the minimization of the collective welfare. But Smith was careful to point out that the Invisible Hand worked only under certain conditions – those in which private property rights were enforced, markets were contestable, people were free to buy from and sell to those who made them the best offer, and public goods such as national defense and certain types of infrastructure are provided collectively.

Sundays. In Florida, a state representative who managed to get a law through the legislature permitting Sunday liquor sales was denounced by liquor dealers. Domestic and global competitive pressures have weakened restrictions on liquor sales and on how long retailers can stay open in countries where those restrictions have been most severe (*The Economist* 2004a). More recently, lagging economies and global competitive pressures have weakened restrictions on how long retailers can stay open in countries where these restrictions have been most severe. For example, see *The Economist* (2004a).

Cartels with lagged demand

Our analysis of cartels has been based on the presumption of a "standard good," one not subject to the forces of lagged demand introduced in chapter 7. Under market conditions of lagged demand, the pricing strategies of a cartel are potentially different. When the market is split among two or more producers, each firm can understand that if it lowers its price, more goods will be sold currently, but even more goods will be sold in the future, when the benefits of the lagged demand/rational addiction kick in. However, each firm can reason that the additional future sales generated by its current price reduction could be picked up by one of the other producers. The benefits are, in other words, external to the firm making the current sacrifice of a lower price. So each producer can reason that it should not incur the current costs of a lower price for the benefit of others. Each producer individually has an impaired incentive to lower the price.

On the other hand, each producer can also see that all the producers have a collective incentive to lower the price currently. Why? To stimulate future demand and to raise their future price and profits. A cartel under such circumstances would be organized to do what all the producers have an interest in doing: Lower the price (not raise the price, as in conventional markets). The problem is that the incentive to go its own way or to chisel on the cartel remains strong for each firm, as is true in the conventional type of cartel, which suggests that consumers may not get the lower current price because of cartel cheating (Lee and Kreutzer 1982).

> A **natural monopoly** is a market structure characterized by a decline in long-run average cost of production within the range of the market demand, which means that the market will be served most cost effectively with only one producer.

The case of the natural monopoly

So far, our discussion of monopoly power has assumed rising marginal costs. One argument for regulation, however, is based on the opposite assumption. Some believe that industries such as electric utilities are **natural monopolies**, meaning that the marginal cost of producing additional units

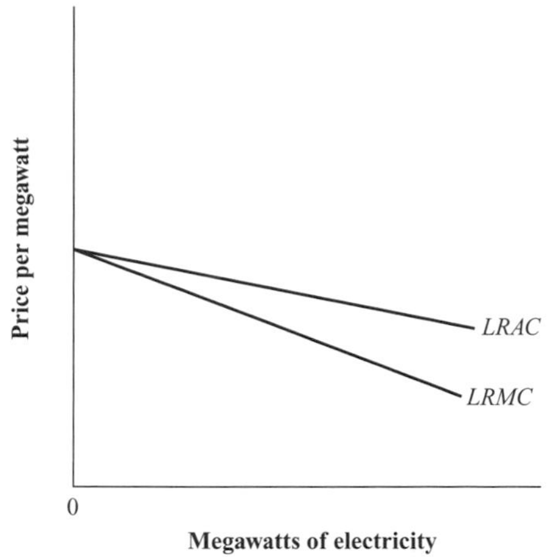

Figure 12.6 Long-run marginal and average costs in a natural monopoly
In a natural monopoly, long-run marginal cost and average costs decline continuously, over the relevant range of production, because of economies of scale. Although the long-run marginal and average cost curves may eventually turn upward because of diseconomies of scale, the firm's market is not large enough to support production in that cost range.

actually decreases over the long run. That is, within the relevant range of the market demand, the long-run marginal cost curve in figure 12.6 slopes downward. Natural monopolies are seen as prime candidates for regulation because their dominance in the market allows them to exert considerable monopoly power, provided that entry is restricted.

Figure 12.7 illustrates the relationship between the long-run average and marginal cost curves and the demand and marginal revenue curves for electric power generation (which is widely thought to be a prime example of a natural monopoly for a wide territory). According to traditional theory, a firm with such decreasing costs will tend to expand production and lower its costs until it becomes large enough to influence price by its production decisions – that is, until it achieves monopoly power. Then it will choose to produce at the point at which all monopolists produce: where marginal cost equals marginal revenue. Thus the monopolistic firm in figure 12.7 will sell Q_m megawatts at an average price of P_m, generating monopoly profits in the process. In other words, firms in decreasing-cost industries tend naturally toward only one producer remaining viable in the market.

Although a firm with decreasing costs can expand until it is the major if not only producer, it will not necessarily be able to price like a monopoly. Suppose a "natural monopoly" flexes its market muscle and charges P_m for Q_m units. Another firm, seeing the first firm's economic profits, may enter the industry,

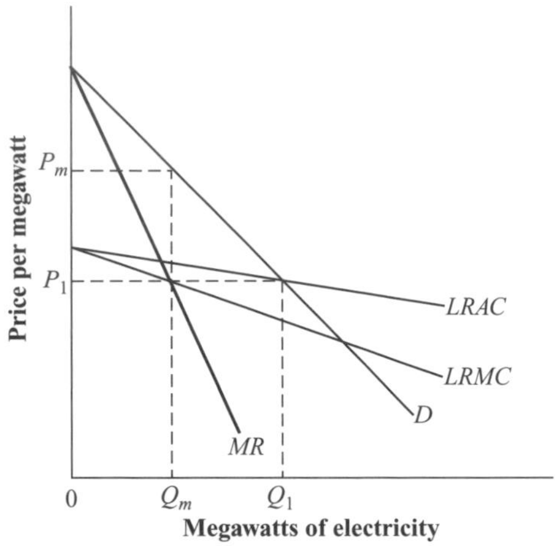

Figure 12.7 Creation of a natural monopoly

Even with declining marginal costs, the firm with monopoly power will produce at the point where marginal cost equals marginal revenue, making Q_m units and charging a price of P_m. Unless barriers to entry exist, however, other firms may enter the market, causing the price to fall toward P_1 and the quantity produced to rise toward Q_1. At that price–quantity combination, only one firm can survive – but without barriers to entry, that firm cannot afford to charge monopoly prices. At a price of P_1, its total revenues just cover its total costs. Economic profit is zero.

expand production, and charge a lower price, luring away customers. To protect its interests, the firm that has been behaving like a monopoly will have to cut its price and expand production to lower its costs. It is difficult to say how far the price will fall and output will rise, but only one firm is likely to survive such a battle, selling to the entire market at a price that competitors cannot undercut. That price will be approximately P_1 in figure 12.7.

If the price does fall to P_1 and only one firm survives, its total revenue will be its price times the quantity produced, Q_1 (or $P_1 \times Q_1$). Notice that at that level, the firm's average cost is equal to P_1. Therefore the total cost of production (the average cost times the quantity sold) is equal to the firm's revenue. The firm is just covering its costs of production, including the owners' risk cost. Now alone in the market, the firm may think it can restrict output, raise its price, and reap an economic profit. Still, it faces the ever-present threat of some other company entering the market and underpricing its product.

Arguments for the regulation of natural monopolies

From a purely theoretical perspective, then, the existence of a natural monopoly is insufficient justification for regulation. Unless there are significant barriers

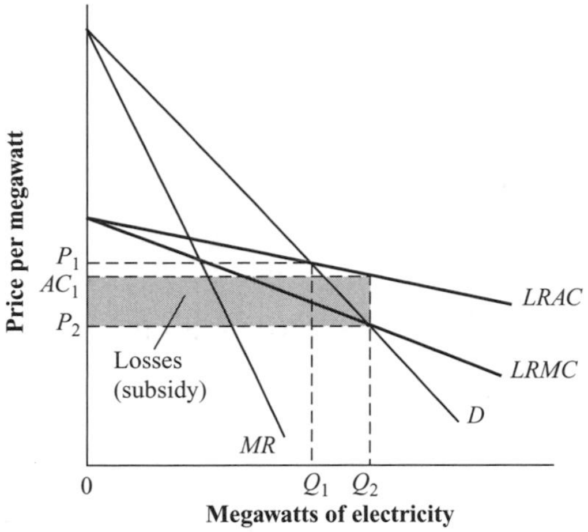

Figure 12.8 Underproduction by a natural monopoly
A natural monopolist that cannot price discriminate will produce only Q_1 megawatts – less than Q_2, the efficient output level – and will charge a price of P_1. If the firm tries to produce Q_2, it will make losses equal to the shaded area, for its price (P_2) will not cover its average cost (AC_1).

to entry into an industry and an inelastic market demand, natural monopolies should not be able to charge monopoly prices. In reply to this argument, proponents of regulation hold that some industries, such as electric utilities, require such huge amounts of capital that no competitor could be expected to enter the market to challenge the natural monopoly. That argument presumes, however, that the generation of electric power must take place on an extremely large scale. Such is not necessarily the case. Furthermore, the capital needed to produce electricity on a profitable scale can be raised by many large corporations, if economic profits exist.

Proponents of the regulation of natural monopolies point also to insufficient output and revenues. Even if an unregulated industry produces Q_1 units and prices that output at P_1 (see figure 12.8), it has not reached the efficient output level. That would be the level at which marginal cost equals marginal benefit – the point at which the marginal cost curve intersects the demand curve. That level is Q_2 in figure 12.8. Why does output fall short?

Given the market demand curve, the firm could sell an output of Q_2 for only P_2, earning total revenues of P_2 times Q_2. Because the average cost of producing at that output level – AC_1 on the vertical axis – would be greater than the price, total costs, at $AC_1 \times Q_2$, would be greater than total revenues. The loss to a firm that tried to produce at the efficient output level is shown by the shaded area on the graph. To produce at the efficient output level, a company would require

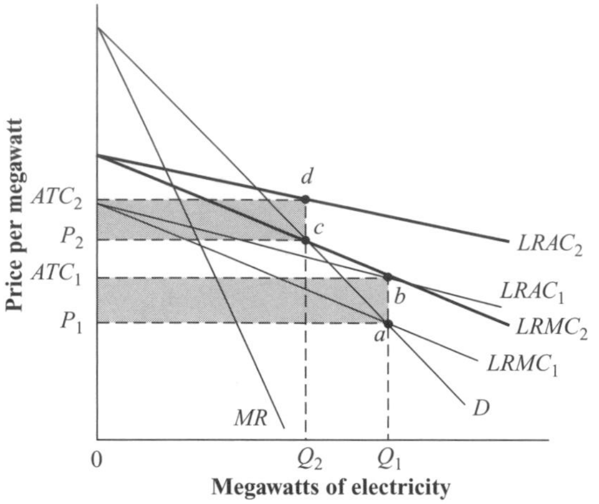

Figure 12.9 Regulation and increasing costs

If a natural monopoly is compensated for the losses it incurs in operating at the efficient output level (the shaded area P_1ATC_1ba), it may monitor its costs less carefully. Its cost curves may shift up, from $LRMC_1$ to $LRMC_2$ and from $LRAC_1$ to $LRAC_2$. Regulators will then have to raise the price from P_1 to P_2, and production will fall from Q_1 to Q_2. The firm will still have to be subsidized (by an amount equal to the shaded area P_2ATC_2dc), and the consumer will be paying more for less.

a subsidy to offset that loss (which creates inefficiencies of its own because of the economic distortions created by the tax necessary to raise the revenue for the subsidy), or it would have to be able to price-discriminate, charging progressively lower prices for additional units sold.

After a firm is given a subsidy, its pricing and production decision must be closely monitored, for its incentive to control costs will be weakened. If the firm allows its cost curves to drift upward, the price it can charge will also rise. In figure 12.9, the firm's long-run marginal and average cost curves shift up from $LRMC_1$ and $LRAC_1$ to $LRMC_2$ and $LRAC_2$. Following the rule that price should be set at the intersection of the long-run marginal cost and demand curves, regulators permit the price to rise from P_1 to P_2. The firm's subsidized losses shrink from the shaded area P_1ATC_1ab to P_1ATC_2cd – but the quantity produced drops also, from Q_1 to Q_2. Consumers are now getting fewer units at a higher price.

Thus, production may be just as inefficient with regulation as without it. Critics point to the US Postal Service as an example of an industry that is closely regulated and subsidized, yet highly inefficient. Yet if the postal industry were truly a natural monopoly, it would be a low-cost producer and would not need protection from competition. Proponents of regulation see the inefficiencies we have just demonstrated as an argument for even more careful scrutiny of a regulated firm's cost – or for government control of production costs through nationalization.

Not all natural monopolies need subsidies to operate at an efficient output level. For all megawatts up to Q_1 in figure 12.8, the unregulated firm can charge up to P_1, a price that just covers its costs on those units. If its product cannot be easily resold, the firm can price-discriminate, charging slightly lower prices for the additional units beyond Q_1. As long as its marginal prices are on or below the demand curve and above the marginal cost curve, the firm will cover its costs while moving toward the efficient output level – and it can do so without giving other firms an incentive to move into its market. If its product can be resold, however, some people will buy at the lower marginal prices and resell to those who are paying P_1, cutting off the firm's profits.

The public interest theory of monopoly regulation

Regulation of monopoly has often been justified on the grounds that it is in the public interest, meaning that it helps to achieve commonly acknowledged national goals. Economists' theories of regulation designed to promote the public interest tend to be based on the goal of increasing market efficiency. (An "economic theory of regulation," under which regulation is demanded by firms that want to suppress competition and supplied by politicians seeking a portion of the resulting monopoly profits from the regulation, will be considered in chapter 13 on "public choice" economics, or the application of economic theory to politics.)

Figure 12.10 shows a cartelized industry producing at an output level of Q_m and selling at a price of P_m. That output level is inefficient because the marginal benefit of the last unit produced (equal to its price) is greater than its marginal cost. Although consumers are willing to pay more than the cost of producing additional units, they are not given the chance to buy those units. The cartel's price–quantity combination not only creates economic profit for the owners, which may be considered inequitable or unjust, but also results in the loss of net benefits, or dead-weight welfare loss, equal to the shaded triangular area *abc*.

Regulation can force firms to sell at lower prices and to produce and sell larger quantities. Ideally, firms can be made to produce Q_c units and to sell them at price P_c, which is the same price–quantity combination that could be achieved under highly competitive conditions. At that output level, the marginal benefit of the last unit produced is equal to its marginal cost.

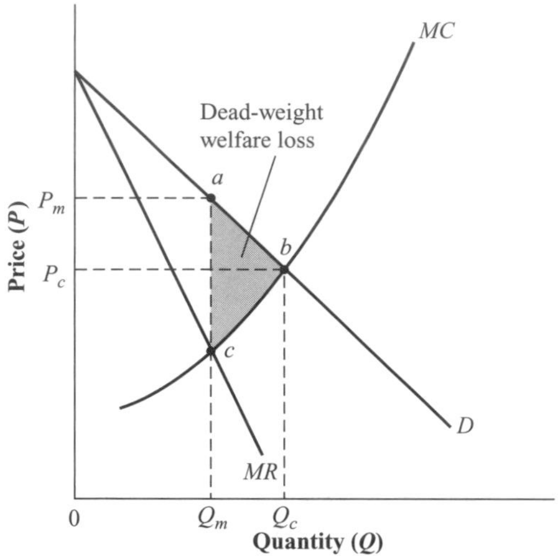

Figure 12.10 The effect of regulation on a cartelized industry
The profit maximizing cartel will equilibrate at point *a* and produce only Q_m units and sell at a price of P_m. In the sense that consumers want Q_c units and are willing to pay more than the marginal cost of production for them, Q_m is an inefficient production level. Under pure competition, the industry will produce at point *b*. Regulation can raise output and lower the price, ideally to P_c, thereby eliminating the dead-weight welfare loss that is equal to the shaded triangle *abc* and which results from monopolistic behavior.

Government regulators need not demand that a company produce Q_c units. All they have to do is require it to charge no more than P_c. After that order has been given, the portion of the demand curve above P_c, along with the accompanying segment of the marginal revenue curve, becomes irrelevant. The firm simply is not allowed to choose a price–quantity combination above point *b* on the demand curve. Then the profit maximizing producer will choose to sell at P_c, the maximum legal price. With marginal revenue guaranteed at P_c, the firm will equate marginal revenue with marginal cost and produce at Q_c, the efficient output level.

Ideal results cannot be expected from the regulatory process, however. The cost of determining the ideal price–quantity combination can be extraordinarily high, if not prohibitive. Because regulators do not work for regulated industries, they will not know the details of a company's marginal cost or demand elasticity. The problem is particularly acute for regulators of monopolies, because there are no competitors from which alternative cost estimates can be obtained. Furthermore, if prices are adjusted upward to allow for a company's higher costs, a regulated firm may lose its incentive to control costs.

The regulated price could conceivably end up being the monopoly price, with the would-have-been monopoly profits being converted into added costs (for example, higher pay and perks for managers of the regulated firm).

The cost of the regulatory process must be emphasized. If regulation is truly to serve the public interest, it must increase the efficiency of the entire social system. That is, its benefits must exceed its costs. Too often, regulation protects large and politically influential firms and industries against competition of small firms by imposing regulations that raise the costs of small firms by more than those of large firms. Though most people assume that businesses are against regulation, the truth is that much regulation of business is favored by the most politically influential of the businesses being regulated. As discussed earlier in this chapter, the major airlines fought against the elimination of regulation in the 1970s. According to a recent study, businesses spent $348 billion in 2000 resisting changes in regulation (both reductions and increases in regulation) because they benefited from the existing regulations (Crain and Hopkins 2001).

Perspective The Value of "Mistreating" Customers

Under perfect competition, there is no issue of how sellers deal with buyers. The good subject to analysis is given, leaving only price as the means of competition. In imperfect markets, sellers have some latitude to define how they will compete, including the way they deal with their buyers. Have you ever heard of a business consultant recommending to her clients that they mistreat their customers? Probably not. The standard recommendations consist of such advice as give customers what they want, pamper them, treat them as individuals, and never attempt to force them to do things they don't want to do. Most of the time this surely is sound advice – but not always. It is often true that businesses can provide more value to their customers by mistreating them – by giving them what they individually don't want, by ignoring their individual desires, by requiring that they do things they would not voluntarily do, and by charging them high prices for frills that cost more than they are worth.

If people always consumed services individually, with the value they received from their consumption being unaffected by what others do, then mistreating them would seldom be a good business strategy. But many services are consumed either together or in the presence of others. When this is the case, suppliers should always be alert to the possible *collective* benefits they can provide their customers by mistreating them on an *individual* basis. And because such mistreatment increases the collective benefits a firm can provide their customers, it also increases the firm's profits.

Private schools face serious competition attracting customers. They have to cover their costs of educating students with tuition payments from parents who have the option of sending their children to public schools they have already paid for with taxes. Obviously, private schools have to treat their customers well if they are to survive. But some of the most successful private schools recognize that treating their customers well as a group can require mistreating them individually. In many respects the education of children is a collective enterprise in which the best results require that all customers be required to do things that many would not voluntarily choose to do.

Consider the example of a private school in Nanuet, New York, that has done very well in part because it has come up with a creative way of mistreating its customers. Love Christian Academy required that all the parents have monthly meetings with their children's teachers and volunteer to work at the school at least one day a year. If parents missed a meeting, or even came late for a meeting, they were fined $100. Parents who were fined often felt mistreated. One parent was quoted as being "not pleased" with receiving a fine for violating one of the rules, and some parents have removed their children from the school because of the strict rules. But the school has thrived because most parents felt more than compensated by knowing that their children were attending a school with other children whose parents were actively involved in their education (Stecklow 1994, A1).[7]

Manufacturers who sell their products through independent dealers often impose restrictions on the price the dealers can charge for the products or the number of dealers who can sell them in a given area. These restrictions are referred to respectively as "resale price maintenance (RPM) agreements"

[7] Similarly, few parents want their children spanked at school. But if the choice is between sending their children to a school where none of the students is spanked or to one in which any student who misbehaves is spanked, including their own, many parents prefer the latter. This is recognized by many private schools that advertise the fact that they believe in maintaining discipline in the classroom by subjecting unruly students to an old-fashioned spanking. Dr. Connie Sims, the superintendent of Love Christian Academy, made clear that before students are accepted their parents must accept the school's disciplinary policy (Stecklow 1994, A1). We want to emphasize that our concern here is not whether or not spanking is the best, or even a good, way of disciplining children. The point is that many schools can attract business with practices that each of their customers would find objectionable if applied only to their children, but which they appreciate when applied to all students.

and "exclusive-dealing arrangements." The effect of these restrictions is to increase the price that consumers pay, and for a long time the conventional view of policy critics was that the price maintenance agreements and exclusive dealerships allowed sellers to profit at the consumers' expense. But, as in the previous examples, a policy that at first glance appears to be mistreating customers may actually be in the customers' best interest by allowing them to overcome a Prisoner's Dilemma.

In certain cases, requiring retailers to charge higher prices (price maintenance) or allowing them to charge higher prices (exclusive territory) makes it possible for a manufacturer to benefit customers, because without these restrictions each customer would find it individually rational to behave in ways that are collectively harmful. Consider a product on which customers are able to make a more informed choice when the product is properly displayed. One example is furniture, which is best examined in a well-appointed setting containing other pieces of complementary furniture.

Another example is sound equipment that consumers would like to evaluate in sound rooms before purchasing. But without the manufacturer being able to impose some restrictions on the retailer, it is unlikely that the consumer will benefit from such helpful displays. The retailer who went to the expense of properly displaying a product or having experts on hand to answer questions of potential customers would be vulnerable to the price competition of retailers who did not provide and incur the cost of these services. A retailer with a warehouse and a toll-free number, or a Web site could (and many have) run advertisements suggesting that customers visit retailers with showrooms and experts to decide what they want to buy, and then order from their warehouse at a discount price.

The problem is that although it makes sense for each customer to take advantage of such offers, if many customers do so they will end up collectively worse off as the retailers with showrooms go out of business. So retail price maintenance agreements and exclusive-dealing arrangements can be thought of as ways of protecting consumers against their own Prisoner's Dilemma temptations.[8]

[8] If price competition is not permitted, retailers must compete through the display, service, and sales expertise that make the product more valuable to consumers. Similarly, by providing one retailer the exclusive right to sell its product in a market area, a manufacturer prevents, or at least reduces the ability of, some retailers to free-ride on that retailer's efforts. A retailer with the exclusive right to sell a product in an area has a strong motivation to provide the combination of display and service that consumers find most attractive. And with each consumer able to secure the advantages of good displays and service only by paying for them, they are no longer in a Prisoner's Dilemma.

Our discussion of firms with monopoly power might suggest that "high prices" are always and everywhere "bad" for consumers. But is that true when the benefits a person receives from consuming a good or service can be significantly influenced by whom the other consumers are? Consider a rather extreme example. There are two hotels in the town you are visiting that are identical except for their customers. One is patronized by low-income and poorly behaved rowdies who create loud disturbances all night, whereas the other is patronized by affluent, well-behaved folks who are careful not to disturb their neighbors. Which hotel would you prefer? Preferences differ, and no doubt some would prefer the "action" that is more likely available at the first hotel. But it is a safe bet that most affluent, well-behaved people would prefer, and be willing to pay more for, the second.

How can a hotel do a reasonable job filtering out less desirable customers that does not violate antidiscrimination laws, and increase its profit as a result? Just charge higher prices than the other hotel, even though it is physically identical. The less desirable customers will tend to take their business to the other, lower-priced hotel, which makes your hotel more valuable to those who can afford to pay extra to avoid the less affluent and/or unruly guests. This strategy won't work perfectly. It does not, for example, screen out rock bands that may be affluent but very unruly. But though imperfect, high prices do have the virtue of generally doing a good job of screening out less desirable guests, and this is clearly a case in which virtue is its own reward (Lee and McKenzie 1998).

The business of MBA education is another example of the importance of the client. MBA students who attend a university with other students who are capable and enthusiastic and have lots of business experience will typically get a far better education than do those who attend a university with students who are poorly prepared, uninterested, and inexperienced, even though the universities are of similar quality in terms of faculty and facilities. Students learn not only from their classroom experiences, but also from their after-class interaction with other students. This suggests that the high tuition charges in many executive MBA programs can be explained, at least in part, by the value they create as screening devices.

Indeed, if customers are given too much consideration, some will abuse it at the expense not just of the business, but of customers in general. Consider refund policies. Most retail stores allow customers to return merchandise that they feel doesn't suit their needs as well as they anticipated. Within reasonable limits, such policies benefit all customers and build goodwill and profitability for the business. Some retailers have pushed those limits, however, with almost no restrictions on refunds. Apparently, some retailers are now having second thoughts as more and more customers are taking advantage of generous refund policies.

For example, in early 2005, Blockbuster thought that it would be nice to its customers by abolishing its usual late fees on movie rentals – so long as the movie was returned within a week of the established due date (which could vary with the movie rented).[9] As a consequence of the longer grace period without any extra charge, customers starting hoarding the movies they rented, the net result of which was that the shelves began emptying out with greater frequency, with many customers having to incur the added cost of returning repeatedly to their local Blockbuster checking for movies they wanted to see. At times, customers had to delay getting the movies they wanted for two and three weeks (Luna 2005). You can just about bet that by the time this book is published, Blockbuster will have reinstituted a more restrictive late fee – as a way of more effectively using its stock of movies and as a way of lowering the total cost of movie rentals (including the cost of customers having to return to their local stores to find the movies they want).[10] In the mid-1990s, Best Buy (and many other stores) stopped giving refunds unless the customer had a sales receipt, and even then the customer had to pay a "restocking fee" of 15 percent of the purchase price if the package in which the product came had been opened (Lee 1996). Before the change in policy, one Best Buy customer received a refund on a video

[9] If the movie is not returned within a week of the due date, Blockbuster charges customers the price of the movie minus the rental charge (usually about $8, Flint 2005). If the movie is returned within thirty days, the second charge is removed, but the customer would be charged a $1.25 restocking fee. Franchises were not required to adopt the no-late-fee policy (Luna 2005).

[10] Blockbuster may be pressed to reinstate its previous late-fee policy because of lawsuits. New Jersey's attorney general has filed suit against Blockbuster for deceptive advertising since the company has "not told customers about the big fees they are charged if they keep videos and games for more than a week after they are due." Blockbuster responded by arguing that their policy was to call customers with overdue rentals to warn them of the additional charge (Flint 2005). Subsequently, Blockbuster settled its deceptive advertising suits by paying a total of $630,000 to forty-seven states and the District of Columbia. It also agreed to give refunds to customers charged for movies not returned and for restocking fees and to provide a better explanation of its "no-late-fees" policy (Muñoz 2005). Of course, by the time this book is published, the Blockbuster retail store business may be a shadow of its former self, given the growing competition its bricks-and-mortar stores face with the emergence of online movie rental sites (its own and others'– Netflix, for example), from the plunging prices of purchased DVDs (discount stores at the time of writing offer racks of DVDs for under $10, with some under $5 or $6 dollars), and from digital TiVo-type recording of television programs.

recorder that he claimed was defective. Indeed, it was defective for a reason the Best Buy repair technicians discovered when they played back the tape inside and saw the splash of water as the camera fell into a swimming pool and sank to the bottom. It was at the bottom when the recording stopped. At about the same time, Wal-Mart, the world's biggest retailer, similarly moved away from its open-ended return policy by imposing on most items a 90-day maximum beyond which no refund would be made. Before this restriction went into effect, a customer got a refund for a beat-up thermos that Wal-Mart later learned from the manufacturer had been purchased in the 1950s, long before there was a Wal-Mart. Another retailer that has decided to halt its no-questions-asked policy on returns is the catalog store L.L. Bean, Inc. According to a spokeswoman for the firm, some customers were returning clothes that had been purchased at garage sales or found in the closets and attics of deceased relatives (Lee 1996). As this book is being written, it is hard to find a retailer that hasn't tightened its return policy. Most retailers of electronic products now have restocking fees.

Most customers may be honest, and a largely unrestricted return policy would be appropriate for them. But honest people can be the most supportive and appreciative of restrictions when a liberal return policy begins to be abused. And there is a tendency for the number who take advantage of a generous return opportunity to grow over time as some of those who do not initially return items that shouldn't be returned see others doing so. The cost of paying people for fraudulent, or at least highly questionable, returns is soon reflected in the price that everyone has to pay. Imposing strict limits on all customer returns will seem like mistreatment to some, but it is really little different than imposing restrictions on the hours of stores in a mall or fines on parents who are late for meetings with their children's teachers. Without such restrictions, each consumer will have an opportunity to gain by engaging in behavior that is collectively harmful.

When bosses repeat the refrain "The customer is always right," workers may be led to believe that the unspoken rule is that they should take whatever the customers throw at them in the way of abuse. As we have seen, the bosses' advice might be a reasonable working rule, but it is also likely to be advice that the boss doesn't want employees to take with complete seriousness. The rule overlooks the fact that abusive customers can make work a form of "hell" for the workers. If forced to take excessive abuse, the workers would, no doubt, demand higher wages to compensate them for this abuse. At some point, as more and more abuse is encountered, it is altogether reasonable to expect that the higher wages the workers require will exceed the value received by the firm from accommodating abusive customers. Any tolerably reasonable boss will, at some point, ask workers to stand their ground and return the "fire" of their customers. Otherwise, firm profits can be impaired.

The founding president of Southwest Airlines, Herb Kelleher, understood the (economic) principles at stake. He has written letters to customers who had been abusive to his workers, telling those customers that they should take their business elsewhere. Southwest might have lost some business, but the company could also have expected higher profits because it could then have a total wage bill that would be lower than otherwise and could more than compensate the company for the lost business. Also, the policy may have screened out unruly passengers, thus making Southwest more attractive to well-behaved passengers.

PART II ORGANIZATIONAL ECONOMICS AND MANAGEMENT

"Hostile" takeover as a check on managerial monopolies

It may appear that our discussion of monopolies applies only to "markets" and has little or nothing to do with the management of firms. Indeed, the theory of monopolies is directly applicable to management problems. This is because firms often rely exclusively on internal departments (and their employees) for the provision of a variety of services, such as legal, advertising, and accounting, as well as for the production of parts that are assembled into the firm's final goods sold to consumers. In such cases, the internal departments can begin to act like little monopolies, cutting back on what they could produce and demanding a higher price (through their firm's budgetary processes) for what they do than is required. One reason a firm might want to outsource its services is to avoid becoming subjected to the inefficiencies of internal monopolies. The firm can always seek competitive bids from alternative outside suppliers. The act of outsourcing some services can also keep the outsourcing threat alive for other internal departments that might try to act like internal monopolies.

Outsourcing can thus improve a firm's profitability in two ways: First, it offers firms the opportunity to get some of their services cheaper from competitive outside bids. Second, it can make remaining inside departments work more efficiently, since they will then be alerted to the prospects of their being replaced by more competitive outside suppliers. For example, in 2004, Western Michigan University took bids to provide its needed custodial care from the union of its sixty custodial workers and from five outside private custodial firms. The university replaced its in-house custodial workers with workers employed by Commercial Sanitation Management Services because that company's bid reduced the university's maintenance cost by $1.5 million a year (Davis 2005).

Still, managers can become complacent in managing their departments, allowing their departments to act monopolistically – and inefficiently. And, of course, managers can become lax for other reasons, such as by spending more on office perks than necessary, and expanding the size of the firm beyond its core competencies – and generally being too lavish with shareholder profits. The temptation is for top management to take advantage of the Prisoner's Dilemma which each shareholder finds herself in with respect to monitoring the behavior of the managers of the firm they (the shareholders) own. Corporate takeovers, however, represent an important check on management discretion by threatening the jobs of management teams that do not pay enough attention to the interests of their shareholders.

Reasons for takeovers

There are many reasons for corporate takeovers, and different ways for them to occur. There may be complementarities in the production and distribution of the products of two firms that can be best realized by one firm. For example, Microsoft produces applications that can be run on Windows. Or, as was commonly the case in earlier manufacturing mergers, two firms may find that they can realize economies of scale by combining their operations. And one firm may be supplying another firm with the use of highly specific capital, and a merger between the two reduces the threat of opportunistic behavior that can be costly to both (a subject covered in chapter 6).

Most takeovers are what are referred to as "friendly." A friendly takeover occurs when the management of the two firms works out an arrangement that is mutually agreeable. The takeover of ABC by Disney was a friendly one. Indeed, takeovers occur for the same reason that all market transactions occur: Generally speaking, efficiencies are expected, meaning that both parties can be made better off. So it should not be surprising that most takeovers are friendly.

But there are takeovers that are opposed by the management of the firms being taken over, as was the case, at least initially, in Oracle's takeover of PeopleSoft in late 2004. These takeovers are referred to as "hostile" and are commonly seen as undesirable and inefficient. "Hostile" takeovers are depicted as the work of corporate "raiders" who are interested only in turning a quick profit and who disrupt productivity by forcing the management of the targeted firms to take expensive defensive action and distracting them from long-run concerns.

If managers of target corporations always acted in the interest of their shareholders (the real owners of the corporation), then a strong case could be made for regarding so-called hostile takeovers as inefficient. Managers of the target corporation would then oppose a takeover only if it could not be made in a way that benefited their shareholders, as well as those of the acquiring corporation. But if managers could always be depended upon to act in the interest of their shareholders, then there would be no need for many of the corporate arrangements that have been discussed in this book.

The market for corporate control

The strongest argument in favor of "hostile" takeovers is that they bring the interests of managers more in line with those of shareholders than would otherwise be the case. There is a so-called "market for corporate control" that allows people who believe that they can do a better job of managing a company and maximizing shareholder return to oust the existing management by outbidding them for the corporate stock. Although there are not a large number of such takeover attempts, and not all attempts are successful, just the threat of a "hostile" takeover provides a strong disincentive for managers to go as far as they otherwise would like in pursuing personal advantages at the expense of their shareholders. This disincentive suggests that there are efficiency advantages deriving from the possibility of "hostile" takeovers. The issue of efficiency is not unrelated, however, to the primary concern of this section, which is why "hostile" takeovers are less hostile than they are commonly depicted.

A takeover is often considered hostile for the very reason that it promotes efficiency. A management team that is doing a good job of managing a firm efficiently has little to fear from being taken over by a rival management team. The stock price of a well-managed firm will generally reflect that fact, and it will not be possible for a corporate raider to profit by buying that firm's stock in the hope of increasing its price through improved management. Only when the existing managers are not running the firm efficiently – because of incompetence, the inability to abandon old ways in response to changing conditions, or by intentionally benefiting personally at the expense of shareholders – is a takeover likely. But under these circumstances, a takeover that promises to increase efficiency will not be popular with existing managers, because it puts them out of work. Not surprisingly, managers whose jobs are threatened by a takeover will see it as "hostile."

The fact that pejorative terms such as "hostile takeover" and "corporate raiders" are so widely used testifies to the advantage existing managers have over shareholders at promoting their interests through public debate. The costs from a "hostile" takeover are concentrated on a relatively small number of people, primarily the management team that loses its pay, perks, and privileges. Each member of this team will lose a great deal if the team is replaced and so has a strong motivation to oppose a takeover. And even a grossly inefficient management team can be organized well enough to respond in unison to a takeover threat, and to speak with one voice. That voice will usually characterize a takeover as hostile to the interests of the corporation, the shareholders, the community, and the nation, and we might expect managers to be more vociferous the more inefficient the management.

But if a takeover is actually efficient, what about the voice of those who benefit? Why is the media discussion of takeovers dominated by the managers who lose rather than by the shareholders who win? And there is plenty of evidence that the shareholders of the target company in a hostile takeover do win. For example, during the takeover wave in the 1980s, it was estimated that stock prices of targeted firms increased about 50 percent because of hostile takeovers, which suggests that the managers of the targeted firms may have destroyed a considerable amount of their corporations' value before being targeted for takeover (Jensen 1988).

As will be discussed later in this section, this increase in stock values does not necessarily *prove* that a takeover is efficient. The takeover could depress the stock prices of the firm that is taking over the target firm, for example.[11] But even if the takeover is not efficient, the shareholders of the target firm should favor it and counter the negative portrayal put forth by their managers. This seldom happens, however, because there are typically a large number of shareholders, with few, if any, having more than a relatively small number of shares. Most shareholders have a diversified portfolio and are only marginally

[11] However, Michael Jensen minces few words on what the data implies: "[T]he fact that takeover and LBO premiums [or added prices] average 50% above market price illustrates how much value public-company managers can destroy before they face a serious threat of disturbance. Takeovers and buyouts both create value and unlock value destroyed by management through misguided policies. I estimate that transactions associated with the market for corporate control unlocked shareholder gains (in target companies alone) of more than $500 billion between 1977 and 1988 – more than 50% of the cash dividends paid by the entire corporate sector over this same period" (Jensen 1989, 64–5).

affected by changes in the price of any particular corporation's stock. The probability that the actions of a typical individual stockholder will have an impact is very low, approaching zero. So even if the gain to shareholders far exceeds the loss to management, the large number of shareholders and their diverse interests make it extraordinarily difficult for them to speak in unison. As indicated earlier, shareholders are disadvantaged because they are in a Prisoner's Dilemma with respect to influencing the terms of the debate on behalf of their collective benefit.

If shareholders and management were on equal footing at influencing the public perception of hostile takeovers, almost no takeovers would be reported as hostile. Consider a hypothetical situation that is similar to what is commonly seen as a hostile takeover.

Assume that you are the owner of a beautiful house on a high bluff overlooking the Pacific Ocean near Carmel, California. You are extremely busy as a global entrepreneur and unable to spend much time at this house. Because the house and grounds require full-time professional attention, you have hired a caretaker to manage the property. Assume that you pay the caretaker extremely well (mainly because you want him to bear a cost from being fired for shirking and engaging in opportunism), and give him access to many of the amenities of the property. He's very happy with the job, and you are pleased enough with his performance.

But one day a wealthy CEO who is planning to retire in the Carmel area makes you an offer on the house of $15 million, about 50 percent more than you thought you could sell it for. Although you were not interested in selling at $10 million, you find the $15 million offer very attractive. For whatever reason, the house is worth more to the retiring CEO than to you. It could be that the CEO values the property more than you simply because she will have more time to spend living in and enjoying the house. Or it could be because the CEO believes that a profit can be made on the house by bringing in a caretaker who will do a far better job managing the property, thus increasing its value to above $15 million. But it really makes little difference to you why the CEO values the house more than you do, and you are quite happy to sell at the price offered whatever the reason.

Imagine how surprised you would be if, as the sale of your house was being negotiated, the news media reported that your property was the target of a hostile takeover by a "house raider" interested only in personal advantage. What's so hostile about being offered a higher price for your property than you thought it was worth? And are you somehow worse off because the buyer also sees private benefit in the exchange?

But the media wasn't interested in your opinion. Instead, reporters had been talking to your caretaker, who knew he would lose his job if the sale went through. So the caretaker was reporting that the sale of the property was the result of a hostile move by an unsavory character. Obviously this is silly, and the media is not likely to report this, or any similar sale of a house, as a hostile takeover. But is this any sillier than reporting a corporate takeover as hostile when the owners of the corporation (the shareholders) are being offered a 50 or 100 percent premium to sell their shares?

The two situations are not exactly the same, but they are similar enough to call into question the "hostility" of most hostile takeovers. One important difference between the two situations is that if such a report did start to circulate about the sale of your house, and somehow threatened that sale, you would have the motivation and ability to clearly communicate that it was your house, that you found the offer attractive, and that there was nothing at all hostile about the sale. This difference explains why our example should not be taken as a criticism of the press. When there is one owner (or a few), as in the case of a house, the press can easily understand and report that owner's perspective. But when there are thousands of owners, as in the case of corporations, it is much easier for reporters to obtain information about a corporation from its top managers.

The fact that there are a multitude of owners in the case of corporations is the basis for other differences between the sale of a house and the sale of a corporation. Just as reporters find that it is easier to rely on top management for information on a corporation, so do the owners of a corporation find it easier to rely on management to make most corporate decisions, even major decisions such as those that affect the sale of the corporation. Obviously, the reason for granting a management team the power to act somewhat independently of shareholders is that shareholders are so large in number, so dispersed in location, and so diverse in interests, that they cannot make the type of decisions needed to manage a corporation, or much else, for that matter. But as we have discussed in detail throughout this text, there are risks associated with letting agents (managers) act on behalf of principals (owners/shareholders). As the owner of the house outside Carmel, would you want your caretaker to negotiate the sale for you? Only if the caretaker were subject to a set of incentives that go a long way in aligning his interests in the sale with yours.

The efficiency of takeovers

Are hostile takeovers efficient? Not everyone believes they are. Hostile takeovers are commonly seen as ways to increase the wealth of people who are already rich at the expense of the corporation's average workers (not just its managers), the corporation's long-run prospects, and the competitiveness of the general economy. For example, responding to a hostile takeover bid for Chrysler Corporation in the mid-1990s by Kirk Kerkorian, a major newspaper ran an editorial: "[W]hen Kerkorian was complaining about insufficient return to stockholders, the value of [his] investment in Chrysler had more than tripled, to $1.1 billion. That's not good enough? To satisfy his greed, Kerkorian seems prepared to endanger the jobs of thousands of Americans and the health of a major corporation so important to the economy" (*Atlanta Journal – Constitution* 1995).

This editorial comment ignores the efficiency effects of a corporate takeover. But at the same time, the effect of a hostile takeover on economic efficiency is more complicated than has been suggested in this chapter so far. The stockholders of the corporation being taken over do gain (see Grinblatt and Titman 2002, for a review of the extensive literature on this topic). But what about the common stockholders (whose earnings can vary with the success of their companies since they are residual claimants) and bondholders (whose earnings are set by fixed interest rates) of the takeover corporation? Don't they lose as their firm runs up lots of debt to pay high prices for the stock of the acquired firm? Also, doesn't the threat of a hostile takeover motivate managers to make decisions that boost profits in the short run but which harm the corporation's long-run profitability? And what about the fact that important parts of an acquired firm are often spun off after a hostile takeover, leaving a much smaller firm, with many of its workers being laid off? Shouldn't these losses be set against any gains that the shareholders of acquired firms receive, and isn't it possible that the losses are larger than the gains?

The evidence from the 1980s, when hostile takeovers were at their peak, suggests that the magnitude of the gains to the shareholders of a corporation that is targeted for a takeover are quite large.[12]

[12] A study by the Office of the Chief Economist of the Securities and Exchange Commission (SEC) looked at 225 successful takeovers from 1981–4 and found that the average premium to shareholders was 53.2 percent. In a follow-up study for 1985 and 1986, the premium was found to have dropped to an average of 37 and 33.6 percent, respectively. These averages probably understate the gains because they compare the stock price one month before the announcement of a takeover bid with the takeover price, and often the price begins increasing in response to rumors long before a formal offer is tendered (Jarrell, Brickley, and Netter 1988). These percentages represent huge gains in total dollars, amounting to $346 billion over the period 1977–86 (in 1986 dollars), according to one study (Jensen 1988, 21). We should point out that this estimate applied to all mergers and acquisitions (M&As), not just "hostile" takeovers. But "hostile" or not, takeovers consistently increase the value of the acquired firm's stock, and probably increase it more when the takeover is opposed by management than otherwise, because offering a higher price is a way around a reluctant management.

Winner's curse

Those who own something that others are bidding for should be expected to see their wealth increase. So it is not really surprising that takeover bids increase the wealth of the corporation's stockholders, although the magnitude of the gains are impressive. But that is not necessarily true for the stockholders of a corporation mounting a takeover bid. In a competitive bidding process it is possible to bid too much, and some believe that this is particularly true of the corporation making the winning bid. The winning bid is typically made by the bidder who is most optimistic about the value of the object of the bidding (see Thaler 1992). This is no problem when bidding for something the bidder wants for its subjective value (say, an antique piece of furniture), because the object probably is worth more to the winning bidder than to others. But when bidding for a productive asset (such as an offshore oil field) that is valued for its ability to generate a financial return, the value of the object is less dependent on who owns it.[13] Therefore, if the average bid is the best estimate of the value of the object, then there is a good chance that the winning bid is too high.

Economists have referred to this possible tendency to overbid as the "winner's curse." But for two very good reasons, the winner's curse may not be all that prevalent. First, people who are prone to fall victim to this curse are not likely to acquire (or retain) the control over the wealth necessary to keep bidding on valuable property, certainly not property as valuable as a corporation. Second, in many bidding situations, each bidder often receives information on how much others are willing to pay as the bidding process takes place and then adjusts their evaluation of the property accordingly. This is the case in corporate takeovers when offers to pay a certain price for a corporation's stock are made publicly.

So, we should expect that the winning bid for the stock of a corporation targeted for a takeover will fairly accurately reflect the value of that corporation to the winner and therefore will not greatly affect the wealth of the acquiring corporation's stockholders; we should also expect that the more competitive the bidding process, the closer the bid price to the actual stock value. And that is exactly what the evidence suggests.[14]

[13] In general, of course, the value of the asset will depend to some degree on who owns it. The highest bidder will likely have good reason to believe that she is better able to utilize the asset to create value. In the case of an oil field, the possibilities for one owner to obtain more wealth than another are probably quite limited. In the case of a corporation, the importance of management no doubt provides more opportunity for some owners to run the business more profitably than others.

[14] According to a 1987 study by economists Gregg Jarrell and Annette Paulsen, stockholders of acquiring corporations realized an average gain of between 1 and 2 percent on 663 successful

Bondholders

What about the possibility that the additional value realized by shareholders of the target corporation is paid for by losses to bondholders? For example, a takeover could increase the risk that either the acquiring or the acquired firm will suffer financial failure, while also increasing the possibility that one or both will experience very high profits. Shareholders stand to benefit from the high profits if they occur, and so they can find the expected value of their stock increasing because of the increased risk. The additional risk cannot generate a similar advantage for bondholders because the return to bondholders is fixed. They lose if the corporation goes bankrupt, but they don't share in any increased profits if the corporation does extremely well. According to several studies of takeovers from the 1960s–1980s, however, takeovers do not impose losses on bondholders (Dennis and McConnell 1986; and Lehn and Paulsen 1987). No doubt some bondholders suffer small losses while others realize small gains, but the best conclusion is that, even in the worst case, any losses to bondholders do not come anywhere close to offsetting the gains to stockholders.

Takeover mistakes

So far, we have been discussing the average wealth effect on shareholders and bondholders from takeovers. Just because the average wealth effect of a hostile takeover is positive does not mean that all such takeovers create wealth. People make mistakes in the market for corporate takeovers, just as they do in other markets and in all aspects of life. The question is not whether people make mistakes, but whether they are subjected to *self-correcting forces* when they do. The bidders subject to the winner's curse should themselves be the target of a takeover. The evidence suggests that in the case of hostile takeovers, they are. Economists Mark Mitchell and Kenneth Lehn asked, "Do Bad Bidders Become Good Targets?" (Mitchell and Lehn 1990). Looking at takeovers over the period January 1980–July 1988, they found that those firms resulting from takeovers that were wealth-reducing (according to the response of stock prices) were more likely to be challenged with a subsequent takeover than were firms whose takeovers had proven to be wealth-increasing. The market for corporate control does not prevent mistakes from being made, but it creates the information and motivation vital for correcting them when they occur (Mitchell and Lehn 1990).

bids from 1962 to 1985. Interestingly, and not surprisingly, as takeover activity increased, the return to acquiring firms decreased, with the average percentage return being 4.95 in the 1960s, 2.21 in the 1970s, and −0.04 (but statistically insignificant) in the 1980s (Jarrell and Paulsen 1989).

Short-run vs. long-run profits

If you are a corporate manager, you may be thinking that the threat of a takeover could motivate you to act in ways that increase the value of the corporate stock in the short run, but which are harmful to the profitability of the corporation in the long run. Is it true that managers are less likely to be ousted in a hostile takeover if they concentrate on short-run profits at the expense of long-run profits?

The answer might be "Yes" if the prices of corporate stock reacted only to short-run profits, but should we expect only short-run performance reports to control stock prices? If they did, then there would be money to be made by investors who took the long view. If a stock's price were inflated by short-run gains that were not likely to continue into the future, then investors could sell the stock in anticipation that future performance wouldn't likely match current performance, which means that investors could buy the stock back when its price declined with dampening future gains, pocketing a capital gains between the difference in the current sell price and the future buy-back price. If the stock were depressed because of the impact of current poor earnings that were not expected to continue into the future, then investors could buy the stock currently at the depressed price and sell the stock when its price reflected higher earnings in the future. The buying and selling of the stock would mean that the company's long-term prospects would necessarily be taken into account in the market price of the stock (perhaps not perfectly, but only because of the costs of information on what will happen in the future and because of ever-present uncertainties about what the future will bring).

How should managers of the company be expected to make their decisions relating to short-run and long-term market forces? Consider a decision facing you as a manager on whether to commit to an expensive research and development project that will reduce profits over the near term but is expected to more than offset this loss with higher profits in the future. Should you be fearful that investing in this project will, because of the reduction in current profits, drive the price of your stock down, making your corporation more vulnerable to a hostile takeover? The answer is probably "No", if your estimate of the long-run profitability of the project is correct. There are two good reasons that a takeover wouldn't be likely. First, the obvious fact that price–earnings ratios vary widely between different stocks provides compelling evidence that stock prices reflect more than current profits. Second, studies indicate that a corporation's stock price generally increases when the corporation announces increased spending on investment, and generally decreases when a reduction in investment spending is announced (McConnell and Muscarella 1985). A study by Brownyn Hall found that, over the period 1976–85, the firms taken over by other firms did not have a higher research and development-to-sales ratio than did firms in the same industry that were not taken over.[15] There is no reason for managers to become short-sighted because of the threat of a hostile takeover. Indeed, the best protection against a takeover, hostile or otherwise, is to make decisions that increase the long-run profitability of the corporation, even if those decisions temporarily reduce profits.

Break-ups

What about the fact that after a corporation is taken over it is sometimes broken up as the acquiring firm sells off divisions, often ones that have been profitable? Isn't this disruptive and inefficient? There is no doubt that takeovers are disruptive, particularly when they result in parts of the acquired firm being spun off. But disruption is not necessarily inefficient. Indeed, any economy has to motivate a rapid response to changing circumstances if it is to be efficient, and such a response is necessarily disruptive. Making the best use of resources in a world of advancing technologies, improved opportunities, and global competition requires continuous disruption. The alternative is stagnation and relative decline.

Many of the mergers that took place in the 1960s and 1970s created large conglomerate structures that, even if efficient at the time, soon ceased to be efficient. Increased global competition began rewarding smaller firms with quicker response times to changing market conditions. Technology reduced the synergies that might have existed at one point by having different products produced within the same firms. It became less costly for firms to buy inputs and components from other firms, thus increasing the ability to specialize in their core competencies (in the vernacular of earlier chapters, transaction costs fell).

In many cases, these changes made the divisions of the corporation worth more as separate firms than as parts of the whole. Many managers, however, prefer to be in charge of a large firm rather than a small one and are reluctant to divest divisions that are worth more by themselves or as part of another organizational structure. This managerial reluctance of the 1960s, 1970s, and into the 1980s was partly responsible for the depressed stock prices of which corporate raiders were able to take advantage by buying a controlling interest

[15] Hall's study is discussed by Jensen (1988).

in conglomerates and then increasing their total value by spinning off some of their divisions.[16]

Laid-off workers

Another complaint about the spinning off of divisions and downsizing that often accompanies takeovers is that workers are laid off. The claim is made that although stockholders may come out ahead, they do so at the expense of workers who lose their jobs. But the questions we need to consider are:

- Is this a valid criticism of takeovers?
- Which workers are most likely to be laid off and how big is the cost to the workers when compared against the gain to shareholders?

The fact that workers are laid off after hostile takeovers is consistent with the view that these takeovers promote *efficiency*. The most natural thing in the world for managers to do when sheltered against the full rigors of competition is to let the workforce grow larger than efficiency requires.[17]

Economic progress occurs most rapidly when there are strong pressures to produce the same output with less effort – that is, to lay off workers when they are no longer needed. Taking this measure often causes dislocations in the short run, but in the long run it increases the availability of the most valuable resource (human effort and brainpower) to expand output elsewhere in the economy. So, a strong case can be made for arguing that one of the advantages of the market for corporate control is the increased pressure on managers to keep the size of their workforce under control.

Some of the efficiencies derived from hostile takeovers (and therefore some of the benefits to corporate shareholders) are the result of workers losing their jobs, but the evidence suggests that the workers most likely to lose their jobs are executives and managers, not line workers.[18] Moreover, even if many line workers

[16] Others have explained the advantages of moving toward smaller and more focused firms with the existence of improved, more efficient capital markets that have made it attractive for firms to substitute reliance on external capital markets for internal capital markets, which favor multidivision firms. See Bhide (1990).

[17] This is most evident in what are often referred to as "bloated government bureaucracies," a fact that is partially attributable to the absence of the takeover option.

[18] In one study, sixty-two hostile takeover attempts (fifty of which were successful) from 1984 to 1986 were examined (Bhagat, Shleifer, and Vishny 1990). According to this study, layoffs were common, but seldom exceeded 10 percent of the workforce and were typically far less than that. Also, it was estimated that the probability of being laid off was 70 percent higher for white-collar workers than for blue-collar workers. The jobs of managers, not those of workers on the line, were most at risk. In addition, layoffs at targeted firms that were not taken over

are harmed in the case of losing their jobs from a hostile (and friendly) takeover, it does not mean that most of the workers harmed are necessarily made worse off by a *system* that encourages (or doesn't discourage) takeovers. Workers harmed in the case of their firm's takeover can receive offsetting benefits from the efficiency improvements they, the workers, realize through the lower price of the goods they buy. The lower prices can result because a multitude of other firms are taken over (or feel the threat of a takeover), the result of which is that their costs are more tightly controlled than would otherwise be the case.

Takeover defenses

Even if it we accept that hostile takeovers are generally efficient, it doesn't follow that there should be no corporate defenses against such takeovers. Ideally there should be some resistance to takeover offers, but not "too much." Neither efficiency nor the interest of stockholders would be served if the managers of a corporation simply acquiesced to the first takeover bid that offered more for the corporation's stock than the current price. The first bidder is not necessarily the one best able to improve the performance of the target corporation, and therefore the first bidder is not necessarily the one who can make the best overall offer. By being able to mount some defense against hostile offers, corporate managers can stimulate an aggressive auction that results in a winning bid that more accurately reflects the value of the corporation. For example, PeopleSoft fought the hostile takeover bid by Oracle for a year and a half, until Oracle finally won control in December 2004. Oracle initially offered $16 a share for PeopleSoft in June 2003, which PeopleSoft Managers rejected. The result was that Oracle increased the price it offered as it met intense resistance. Even when PeopleSoft shareholders voted to accept an Oracle offer of $24 a share, which was a healthy premium over PeopleSoft's share price at the time, PeopleSoft's manager continued to resist. This led to PeopleSoft shareholders ending up with a price of $26.50, several billion dollars more than they would have received from the initial offer (*The Economist* 2004a).

On the other hand, efficiency and the interests of shareholders can be harmed if the defenses against takeover bids are too impenetrable. If a takeover looks impossible, no one will make the effort to acquire control of even the most poorly managed corporation. A significant investment is also involved on the

were greater (as a percentage of the workforce) than those in firms that were taken over. This latter fact suggests that the threat of a takeover provides a strong incentive for efficiencies even when no takeover actually occurs.

part of an outsider to determine the potential for improving the management of a target corporation and the maximum price that can be paid for its stock and still make the takeover pay. There is little motivation to incur the cost of this investment unless it gives those who do so a bidding advantage. So, takeover defenses that go "too far" in requiring the initial bidder firm to make its information generally available can discourage takeover efforts to the point of reducing the amount of the winning bid.

No one can know exactly what the best defense is against a hostile takeover from the efficiency perspective. Obviously the most efficient defense is efficient management, that provides shareholders with a competitive return on their investment. But there are other ways to discourage takeover attempts, with the best one varying from situation to situation. They also vary in how efficient they are.

Greenmail

Interestingly, there is evidence that bringing litigation against bidders increases the amount that is ultimately paid for the stock of the target corporation, assuming that the target corporation loses the case.[19] Managers of the target corporation can also defend against a takeover by offering to repurchase the stock acquired by a raider at a premium, a practice known as "greenmail." Some studies indicate that greenmail imposes significant negative returns on shareholders of the target (repurchasing) firm, but other studies indicate that greenmail can result in small gains for the repurchasing firm's shareholders (Jensen and Ruback 1983; Mikkelson and Ruback 1985). Managers of the target corporation will want to be careful, however, if considering a policy of greenmail, because any gain to shareholders probably comes by encouraging others to attempt a takeover in the hope of extracting it. Paying greenmail on a consistent basis is obviously not a way of promoting the long-run profitability of a firm.

Poison pills

A very effective way for managers of a corporation to defend against a takeover is through what is referred to as "poison pills." A poison pill is a rule that allows shareholders of the target corporation to acquire additional shares at attractive

[19] Unless otherwise indicated, the studies cited are discussed in Jarrell, Brickley, and Netter (1988).

prices, which serves to dilute the stockholding of the acquiring corporation. Although there are different types of poison pills, studies indicate that they are in general harmful to the wealth of the target corporation's shareholders (Malatesta and Walkling 1988).

Anti-takeover regulations

Managers can also protect themselves against takeovers by lobbying for legislation that reduces the chances that any takeover will be successful. Such legislation imposes a variety of regulations on takeover activity, but the studies that have been done suggest that, in general, they reduce shareholder wealth. The stock price of firms typically declines relative to the general stock prices when the state in which they are incorporated passes anti-takeover legislation (Ryngaert and Netter 1988).

Golden parachutes

Obviously, the interests of managers and those of shareholders are not in perfect alignment in the case of takeovers. But there are possibilities for overlap that are worth noting. A justification for a controversial severance-pay contract for top managers is based on the desirability of reducing management opposition to takeover bids that benefit shareholders. Top corporate managers are commonly granted what are referred to as "golden parachutes," which provide them with handsome compensation when they leave the corporation. Such compensation can be particularly useful in cases in which top managers have to invest heavily in knowledge that is highly specific to the corporation, and therefore worth little elsewhere. Golden parachutes can also encourage executives to take greater risks, given that they know that they will receive a significant severance-pay package if the risks they take result in losses and they lose their jobs.[20] The argument is that when these managers are offered generous severance pay they are less likely to oppose a takeover offer that promotes efficiency and increases

[20] In the absence of some form of handsome severance-pay package, managers may be inclined to take too little risk, or less risk than the stockholders may want them to take. The stockholders can have diversified portfolios of stocks and companies over which they can spread their risks. Managers, on the other hand, can have a fairly narrowly invested portfolio, given that their talent, one of their biggest investments, is typically invested in one firm. Without some incentive to do otherwise, managers may be inclined to protect their investments by investing their firm's assets in safe ventures.

shareholder wealth. Golden parachutes help bring the interests of top managers more in line with those of their shareholders.

But as with all incentives, care has to be exercised. Golden parachutes should not be so lucrative that they make executives indifferent about keeping their jobs or losing them (see Jensen and Ruback 1983). Neither should the parachutes be so "golden" that board members are reluctant to replace executives whom they believe are managing their companies poorly, or not in the best interest of stockholders. For example, we noted in chapter 9 that in 2005 so-called "corporate raider" Carl Icahn (who had mounted takeovers of Texaco, TWA, RJR-Nabisco, Kerr-McGee, and Myland Laboratories in the 1990s only to impose restructuring demands on the companies) sought early that year to gain control of the board of directors of Blockbuster for the purpose of stopping the then-CEO and board chairman John Antioco from seeking to move the company into the Internet-based movie rental business. In his efforts to garner sufficient proxy votes to have his slate of board members elected, Icahn characterized Antioco's 2004 compensation package of $7 million in salary and $27 million in restricted stock as "egregious" (Peers and Zimmerman 2005). Still, when Icahn won the proxy fight, and Antioco lost his board seat, Icahn supported a move by board members to appoint Antioco as chairman of the board because "we don't want him [Antioco] to have the right" to collect the $54 million severance package to which he would have been entitled were he to be fired (Peers and Zimmerman 2005).

As with all arrangements, golden parachutes can be poorly designed and abused. It may make sense to provide golden parachutes to no more than just the CEO of a corporation and those few members of the top-level management team who can smooth or obstruct the transfer of control. But there is no reason to extend golden parachutes to managers not involved in such a transfer. Also, although golden parachutes can be too stingy to promote the shareholder interests, they can also be too generous, from the shareholders' perspective. Ideally, golden parachutes will be provided only to those managers whose responsibilities are relevant to a takeover, and the severance compensation provided will be tied to premiums in share prices generated by the takeover.

There is at least tentative support for the proposition that golden parachutes, across a range of companies, tend to promote the interests of shareholders. According to one study of corporations that adopted them, corporate stock increases an average of about 3 percent when the adoption is announced. One interpretation of this result is that the golden parachutes tended to strengthen the connection between the interests of shareholders and managers since golden parachutes offer executives protection for taking risks over a portfolio of business ventures. It is possible, of course, that part of the increased stock value resulted from the belief that the announcement indicated that management was expecting a takeover bid and wanted to protect themselves against it. But going beyond golden parachutes, it has been argued that one reason that there have been fewer hostile takeover attempts in recent years is that in response to the hostile takeovers of the 1970s, 1980s, and early 1990s, corporations have done a better job aligning the interests of managers with the interests of shareholders when facing a takeover. The result is more friendly takeovers (Holmstrom and Kaplan 2001).

THE BOTTOM LINE

The key takeaways from chapter 12 are the following:

(1) Firms in monopolistically competitive and oligopoly markets will follow the same production rule for profit maximization that perfect competitors and pure monopolies follow: They will produce where marginal cost and marginal revenue are equal.
(2) Monopolistic competitors may earn zero economic profits in the long run, but they will not produce at the minimum of their long-run average cost curve.
(3) The downward sloping demand faced by a dominant producer in a market can be derived from the gaps between the quantity demanded and supplied at various prices by all other smaller producers.
(4) The profit incentive firms have to cartelize their markets is a cause of cartels falling apart as members cheat on cartel production and pricing agreements.
(5) At times, producers demand government regulation because such regulation can enable the producers to restrict their aggregate production and charge above-competitive prices.
(6) Although the analysis of imperfect competition tells us something about the working of real-world markets, it does not answer all the questions economists have asked. The theories presented here have by no means done a perfect job of predicting the consequences of imperfect competition. Thus our conclusions regarding the pricing and production behavior of firms in monopolistically competitive and oligopolistic markets are tentative at best.
(7) Economists seeking to make solid, empirically verifiable predictions about market behavior rely almost exclusively on supply and demand and monopoly models.

Although predictions based on those models may sometimes be wrong, they tend to be easier to use and may be more reliable than predictions based on models of imperfect competition. Predictions aside, it is important to remember that most markets are imperfect.

(8) The competitiveness of the capital market – including the market for entire firms – will act as a discipline on managers who might believe that they can take advantage of their discretionary authority. Capital markets also induce managers to find the most cost-effective methods of production.

REVIEW QUESTIONS

(1) Under what circumstances could a monopolistic competitor earn an economic profit in the long run?

(2) To achieve the efficiency of perfect competition, must a market consist of numerous producers? If not, what other conditions are required?

(3) How does the number of producers in a market affect the chances of forming a workable cartel?

(4) How do the costs of entering a market affect the chances of forming a workable cartel?

(5) Must a monopolist employer share the monopoly profits with the managers and workers? If not, why not? If so, what does "profit sharing" do to the monopolist's output level? Prices?

(6) Should antitrust law attempt to eliminate all forms of imperfect competition? Why or why not?

(7) "In an economy in which resources can move among industries with relative ease, a cartel attempting to maximize short-term profits will sow the seeds of its own destruction." Explain.

(8) How would a cartel in a market for a network good collude on price? Explain.

(9) Suppose that the managers of a firm allowed their internal departments to act as little monopolies or suppose that the managers paid their workers more than the labor market would bear. What would happen in capital markets? To the firm?

(10) Why would you expect the market for corporate control not to work very well when there is a stock market bubble of the type experienced in the late 1990s and into 2000? Can you explain some of the unethical management behavior and deceptive accounting practices that came

to light in the early 2000s as, at least partially, the result of a breakdown in the market for corporate control?

(11) Would you expect government-run organizations to be more or less efficient than privately owned firms? Explain your answer with reference to capital markets.

Appendix: antitrust laws in the United States

As we saw in the chapter, monopoly power often leads to market inefficiencies, or a misallocation of resources. Reductions in monopoly power should therefore improve consumer welfare. The US government's antitrust policy, which is one of the oldest forms of government regulation of business, is designed, ostensibly, to improve market efficiency by reducing barriers to entry, breaking up monopolies, and reducing the monetary benefits of conspiring to reconstruct production or raise prices. It is based on three major laws, which have been amended and modified by court decisions: the Sherman, Clayton, and Federal Trade Commission Acts.

The Sherman Act

The Sherman Act was passed in 1890, after a series of major corporate mergers. It contains two critical provisions. The first, section 1, declares illegal "every contract, combination in the form of trust or otherwise, or conspiracy, in restraint of trade or commerce among several states or with foreign nations." The second, section 2, declares that "every person who shall monopolize, or conspire with any other person or persons to monopolize any part of trade or commerce among the several states, or with foreign nations, shall be guilty of a misdemeanor." In short, section 1 outlaws any form of cooperative behavior that restrains competition; section 2 outlaws monopolization or any attempt to acquire monopoly power.

The language seems clear enough, yet the courts were initially reluctant to rule against violations of the law, citing prosecutors' loose interpretation of the words "restraint of trade" and "conspire . . . to monopolize." In 1911, however, the Supreme Court ruled that Standard Oil Company, which then controlled 90 percent of the nation's refinery capacity, should be broken up. By dividing the firm along geographical lines (which explains the names Standard Oil of Ohio and Standard Oil of California), the court effectively nullified the economic benefits of the break-up. In place of one large monopoly, the justices created smaller monopolies. Later, the court broke up the United States Steel Corporation and American Can Company on the grounds that they followed "unfair and unethical" business practices.

A **tying contract** is an agreement between seller and buyer that requires the buyer of one good or service to purchase some other product or service.

An **exclusive dealership** is an agreement between a manufacturer and its dealers that forbids the dealers from handling other manufacturers' products. The Clayton Act is applicable only to exclusive dealerships that reduce competition "substantially," however.

A **horizontal merger** is the joining of two or more firms in the same market – for example, two car companies – into a single firm.

The Clayton Act

Because the Sherman Act did not specify what constituted unfair and unethical business practices, and because the courts generally took a very narrow view of what constituted restraint of trade and commerce, Congress passed a new law in 1914. The Clayton Act listed four illegal practices in restraint of competition. It outlawed price discrimination, or the use of price differences not justified by cost differentials to lessen competition or create a monopoly. This provision was intended to prevent firms from cutting prices below cost in a particular geographical region in order to drive competitors out of the market. Railroads and department stores were allegedly involved in such "predatory competition."

The Clayton Act also forbade **tying contracts** and **exclusive dealership**. If IBM tried to force buyers of home computers to purchase only IBM software, for example, its purchase and sale agreement with customers might be considered a tying contract. As long as other manufacturers' products are sold in the same area, manufacturers may organize exclusive dealerships covering designated territories, as is common in the automobile industry. Since 1985, the antitrust enforcement agencies and the courts have been more lenient toward such nonprice vertical restraints as tying contracts and exclusive dealerships.

Section 7 of the Clayton Act forbids mergers, or the acquisition by a firm of its competitors' stock, if the effect of the merger is to reduce competition substantially. The act applies only to **horizontal merger**, however. **Vertical mergers** were excluded from the act. For example, the Clayton Act would permit the merging of an oil-drilling firm with a refining firm, forming a **conglomerate**. The combining of firms from two entirely different markets – washing machines and light bulbs, for instance – would be considered a conglomerate merger. These loopholes in the Clayton Act – vertical and conglomerate mergers – were closed in part by the Celler–Kefauver Antimerger Amendment, passed in 1950. Although the Clayton Act has since been applied to vertical mergers, it has never been applied to conglomerates.

Finally, the Clayton Act declared **interlocking directorate** illegal. If the same people direct competing firms and advise policies that effectively reduce industry output, they constitute a *de facto* monopoly. Section 8 of the Clayton Act prohibits such arrangements if they "substantially reduce" competition.

The Federal Trade Commission Act

The original purpose of the Federal Trade Commission Act, passed in 1914, was to thwart "unfair methods of competition" among firms. The act empowered the FTC to investigate cases of industrial espionage, bribery for the purpose of obtaining trade secrets or

A **vertical merger** is the joining into a single firm of two or more firms that perform different stages of a production process.

A **conglomerate** is a firm that results from the merging of several firms from different industries or markets.

An **interlocking directorate** is the practice of having the same people serve as directors of two or more competing firms.

gaining business, and boycotts.[21] Later, the Wheeler–Lea Amendment expanded the commission's mandate to cover "unfair or deceptive acts or practices" that harmed customers, including the sale of shoddy merchandise and misleading or deceptive advertising.

The purposes and consequences of antitrust laws

The professed purpose of all these laws is to fight monopoly power by outlawing business practices that prevent or retard competition. By forcing firms to restrict production or fix prices surreptitiously, antitrust legislation makes collusion among competitors more costly. Violations of the law carry fines and penalties on conspiring firms and their employees.

Although many economists believe that antitrust law has achieved some of these objectives, critics complain of its inefficiency and have argued that the purpose of antitrust laws has been to thwart competition from large and growing firms that are more efficient than their competitors who complain of antitrust violation (see Di Lorenzo 1985; Armentano 1990). Detecting violators and bringing legal action against them takes time. Often, market forces erode monopoly power before the government can prosecute. The result can be a huge waste of legal resources. As noted in chapter 11, the Department of Justice spent more than twelve years prosecuting IBM for its dominance in the mainframe computer market, with questionable results.

In attempting to determine which firms possess monopoly power, the Department of Justice and the FTC have sometimes relied on "concentration ratios," or estimates of the percentage of industry sales controlled by the largest domestic firms. The arbitrary use of such ratios can be misleading. The top four firms in steel, for example, may have little monopoly power, for they must compete with producers of fiberglass, aluminum, and wood as well as with each other. Moreover, large market shares may be the result of superior efficiency, a higher-quality product, or good luck. Nevertheless, to avoid the appearance of impropriety, firms may decide to operate on a smaller scale than cost efficiency would normally dictate.

Economic consequences of treble damages

One of the antitrust laws in the United States – the Clayton Act – gives private firms the power to initiate antitrust suits. If an antitrust violation is proven, prosecuting firms receive a reward equal to three times the computed damages. Critics charge that firms may use antitrust suits as a means of diverting their competitors' resources away from

[21] Not all boycotts are prohibited, of course – only efforts designed to prevent goods from reaching their intended designation. That is, a union cannot prevent goods from crossing its picket lines, and firms cannot organize restrictions on the purchase of other firms' products.

production. The mere threat of an antitrust suit may be enough to keep some large firms from competing actively through better product design and lower prices.

Section 4 of the Clayton Act states that:

> Any person who shall be injured in his business or property by reason of anything forbidden in the antitrust laws may sue therefore in any district court of the United States in the district in which the defendant resides or is found or has an agent, without respect to the amount in controversy, and shall recover threefold the damages by him sustained, and the cost of suit, including a reasonable attorney's fee.

In other words, the successful private plaintiff in an antitrust case is to be paid treble the damages done to him by the defendant. This provision of the Clayton Act means that thousands of private firms and individuals join the Department of Justice and the FTC in the enforcement of antitrust laws. For many years the treble damages provision generated no controversy; it accorded well with the notion that victims should be compensated and apparently served an important deterrent to potential violators. Beginning in the 1970s, however, criticism of treble damages began to appear in the law and economics literature.

Critics have pointed out that the law has costs as well as benefits. A proper assessment must take account of both costs and benefits. Economists William Breit and Kenneth Elzinga find three principal costs of treble damage suits:

- *Perverse incentives* Treble damages can reduce the incentives of consumers to take private steps to avoid the harm done by the monopolistic firm. If the expected gains from the successful antitrust suit are high relative to the costs of buying from a monopoly seller, the buyer has a positive incentive not to avoid the monopoly seller, even if it is possible to do so. To put it another way, the treble damage provision encourages private enforcement of antitrust laws but discourages the private prevention of monopoly behavior.
- *Misinformation* A private party has an incentive to claim damages from anticompetitive behavior even when such behavior has not taken place. The treble damages provision generates many "nuisance suits" in which the plaintiff sues in the hope of forcing an out-of-court settlement. Such tactics have a fair chance of success in antitrust cases because in many instances the definition of "anticompetitive behavior" is quite vague. Moreover, in a jury trial anything can happen, giving the defendant (even if innocent) a strong incentive to settle before going to court.
- *Reparations costs* Considerable resources are devoted to determining and allocating damages in private antitrust suits. The judicial, clerical, and legal costs associated with compensating private plaintiffs all represent costs incurred solely because of the private enforcement provisions of the antitrust laws.

Although treble damages have their defenders, many students of law and economics have suggested that the provision be done away with or for awards to be restricted to the amount of the actual damages (Posner 1974), while others have supported severely limiting the types of cases subject to the treble damage provision (Breit and Elzinga 1985). The courts themselves seem to have grown wary of treble damages. At the time of writing, judges had in several recent rulings reduced damage awards in treble damage cases. The behavior of the judges in such cases may reflect the belief that the broad application of the treble damage provision generates more costs than benefits to the economy (Breit and Elzinga 1985).

CHAPTER

13

Competitive and monopsonistic labor markets

Labour, like all other things which are purchased and sold, and which may be increased or diminished in quantity, has its . . . market price.
David Ricardo

Professional football players earn more than ministers or nurses. Social workers with college degrees generally earn less than truck drivers, who may not have completed high school. Assistant professors of accounting typically earn more than full professors of history. Even the best history teacher and researcher probably earns less than a mediocre teacher and researcher in accounting on most campuses.

Why do different occupations offer different salaries? Obviously not because of their relative worth to us as individuals. Just as there is a market for final goods and services – calculators, automobiles, dry cleaning – there is a market for labor as a resource in the production process. In competitive labor markets, the forces of supply and demand determine the wage rate workers receive.

By concentrating on the economic determinants of employment – those that relate most directly to production and promotion of a product – we do not mean to suggest that other factors are unimportant. Many noneconomic forces – such as social status, appearance, sex, race, and personal acquaintances – influence who is employed at what wage. Our purpose is simply to show how economic forces affect the wages paid and the number of employees hired. Such a model can show not only how labor markets work but also how attempts to legislate wages, such as minimum-wage laws, affect the labor market.

The general principles that govern the labor market also apply to the markets for other resources, principally land and capital. The use of land and capital has a price, called *rent* or *interest*, which is determined by supply and demand. Furthermore, land, capital, and labor are all subject to the law of diminishing marginal returns. Beyond a certain point and given a fixed quantity of at least one resource, more land, labor, or capital will produce less and less additional output.

But because workers have minds of their own, with their own interests which are not the same as those who hire them, there are important differences in the market for labor and the market for, say, turbines or asphalt, that warrant a separate consideration of labor markets. We discussed some of those considerations in chapters 2 and 4 by examining how the way workers are paid, as well as how much, can motivate improved performance. This chapter exams labor markets in more detail.

PART I THEORY AND PUBLIC POLICY APPLICATIONS

The demand for and supply of labor

The **demand for labor** is the inverse relationship between the real wage rate and the quantity of labor employed during a given period, everything else held constant.

Labor is a special kind of commodity, one in which people have a personal stake. The employer buys this commodity at a price: the *wage rate* the laborer receives in exchange for his or her efforts. In a competitive market, the price, or wage rate, of labor is determined just as other prices are, by the interaction of supply and demand. To understand why people earn what they do, we must first consider the determinants of the demand and supply of labor.

The **demand for labor**

As with a demand curve for a product, the demand curve for labor generally slopes downward. At higher wage rates, employers will hire fewer workers than at lower wage rates.

The demand for labor is derived partly from the demand for the product produced. If there were no demand for mousetraps, there would be no need – no demand – for mousetrap makers. This general principle applies to all kinds of labor in an open market. Plumbers, textile workers, and writers can earn a living because there is a demand for the products and services they offer. The greater the demand for the products and the greater the demand for the labor needed to produce it – and the greater the demand for a given kind of labor, everything else held equal – the higher the wage rate.

Labor productivity is how much a worker can produce per unit of time (per hour, week, month).

Labor productivity – that is, the quantity of work a laborer can produce in a given unit of time – is another critically important determinant of the demand for labor. The price of the final product puts a value on a laborer's

Table 13.1 *Computing the marginal value of labor*

Units of labor (1)	Marginal product of each laborer (per hour) (2)	Price of mousetraps in product market (3) ($)	Value of each laborer to employer (value of the marginal product) ((2) × (3)) (4) ($)
First laborer	6	2	12
Second laborer	5	2	10
Third laborer	4	2	8
Fourth laborer	3	2	6
Fifth laborer	2	2	4
Sixth laborer	1	2	2

output, but her productivity determines how much she can produce. Together, labor productivity and the market price of what is produced determine the market value of labor to employers, and ultimately the employers' demand for labor.

We can predict that the demand for labor will rise and fall with increases and decreases in both productivity and product price. Suppose, for example, that mousetraps are sold in a competitive market, in which their price is set by the interaction of supply and demand. Assume also that mousetrap production is subject to diminishing marginal returns. As more and more units of labor are added to a fixed quantity of plant and equipment, output expands by smaller and smaller increments.[1]

Column (2) of table 13.1 illustrates diminishing returns. The first laborer contributes a marginal product – or additional output – of six mousetraps per hour. From that point on, the marginal product of each additional laborer diminishes. It drops from five mousetraps to four to three, and so on, until an extra laborer adds only one mousetrap to total hourly production.

The employer's problem, after production has reached the range of marginal diminishing returns, is to determine how many laborers to employ. She does so by considering the value of the marginal product of labor. Column (3)

[1] You may recall from chapter 10 that while there maybe increasing marginal returns initially when a variable resource is added to a fixed quantity of another resource, the additional returns to additional units of the variable resource must, eventually, reverse course. This is a technological fact of life, not a matter of economic logic. We showed in chapter 10 that in competitive markets, firms would produce in the range where their marginal cost curves are upward sloping. That is, they will produce where they encounter diminishing returns. This is a matter of economic logic and the conceptual foundation for our assumption that firms will confront diminishing returns when they contemplate hiring additional units of labor when the wage rate falls.

shows the market price of each mousetrap, which we assume here remains constant at \$2. By multiplying that dollar price by the marginal product of each laborer (column (2)) the employer arrives at the value of each laborer's marginal product (column (4)). This is the highest amount that she will pay each laborer. She is willing to pay less (and thereby gain profit), but she will not pay more.

If the wage rate is slightly below \$12 an hour, the employer will hire only one worker. She cannot justify hiring the second worker if she has to pay him \$12 for an hour's work and receives only \$10 worth of product in return. If the wage rate is slightly lower than \$10, the employer can justify hiring two laborers. If the wage rate is lower still – say, slightly below \$4 – the employer can hire as many as five workers.

Following this line of reasoning, we can conclude that the demand curve for mousetrap makers slopes, as do the demand curves for other goods, downward. That is, the lower the wage rate, everything else held constant, the greater the quantity of labor demanded. Theoretically, what is true of one employer must be true of all. That is, the market demand curve for a given type of labor must also slope downward (see figure 13.1).[2] Thus, profit maximizing employers will not employ workers if they have to pay them more, in wages and fringe benefits, than they are worth. What they are worth depends on their *productivity* and the *market value* of what they produce.

If the price of the product, mousetraps in this example, increases, the employer's demand for mousetrap makers will shift – say, from D_1 to D_2 in figure 13.1. Because the market value of the laborers' marginal product has risen, producers now want to sell more mousetraps and will hire more workers to produce them. Look back again at table 13.1. If the price of mousetraps rises from \$2 to \$4, the value of each worker's marginal product doubles. At a wage rate of \$10 an hour, an employer can now hire as many as four workers. (Similarly, if the price of the final product falls below \$2, the demand for workers will also fall – with the demand curve shifting from D_1 to D_3 in figure 13.1).

When technological change improves worker productivity, the demand for workers may increase. If workers produce more, the value of their marginal product may rise, and employers may then be able to hire more of them. Such is not always the case, however. Sometimes an increase in worker productivity

[2] The reader may get the impression that the market demand curve for labor is derived by horizontally summing the value of marginal product curves of individual firms, which are derived directly from tables such as table 13.1. Strictly speaking, that is not the case. However, these are refinements of theory that are considered in other, more advanced textbooks and courses.

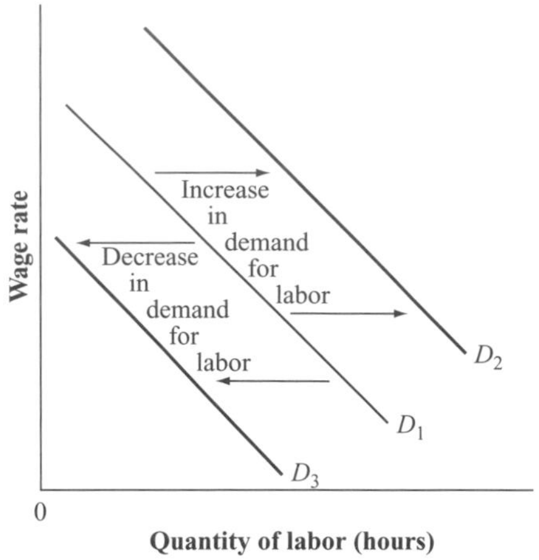

Figure 13.1 Shift in demand for labor
The demand for labor, as with all other demand curves, slopes downward. An increase in the demand for labor will cause a rightward shift in the demand curve, from D_1 to D_2. A decrease will cause the leftward shift, to D_3.

decreases the demand for labor. For instance, if worker productivity increases throughout the industry, rather than in just one or two firms, more mousetraps may be offered on the market, depressing the equilibrium price. The drop in price reduces the value of the workers' marginal product and may outweigh the favorable effect of the increase in productivity. In such cases the demand for labor will fall. Consumers will pay less, but employees in the mousetrap industry will have fewer employment opportunities and earn less.

> The **supply of labor** is the assumed positive relationship between the real wage rate and the number of workers (or work hours) offered for employment during a given period, everything else held constant.

The **supply of labor**

The supply curve for labor generally slopes upward. At higher wage rates, more workers will be willing to work longer hours than at lower wage rates (see figure 13.2). If you survey your MBA classmates, for example, you will probably find that more of them would be willing to work at a job that paid $50 an hour than would work for $20 an hour. (At $500 an hour, most would be willing to work without hesitation, aside from a few lawyers, surgeons, and consultants whose opportunity cost exceeds $500 an hour!)

The supply of labor depends on the opportunity cost of a worker's time. Workers can do many different things with their time. They can use it to construct mousetraps, to do other jobs, to go fishing, and so on. Weighing the opportunity cost of each activity, the worker will allocate her time so that the

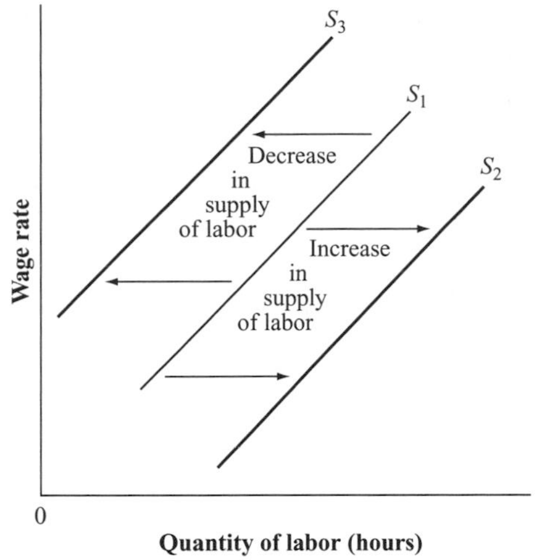

Figure 13.2 Shift in the supply of labor
The supply curve for labor slopes upward. An increase in the supply of labor will cause a rightward shift in the supply curve from S_1 to S_2. A decrease in the supply of labor will cause a leftward shift in the supply curve, from S_1 to S_3.

marginal benefit of an hour spent doing one thing will equal the marginal benefit of time that could be used elsewhere. Because some kinds of work are unpleasant, workers will require a wage to make up for the time lost from leisure activities such as fishing. To earn a given wage, a rational worker will give up the activities she values least. To allocate even more time to a job (and give up more valuable leisure-time activities), a worker will require a higher wage.

Given this cost–benefit trade off, employers who want to increase production have two options. They can hire additional workers or ask the same workers to work longer hours. Those who are currently working for \$20 an hour must value time spent elsewhere at less than \$20 an hour. To attract other workers, people who value their time spent elsewhere at more than \$20 an hour, employers will have to raise the wage rate, perhaps to \$22 an hour. To convince current workers to put in longer hours – to give up more attractive alternative activities – employers will also have to raise wage rates. In either case, the labor supply curve slopes upward. More labor is supplied at higher wages.[3]

[3] We note in passing that it is possible for the labor supply curve to bend backwards beyond some high wage rate. That is, beyond some wage rate, workers will choose to use some of their higher incomes to "buy" additional leisure, which means they will provide a lower quantity of labor on the market. While such a backward bending supply curve of labor is possible, we focus our attention on the upward sloping curve because that is the usual case.

The supply curve for labor will shift if the value of employees' alternatives changes. For example, if the wage that mousetrap makers can earn in toy production goes up, the value of their time will increase. The supply of labor to the mousetrap industry should then decrease, shifting upward and to the left from S_1 to S_3 in figure 13.2. This shift in the labor supply curve means that less labor will be offered at any given wage rate, in a particular labor market. To hire the same quantity of labor – to keep mousetrap makers from going over to the toy industry – the employer must increase the wage rate.

The same general effect will occur if workers' valuation of their leisure time changes. Because most people attach a high value to time spent with their families on holidays, employers who want to maintain operations then generally have to pay a premium for workers' time. The supply curve for labor on holidays lies above and to the left of the regular supply curve. Conversely, if for any reason the value of workers' alternatives decreases, the supply curve for labor will shift down to the right. If wages in the toy industry fall, for instance, more workers will want to move into the mousetrap business, increasing the labor supply in the mousetrap market.

Equilibrium in the labor market

A competitive market is one in which neither the individual employer nor the individual employee has the power to influence the wage rate. Such a market is shown in figure 13.3. Given the supply curve S and the demand curve D, the wage rate will settle at W_1, and the quantity of labor employed will be Q_2. At that combination, defined by the intersection of the supply and demand curves, those who are willing to work for wage W_1 can find jobs.

The equilibrium wage rate is determined much the same way as the prices of goods and services are established. At a wage rate of W_2, the quantity of labor employers will hire is Q_1, whereas the quantity of workers willing to work is Q_3. In other words, at that wage rate a *surplus* of labor exists. Note that all the workers in this surplus group except the last one are willing to work for less than W_2. That is, up to Q_3, the supply curve lies below W_2. The opportunity cost of these workers' time is less than W_2. They can be expected to accept a lower wage, and over time they will begin to offer to work for less than W_2. Other unemployed and employed workers must then compete by accepting still lower wages. In this manner, the wage rate will fall toward W_1. In the process, the quantity of labor that employers want to hire will expand from Q_1 toward Q_2.

Meanwhile, the falling wage rate will convince some workers to take another opportunity, such as going fishing or getting another job. As they withdraw

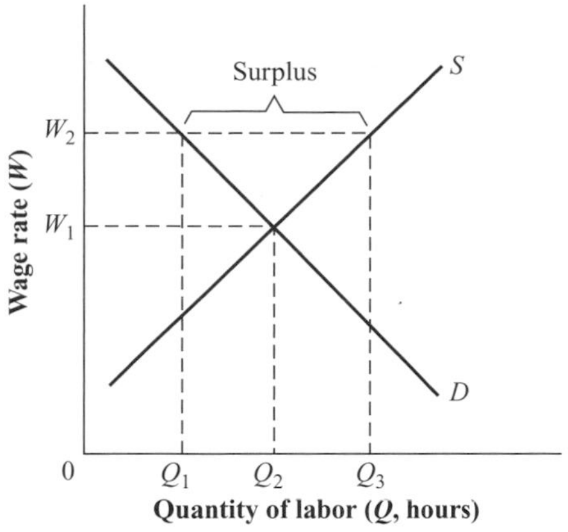

Figure 13.3 Equilibrium in the labor market
Given the supply and demand curves for labor S and D, the equilibrium wage will be W_1 and the equilibrium quantity of labor hired Q_2. If the wage rate rises to W_2, a surplus of labor will develop, equal to the difference between Q_3 and Q_1.

from this market, the quantity of labor supplied will decline from Q_3 toward Q_2. The quantity supplied will meet the quantity demanded – meaning no labor surplus – at a wage rate of W_1.

In practice, the money wage rate – the number of dollars earned per hour – may not fall. Instead, the general price level may increase while the money wage rate remains constant. But the real wage rate – that is, what the money wage rate will buy – still falls, producing the same general effects: fewer laborers willing to work, and more workers are demanded by employers. When economists talk about wage increases or decreases, they mean changes in the real wage rate, or in the purchasing power of a worker's paycheck.

Conversely, if the wage rate falls below W_1, the quantity of labor demanded by employers will exceed the quantity supplied, creating a *shortage*. Employers, eager to hire more workers at the new cheap wage, will compete for the scarce labor by offering slightly higher wages. The quantity of labor offered on the market will increase, but at the same time these slightly higher wages will cause some employers to cut back on their hiring. In short, in a competitive market, the wage rate will rise toward W_1, the equilibrium wage rate.

Why wage rates differ

In a world of identical workers doing equivalent jobs under conditions of perfect competition, everyone would earn the same wage. In the real world, of course, workers differ, jobs differ, and various institutional factors reduce the competitiveness of labor markets. Some workers therefore earn higher wages than others. Indeed, the differences in wages can be inordinately large. (Compare the hourly earnings of actor Tom Hanks to those of elementary school teachers.) Wages differ for many reasons, including differences in the nonmonetary benefits (or costs) of different jobs. Conditions in different labor markets may differ in such a way as to cause wages to differ. Differences in the inherent abilities and acquired skills of workers can generate substantial differences in wages. Finally, discrimination against various groups often lowers the wages of people in those groups.

Differences in nonmonetary benefits

So far, we have been speaking as though the wage rate were the key determinants of employment. What about job satisfaction and the way employers treat their employees – are these issues not important? Some people accept lower wages in order to live in the Appalachians or the Rockies. College professors forgo more lucrative work to be able to teach, write, and set their own work schedules. The congeniality of colleagues is another significant nonmonetary benefit that influences where and how much people work. Power, status, and public attention also figure in career decisions.

The trade-offs between the monetary and nonmonetary rewards of work will affect the wage rates for specific jobs. The more value people place on the nonmonetary benefits of a given job, the greater the labor supply. Added to wages, nonmonetary benefits could shift the labor supply curve from S_1 to S_2 in figure 13.4, lowering the wage rate from W_2 to W_1. Even though the money wage rate is lower, however, workers are better off according to their own values. At a wage rate of W_1, their nonmonetary benefits equal the vertical distance between points *a* and *b*, making their full wage equal to W_3. The *full wage rate* is the sum of the money wage rate and the monetary equivalent of the nonmonetary benefits of a job.

Workers who complain that they are paid less than workers in other occupations often fail to consider their full wages (money wage plus nonmonetary benefits). The worker with a lower monetary wage may be receiving more nonmonetary rewards, including comfortable surroundings, freedom from intense pressure, and so on. The worker with the higher money wage may actually be earning a lower full wage than the worker with nonmonetary income. Certainly many executives must wonder whether their high salaries compensate them for their lost home life and leisure time, and teachers who envy the higher salaries

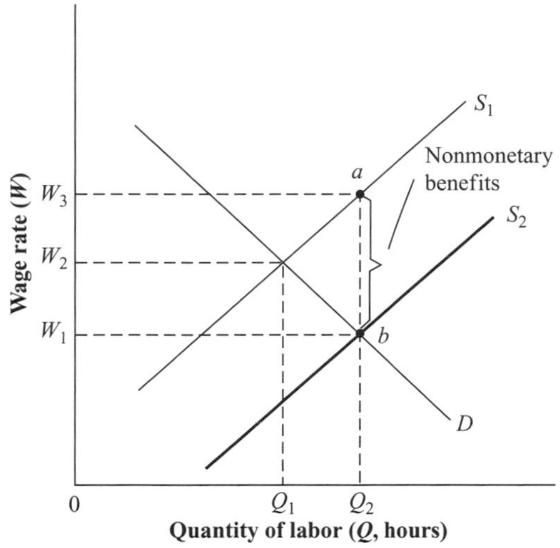

Figure 13.4 The effect of nonmonetary rewards on wage rates
The supply of labor is greater for jobs offering nonmonetary benefits – S_2 rather than S_1. Given a constant demand for labor, the wage rate will be W_2 for workers who do not receive nonmonetary benefits and W_1 for workers who do. Even though wages are lower when nonmonetary benefits are offered, workers are still better off; they earn a total wage equal, according to their own values, to W_3.

of coaches should recognize that a somewhat higher wage rate is necessary to offset the increased risk of being fired that goes with coaching.

Employers can benefit from providing employees with nonwage benefits. A favorable working climate attracts more workers at lower wages. Although providing benefits can be costly, doing so is worthwhile as long as they lower wages more than they raise other labor costs. Some nonwage benefits, such as air conditioning and low noise levels, also raise worker productivity. Needless to say, an employer cannot justify unlimited nonwage benefits. Employers will not pay more in wages – monetary or nonmonetary – than a worker is worth. In a competitive labor market they will tend to pay all employees a wage rate equal to the value added by the marginal employee – the last one hired.

Differences among markets

Differences in nonmonetary benefits explain only part of the observed differences in wage rates. Supply and demand conditions may differ between labor markets. As figure 13.5(a) shows, given a constant supply of labor, S, a greater demand for labor will mean a higher wage rate. Conversely, given a

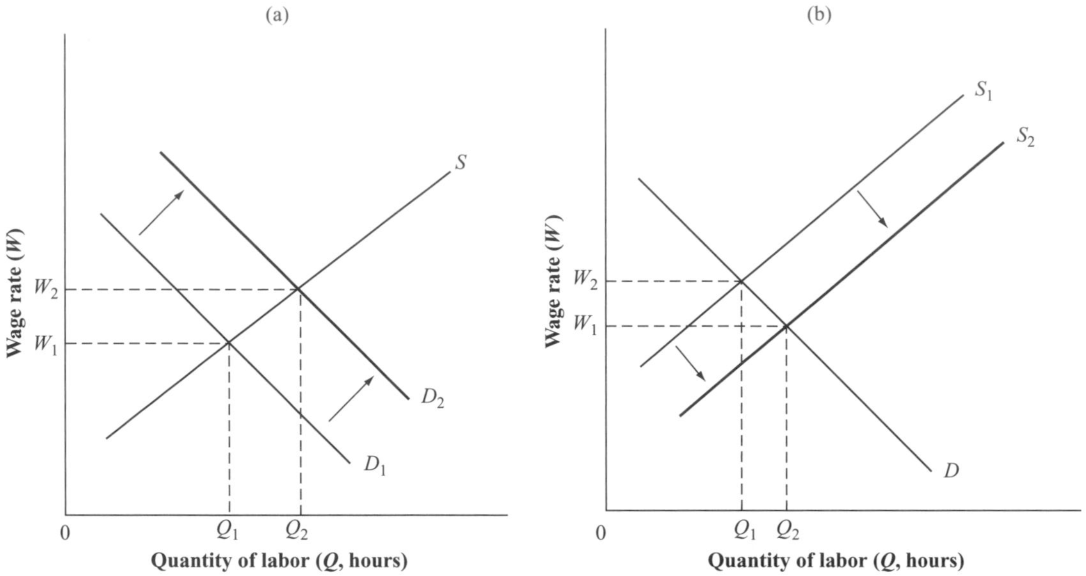

Figure 13.5 The effect of differences in supply and demand on wage rates
In competitive labor markets, higher demand for labor (D_2 in panel (a)) will bring a higher wage rate. A higher supply of labor (S_2 in panel (b)) will bring a lower wage rate.

constant demand for labor, a greater supply of labor will mean a lower wage rate. Depending on the relative conditions in different markets, wages may – or may not – differ significantly.

People in different lines of work may also earn different wages because consumers value the products they produce differently. Automobile workers may earn more than textile workers because people are willing to pay more for automobiles than for clothing. Consumer preferences contribute to differences in the value of the marginal product of labor and ultimately in the demand for labor.

By themselves, relative product values cannot explain long-run differences in wages. Unless textile work offers compensating nonmonetary benefits, laborers in that industry will be attracted to higher wages elsewhere, perhaps in the automobile industry. The supply of labor in the automobile industry will rise and the wage rate will fall. In the long run, the wage differential will decrease or even disappear.

Certain factors may perpetuate the money wage differential in spite of competitive market pressures. Textile workers who enjoy living in North or South Carolina may resist moving to Detroit, Michigan, where automobiles are manufactured. In that case, the nonmonetary benefits associated with textile work offset the difference in money wages. In addition, the cost of acquiring the skills needed for automobile work may act as a barrier to movement between industries – a problem we shall address shortly.

Differences among workers

Differences in labor markets do not explain wage differences among people in the same line of work. *Differences among workers* must be responsible for that disparity. Some people are more attractive to employers. Employers must pay such workers more because their services are eagerly sought after, but they can afford to pay them more because their marginal product is greater.

Barry Bonds earns an extremely high salary. The San Francisco Giants are willing to pay him so well both because of his popularity among fans – Bonds' presence in the line-up attracts bigger crowds – and because he is a successful hitter. Because a winning team generally attracts more support than a losing one, Bonds' presence indirectly boosts the team's earnings. In other words, Bonds is in a labor submarket like that shown by curve D_2 in figure 13.5(a). Other players are in submarket D_1.

Human capital is the acquired skills and productive capacity of workers.

Differences in skill may also account for differences in wages. Most wages are paid not just for a worker's effort but also for the use of what economists call **human capital**. We usually think of capital as plant and equipment – for instance, a factory building and the machines it contains. A capital good is most fundamentally defined, however, as something produced or developed for use in the production of something else. In this sense, capital goods include the education or skill a person acquires for use in the production process. The educated worker, whether a top-notch mechanic or a registered nurse, holds within herself capital assets that earn a specific rate of return. In pursuing professional skills, the worker, in much the same way as the business entrepreneur, takes the risk that the acquired assets will become outmoded before they are fully used. Students who have majored in history expecting to teach have all too often found that their investment in human capital did not pay off. Many were unable to get teaching jobs in their chosen field. Some have ended up as bartenders and cab drivers.

Finally, wage differences can result from *social discrimination* – whether sexual, racial, religious, ethnic, or political. Potential employees are easily grouped according to identifiable characteristics, such as sex or skin color. If employment decisions are made primarily on the basis of the group to which the individual belongs, rather than on individual merit, a form of discrimination (called "statistical discrimination") has occurred. Thus a qualified woman may not be considered for an executive job because women as a group are excluded. To the extent that employers prefer to work with certain groups, such as whites or men, the labor market will be segmented. Employees in different submarkets, with different demand curves and wage differentials, will be unable to move easily from one market to another. The barriers to the free movement of workers allow wage differences that have little to do with productivity to persist.

Competition among producers in the market for final goods can weaken (but not necessarily eliminate) discriminatory practices. Suppose that employers harbor a deep-seated prejudice against women, which depresses the market demand and wage rates for female workers. If women are just as productive as men, an enterprising producer can hire women, pay them less, undersell the other suppliers, and take away part of their markets. Under competitive pressure, employers will start to hire women in order to keep their market shares. As a result, the demand for women workers will rise whereas the demand for men will fall. Such competition may not eliminate the wage differential between men and women, but it can reduce it. In industries in which employers face little competition, employment discrimination is more likely, according to a substantial number of econometric studies.[4]

Monopsonistic labor markets

Competition is bad for those who have to compete. Not only as producers but as employers, firms would rather control competitive forces than be controlled by them. They would like to pay employees less than the market wage – but competition does not give them that choice.

Similarly, workers find that competition for jobs prevents them from earning more than the market wage. Thus doctors, truck drivers, and barbers have an interest in restricting competition in their labor markets. Acting as a group, they can acquire some control over their employment opportunities and wages.

Such power is difficult to maintain without the support of the law or the threat of violence, whether real or imagined. It comes at the expense of the consumer, who will have fewer goods and services to choose from at higher prices. As always, the exercise of power by one group leads not only to market

[4] For reviews of the economic literature on labor market discrimination, see Alexis (1974), Marshall (1974), Cain (1986), and Gunderson (1989).

inefficiencies but also to attempts by other groups to counteract it. The end result can be a reduction in the general welfare of the community.

This section examines both employer and employee power in the labor market; the conditions that allow it to persist; its influence on the allocation of resources; and its effects on the real incomes of workers, consumers, and entrepreneurs.

The monopsonistic employer

Power is never complete. It is always circumscribed by limitations of knowledge and the forces of law, custom, and the market. Within limits, employers can hire and fire and can decide what products to produce and what type of labor to employ. Laws restrict the conditions of employment (working hours, working environment) they may offer, however, as well as their ability to discriminate among employees on the basis of sex, race, age, or religious affiliation. Competition imposes additional constraints. In a highly competitive labor market, an employer who offers very low wages will be outbid by others who want to hire workers. Competition for labor pushes wages up to a certain level, forcing some employers to withdraw from the market but permitting others to hire at the going wage rate.[5]

A **pure monopsony** is the sole buyer of a good, service, or resource protected by barriers to entry by other employers or barriers to exit by employees.

For the individual employer, then, the freedom of the competitive market is a highly constrained freedom. Not so, however, for those lucky employers who enjoy the power of a **monopsony**. (Monopsony should not be confused with *monopoly*, the single seller of a good and service.) The term is most frequently used to indicate the sole or dominant employer of labor in a given market. A good example of a monopsony is a large coal-mining company in a small town with no other industry. A firm that is not a sole employer but that dominates the market for a certain type of labor is said to have **monopsony power**. By reducing the demand for workers' services, monopsony power allows employers to suppress the wage rate.

Monopsony power is the ability of a producer to alter the price of a resource by changing the quantity employed.

The cost of labor

Monopsony power reduces the costs of competitive hiring. Assume that the downward sloping demand curve *D* in figure 13.6 shows the market demand

[5] Competitors who do not hire influence the wage rate just as much as those who do; their presence on the sidelines keeps the price from falling. If a firm lowers its wages, other employers may move into the market and hire away part of the workforce.

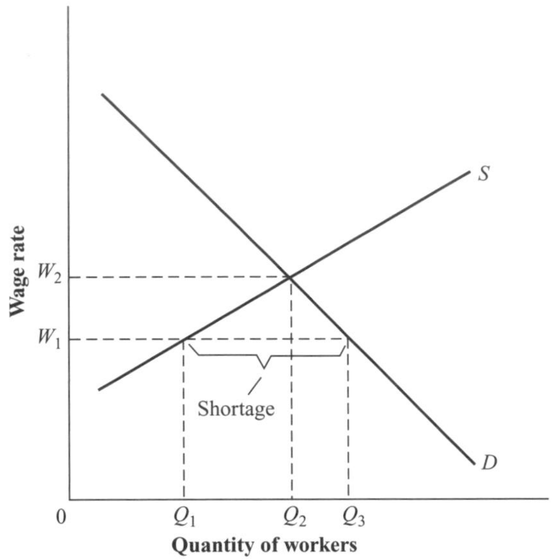

Figure 13.6 The competitive labor market
In a competitive market, the equilibrium wage rate will be W_2. Lower wage rates, such as W_1, would create a shortage of labor, and employers would compete for the available laborers by offering a higher wage. In pushing up the wage rate to the equilibrium level, employers impose costs on one another. They must pay higher wages not only to new employees but also to all current employees, in order to keep them.

for workers, and the upward sloping supply curve S shows the number of workers willing to work at various wage rates. If all firms act independently – that is, if they compete with one another – the market wage rate will settle at W_2, and the number of workers hired will be Q_2. At lower wage rates, such as W_1, shortages will develop. As indicated by the market demand curve, employers will be willing to pay more than W_1. If a shortage exists, the market wage will be bid up to W_2.

An increase in the wage rate will encourage more workers to seek jobs. As long as there is a shortage, however, the competitive bidding imposes costs on employers. The firm that offers a wage higher than W_1 forces other firms to offer a comparable wage to retain their current employees. If those firms want to acquire additional workers, they may have to offer an even higher wage. As they bid the wage up, firms impose reciprocal costs on one another, as at an auction.

Because any increase in wages paid to one worker must be extended to all, the total cost to all employers of hiring even one worker at a higher wage can be

Table 13.2 *Market demand for workers*

No. of workers willing to work (1)	Annual wage of each worker (2) ($)	Total wage bill ((1) × (2)) (3) ($)	Marginal cost of additional worker (Change in (3)) (4) ($)
1	20,000	20,000	20,000
2	22,000	44,000	24,000
3	24,000	72,000	28,000
4	26,000	104,000	32,000
5	28,000	140,000	36,000
6	30,000	180,000	40,000

substantial when the employment level is already large. If the wage rises from W_1 to W_2 in figure 13.6, the total wage bill for the first Q_1 workers rises by the wage increase $W_2 - W_1$ times Q_1 workers. Table 13.2 shows how the effect of a wage increase is multiplied when it must be extended to other workers. Columns (1) and (2) reflect the assumption that as the wage rate rises, more workers will accept jobs. If only one worker is demanded, he can be hired for $20,000. The firm's total wage bill will also be $20,000 (column (3)). If two workers are demanded, and the second worker will not work for less than $22,000, the salary of the first worker must also be raised to $22,000. The cost of the second worker is therefore $24,000 (column (4)): $22,000 for his services plus the $2,000 rise that must be given to the first worker.

The cost of additional workers can be similarly derived. When the sixth worker is added, she must be offered $30,000 and the other five workers must each be given a $2,000 rise. The cost of adding this new worker, called the **marginal cost of labor**, has risen to $40,000. Note that as the number of workers hired increases, the gap between the marginal cost of labor and the going wage rate expands. When two workers are hired, the gap is $2,000 ($24,000 – $22,000). When six are employed, it is $10,000 ($40,000–$30,000).

The **marginal cost of labor** is the additional cost to the firm of expanding employment by one additional worker.

Figure 13.7, based on columns (1) and (4) of table 13.2, shows the marginal cost of labor graphically. The marginal cost curve lies above the supply curve because the cost of each new worker hired (beyond the first worker) is greater than the worker's salary.

The monopsonistic hiring decision

The monopsonistic employer does not get caught in the competitive bind. By definition, it is the only or dominant employer. Like a monopolist, the

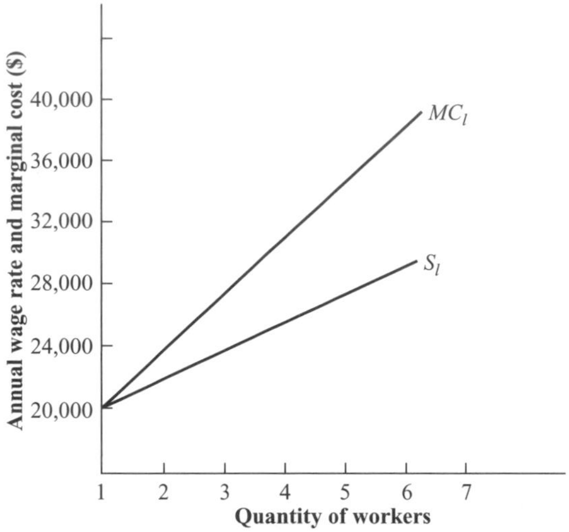

Figure 13.7 The marginal cost of labor

The marginal cost of hiring additional workers is greater than the wages that must be paid to the new workers. Therefore the marginal cost of labor curve lies above the labor supply curve.

monopsonist can search through the various wage–quantity combinations on the labor supply curve for the one that maximizes profits. The monopsonist will keep hiring more workers as long as their contribution to revenues is greater than their additional cost, as shown by the marginal cost of labor curve *MC* in figure 13.8. To maximize profits, in other words, the monopsonist will hire until the marginal cost of the last worker hired (*MC*) equals his marginal value, as shown by the textiles market demand curve for labor. Given the demand for labor, *D*, the monopsonist's optimal employment level will be Q_2, where the marginal cost and demand for labor curves intersect. Note that that level is lower than the competitive employment level, Q_3.

Why hire where marginal cost equals marginal value? Suppose the monopsonist employed fewer workers – say, Q_1. The marginal value of worker Q_1 would be high (point *a*), while her marginal cost would be low (point *b*). The monopsonist would be forgoing profits by hiring only Q_1 workers. Beyond Q_2 workers, the reverse would be true. The marginal cost of each new worker would be greater than her marginal value. Hiring more than Q_2 workers would reduce profits.

After the monopsonist has chosen the employment level Q_2, it pays workers no more than is required by the labor supply curve, *S*. In figure 13.8, the monopsonist must pay only W_1 – much less than the wage that would be paid

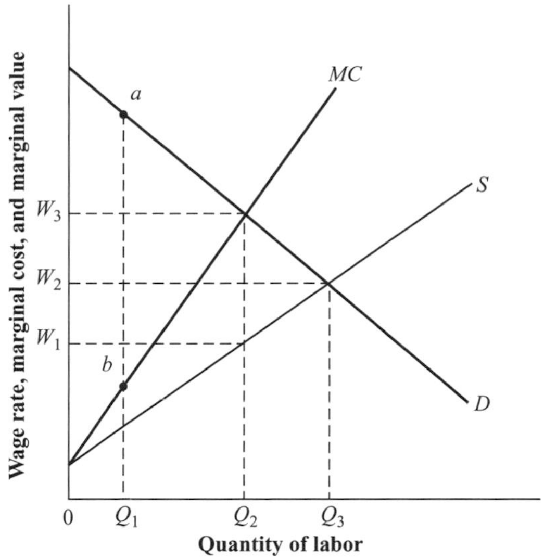

Figure 13.8 The monopsonist
The monopsonist will hire up to the point at which the marginal value of the last worker, shown by the demand curve for labor, equals his or her marginal cost. For this monopsonistic employer, the optimum number of workers is Q_2. The monopsonist must pay only W_1 for that number of workers – less than the competitive wage level, W_2.

in a competitive labor market, W_2. In other words, the monopsonist hires fewer workers and pays them less than does an employer in a competitive labor market.

It is the monopsonistic firm's power to reduce the number of workers hired that enables it to hold wages below the competitive level. In a competitive labor market, if one firm attempts to cut employment and reduce wages, it will not be able to keep its business going, for workers will depart to other employers willing to pay the going market wage. The individual firm is not large enough in relation to the entire labor market to exercise monopsony power. It therefore must reluctantly accept the market wage, W_2, as a given.

Employer cartels: monopsony power through collusion

Envying the power of the monopsonist, competitive employers may attempt to organize a cartel. An *employer cartel* is any organization of employers that seeks to restrict the number of workers hired in order to lower wages and increase profits.

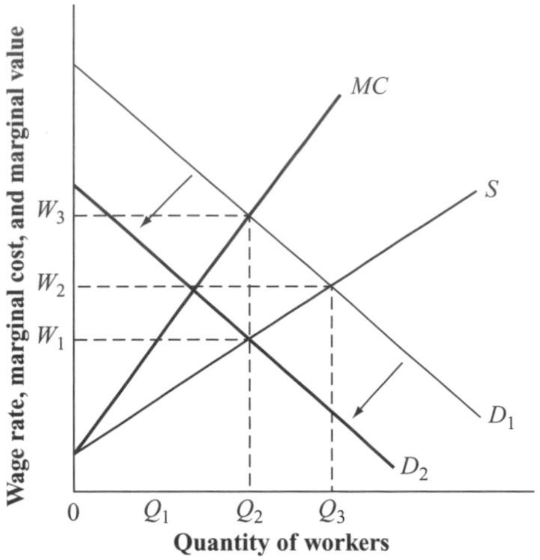

Figure 13.9 The employer cartel

To achieve the same results as a monopsonist, the employer cartel will devise restrictive employment rules that artificially reduce market demand to D_2. The reduced demand allows cartel members to hire only Q_2 workers at wage W_1 – significantly less than the competitive wage, W_2.

The usual way of lowering employment is to establish restrictive employment rules that limit the movement of workers from one job to another. Such rules tend to reduce the demand for labor. In figure 13.9, demand falls from D_1 to D_2. As a result, the wage rate drops, from W_2 to W_1, and employment falls, from Q_3 to Q_2. Although the method of limiting employment is different from that used in monopsony, the effect is the same. Whether the monopsonistic firm equates marginal cost with marginal value (shown by curve D_1) or the employer cartel reduces the demand for labor (to D_2), employment still drops to Q_2. In both cases, workers earn a wage rate of W_1 – less than the competitive wage.

One industry in which employers have tried to cartelize the labor market is professional sports. Owners of teams have developed complex rules governing the hiring of athletes. In the National Football League (NFL), for example, teams acquire rights to negotiate with promising college players through an annual draft. After one team has drafted a player, no other team in the league can negotiate with him (unless he remains unsigned until the next year's draft). Teams can buy and sell draft rights as well as rights to players already drafted, but within leagues they are prohibited from competing directly with one another for players' services. Violations of these rules carry stiff penalties, including revocation of a team's franchise.

Perspective Monopsony and the Minimum Wage

In chapter 5, we discussed at length the impact of the imposition of a federal minimum wage on competitive labor markets. We noted there how a minimum wage would curb employment and cause employers to try to offset the added labor costs associated with a minimum wage with reductions in fringe benefits and hikes in work demands. The analysis of a minimum wage under monopsony market conditions is much more straightforward. However, the employment consequence of an imposed minimum wage may be surprising.

Consider again figure 13.9, used in our analysis of an employer cartel. Suppose that the monopsony (or the employer cartel) restricts labor market demand and pays a wage of W_1 and hires Q_2 workers, because ite marginal cost of labor is the *MC* curve. Now, suppose that the government imposes a minimum wage equal to the competitive wage rate, W_2. W_2 then becomes the monopsonist's marginal cost of labor curve up to where W_2 intersects D_1.

If the monopsony weights off its marginal cost of labor, now W_2, it can increase its profits by hiring labor up to Q_3, the competitive equilibrium employment level. Note that, perhaps surprisingly, the imposition of the minimum wage under monopoly causes employment to rise from Q_2 to Q_3. The monopsonist expands employment beyond Q_2 because by doing so it can make additional profits (over and above what they would otherwise have been, not over and above what they would have been had the monopsonist remained unconstrained in the wage rate now paid by the minimum wage). Moreover, there are no adjustments in fringe benefits or work demands that the monopsonist can make to mute the impact of the minimum wage. You may recall that, in chapter 5, competitive employers adjusted their fringe benefits and work demands in response to the minimum wage, but that was only because the minimum wage set up an initial disequilibrium in the labor market in the form of a shortage. In the case of the monopsonist, the monopsonist does not end up in a disequilibrium: The quantity of labor demands at W_2 is exactly equal to the quantity of labor supplied at W_2.

Does this mean that the minimum wage does not undercut the employment opportunities for the covered workers? No, not necessarily. First, the minimum wage could be set so high – say, above W_3 in figure 13.9 – that even monopsonies would curb their employment when faced with a minimum wage. Second, monopsonies could control a minor portion of all labor markets, meaning that the negative employment effects in competitive labor markets more than offset any possible positive employment effects in the more limited monopsony-controlled labor markets. The presence of some monopsonized markets could help explain why, as mentioned in chapter 5, the measured negative employment effects of minimum-wage increases have generally been small.[6]

PART II ORGANIZATIONAL ECONOMICS AND MANAGEMENT

Paying for performance

Up to this point in the chapter, our discussion has focused on how labor "markets" work, and our interest has been on how the wage rate and other benefits are determined by the broad forces of supply and demand. However, markets must ultimately work with the interests of workers in mind. The problem most firms must solve is how to get workers to do what they are supposed to do, which is work effectively and efficiently together for the creation of firm profits. This is an extraordinarily difficult task. There is a lot of trial and error in business, especially as it relates to how workers are paid. At the same time, thinking conceptually about the payment/incentive problem can help firms moderate the extent of errors in business.

One of the most fundamental rules of economics, and the *raison d'être* for the discussions in the "Organizational economics and management" sections, is that if you offer people a greater reward, then they will do more of whatever is being rewarded, everything else equal. Many people find this proposition to be objectionable, because it implies that people can, to one degree or another, be "bought." Admittedly, incentives may not matter in all forms of behavior. Some people will sacrifice their lives rather than forsake a strongly held principle. However, the proposition that incentives matter applies to a sufficiently wide range of behavior to be considered a "rule" that managers are well advised to keep in mind: Pay someone a higher wage – such as time and a half – and they will work longer days. Pay them double time, and they will even work holidays. There is some rate of pay at which a lot of people will work almost any time of the day or night on any day of the year.

[6] See chapter 5 for references to the econometric studies on the employment effects of the minimum wage.

This rule for incentives is not applicable only to the workplace. Parents know that one of the best ways to get their children to take out the garbage is to tie their allowance to that chore. According to research, if mentally ill, institutionalized patients are paid for the simple tasks they are assigned (for example, sweeping a room or picking up trash), they will perform them with greater regularity.[7]

Even pigeons, well known for having the lowest form of birdbrain, respond to incentives. Granted, pigeons may never be able to grasp the concept of monetary rewards (offering them a dollar won't enlist much of a response), but pigeons apparently know how to respond to food rewards (offer a nut in the palm of your outstretched hand and a whole flock will descend, and maybe leave their mark, on your shoulder). From research, we also know that pigeons are willing to work – measured by how many times they peck colored levers in their cages – to get food pellets, and they will work harder if the reward for pecking is raised. Researchers have also been able to get pigeons to loaf on the job, just as humans do. How? Simply lower their rate of "pay."[8]

The "right" pay

It would appear that rules of incentives would lead managers everywhere to make sure that workers have the right incentives by always tying pay to some measure of performance. Clearly, as noted earlier in this book, the lone worker in a single proprietorship has the "right" incentive. His or her reward is the same as the reward for the whole firm. The full cost of any shirking is borne by the worker/owner. However, such a congruence between the rewards of the owners and workers is duplicated nowhere else. Opportunities to shirk abound in large organizations.[9]

7 For a review of the experimental literature on the connection between pay and performance of institutionalized patients, see McKenzie and Tullock (1994, chapter 4).

8 For a review of the relevant literature, again see McKenzie and Tullock (1994, chapter 4).

9 There are always "gaps" between the goals of the owners and the workers, and the greater the number of workers, typically, the greater the gap in incentives. In very large firms, workers have greatly impaired incentives to pursue the goals of the owners. The workers are far removed from the owners by layers of bureaucracy, communications about the firm's goals are often imperfect, and each worker at the bottom of the firm's pyramid can reason that her contributions to the firm's revenues and goals, or the lack of them, can easily go undetected. A recurring theme of this book is that when monitoring is difficult, one can expect many workers to exploit opportunities to improve their own wellbeing at the expense of the firm and its owners. And the opportunities taken can result in substantial losses in worker output. Management specialist Edward Lawler reported that during a strike at a manufacturing firm, a secretary was asked to take over a factory job and was paid on a piece-rate basis. Despite no previous experience, within days she was turning out 375 percent more output than the normal worker who had spent ten years on the job and was constantly complaining that the

How can managers improve incentives, reduce shirking, and increase worker productivity? The well-known management guru Frederick Taylor (1895) strongly recommended piece-rate pay as a means of partially solving what he termed the "labor problem," but he was largely ignored in his own time by both management and labor, and for the good reasons discussed in this chapter. As indicated by the story in the previous paragraph, paying workers on a piece rate doesn't guarantee diligent performance.

There is a multitude of ways of getting workers to perform that don't involve money pay, and many of them are studied in various disciplines, one being organizational behavior, which draws on the principles of psychology. Managers do need to think about patting workers on the back once in a while, clearly defining corporate goals, communicating goals in a clear and forceful manner, and exerting leadership.

Southwest Airlines, one of the more aggressive, cost-conscious, and profitable airlines, motivates its workers by creating what one analyst called a "community . . . resembling a 17th century New England town more than a 20th century corporation." The airline *bonds* its workers with such shared values as integrity, trust, and altruism (Lee 1994). But a company with a productive corporate culture is almost surely a company with strong incentives in place to reward productivity. Without taking anything away from the corporate culture at Southwest Airlines, it should be pointed out that one reason that it has the lowest cost in the business is that its pilots and flight attendants are paid by the trip. This, along with a strong corporate culture, explains why Southwest's pilots and flight attendants hustle when the planes are on the ground. Indeed, Southwest has the shortest turn-around time in the industry. It pays for the crews to do what they can to get their planes back in the air quickly (Banks 1994, 107). Motorola organizes its workers into teams and allows them to hire and fire their cohorts, determine training procedures, and set schedules. Federal Express' corporate culture includes giving workers the right to evaluate their bosses and to appeal their own evaluations all the way to the chairman. It's understandable why Federal Express delivery people move at least twice as fast as US postal workers: FedEx workers have incentives to do so, whereas postal workers do not.[10]

work standards were too demanding (Lawler 1990, 58). Obviously, the striking worker had been doing something other than working on the job.

[10] FedEx actually tracks its delivery people on their routes, and the workers understand that their pay is tied to how cost-effective they are in their deliveries. Postal workers understand that they are not being so carefully monitored, mainly because there are no stockholders who can claim the profits from getting more work done.

We don't want to criticize the traditional, nonincentive methods for getting things done in business. Indeed, we have discussed the issue of "teams" much earlier in the book, and the importance of virtues such as "trust" are raised before we conclude this chapter. At the same time, we wish to stress a fairly general and straightforward rule for organizing much production: *Give workers a direct, detectable stake in firm revenues or profits in order to raise revenues and profits: Pay for performance.* One means of doing that is to make workers' pay conditional on their output: the greater the output from each worker, the greater the individual worker's pay.

Ideally, we should dispense with salaries, which are paid by the week or year, and always pay by the "piece" – or "piece rate." Many firms – for example, hosiery mills – do pay piece rates: they pay by the number of socks completed. Piece rates can be expected to raise the wages of covered workers for two reasons: First, the incentives can be expected to induce workers to work harder for more minutes of each hour and for more hours during the workday.

Second, the piece-rate workers will be asked to assume some of the risk of production, which is influenced by factors beyond the workers' control. For example, how much each worker produces will be determined by what the employer does to provide workers with a productive work environment and what other workers are willing to do. So, piece-rate workers can be expected to demand, and receive, a *risk premium* in their paychecks. One study has, in fact, shown that a significant majority of workers covered under "output-related contracts" in the nonferrous foundries industry earn between 5 percent and 12 percent, depending on the occupation, more than their counterparts who are paid strictly by their time at work. Of that pay differential, about a fifth has been attributable to risk bearing by workers, which means that a substantial share of the pay advantage for incentive workers is attributable to the greater effort expended by the covered workers (Petersen 1991).

However, such a rule – paying by the piece – is hardly universally adopted. Indeed, piece-rate workers make up a fairly small portion of the total work force (though we have not been able to determine precisely how prevalent piece-pay systems are). Many automobile salespeople, of course, are paid by the number of cars sold. Many lawyers are paid by the number of hours billed (and presumably services provided). Musicians are often paid by the number of concerts played.

But there are relatively few workers in manufacturing and service industries whose pay is directly tied to each item or service produced. Professors are not paid by the number of students they teach. Office workers are not paid by the number of forms processed or memos sent. Fast-food workers are not paid by the number of burgers flipped. Most people's pay is directly and explicitly tied to time on the job: They are generally paid by the hour or month or year.

Admittedly, the pay of most workers has some indirect and implicit connection to production. Many workers know that if they don't eventually add more to the revenues of their companies than they take home in pay, their jobs will be in considerable jeopardy. The question we find interesting is why a "piece rate" – or direct "pay for performance" – is not a more widely employed pay system, given the positive incentives it potentially provides.

Many explanations for the absence of a piece-rate pay system are obvious and widely recognized.[11] The output of many workers cannot be reduced to "pieces." In such cases, no one should expect pay to be tied to that which cannot be measured with tolerable objectivity. Our work as university professors is hard to define and measure. In fact, observers might find it hard to determine when we are working, given that while at work, we may be doing nothing more than staring at a computer screen or talking with colleagues in the hallway. Measuring the "pieces" of what secretaries and executives complete is equally, if not more, difficult. We noted early in this book that Lincoln Electric, which has had considerable success with its pay-for-performance (as explained below), once tried to pay its typists by the keystroke, but the company quickly terminated the typists' "piece-rate pay" when one typist was caught constantly hitting a single key while she ate her sandwich on her lunch break (Roberts 2004, 42).

If a measure of "output" is defined when the assigned tasks are complex, the measure will not likely be all-inclusive. Some dimensions of the assigned tasks will not be measured, which means that workers' incentives may be grossly distorted. They may work only to do those things that are defined and measured – and related to pay – at the expense of other parts of their assignments. If workers are paid by the number of parts produced, with the quality of individual parts not considered, some workers could be expected to sacrifice quality in order to increase their production count. If professors were paid by the number of students in their classes, you can bet they would spend less time at research and in committee meetings (which would not be all bad). If middle managers were paid solely by units produced, they would produce a lot of units with little attention to costs. There is an old story from the days before the fall of communism in the former Soviet Union. According to the story, the managers

[11] For a review of arguments offered by psychologists against incentive pay plans, see Kohn (1993a, 1993b). Kohn sums up his argument as follows: "Do rewards motivate people? Absolutely. They motivate people to get rewards" (Kohn 1993b, 62), suggesting that the goals of the firm might not be achieved in the process, given the complexity of the production process and the margins workers can exploit.

of a shoe factory were given production quotas for the number of shoes they had to make, and they were paid according to how much they exceeded their quota. What did they do? They produced lots of shoes, *but only left ones!*

Much work is the product of "teams," or groups of workers, extending at times to the entire plant or office. Pay is often not related to output because it may be difficult to determine which individuals are responsible for the "pieces" that are produced. Because we took up the problems of forming and paying teams in chapter 10, here we remind readers only that team production creates special incentive problems. Making the teams "small" is one way to enhance incentives by making the contributions, or lack thereof, of each team member visible to others on the team.

Piece-rate pay and worker risk

When workers are paid by salary, they are given some assurance that their incomes will not vary with firm output, which can go up and down for many reasons that are not under the workers' control. For example, how many collars a worker can stitch to the body of shirts is dependent upon the flow of shirts through the plant, over which the workers who do the stitching may have no control. When workers are paid by the piece, they are, in effect, asked to assume a greater risk, that shows up in the variability of the income they take home. This means that piece-rate workers have to be paid a higher *average* income than if they were offered a predictable wage. Without the higher average income for those working at a piece rate, workers would choose to work for employers paying a predictable wage and those paying a piece rate would either be unable to hire anyone, or have to hire poorly skilled workers. So in order for the piece-rate system to work – and be profitable for the firm – the increase in expected worker productivity has to exceed the *risk premium* that risk averse workers would demand. This means that a piece rate (or any other form of incentive compensation) is often not employed in many firms simply because the risk premium workers demand is greater than their expected increase in productivity. This is often the case because workers tend to be risk averse (or reluctant to take chances, or assume the costs associated with an uncertain and variable income stream).

Even if workers are not more risk adverse than employers, piece-rate pay systems may also be avoided because employers are likely to be in a better position to assume the risk of production variability than their employees are. This is because much of the variability in the output of *individual* workers will be "smoothed out" within a whole *group* of employees. When one worker's output is down, then another worker's output will be up. Workers will, in effect, be able to buy themselves out of the risk. If each of the workers sees the risk cost of the piece-rate system at $500 and the employer sees the risk cost at $100, then each worker can agree to give up, say, $110 in pay for the rights to a constant income. The worker gains, on balance, $390 in nonmoney income ($500 in risk cost reduction minus the $110 reduction in money wages). The employer gives up the piece-rate system simply because it can make a profit – $10 in this example – off each worker ($110 reduction in worker money wages minus the $100 increase in risk cost). One would therefore expect, other things being equal, for piece-rate pay schemes to be more prevalent in "large" firms than in "small" ones. Large employers are more likely to be able to smooth out the variability.

If paid by the work done, workers would also have to worry about how changes in the general economy would affect their workloads and production levels. A downturn in the economy, due to forces that are global in scope, can undermine worker pay when pay is tied to output. When DuPont introduced its incentive compensation scheme for its fibers division in the late 1980s – under which a portion of the workers' incomes could be lost if profit goals were not achieved, but would be multiplied if profit goals were exceeded – the managers and employees expected, or were told to expect, substantial income gains (Hayes 1988). However, when the economy turned sour in 1990, employee morale suffered as profits fell and workers were threatened with reduced incomes. The incentive program was cancelled before the announced three-year trial period was up (Koening 1990). DuPont obviously concluded that it could buy back worker morale and production by not subjecting pay to factors that were beyond worker control. Each individual employee could reason that there was absolutely nothing she could do about the national economy or, for that matter, about the work effort expended by the 20,000 other DuPont workers who were covered by the incentive program. They could rightfully fear that their incomes were being put at risk by the free-riding of all other workers.

Piece-rate (and other forms of incentive) pay schemes will also more likely to be used in situations where the risk to workers is low relative to the benefits of the improved incentives. This means that they will tend to be used where production is not highly variable and where, in the absence of piece-rate pay, workers can easily exploit opportunities to shirk – where workers cannot be easily monitored. For example, salespeople who are always on the road (which necessarily means that no one at the home office knows much about what they do on a daily basis) will tend to be paid, at least in part, by the "piece," in some form or another, say, by the sale.

Piece-rate pay systems can also be used only when and where employers can make credible commitments to their workers to abide by the pay system that they establish and not to cut the *rate* in the *piece rate* when the desired results are achieved. Unfortunately, managers are all too often unable to make the credible commitment for the same reason that they might find, in theory, the piece-rate system to be an attractive way (in terms of worker productivity and firm profits) to pay workers. The basic problem is that both workers *and* managers have incentives to engage in opportunistic behavior to the detriment of the other group.

Managers understand that many workers have a natural inclination to shirk their responsibilities, to loaf on the job, and misuse and abuse company resources for personal gain. Managers also know that if they tie their workers' pay to output, then output may be expected to expand: Fewer workers will exploit their positions and loaf on the job. At the same time, the workers can reason that incentives also matter to managers. As is true of workers, managers are not always angels and can be expected, to one degree or another, to exploit their positions, achieving greater personal and firm gain at the expense of their workers.

Hence, workers can reason that if they respond to the incentives built into the piece-rate system and produce more for more pay, then managers can change the deal. The managers can simply raise the number of pieces that the workers must produce in order to get the previously established pay, or managers can simply dump what will then be excess workers. Recall our earlier example (in n. 9) of the secretary who, when asked during a strike to take over a job that had been done by a piece-rate worker with ten years' experience, quickly began producing 375 percent more that the experienced worker had. Workers in that firm were obviously shirking despite the piece-rate pay because they were afraid that the employer would reduce the per piece rate if they produced as much per hour as they could.

To clarify this point, suppose a worker is initially paid $500 a week, and during the course of the typical week, she produces 100 pieces – for an average pay of $5 per piece. Management figures that the worker is spending some time goofing off on the job and that her output can be raised if she is paid $5 for each piece produced. If the worker responds by increasing her output to 150 pieces, management can simply lower the rate to $3.50 per piece, which would give the worker $525 a week and would mean that the firm would take the overwhelming share of the gains from the worker's – not management's – greater efforts. The worker would, in effect, be working harder and more diligently with little to show for what she has done. By heeding the piece-rate incentive, the worker could be inadvertently establishing a higher production standard.

These threats are real. In the 1970s, managers at a General Motors panel stamping plant in Flint, Michigan, announced that the company would allow workers to leave after they had satisfied daily production targets. Workers were soon leaving by noon. Management responded by increasing production targets. The result was a bitter workforce (Klein, Crawford, and Alchian 1978).

So, one reason that piece-rate systems aren't more widely used is that the systems can be abused by managers, which means that workers will not buy into them at reasonable rates of pay. Indeed, the piece-rate system can have the exact opposite effect of the one intended. We have noted that workers can reason that their managers will increase the output demands if they produce more for any given rate. However, the implied relationship between output and production demands should also be expected to run the other way: That is, the workers can reason that if managers will raise the production requirements when they produce more in response to any established rate, then managers should be willing to lower the production requirements when the workers lower their production after the piece-rate system is established. Hence, the establishment of the piece-rate system can lead to a reduction in output as workers cut back on production.

The lesson of this discussion is not that piece-rate pay incentives can't work. Rather, the lesson is that getting the piece-rate pay system right can be tricky. Managers must convincingly *commit* themselves to holding to the established piece rate and not exploiting the workers. The best way for managers to be believable is to create a history of living up to their commitments, which means creating a valuable reputation with their workers, which is all the more important when performance targets are imprecise (Baker, Gibbon, and Murphy 1994).

Lincoln Electric's pay system

Lincoln Electric, a major producer of arc-welding equipment in Cleveland, makes heavy use of piece-rate pay. As Roberts (2004) and Miller (1992) have stressed, the Lincoln Electric pay system continues to contribute to worker productivity for several reasons:

- First, the company has a target rate of return for shareholders, with deviations from that target either adding to or subtracting from their workers' year-end bonuses, with the bonus often amounting to 100 percent of workers' base pay.

- Second, employees largely own the firm, a fact that reduces the likelihood that piece rates will be changed.
- Third, management understands the need for credible commitments. According to one manager, "When we set a piecework price, that price cannot be changed just because, in management's opinion, the worker is making too much money . . . Piecework prices can only be changed when management has made a change in the method of doing that particular job and under no other conditions. If this is not carried out 100 percent, piecework cannot work" (Miller 1992, 117).
- Fourth, Lincoln pursues a permanent employment policy. Permanent employees are guaranteed only 75 percent of normal hours, and management can move workers into different jobs in response to demand changes. Also, workers have agreed to mandatory overtime when demand is high (meaning that the firm doesn't have to hire workers in peak demand periods). In other words, workers and management have agreed to share some of the risk.
- Fifth, to combat quality problems, each unit produced is stenciled with the initials of the workers who produced it. If a unit fails after delivery because of flaws in production, the responsible workers can lose as much as 10 percent of their annual bonus.
- Sixth, large inventories are maintained to smooth out differences in the production rates of different workers.

Finally, with its reward system heavily weighted to performance pay, workers who are motivated by monetary rewards and who are willing to work hard have been attracted to Lincoln. Workers who aren't so motivated don't apply to Lincoln or, if they try working at Lincoln and find that they aren't willing to keep up with the pace of the coworkers, tend to resign and work elsewhere.

The importance of the self-selection of workers in Lincoln's Cleveland plant became clear to Lincoln management when the company bought plants in other countries and instituted its piece-rate pay system, only to learn that the workers at the foreign plants had not self-selected to respond to Lincoln's pay system. The result was that the company's acquisitions were failures simply because its piece-rate system did not inspire the effort response experienced in the Cleveland plant (Bartlett and O'Connell 1998).

When managers can change the rate of piece-rate pay

Does this mean that managers can never raise the production standard for any given pay rate? Of course not. Workers should be concerned only if the standard is changed because of something *they* – the workers – did. If management in some way increases the productivity of workers (for example, introduces computerized equipment or rearranges the flow of the materials through the plant), independent of how much effort workers apply, then the piece rate pay standard can be raised. Workers should not object. They are still getting their value for their effort. They are not being made worse off. What managers must avoid doing is changing the foundations of the work and then taking more in terms of a lower *pay rate* than they are due, which effectively means violating the contract or commitment with their workers.

There is a powerful lesson in what the manager at Lincoln Electric said, making his words worthy of a repeat. "Piecework prices can only be changed when management has made a change in the method of doing that particular job and under no other conditions" (Miller 1992, 117). Otherwise, piece-rate pay can have the exact opposite effect of the one intended.

Two-part pay systems

There are innumerable ways of paying people to encourage performance. The two-part pay contract – *salary plus commission* – is obviously a compromise between straight salary and straight commission pay structures. For example, a worker for a job placement service can be paid a salary of $4,000 a month, plus 10 percent of the fees received for any placement. If the recruiter can be expected to place two workers a month and the placement fee is $15,000, the worker's expected monthly income is $7,000 ($4,000 plus 10 percent of $30,000).

This form of payment can be mutually attractive to the placement firm and its recruiters because it accomplishes a couple of important objectives. First, the system can be a way by which workers and their employers can share the risks to reflect the way the actual placements depend on the actions of both the workers and their employers. Whereas each worker understands that her placements are greatly affected by how hard and smart she personally works, each also knows that often, to a nontrivial degree, the placements are related to what all other workers and the employer do. Worker income is dependent on, for example, how much the employer advertises, seeks to maintain a good image for the firm, and develops the right incentives for *all* workers to apply themselves.

Workers have an interest in everyone in the firm working as a team, and working productively, just as the employer does. Productive work by all can increase firm output, worker pay, and job security. As a consequence, although each worker may, in one sense, "prefer" all income in the form of a guaranteed fixed monthly check, the worker also has an interest in commission pay – *if everyone else is paid commission and if perverse incentives are avoided.* Hence, a pay system that is based, to a degree, on commission can raise the incomes of all workers. Put another way, to the extent that one worker's income is dependent upon other workers' efforts, we should expect workers to favor a pay system that incorporates strong production incentives for all workers.

With the two-part pay system, workers are given some security in that they can count on, for some undetermined amount of time, a minimum income level – $4,000 per month in our example. The workers shift some of their risk to their employer, but the risk assumed by the employer need not equal the sum of the risk that the workers avoid. This is because, as noted earlier, the employer usually hires a number of people, and the variability of the income of the employer is, therefore, not likely to be as great as the variability of the individual workers' income.

Why incentive pay equals higher pay

Of course, firms can expect that incentive schemes that enhance firm profits do not come free of charge. According to one early study, some 200 punch-press operators in Chicago who were paid piece rate earned, on average, 7 percent more than workers who did much the same jobs but who were paid a straight salary (so much per unit of time– for example, hour, week, or month) (Pencavel 1977). According to another study involving more than 100,000 workers in 500 manufacturing firms within two industries, the incomes of the footwear workers on some form of piece-rate or salary-plus-commission pay averaged slightly over 14 percent more than the workers on salaries (with the differential ranging up to 31 percent for certain types of jobs). The workers in the men's coats and suits industry on piece rate averaged between 15 and 16 percent more than the salaried workers (Seiler 1984). And the best evidence available suggests that the more workers' incomes are based on incentive pay, the greater the income differential between those who earn piece-rate pay (or any other form of incentive pay) and those who don't.

Of course, it may be that the income differential between incentive-paid and salaried workers is a matter of the difference in the demands of the jobs incentive-paid workers and salaried workers take. Incentive-paid jobs may pay more because they are the jobs the most competent workers are most anxious to take. However, the studies cited have attempted to either look at incentive-paid and salaried workers in comparable jobs or have adjusted (by statistical, econometric means) the pay gaps for differences in the "quality" of the different jobs.[12]

One of the more obvious explanations for why incentive-paid workers earn more than salaried workers is that the incentive-paid workers accept more risk. After all, the incomes of the incentive-paid workers can vary not only with the workers' effort, but also with the promotional efforts of their firms and general economic conditions in the market, among a host of other factors. A firm's ad campaigns can complement a worker's efforts to sell a product or service. A downturn in the national economy can make selling more difficult, effectively dropping the workers' rates of pay per hour (albeit for a long or short period of time). The incentive-paid workers' greater average pay amounts to a risk premium intended to account for the prospects that income may not always match expectations.

The business lesson is simple: To get workers to accept incentive pay, employers have to raise the pay. If both incentive-paid and salaried jobs were paid the same, workers would crowd into the salaried jobs, increasing the number of workers available to work for salaries and reducing the number of workers available to work on commission. The incomes of the salaried workers, everything else being equal, would tend to fall, whereas the incomes of the incentive-paid workers would tend to rise. If there were no considerations other than risk under the different pay schemes, the wage differential would continue to widen until the income difference were about equal to the difference in the added "risk cost" the incentive-paid workers suffered. That is to say, if the risk cost (or premium) were deducted from the pay of incentive-paid workers, the resulting net pay of the incentive-paid workers would be about the same as the pay of salaried workers.

But risk doesn't explain the entire differential. One of the studies mentioned at the start of this discussion found that the "risk premium" accounted for only a little more than 3 percentage points of the pay differential in the footwear industry and only 6 percentage points of the difference in men's clothing (with a great deal of variance reported across occupational categories) (Seiler 1984). Another important portion of the differential can be explained by the dictum that is central to all the "Organizational economics and management" sections of this book: Incentives matter! Incentive-paid workers simply gain more from extra work than do their salaried counterparts. A salaried worker is no doubt

[12] The study by Pencavel (1977) adjusts data for differences in education, experience, race, and union status. The second study by Seiler (1984) adjusts for differences in union status, gender, location of employment, occupation, type of product, and method of production, among other variables.

required to apply a given, minimal level of effort on the job. Salaried workers can choose to work more and produce more for the company. Their extra work might have some reward – a future rise or promotion – but such prospects are never certain. Many workers believe, with justification, that their rises are more directly tied to the number of years they survive at their firms than to how much extra they work and produce.

By way of contrast, the rewards of incentive-paid workers are much more immediate, direct, and contractual. Incentive-paid workers know that if they produce or sell more for their firms, their incomes will rise immediately and by a known amount. Accordingly, they have a greater incentive to apply themselves. One study in the early 1960s found that incentive pay improved worker productivity by as much as 40 percent, not all of which, as will be argued, is necessarily due to extra effort (Mangum 1962).

Incentive pay does more than just motivate greater effort. Different methods of pay are likely to attract different workers (Lazear 2000). Workers who are relatively unproductive, or who just don't want to compete aggressively, are likely to opt out of incentive-paid work. They will tend to crowd into salaried jobs, where many other relatively unproductive and less ambitious workers are. In short, workers who tend to be more productive than average can be expected to self-select into jobs with incentive pay. We should expect some firms to use incentive pay elements in many jobs simply to cull the unproductive workers. Incentive pay allows job applicants who know that they are willing to work hard to convincingly communicate this willingness to prospective employers by their willingness to accept the challenge of incentive pay.

If business becomes more uncertain, less predictable – as many seem to think it has since the 1980s with the growing complexity and globalization of business – we would expect the income gap between incentive-paid and salaried workers to widen. Employers will want to increase their competitive positions by giving their workers a greater incentive to work harder and smarter. Employers will want to shift a share of the growing business risk to their workers, at a price, of course, through greater reliance on commissions. At the same time, relatively speaking, more workers might seek to avoid the greater risk by trying to move to salaried jobs. However, their efforts will simply hold salaries down, widening the gap between incentive-paid and salaried jobs.

Honest dealing

It is important to elaborate further on a problem that can be crucial to the performance of managers: Getting the workers to deal honestly when their pay

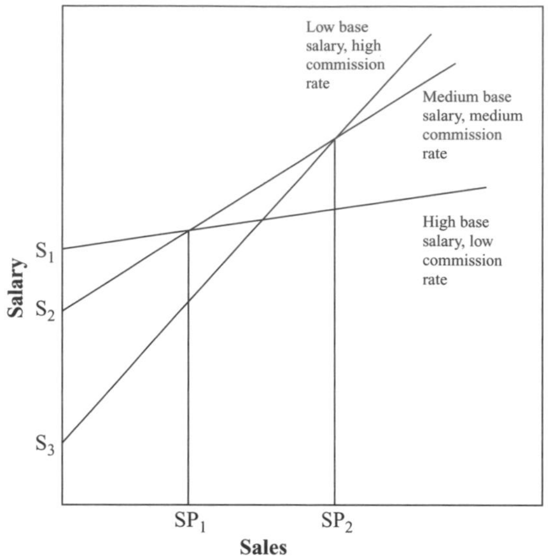

Figure 13.10 Menu of two-part pay packages
By varying the base salary and the commission rate, employers can get salespeople to reveal more accurately the sales potential of their districts. A salesperson who believes that the sales potential of his district is great will take the income path that starts at a base salary of S_3. The salesperson who doesn't think the sales potential of his district is very good will choose the income path that starts at S_1.

is at stake. For example, consider the manager who has to deal with a salesforce that works out in the "field," far removed from headquarters. The salespeople are hard to monitor. They know a great deal more about their territories in terms of sales potential than the managers can back at headquarters. How do the managers get the sales people to reveal the sales potential of their districts? This question is especially troublesome when the salespeople know that their revealed information will affect their sales performance criteria and the combination of the salary and commission components of their compensation package. If the manager at headquarters simply asks the salespeople how much they can sell in their areas, there is a good chance the salespeople will understate the sales potential. After all, some understatement harbors the potential of raising the salary and commission rate.

Fortunately, there is a way for managers to get honest responses on the potential sales in different territories. The manager can offer the sales personnel a menu of combinations of salary and commission rates. Consider the set of three salary–commission rate combinations illustrated in figure 13.10, which has pay on the vertical axis and sales on the horizontal axis. One pay package has a high salary, S_1 and a low commission rate, which is described by the low slope of the straight, upward sloping compensation line that emerges from S_1 on the vertical axis. Another pay package has a lower salary component, S_2 and a higher commission rate, and yet a third has an even lower salary, S_3 and an even higher commission rate.

What's a sales person to do? Lying about the sales potential of his or her territory won't help. Indeed, the sales person isn't even asked to lie. All she must do is choose from among the compensation packages in a way that she, not the manager, believes will maximize total pay. The salesperson who sees little prospect for sales will choose the package with the salary of S_1. The salesperson will be compensated for the limited sales potential by a high salary. The salesperson who believes that the sales potential will be greater than SP_1 (on the horizontal axis) but less than SP_2 will choose the package with a salary of S_2. The salesperson who believes that the "sky is the limit" (meaning a sales potential greater than SP_2) will choose the package with the low salary of S_3. This is the approach for establishing salary–commission rate pay contracts at IBM (Milgrom and Roberts, 1992, 400–2). It's not a sure-fire way of making sales people totally honest, but it can improve the managerial decision, and that's all that real-world managers can hope to achieve.

Incentives in the Irvine Company rental contracts

Because risk sharing and risk-reducing contracts can be mutually beneficial, we should not expect two-part payment schemes to be restricted to payments by employers to workers. They can also be a part of the payments made by tenants to landlords. Rental agreements have something in common with agreements between employers and employees since they include paying for performance. Both the landlord and tenant are intent on having an agreement that will ensure that the other will "perform" as specified. The landlord wants the rent and behavior by the tenant that maintains the value of the property. The tenant wants a nice living environment – or, in the case of retail space, wants a profitable business environment. Each wants to get as much as possible from the other.

Consider the nature of rental payments within and near the city of Irvine, California, which is situated along the coast between Los Angeles and San Diego. Irvine is a totally planned community with close to 200,000 residents within an area of approximately 180,000 acres (42 square miles). It has been planned and developed not by the usual government planning boards, but by a private wealth maximizing firm, the Irvine Company, which was once (in the early 1960s and before) the Irvine Ranch.

One of the more interesting features of the city is that much of the commercial property continues to be owned and managed by the Irvine Company, which has an interesting contract with its commercial tenants. The contract requires that tenants make a three-part payment: a fixed monthly rental payment; a fixed monthly payment for upkeep of the common areas within the community shopping areas; and a payment based on a percentage of their revenues. We are told that these payments can be quite stiff. For example, for a 1,000 square foot store in the nearby upscale shopping center called Fashion Island, the rent can apparently be several thousand dollars a month, plus several percentage points of the store's revenues, plus several hundred dollars a month in maintenance fees.[13]

How can the Irvine Company charge so much and then take a part of the store's revenues? It is all too tempting to conclude, as many have, that the contract is "exploitive," reflecting the monopoly power of the Irvine Company. Maybe so, to a degree. The owners and executives of the Irvine Company are wealthy. But, at the same time, there are good reasons to believe that the stores also benefit from the contract, especially from a provision in it that gives the Irvine Company a stake in the revenues of the stores in their shopping centers.

Naturally, any given store would love to retain the benefits of being in Fashion Island and, at the same time, pay no rent whatsoever. On reflection, however, the store owner could easily see that such a deal would be a loser, unless it was virtually the only store that got such a deal. Each store owner can reason that the payment for the upkeep of the grounds can clearly be in her best interests, given that the upkeep payments can make the whole center attractive to customers, increasing the traffic in all stores. These mandatory payments force each store owner to contribute to the general upkeep of the mall, overriding the inclination of each one to shirk on that upkeep. The store owners are, in effect, employing the Irvine Company to overcome the Prisoner's Dilemma problem they would otherwise face. They want the Irvine Company to perform with the interests of the stores in mind, as well as the interest of the Irvine Company's stockholders. Of course, there is a clear tie-in between the store owners' interests and those of the Irvine stockholders. The better the store owners do, the better the Irvine

[13] We are not privileged to know the particulars of the contracts, but the exact dollars involved are irrelevant to our discussion. Actually, the contract terms vary, as should be expected.

Company does, and that is the kind of performance tie-in that the store owners should seek.

The store owners can also reason that the high rental payments accomplish a couple of objectives. They ensure that all stores are high-value stores, with a focused appeal to upscale shoppers. Low-valued stores are not likely to be able to meet the stiff rental payments. The high payments also ensure that prices will be somewhat higher at Fashion Island than at other shopping centers, thus causing downscale shoppers to go elsewhere (permitting upscale shoppers freer access to the stores). The high rental payments also reflect the fact that the demand for the space at Fashion Island is high, partially because the Irvine Company has done a good job of enabling the store owners to make high profits. Stores, in other words, don't always want low rents, because low rents can (and frequently do) go hand-in-hand with low profits (because the low prospect of profits feeds into the demand for the rental property).

But why would the stores ever *want* to sign a contract that enables the Irvine Company to share in its revenues? Store owners understand that the Irvine Company controls much of the commercial space in the Fashion Island/Irvine area. The Irvine Company greatly influences the overall order of things in the area, including the income levels of residents, the distribution of various shopping centers within the area, and the distribution of stores within and across the shopping centers. The company has a substantial impact on the "look and feel" of the community, which means that the company can greatly influence the degree of success of individual store owners.

Taken together, we should not be surprised that the Irvine Company takes a share of the stores' revenues and that the store owners (collectively) *want* them to do just that. The percentage take gives the Irvine Company a direct incentive to operate in the interests of the store owners. If the Irvine Company allows the community to deteriorate or allows "too many" direct (or even indirect) competitors into their shopping centers, then the company will suffer an income and wealth loss (given that the value of their shopping centers are a function of the stores' profitability). The revenue percentage is a way the store owners can "pay for performance" on the Irvine Company's part.

We also should not be surprised that in many other areas of the country landlords do not include the percentage take. This is because in so many other areas, property ownership is often fragmented among a number of owners, with no one dominant property owner who is capable of determining, to a significant degree, the "look and feel" and profitability of individual store owners. As a consequence, store owners are unlikely to give a percentage of their revenues to their landlords when in fact each landlord can do little to earn the take. The landlord is unlikely to demand a percentage take because then the landlord would have to accept a lower fixed rental payment and would be at the mercy of the store owner, who has complete control over the store's profitability. There are simply no mutual gains to be divided.

Put another, perhaps more instructive, way, we should expect percentage takes to be a part of lease contracts where the landlords have a significant impact on store sales–for example, in shopping malls and other planned communities. The more fragmented the property, the less likely (or the lower) the percentage take.

THE BOTTOM LINE

The key takeaways from chapter 13 are the following:

(1) The demand for labor is influenced by the laborer's productivity and the price of the laborer's product. The supply of labor is influenced by workers' opportunity costs.

(2) In a competitive labor market, wage rates are determined by the interaction of willing suppliers of labor (employees) and demanders of labor (employers).

(3) Suppliers of labor (workers) are influenced significantly by the nonmonetary benefits of employment, as well as by the value they place on their next-best alternative employment. Differences in money wage rates may not reflect true differences in full wage rates.

(4) In competitive labor markets, wage rates above the intersection of supply and demand give rise to market surpluses, which can cause the wage rate to fall toward equilibrium. Wage rates below the intersection of supply and demand give rise to market shortages, which can cause the wage rate to rise.

(5) Monopsonists will maximize profits by hiring workers up to the point that the marginal cost of the last worker equals her marginal value. Monopsonists can pay less than the competitive wage rate because it can restrict the market demand for labor.

(6) A minimum wage imposed on monopsony labor markets can cause an increase in the number of workers hired.

(7) Workers who are paid for performance incur a risk cost, which can explain why they often earn more than workers who are paid a straight salary. In addition,

workers who are paid for performance are also induced to produce more, which enables them to earn more.

(8) In order for piece-rate pay systems to result in an increase in worker production, employers must be able to credibly commit themselves to not lowering the rate of pay when workers increase their output.

(9) Although paying for performance has a nice ring to it, providing the "right" pay for the "right" performance is a serious, not always easily resolved problem for managers. Accordingly, there are profits to be made from getting incentives right as surely as there are profits to be made from getting product designs right.

(10) One reason for employers paying workers in two parts – salary plus some form of commission (or tie-in to performance) – is that both employer and employee can gain. The employer can accept the risk associated with having to meet a regular, contracted salary payment, and the employee can want the salary because it reduces her risk and, at the same time, gives the employer an incentive to work hard at keeping the work going (in order that the salary can be met with relative ease).

REVIEW QUESTIONS

(1) The government requires employers to pay time and a half for labor in excess of forty hours a week. How should managers be expected to react to that law? What effect should such a law have on the quantity of labor demanded? Why?

(2) Does union support of laws outlawing child labor square with the private interests of union members? How could the minimum wage rate and migrant housing standards affect the wages of union members? How can they be expected to affect the prices of consumer goods? Explain, using supply and demand graphs.

(3) Suppose the government requires employers to pay a minimum wage of $10 per hour to workers over twenty-two years of age. What effect should such a law have on the employment opportunities and wage rates of persons under twenty-two?

(4) How can government mandates requiring that employers provide their workers with particular fringe benefits make workers worse off? How do such mandates affect the supply and demand curves for labor? What happens to the market wage and employment level?

(5) Are there reasons for believing that it is unlikely that minimum-wage laws would benefit workers even in the case of some monopsony power by the employer?

(6) Workers paid on a piece-rate basis often use the term "rate buster" for someone who responds to the piece rate by turning out lots of output. Is "rate buster" a term of endearment here? How does a reputation by management for honesty and credibility help eliminate the problem reflected by the term "rate buster?"

CHAPTER 14

Problems in collective decision making

I have no fear, but that the result of our experiment will be, that men may be trusted to govern themselves without a master. Could the contrary be proved, I should conclude, either that there is no God, or that he is a malevolent being. **Thomas Jefferson**

Previous chapters (most notably chapters 5, 8, and 13) have discussed the effects of various government policies on the market system in general and the firm in particular. We looked at government efforts to control the external costs of pollution. We considered the economic impact of price controls, for example, on final goods market and on minimum wages for labor markets. Throughout the analysis we have focused on assessing the *economic efficiency* of government policy. We have said little about how government policies are determined or why government may prefer one policy to another.

In this chapter, we shift our focus to the functioning of government itself. Using economic principles, we examine the process through which government decisions are made and carried out in a two-party democratic system, and we consider that system's consequences. Today, when government production accounts for a substantial portion of the nation's goods and services, no student of economics and business can afford to ignore these issues.

A study of the political process is especially important for many MBA students, mainly because a nontrivial amount of your time will be involved with seeking to respond to, or change, one governmental policy or another. Moreover, politics is also endemic to many businesses. Our discussion of the "economics of politics" has various implications for how businesses can be expected to operate, especially those that rely on "participatory management" processes (which are necessarily democratic, to one extent or another).

PART I THEORY AND PUBLIC POLICY APPLICATIONS

The central tendency of a two-party system

In a two-party democratic system, elected officials typically take middle-of-the road positions. Winning candidates tend to represent the moderate views of many voters who are neither strongly liberal nor strongly conservative. For this reason, there is often not a lot of difference between Republican and Democratic candidates. Even when the major parties' candidates differ strongly, as George W. Bush and John Kerry did at the start of the 2004 presidential campaign, they tend to move closer together as the campaign progresses.

Presidential candidates from both major political parties have, of course, talked a lot since the 1970s about the role of the federal government in the economy. Successful Democratic presidential candidates – Jimmy Carter and Bill Clinton – portrayed themselves as socially warm hearted and advocated more government expenditures on an expanded array of government programs during their presidential campaigns. In contrast, successful Republican candidates – Ronald Reagan, George H. W. Bush (hereafter, Bush I), and George W. Bush (hereafter, Bush II) – were more skeptical of government and stressed the need to contain, if not reduce, government programs on many fronts (except for defense).

From all the rhetoric, voters might expect the fiscal records of presidents to be radically different, depending on their political parties. The presidential records on expenditures belie these usual quick-and-easy assessments. One important record to consider is federal government expenditures as a percent of gross domestic product (GDP). Such a statistic should be telling because government expenditures are the real tax on the economy. They soak up resources that could otherwise be used in the private sector. Surprisingly, by this measure – federal spending divided by GDP – there hasn't been much difference in the actual track records of Democratic and Republican presidents, despite the differences in their rhetoric.

Through the twelve years of Democrats in the White House – Carter's one term and Clinton's two – federal government expenditures averaged 20.1 percent of GDP. Through the sixteen years of Republicans in the White House – Reagan's two terms, Bush I's one term, and Bush II's first term – federal expenditures were actually higher, averaging 21.6% of GDP. This means that while the difference was small, Republican presidents stood witness to a 7.5 percent greater average share of GDP being soaked up by the federal government than the Democratic presidents did.[1]

Agreed, these recorded minor differences in the spending records of presidents can be attributable to the fact that Republic and Democrats in the White House and Congress hold each other in check. But the minor differences could also be chalked up to the political incentives presidential candidates have to move close to the fiscal positions of the opposition, which can be illustrated in figure 14.1. The bell shaped curve shows the approximate distribution of voters along the political spectrum from very liberal to very conservative. A few voters have views that place them in the "wings" of the distribution, but most cluster near the center. Assuming that citizens will vote for the candidate who most closely approximates their own political position, a politician who wants to win the election will not choose a position in the "wings" of the distribution.

Suppose, for instance, that the Republican candidate chooses a position at R_1. The Democratic candidate can easily win the election by taking a position slightly to the left, at D_1. Although the Republican will take all the votes to the right of R_1 and roughly half the votes between R_1 and D_1, the Democrat will

[1] Of course, Republicans are supposedly more inclined to favor defense over social program spending. If only non-defense federal spending is considered, the Republican presidents still outpaced their Democratic counterparts, albeit slightly, which carries an element of surprise because, again, of the sharp contrast in Democratic and Republican presidential rhetoric. Nondefense federal spending during the twelve years of Democrats in the White House averaged 16.3% of GDP. During the sixteen years of Republicans in the White House, nondefense federal spending averaged 16.5% of GDP. Reagan and Clinton tied, with nondefense spending during each of their eight years at 16.3%. During each of their second terms in office, nondefense federal spending averaged 15.7% of GDP. Bush I and Bush II, each pushing his own brand of "fiscal conservatism," managed to reverse the relative shrinkage of nondefense federal spending orchestrated by their respective predecessors, Reagan and Clinton: not exactly what one would expect from their political rhetoric. Of course, every president must yield to the demands of Congress and, hence, cannot be given total blame or credit for what happens to federal spending during his term of office. During the eleven years the Democrats controlled both houses of Congress (regardless of which party controlled the White House), nondefense federal spending represented 16.4% of GDP. During the nine years the Republicans controlled both houses, nondefense federal spending represented 16.2% of GDP. Nondefense federal spending represented 16.3% when the Democrats controlled both houses of Congress and the White House and 16.2% when the Republicans controlled both houses and the White House: again, hardly what would be expected given the sharp contrast in the parties' fiscal rhetoric. When the Democrats controlled the White House and the Republicans controlled both Houses of Congress, nondefense federal spending represented 16.2% of GDP. When Republicans controlled the White House and the Democrats controlled both houses, nondefense federal spending constituted 16.4% of GDP. No matter how the data is turned, the overall level of federal spending as a percentage of the national economy certainly hasn't been affected as much as partisan election rhetoric might suggest. There is probably a dime's worth of difference in the fiscal inclinations of elected Democrats and Republicans, but certainly not more than a dime.

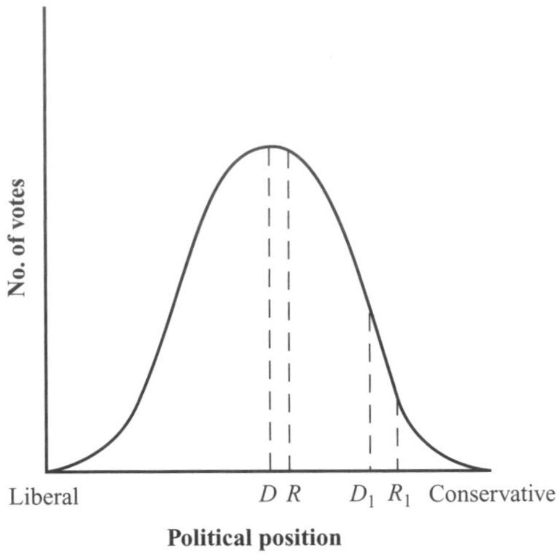

Figure 14.1 The political spectrum
A political candidate who takes a position in the "wings" of a voter distribution, such as D_1 or R_1, will win fewer votes than a candidate who moves toward the middle of the distribution. In a two-party election, therefore, both candidates will take middle-of-the-road positions, such as D and R.

take all the votes to the left. Clearly, the Democrat will win an overwhelming majority.

The smart politician will therefore choose a position near the middle. Then the opposing candidate must also move to the middle, or accept certain defeat. Suppose, for instance, that the Republican candidate chooses position R, but the Democrat remains at D_1. The Republican will take all the votes to the left of R and roughly half the votes between R and D_1. She will have more than the simple majority needed to beat her Democratic opponent. In short, both candidates will improve their vote total by moving toward the middle of the distribution. Does this mean that both candidates will end up at the same point – exactly in the middle of the distribution? Probably not.

> The **median voter** is the person in the exact middle of the political distribution.

Politicians can misinterpret the political climate. Even with polls, no one can be certain of the distribution of votes before an election. Just as producers find the optimum production level through trial and error, so might politicians suffer several defeats before finding the true center of public opinion. Inevitably, however, political competition will drive them toward the middle of the distribution, where the **median voter** group resides.

The history of presidential elections illustrates how politicians play to the views of the median voter. After an election in which the successful candidate won by a wide margin, the losing party moved toward the position of the winning party. After Barry Goldwater lost by a wide margin to Lyndon Johnson in 1964, the Republican Party made a deliberate effort to pick a more moderate candidate. As a result, the contest between Richard Nixon and Hubert Humphrey in 1968 was practically a dead heat. After the far-left George McGovern was defeated in a landslide by Richard Nixon in 1972, Democrats realized they, too, needed a less extreme candidate. Their choices in 1976 and 1984, Jimmy Carter and Walter Mondale, were more moderate. After Ronald Reagan soundly defeated Jimmy Carter and Walter Mondale and George Bush I beat Michael Dukakis in 1988, the Democrats began what appeared to be a move back toward the center, picking Bill Clinton, a centrist candidate whose policies, in many ways, have been more conservative than were Bush I's or Bush II's.

Ronald Reagan's two victories may seem at variance with the median voter result, since he took what most considered positions well to the right of most voters. This could represent another reason why both presidential candidates don't end up in the same position. Politicians can influence public opinion as well as simply respond to it. Reagan was known as "The Great Communicator," and he was no doubt able to pull the median voter in his direction. But it was also probably true that world and domestic events were causing public opinion to shift in a more conservative direction, and Reagan was better positioned politically to take advantage of that shift.

The economics of the voting rule

So far, we have been assuming that a winning candidate must receive more than 50 percent of the vote. Although most issues that confront civic bodies are determined by simple-majority rule, not all collective decisions are made on that basis, nor should they be. Some decisions are too trivial for group consideration. The cost of a bad decision is so small that it is uneconomical to put the question up for debate. Other decisions are too important to be decided by a simple majority. Richard Nixon was elected president with only 43 percent of the popular vote in 1968 (when a third-party candidate, George Wallace, took almost 14 percent), but Nixon's impeachment would have required more than a majority of the Senate and the House of Representatives. In murder cases, juries are required to reach unanimous agreement. In such instances, the cost of a misguided decision is high enough to justify the extra time and trouble required to achieve more than a simple majority.

The voting rule that government follows helps to determine the size and scope of government activities. If only a few people need to agree on budgetary proposals, for example, the effect can be to foster "big government." Under such an arrangement, small groups can easily pass their proposals, expanding the scope of government activity each time they do so. However, under a voting rule that requires unanimous agreement among voters – a unanimity rule – very few proposals will be agreed to or implemented by government. There are very few issues on which everyone can agree, particularly when many people are involved.

A unanimity rule can be exploited by small groups of voters. If everyone's vote is critically important, as it is with a unanimous voting rule, then everyone is in a strategic bargaining position. Anyone can threaten to veto the proposed legislation unless she is given special treatment. Such tactics increase the cost of decision making.

Government represents the people's collective interest, but the type of voting rule used determines the particular interests represented and the extent to which they are represented.

The inefficiencies of democracy

As a form of government, democracy has some important advantages. It disperses the power of decision making among a large number of people, reducing the influence of individual whim and personal interest. Thus it provides some protection for individual liberties. Democracy also gives political candidates an incentive to seek out and represent a broad sector of public opinion and interests. Competition for votes forces candidates to reveal what they are willing to do for various interest groups. As does any system, however, including the market system, the democratic system has some drawbacks as well. In particular, democracy is less than efficient as a producer of some goods and services.

The fact that the democratic form of government is inefficient in some respects does not mean that we should replace it with another decision making process, any more than we should replace the market system, which is also less than perfectly efficient. Instead, we must measure the costs of one type of production against the other, and choose the more efficient means of production in each particular case. We must weigh the cost of externalities in the private market against the cost of inefficiencies in the public sector. Neither system is perfect, so we must choose carefully between them.

Median voter preferences

When you buy a good such as ice cream in the marketplace, you can decide how much you want. You can adjust the quantity you consume to your individual

Table 14.1 *Costs and benefits of a public park for five people, case I*

Individuals (1)	Dollar value of benefits to each person (2) ($)	Tax levied on each person (3) ($)	Net benefit (+) or net cost (−) ((2)–(3)) (4) ($)	Vote for or against (5)
A	200	100	+100	For
B	150	100	+50	For
C	125	100	+25	For
D	50	100	−50	Against
E	25	100	−75	Against
Total	**550**	**500**		

preferences and your ability to pay. If you join with your neighbors to purchase some public service, however, you must accept whatever quantity of service the collective decision making process yields. How much of a public good government buys depends not only on citizens' preferences but also on the voting rule that is used.

Consider police protection, for instance. Perhaps you would prefer to pay higher taxes in return for a larger police force and lower crime rate. Your neighbors might prefer a lower tax rate, a smaller police force, and a higher crime rate, but public goods must be purchased collectively, no matter how the government is organized. If preferences differ, you cannot each have your own way. Under a democracy, the preferences of the median voter group will tend to determine the types and quantities of public goods produced. If you are not a member of that group, the compromise that is necessary to a democracy inflicts a cost on you. You probably will not receive the amount of police protection you want.

The simple-majority voting rule

Any decision that is made less than unanimously can benefit some people at the expense of others. Because government expenses are shared by all taxpayers, the majority that votes for a project imposes an external cost on the minority that votes against it. Consider a democratic community composed of only five people, each of whom would benefit to some degree from a proposed public park. If the cost of the park, $500, is divided evenly among the five, each will pay a tax of $100. The costs and benefits to each taxpayer are shown in table 14.1. Because the total benefits of the project ($550) exceed its total cost ($500), the

Table 14.2 *Costs and benefits of a public park, case II*

Individuals (1)	Dollar value of benefits to each person (2) ($)	Tax levied on each person (3) ($)	Net benefit (+) or net cost (−) ((2)−(3)) (4) ($)	Vote for or against (5)
A	140	100	+40	For
B	130	100	+30	For
C	110	100	+10	For
D	50	100	−50	Against
E	0	100	−100	Against
Total	**430**	**500**		

measure will pass by a vote of three to two, but the majority of three imposes net costs of $50 and $75 on taxpayers *D* and *E*.

When total benefits exceed total costs, as in this example, decision by majority rule is fairly easy to live with. The vote on the next cost-effective project may favor *D* and *E*. But projects can easily pass even though their cost exceeds benefits. Table 14.2 illustrates such a situation. Again, the $500 cost of a proposed park is shared equally by five people. Total benefits are only $430, but again they are unevenly distributed. Taxpayers *A*, *B*, and *C* each receive benefits that outweigh a $100 tax cost. Thus *A*, *B*, and *C* will pass the project, even though it cannot be justified on economic grounds.

It is conceivable that many different measures, each of whose costs exceed its benefits, could be passed by separate votes. If all the measures were considered together, however, the package will more likely be defeated. Consider the costs and benefits of three proposed projects – a park, a road, and a school – shown in table 14.3. If the park is put to a vote by itself, it will receive the majority support from *A*, *B*, and *C*. Similarly, the road will pass with the support of *A*, *C*, and *E*, and the school will pass with the support of *C*, *D*, and *E*. If all three projects are considered together, however, they will be defeated. Voters *A*, *B*, and *D* will reject the package (see column (4)).

Many, if not most, measures that come up for a vote in a democratic government benefit society more than they burden it. Moreover, voters in the minority camp can use "logrolling" (vote trading) to defeat some projects that might otherwise pass. For instance, referring to table 14.3, voter *A* can agree to vote against the park if voter *D* will vote against the school. Our purpose here is simply to demonstrate that, in *some* (not all) instances, the democratic process can be less than cost-efficient.

Table 14.3 *Costs and benefits of a public park for five people, case III*

	Park (1)			*Road (2)*			*School (3)*			*Total, 3 Projects (4)*		
Individuals	Benefit ($)	Cost ($)	Vote	Benefit ($)	Cost ($)	Vote	Benefit ($)	Cost ($)	Vote	Benefit ($)	Cost ($)	Vote
A	120	100	For	250	200	For	50	400	Against	420	700	Against
B	120	100	For	50	200	Against	50	400	Against	220	700	Against
C	120	100	For	250	200	For	500	400	For	870	700	For
D	50	100	Against	50	200	Against	500	400	For	600	700	Against
E	50	100	Against	250	200	For	500	400	For	800	700	For
Total	**460**	**500**		**850**	**1,000**		**1,600**	**2,000**		**2,910**	**3,500**	

Political ignorance

In some ways, the lack of an informed citizenry is the most severe problem in a democratic system. The typical voter is not well informed about political issues and candidates because being well-informed politically is not worth much to the average person.

A simple experiment will illustrate this point. Ask everyone in your class to write down the name of his or her congressional representative. Then ask them for the name of the opposing candidate in the last election. You may be surprised by the results. In one survey, college juniors and seniors, most of whom had taken several courses in economics, political science, and sociology, were asked how their US senators had voted on some major bills. The students scored no better than they would have done by guessing (McKenzie 1977). In the 1980s, 70 percent could not name any congressional candidate in their district in the middle of the election campaign (Neumann 1986, 15–16). In the United States, most voters do not even know which party controls Congress (Stokes and Miller 1962; Neumann 1986; Carpini and Keeter 1996) and public opinion polls indicate that most voters greatly underestimate the cost of programs such as Social Security (Browning 1974). In 2000, one week before the Republican convention, a survey group of voters found that 75 percent of Americans didn't know when the convention would be held; 25 percent couldn't name their governor; 50 percent couldn't name their congressman (Goldberg 2003). When it comes to knowing about (much less understanding the consequences of) current government policies, the political ignorance of Americans is stark, according to Ilya Somin (2003) who has summarized the findings of a number of studies:

- In 2004, 70 percent of Americans interviewed did not know that Congress and the president had provided a substantial prescription drug benefit to the Medicare program for the elderly (Princeton Survey Research Associates 2004).
- In 2004, 60 percent of survey respondents did not know that the then recent rapid growth of the federal deficit was in a major way attributable to the large increase in federal spending (not just to Bush II's tax rate reductions) (Pew Research Center Survey 2004).
- In 2004, 62 percent of respondents did not know that Social Security was one of the two largest expenditure categories in the federal budget (Princeton Survey Research Associates 2004). Some 43 percent did not know that defense

spending was the other largest federal budget category (Princeton Survey Research Associates 2004).[2]

If voters were better informed on legislative proposals and their implications, government might make better decisions. In that sense, political information is a public good that benefits everyone. Nevertheless, as we have seen before, in large groups people have little incentive to contribute anything toward the production of a public good. Their individual contributions simply have little effect on the outcome and each can hope to free-ride off the contribution of others.

The result is that they often cast their votes on the basis of impressions received from newspaper headlines or television commercials – impressions carefully created by advertisers and press secretaries. (See the Perspective later in the chapter, that explains economists' views on voters' incentives, or lack thereof, to vote and become informed on policy issues central to elections.)

Special interests

The problem of political ignorance is especially acute when the benefits of government programs are spread more or less evenly, so that the benefit to each person is relatively small. Benefits are not always spread evenly: Subgroups of voters – farmers, labor unions, or government workers – often receive more than their proportional share. Members of such groups thus have a special incentive to acquire information on the legislative proposals that affect them. Farmers can be expected to know more about farm programs than will the average voter. Government workers will keep abreast of proposed pay increases and fringe benefits for themselves, and defense contractors will take a strong interest in the military budget.

Congressional representatives, knowing they are being watched by special-interest groups, will tend to cater to their wishes. As a result, government programs will be designed to serve the interest of groups with political clout, not the public as a whole. This is especially true when voters in general are "politically ignorant."

[2] Dozens of other studies revealing widespread political ignorance among Americans on several dozen economic and social policies are summarized in Somin (2003, 6–7).

Rent seeking

As long as long as there are monopoly rents to be garnered from market-entry restrictions or there is a payoff from government subsidies, political entrepreneurs can be expected to compete for the rents through *lobbying* (for example, providing political decision makers with lavish dinners and junkets to exotic locations for "working vacations"), campaign contributions, and outright bribes (see Tullock 1967; Krueger 1974; McChesney 1997). Rent seekers can be expected to assess their rent seeking expenditures as investments, ensuring as best they can that the rates of return on such investments are no less than their investments on other business ventures.

In the process of seeking rents through government protections and subsidies, the rent seekers can collectively devote more valuable resources to rent seeking than the expected rent is worth. In such case, the inefficiency of monopoly is greater than the inefficiency or dead-weight-loss triangle identified in figure 11.6 (p. 437) . The net welfare loss from monopoly (or a subsidy) can, at the limit, include that dead-weight-loss triangle plus the profit rectangle (Tullock 1967)

Rent seeking is epitomized by the various individual companies and business trade associations in the capitals of the world, whose lobbyists are constantly knocking on the doors of key politicians, but rent seeking is not restricted to private businesses. Universities in the United States have since the 1980s learned that they also can engage in rent seeking, lobbying for so-called federal "legislative earmarks," or special appropriations for university projects (buildings and curriculum development) that are attached to (and buried in) budget bills. In fiscal year 2003, the *Chronicle of Higher Education* found that 716 US colleges and universities benefited from 1,964 "legislative earmarks" worth $2 billion (Krueger 2005). Economists from UCLA and the University of Toronto found that a $1 increase in lobbying expenditures can be expected to lead to $1.56 increase in "earmarks." However, for those universities who have a member of Congress on either the House or Senate Appropriation Committee, a $1 increase in lobbying leads to a $4.50 increase in "earmarks." This means that universities' fortunes rise and fall with changes in the membership of the appropriation committees (Krueger 2005).

Cyclical majorities

In their personal lives, most people tend to act consistently on the basis of rational goals. If an individual prefers good *A* to good *B*, and good *B* to good *C*,

Table 14.4 *Collective preference orderings for voters*

Individual	Order of preference (ranked from high to low)
I	*A*, *B*, *C*
II	*B*, *C*, *A*
III	*C*, *A*, *B*

the rational individual will repeatedly choose *A* over *C*. Collective decisions made by majority rule are not always so consistent. Consider a community of three people (I–III), whose preferences for goods *A*, *B*, and *C* are as in table 14.4.

Suppose these three voters are presented with a choice between successive pairs of goods, *A*, *B*, and *C*. If the choice is between good *A* and good *B*, which will be preferred collectively? The answer is *A*, because individuals I and III both prefer *A* to *B*. If *B* is pitted against *C*, which will be preferred? The answer is *B*, because individuals I and II both prefer *B* to *C*. Because the group prefers *A* to *B* and *B* to *C*, one might think it would prefer *A* to *C*, but note that if *A* and *C* are put up to a vote, *C* will win since both II and III prefer *C* to *A*. A cyclical, or revolving, majority has developed in this group situation. This phenomenon can lead to continual changes in policy in a government based on collective decision making and has been called the "paradox of voting," or the "Arrow paradox" (after Kenneth Arrow, who first made the demonstration in 1951; see Arrow 1963).

Although there is no stable majority, the individuals involved are not acting irrationally. People with perfectly consistent personal preferences can make inconsistent collective choices when acting as a group. Fortunately, the larger the number of voters and issues at stake, the less likely a cyclical majority is to develop. Still, citizens of a democratic state should recognize that the political process may generate a series of inconsistent, or even contradictory, policies.

The economics and politics of business regulation

Name an industry that has not, in some way, been under the authority of a government regulatory agency at some time. At the start of the twentieth century such a task would have been relatively simple. Today, with government extending its activities in all directions, it is not. Almost every economic activity either is or has been at some time in the past, subject to some type of regulation at one stage or another. The list of federal regulatory agencies virtually spans the alphabet – FAA, FDA, FEA, FPC, FRS, FTC, ICC, NTHSA, OSHA, SEC – to say nothing of the various state utilities commissions, licensing boards, health departments, and consumer protection agencies. As a result, it is much easier to list regulated industries than to name an unregulated one. Air transport, telephone service, trucking, natural gas, electricity, water and sewage systems, stock brokering, health care, taxi services, massage parlors, pharmacies, postal services, television and radio broadcasting, toy manufacturing, beauty shops, ocean transport, legal advice, slaughtering, medicine, embalming and funeral services, optometry, oyster fishing, banking, and insurance – all are regulated. In the 1960s and 1970s especially, regulation was one of the nation's largest growth industries (although there was something of a "recession" in regulations in the 1980s). Why have people been willing to substitute the visible foot of government for the invisible hand of competition?

Explaining regulation – why and how it happens – is a major challenge to economists. Although several insightful theories have been proposed, statistical tests of those theories are incomplete and are at times based on crude data. Some instances of regulation or changes in regulatory policy cannot be explained by current theories. At best, we can only review the two major lines of explanation for the existence of so much regulation – the public interest theory and the economic theory of regulation.

The public interest theory of regulation

Much of our discussion of government involvement in the economy has been organized around discussions of how regulation can improve market efficiency. In chapter 5, we discussed how *externalities* – external costs and benefits – can cause market inefficiencies and how tax or regulatory regimes can increase the efficiency of markets. For example, shock-absorbing bumpers benefit not only the person who buys a car but also those who may be involved in a collision with the buyer. If John collides with Mary's car which is protected by shock-absorbing bumpers, he may sustain less damage than he would have otherwise, without having paid for the protection received. He free-rides on Mary's purchase. Because of the externality, the quantity of shock-absorbing bumpers purchased in an unregulated market will fall short of the economic optimum. Hence the need for regulation of safety equipment such as shock-absorbing bumpers, headlights, and mud flaps on trucks to prevent rocks from being propelled through windshields.

In chapter 10, we stressed the extent to which monopolies can generate inefficiency in the allocation of resources. We noted in chapter 12 how production and price controls can enhance consumer welfare. At every point, we stressed how the cost of regulation can restrict its extent. If regulation is truly to serve the public interest, it must increase the efficiency of the entire social system: That is, its benefits must exceed its costs.

Too often, the net benefits of regulation are overestimated because of the failure to consider its costs, which were estimated to be $843 billion in the United States in 2000 (Crain and Hopkins 2001). And, all too often, regulation seems to serve the interest of the regulated industry, not the broader "public interest," which is why economists began several decades ago to become skeptical of the public interest theory of regulation, in favor of an industry-centered view. Instead of seeing regulation as something thrust on firms, they began to view it as a government-provided service frequently sought by those who are regulated.

The supply and demand for regulation

Beginning in the 1960s, many economists began to see regulation as a product of the supply of and demand for politically provided benefits (Stigler 1971; Breyer 1985). Government is seen as a supplier of regulatory services to industry. Such services can include price fixing, restrictions on market entry, subsidies, and even suppression of substitute goods (or promotion of complementary goods). For example, regulation enabled commercial television stations to get the Federal Communication Commission (FCC) to delay the introduction of cable television.

These regulatory services are not free; they are offered to industries willing to pay for them. In the political world, the price of regulatory services may be campaign contributions or lucrative consulting jobs, or votes and volunteer work for political campaigns. Regulators and politicians allocate the benefits among all the various private interest groups so as to equate political support and opposition at the margin.

Firms demand regulation that serves their private interest. As we have seen, forming a cartel in a free market can be difficult, both because new firms may enter the market and because colluders tend to cheat on cartel agreements. The cost of reaching and enforcing a collusive agreement can be so high that government regulation is attractive by comparison.

The view that certain forms of regulation emerge from the interaction of government suppliers and industry demanders seems to square with much historical evidence. As Richard Posner has observed:

> The railroads supported the enactment of the first Interstate Commerce Act, which was designed to prevent railroads from price discrimination because discrimination was undermining the railroad's cartels. American Telephone and Telegraph pressed for state regulation of telephone service because it wanted to end competition among telephone companies. Truckers and airlines supported extension of common carrier regulation to their industries because they considered unregulated competition excessive. (Posner 1974, 337)

Barbers, beauticians, lawyers, and other specialists have all sought government licensing, which is a form of regulation. Farmers have backed moves to regulate the supply of the commodities they produce. Whenever deregulation is proposed, the industry in question almost always opposes the proposal. Gasoline retailers in North Carolina (and a dozen other states) got a state statute passed that restricts gas stations from selling gasoline below their "wholesale price" (except for ten days during the grand opening of a new station). Through the threat and actuality of lawsuits by mom-and-pop gas stations, the law obviously places a lower bound on price competition and restrains the creative efforts of convenience stores from using gasoline pricing as a means of bringing in customers who buy higher-margin nongasoline products on their refueling stops (Associated Press 2005a).

To the extent that regulation benefits all regulated firms, whether or not they have contributed to the cost of procuring it, industries may consider regulation a public good. This creates a free-rider problem, which occurs when people can enjoy the benefits of a scarce good or service without paying directly for it by pretending not to want it. Some firms will try to free-ride on others' efforts to secure regulation. If all firms free-ride, however, the collective benefits of regulation will be lost.

The free-rider phenomenon is particularly noticeable in large groups, whose cost of organizing for collective action can be substantial. Someone must bear the initial cost of organization. Yet because the benefits of organization are spread more or less evenly over the group, the party that initiates the organization may incur costs greater than the benefits it receives. Thus collective action may not be taken. Free-riding may explain why some large groups, such as secretaries, have not yet secured government protection. Everyone may be waiting for everyone else to act. Small groups may have much greater success because of their proportionally smaller organizational costs and larger individual benefits. Perhaps it was because only a few railroad companies existed in the 1880s that they were able to lobby successfully for the formation of the ICC.

There are some exceptions to this rule. Several reasonably large groups, including truckers and farmers, have secured a high degree of government regulation, whereas many highly concentrated groups, such as the electrical appliance industry, have not. In highly concentrated industries, it may be less costly to develop private cartels than to organize to secure government regulation. In industries composed of many firms, on the other hand, any one firm's share of the cost of securing regulation may be smaller than its share of the costs of establishing and enforcing a private cartel. Large groups also control more sizable voting blocks than do small groups. Large groups may have the advantage of established trade associations, whose help can be enlisted in pushing for protective legislation (Olson 1971, chapters 1, 2).

In broad terms, the economic theory of regulation explains much about government policy – but that is one of its weaknesses. The theory is so broad that its usefulness as a predictor is limited. It does not enable economists to forecast which industries are likely to seek or achieve government regulation. Nor does it explain the political movement to deregulate the trucking and banking industries, or to regulate the environment. Neither of these trends appears to meet directly the demand of any particular business interest group. In general, any self-interested group will be better represented the larger its interest in the outcome, the smaller its size, the more homogenous its position and objectives, and the more certain the outcome.

The efficiency of competition among governments

In the private sector, competition among producers keeps prices down and productivity up. A producer who is just one of many knows that any independent attempt to raise prices or lower quality will fail. Customers will switch to other products or buy from other producers, and sales will fall sharply. To avoid being undersold, therefore, the individual producer must strive continually to keep its production cost as low, or lower, than other producers striving to do the same. Only a producer who has no competition – that is, a monopolist – can hope to raise the price of a product without fear of losing profits.

These points apply to the public as well as the private sector. The framers of the Constitution, in fact, bore them in mind when they set up the federal government. Recognizing the benefits of competition, they established a system of competing state governments loosely joined in federation. As James Madison described in *The Federalist* papers, "In a single republic, all the power surrendered by the people is submitted to the administration of a single government: and the usurpations are guarded against by a division of the government into distinct and separate departments" (Hamilton, Jay, and Madison 1964).

Under the federal system, the power of local governments is checked not just by citizens' ability to vote but also by their ability to move somewhere else. If a city government raises its taxes or lowers the quality of its services, residents can go elsewhere, taking with them part of the city's tax base. Of course, many people are reluctant to move, and so government has a measure of market power, but competition among governments affords at least some protection against the abuses of that power. It doesn't take many people and businesses to move out of a political jurisdiction to send a strong signal to the political authorities that they have to be more competitive.

Local competition in government has its drawbacks. Just as in private industry, large governments can realize economies of scale in the production of services. Garbage, road, and sewage service can, up to a point, be provided at a lower cost on a larger scale. For this reason, it is frequently argued that local governments, especially in metropolitan areas, should consolidate. Moreover, many of the benefits offered by local governments spill over into surrounding areas. For example, people who live just outside San Francisco may benefit from its services without helping pay for them. One large metropolitan government, including both city and suburbs, could spread the tax burden over all those who benefit from city services.

Consolidation can be a mixed blessing, however, if it reduces competition among governments. A large government restricts the number and variety of alternatives open to citizens and increases the cost of moving to another locale by increasing the geographical size of its jurisdiction. Consolidation, in other words, can increase the government's monopoly power. As long as politicians and government employees pursue only the public interest, no harm may be done. But the people who run government have interests of their own. So the potential for achieving greater efficiency through consolidation could easily be lost in bureaucratic expansion and red tape. Studies of consolidation in government are inconclusive, but it seems clear that consolidation proposals should be examined carefully.

The economics of government bureaucracy

Bureaucracy is not limited to government. Large corporations such as General Motors and Wal-Mart employ more people than do the governments of some nations. They are bigger than the major departments of the federal government – although no company, of course, is as large as the federal government as a whole. Yet corporate bureaucracy tends to work more efficiently than government bureaucracy. The reason may be found in the fact that firms pursue one simple objective – profit – that can be easily measured in dollars and cents. Governments have a multiplicity of often ill-defined objectives.

Certainly the reason cannot be that stockholders are better informed than voters. Most stockholders are rationally ignorant of their companies' doings, for the same reason that voters are rationally ignorant of government policy – the personal cost of becoming informed outweighs the personal benefits. Even in very large corporations, however, some individuals hold enough stock to make the acquisition of information a rational act. Often, such stockholders sit on the company's board of directors, where their interest in increasing the value of their own shares makes them good representatives of the rest of the stockholders. The crucial point is that this informed stockholder has one relatively simple objective – profit – and can find out relatively easily whether the corporation is meeting it. The voter, on the other hand, has a complicated set of objectives and must do considerable digging to find out whether the objectives are being met.

Because most corporations face competition, the stockholder's drive toward profit is reinforced. General Motors knows that its customers may switch to Toyota if it offers them a better deal. In fact, stockholders can sell their General Motors stock and buy stock in Toyota. Corporate executives thus have a strong incentive to make decisions on the basis of the consumer's wellbeing – not because they wish to serve the public good, but because they want to make money.

Government bureaucracies, however, tend to produce public goods and services for which there is no competition. No built-in efficiencies guard the taxpayer's interests in a government bureaucracy. Both government bureaucrats and corporate executives base their decisions on their own interests, not those of society, but competition ensures that the interests of corporate decision makers coincide with those of consumers. No such safeguards govern the operations of government bureaucracies. Bureaucracies are constrained by political, as opposed to market, forces.

From the economist's point of view, one of the advantages of the profit maximizing goal of competitive business is that it enables predictions. Although some business people pursue other goals – personal income, power, respect in the business – their behavior can generally be explained quite well in terms of a single objective – profit. No single goal such as profit drives the government bureaucracy. Different bureaucracies pursue different objectives. We do not have time or space to consider all the possible objectives of bureaucracy, but we touch on two: monopolistic profit maximization and size maximization.

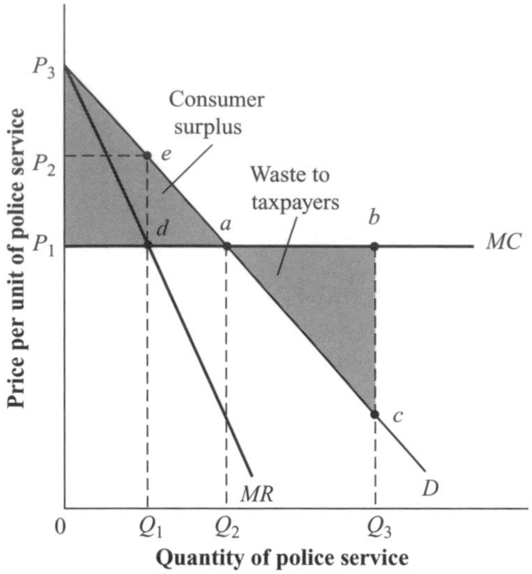

Figure 14.2 Bureaucratic profit maximization

Given the demand for police service, D, and the marginal cost of providing it, MC, the optimum quantity of police service is Q_2. A monopolistic police department interested in maximizing its profits will supply only Q_1 service at a price of P_2, however. (A monopolistic bureaucracy interested in maximizing its size would expand police service to Q_3.)

Profit maximization

Assume that police protection can be produced at a constant marginal cost, as shown by the horizontal marginal cost curve in figure 14.2. The demand for police protection is shown by the downward sloping demand curve D. If individuals could purchase police service competitively at a constant price of P_1, the optimum amount of police service would be Q_2, the amount at which the marginal cost of the last unit of police service equals its marginal benefit. The total cost would be $P_1 \times Q_2$ (or the area $0P_1 a\ Q_2$), leaving a consumer surplus equal to the triangular area $P_1 P_3 a$. Notice that there is no economic profit being realized by the police in this case.

Police protection is usually delivered by regional monopolies, however. That is, all police services in an area are supplied by one organization. These regional monopolies have their own goals and their own decision making process, which do not necessarily match the individual taxpayers'. If police service must be purchased from such a profit maximizing monopoly, service will be produced to the point at which the marginal cost of the last unit produced equals its marginal revenue: Q_1. The monopolist will set that quantity above cost at price P_2, making a profit equal to the rectangular area $P_1\ P_2 ed$.

At the monopolized production level, there is still some surplus – the triangular area P_2P_3e – left for consumers, but they are worse off than under competitive market conditions. They get less police protection (Q_1 instead of Q_2) for a higher price (P_2 instead of P_1).

This analysis presumes that the police are capable of concealing their costs. If taxpayers know that P_2 is an unnecessarily high price, the outcome might be the same as that under competition. They might force the police to produce Q_2 protection for a price of P_1. But then governments may simply allow their costs to rise. Not having other sources of supply on which to compare costs, taxpayers may not know that costs are inflated and, hence, that the efficient output level is Q_2.

Size maximization

In fact, a government bureaucracy is unlikely to take profit as its overriding objective, if only because bureaucrats do not get to pocket the profit. Instead, government monopolies may try to maximize the size of their operations, because if a bureaucracy expands those who work for it will have more chance of promotion, their power, influence, and public standing will improve, and they will likely get nicer offices and better equipment.

What level of protection will a police department produce under such conditions? Instead of providing Q_1 service and misrepresenting its cost at P_2, it will probably provide Q_3 service – more than taxpayers desire – at the true price of P_1. The bill will be $P_1 \times Q_3$, or the area $0P_1bQ_3$ in figure 14.2. Note that the net waste to taxpayers, shown by the shaded area *abc*, exactly equals the consumer surplus, P_1P_3a. By extending service to Q_3, the police have squeezed out the entire consumer surplus and spent it on themselves.

Fortunately, government bureaucracies do not usually achieve perfect maximization of size and the waste that would result. For one thing, most legislatures have at least some information about the production costs of various services, and bureaucrats may not be willing to do the hard work necessary to exploit their position fully. If bureaucracy does not manage to capture the entire consumer surplus, citizens will realize some net benefit from their investment.

Making bureaucracy more competitive

What can be done to make government bureaucracy more efficient? Perhaps the development of managerial expertise at the congressional level would encourage more accurate measurement of the costs and benefits of government programs. Cost–benefit analysis alone, however, will not necessarily help. As long as special-interest groups, including those of government employees, exist, the potential for waste can be substantial.

A better solution to bureaucratic inefficiency may be to increase competition in the public sector. In the private marketplace, buyers do not attempt to discover the production costs of the companies they buy from. They simply compare the various products offered, in terms of price and quality, and choose the best value for their money. A monopoly of any kind, of course, makes that task difficult, if not impossible, but the existence of even one competitor for a government bureaucracy's services would allow some comparison of costs. The more sources there are of a service, the flatter the demand curve that each source faces, and the more efficient each must be to stay in business.

How exactly can competition be introduced into bureaucracy? First, proposals to consolidate departments should be carefully scrutinized. What appears to be wasteful duplication may actually be a source of competition in the provision of service. In the private sector, we would not expect the consolidation of General Motors, Ford, and Daimler-Chrysler to improve the efficiency of the auto industry. If anything, we would favor the break-up of the large firms into separate, competing companies. Why, then, should we merge the sanitation departments of three separate cities?

A second way to increase the competitiveness of government services is to contract for them with private producers. Many government activities that must be publicly financed need not necessarily be publicly produced. In the United States, highways are usually built by private companies but repaired and maintained by government. Competitive provision of maintenance as well as construction might reduce costs. Other services that might be "privatized" are fire protection, garbage collection, and education.

Because of tight state budgets that were expected to extend into the future, universities in Michigan had to start getting serious about controlling costs, which led them to "privatizing," or contracting out or outsourcing, a variety of services. Of the ten out of fifteen Michigan universities that responded to a survey in 2005, 90 percent had contracted out garbage and sanitation services, 80 percent had contracted out their bookstore operations, and 70 percent had contracted out their vending machine needs, as well as other services (legal, utilities, food, busing, laundry, and maintenance services). Why? Mainly to save money and tap into the expertise of outside vendors. We noted in chapter 12 how Western Michigan State University reduced its annual maintenance costs by $1.5 million by contracting out its custodial services. Ferris State University reported contracting out its vending services, with the result that the university went from losing $85,000 a year on its vending machines to making an annual profit of the same amount from the outside vending machine company (Davis 2005).

Finally, competition can be increased simply by dividing a bureaucracy into several smaller departments with separate budgets, thus increasing competition. Such a change would eliminate a dissatisfied consumer of a government service from having to move to a different political jurisdiction to get better or cheaper government services. The consumer/taxpayer could simply switch to a different government provider of a service in the same jurisdiction. The loss (or threat of loss) of customers can put pressure on a government agency to improve its performance.

Perspective The Mathematics of Voting and Political Ignorance

Gordon Tullock (1992, 111–14, with permission)

Gordon Tullock (1992, 111–14, with permission) Public problems are normally more important than private problems, but the decision by any individual on a private problem is likely to be more important than her decision on a public problem, simply because most peoples' decisions on public matters make almost no difference. It is rational, therefore, for the average family to put a great deal more thought and investigation into a decision such as what car to buy than into a decision on voting for president. As far as we can tell, families, in fact, act quite rationally in this matter, and the average family devotes almost no time to becoming informed on political matters but will carefully consider the alternatives when buying a car. Why is that the case?

In order to address the question we need first to ask a more basic question: What is the payoff to the individual from voting? Assume that you are in possession of some information and have decided that you favor the Democratic Party or, if it is a primary, some particular candidate. The payoff could be computed from the following expression:

$$BDA - C_v = P$$

B = benefit expected to be derived from success of your party or candidate
D = likelihood that your vote will make a difference
A = your estimate of the accuracy of your judgment + $(-1 < A < +1)$
C_v = cost of voting
P = payoff

Certain aspects of this expression deserve a little further discussion. The B refers, of course, not to the absolute advantage of having one party or candidate in office, but the difference between the candidate and her opponent. The factor labeled A, the estimate of the accuracy of the voter's judgment, is included here because we are preparing to consider the amount of information held by the individual, and the principal effect of being better informed is that your judgment is more likely to be correct. The factor labeled A can take any value from -1, which represents a certainty that the judgments will be wrong, to $+1$, which indicates that the voter is sure she is right. The choice of this rather unusual way of presenting what is really a probability figure is due solely to its use in the particular equation, not to any desire to change the probability notational scheme. For the equation to give the right answer, it is necessary that A have a value of zero when the individual thinks that she has a fifty-fifty chance of being right.

The factor labeled D is the likelihood that an individual's vote will make a difference in the election; that is, the probability that the result if she were to vote would be different than it would be if she were not to vote. For an American presidential election, this is less than one in 10 million even in an election that is expected to be close. C_v is the cost, in money and convenience, of voting. For some people, of course, it may be negative. They may get pleasure, or at least the negative benefit of relief of social pressure, from voting. If we view voting as an instrumental act, however – something we do not because it gives us pleasure directly but because we expect it to lead to some desirable goal – then our decision to vote or not will depend on weighing the costs and benefits.

Let us put a few figures into our expression. Suppose I feel that the election of the "right" candidate as president is worth \$10,000 to me. I think I am apt to be right three times out of four, so the value of A will be 0.5, D will be figured as 0.0000001. Assuming that my cost of voting is \$1.00, the expression gives $(\$10{,}000 \times 0.5 \times 0.0000001) - \$1.00 = \$0.9995$. The payoff to voting is negative, and so it follows from this that I have no reason to vote.

It will, however, be worthwhile to consider a few variations on the expression. In the first place, it is frequently argued that this line of reasoning would lead to no one voting. This is not true. If people began making these computations and then refraining from voting, this would raise the value of D, since the fewer the voters, the more likely that any given vote will affect the outcome. As more and more people stopped voting, D would continue to rise until the left-hand side of the expression equaled the right. At this equilibrium there would be no reason for nonvoters to begin to vote or for voters to stop. Presumably the people voting would be those among the population who were most interested in politics, since D would have the same value for everyone but $(B \times A)$ would approximate a positive function of political interest.

The equation, if it is thought to be in any way descriptive of the real world, would imply that people would be more likely to vote in close elections. This hypothesis has been tested and found to be correct.

Let us now complicate our model. An additional factor, C_I, the cost of obtaining information, has been included in the first equation noted above:

$$BDA - C_v - C_I = P$$

This is, of course, the cost of obtaining additional information, since the voter will have at least some information on the issues as a result of her contact with the mass media. Of course, A is a function of information ($A = (I)$), and hence each increase in information held will increase A and thus raise both the benefits and the costs. The problem for the rational individual contemplating whether or not she should vote would be whether there are any values of C_I that would lead to a positive value payoff.

Suppose, for example, that the investment of \$100.00 (mostly in the form of leisure forgone) in obtaining more information would raise the value of A from 0.5 to 0.8. Using the same amounts for the other values as we used previously, $P = -\$100.9992$. Clearly, this is even worse than the original outcome. Furthermore, these figures are realistic. The cost of obtaining enough information to significantly improve your vote is apt to very much outweigh the effect of the improvement. This is particularly true for the average voter, who does not have much experience or skill in research and who would put a particularly high negative evaluation on the time spent in this way.

A further implication of our reasoning must be pointed out. There may be social pressures that make it wise for the individual to make the rather small investment necessary for voting. In terms of our equation, C_v may be negative. In these cases, voting would always be rational. Becoming adequately informed, however, is much more expensive. Further, it is not as easy for your neighbors (or your conscience) to see whether you have or have not put enough thought into your choice. Thus, it would almost never be rational to engage in much study in order to cast a "well-informed" vote. For certain people (and presumably most readers of this book will fall within this category) *A* may already be quite high. For intellectuals interested in politics, the amount of information acquired about the different issues for reasons having nothing to do with voting may be quite great. Further, for this group of people, the value put on the wellbeing of others may be higher than in the rest of the population. It may be, then, that these people would get a positive payoff from voting even though the average citizen would get negative returns from taking the same action. Thus, for many of the readers of this book, voting may be rational. I have my doubts, however. The value put on the wellbeing of others must be extremely great. Further, my own observation of intellectuals interested in politics would not confirm that *A* is high for them. They may have a great deal of information, but this seems to have been collected to confirm their basic position, not to change it.

PART II ORGANIZATIONAL ECONOMICS AND MANAGEMENT APPLICATIONS

Why professors have tenure and business people don't

Tenure is nothing short of a Holy Grail for newly employed assistant professors in the country's colleges and universities. Without tenure, faculty members must, as a general rule, be dismissed after seven years of service, which means they must seek other academic employment or retreat from academic life. With tenure, professors have the equivalent of lifetime employment. Rarely are they fired by their academies, even if they cease to perform adequately as teachers and/or researchers.

Business people rarely, if ever, have the type of tenure protection that professors do. Why the different treatment? Is it that universities are stupid, bureaucratic organizations in which professors are able to obtain special treatment? Maybe so, but we would like to think not. (Indeed, we think our universities have shown great wisdom in granting us both tenure in our current positions, from which we could not be dislodged with anything short of a direct nuclear hit!) We suggest that our explanation for why professors have tenure will help us understand why some form of tenure will gradually find its way into businesses that have begun to rely progressively more on "participatory management" (with low-ranking managers and line workers having a greater say in how the business is conducted).

The nature of tenure

Professors do not, of course, have complete protection from dismissal, and the potential for being fired is surely greater than that reflected in the number of actual firings. However, when professors are fired it is generally for causes unrelated to their professional competence. The most likely reasons for dismissal are "moral turpitude" (which is academic code for sexual indiscretions with students) and financial exigencies (in which case, typically, whole departments are eliminated).

Most opponents and supporters of academic tenure express their views in emotional terms: "Tenure is sloth" or "Tenure protects academic freedom." We suggest that tenure be thought of as a part of the employment relationship. It amounts to an employment contract provision that specifies, in effect, that the holder cannot easily be fired. To that extent, tenure provides some but by no means perfect employment security. A university may not be able to fire a faculty member quickly, but it can repeatedly deny salary increases and gradually increase teaching loads until the faculty member "chooses" to leave.[3]

The costs and benefits of tenure to universities, professors, and students

Clearly, tenure has costs that must be suffered by the various constituencies of universities. Professors sometimes do exploit tenure by shirking their duties in the classroom, in their research, and in their service to their universities. However, tenure is not the only contract provision that has costs. Health insurance (as well as a host of other fringe benefits) for professors imposes costs directly on colleges or universities and indirectly on students. Nonetheless, health insurance costs continue to be covered by universities because the benefits matter, too – not just the costs. Health insurance survives as a fringe benefit because it represents, on balance, a mutually beneficial trade for the various constituencies of universities. Universities (which can buy group insurance policies more cheaply than can individual faculty members) are able to lower their wage bills by more than enough to cover the insurance costs because they provide health insurance. By the same token, professors pay for tenure just as they do other fringe benefits; presumably, tenure is worth more to them than the value of the forgone wages.

[3] Accordingly, the degree of protection that tenure affords is a function of such variables as the inflation rate. That is, the higher the inflation rate, the more quickly the real value of the professor's salary will erode each time a rise is denied.

Why tenure? Any reasonable answer must start with the recognition that academic labor markets are tolerably, if not highly, competitive, with thousands of employers and hundreds of thousands of professors, and wages and fringe benefits respond fairly well to market conditions. If, in fact, tenure were not a mutually beneficial trade between employers and employees, universities – which are constantly in search of more highly qualified students, faculty at lower costs, and higher recognition for their programs – would be expected to alter the employment contract, modify the tenure provision, increase other forms of payment, and lower overall university costs.[4]

The analysis continues with the recognition that jobs vary in difficulty, in time and skills required, and in satisfaction. "Bosses" can define many jobs, and they are generally quite capable of evaluating the performance of those they hire for those jobs. In response to sales, for example, supervisors in fast-food restaurants can determine not only how many hamburgers to cook but also how many employees are needed to flip those hamburgers (and assemble the different types of hamburgers). Where work is relatively simple and routine, we would expect it to be defined by and evaluated within an authoritarian/hierarchical governance structure of firms, as is generally true in the fast-food industry.

Academic work is substantially different, because many forms of the work are highly sophisticated, its pursuit cannot be observed directly and easily (given the reliance on thinking skills), and it involves a search for new knowledge that, when found, is transmitted to professional and student audiences. (Academic work is not the only form of work that is heavily weighted with these attributes, a point that is further considered later.) Academic supervisors may know in broad terms what a "degree" should consist of and roughly what courses should be required for a major in particular subjects. However, academic supervisors must rely extensively on their workers/professors to define their own specific research and classroom curriculums and to change the content of degrees and majors as knowledge in each field evolves. Academic administrators employ people to conduct research and explore uncharted avenues of knowledge that the administrators themselves cannot conduct or explore because they lack knowledge of a field, have no time, or are not so inclined.

[4] Granted, tenure may be required by accrediting associations. However, there is no reason that groups of universities could not operate outside accrediting associations or organize their own accrediting associations without the tenure provision – if tenure were, on balance, a significant impairment to academic goals. In many respects, the accrediting association rules can be defended on the same competitive grounds that recruiting rules of the National Collegiate Athletic Association are defended. See McKenzie and Sullivan (1987).

Fast-food restaurants can be governed extensively (but not exclusively) by commands from supervisors, and there is an obvious reason why this is possible. Again, the goods and services produced are easily valued and sold, with little delay between the time they are produced and the time the value is realized and easily evaluated. Workers in such market environments would be inclined to see supervisors as people who increase the income of stockholders *and* workers mainly by reducing the extent to which workers shirk their agreed-upon duties.

Worker-managed universities and academic politics

Academe, however, is a type of business that tends to be worker-managed and controlled, at least in many significant ways. This aspect of the academic marketplace solves many decision making problems but introduces other serious problems that can be moderated by providing professors with contractual job security of the type associated with tenure. Professors are extensively called upon to determine what their firms (universities) produce (what research will be done, what courses will be required, what the contents of the various courses will be, and even who will be taught). In addition, they help to determine who is hired to teach identified courses and undertake related research, how workers are evaluated, and whether a worker/professor is competent enough to have her employment continued.

Our argument begins with the plausible view that the more sophisticated, esoteric, and varied the job to be done is, the more likely it is for managerial control to be shifted to a meaningful degree to the workers themselves who are the experts in what "good performance" consists of, and the more democratic the decision making will be.[5] This supports the view that universities have reason to "supply" tenure since, for one reason, existing professors are called upon to select who is hired to be professors, which stands in sharp contrast to the way hiring decisions are made in business as well as in sports (Carmichael 1988). In baseball, for example, the owners through their agents determine who plays in what position on the team. Baseball is, in this sense, "owner-managed."

[5] Of course, not all academic environments share the same goals or face the same constraints. Some universities view pushing back the frontiers of knowledge as central to their mission, whereas others are intent on transmitting the received and accepted wisdom of the times, if not the ages. Some universities are concerned mainly with promoting the pursuit of usable (private goods) knowledge, that which has a reasonable probability of being turned into salable products, whereas other universities are interested in promoting research, the benefits of which are truly public, if any value at all can be ascertained.

In academe, the incumbent professors select the team members and determine which positions they play. Academe is, in this sense, "labor-managed."

In baseball, the owners' positions are improved when they select "better players." On the other hand, in academe, without tenure, the position of the incumbent decision makers could be undermined by their selection of "better professors," those who could teach better and undertake more and higher-quality research for publication in higher-ranking journals.[6] Weaker department members would fear that their future livelihoods (as well as prestige) would be undermined if they supported the prospective hires who they honestly thought would be the best teachers and researchers. Thus, tenure can be construed as a means employed by university administrators and board members – who want the most promising professors to be hired but must delegate decision making authority to the faculty – to induce faculty members to honestly judge the potential of the new recruits. In effect, university officials and board members strike a credible bargain with their professor decision makers: If you select new recruits who are better than you are, you will not be fired.

Universities have reason to *supply* tenure, but what reason do professors have to *demand* it? We don't buy the argument that most faculty members worry that their freedom to pursue research will be violated by public opinion. Too few faculty members ever go public with their work or say anything controversial in their classes for them to want to give up very much in the way of pay for protection from external forces. Rather, we believe that tenure is designed to protect professors from their colleagues in a labor-managed work environment operating under the rules of academic democracy. That is, the real worry a professor has is that her research and teaching will prompt a hostile reaction from her colleagues, not from politicians or the public.

Academic work is often full of strife, and the reasons are embedded in the nature of the work and the way work is evaluated and rewarded, a point one of the authors has discussed in detail elsewhere (McKenzie 1996). Suffice it to say here that tenure is a means of putting some minimum limits on political infighting. It increases the costs that predatory faculty members must incur to be successful in having more productive colleagues dismissed.

In addition, professors understand that the relative standing of their positions and ranking of their research can change over time with changes in the cast of decision makers, who are likely to adjust their assessments from time to

[6] "[T]enure is necessary," Carmichael concludes, "because without it incumbents would never be willing to hire people who turn out to be better than themselves" (1988, 454).

time. The ranking of their research can also change with shifts in the relative merit that department members assign to different types and forms of academic work. For example, a macro person understands that even though his or her publications may now be highly valued (relatively) within the department, the ranking can easily change because changes occur in the way evaluations are made, existing department members periodically reassess the relative worth of different types of work, and the cast of decision makers changes. When the decision making unit is multi-disciplinary, shifts in the relative assessments of the worth of individual professors' work in the different disciplines can fluctuate even more dramatically, given that each professor is likely to have allegiance first to her own discipline and then to other, closely related disciplines.

Within schools of business, for example, accounting faculty members may have, on the margin, an incentive to depreciate the work of marketing professors, given that such depreciation may shift positions to accounting – and vice versa. Even more fundamentally, organizational theorists in the management department steeped in behavioral psychology may have an incentive to depreciate the work of professors in finance – which is grounded in economics – given that negative shifts in the relative evaluation of economics-based work can marginally improve the chances of positions being shifted to the management department. Like-minded faculty members can be expected to coalesce to increase their political effectiveness in shaping decisions that can, in turn, inspire the formation of other coalitions, thus motivating all coalitions to increase their efforts. The inherent instability of coalitions can, of course, jeopardize anyone's job security and long-term gains.

Universities also realize, given the nature of academic democracy and the threat it poses, that faculty members have inherent reasons for demanding tenure, and these make it possible to recoup the cost of tenure by reducing professorial wages to less than what they would have to be if the professors did not share a need for job security.

Of course, this line of analysis leads to a number of deductions:

- If the work of professors were less specialized, professors would be less inclined to demand tenure. For example, in colleges in which the emphasis is on teaching rather than research, tenure would be less prevalent, and/or less protective. So we would expect that any pressure to eliminate tenure would be stronger in teaching colleges than in research universities.
- As a group of decision makers or a discipline becomes more stable, we would expect faculty to consider tenure less important and to be less willing to forgo wages and other fringe benefits to obtain tenure.

- If there is a close to even split on democratic decisions related to employment, merit rises, and even tenure, faculty members will assign more value to tenure, given that a more or less evenly split vote may change with slight shifts in the composition of the decision making group.
- The further below market are the wages of faculty during the probation period and the further above market are the wages after tenure, the more valuable tenure is to faculty members.
- As the diversity within a decision making unit increases (more disciplines included with more divergent views on how analyses should be organized and pursued), the demand for tenure will increase.

Why business people don't have tenure

If professors have tenure, why don't business people have provision for the same kind of job security? The quick answer to that question is that businesses, in contrast to universities, are not typically labor-managed. As already noted, in business goals are usually well defined. Perhaps more important, success can usually be identified with relative ease by using an agreed-upon measure, that is, profit (or the expected profit stream captured in the market prices of traded securities). The owners, who are residual claimants, have an interest in maintaining the firm's focus on profits. Moreover, people who work for businesses tend to have a stake in honest evaluations of potential employees, given that their decisions on "better" recruits can increase the firm's profits and the incomes and job security of all parties.

Admittedly, real-world businesses do not always adhere to the process as described. They use, to a greater or lesser degree, participatory forms of management, and for some businesses, profit is not always the sole or highest priority goal. "Office politics" is a nontrivial concern in many firms. The point is, however, that in business the need for tenure is not as great as it is within academe. Employees in business do not have the incentive that professors have to demand tenure, primarily because business employees do not experience the problems inherent in democratic management that derive from imprecise and shifting goals and from esoteric and often ill-defined research projects. Tenure is seldom found in firms, for the simple reason that in business granting tenure to employees is less likely to be done in a way that is mutually beneficial to both employees and employers than in college and university settings.

But in some cases, for-profit businesses are similar enough to make tenure-type arrangements beneficial to employees and the firm. Consider law firms, accounting firms, and consultant firms. These firms are often organized as partnerships, which are in effect worker-managed firms, with new hires being chosen by the existing partners, just as in universities new hires are chosen by the existing professors. And much like the situation in universities, in these partnerships new employees who after a number of years are judged that they do not have the dedication and ability to contribute significantly to the firm are dismissed (or relegated to low-status and low-paid employment), while those who are judged worthy are made a partner in the firm, which comes with higher income and greatly increased job security – much like university tenure.

Tenure as a tournament

The granting of tenure can be seen as another form of a tournament used to determine who can best other competitors for some prize, in this case a lifetime employment contract (Lazear and Rosen, 1981). Tenure decisions are a way of allowing faculty members to reveal their skills. An employer cannot depend on a potential employee to be fully objective or honest in presenting her qualifications. The graduate school records of new doctorates provide useful information on which to base judgments of potential recruits for success as university teachers and researchers. However, such records are of limited worth in instances when a professor's research is at the frontier of knowledge in her discipline. The correlation between a person's performance as a student, as a prospective professor, as a teacher, and as a researcher is, at best, imperfect.

To induce promising faculty members to accurately assess their abilities and confess their limits, the competitors (new assistant professors) are effectively told that only some among them will be promoted and retained. Because standards for tenure differ from one university to another, universities offer prospective faculty members an opportunity to, in effect, self-select and go to a university where they think they are likely to make the tenure grade. The prospects of being denied tenure will encourage weak candidates to avoid universities with tough tenure standards, given the probability that they would have to accept wages below the market during the probation period. The lost wages amount to an investment that probably will not be repaid with interest (in terms of wages above the market after the probation period when tenure is acquired). Thus, the tenure tournaments can reduce to some extent the costs that universities incur in gathering information and making decisions, because they force recruits to be somewhat more honest in their claims.

Competition for the limited number of "prized positions" often will drive new faculty members to exert a level of effort and produce a level of output that exceeds the value of their current compensation. To induce prospective faculty to exert the amount of effort necessary to be ability-revealing, universities must offer a "prize" that potential recruits consider worth the effort. That is, the recruits must expect the future (discounted) reward to compensate them for the extra effort they expend in the tournament and for the risk associated with not "winning." One approach for universities to use to encourage recruits to exert a reasonable level of effort in the competition is to offer those who win the prospect of substantially greater compensation in the future (at least enough to repay the costs of assumed risk and of interest lost on delayed compensation). Another approach that offers future compensation as an incentive is to increase the security of continued employment and compensation after the tournament has ended and the winners have been determined. That is, tenure can be offered as the "prize."[7]

After all is said and done, tenure is nothing more than another contract provision that faculty members prize, universities provide, and just about everyone else criticizes. Business people could also have tenure. All they would have to do is "pay" for it in terms of lost wages. However, business people typically don't have the same strong reasons for wanting tenure as do professors although, as we have seen, some do. Tenure survives in the academies of the country mainly because faculty members aggressively demand it (even those who believe strongly in the value of markets) and because universities voluntarily negotiate it. Tenure's long-term survival and the competitiveness of university labor markets suggest that the trade is mutually beneficial.

THE BOTTOM LINE

The key takeaways from chapter 14 are the following:

(1) Political parties in two-party systems will tend to gravitate toward the middle of the voter distribution, that is, will tend to represent the views of the "median voter."
(2) Simple-majority voting rules can result in governments undertaking projects the costs of which are greater than their collective worth.

[7] After tenure is awarded, faculty efforts should be expected to decline while their pay simultaneously rises. In the midst of the tournament, the new faculty members will exert unduly high amounts of effort, simply because of the prospect of being rewarded in the future by higher pay and greater job security. Also, the rise in compensation and fall in effort that accompany tenure may correlate with the fact that the added money makes it possible for faculty members to buy more of most things, including great leisure (or leisure-time activities). If we did not expect new faculty members to anticipate relaxing somewhat after attaining tenure and enjoying, to a degree, being "overpaid," we could not expect the tenure tournament to be effective as a means to an end, which is disclosure of the limits of the new faculty members' true abilities.

(3) Voters in "large" electorates have an impaired incentive to be informed on the issues and candidates' positions in elections. Special interests can have undue political influence in democracies because of the concentrated benefits they receive from government programs they advocate, especially since the general public may be politically ignorant of the economic consequences of many government programs.
(4) Cyclical majorities are an ever-present prospect in democracies.
(5) In government as well as private industry, producers in a monopolistic market position will tend to exploit the lack of competition for their service. A government bureau that has no competitors is in an enviable bargaining position *vis-à-vis* legislators and taxpayers. As the sole producer of a service, it can charge higher prices and deliver poorer service than competitive producers would. Performance of government bureaucracies can be improved by the introduction of competition for their services.
(6) The democratic system provides checks and balances to control the exploitation of power in government. Voters can vote against re-electing officeholders who abuse the public trust. They may not do so reliably, however, because of imperfect information.
(7) The problems with government decision making are reflections of the more general problems associated with all collective decision making – decisions that are made by a group rather than by an individual and which, once made, apply to everyone in the group.
(8) Collective decision problems exist inside all organizations, whether government agencies, non-profit firms, or private for-profit firms.
(9) Tenure for professors can be viewed a fringe benefit (job security) that has the effect of lowering professors' money wages. Tenure can be seen as a form of job protection from internal political forces inside the labor-managed firm. Business people do not commonly have tenure because they are unwilling to pay for tenure, and they are unwilling to pay for it because of the constraining influence of profits on what firms can do.

REVIEW QUESTIONS

(1) Is it desirable, in your opinion, that government generally adopts policies intended to please the median voter group? Why or why not?
(2) It is sometimes said that a rational decision must be based on perfect information. Would it be rational for a voter to acquire perfect information about politics? Would it be rational for a consumer to acquire perfect information about the products she is thinking of buying? In

which of the two situations above would it be rational to acquire the most information?

(3) What effect does increased competition have on the slope of an individual firm's demand curve? Why? How does a change in the slope of a firm's demand curve affect its efficiency? How do these effects apply to government bureaucracies?

(4) "Competition forces producers to reveal what they are willing to do at the limit, not just what they want to do." How does this statement apply to government bureaucracy, and to legislators' ability to control it?

(5) Write down all the government-provided services you can think of. Which of them *must* be provided by government bureaucracy? Which could be provided through a competitive contract? Why?

(6) When would workers want and not want democratic governance in the workplace?

(7) Can you think of employment situations, other than those discussed in this chapter, in which there exists some form of tenure (granted to employees who perform well over some initial probation period)? Does the tenure granted in these situations provide as much job security as does university tenure for professors?

CHAPTER 15

International trade and finance

It can be of no consequence to America, whether the commodities she obtains in return for her own, cost Europeans much, or little labor; all she is interested in, is that they shall cost her less labor by purchasing than by manufacturing them herself.
David Ricardo

International trade can be misleading in capturing the growing volume of exchanges across national boundaries. Nations never really trade; people do. This simple point is important, because it allows us to approach international trade as an extension of trading models already developed. In earlier chapters, our discussion of trade presumed that if markets were bounded by geography, they were local or national marketplaces in scope. In this chapter, our marketplace is the world. We divide our discussion of international economics into its major subdivisions: *international trade* (mainly dealing with the exchange of real goods and services across national boundaries and their terms of trade) and *international finance* (mainly dealing with the exchange of national currencies and their exchange rates, which facilitate the trade of real goods and services).

Of course, differences exist between international and domestic trade – enough to make international economics an important subdiscipline of the profession. Some differences are obvious, such as the many different national currencies, cultures, institutions, laws, languages, artificial trade barriers (tariffs, quotas, embargoes, and health regulations), and monetary and fiscal policies of various countries that unavoidably affect international exchanges. Other differences go largely unrecognized. An intangible but significant factor is the difference in people's attitudes toward domestic and international trade, differences that result largely from cultural, ethnic, and nationalistic ties. As Abraham Lincoln supposedly said, "Domestic trade is among us; international trade is between us and them." Yet people all over the world trade with each other for the same reason: They stand to gain from the transaction in spite of the location or nationality of their trading partners.

Understanding that trade is between people, not nations, is important for another reason. If we focus solely on gains from trade to nations taken as unified political entities, we may overlook the *distributional effects* of international commerce – the gains and losses to individuals. As we shall show, even though international trade increases a *nation's* total income, it can reduce some individuals' incomes while it increases others' incomes. To evaluate objections to free trade among nations in proper perspective, we must recognize these individual gains and losses.

Objections to free trade can easily be explained in terms of market theory. A major principle of economic theory is that each individual competitor has a vested interest in reducing the competition she faces. Competition forces product prices down, forces constant product development and improvement, and in the long run restricts business profits to only the risk-adjusted profit opportunities available elsewhere. It is thus understandable why domestic firms seek protection from their foreign competitors. However, explaining the passage of restrictions on competition from abroad involves the application of principles developed in earlier chapters. This is because, as will be shown, restricting foreign imports increases the prices consumers must pay. A policy of general protection against imports based on the narrow interests of particular sectors of the economy can reduce everyone's income. On this basis rests the case for free international trade as a guiding policy philosophy.

In Part I, after first examining the advantages of international trade from a purely national perspective, we turn to the distributional, or individual, effects of trade, which will help us understand the political pros and cons of protectionism. We then turn to how trade is financed and lubricated by the exchange of national currencies through international money markets. In Part II, we take up how the growing mobility of financial and real capital has affected the cross-national competition among firms *and* governments, leading to organizational and policy constraints on managers in business and policy makers in governments. We sandwich in between Parts I and II the classic (satirical) case for free trade made with a touch of humor by the nineteenth-century French economist Frédéric Bastiat.

PART I THEORY AND PUBLIC POLICY APPLICATIONS

International microeconomics theory has two major divisions: (1) the theory of the cross-national trade in *real goods and services* and (2) the theory of cross-national trade in *currencies*, which are both affected by, and affect, the volume of trade in goods and services and in capital flows and affect the volume of trade in goods and services and capital flows. We consider each division in turn.

International trade in goods

There are two distinguishable dimensions to international trade that need to be considered separately: (1) the *collective or aggregate gains* from international trade to countries as a whole and (2) the *distributional effects* within countries among those who must compete with imports (both owners and their workers) and those who produce exports. Support for international trade restrictions emanates mainly from so-called "protectionists" in the first group, and opposition to trade restrictions emanates mainly from so-called "antiprotectionists" (exporters and domestic consumers) in the second.

Collective gains from trade

Most of the gains from trade result from producing goods at a minimum cost in term of sacrificed alternatives and the distribution of what is produced to those who value it most. With nations producing and selling those things which they can produce at the lowest opportunity costs, joint output is maximized and consumption opportunities are enhanced. Adam Smith told us in the 1770s about the nature of the gains from trade: "It is a maxim of every prudent master, never to attempt to make at home what it will cost him more to make than to buy" (Smith 1937, 422). Cost savings in individual countries on producing any given output level necessarily imply that more can be produced with any given resource base cross-nationally.

Trade also allows a greater variety and wider choice of available products. The gains from it are clearest when no domestic substitute exists for an imported good. For example, the United States does not have any known reserves of chromium, manganese, or tin. For those basic resources, which are widely used in manufacturing, American firms must rely on foreign suppliers. The gains from trade are also clear for goods that are very costly or difficult to produce in the United States. For example, cocoa and coffee can be raised in the United States, but only in greenhouses. Obviously it is less costly to import coffee in exchange for some other good, such as wheat, for which the US climate is better suited.

Foreign competition also offers benefits to the American consumer. By challenging the market power of domestic firms, foreign producers who market their goods in the United States expand markets supplies, reduce product prices, and expand domestic consumption (which means that consumer surplus value from consuming imported goods can rise), not to mention the fact that foreign competition also increases the variety of goods available. Without competition from the thirty or more foreign automobile producers who sell in the American market, US domestic auto makers would each get a much larger percentage of the market. They would be less hesitant to raise their prices if consumers had fewer alternative sources of supply. Collusion among major manufacturers would also be much more likely without the presence of foreign competitors. There would be less competitive pressures for domestic producer to improve their organization design and management policies as well as improve their products.

An **absolute advantage** in production is the capacity to produce more units of output than a competitor can for any given level of resource use.

A **comparative advantage** in production or cost is the relative advantage based on comparative ratios such that either the absolute advantage is greatest or the absolute disadvantage is smallest.

International trade also promotes specialization, the benefits of which should now be fairly clear (given that they were considered earlier in this book). By concentrating on producing a small number of goods and selling to the world market, a nation can reap the benefits of greater worker and firm proficiency in production. The resulting cost savings can result in *greater aggregate production* in both trading nations – even when production in all goods in one trading nation is more efficient than elsewhere in the world, as shown with the following example (that involves a review of material covered for trade among individuals in chapter 1).

Consider a world in which only two nations, the United States and China, produce only two goods, textiles and beef. Assume that the United States produces both textiles and beef more efficiently than China. That is, with the same resources, the United States can produce more units of beef and more units of textiles than China can. The United States has an **absolute advantage** in the production of both goods. However, a country's **comparative advantage** is more important for trade than is its absolute advantage. As long as the relative productivities or costs differ between individuals, regions, or nations, the participants can engage in mutually beneficial trade.

Table 15.1 shows these absolute and comparative differences for the United States and China. With the same labor, capital, or other resources, the United States can produce thirty units of textiles; China can produce twenty-five.

Table 15.1 *Comparative cost advantages, beef and textiles, United States and China*

	Maximum units of textiles (zero beef units)	Maximum units of beef (zero textile units)	Domestic cost ratios in each nation	Mutually beneficial trade ratio, both nations
United States	30	90	1 textile costs 3 beef	1 textile trades for 2 beef
China	25	25	1 textile costs 1 beef	

If the same resources are applied to beef production, the United States still outproduces China, by ninety units to twenty-five. Under such conditions, one might think that trade with China could not possibly benefit the United States since the United States is more productive in everything. The relevant question, however, is not how efficient the United States is in absolute terms, but whether the people in the United States can make a better deal by trading with China than they can make by trading among themselves.

This question can be addressed by examining the comparative advantage, or the ratios of differences in relative productivities and, hence, costs of textile and beef production in the two countries. Keep in mind that a nation, like an individual, has a comparative advantage where (1) its absolute advantage in production is greater or (2) its absolute disadvantage is smaller. Generally, a nation will have a comparative advantage in those products whose production requires a large proportion of factors that are relatively abundant and inexpensive in that nation; and a comparative disadvantage in products whose production requires a large proportion of productive factors that are relatively scarce and expensive in that nation. It is a technological fact that different products generally require different proportions of factors in their production.

To determine the comparative advantages, we must compare the *relative productivities* in the United States and China. The United States is only 20 percent more productive in textiles than is China, whereas it is 260 percent more productive in beef. Its relatively greater productivity – its comparative advantage – is in beef. By the same comparative framework, China is 83 percent as productive in textiles and 28 percent as productive in beef as the United States. China's relatively greater productivity – its comparative advantage – lies in textile production. The "law of comparative advantage" tells us that if the countries specialize in the production of that good in which they have a comparative advantage, then trade can be mutually beneficial.

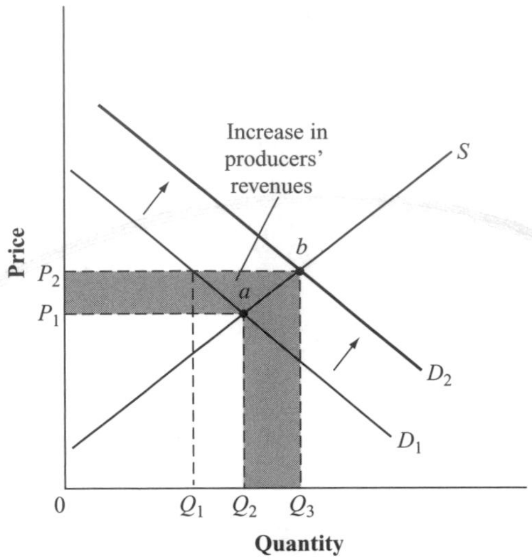

Figure 15.1 Gains from the export trade

Opening up foreign markets to US producers increases the demand for their products, from D_1 to D_2. As a result, domestic producers can raise their price from P_1 to P_2 and sell a larger quantity, Q_3 instead of Q_2. Revenues increase by the shaded area $P_2bQ_3Q_2aP_1$. The more price-elastic or flatter the supply function (S), the larger the change in quantity and the smaller the change in price.

We can come to the same conclusion by comparing the two countries' relative costs of producing textiles and beef. We know that economic resources are unevenly distributed among nations, thereby producing differences in productive capacities. Remember that a comparative advantage is the capacity to produce a product at a lower cost than a competitor's, in terms of the goods that must be given up. In the illustration captured in figure 15.1, the United States must forgo fewer units of textiles to obtain a unit of beef. In the United States 1 unit of beef costs one-third units of textiles. In China, 1 unit of beef costs one unit of textiles. Although a single nation could theoretically have an absolute advantage in all commodities, it could not have a comparative advantage in all commodities. With two nations and two commodities, *if a nation has a comparative advantage in one commodity it must have a comparative disadvantage in the other commodity.* Having a comparative advantage in beef necessarily means the United States cannot have a comparative advantage in textiles.

In a sense, the United States trades with itself every time it produces either beef or textiles. If it produces beef, it incurs an opportunity cost; it gives up some of the textiles it could have produced. If it produces textiles, it gives up some beef. As table 15.1 indicates, every time the United States produces one unit of textiles, it gives up three units of beef (because it can produce either 30 units of textiles or 90 of beef – a ratio of 1 to 3). Thus the United States can benefit by trading beef for textiles if it can give up fewer than 3 units of beef for each unit of textiles it gets from China.

China, on the other hand, gives up 1 unit of beef for each unit of textiles it produces. If China can get more than 1 unit of beef for each unit of textiles it trades it, too, can gain by trading. In short, if the trade ratio is greater than 1 unit of beef for 1 unit of textiles but less than 3 units of beef for 1 unit of textiles, trade will benefit both countries. For example, at an exchange ratio of 1 unit of textiles to 2 units of beef, the United States will gain because it has to give up fewer units of beef – 2 instead of 3 – than if it tried to produce the textiles itself. It can produce 3 units of beef (giving up 1 of textiles). Then it can trade two of its three units of beef produced in exchange for the 1 unit of textiles that it did not produce. It will, after trade, have 1 extra beef unit left over. (Alternatively, it could trade all 3 units of beef for 1.5 units of textiles.) China can produce 1 unit of textiles and trade it for 2 units of beef, gaining 1 beef unit in the process.

Both nations can gain from such a trade because each is specializing in the production of a good for which it has a *comparative opportunity cost advantage.*[1] Because of economies of specialization, both countries can reap additional benefits as they become more focused, knowledgeable, and proficient in the production of a more limited array of goods.

Table 15.2 shows the gains in production each nation can realize under such an arrangement. Before trade, the United States produces 15 units of textiles and 45 of beef; China produces 3 units of textiles and 22 of beef. Before trade, total production for the two countries combined is therefore 18 units of textiles and 67 units of beef. With trade and specialized production, the United States produces 90 units of beef and China produces 25 units of textiles. At an international trade ratio of 1 unit of textiles to 2 units of beef, suppose the two nations agree to trade 40 units of beef for 20 units of textiles. The United States gets more beef – 50 units as opposed to 45 – and more textiles – 20 units as opposed to 15. China also gets more of both commodities. Similarly, China ends up after trade with more of both goods – 40 units of beef instead of 22 and 5 units of textiles instead of 3.

[1] Specialization in production for the United States and China will likely be partial with increasing marginal production costs. With constant cost or decreasing cost, the specialization of production may be complete.

Table 15.2 *Mutual gains from trade in beef and textiles, United States and China*

	United States	China	Total, United States and China
Production and consumption levels before international trade	15 textiles 45 beef	3 textiles 22 beef	18 textiles 67 beef
Production levels in anticipation of international trade (complete specialization assumed)	0 textiles 90 beef	25 textiles 0 beef	25 textiles 90 beef
At an exchange ratio of 2 beef for 1 textile, United States and China agree to trade 40 beef for 20 textiles			
Consumption levels after international trade	20 textiles 50 beef	5 textiles 40 beef	25 textiles 90 beef
Increased consumption (before-trade consumption levels subtracted)	5 textiles 5 beef	2 textiles 18 beef	7 textiles 23 beef

Thus, by engaging in international trade according to comparative advantage, trading countries can gain in the sense that they can have more of all goods, those that are subject to trade and those that are not. By reducing the opportunity cost of production, trade frees up resources that would be absorbed in the domestic production of the imported goods, which means that imports release resources that can be used elsewhere in the domestic economy. In more concrete terms, if less labor is used in China to produce beef Chinese consumers buy, then there is more labor available for the production of textiles that are exported and for the production of, say, healthcare services that cannot be subject to international trade.

The **terms of trade** is the ratio at which one commodity can be traded or exchanged for another commodity internationally; or, on an aggregate basis, it is the ratio of the price of exports to the price of imports.

As we have seen, even a nation that has an absolute advantage in every product can benefit from trade. In reality, no such nation exists, but that just underscores the point that even in the unlikeliest of conditions, trade can be mutually beneficial. Furthermore, if voluntary trade takes place, we must assume that both parties perceive that they will gain. Why else would they agree to the arrangement?

How much each nation gains in the aggregate from international trade depends on the **terms of trade**. The more favorable a nation's terms of trade, and therefore its exchange rate, the larger its share of gain from trade. In terms of table 15.1, the closer the exchange ratio is to 1 textile for 1 beef (the US limit), the more China gains from trade with the United States. The closer the exchange rate is to 1 textile for 1 beef (China's limit), the more the United States gains from trade with China.

The distributional effects of trade

International trade remains a controversial subject in policy circles and among media pundits. This is because firms – their owners and workers – within nations may not all gain from trade. Individual gains tend to go to domestic firms that produce goods and services for export; losses tend to go to domestic firms that produce goods and services that are imported. It should be kept in mind that this is true of any trade, domestic as well as foreign. If more American consumers decide that they prefer to buy Dell computers assembled in the United States to those assembled by Lenovo (the Chinese computer maker that finalized its $1.75 billion purchase of IBM's personal computer and laptop divisions in 2005 to become the world's third largest computer maker with 5 percent of world personal computer sales, *New York Times*, May 5, 2005), those Americans who assemble the Dell computers and who own stock in Dell will benefit, but those working for and owning stock in Lenovo will be harmed, although the harm may be temporary.

Gains to exporters

Exporters of domestic goods gain from international trade because the market for their goods expands, increasing demand for their products, thus raising their output and the prices they can charge. The increase in their revenue can be seen in figure 15.1. When the demand curve shifts from D_1 to D_2 because of the added foreign demand, producers' revenues rise from $P_1 \times Q_2$ (point *a*) to $P_2 \times Q_3$ (point *b*). (The more price-elastic or flatter the supply function (S), the larger the change in quantity and the smaller the change in price.) The increase in revenues is equal to the shaded L shaped area bounded by $P_2bQ_3Q_2aP_1$. Producers benefit because they receive greater profits, equal to the shaded area above the supply curve, P_2baP_1 (that portion of the increased revenues that is not additional cost). Workers and suppliers of raw materials benefit because their services are in greater demand, and therefore more costly. The cost of producing additional units for export is equal to the shaded area below the supply curve between Q_2 and Q_3, Q_2abQ_3.

In 2004, a devastating tsunami hit a number of countries in Southeast Asia, killing over 200,000 people, leaving millions of people homeless, and wiping out much of the area's food producing potential. As a consequence, many farmers in unaffected areas of the world stood witness to an increase in the demand for their products at some minor increases in the prices of the goods they produced as governments and private groups worked to move food to the area affected by the tsunami. Consumers in areas unaffected directly by the tsunami, of course, were indeed adversely affected by it, albeit indirectly. They had to pay higher prices for their foodstuff from nontsunami areas as well as pay higher prices for imports of food from the directly affected area.

Figure 15.1 suggests why farmers supported the sales of wheat to the Soviet Union that began in the early 1970s. They complained loudly when the US government temporarily suspended sales for political reasons in the late 1970s. Many consumers and members of Congress objected to the wheat sales, however, on the grounds that they would increase the domestic price of wheat, and therefore of bread.

In a narrow sense, consumers of exported products have an interest in restricting their exportation. Yet in the broad context of international trade, restrictions can work against the private interests of individuals, including consumers of bread. Trade is ultimately a two-way street. To import goods and services that can be produced more cheaply abroad than at home, a nation must export something else. No nation will continually export part of what it produces without getting something in return. So when exports are restricted to benefit a special-interest group, imports of other commodities are also restricted. Restrictions on the exportation of wheat may hold down the price of bread, but they can also increase the price of imported goods, such as radios and television sets.

Losses to firms competing with imports

Government policy is more likely to restrict imports than exports. Whereas consumers gain from increased imports, domestic producers often lose from the increased competition. Foreign producers can gain a foothold in the domestic market in three ways:

1. By providing a better product than domestic firms do
2. By selling essentially the same product as that of domestic firms, but at a lower price
3. By providing a product previously unavailable in the domestic market.

Most domestic buyers (consumers who buy final products and producers who buy inputs) welcome the importation of previously unavailable products, but domestic producers who face competition from foreign suppliers have an incentive to object to importation. If imports are allowed, the domestic supply

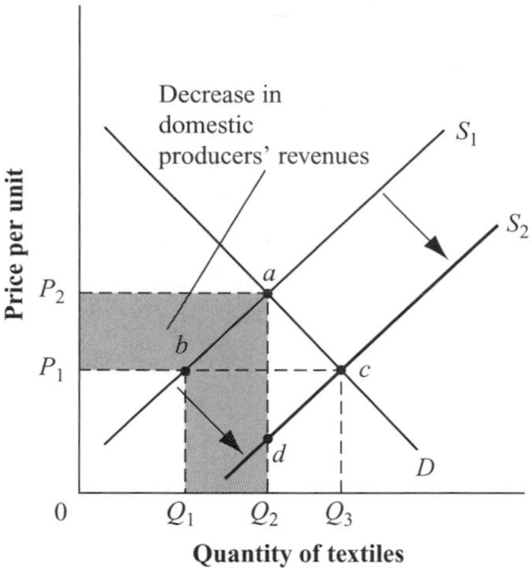

Figure 15.2 Losses from competition with imported products

Opening up the market to foreign trade increases the supply of textiles from S_1 to S_2. As a result, the price of textiles falls from P_2 to P_1, and domestic producers sell a lower quantity, Q_1 instead of Q_2. Consumers benefit from the lower price and the higher quantity of textiles they are able to buy, but domestic producers, workers, and suppliers lose. Producers' revenues drop by an amount equal to the shaded area $P_2aQ_2Q_1bP_1$. Workers' and suppliers' payments drop by an amount equal to the shaded area Q_2abQ_1. Starting at point *c*, a tariff or tax equal to *ad* is levied, shifting the supply curve from S_2 to S_1. In an industry whose costs are increasing, the increase in price from P_1 to P_2 in the importing country is less than the increase in the tariff (*ad*), because a price fall in the exporting country absorbs some of the burden of the duty.

of a good increases. Domestic competitors will sell less, and they may have to sell at a lower price. In short, the business opportunities and the employment opportunities of their workers and suppliers decline as a result of foreign competition, with a potential reduction in their real incomes.

Figure 15.2 shows the effects of importing foreign textiles. Without imports, demand is *D* and supply is S_1. In a competitive market, producers will sell Q_2 units at a price of P_2. Total receipts will be $P_2 \times Q_2$. The importation of foreign textiles increases the supply to S_2, dropping the price from P_2 to P_1. Because prices are lower, consumers increase their consumption from Q_2 to Q_3 and get more for their money. (The more price-elastic or flatter the demand curve (*D*), the greater the change in quantity and the smaller the change in price.)

Domestic firms, their employees, and their suppliers lose. Because the price is lower, domestic producers must move down their supply curve (S_1) to the lower quantity Q_1. Their revenues fall from $P_2 \times Q_2$ to $P_1 \times Q_1$. In other words, the revenues in the shaded L shaped area bounded by $P_2aQ_2Q_1bP_1$ are lost. Of this total loss in revenues, owners of domestic firms lose, on balance, the area above the supply curve, P_2abP_1, representing profits. Workers and suppliers of raw materials lose the area below the supply curve, Q_2abQ_1. This is the cost domestic firms do not have to incur when they reduce domestic production from Q_2 to Q_1, the payments that would be made to domestic workers and suppliers in the absence of foreign competition. If workers and other resources are employed in textiles because it is their best possible employment, the introduction of foreign products can be seen as a restriction on some workers' employment opportunities. In summary, although international trade lowers import prices and raises export prices in the domestic nation, the net impact is a reduced social opportunity cost curve that expands total output and consumption opportunities.

A **tariff** is a special tax or duty on imported goods that can be a percentage of the price (*ad valorem* duty) or a specific amount per unit of the product (specific duty).

The effects of trade restrictions

The fact that foreign competition in particular hurts some domestic firms of those products provides an incentive for their owners, workers, and suppliers to seek government restrictions on the imports of tradable goods. Of course, some industries, such as communications, services, and utilities, are largely insulated from foreign competition, although technological advances are making some of these goods tradable as well. For example, because it is now possible for people halfway around to world to ask questions and fill out a form electronically as cheaply as someone next door, the marketing research industry is no longer a strictly domestically based industry, as evidenced by the number of times people in one country – say, France – receive telephone calls from telemarketers working in India for firms based in Canada.

A **quota** is a physical or dollar value limit on the amount of a good that can be imported or exported during some specified period of time.

Two forms of protection are commonly used: a **tariff** and a **quota**. A tariff may be imposed to raise money for the levying country – or, as is the more likely case, to protect some industry against the discipline of competition. There are other nontariff barriers (NTBs) such as controlling the flow of foreign exchange, licensing requirements, health, quality, or safety restrictions and regulations on products.

Since the 1970s, countries such as the United States and those in the European Union (EU) have also restricted trade by negotiating "voluntary" limits on exports from countries like China. Of course, the bargaining hand of the countries wanting the trade restriction is fortified by the often explicit threat of the imposition of tariffs and quotas. After quotas on Chinese textile imports into Europe were lifted in 2005, various categories of Chinese textile imports into both the European Union and the United States jumped dramatically, between 51 and 534 percent over the course of only the first four months of the year, according to early reports (Miller 2005). Politicians on both continents began advocating renewed quotas on Chinese imports, if China did not restrain its exports "voluntarily." In April 2005, China responded to the political threats by imposing 2 and 3¢ taxes on many of its textile exports and was, at the time of writing, considering sharply higher export duties, mainly to fend off the reimposition of foreign quotas (Miller 2005).[2] Nevertheless, a month later, the George W. Bush administration reimposed quotas on several major categories of apparel products, pants, shirts, and underwear, arguing that the restrictions demonstrate "this administration's continued commitment to America's textile manufacturers and their employees" (Los Angeles Times Wire Service 2005).

The distributional impact of various forms of protection can be assessed by considering the impact of tariffs. If tariffs are imposed on a foreign good such as textiles, the supply of textiles will decrease – say, from S_2 to S_1 in figure 15.2 – and the price of imports will rise. Domestic producers will raise their prices, too, and domestic production will go up. If the tariff is high and all foreign textiles are excluded, the supply will shift all the way back to S_1. A lower tariff will have a more modest effect, shifting the supply curve only part of the way back toward S_1. The price of textiles will rise and domestic producers will expand their production, but imports will continue to come into the country. How much the price rises and the quantity falls after the imposition of the tariff depends not only on how high the tariff is, but also on how price-elastic the demand curve (D) is. The more elastic D is, the greater the fall in quantity and the less the rise in price for any given tariff.

A quota has the same general effect as a tariff, although its price–cost effect can be much more drastic. Both tariffs and quotas reduce the market supply, raise the domestic market price, and encourage domestic production, thereby helping domestic producers and harming domestic consumers.

A quota, however, can sever international price–cost links because the functioning of the market mechanism for relating the prices of goods in different nations is artificially impaired. Nonetheless, quotas are sometimes imposed by nations because they are a more certain and precise technique of control, and can be changed by administrative decree. Quotas have a revenue-raising potential only when the issuing government decides to sell the quotas to importers

[2] The threat of reinstated quotas was very real in early 2005. In April, a US appeals court ruled that the US Department of Commerce could consider petitions from the US textile industry to have quotas reimposed on $1.3 billion worth of Chinese clothing (*Washington Post* 2005). China could easily reason that it would be better for it to tax its exports than to have other countries tax them through tariffs or raise the prices of China's goods in the United States with quotas, with the benefits going to the holders of the quotas. With a tax on its exports, China at least could get the benefits of the tax revenues.

(which can be done because the quotas restrict imports, raise the prices of the goods imported, and thus give the quotas a monetary value, which is why foreign exporters and domestic importers seek to "own" them).

Three main differences exist between quotas and tariffs. First, quotas firmly restrict the amount of a product that can be imported, regardless of market conditions. A quota might specify how much oil may be imported each day or how much sugar may be imported each year. Tariffs, on the other hand, permit any level of importation for which consumers are willing to pay. Thus, if demand for the product increases, imports may rise.[3]

While espousing an economic and political philosophy of "free trade" as the route to prosperity, Ronald Reagan imposed quotas on steel, copper, textiles, and autos from Japan (Karstensson 2003). In 1984, the so-called "voluntary restraint" program forced Japan to restrict auto sales in the United States to 1.84 million cars. Because Japanese supply was not allowed to keep pace with the rapidly expanding US demand at the time, the price of Japanese cars rose, more expensive (and profitable) models were imported, and consumers faced longer waiting lists for Japanese cars. The price of American cars also rose. These consequences led to the termination of the voluntary restraint program in 1985. But George W. Bush followed Reagan's lead in 2002, a year after he took office: Bush talked free trade but reimposed tariffs and quotas on imported steel, with much the same unavoidable consequences: Higher prices on imported and domestic steel and higher prices on American-made products that used steel (Greenville and MacAulay 2004).

The second major difference between tariffs and quotas is that quotas are typically specified for each important foreign producer. Otherwise, all foreign producers would rush to sell their goods before the quota was reached. When quotas are rationed in this way, more detailed government enforcement is required. Tariffs place no such restrictions on individual producers. Moreover, the tariff is collected by the government in custom duties, whereas price enhancement with a quota goes as a windfall gain to the fortunate few with import quotas.

Finally, quotas enable foreign firms to raise their prices and extract more income from consumers. One economist estimated that the Reagan administration's voluntary restraint program permitted Japanese auto producers to raise their prices high enough to take an additional $2,500 per car, or $5 billion, out of the American market (Crandall 1985). As a result of the protectionist

[3] A hybrid of a tariff and quota, called a "tariff quota," imposes a tax on imported goods but also sets a fixed quantity limit on importation of the imported good.

shield, US auto makers raised domestic car prices $1,000 per car, or $8 billion per year, in 1984 and 1985. Tariffs, on the other hand, force foreign firms to lower their prices to offset the increase from the tariff. They also generate income for the federal government.

Although tariffs and quotas promote a less efficient allocation of the world's scarce resources, because of the private benefits to be gained from them by domestic producers we should expect those producers to seek them as long as their market benefits exceed the political cost of acquiring protection. Politicians are likely to expect votes and campaign contributions in return for tariff legislation that generates highly visible benefits to special interests. Producers (and labor) will usually make the necessary contributions, because the elimination of foreign competition promises increased revenues in the protected industries. The difference between the increase in profits caused by import restrictions and the amount spent on political activity can be seen as a kind of profit in itself. That is, the potential for the imposition of tariffs and quotas can be expected to lead to the kind of *rent seeking* we discussed in chapter 13, the net effect of which can be expected to hike the dead-weight loss from the import protection.

In contrast to producers, consumers have reason to oppose tariffs or quotas on imported products. Such legislation inevitably causes prices to rise, because a tariff amounts to a subsidy to the domestic producer of the dutiable product and is paid for largely by the consumers of that product in the form of higher prices. Consumers typically do not offer very much resistance, however, because the effects of tariffs and quotas are hard to perceive. In contrast to a sales tax, the cost of a tariff is not rung up separately at the cash register, and many consumers do not reason through its complex effects on consumer prices. In fact, many if not most consumers feel that tariffs on foreign automobile, steel, or copper producers are good for the nation and for themselves. "Buy American" slogans and advertisements emphasizing the need to preserve American jobs are generally effective in swaying public opinion.[4]

As a group, consumers have less incentive to oppose tariffs than industry has to support them, because the costs to individual consumers and taxpayers are negligible and largely hidden (again, a point we developed with reference to

[4] How costly is protectionism? Estimates for the cost of protectionism in the United States vary substantially. One comprehensive investigation showed that protection in thirty-one countries cost consumers $53 billion in 1984, yet provided only $40 billion in benefits to the producers (Hufbauer *et al.* 1986). However, one survey of the econometric literature suggests that the cost estimates in many studies are "embarrassingly low," given how much emphasis economists place on the costs of tariffs and quotas (Feenstra 1992).

interest-group politics in general in chapter 13). The benefits of a tariff accrue principally to a relatively small group of firms, whose lobbyists may already be well entrenched in Washington. These firms have a strong incentive to be fully informed on the issue and to make campaign contributions, but the harmful effects of a tariff are diffused over an extremely large group of consumers. The financial burden that any one consumer bears may be very slight, particularly if the tariff in question is small, as most tariffs are. As a result, the individual consumer has little incentive to become informed on tariff legislation or to make political contributions to lobby against such legislation.

Although consumers as a whole may share an interest in opposing tariffs, collective action must still be undertaken by individuals – and individuals will not incur the cost of organizing unless they expect to receive compensating private benefits.

At some level of increased cost, of course, consumers will find the necessary incentive to oppose tariff legislation. For this reason Congress rarely passes tariffs high enough to make importation totally unprofitable. Even low tariffs reduce the nation's real income while redistributing it toward protected sectors. The size of the pie is reduced, but the protected few get a bigger slice. In spite of all the impediments to free trade imposed by governments around the world, the dollar volume of US imports and exports has increased at a progressively faster rate since the 1960s. Similarly, total world trade has increased at progressively faster rates. Between 1980 and 1990, total world trade in goods expanded at a rate of 5.25 percent a year (two-thirds faster than real world GDP). Between 1990 and 2000, total world trade in goods expanded at an average rate of 6.20 percent (nearly 200 percent faster than the growth in real world GDP) (White 2002).[5]

Accordingly, the case against protectionism, already described above as a negative-sum game in which the losing consumers lose more than the protected producers win, involves four additional problems:

- First, protectionism allows the survival of high-cost producers that would otherwise fail.
- Second, trade restrictions have a habit of affecting other industries. For example, automobiles need protection because the ball bearings, steel, and textiles that provide inputs to automobiles are protected and are more costly because of the import protection.
- Third, foreign nations often retaliate against protectionism. Tit-for-tat is the *modus operandi* in international trade: Country *A* raises barriers on product

[5] World trade in services expanded at even faster rates for the periods 1980–90 and 1990-2000 – 7.92 percent and 6.25, respectively (White 2002).

X from country *B* because Country *B* imposed a tariff on Country's *A*'s product *Y*.

- Fourth, trade restrictions aren't really job-saving or job-creating (on balance), but job-swapping. Protectionism raises the exchange rate, hurting exports in unprotected industries. Because in the long run the value of exports must be equal to the value of imports, we end up swapping jobs, ending up with more jobs in inefficient protected industries and with fewer jobs in efficient unprotected industries (Blinder 1987, 118–19). Moreover, a relatively small percentage (3 percent) of all jobs lost each year in the United States are lost to the so-called "offshoring" of work, and trade restrictions that seek to prevent offshoring of jobs imposed considerable costs on the American economy (perhaps more than $100,000 per job saved) (Balaker and Moore 2005).

The case for free trade

We have seen how international trade can on balance increase the total incomes of the nations engaged in it, although export producers gain and producers that provide substitutes for imports lose. And even those who work for and receive profits from a domestic industry that is harmed by having to compete with foreign imports are generally better off in an economy where all domestic industries are subject to foreign competition than they would be in an economy where all industries are protected against that competition. By extension, we can conclude that anything that restricts the scope of trade between nations generally reduces those nations' real incomes. To the extent that trade is a two-way street – that exports trade for imports, at least in the long run – a reduction in imports brings a reduction in exports. From US imports, the Chinese get the dollars they need to buy US exports. If the US reduces its imports, the Chinese will have fewer funds with which to buy from the United States. For this reason, US farmers, who sell approximately one-third of their crops in foreign markets, actively opposed the protectionist movement led by textiles, steel, and copper firms.

Yet what is true for one sector of the economy is not necessarily true for all. As just indicated, if all sectors are protected by tariffs, it is possible (but not inevitable) that all will experience a drop in real income. Figure 15.3 illustrates the case of an economy with two industries – automobiles and textiles – in a game theoretic framework. Both industries must compete with imports. If neither seeks protection, both will operate in cell I, at a combined real income of $50 ($20 for the textiles industry and $30 for the automobile industry). If the textiles industry receives protection but the auto industry does not, they

	Textile industry without tariff protection		Textile industry with tariff protection	
Automobile industry without tariff protection	Cell I		Cell II	
	Real income, textile	Real income, auto	Real income, textile	Real income, auto
	$20	$30	$23	$25
Automobile industry with tariff protection	Cell III		Cell IV	
	Real income, textile	Real income, auto	Real income, textile	Real income, auto
	$15	$34	$17	$26

Figure 15.3 Effects of tariff protection on individual industries: case 1

If neither the textiles nor the automobile industry obtains tariff protection, the economy will earn its highest possible collective income (cell I), but each industry has an incentive to obtain tariff protection for itself. If the textiles industry alone seeks protection (cell II), its income will rise while the auto industry's income falls. If the auto industry alone seeks protection, its income will rise while that of the textiles industry falls. If both obtain protection, the economy will end up in cell IV, its worst possible position. Income in both sectors will fall.

will move to cell II, where tariffs raise the textiles industry's income from $20 to $23. The automotive sector's income falls to $25, so that the two industries' combined real income falls to $48. Consumers get fewer textiles at a higher price and the automobile sector exports fewer cars.

Similarly, if the auto industry receives protection while the textiles industry does not, the economy will move from cell I to cell III. Again, total real income falls, this time from $50 to $49, with the auto industry better off. Its income rises from $30 to $34, but the textiles industry's income falls to $15. Obviously, if one industry seeks protection, the other has an incentive to follow suit. If the textiles industry counters with a tariff of its own, the economy will move from cell III to cell IV, and the industry's real income will rise from $15 to $17.

Without some constraint on both sectors, then, the two industries are in the kind of Prisoner's Dilemma considered throughout this book, where each has an interest in seeking protection regardless of what the other does. Yet if the economy winds up in cell IV, total real income will be lower than under any other conditions: only $43. Obviously the best course for the economy as a whole is to prohibit tariffs altogether, and in an economy with only two sectors, the cost of reaching an agreement is manageable. The real world, however, has many economic sectors, and the costs of reaching a decision are much greater.

In figure 15.3, both industries end up with lower real incomes in cell IV, but in reality, the effects of multiple tariffs will be different in different sectors of the economy. Although total real income will fall, several sectors may realize individual gains. Consider figure 15.4. Although total real income falls from cell I ($50) to cell IV ($48), the auto sector's income rises (from $30 to $31). In this case, the textile sector bears the brunt of tariff protection and the auto sector has a compelling interest in obtaining protective tariffs. The sectors of the economy that are most adept at manipulating the political process will be the least willing to accept free trade.

Although it is true that for a nation some trade is better than no trade, it is not necessarily true that free trade is better than restricted trade. Even though protectionism promotes economic inefficiency in the aggregate, a nation may under certain conditions act like a monopolist and improve its share of the gains through trade restrictions. Similarly, the owners of relatively scarce factors of production may be better off with restricted trade. But even in this case, world income is reduced by the trade restrictions. What one country gains, other countries lose. And if all countries try to benefit from trade restriction, they all lose.

Economists generally choose free trade for all because of its obvious benefits to the nation as a whole, or certainly the world as a whole. For example, two economists estimate that because the US average tariff rate fell from 40 percent in 1946 to 4 percent in 2005 and because of the greater international mobility of resources and goods and services, US income grew by roughly $1 trillion, or 10 percent of GDP, which implies that "after a half-century of shrinking distances and commercial liberalization, the average American household enjoys an income gain of about $10,000 per year" (Hufbauer and Grieco 2005). However, as we note in the next section, the case for free trade

	Textile industry without tariff protection	Textile industry without tariff protection
Automobile industry without tariff protection	Cell I Real income, textile: $20 Real income, auto: $30	Cell II Real income, textile: $23 Real income, auto: $25
Automobile industry with tariff protection	Cell III Real income, textile: $15 Real income, auto: $34	Cell IV Real income, textile: $17 Real income, auto: $31

Figure 15.4 Effects of tariff protection on individual industries: Case 2
In this case, the auto industry gains from tariff protection, even if both sectors are protected (cell IV). The textiles industry's income falls from $20 (cell I) to $17 (cell IV), but the auto industry's income rises from $30 (cell I) to $31 (cell IV). Thus the auto industry has no incentive to agree to the elimination of tariffs.

has several legitimate exceptions. Yet even the trade restrictions necessary for the achievement of public benefit can be abused by those who would seek to obtain trade protection for private purposes.

The case for restricted trade

Proponents of tariffs rarely argue that they will serve their private interests at the expense of the public by raising prices, and reducing the availability of goods. Instead, they typically advocate tariffs as the most efficient means to accomplish some national objective. Any private benefits that would accrue to protected industries are generally portrayed as insignificant side-effects.

Although most arguments in favor of tariffs camouflage the underlying issues, one is at least partially valid. It has to do with the maintenance of national security.

The need for national security

Pro-tariff arguments based on national or military security stress the need for a strong defense industry. If imports are completely unrestricted, certain industries needed in time of war or other national emergency could be undersold and run out of business by foreign competitors. In an emergency, the United States could then be dependent on possibly hostile foreign suppliers for essential defense equipment.[6] Tariffs may create inefficiencies in the allocation of world resources, but that is one of the costs a nation must bear to maintain military self-sufficiency and hence a strong national defense.

Given the wavering popularity of US foreign policy and the uncertain support of allies, this argument has some merit. Other nations, such as Israel, have found that they cannot count on the support of all their allies in time of war. Because France disagreed with Israeli policy in the Middle East it has, at times, held up shipment of spare parts for planes it had earlier sold to Israel. The United States could conceivably find itself in a similar position if it relied excessively on foreign firms for planes, firearms, and oil.

But even though the national defense argument has some validity, it is one that special-interest groups can easily abuse for private gain. The textile industry, for example, promotes itself as a ready source of combat uniforms during wartime. In years past, US oil producers, contending that a healthy domestic oil industry is vital to the national defense, have lobbied for protection from foreign oil in wartime. But the effects of a tariff are not necessarily what are claimed for them. By making foreign oil more expensive, a tariff increases consumption of domestic oil stocks. Because oil is a finite resource, a tariff can ultimately make the United States more dependent on foreign energy sources in time of emergency. Also, it might be more efficient in many cases to buy products that are important for national defense from foreign suppliers and store sufficient quantities of them for emergencies. Since the United States is dependent on foreign oil, it stores large amounts of petroleum in the Strategic Petroleum Reserve as an emergency reserve.

[6] The nation could convert to the production of war-related goods, but the conversion process might be prohibitively lengthy and complex.

Comparative wages

Politicians, pundits, and industry lobbyists often argue for protection on the grounds that because workers are paid less in foreign countries, US industries cannot hope to compete with foreign imports. They fail to realize that trade depends on the *relative costs of production*, not absolute wage rates in various nations. US wages may be quite high in either absolute or relative terms, but the output of some worker groups that have relatively lower total production costs can still be exported. If some products from high-wage domestic workers are exported, then other products from other high-wage worker groups must be imported.

The important point is what tariffs do to trade. In our earlier hypothetical example of trade in textiles and beef, the United States was more efficient than China in the production of both products. That is, generally speaking, fewer resources were required to produce those goods in the United States than in China. Very possibly, the incomes of textiles and beef workers would be higher in the United States than in China, but because Chinese firms had a comparative cost advantage in textiles (measured in terms of the number of units of beef forgone for each textiles unit), they were able to undersell textiles firms in the United States. If the United States imposed tariffs or quotas on imported textiles because China had a comparative advantage in that product, it would destroy the basis for trade between the two nations. Reducing imports will tend to reduce exports, at least in the long run.

Who gets the money

A further questionable argument for tariffs is based on the faulty idea that the United States necessarily loses when money flows overseas in payment for imports. As Abraham Lincoln is reported to have said, "I don't know much about the tariff, but this I do know. When we trade with other countries, we get the goods and they get the money. When we trade with ourselves, we get the goods and the money."

Lincoln was clearly right when he said he did not know much about the tariff. He failed to recognize the real income benefits of international trade, which are reduced by tariffs. He seems to have confused the nation's welfare with its monetary holdings. It is true that if Americans buy goods from abroad, Americans get the goods and foreigners get the money.[7] But what are foreigners going to do with the money they receive? If they never spend the money they get

[7] Actually, the transaction may not involve the transfer of paper money. It is more likely – as explained later in this chapter – that payment will be made by transferring funds from one bank account to another. The importer's bank balance will drop, and the exporter's bank balance will increase.

from imports, Americans will be better off, for they will have obtained some foreign goods in exchange for some paper bills, which are relatively cheap to print (or, more likely, electronic blips on some bank's computer). At some point, however, foreign exporters will want to get something concrete in return for their labor and materials. They will use their dollars to buy goods (or bonds and stock) from US manufacturers. Again, trade is a give-and-take process, in which benefits flow to both sides.

Lost jobs

The textile industry has complained (for what seems an eternity) that foreign imports of textile products are *the* cause of lost jobs in the US textile industry. It is true that American textile firms have closed lots of plants and laid off hundreds of thousands of textile workers since the 1960s, and textile imports are much higher today than they were in, say, the early 1970s. But are imports from China, Malaysia, the Philippines, and elsewhere fully to blame for lost US jobs? There are several considerations that need to be kept in mind:

- First, domestic textile firms have to compete with domestic competitors as well as foreign competitors. Without much question, many aggressively competitive American firms have helped to run many not-so-competitive American firms out of business over the years.
- Second, the textile industry, pressed by the forces of domestic and foreign competition, went through a technological revolution in the 1970s and 1980s, dramatically increasing their output per worker because of the replacement of fly shuttle-looms with water-jet and air-jet looms. From research conducted by one of the authors, this increase in productivity is responsible for a substantial share of employment loss in the industry (McKenzie 1987).
- Third, many American textile firms have closed because their cost of production has risen as the wages they have had to pay has risen (relative to wages elsewhere in the world). One of the reasons that wages in textiles have risen relatively is that the economies of key textile producing states (North and South Carolina) have progressed economically with the expansion of their nontextile sectors, which has put upward pressures on the wages textile firms have had to pay. In short, the expansion of nontextile American industries has played a role in the contraction of the number of plants and employment in the American textile industry.

Tit-for-tat

A third argument often made is that foreign nations impose tariffs on US goods. Unless we respond in kind, foreign producers will have the advantage in both markets. This argument has a significant flaw. By restricting their imports, foreign nations reduce their ability to sell to the United States and other nations. To buy Chinese goods, for instance, Americans need yuan. They get yuan by selling to China. If China reduces its imports from the United States, Americans will have fewer yuan to buy Chinese goods. So, the Chinese are restricting their own exports with their tariffs: They harm themselves as well as Americans. If Americans respond to their actions by imposing tariffs of their own, they will reduce trade even further. The harm is compounded, not negated.

Nevertheless, "trade wars" can, and do, break out. The result is that nations impose restrictions on each other. Such wars can be mutually beneficial, but only if they make trading partners realize the universal benefits of free trade and move to negotiate bi- or multi-lateral reductions in the trade restrictions they have imposed.

Infant industries

Finally, tariff advocates sometimes claim that new industries deserve protection because they are too small to compete with established foreign firms: they are the so-called "infant industries." If protected by tariffs, these new infant industries can expand their scale of production, lower their production costs, and eventually compete with foreign producers. The problem with this argument is that it is very difficult for a government to determine which new industries may eventually be able to compete with foreign rivals. Over the long period of time that an industry may need to mature conditions, including the technology of production, may change significantly. For an infant industry to become truly competitive, it must do more than become more productive and cost-effective through the achievement of scale economies: It must develop a comparative cost advantage.

Moreover, the mere likelihood that a firm will eventually be able to compete with its foreign rivals does not in itself warrant protection. Not until firms have become established will consumers receive the benefit of lower prices. In the interim, tariff protection hurts consumers by raising the prices they must pay. Proponents of protection must be able to show that the time-discounted future benefits to be gained by establishing an industry exceed the current costs of protecting it. Also, if an infant industry has enough political influence to get tariff protection when it is small, it will probably have enough to keep that protection when it gets larger. The steel industry has managed to keep its protection against imports for many decades after it justified that protection by claiming that it was necessary to become established.

Finally, if a firm can expand, cover all its costs of production, and eventually compete with its foreign rivals, private entrepreneurs as well as government officials can be expected to see the eventual economies. Entrepreneurs are not likely to miss the opportunity to invest in companies that have the chance of achieving the required comparative advantages. Through the stock and bond markets, firms with growth potential will be able to secure the funds they need for expansion. If a firm cannot raise capital from private sources, it may be because the return on the investment is too low in relation to the risk. Why should the government accept risks that the private market will not accept? Should anyone really expect policy makers and government workers to be better at assessing profitable opportunities than private entrepreneurs?

China's trade surplus with the United States

During the 1990s and early 2000s, the United States had a growing deficit in the trade of goods with China. In 1994, the goods deficit was between $29 and $30 billion. By 2000, it had risen to almost $83 billion. By 2004, it had reached almost $162 billion (Frauenheim 2005). Proponents of tariffs and quotas on Chinese imports, especially textile imports, pointed to how China had pegged its currency, the yuan, against the dollar. This meant that while the dollar rose and fell with respect to other currencies, the yuan price of the dollar remained more or less stable. Proponents of US protectionism argued that one of the reasons for the "invasion" of Chinese goods into the United States is that China had chosen an exchange rate that artificially hiked the yuan price of the dollar, making Chinese goods artificially cheap in the United States. Hence, according to critics of China's exchange rate policy, US textile manufacturers, especially, needed protection to offset the inflated value of the dollar (Frauenheim 2005; Los Angeles Times Wire Service 2005).

International finance

People rarely use barter in trade. Exchanging one toy for two pens or three pots for the rear end of a steer simply is not practical. Because the bartering seller must also be a buyer, buyers and sellers may have to incur very substantial costs to find one another, even in the domestic market. When people are hundreds or thousands of miles apart and separated by national boundaries and foreign cultures and languages, barter is all the more complicated. We rarely see exporters acting as importers, exchanging specific exports for specific imports (although barter is not absent in international trade, mainly as a means of avoiding trade restrictions and taxes).

The process of international monetary exchange

The **international exchange rate** is the price of one national currency (such as the euro) stated in terms of another national currency (such as the dollar). In other words, the international exchange rate is the dollar price you must pay for each euro you buy.

Imagine you own a small gourmet shop that carries special cheeses. You may buy your cheese either domestically – cheddar from New York, Monterey Jack from California – or abroad. If you buy from a domestic firm, it is easy to negotiate the deal and make payment. Because the price of cheese is quoted in dollars and the domestic firm expects payment in dollars, you can pay the same way you pay other bills – by writing a personal check. Only one national currency is involved.

Purchasing cheese from a French cheese maker is a little more complicated, for two reasons. First, the price of the cheese will be quoted in euros (or francs). Second, you will want to pay in dollars, but the French cheese maker must be paid in euros. Either you must exchange your dollars for euros, or the cheese maker must convert them to euros. At some point, currencies must be exchanged at some recognized *foreign exchange rate.* Before you buy, you will want to compare the prices of French and domestic cheeses. To do so, you must convert the euro price of cheese into its dollar equivalent. To do that, you need to know the **international exchange rate** between dollars and euros. Once you know the current exchange rate, conversion of currencies is not difficult.

Assume that you want to buy €5,000 (read "5,000 euros") worth of cheese, and that the international exchange rate between dollars and euros is $1.25 (that is, $1.25 buys €1), roughly the exchange rate as this chapter was being finalized. €5,000 will cost you $6,250.

A **depreciation** of a national currency, such as the dollar, is a reduction in its exchange value or purchasing power, brought about by market forces, in relation to other national currencies.

The international exchange rate determines the dollar price of the foreign goods you want to buy. A different exchange rate would have changed the dollar price of cheese. For instance, suppose the exchange rate rose from $1.25 = €1 to $2.00 = €1. In the jargon of international finance, such a change represents a **depreciation** of the dollar. The dollar has depreciated relative to the euro because it now takes more dollars to buy one euro, or a single dollar now buys fewer euros. This necessarily means that the euro has *appreciated* relative to the dollar because it now takes fewer euros to buy a dollar (0.5 euros now buys a dollar as opposed to 0.8 before).

As an American, your willingness to buy French cheese obviously depends on the euro price of cheese and the exchange rate between dollars and euros. If the euro price of cheese increases or decreases, your dollar price increases

Table 15.3 *Likely long-run effects of depreciation and appreciation of the dollar on US exports and imports*

	Depreciation of dollar	Appreciation of dollar
Price of exports	Decrease	Increase
Total dollar value of exports	Increase	Decrease
Price of imports	Increase	Decrease
Total dollar value of imports	Decrease	Increase

or decreases at any given exchange rate. If the dollar depreciates relative to euros, the dollar price of French cheese rises. It is very likely you (and other Americans) will be inclined to import less, because at the higher price American cheese consumers will buy less. One the other hand, if the dollar appreciates (that is, if a dollar buy more euros), the dollar price of French cheese falls. Very likely, you will import more because you can lower your own price and sell more.

In general, a depreciation of the dollar discourages imports and encourages exports, which reduces a merchandise balance of trade deficit, or increases a merchandise balance of trade surplus in the long run.[8]

These long-run consequences of changes in the international rate of exchange are summarized in table 15.3. In the (very) short run, however, a depreciation in the dollar can increase the dollars we spend on imports and reduce the dollars we receive from our exports because we will have to spend more dollars on each imported item and we will receive fewer dollars on each exported item. In the (very) short run we will not have enough time to reduce how much we import very much and foreigners will not have enough time to increase how much they import from us very much. Recall that price elasticities of demand are smaller in the short run than the long run. Given more time to

[8] The merchandise balance of trade is what we hear on business news programs referred to somewhat misleadingly as our "trade balance." However, strictly speaking, the *merchandise* trade balance refers only to a country's exports and imports of goods that flow in and out of the country. For example, a French family flies to America and spends $5,000 on hotels, meals, rental cars, scuba lessons, fishing trips, and Disney World tickets. While at Disney World, the family buys a Mickey Mouse hat for $8.50, which is all they take back to France. Only the $8.50 spent on the hat of their total $5,008.50 spending will be treated as an import in the merchandise balance of trade. If we counted just this French family's expenditures in America and an American family's expenditure of $20.00 on French cheese, the official figures would show the United States running a *merchandise trade deficit* with France. But the merchandise trade deficit misses the French family's expenditures on American services, which are just as important for the prosperity of the country as the family's expenditure on the Mickey Mouse hat.

adjust, however, it is more likely that a depreciation in the dollar will reduce (increase) our merchandise trade deficit (surplus).[9]

The exchange of national currencies

Assume that as a cheese importer you have figured the dollar price of French cheese using the exchange rate, and you find it satisfactory. Because your American customers pay for their groceries in dollars, that is the currency you receive when you sell the cheese. Yet cheese makers in France want euros since that is what they need to pay for their mortgages and groceries. How do you convert your dollars into euros? (Many MBA students are well versed in converting currencies, because they do so much international business and travel. If you understand currency conversions, you might wish to skip to the next section. However, those who are new to international business and travel will find this section instructive.)

Again, if you want to buy French cheese and need euros, a bank will exchange your dollars for you. Banks deal in different currencies for the same reason that business people trade in commodities, to make money. An automobile dealer buys cars at a low price with the hope of selling them at a higher price. Banks do the same thing, except that their commodities are currencies. They buy dollars and pay for them in euros, pounds, and yen, with the idea of selling them at a profit. So you can use dollars to buy the euros you need from an American bank, and have those euros transferred to the account of the French cheese maker. Or you can pay for your French cheese by writing a check against your dollar checking account in the United States and send the check to the French firm.[10] The French cheese maker will accept the check knowing that your dollars can be traded for euros (that is, sold to a French bank) at the rate of exchange. Of course, if you expect the French cheese maker to accept a check in dollars, you will have to pay more to compensate him for the cost of converting the dollars into euros. Either way, you will have to pay a premium for the euros since, as indicated, banks are in the business of selling currencies for a profit.

[9] This short-run reduction in revenue from exports after a depreciation in the dollar, followed by a long-run increase in revenue from exports, is often referred to as the "J-curve phenomenon" (Dornbush and Krugman 1976). Thus, although a depreciation in the exchange rate will eventually achieve a balance of trade equilibrium as shown in table 15.3, it may take some time.

[10] Instruments of exchange other than checks are often used in international transactions. The process, however, is the same.

This hypothetical purchase of French cheese leads to an important observation. Be it cheese, or watches, or anything else, a US import will increase the dollar holdings of foreign banks. So will American expenditures abroad, whether for tours or for foreign stocks and bonds. Americans must have euros to buy goods and services in most European countries; therefore, they must offer American dollars in exchange. Foreign banks end up holding some of the dollars that Americans have used to buy euros, and other foreign currencies. And as these purchases increase the dollars they are holding relative to other currencies, the value of dollars declines relative to the value of other currencies on the foreign exchange market.

In the same way, US exports reduce the dollar holdings of foreign banks. Exports are typically paid for out of the dollar accounts of foreign banks. Foreign expenditures on trips to the United States or on the stocks and bonds of US corporations have the same effect. They reduce the dollar holdings of foreign banks and increase the foreign currency holdings of US banks. In this case, the value of dollars increases relative to the value of other currencies on the foreign exchange market.

As the dollar depreciates or appreciates, market forces come into play that counteract the move in the dollar's value. For example, depreciation of the US dollar in the exchange rate will have several effects, all tending to reduce the number of dollars coming onto the international money market. As explained earlier, the exchange will make French goods more expensive for Americans to buy. Thus it will tend to reduce US imports and, accordingly, the number of dollars that must be exchanged for foreign currencies. Depreciation will also tend to reduce the price of American goods to foreigners. For instance, at an exchange rate of $1.25 for €1, the euro price of a $1 million American computer is €800,000. At an exchange rate of $1.50 for €1, the euro price of the same computer is €666,667 – a substantial reduction in price. To buy American goods at the new lower euro price, the French will increase their demand for dollars. Again, the quantity of dollars being offered on the money market will fall, and the growth in foreign dollar holdings will be checked.

A free **exchange rate system** is one in which the prices of all national currencies in terms of other national currencies are determined by the unfettered forces of the supply of and demand for national currencies.

Determination of the exchange rate

As with the price of anything, exchange rates are determined by the forces of demand and supply, although governments may interfere to alter the rate from what market forces alone would have produced. When there is no government interference, the rates are dubbed "**free**" or "floating."

When government intervenes, by having the central bank, or some other government agency, buy or sell currency in the foreign exchange markets, the exchange rates are dubbed "**fixed**" (also "pegged"), or kept within specified limits. From 1945 to 1971, the dollar exchange rate for all currencies were basically fixed. Since 1971, however, rates have been set flexibly, with some government intervention in a "dirty," or *managed*, floating exchange rate system, in which the prices of currencies are partly determined by competitive market forces and partly determined by official government intervention. That is, governments may not prevent minor exchange rate movements in exchange rates, but will try to keep the exchange rate from changing substantially during any short period of time.

A **fixed exchange rate system** is one in which the prices of currencies are established and maintained by government intervention. Under such systems, governments become active traders in their currencies.

National currencies have a *market value* – that is, a price – because individuals, firms, and governments use them to buy foreign goods, services, and securities. There is a market demand for a national currency such as the euro. Furthermore, the demand for the euro (or any other currency) slopes downward, like curve *D* in figure 15.5. To see why, look at the market for euros from the point of view of US residents. As the dollar price of the euro falls (it takes fewer dollars to buy €1, or more euros can be bought for $1), the price Americans must pay for European goods also falls. As a result, Americans will want to buy more European goods. They will require a larger quantity of euros to complete their transactions. Therefore, the demand curve for euros is downward sloping, as shown by curve *D* in figure 15.5. As the price of euros goes down, the quantity demanded of euros goes up – and correspondingly, as the price of euros goes up, the quantity demanded of euros goes down.

The supply of euros coming onto the market reflects the European demand for American goods, services, and securities. To get American goods, Europeans need dollars. They must pay for those dollars with euros, and in doing so they supply euros to the international money market. As the dollar price of the euro increases, the price of American goods to the Europeans falls. To take advantage of the increased dollar price of euros, Europeans buy a larger quantity of American goods, which means that they need more dollars and must offer more euros to get them. Therefore, the quantity of euros supplied on the market rises as the dollar price of euros rises. Thus, the supply curve for euros slopes upward to the right, like curve *S* in figure 15.5.

The buyers and sellers of euros make up what is loosely called the *international money market* in euros. Banks are very much involved in such markets. They buy euros from the sellers (suppliers) and sell them to the buyers (demanders). As in other markets, the interaction of suppliers and demanders

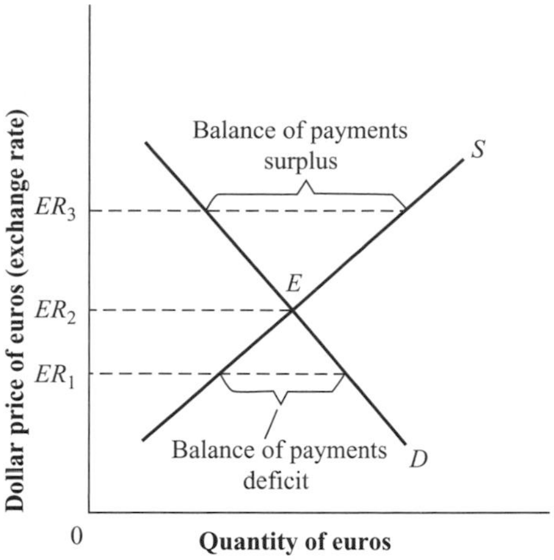

Figure 15.5 Supply and demand for euros on the international currency market
The international exchange rate between the dollar and the euro is determined by the forces of supply and demand, with the equilibrium at *E*. If the exchange rate is below equilibrium, say at ER_1, the quantity of euros demanded, shown by the demand curve, will exceed the quantity supplied, shown by the supply curve. Competitive pressure will push the exchange rate up. If the exchange rate is above equilibrium, say, ER_3, the quantity supplied will exceed the quantity demanded and competitive pressure will push the exchange rate down. Thus the price of a foreign currency is determined in much the same way as the price of any other commodity.

determines the market price. That is, given the supply and demand curves in figure 15.5, in a competitive market the dollar price of the euro will move toward the equilibrium point at *E* involving the intersection of the supply and demand curves. The equilibrium price, or exchange rate, will be ER_2, the price at which the quantity of euros supplied exactly equals the quantity of euros demanded.

At the market equilibrium point, no build-up of dollars or euros occurs in the accounts of foreign banks. European and US banks have no reason to modify the exchange rate to encourage or discourage the purchase or sale of either currency. In the language of finance, the net balance of payments coming into and going out of each country is zero.

If the exchange rate is below equilibrium level – say, ER_1 – the quantity of euros demanded will exceed the quantity supplied. An *imbalance of payments* will develop. Again in the jargon of international finance, the United States will develop a *balance of payments deficit* – a shortfall in the quantity of a foreign currency supplied. (This is a conceptual definition. When it comes to defining the balance of payments deficit in a way that can be measured by the Department of Commerce, economists are in considerable disagreement.)

As in other markets, this imbalance will eventually right itself. Because of the excess demand for euros, European banks will accumulate excess dollar balances – they will want to buy more euros than they can at the prevailing dollar price for euro, which is the same as wanting to sell more dollars than they can at the prevailing euro price for dollars. Competitive pressure will then push the exchange rate back up to ER_2. People who cannot buy euros at ER_1 will offer a higher price. As the price of euros rises, French goods will become less attractive to Americans, and the quantity of euros demanded will fall. Conversely, American goods will become more attractive to the French, and the quantity of euros supplied will rise.

Similarly, at an exchange rate higher than ER_2 – say, ER_3 – the quantity of euros supplied will exceed the quantity demanded (see figure 15.5). The surplus of euros will not last forever, however. Eventually the exchange rate will fall back toward ER_2, causing an increase in the quantity of euros demanded and a decrease in the quantity supplied. In short, in a free foreign currency market, the price of a currency is determined in the same way as the prices of other commodities.

The two major advantages of a floating system are (1) that exchange rates are automatically determined exclusively by free market forces, without government intervention, controls, or regulations; and (2) external adjustment, under favorable conditions, is attained without requiring major domestic or internal price, income, or employment changes. A floating system's one major disadvantage is that instability in the form of possible frequent, hard-to-predict, and large fluctuations could discourage international trade, transactions, and investment.[11]

Market adjustment to changes in money market conditions

By modifying exchange rates to correct for imbalances in payments, the money market can accommodate vast changes in the economic conditions of nations engaged in trade. A good example is the way the market handles a change in consumption patterns. These changes in consumption, and hence in foreign exchange rates, can be caused by changes in a nation's tastes and preferences,

[11] However, it needs to be noted that since flexible exchange rates were reintroduced in 1971, the volume of world trade has significantly increased, despite considerable volatility in exchange rates. At the same time, the realized volume of trade could be lower than what would have occurred without the shift from fixed to flexible exchange rates.

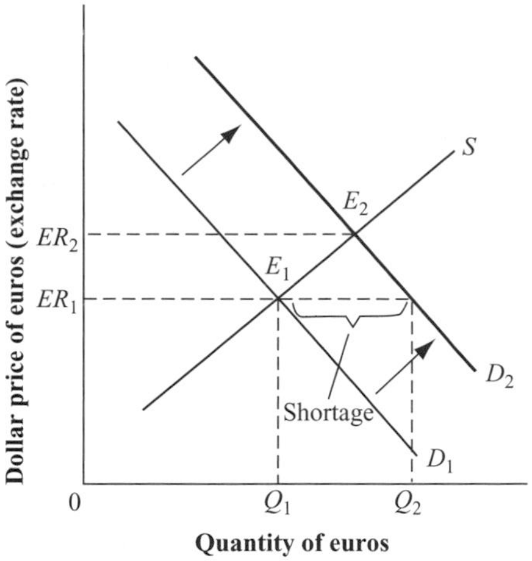

Figure 15.6 Effect of an increase in demand for euros

An increase in the demand for euros will shift the demand curve from D_1 to D_2, pushing the equilibrium from E_1 to E_2. At the initial equilibrium exchange rate ER_1, a shortage will develop. Competition among buyers will push the exchange rate up to the new equilibrium level, ER_2.

real income, level of prices (including interest rates), costs, and expectations as to future exchange rates.

Suppose that American preferences for French goods – say, wines and perfumes – increase for some reason. The demand for euros will increase because Americans will need more of them at every dollar price to buy the additional French goods they desire. If, as in figure 15.6, the US demand for euros shifts from D_1 to D_2, the quantity of euros demanded at the old equilibrium exchange rate of ER_1 will exceed the quantity supplied. Those who cannot buy more euros at ER_1 will offer to pay a higher price. The exchange rate will rise toward the new equilibrium level of ER_1 as the equilibrium point shifts from E_1 to E_2. As the dollar depreciates in value, which is the same as an increase in the dollar price for euros, the imbalance in payments is eliminated.

Now suppose that Americans' real incomes rise. Assuming that the consumption of goods and services goes up with real income – we called these "normal" goods and services in chapter 7 – Americans will be likely to demand more foreign imports, both directly and in the form of domestic goods that incorporate foreign parts or materials. Either way, an increase in real incomes leads to an increase in the demand for foreign currencies. Again the demand for euros will rise, as in figure 15.6. The dollar price of euros will rise with it to bring the quantity supplied into line with the quantity demanded.

A change in the rate of inflation can have a similar effect on the exchange rate. If the inflation rates are about the same in two nations that trade with each other, the exchange rate between their currencies will remain stable, every thing held constant.[12] Because the relative prices of goods in the two nations stay the same, people will have no incentive to switch from domestic to imported goods, or vice versa. If one nation's inflation rate exceeds another's, however, the relative prices of foreign and domestic goods change. If prices increase faster in the United States, for example, Americans will want to buy more foreign goods and fewer domestic goods. Foreigners, on the other hand, will have an incentive to buy more goods from their own countries, where prices are not rising as fast as in the United States. In sum, a higher US inflation rate spells a rise in the demand for foreign currencies, a fall in their supply, and a depreciation of the dollar. This increases the dollar price of foreign currencies and, therefore, increases the dollar price of foreign goods. Similar flows occur when interest rate differentials exist between nations.

Control of the exchange rate: risk reduction through hedging

To understand the argument that a properly working fixed-exchange rate system can be better than a floating-rate system, consider the problems that would arise if *each state* in the United States had its own currency. The exchange rate would vary among all the states. The resulting risks and inconveniences would severely hamper interstate trade. For instance, a worker in New York City who commutes from New Canaan, Connecticut, would have to face fluctuating exchange rates on a daily basis when riding subways, buying gas, eating lunch, and making a large number of other transactions.

So the fixed exchange rate has one advantage over the floating rate: *stability.* Because even a small change in the exchange rate can cause significant losses to people who have already concluded business deals, a flexible exchange rate can increase the risks involved in international trade. For example, suppose you agree to purchase cheese at an exchange rate of $1.25 = €1. You promise to pay the exporter $500, and the French cheese maker expects to receive €400. ($500 ÷ 1.25). By the time you send the check, however, the rate has moved to $1.30 = €1. The exporter will now receive only €384.61 ($500 ÷ 1.30). She loses €15.39. If the exchange rate moves in the opposite direction, of course, the exporter will gain.

[12] This is a point made under the so-called "purchasing power parity (PPP) theory" of exchange rate determination, which is subject to dispute among economists for reasons that would take us beyond the scope of this textbook.

The French cheese maker can hedge against the risk of selling cheese for dollars, when she needs euros to spend, by selling dollars short on the forward exchange market (selling dollars that she borrows at today's price in euros) and buying them when the dollars arrive. For example, assume she is selling a total of $100,000 worth of cheese, which she expects to convert into €80,000, given that the current exchange rate is $1.25 = €1. To hedge against the value of the dollar declining while waiting for them to arrive, she could sell $100,000 short, receiving €80,000 for them. When her $100,000 arrives she can then pay for the $100,000 at the exchange rate that exists then. If the dollar has fallen in value, say to $1.30 = €1, then the dollars she receives will be worth €3,077 less than she expected, €76,923 instead of €80,000. But we can now buy back the $100,000 she sold for €80,000 for €76,923, making a profit of €3,077. So what she lost by selling cheese for dollars she made up by selling dollars short. If the dollar's value relative to euros increased while the cheese merchant is waiting for her dollars, she makes more money than she expected from selling cheese, but loses the gain by selling dollars short. This hedging doesn't work perfectly, since there are transactions costs associated with selling and buying dollars on foreign exchange markets, but it still reduces the risk associated with fluctuations in the value of foreign currency.

But the most anyone can ever hope to do is reduce risk, not eliminate it. Even if governments fix foreign exchange rates, risks remain. Problems can develop when market conditions change but the exchange rate is fixed. If the demand for euros increases while the dollar price of euros is fixed, a shortage of euros will develop on the international money market (and the United States will run a balance of payments deficit). All those who want euros at the fixed price will be unable to get all the euros they want, which means that they will not be able to buy all the European goods they want. To keep the dollar price of euros from rising (and keeping the dollar from depreciating), the US government will have to fill in the market shortage by drawing down its reserve of euros. Otherwise, the US government will have to set up an elaborate mechanism for rationing the available euros and for policing the market against black marketeering, which creates further risks and costs. Obviously, the US euro reserves will limit its ability to keep the dollar from depreciating.

If the US demand for euros drops while the dollar price of euros is fixed, there will be a surplus of euros (while the United States will run a balance of payments surplus). To keep the dollar price of euros from falling (and keeping the dollar from appreciating), the US government will have to buy up the excess euros. Of course, the US government can create the dollars that it uses to buy the euros, but that means that European governments will have to accumulate the dollars, which ultimately means that European economies are exporting goods for a store of dollars that they do not use to buy goods from the United States.

And even with government attempts to fix currency rates, if the shifts in market conditions are large enough, the controls will break down and foreign exchange rates will change. Instead of changing fairly gradually as conditions change, foreign exchange rates are more likely to change suddenly and dramatically when government price fixing attempts become too difficult to continue.

Perspective Bastiat's Satirical Case for Free Trade: "A Petition"

Frédéric Bastiat was a nineteenth-century French economist who had a penchant for enhancing the power of economic arguments with satire. Here, in the following short essay, Bastiat is at his best, showing with unusual clarity the fundamental problems with the case made by protectionists. In this essay, which is written as a "petition" to the French Chamber of Deputies in 1845, he pretends to represent candle makers (and everyone else involved in the production of artificial sources of light), he wrote to the French Chamber of Deputies in 1845:

From the Manufacturers of Candles, Tapers, Lanterns, Candlesticks, Street Lamps, Snuffers, and Extinguishers, and from the Producers of Tallow, Oil, Resin, Alcohol, and Generally of Everything Connected with Lighting.

To the Honorable Members of the Chamber of Deputies.

Gentlemen:

You are on the right track. You reject abstract theories and have little regard for abundance and low prices. You concern yourselves mainly with the fate of the producer. You wish to free him from foreign competition, that is, to reserve the *domestic market* for *domestic industry.*

We come to offer you a wonderful opportunity for applying your – what shall we call it? Your theory? No, nothing is more deceptive than theory. Your doctrine? Your system? Your principle? But you dislike doctrines, you have a horror of systems, and, as for principles, you deny that there are any in political economy; therefore we shall call it your practice – your practice without theory and without principle.

We are suffering from the ruinous competition of a foreign rival who apparently works under conditions so far superior to our own for the production of light that he is *flooding* the *domestic market* with it at an incredibly low price; for the moment he appears, our sales cease, all the consumers turn to him, and a branch of French industry whose ramifications are innumerable is all at once reduced to complete stagnation. This rival, which is none other than the sun, is waging war on us so mercilessly that we suspect he is being stirred up against us by perfidious Albion (excellent diplomacy nowadays!), particularly because he has for that haughty island a respect that he does not show for us.

We ask you to be so good as to pass a law requiring the closing of all windows, dormers, skylights, inside and outside shutters, curtains, casements, bull's-eyes, deadlights, and blinds – in short, all openings, holes, chinks, and fissures through which the light of the sun is wont to enter houses, to the detriment of the fair industries with which, we are proud to say, we have endowed the country, a country that cannot, without betraying ingratitude, abandon us today to so unequal a combat.

Be good enough, honorable deputies, to take our request seriously, and do not reject it without at least hearing the reasons that we have to advance in its support.

First, if you shut off as much as possible all access to natural light, and thereby create a need for artificial light, what industry in France will not ultimately be encouraged?

If France consumes more tallow, there will have to be more cattle and sheep, and, consequently, we shall see an increase in cleared fields, meat, wool, leather, and especially manure, the basis of all agricultural wealth.

If France consumes more oil, we shall see an expansion in the cultivation of the poppy, the olive, and rapeseed. These rich yet soil-exhausting plants will come at just the right time to enable us to put to profitable use the increased fertility that the breeding of cattle will impart to the land.

Our moors will be covered with resinous trees. Numerous swarms of bees will gather from our mountains the perfumed treasures that today waste their fragrance, like the flowers from which they emanate. Thus, there is not one branch of agriculture that would not undergo a great expansion.

The same holds true of shipping. Thousands of vessels will engage in whaling, and in a short time we shall have a fleet capable of upholding the honor of France and of gratifying the patriotic aspirations of the undersigned petitioners, chandlers, etc.

But what shall we say of the *specialties of Parisian manufacture?* Henceforth you will behold gilding, bronze, and crystal in candlesticks, in lamps, in chandeliers, in candelabra sparkling in spacious emporia compared with which those of today are but stalls.

There is no needy resin-collector on the heights of his sand dunes, no poor miner in the depths of his black pit, who will not receive higher wages and enjoy increased prosperity.

It needs but a little reflection, gentlemen, to be convinced that there is perhaps not one Frenchman, from the wealthy stockholder of the Anzin Company to the humblest vendor of matches, whose condition would not be improved by the success of our petition.

We anticipate your objections, gentlemen; but there is not a single one of them that you have not picked up from the musty old books of the advocates of free trade. We defy you to utter a word against us that will not instantly rebound against yourselves and the principle that guides your entire policy.

Will you tell us that, though we may gain by this protection, France will not gain at all, because the consumer will bear the expense?

We have our answer ready:

You no longer have the right to invoke the interests of the consumer. You have sacrificed him whenever you have found his interests opposed to those of the producer. You have done so in order *to encourage industry and to increase employment.* For the same reason you ought to do so this time too.

Indeed, you yourselves have anticipated this objection. When told that the consumer has a stake in the free entry of iron, coal, sesame, wheat, and textiles, "Yes," you reply, "but the producer has a stake in their exclusion." Very well! Surely if consumers have a stake in the admission of natural light, producers have a stake in its interdiction.

"But," you may still say, "the producer and the consumer are one and the same person. If the manufacturer profits by protection, he will make the farmer prosperous. Contrariwise, if agriculture is prosperous, it will open markets for manufactured goods." Very well! If you grant us a monopoly over the production of lighting during the day, first of all we shall buy large amounts of tallow, charcoal, oil, resin, wax, alcohol, silver, iron, bronze, and crystal, to supply our industry; and, moreover, we and our numerous suppliers, having become rich, will consume a great deal and spread prosperity into all areas of domestic industry.

Will you say that the light of the sun is a gratuitous gift of Nature, and that to reject such gifts would be to reject wealth itself under the pretext of encouraging the means of acquiring it?

But if you take this position, you strike a mortal blow at your own policy; remember that up to now you have always excluded foreign goods *because* and *in proportion as* they approximate gratuitous gifts. You have only *half* as good a reason for complying with the demands of other monopolists as you have for granting our petition, which is in *complete* accord with your established policy; and to reject our demands precisely because they are *better founded* than anyone else's would be tantamount to accepting the equation: $+\times=+-$; in other words, it would be to heap *absurdity* upon *absurdity*.

Labor and Nature collaborate in varying proportions, depending upon the country and the climate, in the production of a commodity. The part that Nature contributes is always free of charge; it is the part contributed by human labor that constitutes value and is paid for.

If an orange from Lisbon sells for half the price of an orange from Paris, it is because the natural heat of the sun, which is, of course, free of charge, does for the former what the latter owes to artificial heating, which necessarily has to be paid for in the market.

Thus, when an orange reaches us from Portugal, one can say that it is given to us half free of charge, or, in other words, at *half price* as compared with those from Paris.

Now, it is precisely on the basis of its being *semigratuitous* (pardon the word) that you maintain it should be barred. You ask: "How can French labor withstand the competition of foreign labor when the former has to do all the work, whereas the latter has to do only half, the sun taking care of the rest?" But if the fact that a product is *half* free of charge leads you to exclude it from competition, how can its being *totally* free of charge induce you to admit it into competition? Either you are not consistent, or you should, after excluding what is half free of charge as harmful to our domestic industry, exclude what is totally gratuitous with all the more reason and with twice the zeal.

To take another example: When a product – coal, iron, wheat, or textiles – comes to us from abroad, and when we can acquire it for less labor than if we produced it ourselves, the difference is a *gratuitous gift* that is conferred upon us. The size of this gift is proportionate to the extent of this difference. It is a quarter, a half, or three-quarters of the value of the product if the foreigner asks of us only three-quarters, one-half, or one-quarter as high a price. It is as complete as it can be when the donor, like the sun in providing us with light, asks nothing from us. The question, and we pose it formally, is whether what you desire for France is the benefit of consumption free of charge or the alleged advantages of onerous production. Make your choice, but be logical; for as long as you ban, as you do, foreign coal, iron, wheat, and textiles, *in proportion* as their price approaches *zero*, how inconsistent it would be to admit the light of the sun, whose price is zero all day long! Bastiat (1996, emphases in the original). Foundation for Economic Education, Inc., reprinted with permission from FEE.

PART II ORGANIZATIONAL ECONOMICS AND MANAGEMENT

The consequences of "quicksilver capital" for business and government

Economists and policy makers alike widely acknowledge that capital (meaning real capital in the form of plant and equipment, as well as financial capital) has become more mobile on a global basis. Consider that the mobility of much capital is inversely related to its size, and then consider the continuing effect technology is having on the size of capital. We cannot possibly recount here all of the details of recent technological and restructuring trends, but a few observations may be helpful in describing the trends we have in mind.[13] The most dramatic example of the downsizing of capital is found in the computer field. When universities bought their first mainframe computers in the early 1960s, they filled suites of offices and had a meager 8K of internal memory. Today, a good desktop computer has more memory and computing power than big university mainframes in the mid-1990s.

With the miniaturization of computers has come the downsizing of other types of capital. Factories made of steel and concrete still dot the landscape, but their economic dominance seems to be more a feature of the underdeveloped economies of Eastern Europe than of the western world. Capital has turned into something of a butterfly. The critical assets of companies are no longer just, or even primarily, steel and buildings. They are increasingly the information and the brainpower at the companies' disposal for creating the quintessential company asset – good ideas for doing things better, faster, cheaper, and more profitably at the most favorable location.

[13] See McKenzie and Lee (1991); McKenzie (1997).

In general, the late Walter Wriston, long-time CEO of Citicorp declared:

> Money moves over, around and through them [national borders] with the speed of light. The flows of capital are now in the range of 30 to 50 times greater than world trade. The world's capital market that moves along this electronic highway goes where it is wanted and it stays where it is well-treated . . . As long as our free-market system permits and delivers an acceptable rate of return on investment in an environment of political stability that is competitive with other areas of investment, the capital will keep coming. (Wriston 1989)

Knowledge is not only the major productive input in many firms, it is often the primary output as well. As George Gilder recognized before many other technology watchers, "The displacement of materials with ideas is the essence of all real economic progress" (Gilder 1989, 63). Management guru Tom Peters drove home the transformation of production by noting in one of his seminars for business people, "Welcome to a world where, in the words of one executive I know, 'If you can touch it, it's not real.' I don't know about you, but that's a tough concept for an old (me) civil engineer (me, again) to get" (Peters 1994, 13). With information, knowledge, and ideas now representing some of the most productive capital and resources, consumers of business obviously benefit. Productive capacity can be moved around the globe literally with a few keystrokes on a computer and at the speed of electrical impulses, allowing those firms who can produce the best products at the lowest price to attract productive capital and resources from all over the world and sell their products to consumers all over the world.

Trade and mobility of capital increase our standard of living by making businesses more competitive. With the emergence of a global economy, consumers are no longer as dependent as they once were on local suppliers. Producers can move their capital to locations where the resources they need for production are relatively more abundant than in their national markets. Then with modern telecommunications technology, managers can, at much lower cost than at any time in human history, stay in touch with their home offices. Of course, with the same technology, including wireless phone and Internet connections, consumers can buy what they want from producers abroad who have relatively lower costs and can, again, do so with a few strokes on their computers. Moreover, the expanded competition from international sources can be expected to undermine the market power of local/national firms.

Not surprisingly, between 1997 and 2005, the prices of goods in the US market subject to international trade and competition fell dramatically. For example, prices of computers and peripherals fell 86 percent; video equipment,

68 percent; toys, 36 percent; women's outerwear, 20 percent; and men's shirts and sweaters, 17 percent. The prices of many goods not as subject to international competition rose: college tuition, 53 percent; cable television, 41 percent; prescription drugs, 37 percent. According to the president of the Federal Reserve Bank of Dallas, open markets were a major reason that the US inflation rate had been held to about 2 percent for several years in the late 1990s and early 2000s (Fisher 2005).

Capital mobility and business competitiveness

The very technology lauded for expanding investment and market opportunities has a downside for firms, their workers, and governments: Workers in different nations are pitted against one another for wages and fringe benefits. If they seek payment bundles (wages and fringe benifits) that are out of line with their productivity and drive up the relative costs of their firms *vis-à-vis* firms in other countries, imports can be expected to flow into their country from abroad, undermining their job security. Businesses can also be expected to move their capital to countries where their costs are contained by the relative abundance of workers who control their wages.

Capital mobility literally can force managers to trim the "fat" out of their organizations and seek worker incentive systems that can drive up the demands managers impose on their workers. If firms in the domestic economy can outsource a portion or all of their production to foreign countries, then the more mobile capital is, the greater the pressure to outsource. If firms can outsource but don't outsource to lower-cost foreign venues, then their market positions are subject to being undermined by firms that do take opportunities to outsource. Greater capital mobility, in other words, intensifies the Prisoner's Dilemmas faced by businesses and their workers, making them global in scope.

Capital mobility and government competitiveness

Less obvious, but just as true, the growth in capital mobility can also benefit consumers/taxpayers by subjecting government to more competitive pressures. We are all consumers of not just the output of businesses, but also of the output of governments. We pay for government services through taxes, and hope to get good value for the money we spend. Unfortunately, we have far less control, as consumers, over the cost and quality of government services since we cannot easily reduce the amount we pay for what we get from one government by shifting our patronage to another. Governments have not faced nearly as much competition for their consumers'/taxpayers' dollars as businesses have. But the technological improvements that are putting more competitive pressures on businesses to service the interest of consumers are also putting the same pressures on governments.

What does the growing mobility of capital on a global scale mean for governments and the policies they choose? Our answers must, to a degree, be speculative, although a few observations seem to be rock solid. First and foremost, governments must face up to the fact that governments do business within a *given* parcel of land. On the other hand, a growing number of businesses can do business – and must do business – on practically *any* parcel of land. All the while businesses must treat governmentally imposed taxes and regulations like any other cost of doing business and must respond accordingly – that is, move elsewhere if governmentally imposed cost conditions warrant it.

What does that critical observation mean for different levels of government? For state and national governments? For city governments? In general, national and state governments must realize that their role is now, more than ever, one of "greasing the skids" for businesses who operate or might operate in their jurisdictions; it is one of making sure that state and local policies do not hamper the competitiveness of the businesses that operate inside their borders. To do otherwise can mean that capital and jobs go elsewhere.

In bygone eras, politicians and policy makers could sit around glibly chatting about what they *wanted* to do, or what their constituents would allow them to do, with little regard for what other governments in other parts of the country were doing. They could tax and regulate in the knowledge that capital could not move, except at a snail's pace and at great cost. If an interest group wanted an added tax or a subsidy, the only relevant issue was typically whether the politicians had the votes. Now governments have to think twice, or more carefully than before, about such matters.

More to the point, they must think *competitively*, which is something many governments around the world are not yet experienced at doing. Politicians and policy makers must, like all good businesses, begin to ask, "What are our competitors (other governments) doing?" For that matter, "Who are the relevant competitors?", "What will the "market" bear in terms of the types and levels of taxes and regulations we can impose?", "What is the responsiveness of our customer/citizen base to higher tax rates and greater regulatory costs?"

It used to be true that political leaders and policy makers didn't have to worry much about how efficient they were compared to other governments in their state, or even their country. As a result, few governments were very efficient (especially since they often are monopoly suppliers and since they are not subject to the pressures of corporate takeover markets, topics covered in chapters 11 and 12). But now these political authorities must begin to look around the world to determine who has the very highest standards for government performance and seek to meet those standards. This is because, as in business, governments are, as never before, in competition with "the very best" in the world for the capital they need. They must realize, at the very least, that the growing mobility of capital necessarily makes cuts in tax rates potentially more attractive. Why? Because the greater responsiveness of capital means that they will have more capital in their jurisdictions with the greater prospects that the expanded base, potentially at least, will more than offset the impact of the rate cuts. The converse also applies.

For that matter, everyone associated with government – all those who draw from government in various forms (the authors of this textbook included) – must accept the tightening grip of the *economic*, as distinct from *political*, limits to what governments can do. Hence, every proposed program must be evaluated to a greater extent than ever before in terms of the other programs that will have to be given up. To work within those limits, people of all political persuasions must begin to ask how government services can be provided more effectively and at lower cost, not so much because that is a way of reducing government involvement in the economy (which might be helpful), but as a way of government doing more for the benefit of those operating within its borders, for the purpose of attracting more capital and of inducing the creation of more home-grown capital that will have less reason to leave. This greater concern over providing the best service for the lowest taxes and least costly regulation will not primarily benefit business, but consumers, who will now find that businesses can provide their goods and services at less cost, and will be required to do so because of global competition.

Many commentators have suggested that the ongoing long-term decline in national tariff barriers around the world, less regulation, lower marginal tax rates, and more privatization is evidence of how political leaders (following the lead of Ronald Reagan and Margaret Thatcher) have adopted a free-trade ideology. Perhaps that is the case, but we suspect that the growing mobility of capital (and production and jobs) has contributed to political leaders seeing the necessity of freeing up markets and international trade in order to contain production costs within their jurisdictions.

Proponents of privatization of various government services – from garbage collection to the distribution of public housing units to the provision of education – make an important point: Just because a service must be funded by the public treasury, it need not be delivered by public agencies. The proponents' goal is to make government more efficient by choosing from an array of alternative delivery systems (government included), the purpose of which must be to make governmental jurisdictions more competitive *vis-à-vis* other governmental jurisdictions and to increase the likelihood of the existing capital base remaining and additional capital flowing in.

The downside of capital mobility

Of course, not all effects of the ongoing growth in a capital mobility can be expected to be efficiency-enhancing. For example, if some governments take it upon themselves to tighten their pollution controls that have global, as well as local, benefits, then in order to control production costs, including pollution-control costs, many mobile firms can be expected to move their plant, equipment, and jobs to governmental jurisdictions where pollution controls are not so tight (and costly).[14] Many firms may have to move to where they can pollute more freely. Otherwise, their prices and market shares can be undercut by firms that are willing to move. The competitive pressures to control costs can undercut governmental efforts to clamp down on polluters.

Moreover, firms who can produce their wares in multiple locations are in something of a "sellers" position with local and national governments, enhanced by capital mobility. They can effectively offer their capital (plants) and jobs up for auction with governments as the bidders.

In 2004, for example, Dell Computers (which has plants in Brazil, China, Ireland and Malaysia) was the latest in a long string of firms to pick multiple communities in different states in which the company indicated a willingness to build a 500,000 square foot plant that would employ up to 1,700 workers, with the company's investment in the project expected to run $100 million. Winston-Salem, North Carolina "won" the bidding for the plant, but only after Winston-Salem, Forsyth County, and the State of North Carolina agreed to provide nearly $280 million to cover Dell's cost for land and its improvements and the training of Dell workers (cited as "incentives" by government officials and in news reports (Hewitt 2004, Cherrie 2005). In having states and communities bid for its plant, Dell was following a well-worn tactic followed in the 1990s by a host of companies, not the least of which are BMW and Mercedes Benz, luxury car companies that were able to extract hundreds of millions of dollars in tax breaks and cost coverage from South Carolina and Alabama, respectively, for their proposed expansion plants (McKenzie 1997, chapter 6).

[14] Alternatively, they can simply close their own plants down and outsource production to firms in countries with more lenient pollution controls.

Of course, policy makers and managers in local and state governments must realize that once they start paying companies to move into their jurisdictions, many mobile companies already there can be expected to use their mobility to threaten to move elsewhere if some of their costs are not covered by local and state governments. And competition will pressure management to pit states in a "bidding war" for their capital and jobs. If they don't seek competitive bids on their threats to move out, then competitors that do obtain "incentives" will have a cost advantage in the final products market. Governments can find their costs rising as the bidding wars are extended.

In 2005, Airbus, owned by the European Aeronautic Defense and Space Company, sought to win a then-pending $5 billion-plus contract from the US Air Force for refueling tankers. No doubt, Airbus figured that to have a chance of getting the contract over rival Boeing, it would have to have a major plant presence in the United States. But the company understood that it could minimize its location costs by pitting states and communities against one another. Accordingly, it held hearings at seventy possible sites, allowing state and local officials a chance to make presentations. It then selected airports in Mobile, Alabama; Kiln, Mississippi; and North Charleston, South Carolina for the final competition. It planned to make its location decisions by the end of 2005 (Associated Press 2005b).

Michigan has for a long time indicated a willingness to pay firms to move in, and stay put, and regularly has used its power of eminent domain to condemn property in its competitive struggle to attract and retain businesses. That fact obviously didn't escape the attention of General Motors, which in 1980 announced plans to close two of its Fisher Body plants in Detroit and replace them with a new $630 million Cadillac plant. Its plant-closing announcement was accompanied by none-too-subtle threats to move the plant out of the city, unless a suitable site could be found. Six thousand jobs were at stake, a fact that caused state and city officials to launch a campaign that ended with the condemnation (with the approval of Michigan's State Supreme Court in a landmark ruling) of a section of the city known as Poletown, encompassing 327 acres, 127 businesses, sixteen churches, and 1,753 residences – and the expenditure of tens of millions of federal, state, and city tax dollars, partially for the benefit of GM stockholders (Richman 1981).[15]

[15] Detroit bought the property for about $200 million ($150 million of this amount coming from the federal government) and sold the property to GM for slightly more than $8 million (Richman 1981). The Michigan State Supreme Court in 2004 unanimously overturned its landmark Poletown decision "in order to vindicate our constitution, protect the people's property right and preserve the legitimacy of the judicial branch as the expositor, not creator,

Firms that remain immobile may find themselves taxed more heavily to cover the business costs of other firms who are more mobile.

THE BOTTOM LINE

The key takeaways from chapter 15 are the following:

(1) Trade can be mutually beneficial so long as the traders specialize in the production of the good(s) in which they have a comparative advantage. That is to say, even a trader who is less productive than everyone else in everything can find trade beneficial.
(2) Generally speaking, tariffs and quotas reduce the aggregate real incomes of the countries that impose them, as well as countries that are subject to them, because they deny mutually beneficial trades.
(3) Those industries protected by tariffs and quotas can gain from them, but only at the expense of consumers who must pay higher prices for the protected goods and at the expense of exporters who are not able to export as much as they would be able to absent the trade protections.
(4) International exchange rates are determined by the forces of supply and demand for various currencies.
(5) Exchange rate controls can lead to imbalances in the balance of trade and capital flows.
(6) The growth in capital mobility across national boundaries has increased the competitiveness of businesses and impaired the ability of governments to impose burdensome taxes, regulations, and international trade restrictions.

REVIEW QUESTIONS

(1) Using supply and demand curves, show how a US tariff on a foreign-made good will affect the price and quantity sold in the country of origin.

of fundamental law" (as reported by Gallagher 2004). The reversal did nothing to change the fate of Poletown or the gains received by GM by threatening to move elsewhere more than two decades earlier. The new decision, however, should restrict the ability of Michigan to compete for plants and jobs, driving down the "price" firms can receive from the state of Michigan and local governments in Michigan for any new proposed plants and jobs.

(2) How will an import quota on sugar affect (a) the price of sugar produced and sold domestically, (b) Sugar produced domestically and sold abroad?

(3) If a tariff is imposed on imported autos and the domestic demand for autos rises, what will happen to auto imports? If a quota is imposed on imported autos and the demand for autos increases, what will happen to auto imports?

(4) Consider the following production capabilities of France and Italy for cheese and bread for a given use of inputs. Which nation will export cheese to the other? What might be a mutually beneficial exchange rate for cheese and bread?

	Cheese units		Bread units
France	40	or	60
Italy	10	or	5

(5) "Tariffs on imported textiles increase the employment opportunities and incomes of domestic textiles workers. They therefore increase aggregate employment and income." Evaluate this statement.

(6) Because the balance of payments must always balance, how can a disequilibrium situation occur?

(7) How much would a business spend to get a tariff? What economic considerations will have an impact on the amount spent?

REFERENCES

Abowd, John M., 1990. Does performance-based managerial compensation affect corporate performance?, *Industrial and Labor Relations Review* 43: 52S–3S

Adam, Scott, 1995. Manager's journal: the Dilbert principle, *Wall Street Journal*, May 22: A14

Akerlof, George A., 1970. The market for lemons: qualitative uncertainty and the market mechanism, *Quarterly Journal of Economics* 84: 488–500

Alchian, Armen A. and Harold Demsetz, 1973. The property rights paradigm, *Journal of Economic History* 33: 17

Alexis, M., 1974. The political economy of labor market discrimination: synthesis and exploration, in A. Horrwitz and G. von Furstenberg (eds.), *Patterns of Discrimination*, Lexington, MA: D.C. Heath/Lexington Books

Alonzo-Zaldivar, Ricardo, 2005. Insurance option has workers pay more, *Los Angeles Times*, May 23: A1.

Alpert, William T., 1986. *The Minimum Wage in the Restaurant Industry*, New York: Praeger

Amihud, Y. and B. Lev., 1981. Risk aversion as a managerial motive for conglomerate mergers, *Bell Journal of Economics* 12: 605–17

Aristotle, *Ethics*, vol. 8, no. 9

Armentano, Dominick T., 1990. *Antitrust and Monopoly: Anatomy of a Policy Failure*, Oakland, CA: Independent Institute

Arrow, Kenneth, 1963. *Social Choice and Individual Values*, New York: Wiley

Arthur, W. B., 1996. Increasing returns and the new world of business, *Harvard Business Review*: 100–9

Associated Press, 2005a. Store says two others selling gas too cheap, *Winston-Salem Journal*, May 5: B5

2005b. North Carolina fails to make cut for US airbus factory, *Winston-Salem Journal*, May 6, available on May 9, 2005 at http://www.journalnow.com/servlet/Satellite?pagename = WSJ/MGArticle/WSJ_BasicArticle&c = MGArticle&cid = 1031782569685

2005c. Senate looks at raising minimum wage, *Wall Street Journal*, March 6: A17

Atlanta Journal – Constitution, 1995. Long-term risk (editorial), April 15: A10

Baker, George, 2000. The use of performance in incentive contracting, *American Economic Review* 90(2): 415–20

Baker, George, Robert Gibbon and Kevin Murphy, 1994. Subjective performance measures in optimal incentive contracts, *Quarterly Journal of Economics* 109: 1125–56

Balaker, Ted and Adrian T. Moore, 2005. *Offshoring and Public Fear: Assessing the Real Threat to Jobs*, Santa Monica, CA: Reason Foundation, Policy Study 33, available on May 19, 2005 at http://www.rppi.org/ps333.pdf

Banks, Howard, 1994. A sixties industry in a nineties economy, *Forbes*, May 9: 107–12

Barham, Catherine and Nasima Begum, 2005. Sickness absence from work in the UK, *Labour Market Trends*, London: Office for National Statistics, Labour Market Division, April: 149–58

Bartlett, C. A. and J. O'Connell, 1998. Lincoln Electric: venturing abroad, Boston: Harvard University Graduate School of Business, Case 3-398-095

Bastiat, Frédéric, 1996. *Economic Sophisms*, Irvington-on-Hudson, NY: The Foundation for Economic Education, Inc., trans. and ed. Arthur Goddard, Library of Economics and Liberty, available on January 4, 2004 at http://www.econlib.org/library/Bastiat/basSoph3.html>

Baumol, William J., 1982. Contestable markets: an uprising in the theory of industry structure, *American Economic Review* 72: 1–15

Becker, Gary S., 1971. *Economic Theory*, New York: Alfred A. Knopf

Becker, Gary S. and Kevin M. Murphy, 1988. A theory of rational addiction, *Journal of Political Economy* 96(4): 675–700

Bennett, James T. and Manuel H. Johnson, 1983. *Better Government at Half the Price*, Ottawa, IL: Carolina House

Bentley, Arthur, 1967. *The Process of Government*, Cambridge, MA: Belknap Press, Harvard University Press

Bethel, Tom, 1998. *The Noblest Triumph: Property and Prosperity Through the Ages*, New York: St. Martin's Press

Bhagat, Sanjai, Andrei Shleifer, and Robert W. Vishny, 1990. Hostile takeovers in the 1980s: the return to corporate specialization, in Martin N. Bailey and Clifford Winston (eds.), *Brookings Papers on Economic Activity*, Washington, DC: Brookings Institution: 1–72

Bhide, Amar, 1990. Reversing corporate diversification, *Journal of Applied Corporate Finance* 3: 70–81

Black, William K., Kitty Calavita, and Henry N. Pontell, 1995. The savings and loan debacle of the 1980s: white-collar crime or risky business?, *Law & Policy* 17(1): 23–55

Blalock, Garrick, Vrinda Kadiyali, and Daniel H. Simon, 2005a. The impact of post 9/11 airport security measures on the demand for air travel, Ithaca, NY: Economics Department, Cornell University, Working Paper, February 23 version

2005b. The impact of 9/11 on road fatalities: the other lives lost to terrorism, Ithaca, NY: Economics Department, Cornell University, Working Paper, February 2 version

Blinder, Alan, 1987. *Hard Heads, Soft Hearts*, Reading, MA: Addison-Wesley

Boehm, Christopher, 1993. Egalitarian behavior and reverse dominance hierarchy, *Current Anthropology* 14: 227–54

Boulding, Kenneth E., 1970. *Economics as a Science,* New York: McGraw-Hill

Bowles, Samuel and Herbert Gintis, 2001. The evolution of strong reciprocity, Amherst, MA, Department of Economics, University of Massachusetts, Working Paper

Brandenburger, Adam M. and Barry J. Nalebuff, 1996. *Coopetition*, New York: Currency/Doubleday

Breit, William and Kenneth G. Elzinga, 1985. Private antitrust enforcement: the new learning, *Journal of Law and Economics* 28(2): 405–43

Breyer, Stephen, 1982. *Regulation and Its Reform*, Cambridge, MA: Harvard University Press

Brickley, James A., Sanjai Bhagat, and Ronald C. Lease, 1985. The impact of long-range managerial compensation plans on shareholder wealth, *Journal of Accounting and Economics* 7: 115–29

Brickley, James A. and Frederick H. Dark, 1987. The choice of organizational forms: the case of franchising, *Journal of Financial Economics* 18: 401–20

Brody, Jane E. 2005. As Americans get bigger, the world does, too, *New York Times*, April 19: D1

Brown, Charles, Curtis Gilroy, and Andrew Kohen, 1982. The effect of the minimum wage on employment and unemployment, *Journal of Economic Literature* 20: 487–528

Browning, Edgar, 1974. Why the social insurance budget is too large in a democracy, *Economic Inquiry* 13: 373–88

Buchanan, James M. and Yong J. Yoon, 2000. Symmetric tragedies: commons and anticommons, *Journal of Law and Economics* 43(1): 1–13

Bulow, Jeremy and Lawrence Summers, 1986. A theory of dual labor markets with applications to industrial policy, discrimination and Keynesian unemployment, *Journal of Labor Economics* 4(3): 376–414

Bureau of Labor Statistics, 2004. *The Effect of Outsourcing and Offshoring on BLS Productivity Measures*, March 26, available on August 20, 2004 at http: //www.bls.gov/lpc/lproffshoring.pdf

Burgelman, Robert, 2002. *Strategy is Destiny: How Strategy-Making Shapes a Company's Future*, New York: Free Press

Bush, Winston C., 1972. Individual welfare in anarchy, in Gordon Tullock (ed.), *Explorations in the Theory of Anarchy*, Blacksburg, VA: University Publications, Inc.

Byrne, John A., 1996. Has outsourcing gone too far?, *Business Week*, April 1: 27

Cable, John and Nicolas Wilson, 1989. Profit-sharing and productivity: an analysis of UK engineering firms, *Economic Journal* 99: 366–75

Cain, G. G., 1986. The economic analysis of labor market discrimination: a survey, in O. Aschenfelter and R. Layard (eds.), *Handbook of Labor Economics*, London: Elsevier Science Publishers: 693–785

Cannon, Michael F., 2003. Three avenues to patient power, *Brief Analysis*, Dallas, TX: National Center for Policy Analysis, 430, January 30, Available on August 17, 2004 at http: //www.ncpa.org/iss/hea/2003/pd013003a.html

Card, David and Alan B. Krueger, 1995. *Myth and Measurement: The New Economics of the Minimum Wage*, Princeton, NJ: Princeton University Press

Carmichael, H. L., 1988. Incentives in academics: why is there tenure?, *Journal of Political Economy* 96(2): 453–72

Cartwright, Dorwin, 1968. The nature of group cohesiveness, in Dorwin Cartwright and Alvin Zander (eds.), *Group Dynamics: Research and Theory*, 3rd edn., New York: Harper & Row: 91–109

Cherrie, Victoria, 2005. Dell requests rezoning for new access road in agricultural area, *Winston-Salem Journal*, April 30: B1

Christensen, Clayton. M., 1997, *The Innovator's Dilemma: When New Technologies Cause Great Firms to Fail*. Cambridge, MA: Harvard Business School Press

Coase, Ronald H., 1972. Durability and monopoly, *Journal of Law and Economics* 15: 143–9

1988. *The Firm, the Market, and the Law*, Chicago: University of Chicago Press: 33–55 (reprinted from Ronald H. Coase, The Nature of the Firm, *Economica* 4,1937: 386–405)

Cobb, William E., 1973. Theft and the two hypotheses, in Simon Rottenberg (ed.), *The Economics of Crime and Punishment*, Washington, DC: American Enterprise Institute for Public Policy Research

Cooter, Robert and Thomas Ulen, 1988. *Law and Economics*, Glenview, IL: Scott Foresman

Cosmides, Leda and John Tooby, 1992. Cognitive adaptation for social exchange, in Jerome H. Barkow, Leda Cosmides, and John Tooby (eds.), *The Adapted Mind*, New York: Oxford University Press

Craig, Lynn, 2003. The time cost of children: a cross-national comparison of the interaction between time use and fertility rate, University of New South Wales, Sydney, paper presented at the IATUR Conference on Time Use Research, September 15–17, available on August 17, 2004 at http://www.sprc.unsw.edu.au/people/Craig/Time%20Cost%20of%20Children%20Time%20use%20and%20Fertility.pdf

Crain, W. Mark and Thomas D. Hopkins, 2001. *The Impact of Regulatory Costs on Small Firms: A Report for the Office of Advocacy*, Washington, DC: U.S. Small Business Adminstration, RFP No. SBAHW-00-R-0027, available on March 31, 2005 at http://www.sba.gov/advo/research/rs207.pdf

Crandall, Robert, 1985. Assessing the impact of the automobile export restraints upon US automobile prices, Brookings Institution, December, mimeo

Dahl, Jonathan, 1994. Many bypass the new rules of the road, *Wall Street Journal*, September 29: B1

David, Paul A., 1985. Clio and the economics of QWERTY, *American Economic Review* 75(2): 332–7

Davidow, William and Michael Malone, 1992. *The Virtual Corporation*, New York: HarperCollins

Davis, Laura J., 2005. *Privatization Brings Big Savings to Michigan's State Universities*, Chicago: Heartland Institute, April, available on May 13, 2005 at http://www.heartland.org/Article.cfm?artId=16769

Dawkins, Richard, 1976. *The Selfish Gene*, Oxford: Oxford University Press

Demsetz, Harold, 1964. Toward a theory of property rights, *American Economic Review* 57: 347–59

Deneckere, Raymond J. and R. Preston McAfee, 1996. Damaged goods, *Journal of Economics and Management Strategy* 5(2): 149–74

Dennen, Rodgers Taylor, 1975. *From Common to Private Property: The Enclosure of the Open Range*, PhD dissertation, Seattle: Economics Department, University of Washington

Dennis, Debra K. and John J. McConnell, 1986. Corporate mergers and security returns, *Journal of Financial Economics* 16: 143–87

DLorenzo, Thomas J., 1985. The origins of antitrust: an interest group perspective, *International Review of Law and Economics* 5: 73–90

Dore, Ronald P., 1987. *Taking Japan Seriously*, Stanford, CA: Stanford University Press

Dornbush, Rudiger and Paul Krugman, 1976. Flexible exchange rates in the short run, *Brookings Papers on Economic Activity*, March: 537–75

Drucker, Peter, 2001. *Management Challenges for the 21st Century*, New York: Harper-Business

Dunbar, Robin, 1998. The social brain hypothesis, *Evolutionary Anthropology* 6: 178–90

Dunlap, Al and Bob Andelman, 1996. *Mean Business: How I Save Bad Companies and Make Good Companies Great*, New York: Times Books

Dunn, L. F., 1985. Nonpecuniary job preferences and welfare losses among migrant agriculture workers, *American Journal of Agricultural Economics* 67(2): 257–65

Earley, P. Christopher, 1989. Social loafing and collectivism: a comparison of the United States and the People's Republic of China, *Administrative Science Quarterly* 34(4): 565–82

The Economist, 1999. Lessons from Microsoft, March 6: 21

2004a. Dead firms walking, September 23, available on June 21, 2005 at http://www.economist.com/business/displayStory.cfm?story_id = 3219857

2004b. Low-cost airlines, July 8, available on June 21, 2005 at http://www.economist.com/displaystory.cfm?story_id = S%27%298L%25Q%21%2F%21%20P%23L%0A

The Economist, 2004c. "Turbulent skies," July 8, available on August 21, 2005 at http://www.economist.com/business/displaystory.cfm?story_id = 2897525

Evans, David S., Albert Nichols, and Bernard Reddy, 1999. *The Rise and Fall of Leaders in Personal Computer Software*, Cambridge, MA: National Economic Research Associates, January 7

Farrell, J. and P. Klemperer, 2005. Coordination and lock-in: competition and switching costs and network effects, available on February 25, 2005 at http://paulklemperer.org/, a revised version of which will be published in M. Armstrong and R. H. Porter, *Handbook of Industrial Organization*, New York: Oxford University Press, 2005

Fast, N. and N. Berg, 1971. The Lincoln Electric Company, *Harvard Business School Case*, Cambridge, MA: Harvard Business School Press

Feenstra, Robert C., 1992. How costly is protectionism?, *Journal of Economic Perspective* 6(3): 159–78

Fehr, Ernst and Klaus M. Schmidt, 2002. Theories of fairness and reciprocity – evidence and economic application, *Advances in Economics and Econometrics*, 8th World Congress, eds. M. Dewatripont, L. Hansen, and S. J. Turnovsky, Cambridge: Cambridge University Press

Ferrell, Greg, 2000. Online time at office soars, *USA Today*, February 18: 1A

Fishback, Price V., 1992. *Soft Coal, Hard Choices: The Economic Welfare of Bituminous Coal Miners, 1890–1930*, New York: Oxford University Press

Fisher, Franklin M., 1998. Direct testimony, *US v. Microsoft Corporation*, Civil Action No. 98–1233 (TPJ), filed October 14, available on August 16, 2004 at http://www.usdoj.gov/atr/cases/f2000/2057.pdf

Fisher, Richard W., 2005. Protect us from protectionists, *Wall Street Journal*, April 25: A14

Fitzroy, Felix R. and Kornelius Kraft, 1986. Profitability and profit-sharing, *Journal of Industrial Economics* 35(2): 113–30

1987. Cooperation, productivity and profit sharing, *Quarterly Journal of Economics* 103: 23–36

Fleisher, Belton M., 1981. *Minimum Wage Regulation in Retail Trade*, Washington, DC: American Enterprise Institute

Flint, Joe, 2005. Blockbuster faces state suit over no late fees, *Wall Street Journal*, February 22: D2

Frank, Robert H., 1988. *Passions Within Reason: The Strategic of the Emotions*, New York: W.W. Norton

Frank, Robert H., Thomas Gilgorich, and Dennis T. Regan, 1996. Do economists make bad citizens?. *Journal of Economic Perspectives* 10 GJ: 187–92

Frauenheim, Ed., 2005. Getting tough with China?, *CNET News.com: Tech News First*, May 20, available on May 23, 2005 at http://news.com.com/Getting ± tough ± with ± China/2100-1022-5714390.html?part = dtx&tag = ntop&tag = nl.e703

Friedman, David, 1996. *Hidden Order: The Economics of Everyday Life*, New York: HarperBusiness

Friedman, Milton and L. J. Savage, 1948. The utility analysis of choices involving risk, *Journal of Political Economy* 56: 279–304

Furnham, A., 1993. Wasting time in the board room, *Financial Times*, March 10

Galbraith, John Kenneth, 1967. *The New Industrial State*, Boston: Houghton Mifflin

Ghosn, Carlos, 2005. *Shift: Inside Nissan's Historic Revival*, New York: Doubleday, US edn.

Gibbons, Robert and Kevin J. Murphy, 1992. Optimal incentive contracts in the presence of career concerns: theory and evidence, *Journal of Political Economy* 100(3): 468–506

Gilder, George, 1989. *Microcosm: The Quantum Revolution in Economics and Technology*, New York: Simon & Schuster

Gintis, Herbert, 2000a. *Game Theory Evolving*, Princeton, NJ: Princeton University Press

2000b. Strong reciprocity and human sociality, *Journal of Theoretical Biology* 211: 169–79

Girion, Lisa, 2005. Obesity is costly to state, report says, *Los Angeles Times*, April 6: C1

Gladwell, Malcolm, 2000. *The Tipping Point: How Little Things Can Make a Big Difference*, Boston: Little, Brown & Co.

Gneezy, Uri and Aldo Rustichini, 2000. A fine is a price, *Journal of Legal Studies* 29(1): 1–17

Goldberg, Jonah, 2003. Bah Humbug: blame uninformed voters, Townhall.com, December 26, as available on October 5, 2004 at http://www.townhall.com/opinion/columns/jonahgoldberg/2003/12/26.1606/html

Goodman, John C. and Gerald L. Musgrave, 1992. *Patient Power: Solving America's Health Care Crisis*, Washington, DC: Cato Institute

Goodman, John C., Gerald L. Musgrave, and Devon M. Herrick, 2004. *Lives at Risk: Single-Payer Health Insurance Around the World*, Dallas: National Center for Policy Analysis, July

Gordon, H. Scott, 1954. The economic theory of a common property resource: the fishery, *Journal of Political Economy* 62(2): 124–42

Greenhouse, Steven, 2005. Can't retail behemoth pay more?, *New York Times*, May 4: C1

Greenville, Jared W. and T.G. MacAulay, 2004. Tariffs and steel: the US safeguard actions, Sydney: Agricultural and Resource Economics, University of Sydney, paper presented at the Annual Conference of the Australian Agricultural and Resource Economics Society, Melbourne, February: 11–13

Grinblatt, S.J and S. Titman, 2002. *Financial Markets and Corporate Strategy*, Boston: McGraw-Hill/Irwin

Gunderson, Morley, 1989. Male–female wage differentials and policy responses, *Journal of Economic Literature* 27(1): 46–72

Gurbaxani, Vijay and Seungjin Whang, 1991. The impact of information systems on organizations and markets, *Communication of the ACM* 34(1): 59–73

Halberstam, David, 1986. *The Reckoning*, New York: Avon Books

Hamilton, Alexander, John Jay and James Madison, *The Federalist: A Commentary on the Constitution of the United States*, no. 51, New York: Random House, Modern Library edn. 1964: 338–9

Hansell, Saul, 2005. Wal-Mart ends online video rentals and promotes netflix, *New York Times*, May 20: C3

Hardin, Garrett, 1968. The tragedy of the commons, *Science* 62: 1243–54

Hare, A. Paul, 1952. A study of interaction and consensus in different-sized groups, *American Sociological Review* 17: 261–8

Hashimoto, Masanori, 1982. Minimum wage effects on training to the job, *American Economic Review* 70: 1070–87

Hayek, F. A., 1944. *The Road to Serfdom*, Chicago: University of Chicago Press

1945. The use of knowledge in society, *American Economic Review* 35(3): 519–30

1948. The meaning of competition, in F. Hayek, *Individualism and Economic Order*, Chicago: University of Chicago Press

1960. *The Constitution of Liberty*, Chicago: University of Chicago Press

Hayes, L., 1988. All eyes on DuPont's incentive program, *Wall Street Journal*, December 5: B1

Heller, Michael A., 1998. The tragedy of the anticommons: property in transition, *Harvard Law Review* 111: 621–88

Henrich, Joseph, Robert Boyd, Samuel Bowles, Colin Camerer, Ernst Fehr, Herbert Gintis, and Richard McElreath, 2001. In search of homo economicus: behavioral experiments in 15 small-scale societies, *American Economic Review: Papers and Proceedings* 91: 73–8

Hesson, Robert, 1979. *In Defense of the Corporation*, Stanford, CA: Hoover Institution Press

Hewitt, Michael, 2004. Commissioners pass Dell plant incentives, *Winston-Salem Journal*, December 14, available on April 25, 2005 at http://www.journalnow.com/servlet/Satellite?pagename = WSJ%2FMGArticle%2FWSJ_BasicArticle&c = MGArticle&cid = 1031779670184

Heyne, Paul, 1994. *The Economic Way of Thinking*, New York: Macmillan

Hirsch, Jerry, 2005. Is wholesale change in alcohol pricing on tap?, *Los Angeles Times*, April 11: C1

Hirshleifer, Jack, 1999. There are many pathways to cooperation, *Journal of Bioeconomics* 1: 73–93

Hobbes, Thomas, 1968. *Leviathan*, ed. C. B. Macpherson, Baltimore, MD: Penguin (first published in 1651)

Hoffman, Elizabeth, Kevin A. McCabe, and Vernon L. Smith, 1998. Behavioral foundations of reciprocity: experimental economics and evolutionary psychology, *Economic Inquiry* 36: 335–52

Holmstrom, Bengt, 1979. Moral hazard and observability, *Bell Journal of Economics* 10: 74–1

Holmstrom, Bengt and Stephen Kaplan, 2001. Corporate governance and merger activity in the United States: making sense of the 1980s and 1990s, *Journal of Economic Perspectives* 15(2): 121–44

Homans, George C., 1950. *The Human Group*, New York: Harcourt, Brace, Inc.

Horngren, C. T., 1999. *Cost Accounting: A Managerial Emphasis*, Englewood Cliffs, NJ: Prentice Hall

Howard, Bion B. and Peter O. Dietz, 1969. *A Study of the Financial Significance of Profit Sharing*, Chicago: Council of Profit Sharing Industries

Hufbauer, Gary Clyde and Paul L. E. Grieco, 2005. The payoff from globalization, Washington, DC: Institute for International Economics, May, available on June 2, 2005 at http://www.iie.com/publications/papers/hufbauer0505.htm

Hufbauer, Gary Clyde *et al.*, 1986. *Trade Protection in the United States: 31 Case Studies*, Washington, DC: Institute for International Economics

Husled, Mark, 1995. The impact of human resource management practices on turnover, productivity and corporate financial performance, *Academy of Management Journal* 38(2): 635–72

Ichniowski, Casey, Kathryn Shaw, and Giovanna Prennushi, 1996. *The Effects of Human Resource Practices on Productivity*, Cambridge, MA: National Bureau of Economic Research, Working Paper 5333

Ingrassia, Paul, 2005. Junk cars, *Wall Street Journal*, May 17: A12

James, John, 1951. A preliminary study of the size determinants in small-group interaction, *American Sociological Review* 16: 444–74

Jarrell, Gregg A. and Annette B. Paulsen, 1989. The returns to acquiring firms in tender offers: evidence from three decades, *Financial Management* 18: 12–19

Jarrell, Gregg A., James A. Brickley, and Jeffrey M. Netter, 1988. The market for corporate control: the empirical evidence since 1980, *Journal of Economic Perspectives* 2: 49–68

Jensen, Michael, 1988. Takeovers: their causes and consequences, *Journal of Economic Perspectives* 2(1): 21–48

1989. Eclipse of the public corporation, *Harvard Business Review* 67(5): 61–74

Jensen, Michael and William H. Meckling, 1976. Theory of the firm: managerial behavior, agency costs and ownership structure, *Journal of Financial Economics* 3: 325–8

1979. Property rights and production functions: an application of labor-managed firms and codetermination, *Journal of Business* 52: 469–506

Jensen, Michael and Richard S. Ruback, 1983. The market for corporate control: the scientific evidence, *Journal of Financial Economics* 11(5): 5–50

Johnson, David L., 1974. An analysis of the costs and benefits for criminals in theft, St. Cloud, MN: Economics Department, St. Cloud State College, mimeo

Joskow, Paul, 1985. Vertical integration and long-term contracts: the case of coal-burning electric generating plants, *Journal of Law, Economics, and Organization* 1: 33–80

Kanter, Rosebeth M., 1973. *Commitment and Community: Communes and Utopias in Sociological Perspective*, Cambridge, MA: Harvard University Press

Karstensson, Lewis, 2003. The merchant and Mr. Reagan, *American Journal of Economics and Sociology* 62(3): 568–82

Keller, John J., 1997. Best phone discounts go to hardest bargainers, *Wall Street Journal*, February 13: B1, B12

Kelly, Kevin, 1998. *New Rules for the New Economy*, New York: Viking/Penguin

Kirzner, Israel, 1973. *Competition and Entrepreneurship*, Chicago: University of Chicago Press

Klein, Benjamin, Robert Crawford, and Armen Alchian, 1978. Vertical integration, appropriable rents, and the competitive contracting process, *Journal of Law and Economics* 21: 297–326

Klein, Benjamin and Keith B. Leffler, 1981. The role of market forces in assuring contractual performance, *Journal of Law and Economics* 89(4): 615–41

Klein, Benjamin and Lester F. Saft, 1985. The law and economics of franchise tying contracts, *Journal of Law and Economics* 28: 345–61

Klein, Joel I. *et. al.*, 1998. Complaint, *United States of America v. Microsoft Corporation*, May 20, available on August 20, 2004 at www.usdoj.gov/atr/cases3/micros/1763.htm

Klein, Richard G., 2000. Archaeology and the evolution of human behavior, *Evolutionary Anthropology* 32: 391–428

Knauft, Bruce., 1991. Violence and and sociality in human evolution, *Current Anthropology* 32: 391–428

Knight, Frank H., 1971. *Risk, Uncertainty, and Profit*, Chicago: University of Chicago Press

Koening, R., 1990. DuPont plan linking pay to fibers profit unravels, *Wall Street Journal*, October 25: B1

Kohn, Alfie, 1993a. *Punished by Rewards*, Boston: Houghton Mifflin

1993b. Why incentive plans cannot work, *Harvard Business Review* September–October: 54–63

Kosters, Marvin and Finis Welch, 1972. The effects of minimum wages on the distribution of changes in aggregate employment, *American Economic Review* 62: 323–31

Krueger, Alan B., 2005. Economic scene: the farm-subsidy model of financing academia, *New York Times*, May 26: C2

Krueger, Ann O., 1974. The political economy of the rent-seeking society, *American Economic Review* 64: 291–303

Laband, David N. and Bernard F. Lentz, 1990. Entrepreneurial success and occupational inheritance among proprietors, *Canadian Journal of Economics* 23(3) 101–17

1990. *Strategic Pay: Aligning Organizational Strategies and Pay Systems*, San Francisco: Jossey-Bass

Lazear, Edward, 1979. Why is there mandatory retirement?, *Journal of Political Economy* 87: 1261–84

2000. Performance pay and productivity, *American Economic Review* 90: 1346–61

Lazear, Edward and S. Rosen, 1981. Rank-order tournaments as optimum labor contract, *Journal of Political Economy* 89(3): 841–64

Ledyard, John O., 1995. Public goods: a survey of experimental research, in John H. Kager and Alvin E. Roth (eds.), *Handbook of Experimental Economics*, Princeton, NJ: Princeton University Press

Lee, Dwight R. 1990. Why it pays to have tough profs, *The Margin* September–October: 28–9

Lee, Dwight R. and David Kreutzer, 1982. Lagged demand and a perverse response to threatened property rights, *Economic Inquiry* 20: 579–88

Lee, Dwight R. and Richard B. McKenzie, 1998. How the client effect moderates price competition, *Southern Economic Journal* 64(3): 741–52

Lee, Louis, 1996. Without a receipt you may get stuck with that ugly scarf, *Wall Street Journal*, November 18: A1

Lee, William G., 1994. The new corporate republics, *Wall Street Journal*, September 26: 12

Lehn, Kenneth and Annette B. Paulsen, 1987. Sources of value in leveraged buyouts, in Murray Weidenbaum (ed.), *Public Policy Towards Corporate Takeovers*, New Brunswick, NJ: Transaction

Leighton, Linda and Jacob Mincer, 1981. Effects of minimum wages on human capital formation, in Simon Rothenberg (ed.), *The Economics of Legal Minimum Wages*, Washington, DC: American Enterprise Institute

Lessig, Lawrence, 2001. *The Future of Ideas: The Fate of the Commons in a Connected World*, New York: Random House

Levitt, Stephen D. and Stephen J. Dubner, 2005. *Freakonomics: A Rogue Economist Explores the Hidden Side of Everything*, New York: William Morrow

Lichter, Robert, Linda Lichter, and Stanley Rothman, 1990. *Watching America*, New York: Prentice Hall: 146

Liebowitz, Stan J. and Stephen E. Margolis, 1995. Path dependence, lock-in and history, *Journal of Law, Economics, and Organization* 11(1): 205–26

1999. *Winners, Losers, and Microsoft: How Technology Markets Choose Products*, Oakland, CA: Independent Institute (reprinted from Stan J. Liebowitz and Stephen E. Margolis, The fable of the keys, *Journal of Law and Economics*, 33, 1990: 1–25)

Lisser, Eleena de, 1999. Windows shopping – one-click commerce: what people do now to goof off at work, *Wall Street Journal*, September 24: A1

Locke, John, 1690. *The Second Treatise of Civil Government*, as found on August 10, 2004 at http: //oregonstate.edu/instruct/phl302/texts/locke/locke2/ 2nd-contents.html

Los Angeles Times Wire Service, 2005. More goods from China face limits, *Los Angeles Times*, May 19: C3

Lott, Jr., John R. and Russell D. Roberts, 1991. A guide to the pitfalls of identifying price discrimination, *Economic Inquiry* 29(1): 14–23

Luna, Nancy, 2005. Lack of late fee empties shelves, *Orange County (CA) Register*, February 18: business 1

Malatesta, Paul H. and Ralph A. Walkling, 1988. Poison pill securities: stockholder wealth, profitability, and ownership structure, *Journal of Financial Economics* 20(1): 347–76.

Mangum, G. L., 1962. Are wage incentives becoming obsolete?, *Industrial Relations* 2: 73–96

Manne, Henry G., 1963. Mergers and the market for corporate control, *Journal of Political Economy* 73: 110–20

Marks, Mindy, 2004. Minimum wages and fringe benefits, Economics Department, St. Louis: Washington University, Working Paper

Marshall, Ray, 1974. Economics of racial discrimination, *Journal of Economic Literature*, 12: 849–71

Marwell, Gerald and Ruth Ames, 1981. Economists free ride, does anyone else?, *Journal of Public Economics* 15: 295–310

Maslow, A. H., 1954. *Motivation and Personality*, New York: Harper & Row

Mathewson, G. Frank and Ralph A. Winter, 1985. The economics of franchise contracts, *Journal of Law and Economics* 28: 503–26

McCabe, K. and V. L. Smith, 1999. A comparison of naive and sophisticated subject behavior with game theoretic predictions, *Proceedings of the National Academy of Sciences of the USA* 97: 3777–81

McChesney, Fred S., 1997. *Money for Nothing: Politicians, Rent Extraction and Political Extortion*, Cambridge, MA: Harvard University Press

McConnell, John J. and Chris J. Muscarella, 1985. Capital expenditure decisions and market value of the firm, *Journal of Financial Economics* 14: 399–422

McKenzie, Richard B., 1977. Political ignorance: an empirical assessment of educational remedies, in Gordon Tullock (ed.), *Frontiers of Economics*, Blacksburg, VA.: University Publications

1987. The loss of textile and apparel jobs: the relative importance of imports and productivity *Cato Journal* Winter: 731–46.

1994. *Times Change: The Minimum Wage and the New York Times*, San Francisco: Pacific Research Institute

1996. In defense of academic tenure, *Journal of Institutional and Theoretical Economics* 152(2): 325–41

1997. *The Paradox of Progress*, New York: Oxford University Press

2000. *Trust on Trial: How the Microsoft Case Is Transforming the Rules of Competition*, Boston: Perseus

2004. Monopoly: a game economists love to play – badly!, *Southern Economics Journal* 70(4): 715–30

McKenzie, Richard B. and Roman Galar, 2004. The importance of deviance in intellectual development, *American Journal of Economics and Sociology* 63(1): 19–49

McKenzie, Richard B. and Dwight R. Lee, 1991. *Quicksilver Capital: How the Rapid Movement of Wealth Has Changed the World*, New York: Free Press

McKenzie, Richard B. and Thomas Sullivan, 1987. The NCAA as a cartel: an economic and legal reinterpretation, *Antitrust Bulletin* 3: 373–99.

McKenzie, Richard B. and Gordon Tullock, 1994. *The New World of Economics*, New York: McGraw-Hill

McMillan, John, 2002. *Reinventing the Bazaar: The Natural History of Markets*, New York: W.W. Norton

Metzger, Bertram L., 1975. *Profit Sharing in 38 Large Companies, I & II*, Evanston, ie: Profit Sharing Research Foundation

Meyer, Stephen, 1981. *The Five-Dollar Day: Labor, Management, and Social Control in the Ford Motor Company, 1908–1921*, Albany, NY: State University of New York Press

Micklethwait, John and Adrian Wooldridge, 2003. *The Company: A Short History of a Revolutionary Idea*, New York: The Modern Library

Mikkelson, Wayne H. and Richard S. Ruback, 1985. An empirical analysis of the interfirm equity investment process, *Journal of Financial Economics* 14: 523–53

Milgrom, Paul and John Roberts, 1992. *Economics, Organization and Management* Englewood Cliffs, NJ: Prentice Hall

Miller, Gary J., 1992. *Managerial Dilemmas: The Political Economy of Hierarchy*, New York: Cambridge University Press

Miller, Scott, 2005. WTO urges caution on textile limits, *Wall Street Journal*, April 25: A2

Mises, Ludwig von, 1962. *The Ultimate Foundations of Economic Science: An Essay on Method*, Princeton, NJ: D. Van Nostrand

Mitchell, Mark L. and Kenneth Lehn, 1990. Do bad bidders become good targets?, *Journal of Political Economy* 98(2): 372–98

Mitchell, R., 1994. Managing by values, *Business Week*, August 1

Moore, Gordon E., 1994. The accidental entrepreneur, *Engineering & Science* 62(4): 23–30

Muñoz, Lorenza, 2005. Blockbuster settles state probes into late-fee ads, *Los Angeles Times*, March 30: C1

Nalbantian, Haig R. and Andrew Schotter, 1997. Productivity under group incentives: an experimental study, *American Economic Review* 87(3): 314–41

Nasar, Sylvia, 2001. *A Beautiful Mind*, New York: Simon & Schuster

National Center for Policy Analysis, 1994. Answering the critics of medical savings accounts, *Brief Analysis*, Dallas, TX: National Center for Policy Analysis, September 16

Neumann, W. R., 1986. *The Paradox of Mass Politics*, Cambridge, MA: Harvard University Press

New York Times, 2005. Lenovo of China completes purchase of IBM's PC unit, May 5: C5

Nishiguchi, Toshihiro, 1994. *Strategic Industrial Sourcing: The Japanese Advantage*, New York: Oxford University Press

Nishiguchi, Toshihiro and Masayoshi, Ikeda, 1996. Suppliers' process innovation: understated aspects of Japanese industrial sourcing, in Toshihiro Nishiguchi (ed.), *Managing Product Development*, New York: Oxford University Press

Olson, Mancur, 1971. *The Logic of Collective Action: Public Goods and the Theory of Groups*, Cambridge, MA: Harvard University Press

Ostrom, Eleanor, 2000. Collective action and the evolution of social norms, *Journal of Economic Perspectives* 14: 137–58

Oyer, Paul, 1998. Fiscal year ends and nonlinear incentive contracts: the effect on business seasonality, *Quarterly Journal of Economics* 113: 149–85

Pearce, Jone L., 1987. Why merit pay doesn't work: implications for organization theory, in D. B. Balkin and L. R. Gomez-Mejia (eds.), *New Perspectives in Compensation*, Englewood Cliffs, NJ: Prentice Hall

Peers, Martin, 2005. At Blockbuster, new strategies raise tensions over board seats, *The Weekly Review* (*Wall Street Journal*), April 18, as found on April 22, 2005 at http://online.wsj.com/article_print/0,SB111378718174309203,00.html

Peers, Martin and Ann Zimmerman, 2005. Dissident Icahn wins board seats at Blockbuster, *Wall Street Journal*, May 12: A1

Pencavel, J. H., 1977. Work effort, on the job screening, and alternative methods of remuneration, *Research in Labor Economics*, 225–59

Peters, Thomas J., 1994. *Tom Peters Seminar: Crazy Times Call for Crazy Organizations*, New York: Vintage Books

Petersen, Tron, 1991. Reward systems and the distribution of wages, *Journal of Law, Economics, and Organizations* 7 (special issue): 130–58

Peterson, John M. and Charles T. Stewart, 1969. *Employment Effects of Minimum Wage Rates*, Washington, DC: American Enterprise Institute for Public Policy Research

Pew Research Center Survey, 2004. Roper Center, Accession no. 0448774, February 4–16

Porter, Lyman W. and E. E. Lawyer, 1965. Properties of organization structure in relation to job attitudes and job behavior, *Psychological Bulletin* 77: 23–51

Posner, Richard A., 1974. Theories of economic regulation, *Bell Journal of Economics and Management Science* 5(2): 335–58

Prestowitz, Jr., Clyde V., 1988. *Trading Places: How We Allowed Japan to Take the Lead*, New York: Basic Books: 156–66

Princeton Survey Research Associates, 2004. Roper Center, Accession no. 0454615, April 15

Radford, R. A., 1945. The economic organization of a POW camp, *Economica* 12: 189–201

Ragan, James F., 1977. Minimum wages and the youth labor market, *Review of Economics and Statistics* 59: 129–36

Read, Leonard E., 1983. I, Pencil, *The Freeman* November (originally published in *The Freeman* in 1958), available on July 19, 2004 at http: //www.fee.org/vnews.php?nid = 1321

Richman, Sheldon, 1981. The rape of Poletown, *Inquiry*, August 3, 24

Roberts, John, 2004. *The Modern Firm: Organizational Design for Performance and Growth*, New York: Oxford University Press

Robins, James A., 1996. Why and when does agency theory matter? A critical approach to the role of agency theory in the analysis of organizational control, Irvine, CA: Graduate School of Management, University of California, Irvine, Working Paper

Rubin, Paul H., 1978. The theory of the firm and the structure of the franchise contract, *Journal of Law and Economics* 21(1): 223–33

1990. *Managing Business Transactions: Controlling the Costs of Coordination, Communication, and Decision Making*, New York: Free Press

2002. *Darwinian Politics: The Evolutionary Origin of Freedom*, New Brunswick, NJ: Rutgers University Press

Ryngaert, Michael and Jeffry Netter, 1988. Shareholder wealth effects of the Ohio anti-takeover law, *Journal of Law, Economics, and Organization* 4: 373–83

Scott, Anthony, 1955. The fishery: the objective of sole ownership, *Journal of Political Economy* 63: 116–24

Seiler, Eric, 1984. Piece-rate vs. time-rate: the effect of incentives on earnings, *Review of Economics and Statistics* 66(3): 363–75

Sethi, Rajiv and E. Somanathan, 1996. The evolution of social norms in common property resource use, *American Economic Review* 86: 766–88

Shapiro, Carl and Joseph Stiglitz, 1984. Equilibrium unemployment as a worker discipline device, *American Economic Review* 74(3): 433–44

Shavell, Steven, 1979. Risk sharing and incentives in the principal and agent relationship, *Bell Journal of Economics* 10(1): 55–73

Shepherd, William G., 1984. Contestability vs. Competition, *American Economic Review* 74: 572–87

Simon, Herbert, 1951. A formal theory of employment relationship, *Econometrica* 19: 293–305

Smith, Adam, 1937. *An Inquiry into the Nature and Causes of the Wealth of Nations*, New York: Modern Library: 4–12

Smith, C. and R. Watts, 1982. Incentive and tax effects of executive compensation plans, *Australian Journal of Management* 7: 139–57

Somin, Ilya, 2003. Voter knowledge and constitutional change: The new deal experience, *William and Mary Law Review* 45: 595–615

Spencer, Herbert, 1896. *Principles of Sociology*, London: Williams & Norgate

Stecklow, Steve, 1994. Evangelical schools reinvent themselves by stressing academics, *Wall Street Journal*, May 12: A1

Steiner, Mary C., Natalie D. Munro, Todd A. Surovell, Eitan Tchernov, and Ofer Bar-Yosef, 1998. Paleolithic population growth pulses evidenced by small animal exploitation, *Science* September 25, available at http://www.science mag.org, December 19, 2004

Stephenson, Frederick J. and Richard J. Fox, 1992. Corporate strategies for frequent-flier programs, *Transportation Journal* 32(1): 38–50

Stigler, George J., 1971. The theory of economic regulation, *Bell Journal of Economics* 2(1): 3–21

Stokes, Donald E. and Warren E. Miller, 1962. Party government and the saliency of congress, *Public Opinion Quarterly* 26: 531–46

Taylor, Frederick W., 1895. A piece rate system, *American Society of Mechanical Engineers Transactions* 16: 856–93

Tellis, Gerald and Peter Golder, 2002. *Will and Vision: How Late Comers Grow to Dominate Markets*, New York: McGraw-Hill

Thaler, Richard H., 1992. *The Winner's Curse: Paradoxes and Anomalies of Economic Life*, New York: Free Press

Thomas, Paulette, 1996. Work week: teams rule, *Wall Street Journal*, May 28: A1

Thompson, Donald N., 1971. *Franchise Operations and Antitrust*, Lexington, MA: D.C. Heath

Tichy, Noel M. and Stratford Sherman, 1993. Jack Welch's lessons for success, *Fortune*, January 25: 86–93

Trivers, Robert L., 1971. The evolution of reciprocal altruism, *Quarterly Review of Biology* 46: 35–57

Tucker, William, 1997. How rent control drives out affordable housing, *Policy Analysis*, no. 274 (May 21), Washington, DC: Cato Institute, available on August 17, 2004 at http: //www.cato.org/pubs/pas/pa-274es.html

Tullock, Gordon, 1967. The welfare costs of tariffs, monopolies, and theft, *Western Economic Journal* 5: 224–32

1972. *Toward a Mathematics of Politics*, Ann Arbor, MI: University of Michigan Press

US Department of Labor, 1993. *High Performance Work Practices and Firm Performance*, Washington, DC: Bureau of National Affairs

Veblen, Thorstein, 1902. *The Theory of the Leisure Class: An Economic Study of Institutions*, New York: Macmillan

Wagner, John L. Paul A Rubin, and Thomas J. Callahan, 1988. Incentive payment and non-managerial productivity: an interrupted time series analysis of magnitude and trend, *Organizational Behavior and Human Decision Processes* 42(1): 47–74

Wall Street Journal, 1975. Less regulation of airline sector is urged by Ford, October 9: 3

Warren-Bolton, Frederick R., n.d. Direct testimony, State of New York *ex rel.* Attorney-General Dennis C. Vacco, *et. al. v.* Microsoft Corporation, Civil Action No.

98–1233 (TPJ), p. 21, available on August 20, 2004 at http: //www.usdoj.gov/atr/cases/f2000/2079.htm

Washington Post, 2005. US can consider textile-import limit, April 28: E2

Wauzzinski, Robert A., 2003. *The Transforming Story of Dwelling House Savings and Loan: A Pittsburgh Bank's Fight Against Urban Poverty*, Lewiston, NY: Edwin Mellen

Weisman, Martin L. and Douglas L. Kruse, 1990. Profit sharing and productivity, in Alan S. Blinder (ed.), *Paying for Productivity: A Look at the Evidence*, Washington, DC: Brookings Institution: 95–140

Wessels, Walter J., 1987. Minimum wages: are workers really better off?, paper prepared for presentation at a conference on minimum wages, Washington, DC, National Chamber Foundation, July 29

White, Erin, 2005. To keep employees, Domino's decides it's not all about pay, *Wall Street Journal*, February 17: A-1

White, Harrison C., 1991. Agency as control, in John W. Pratt and Richard J. Zeckhauser (eds.), *Principals and Agents: The Structure of Business*, Boston, MA: Harvard Business School Press: 187–212

White, Lawrence J., 2002. *International Trade in Services: More than Meets the Eye*, New York: Stern School of Business, Working Paper, February 28, available on May 10, 2005 at http://www.stern.nyu.edu/eco/wkpapers/workingpapers02/02-13 White.pdf

Williams, Walter, 2005. Minimum wage, maximum folly, *Capitalism Magazine*, March 23, as available on August 20, 2005 at http://www.capmag.com/article.asp?id4173

Williamson, Oliver E., 1967. Hierarchical control and optimum size firms, *Journal of Political Economy* 75(2): 123–38

Wilson, James Q., 1993. *The Moral Sense*, New York: Free Press

Wirthman, Lisa, 1997. Superior snooping: new software can catch workers goofing off, but some say such surveillance goes too far, *Orange County (Calif.) Register*, July 20: 1, 10

Wriston, Walter B., 1989. On track with the deficit, *Wall Street Journal*, January 6: A-1

INDEX